Anna Mazurkiewicz

Voice of the Silenced Peoples in the Global Cold War

Rethinking the Cold War

Edited by
Kirsten Bönker and Jane Curry

Volume 8

Anna Mazurkiewicz

Voice of the Silenced Peoples in the Global Cold War

The Assembly of Captive European Nations, 1954–1972

DE GRUYTER
OLDENBOURG

ISBN 978-3-11-065705-0
e-ISBN (PDF) 978-3-11-066100-2
e-ISBN (EPUB) 978-3-11-065718-0
ISSN 2567-5311

Library of Congress Control Number: 2020944767

Bibliographic information published by the Deutsche Nationalbibliothek
The Deutsche Nationalbibliothek lists this publication in the Deutsche Nationalbibliografie; detailed bibliographic data are available on the Internet at http://dnb.dnb.de.

Cover image: Façade of the City Hall in Saigon decorated with a poster saying: "Welcome the ACEN Delegation. Discussion of [anti-] Communist refugees of East Central Europe," 26 February 1959 PERMISSION TO USE (photo release form): Roman W. Rybicki, President of the Stefan Korboński Foundation, Warsaw.
Printing and binding: CPI books GmbH, Leck

MIX
Papier aus verantwortungsvollen Quellen
FSC www.fsc.org FSC® C083411

www.degruyter.com

Contents

For Marcjanna and Jakub

List of Charts and Tables

Appendix:

https://doi.org/10.1515/9783110661002-001

Abbreviations

AAN	Archiwum Akt Nowych (Warszawa)
ACEN	Assembly of Captive European Nations
ADST	Association for Diplomatic Studies and Training
AFCN	American Friends of Captive Nations
AFL-CIO	American Federation of Labor and Congress of Industrial Orgnizations
AMCOMLIB	American Committee for the Liberation of the Peoples of Russia
APACL	Asian Peoples Anti-Communist League
BIB	Board for International Broadcasting
CF	Corporate Files
CFR	Council on Foreign Relations
CDUCE	Christian Democratic Union of Central Europe
CFA	Committee for a Free Asia
CIA	Central Intelligence Agency
CREST	CIA Records Search Tool
CUL	Columbia University Libraries
CWIHP	Cold War International History Project
DCI	Director of Central Intelligence (CIG and CIA)
DDEL	Dwight D. Eisenhower Library and Museum
DER	Division of Exile Relations
DP(s)	displaced person(s)
EC	Executive Committee (CIA presence at FEC)
ECOSOC	Economic and Social Council of the United Nations
EE	Division of Eastern European Affairs, Department of State
EPO	Exile Political Organizations (FEC)
EUR	Office of European Affairs, Department of State
FBI	Federal Bureau of Investigation
FEC	Free Europe Committee (National Committee for [a] Free Europe, Free Europe Inc.)
FECS	Free Europe Citizens Service
FEP	Free Europe Press
FEER	Free Europe Exile Relations
FEOP	Free Europe Organizations and Publications
FEUE	Free Europe University in Exile
FOIA	Freedom of Information Act
FRUS	Foreign Relations of the United States
FWOD	Free World Operations Division (FEC)
GC	General Committee (ACEN)
GPO	Government Printing Office
HIA	Hoover Institution Archives
HNC	Hungarian National Council
HSTL	Harry S. Truman Library
ICFTU	International Confederation of Free Trade Unions
ICFTUE	International Centre of Free Trade Unionists in Exile
IJP	Józef Piłsudski Institute of America

https://doi.org/10.1515/9783110661002-002

IHRC	Immigration History Research Center
IDF	International Development Foundation (FEC/CIA)
IOD	International Organizations Division, CIA
IPN	Institute of National Remembrance
IPU	International Peasant Union
IRC	International Rescue Committee
LDUCEE	Liberal Democratic Union of Central Eastern Europe
NARA	National Archives and Records Administration
NATO	North Atlantic Treaty Organization
NCFE	National Committee for a Free Europe, see FEC
NSC	National Security Council
NSCID	National Security Council Intelligence Directive
OCB	Operations Coordinating Board
ORIT	Inter-American Regional Organization of Workers
OSA	Open Society Archives
PCNU	Polish Council of National Unity
PIASA	Polish Institute of Arts and Sciences
PNDC	Polish National Democratic Committee
PPS	Policy Planning Staff
PUL	Princeton University Library
PUWP	Polish United Workers Party
RFA	Radio Free Asia
RFE/RL	Radio Free Europe/Radio Liberty
SUCEE	Socialist Union of Central and Eastern Europe
UN	United Nations
UNCEE	United National Committees and Councils in Exile
USIA	U.S. Information Agency
USIS	U.S. Information Service
WEAC	West European Advisory Group
USSR	Union of Soviet Socialist Republics
ZNiO	Ossoliński National Institute

Preface

It was June 2005 in Gdańsk, Poland. A conference on the sixtieth anniversary of the end of World War II was taking place at the Faculty of History of the University of Gdańsk. I presented a paper on the contacts between representatives of the democratic opposition in Poland with American diplomats and journalists at the time of the Soviet-rigged post-war elections of 1947. The script of the communist takeover was analogous to other countries of East Central Europe. In the three years following the end of World War II, the members of the anti-communist opposition in the Soviet-dominated nations faced similar choices: prison, escape to the West or compromise. At the time of the Gdańsk conference, sixty years after the war, but less than twenty years since Communism's collapse, the historiography was just picking up the story of exile political activities. In most cases, exiles' political résumés came to an abrupt end with their departure from Poland, especially if their migration path led to the United States. During the deliberations of the Gdańsk conference, Józef Łaptos, who presented a paper on the attitude of the Council of Europe to the countries of East Central Europe, mentioned the organization of political refugees in New York, which existed throughout the entire Cold War. In a brief remark he mentioned one name, which over the thirteen years that followed served as nothing less than Ariadne's Thread for my research: Stefan Korboński (1901–1989). Following Korboński – wartime leader of civilian resistance and a member of the anti-communist opposition in Poland in 1945 and 1947 – into exile seemed like a logical continuation of the project that I had just completed.[1]

The organization mentioned by Łaptos was the Assembly of the Captive European Nations (ACEN). Its history begins with the arrival in the United States of the exiled leaders of parties and political groups from East Central Europe. Some of them left during, or right after the War. Others escaped between 1945 and 1948 once it became obvious that the promise of "free and unfettered" elections made at Yalta had become a flagrant sham. In every country that was later represented in the ACEN, except for Estonia, Latvia and Lithuania which were annexed by the Soviets before Yalta, a similar electoral pattern occurred:

---

1 Anna Mazurkiewicz, *Dyplomacja Stanów Zjednoczonych wobec wyborów w Polsce w latach 1947 i 1989* (Warsaw: Neriton, 2007).

https://doi.org/10.1515/9783110661002-003

Albania – the election of December 1945 featured one ballot;
Bulgaria – the elections held in November 1945 were boycotted by the opposition, the ones in October 1946 solidified the rule of the Communist-led Fatherland Front;
Czechoslovakia – the elections of May 1946 served as a test of the Communists' popularity, the façade being dropped following the coup in February 1948;
Hungary – an electoral test took place in November 1945, elections marked by coercion/fraud in August 1947;
Poland – a referendum used as a test held in June 1946, rigged elections in January 1947; and
Romania – coercion and fraud marked the elections of November 1946.

By 1948 there was no room for domestic opposition in any of the countries of the region.

The United States did not recognize the Soviet annexation of the Baltic States. There were no diplomatic relations between Albania and the U.S. between 1946 and 1991. Washington did, however, recognize all other Communist-dominated governments, and diplomatic relations with the Bulgarian government were established after the elections of November 1947 (broken off in 1950, restored in 1959). In the case of the other countries that were represented in the ACEN, Czechoslovakia, Hungary, Poland, and Romania the United States recognized the interim governments (before the first post-war elections took place, 1945–1946).

Most of the political leaders who were able and decided to leave for fear for their lives, facing long prison terms, or not wishing to stand show trials, hoped that they would be able to exert influence on the course of events from abroad. Their plan was often very similar: to gain the support of the free world for the cause of liberation of their homelands from Soviet domination. The gruesome fate of those who stayed, or could not leave in time, provided them with ample evidence that their fears were justified. Looking at the same countries mentioned above in the context of electoral shams, another pattern of prison, torture, judicial murder, and labor camps recurs. In Albania, professor Gjergj Kokoshi, a former minister of education, faced trial in 1946 (he died in prison in 1960). In 1947 the East Central European agrarian leaders were singled out and tried; in Bulgaria (Nikola Petkov, trial and death in 1947), in Romania (Iliu Maniu, three times a prime minister, 1947 show trial, death in internment in 1953), in Hungary (Béla Kovács, sent to a camp in Siberia in 1947, released 1956) etc, etc. In Poland, Jerzy Braun (a Christian Democrat) who replaced Korboński as the last delegate of the Polish government-in-exile to Poland in March (through June) 1945 was imprisoned in 1948, tortured until he lost all teeth and one eye, and released in 1956. In Czechoslovakia, Jan Masaryk's enigmatic defenestration in 1948 epitomized the end of an era. No change was to be effected by martyrdom under the Soviet regime. The exiles assumed the role of surrogate opposition abroad.

As I began to examine the emergence of unusually diverse, highly educated, experienced and well-connected groups of East Central European exiles in the United States, I noticed a certain pattern. In the case of many leaders who became important to the ACEN story, leaving the home country took place with the help of diplomatic representatives or intelligence employees of the United States or Great Britain. The list below represents a select sample of political leaders from East Central Europe who escaped their homelands with the help of the Americans and/or the British and entered the United States. I have chosen those leaders who later played important roles in the ACEN. But these were not the only ones, and some Americans listed below, like James McCargar, were instrumental in extracting tens of political leaders from the Soviet yoke.

- Georgi M. Dimitrov "Gemeto" – left Bulgaria 1945 with the help of the chief of the U.S. mission in Sophia (Maynard Barnes). Died in Washington in 1972.
- Petr Zenkl – left Czechoslovakia in 1948 with the help of the chief of CIA station in Prague (Charles Katek). Died in Raleigh (NC) in 1975.
- Ferenc Nagy – left Hungary in 1947 with the help of James McCargar (The Pond, G-2). Died in Herndon (VA) in 1979.
- Stanisław Mikołajczyk – left Poland in 1947 with the help of the U.S. Embassy's First Secretary George Andrews. Died in Washington D.C. in 1966.
- Constantin Vişoianu – left Romania in 1946 with the help of Ira C. Hamilton and Thomas R. Hall (OSS). Died in Washington D.C. in 1994.

The leader of the Albanian National Committee – Midhat Frashëri – left the country in 1944 and was instrumental in legitimizing MI6 special operations in Albania. He died in New York in 1949. In the case of the Baltic countries which were annexed by the Soviet Union in 1940 and then again in 1944, the exiled political leaders that established the national councils while in exile relied on the support and cooperation of their diplomatic representatives. The Baltic "diplomats without countries" were continuously recognized and supported by the U.S. government.[2] They assisted the efforts of the political leaders of the

2 Povilas Žadeikis (Lithuania), Alfrēds Bīlmanis, since 1948: Jules Feldmans (Latvia), and Johannes Kaiv (Estonia).

three national councils, all of which were in place by 1944; Lithuanian (Vaclovas Sidzikauskas, died in New York 1973), Latvian (Vilis Māsēns, died in New York in 1964), Estonian Leonhard Vahter (died in 1983 also in New York).[3] Thus the relationship with the American authorities must have been of great importance to the nature of the refugees' actions, their positions and the roles they played overseas.

Inquiring into the nature of this relationship, I realized that the early context in which American cooperation with political exiles from East Central Europe was designed and inaugurated deserved a separate and thorough study. The resulting book entitled: *Political Exiles from East-Central Europe in American Cold War Policy, 1948–1954* appeared in Polish in 2016. It covers the immigration of the exiled leaders, the birth of American psychological warfare plans for their employment, a description of the political organizations – committees and councils – established in the West, as well as detailed records of the initial years of American-exile cooperation.[4] It took me more than five hundred pages to explain the early beginnings of this peculiar Cold War alliance and show that they were not particularly encouraging to either side. By 1954 both sides agreed that a transnational, multiethnic representation of exile organizations was the best way to rise above politically fragmented national groups and strengthen its broader appeal.

The ensuing story of "an exile organization speaking in one voice for almost a hundred million silenced peoples"[5] will open with the words of Stefan Korboński, whose biography inspired me to write this book:

> It never occurs to the crowds of New Yorkers passing daily along West 57th Street that, in the heart of Manhattan, at No. 29, there is an island in the American ocean, inhabited by foreigners using many foreign tongues which sound exotic to the American ear. [...] Among them may be met Monsignor Béla Varga, the last post-war Speaker of the Hungarian Parliament and the constitutional Deputy President of Hungary, as he talks to Béla Fabian, a member of the Hungarian parliament imprisoned for five years by the Germans in Auschwitz. Peter Zenkl, former vice Premier of the Czechoslovak government and mayor of the city of Prague, also a prisoner in Auschwitz, hurries past them to the phone. He is regarded by the Czech Communist government as their main enemy. Beyond a partition is the former

3 "Dr. Vilis Māsēns, an Exile Leader. Latvian Chairman in Group of Captive Nations Dies," *The New York Times*, 16 VII 1964, 31; "Vaclovas Sidzikauskas, 80: Sought Liberated Lithuania," *The New York Times*, 3 XII 1973, 42.

4 Mazurkiewicz, *Uchodźcy z Europy Środkowo-Wschodniej w amerykańskiej polityce zimnowojennej (1948–1954)* [Political Exiles from East-Central Europe in American Cold War Policy] (Warsaw-Gdańsk, IPN-University of Gdańsk, 2016).

5 Vilis Māsēns, Speech, 15 III 1957, Immigration History Research Center (IHRC), ACEN Papers 136, b. 23, f. 3.

Romanian Minister of Foreign Affairs, Constantin Vişoianu, who held on in his country to the last minute alongside King Michael and is now discussing current affairs with his younger compatriot, chief of staff of ACEN, Brutus Coste, and his deputy, the Albanian Nuci Kotta. Here also it is possible to meet the president of the Lithuanian National Committee, Minister Vaclovas Sidzikauskas, who like Fabian and Zenkl spent five years in Auschwitz; Vilis Māsēns, the former Latvian diplomat; Leonhard Vahter, former member of the Estonian parliament; Vasil Gërmenji, the Albanian professor; Bolesław Biega, former Polish diplomat; Feliks Gadomski, a district judge from Warsaw; Władysław Michalak, once a trade union leader; and many others [...] a Tower of Babel on a small scale.[6]

6 Stefan Korboński, *Warsaw in Exile* (New York-Washington D.C.: Frederick A. Praeger, 1966), 103–104.

Introduction

The name of the Assembly of Captive European Nations rings a bell to many Americans born in the first half of the twentieth century. Many seem to recall at least some kind of a function, fundraiser, parade featuring people dressed in folk costumes carrying banners that said, for example, “God, save America from Communism,” or “Freedom for the Captive Nations,” or maybe a televised or printed advertisement featuring an image of a radio antenna and young “captives” assiduously listening to the broadcast jammed by the communist regime.

The prevalence of the myth of “captivity vs. freedom” in American culture found an almost unprecedented popularity during the early years of the Cold War. The term “captive peoples” – dominated the American understanding of the Eastern bloc and its inhabitants. “Metaphors of enslavement played a crucial role in transforming the Soviet Union and China from courageous wartime allies into barbarous foes implacably opposed to the ‘free world,’” thus making popular sense of geopolitics since late 1940s – wrote Susan Carruthers in *Cold War Captives*.[1] Yet, when asked about the actual organization’s profile, membership, or origin few Americans can give any details. A combination of buzzwords comes instead: captive nations, freedom radios, anti-Communist crusade, etc. This is not surprising at all. The many organizations that were created in the United States that could fit under these taglines add to the confusion. All American Conference to Combat Communism, Anti-Bolshevik Bloc of Nations, Anti-Communist League of America, Council Against Communist Aggression, National Captive Nations Committee, and many others.[2] However, in this popular image the political exiles from East Central Europe are almost invisible. The focus is clearly to be found in the fate of “the captives,” dangers of communism (in the latter

1 Susan L. Carruthers, *Cold War Captives: Imprisonment, Escape, and Brainwashing* (Berkeley–Los Angeles–London: University of California Press, 2009), 4–5. Although it was not new, the captive narrative gained new strength in 1948. At the time the American media were covering with great interest the story of a Russian chemistry teacher – Olga Kashenkina’s dramatic attempt to escape from the Soviet consulate in New York by jumping out of the window. It was then, Carruthers argues, that in a popular discourse the Cold War was to become a struggle for a rescue, liberation of the captives.

2 Among hundreds of ethnic or exile organizations (more or less radical) were the Conference of Americans of Central-Eastern European Descent, and the American Committee for Liberation from Bolshevism. Some used the term “captive”: Americans to Free Captive Nations, American Friends of Captive Nations, National Captive Nations Committee, Assembly of Captive European Nations.

https://doi.org/10.1515/9783110661002-004

decades evolving into the nuclear scare) mixed with American dedication (and mobilization) for the cause of defending freedom.

The same seems to be true regarding academic interests. While it has garnered some attention in recent years – most notably thanks to Susan Carruthers[3] – the use of "captives" encompassing the East Central European exiles remains rather obscure. The organization that was behind the "truth dollars," "freedom train," "liberty scrolls," "Crusade for Freedom," the one that organized an unprecedented broadcast organization in the form of Radio Free Europe, was the Free Europe Committee (FEC).[4]

The FEC was an organization financed by the U.S. government that enlisted the support of several private entities and prominent Americans. In the words of John Richardson, President of the Committee (1961): "The Free Europe Committee is a privately managed, unattributed instrument of the United States Government, engaged in psychological and political warfare against communism on both sides of the Iron Curtain."[5] This view has been challenged by both former FEC employees as well as scholars.[6] For one, it clearly denied any agency to the people who constituted the basis of this entire operation – the exiles themselves. Just as the FEC objected to overstatements of governmental control of its activities, so did the exiles associated with it.

The FEC sponsored the Assembly of Captive European Nations (ACEN) – an umbrella organization for the ten exile committees and councils from nine East Central European nations – as one of its Cold War psychological/political warfare instruments. While the FEC prioritized informing and influencing East Central Europeans behind the Iron Curtain, it also devoted varying degrees of effort to bringing the lessons of East Central Europe's experience with communism to

3 Carruthers, *Cold War Captives* ...; Carruthers, "Between Camps: Eastern Bloc "Escapees" and Cold War Borderlands," *American Quarterly* 57/3 (2005).

4 The name of the Committee underwent a few changes. At the time of incorporation (May 1949) it was called National Committee for Free Europe. The following year "a" was added before Free Europe (NCFE). By 1954, when the Assembly of Captive European Nations (ACEN) was established it was called: Free Europe Committee (FEC). In 1965 the FEC became Free Europe Inc. (FE). In order to avoid confusion, I refer to the Committee as FEC throughout the book. Mazurkiewicz, *Uchodźcy* ..., 188, footnote 38.

5 John Richardson, The Free Europe Committee. A Description and a proposal, 27 X 1961, DDEL, C.D. Jackson Papers, B. 53, f.: FEC 1961 (1).

6 A. Ross Johnson established that this was a "unique CIA-FEC relationship, which recognized the autonomous prerogatives of the FEC." Johnson, *Radio Free Europe* ..., 26. Justine Faure described FEC as: "intellectually dependent on Department of State directives, financed by the CIA." Justine Faure, "Croisade américaine en 1950: La délivrance des "Nations captives" d'Europe de l'Est," *Vingtième Siècle. Revue d'histoire* 73 (Jan. – March 2002), 6.

peoples of the free world – particularly to those of developing nations and areas vulnerable to Communist subversion. For the reasons explained in this volume, the American state-private network formed under the FEC logo decided to assist in the ACEN's creation, fund its activities for seventeen years and lend its assistance with access to the political and media networks in the U.S. and abroad.

There were multiple reasons why the exiles decided to affiliate themselves with the Americans – with the government, the intelligence services, and private and media organizations. First, there was no other, comparable source of political and financial support for exile political operations anywhere in the world. None of the West European countries wanted to maintain large exile political communities after the war. For those who had to escape their homelands, the association of the FEC with the United States government, assumed by many, was not an obstacle. Rather, it boosted their hopes, potentially offering greater authority, access, and thus the hope of regaining political agency. Should the CIA be behind this effort, many exiles thought this was "even better" because it bore the promise of real action. Naturally, there were also individual reasons for seeking American protection, beginning with personal security, maintaining social prestige, and yes, earning a basic livelihood. Furthermore, the idealistic attitude of being given the means to preserve national culture in exile (via youth programs, publications in native languages and their translations, revived cultural associations, libraries, archives, opportunities to assist refugees) played an important role as well. The exiles could not bypass the possible impact they could have behind the Iron Curtain (via radio, press, books) even if modulated by American political guidelines. After all, there was one common enemy. While the political organizations were excluded from exercising direct influence behind enemy lines (unlike the Radio Free Europe or Free Europe Press), they could hope to become at least the source of news delivered to the "captive nations" – thus projecting "hope" and therefore real assistance to domestic opposition. The political exiles were given a chance to uphold the pre-war political system abroad albeit in a modified form of the national committees and councils. Hence their decision to maintain their political mandates based on the last free elections (before, or immediately after, World War II, before the Communist seizure of power). Alliance with willing American partners (through the state-private network established for this purpose) gave the exiles tools for political lobbying.

The FEC used three terms to describe East Central Europeans it worked with: exiles, émigrés, and ethnics, plus their organizations. The first group was distinguished by their own claim that "they are the representatives of the democratic traditions of their respective countries; they retain their former citizenships; they devote the largest part of their activities to the political struggle for the liberation of their homelands." The émigrés were persons who had "become citizens of Western countries, they have achieved certain prominence in their respective academic, artistic or business fields; they devote the larger part of their energies to the pursuit of their careers; their organizations have, in fact, the character of professional organizations. They are, however, actively interested in the fate of their former countries." The ethnic organizations were composed of rank-and-file members of ethnic ("hyphenated") groups. Such persons were first-generation or second-generation citizens of Western countries, but "their personal, cultural and emotional links with the respective 'old countries' remain alive."[7]

This study focuses on a group of post-World War II refugees – the anti-communist political exiles and émigrés from East Central Europe who arrived in the U.S. in the second half of the 1940s and sought American support for their political agenda related to their homeland. Former members of post-Yalta parliaments (1945–1948), former diplomats, as well as party leaders settled in the U.S. with the intention of continuing their political activities in spite of Soviet domination in East Central Europe. This group was as diverse as the pre-war and wartime experiences of their respective nations. The common features of political leaders in exile included inter alia: a high status held in the country of origin (public office, political or professional positions, economic independence), a shared initial belief that their exile would be temporary, and a desire to continue their national political activities from abroad.[8]

None of the FEC's programs would have been possible without the participation of the willing exiles – from exile political organizations, the Speakers' Bureau, through the Mid-European Studies Center, Free Europe Press, Citizens' Service, or the University in Exile to the single most important, influential and most expensive project: Radio Free Europe (RFE). Through the many information programs, conferences, press, pamphlet and book publications, world travels, the exiles in fact assumed the role of surrogate representative of the "silenced peoples," or "captive nations" in the "free world" (understood as non-commu-

7 Albert D. Kappel to John Richardson, Memorandum: FEC Objectives Paper, 15 VI 1965, HIA, RFE/RL CF: A, b. 192, f. 3; Anna Mazurkiewicz, "Unwilling Immigrants: Transnational Identities of East Central European Exiles during the Cold War," *Studia Migracyjne – Przegląd Polonijny* 4 (158), (2015): 159–171.

8 Annual Report of the President [Shepardson] of Free Europe Committee, Inc. to the Directors and Members of the Committee (FEC President's Report for the Year 1955), Harry S. Truman Library (HSTL), Papers of Charles Hulten, b. 22, f.: RFE (3), 13; Elizabeth K. Valkanier, "Eastern Europe in Exile," *Annals of the American Academy of Political and Social Science* 317 (May 1958), 146–152. See also: Anna D. Jaroszyńska-Kirchmann, *The exile mission: The Polish political diaspora and Polish Americans, 1939–1956*. Athens: Ohio University Press, 2004.

nist countries worldwide, often capitalized). Such terminology, reconstructed in this volume, was in common use throughout the period of the ACEN–FEC's symbiotic relationship.

Initially, the idea that the East Central European exiles were an asset in advancing the American anti-communist agenda in the free world was evidenced in that most of the ACEN's programs were directed towards the United Nations. By the 1955, the first initiative of organizing the ACEN's sessions in Europe surfaced, less than half a year after ACEN's founding. ACEN's offices were soon opened in London, Paris, and Bonn. In 1956, the ACEN activities were dominated by events taking place in East Central Europe (workers' protests in Poland, the Hungarian Revolution). In the following years most of the ACEN's activities involved attempts to force the world (in particular the UN) to act on behalf of the Hungarian peoples. Beginning in 1958 the FEC stepped up programs targeting the "uncommitted" countries which is visible in the growth of ACEN's programs for Latin America and Asia. By 1959 the exile Assembly reached a peak of its activities with the Presidential Proclamation of the Captive Nations Week and the biggest budget allotted to it by the FEC. Yet, the FEC was as vulnerable to the changes in U.S. Cold War policies as the ACEN. With the reorganization of the FEC in 1960 came the first series of significant cuts in exile programs. Within the next few years, the exile Assembly fell out with American policy, facing severe budget cuts by 1965, and being forced to close by January 1972.

This book is divided into chapters that try to mirror the above-mentioned shifts in ACEN activities. However, it must be remembered that most of these programs overlapped. Consequently, there are chronological overlaps in the book. Focusing on the subject matter is the best way to organize ACEN's role in American Cold War politics, or political warfare, since it allows explanations to be grounded in a precise regional or topical context.

The complete story of the Free Europe Committee's operations within the Department of State-CIA framework still awaits its historian.[9] In recent years important works have been published that constitute important contributions to the wide array of FEC activities. In the area of radio broadcasts, the best account to this day was published by A. Ross Johnson, *Radio Free Europe and Radio Lib-*

---

9 The first attempt was undertaken in 1973. The project was discontinued due to author's premature death. Larry D. Collins, "The Free Europe Committee. An American Weapon of the Cold War," Dissertation Presented to the Faculty of the Department of Political Science, Carleton University, November 1973. For a recent attempt see the dissertation by a Czech scholar: Pavel Paleček, "Protikomunistická propaganda ve studené válce. Výbor pro svobodnou Evropu a exil", PhD Dissertation (manuscript), Brno: Masaryk University 2010. See also: Mazurkiewicz, *Uchodźcy* ..., 179–181.

erty. The CIA Years and Beyond (Washington D.C.: Woodrow Wilson Center Press and Stanford, CA: Stanford University Press, 2010). In the area of exile relations the most comprehensive account which also encompasses the survey of the history of the National Committee for a Free Europe was published under an all-telling title: *The Inauguration of Organized Political Warfare: Cold War Organizations Sponsored by the National Committee for a Free Europe/Free Europe Committee*, ed. Katalin Kádár Lynn (New York–Budapest: Helena History Press, CEU-Press, 2013). The volume contains texts about Romanian, Czechoslovak, Baltic, Polish, Hungarian and Bulgarian national committees, as well as chapters about the ACEN, Free Europe's University in Exile, and even the Hungarian National Sports Federation. These organizations were among some 60 others which were supported, and sometimes even established with the help of the FEC. While that volume does not carry a chapter on the American-sponsored Radio Free Europe, this is a deliberate choice made by the editor, in order to direct scholarly attention to the non-radio activities of the FEC, as the RFE continues to be the most widely researched area of the FEC's operations.[10] Alfred Reisch's account of the book distribution project to countries behind the Iron Curtain, partially administered by the FEC, together with Veronika Durin-Hornyik's account of the Free Europe University in Exile, and Piotr H. Kosicki's interest in the FEC's support of the Christian Democrats in exile, further expand our knowledge about the many programs that the Free Europe Committee administered.[11]

While this book does not seek to examine the role of the FEC in the Cold War it is an attempt to examine one of the FEC-sponsored projects to investigate the role of political exiles in the U.S. Cold War politics. Most of its focus is therefore

---

10 The history of radio's role has been written many times already, as it was surely the most extensive, the most effective and the most expensive programs that the FEC initiated in the early 1950s, and which survive to this day (now operating from Prague). In the text, I commonly refer to Johnson, *Radio Free Europe ...*, and Arch Puddington, *Broadcasting Freedom: The Cold War Triumph of Radio Free Europe and Radio Liberty* (Lexington: The University Press of Kentucky, 2015).

11 Alfred Reisch, *Hot Books in the Cold War. The CIA-Founded Secret Western Book Distribution Program Behind the Iron Curtain* (Budapest-New York: CEU Press, 2013); Veronika Durin-Hornyik, "Le Collège de 'Europe libre et la préparation de la construction démocratique de l'Europe de l'Est (1948–1958)/The Free Europe University in Exile: Preparing for democracy in Central and Eastern Europe (1948–1958), *Relations internationales* 180/4 (2019): 13–25; Piotr H. Kosicki, "Christian Democracy's Global Cold War," in: Piotr H. Kosicki, Sławomir Łukasiewicz (eds.), *Christian Democracy Across the Iron Curtain: Europe Redefined* (Cham, Switzerland: Palgrave Macmillan, 2018), 221–255. See also Richard H. Cummings, *Radio Free Europe's "Crusade for Freedom": Rallying Americans behind Cold War Broadcasting, 1950–1960* (Jefferson NC, London: McFarland & Company, 2010). The author, a former RFE employee, who authors a most interesting Cold War Radios Blog: https://coldwarradios.blogspot.com/, accessed 15 VII 2020.

on the FEC's Division of Exile Relations. This division of the FEC also underwent various reorganizations which included changes in its name. The Exile Political Organizations were placed under the National Councils Division, which was later renamed the Division of Exile Relations (DER), and subsequently renamed Free Europe Exile Relations (FEER). DER/FEER was responsible for cooperation with national committees and councils as well as for individual exiles employed to carry out specific projects. In time this also meant support for 'meritorious exiles' based on their previous services or status.

By examining selected areas of the ACEN's activities, within the context of its relationship to the FEC, I hope to move a step closer to establishing the nature of this organization. Was it a Cold War "front"? Did it achieve any success as a joint representation of nine East Central European nations? What was the role assigned to it by the Americans? What did it accomplish? This book is an analysis of how the combined U.S.-exile effort countered Soviet propaganda in the free world.

It must be emphasized, however, that looking for a major impact of exile activities may be a missed point of reference. For example, the case of the ACEN can be related to the study of European Catholic politicians in exile in Britain during World War II, as Wolfram Kaiser assessed: "Transnational cooperation in exile had only a marginal effect on the development of both the new Christian Democrat parties and their transnational co-operation and of western Europe after the war. Post-war Europe was not made in exile."[12] Idesbald Goddeeris studying *Nouvelles Ėquipes internationales* (an umbrella organization of European Christian Democratic parties, movement and leaders) concluded that exile opinion-making among Western elites depended on the Western agenda and recognition of their legitimacy in representing their compatriots, thus "playing a second-rate role in a film that was directed by the West."[13] The purpose of this book is to further explain the symbiotic nature of exile relations with their hosts in the West. Yet, while acknowledging the interdependence of multiple entities, I pay special attention to the agency of exiles. Thus, broader questions are also considered, such as: political control by the Americans, examination of peculiar American-exile partnership reaching beyond the formula of proxy organizations, like legitimizing U.S. propaganda efforts, or political support for authentic exile causes, etc.

---

12 Wolfram Kaiser, "Co-operation of European Catholic Politicians in Exile in Britain and the USA during the Second World War," Journal of Contemporary History 35/3 (2000): 465.

13 Idesbald Goddeeris, "Exiles' Strategies for Lobbying in International Organisations: Eastern European Participation in the *Nouvelles Ėquipes Internationales*," *European Review of History – Revue européenne d'Historie* 11/3 (2004): 383–400.

In the wide context of U.S. foreign policy, the book covers the span of four administrations – Eisenhower, Kennedy, Johnson and Nixon. I study the relationship between the FEC – an organization established by the top governmental structures (the Department of State and CIA) to work with the exiles from East Central Europe to advance U.S. strategic goals. American politics are therefore of interest to the extent that the FEC interpreted U.S. policy goals in its relations with the exiles. My primary interest is in the intersection of public diplomacy, soft power, propaganda with the aim of examining a particular partnership that emerged between the American Cold War political/psychological warfare instrument and the multinational political exile organization that claimed legitimacy to represent a hundred million captive compatriots. At a time when no other free world power would consider offering financial and political support to them, the United States offered ways and means for the continuation of their anti-communist opposition activities from abroad.

While a small element of a much larger scheme, the study of the ACEN offers a firm and steady ground for interpretation of exile political operations, for it existed from 1954 to 1972, and then from 1972 to 1989 as ACEN, Inc. Throughout these years it consisted of the representatives of the same nine countries (and to a large extent the same people). Regardless of Cold War policy fluctuations, the members of ACEN maintained their contacts with members of the U.S. Congress, delegates to the United Nations, the Council of Europe, and members of governments of the free world. As an organization of exiled political leaders, not American citizens, the ACEN had to work out common policy opinions and recommendations before submitting them to any outside political body. As such, it is intriguing to look at as an organization – a case of East Central European political cooperation really – rather than as individual exiles, or particular national or ethnic organizations.

The history of the ACEN offers a unique opportunity to look into a variety of fascinating fields. Political scientists would pay attention to the fact that the exile political activity does not really fit with the relations between the governments and political opposition. Instead it cuts across the domains of national and transnational politics. Therefore, finding a theoretical framework for this kind of study already poses a problem.[14] A recent study on the political parties in exile by Sławomir Łukasiewicz further explains the issue;[15] in the absence of

---

14 Yossi Shain, *The Frontier of Loyalty. Political Exiles in the age of a nation state* (Wesleyan University Press, Hanover and London: University Press of New England, 1989). The book's recent edition, see: Ann Arbor: University of Michigan Press, 2005.

15 Sławomir Łukasiewicz, *Partia w warunkach emigracji. Dylematy Polskiego Ruchu Wolnościowego "Niepodległość i Demokracja" 1945–1994* (Lublin-Warsaw: IPN, 2014). For case studies re-

parliamentary elections the exiles cannot validate the legitimacy of their actions in any credible way other than holding on to their pre-departure mandates. For a scholar studying ethnic groups in the U.S., the relationship between the political exiles and the older diaspora must be addressed, but inter- and intra-exile organizational relations must be analyzed. A historian of East Central Europe must also consider the home regimes' responses to the challenge that political exiles represent which is still a developing field in historical research. These are vast fields to work on, and yet, for a Cold War historian the most important aspect would most likely remain that of the impact of the exile political lobby based on the captive nations discourse. For this book, therefore, I decided to examine the exile activities carried out with the assistance of the FEC on a truly global scale. Rather than examining the internal dynamics, organization and ideological struggles within the ACEN, I venture to find out the convergence between the American psychological warfare and the East Central European exiles' political and propaganda activities. Ultimately, I seek to establish what the ACEN was; its role, and whatever political agency of their actions its members retained.

In addition to seminal works on American efforts to weaken the Soviet Bloc with the means short of war – from public diplomacy to covert operations[16] – recent books on American state–private networks provided a much-needed context for my study.[17] The works that could be considered complementary to my

---

lated to other political groups see: Anna Siwik, *Polska Partia Socjalistyczna na emigracji w latach 1945–1956* (Kraków: Księgarnia Akademicka, 1998); Siwik, *Polskie uchodźstwo polityczne: socjaliści na emigracji w latach 1956–1990* (Kraków: Abrys, 2002).

16 Peter Grose, *Operation Rollback. America's Secret War behind the Iron Curtain* (Boston-New York: Houghton Mifflin Company, 2000); Scott Lucas, *Freedom's War. The American Crusade against the Soviet Union* (New York: New York University Press, 1999); Gregory Mitrovich, *Undermining the Kremlin, America's Strategy to subvert the Soviet Bloc 1947–1956* (Ithaca-London: Cornell University Press, 2000); Kenneth Osgood, *Total Cold War. Eisenhower's Secret Propaganda Battle* (Lawrence, KS: University Press of Kansas, 2006).

17 Helen Laville, Hugh Wilford (eds.), *The U.S. Government, Citizen Groups and the Cold War. The state–private network* (London–New York: Routledge, 2006); Frances Stonor Saunders, *The Cultural Cold War: The CIA and the World of Arts and Letters* (The New Press, New York 2001, 2013); Kenneth A. Osgood, Brian C. Etheridge (eds.), *The United States and Public Diplomacy. New Directions in Cultural and International History* (Leiden–Boston: Martinus Nijhoff Publishers, 2010); Jason C. Parker, *Hearts, Minds, Voices. U.S. Cold War Public Diplomacy and the Formation of the Third World* (New York: Oxford University Press, 2016); Giles Scott-Smith, "The Free Europe University in Strasbourg: U.S. State–Private Networks and Academic 'Rollback,'" *Journal of Cold War Studies* 16/2 (2014); Scott-Smith, *Networks of Empire. The U.S. State Department's Foreign Leader Program in the Netherlands, France, and Britain, 1950–70* (Brussels: Peter Lang, 2008); Scott-Smith, *The Politics of Apolitical Culture. The Congress for Cultural Freedom, the CIA and post-war American hegemony* (London–New York: Routledge, 2002); Scott-Smith, "A

project as they discuss the exiles from the USSR are Simo Mikkonen's article on the Soviet exiles, and the recent thorough examination by Benjamin Tromly of Russian émigré milieus and their cooperation with the CIA.[18] While most authors mention ACEN in passing, usually on the margins of studying particular national group in exile, the exile Assembly is often confused with other organizations.

In the last decade, the study of exile political activities gained more interest among scholars on both sides of the Atlantic. Among collaborative scholarly initiatives offering vital context to the study of the ACEN there are four notable volumes edited by: Ieva Zake (2009), Sławomir Łukasiewicz (2010), Katalin Kádár Lynn's (2013), and the team of three editors: Luc Van Dongen, Stéphanie Roulin and Giles Scott-Smith (2014).[19] Few scholars wrote on the ACEN while studying the activities of its prominent members (like Stefan Korboński, Aleksander Warma, or Petr Zenkl).[20] Among the works that devote particular attention to the ACEN is Piotr Stanek's study based mostly on the Feliks Gadomski archive, as well as chapters and extended mentions offered by other East Central European authors.[21] My focus here is different, as I examine the ACEN-FEC partnership based on their institutional archives. Rather than studying the dynamics

Radical Democratic Political Offensive": Melvyn J. Lasky, Der Monat, and the Congress for Cultural Freedom," *Journal of Contemporary History* 35/2 (2000).

18 Simo Mikkonen, Exploiting the Exiles. Soviet Émigrés in U.S. Cold War Strategy," *Journal of Cold War Studies* 14/2 (Spring 2012): 98–127; Benjamin Tromly, *Cold War Exiles and the CIA. Plotting to Free Russia* (Oxford: Oxford University Press, 2019).

19 *Anti-Communist Minorities: The Political Activism of Ethnic Refugees in the United States*, ed. Ieva Zake (New York: Palgrave Macmillan 2009); *Tajny oręż, czy ofiary zimnej wojny. Emigracje polityczne z Europy Środkowo-Wschodniej*, ed. Sławomir Łukasiewicz (Lublin-Warsaw: IPN, 2010); *Inauguration of Organized ...*; *Transnational Anti-Communism and the Cold War. Agents, Activities, and Networks*, ed. Luc Van Dongen, Stéphanie Roulin and Giles Scott-Smith (New York: Palgrave Macmillan, 2014). See also: Mazurkiewicz (ed.), *East Central European Migrations During the Cold War. A Handbook* (Berlin-Boston: De Gruyter, 2019).

20 Stanek, *Stefan Korboński (1901–1989): działalność polityczna i społeczna* (Warsaw: IPN, 2014); Pauli Heikkilä, *Estonians for Europe: national activism for European unification, 1922–1991* (Brussels: Peter Lang, 2014); Paweł Ziętara, *Anders, Korboński, Sieniewicz ... Szkice z dziejów Drugiej Wielkiej Emigracji* (Łomianki: LTW 2016); Martin Nekola, *Petr Zenkl: politik a člověk* (Prague: Mladá Fronta, 2014).

21 Piotr Stanek, "Powstanie i działalność Zgromadzenia Europejskich Narodów Zjednoczonych (ACEN) w świetle Archiwum Feliksa Gadomskiego," *Prace uczestników studium doktoranckiego. Historia* 9 (2007): 69–99; Józef Łaptos, *Europa marzycieli. Wizje i projekty integracyjne środkowoeuropejskiej emigracji politycznej 1940–1956* (Kraków: Wyd. Nauk. Uniw. Pedagogicznego, 2012); Francis D. Raška, *Fighting Communism from Afar: the Council of Free Czechoslovakia* (Boulder, CO: East European Monographs, 2008); Marian Wolański, Thomas Lane, *Poland and European Integration. The Ideas and Movements of Polish Exiles in the West, 1939–91* (London: Palgrave Macmillan, 2009).

of exile negotiations on a given issue of the Cold War (within, or beyond the national narratives), I look at the ACEN as a global actor in the American struggle for hearts and minds.

Thus far, there was no academic monograph on the ACEN. However, there are a few notable works written by the exiles, and participants or witnesses of the Assembly's operations. Among these I found especially useful were books by Feliks Gadomski, Stefan Korboński,[22] and articles by Miron Butariu and John F. Leich.[23] The memoirs of Aurel Sergiu Marinescu, while overwhelming in size, proved of little value to my research.[24] One other type of publication related to ACEN should be mentioned here – the accounts of exile activities published in the Soviet-dominated countries with the clear purpose of discrediting the members of the ACEN.[25] There were also studies for the use of the communist authorities which are useful in looking at the reception of exile political activities behind the Iron Curtain.[26]

Over the last ten years I have published a number of case studies regarding the ACEN.[27] Since they have been published in English, and relate to the earlier

---

22 Feliks Gadomski, *Zgromadzenie Europejskich Narodów Ujarzmionych. Krótki zarys* (New York: Bicentennial Publishing Corporation-Nowy Dziennik, 1995); Stefan Korboński, *W imieniu Polski walczącej* (Warsaw: Rytm, 1999). In English: *Warsaw in exile* (London: Allen & Unwin, 1966).

23 Miron Butariu, "Assembly of Captive European Nations. The Little United Nations – The Voice of the People," *Journal of the American Romanian Academy of Arts and Sciences* 10 (1987); John F. Leich, "Great Expectations: The National Councils in Exile 1950–1960," *Polish Review* 35 (1990): 183–196.

24 Anca Cristina Irmia and Anna Mazurkiewicz, Review of: Aurel Sergiu Marinescu, *O contributie la istoria exilului românesc: Activități în exil: ANEC și PNL*, (Bucharest: Vremea, 2005), *Studia Historica Gednanensia* 8 (2017): 348–353.

25 Vilhelms Munters, *The own peoples' enemies* (Riga: Zvaigzne, 1965); Edward Prus, *Pannacjonalizm. Polityczna działalność emigracyjna byłych kolaboracjonistów z Europy wschodniej i południowo-wschodniej* (Katowice: Śląski Instytut Naukowy, 1976).

26 Krzysztof Kolęda, ACEN jako ogniwo systemu wojny psychologicznej Stanów Zjednoczonych [for internal use only] (Warsaw: Ośrodek Badania Stosunków Wschód-Zachód, 1972); *Polska emigracja polityczna. Informator*, reprint (Warsaw: Aduitor, 2004).

27 Mazurkiewicz, "Assembly of Captive European Nations: 'The Voice of the Silenced Peoples,'" in: *Anti-Communist Minorities* ..., 167–185; Mazurkiewicz, "'Niejawna ingerencja rządu w swobodną wymianę poglądów' – Zgromadzenie Europejskich Narodów Ujarzmionych w zimnowojennej polityce USA," in: *Tajny oręż* ..., 255–263; Mazurkiewicz, "The Schism within the Polish Delegation to the Assembly of Captive European Nations 1954–1972" in: *The Polish Diaspora in America and the Wider World*, eds. Adam Walaszek, Janusz Pezda, (Kraków: Polish Academy of Arts and Sciences, 2012), 73–110; Mazurkiewicz, "'Join, or Die' – The Road to Cooperation Among East European Exiled Political Leaders in the United States, 1949–1954," *Polish American Studies* 69/2 (2012): 5–43; Mazurkiewicz, "The Relationship Between the Assembly of Captive European Nations and the Free Europe Committee in the Context of U.S. Foreign Policy

period, or mostly to the Polish delegation, I have decided not to repeat those findings here. The two themes about which I published on earlier – on the Strasbourg sessions (in French) and Captive Nations Week (in Polish) – are used here because they precisely fit the scope of this book: the global Cold War.[28] Both articles were updated by new research and re-focused to consider the ACEN's global struggle.

For any scholar seeking to uncover ACEN's effectiveness and the agency of its members, a few traps await. First, there were several exile organizations from many more than just the nine principal countries, and the ACEN was often confused with them (most notably the National Captive Nations Committee headed by Dr. Lev Dobriansky). Second, it is extremely difficult to separate ACEN members' initiatives and actions from the FEC's role – whether by inspiration or control. Finally, the ACEN was often only one of the forums in which the individual exiles carried out their activities. Some were active within ethnic groups, others worked within party internationals, and yet others (usually those with a respectable standing among the American political and diplomatic elites) preferred to act solo on most occasions.

The ACEN papers are available at the Immigration History Research Center at the University of Minnesota. I examined the entire collection (2007–2008) only to realize that it was just the beginning. While a gold mine for ACEN documentation of its activities, with regard to the ACEN's relationship to the FEC the archival collection at the IHRC seemed sanitized. Not many documents related to ACEN-FEC policy discussions remain there. Most of these are stored in the repository of the sponsoring organization – the Free Europe Committee. To call this collection enormous is an understatement. The FEC files consist of broadcast-related materials and the corporate records. The bulk of these files are at the Hoover Institution Archives (with some parts, like the RFE Research Institute, deposited with Open Society Archive in Budapest). For the ACEN story, the key collection was the administrative files of the FEC, located within the Corporate

1950–1960," in: *The Inauguration of Organized ...*, 397–437; Mazurkiewicz, "'The Little U.N.' at 769 First Avenue, New York (1956–1963)," in: *East Central Europe in Exile*. vol. 2: *Transatlantic Identities* (Cambridge-upon-Tyne: Cambridge Scholars Publishing, 2013), 227–245; Mazurkiewicz, "Decisive Factors in the Selection of Place of Residence within the United States by the Post-World War II Political Émigrés from East Central Europe," in: *The United States Immigration Policy and Immigrants' Responses: Past and Present*, ed. A. Małek, D. Praszałowicz (Peter Lang Edition: Frankfurt am Main 2017), 149–167; Mazurkiewicz, "Stosunek emigracji środkowoeuropejskich zrzeszonych w Zgromadzeniu Europejskich Narodów Ujarzmionych (ACEN) do konferencji jałtańskiej" in: *Jałta – rzeczywistość, mit i pamięć*, ed. Sławomir Łukasiewicz (Warsaw: IPN, 2019), 248–270.

28 See chapters: 2 and 5.2 in this volume.

Records. As I have consulted this not entirely processed collection over the years (in 2008, and in 2017–2018), it should be noted that some designations used in my references might have changed. As of 2018 there were at least three sub-collections that contained relevant information: the alphabetical file (most commonly used by scholars, and fully organized with an updated guide), the historical file (in which the box numbers are often temporary), and the FEC, Inc. collection (which is still being processed). These contain documents created mostly by the FEC staff, with several EC (Executive Committee) memoranda, which enable scholars to look into the CIA's role. As Ross Johnson explained: "The FEC correspondence used pseudonyms before 1959, and thereafter was conducted between the 'President' of the Free Europe Committee and the 'Executive Committee' [not to be confused with the FEC directors' own executive committee], i.e., the CIA. References to 'Advisory Council' in this correspondence mean the Department of State."[29]

Looking into the role of the Agency, I conducted research at the CREST database at the National Archives in Washington in 2009. Since then, many of the files have been made available through the CIA FOIA (Freedom of Information Act) electronic reading room. Whenever this is the case, the CIA-RDP number listed in the footnotes will take the reader to the actual document using this website: https://www.cia.gov/library/readingroom/home. Within this collection few documents related to the ACEN are found. Since the ACEN's quarterly reports are not at Hoover, I filed a request with the CIA for their release in 2010, then appealed the CIA's denial of my Mandatory Declassification Request to the Interagency Security Classification Appeals Panel. While the status of my request at the appeals log reads: "materials received from the Agency," I am still awaiting their decision as this book goes to press.

The other crucial collection related to the activities of the FEC-ACEN duo is the Record Group 59 at the National Archives at College Park (Maryland) – the Department of State. In addition to my own archival queries, I am indebted to Christopher Simpson for sharing with me part of the declassified collection of Department of State files which he had obtained. In the text, I refer to these files as: Christopher Simpson Collection. Among the most important collections were also the C.D. Jackson Papers and C.D. Jackson Records at the Dwight D. Eisenhower Presidential Library in Abilene (Kansas). I have also examined relevant collections at the Open Society Archives in Budapest. Other archival collections used in this publication include the personal papers of individual exiles

---

29 Johnson, *Radio Free Europe ...*, 17, n. 31.

and their organizations (mostly at Hoover Institution Archives), interviews, published memoirs, exile periodicals and U.S. press.

Ideally, materials of all institutions, organizations, or individual opinion leaders working with ACEN should be examined. Moreover, more national and regional archives in East Central Europe should have been included. This would have required a different approach, incorporating archival research on a global scope. Second, the activities of the most active ACEN leaders – men like Pál (Paul) Auer, Stefan Korboński and Edmund Gaspar – as well as the Americans, such as Christopher Emmet, Lewis Galantière, or even C.D. Jackson, cannot be fully analyzed and appraised without a thorough examination of their links to U.S. intelligence. While I have examined a number of the personal papers of some of the men listed above, too many questions relating to their activities still remain unanswered. Books published thus far, with regards to their roles within the FEC, and in relation to the exile operations (especially Galantière or C.D. Jackson)[30] are not revealing. Exile memoirs offer another set of problems relating to their questionable objectivity, nationalistic bias and lack of archival base to support their claims. Where possible, these were used to cite their opinions, with their own accounts appropriately marked.

Furthermore, while there are reasons to pay special attention to the Poles in ACEN, since the Polish exiles not only represented the largest country of the region, were the largest diaspora in the U.S., had double representation in the ACEN, and maintained links to the Polish political exiles in London, I understand that my own background might have influenced the narrative. Mindful of my own bias, I have tried to surpass it by focusing on the Assembly – examining joint initiatives, representations, actions, statements, etc., rather than on opinions and actions underwritten by a specific national council or committee. The same applies to the relationship with the FEC. The only departure from this approach that I decided to make is the preface and the epilogue which were tinted with personal comments regarding Stefan Korboński.

For the sake of maintaining clarity in the argument and keeping the story concise I have decided to leave out material pertaining to two areas that are nevertheless worthy of further examination. One is the ACEN's political and ideological world outlook coined in the course of internal discussions within the Assembly, as well as within its member organizations. The Cold War through the eyes of this particular regional assembly, dividing and uniting moments in the near

---

30 John Allen Stern, *C.D. Jackson. Cold War Propagandist for Democracy and Globalism* (Lanham-Boulder-New York-Toronto-Plymouth, UK: University Press of America, Inc., 2012); Mark I. Lurie, *Galantière. The Lost Generation's Forgotten Man* (West Palm Beach, FL: Overlook Press LLC, 2017).

twenty-year-long exile political cooperation, deserves a separate volume focusing on the internal dynamics of this organization. Such a study awaits a researcher willing to reconstruct the political thought developed in exile by the people who – had it not been for the communist takeover – would most likely have had an impact on the policy of the region.

The other portion of the archival material left out at this time relates to the Communists' reaction to the ACEN activities – both public and clandestine. First, this is due to the fact that access to relevant materials in security archives in the multiple countries of the region is largely conditional upon a knowledge of the languages of the region. Second, the collections I examined at the Polish IPN and Hungarian ABTL (Állambiztonsági Szolgálatok Történeti Levéltára, Budapest) suggest that the communist regimes focused their resources on disrupting and discrediting the members of respective political diasporas in the West, neglecting the ACEN as an organization worthy of their special attention. We now know that there were communist agents planted within the exile national and party organizations, but at this time it is impossible for me to confirm if and to what extent their operations may have affected the works of the Assembly. Third, as far as I could establish, the impact of ACEN activities behind the Iron Curtain was negligible. Most of its operations targeted audiences in the free world, advancing the agenda agreed with the Americans.

In the chapters that follow I highlight the successes and failures of the ACEN delegates' contacts with political and public opinion leaders in the free world. Whenever Moscow reacted to ACEN actions, I note such responses. Each of the chapters in this book aims at presenting a different scope, forum, scope and region of ACEN's activities. The first chapter focuses on presenting the organization of the exile assembly as well as on its connections with the FEC. It therefore shows the aims and forms of exile operations as well as attempts at locating the ACEN within the American Cold War psychological warfare and propaganda network. The first chapter explains the symbiotic relationship between the ACEN and the FEC that originated in 1954 and introduces both bodies. The chapter concludes with a brief description of two organizations that assisted the ACEN in its efforts to reach the American public: the Conference of Americans of Central and East European Descent and the American Friends of Captive Nations.

The second chapter locates the ACEN within the transatlantic context and relates its activities to European integration. The ACEN's own presence in Europe is referred to as a regional forum foreshadowing East Central Europe's ambitions, or rather, demanding attention be focused on the enslaved part of the continent. This chapter explains the early ACEN's impact on the discussions held within the Consultative Assembly of the Council of Europe and concludes with the phasing out of the ACEN's political presence in Europe due to political differences with its American sponsors.

The third chapter discusses the ACEN's lobbying efforts midway through 1956 by examining exiles' mobilization of all the available tools and its allies in response to the workers' rebellion in Poznań in June 1956. The ACEN's effort to put political pressure on Warsaw deserves examination because it was a forerunner to the major information campaign following the Hungarian Revolution of October 1956. The diverse activities undertaken by the ACEN over many years in response to the Hungarian Revolution are described mostly in chapter four. While the Polish June is not comparable to the Hungarian Revolution when it comes to the scale and nature of the protest, the character of the Soviet reaction or its consequences, it serves here as a model to highlight the development of lobbying methods employed by the ACEN.

The fourth chapter focuses on ACEN activities in the UN. The United Nations Organization should be considered the most important forum for the ACEN's activities. It was here that the East Central European refugees invested their hopes for drawing the attention of the world, and taking concrete action. It was in the summer and autumn of 1956 that they developed their ally networks, which in subsequent years were used to lobby for the subjugated. The ACEN's actions undertaken with regard to Hungary constituted the single most important operation that the exile assembly conducted on a global scale. A complete picture of all exile initiatives undertaken in this regard should include the many actions of Hungarian exile organizations carried out in cooperation with the ACEN, as well as recent research on the role of Free Europe (Radio and Press divisions). The current book could not possibly contain the entire scope of ACEN's activities in relation to the Hungarian Revolution, and such is not its aim. The purpose of this chapter is to show the mechanisms and lobbying tools used by the ACEN in the UN.

The fifth chapter places ACEN within a larger Cold War discourse. More precisely, it examines the ACEN's role within a U.S. domestic captive nations propaganda/political agenda. As the ACEN never had the means and manpower to attract support among larger sections of American public opinion, it used its allies in the U.S. Congress, as well as friendly organizations, to advance its political agenda. Despite changes in American foreign policy, the ACEN was able to maintain an almost autonomous network of political alliances in the U.S. and could count on public endorsement and support of prominent politicians.

The sixth chapter examines the ACEN's cooperation with non-FEC, and non-U.S. controlled anti-Communist movements, and shifts attention to South-East Asia. ACEN's allies in Taiwan, South Vietnam, South Korea and the Philippines, while not in-exile, formed strong anti-Communist bonds with the East Central

Europeans. Inspired by their operations, the ACEN joined in the celebrations of Asian Peoples Freedom Day and assisted in promotion of the Asian anti-Communist agenda in the United States.

The seventh chapter focuses on the ACEN's work through its regional offices in Latin America. This was part of a larger American effort to reach nations in the developing world. The East Central European exiles were able to establish a network of delegations throughout the continent and undertake a number of public initiatives that met American goals. At the same time, they aimed at rallying support for their own cause in the UN.

The last chapter examines the FEC's relationship with the ACEN in the 1960s – in the face of political, financial and personal crises both at the FEC and ACEN. This part of the book explains when and why the exiles fell out of their previously friendly partnership with their American sponsors and lost their autonomy. The questions regarding exile agency, the ACEN's role and its impact are addressed in the conclusion, while the epilogue describes the transition of the ACEN from a government-supported organization to an independent one.

In the Appendices, the reader will find ACEN's founding documents and a list of ACEN publications issued before the budgetary cuts hampered the programs. Also, for the first time, complete lists of ACEN members and regional delegates from 1954 to 1972 are being published in the form of tables. These sets of data collected from ACEN materials (printed and archival lists of delegates, committee members) were prepared with multiple purposes in mind. First, they demonstrate who was truly active in the ACEN and did not just have their names entered on its roster. This was determined in two ways: by indicating the leaders of national delegations who were entitled to a seat on the ACEN's General Committee, and by indicating who served on one of the ACEN committees. Second, the tables are useful to verify the professional profile of émigrés involved in political activities carried out under the ACEN banner. Third, they serve as an invitation for diaspora scholars to develop a joint project on activities of the émigrés who were active in the ACEN – most likely as one of the many organizations and venues of political operations while in exile. Such a project should include new archival material and publications available in national languages, scattered across both the European and American continents. The information provided in the tables represents the state of knowledge at the time of the ACEN's operations (1954–1972) and was not edited to represent the current state of research on listed individuals. Based on FEC documentation,[31] I added to the

31 Post termination assistance stipendiaries, account 1200, HIA, RFE/RL CF: A, b. 199, f.2; Exile Political Organization Stipendiaries, ibid.

names of the delegates the sums received from the FEC in the form of stipends, as of January 1963, as well as annual salaries received for their work within either the national delegations (council/committee members), paid staff of the committees and of the ACEN, as well as payments to meritorious exiles.[32] These tables constitute a first step of researching the internal activities of the Assembly and should be verified as to accuracy of information provided, as well as to the actual terms of service in the ACEN.

Throughout the book I use East Central Europe to describe the region that the ACEN-associated exiles represented. I decided to adopt it even though Eastern Europe was the term commonly used at the time by Western diplomats, politicians, journalists, and often by the Free Europe Committee as well. Yet, so-called Eastern Europe was an artificial and temporary creation, the existence of which had been continuously questioned by its exiles since the late 1940s – that is since it was coined. Even in the context of the Cold War, calling this area "Eastern Europe" blurs the picture and obscures the complex political nuances involved. It furthermore belittles the efforts of the exiles and denies them agency in the Cold War confrontation. Throughout, their European self-identification included the word *Central.* Thus, the political exiles negotiated their regional identification within the context of American policy. The stunning consequence was that all the exiles cooperating with the FEC (and those that did not) used Central Eastern Europe or East Central Europe in their internal memorandums and correspondence, as well as public releases, proving that this was not a coincidence. Examination of the names of the regional political organizations created in exile further confirms this point.[33] Does this ultimately matter? Yes, for these terms were introduced in the forums to which the exiles gained access, namely the U.S. Congress, the UN, and the Council of Europe. With the word "central" comes the issue of agency, and East Central Europe becomes a subject on the international agenda as an entity separate from the "east," or the "bloc."

---

32 Exhibit IV: Council Members, Exhibit VI: Present Staff Members of Exile Organizations, Exhibit VII: List of Meritorious Exiles (34), all exhibits: 21 III 1960, attached to: Free Europe Organizations and Publications, Reorientation of Exile Organizations, 1 IV 1960, HIA, RFE/RL CF: A, b. 197, f. 8.

33 Socialist Union of Central Eastern Europe; Christian Democratic Union of Central Europe; Liberal Democratic Union of Central Eastern Europe; Central Eastern European Committee; Central Eastern European Conference; International Federation of Free Journalists of Central and Eastern Europe and Baltic and Balkan Countries/from Central and Eastern Europe; Federation of Christian Trade Unions of Central and Eastern Europe or Central European Federation of Christian Trade Unions in Exile, and more.

This book is the result of thirteen years of archival queries, conference and seminar discussions, numerous consultations with scholars specializing in post-war political migration, Cold War political warfare, as well as engagement with historical witnesses – people who took part, or observed ACEN in action. My gratitude goes to them first, for archival resources can only take a scholar born in the mid-1970s so far. I had the privilege of discussing my preliminary findings with, and obtaining additional information from John F. Leich (1920–2016), Ralph Walter (1924–2013), János Horváth (1921–2019) and Zofia Korbońska (1915–2010). They will forever remain in my most affectionate memory. Witnesses who knew or worked with ACEN members: Stanisław Gebhardt, Jadwiga Gadomska, and Roman W. Rybicki all agreed to share their recollections with me.

I would like to thank the staff of the Immigration History Research Center (Minneapolis): Donna Gabaccia, Daniel Necas, Haven Hawley, Halyna Myroniuk; and the Hoover Institution Archives: Irena Czernichowska, Anatol Shmelev, Maciej Siekierski (Stanford); Magdolna Baráth and Robert Parnica (Budapest) for their suggestions and support. Special thanks go to Christopher Simpson who shared his archival collections with me regarding ACEN. I am also indebted to my translators (Teresa and Zdzisław Rymarz, Marcjanna Mazurkiewicz, Mirjam Molnar, Duong Trinh), Peter Simon, and students at the Valdosta State University: Adavia Elow, Jerome Joynes-Walker, Keyana Howard and Sophia S. Tanner, who transcribed the ACEN texts used in the Appendices.

I remain indebted to my esteemed colleagues for their inspiration, advice and constructive criticism: Józef Łaptos, Katalin Kádár Lynn, Sławomir Łukasiewicz, Piotr H. Kosicki, Francis D. Raška, Piotr Stanek, Joanna Wojdon, Marius Petraru and Paweł Ziętara. A. Ross Johnson, whose expertise is a combination of experience of his service at the RFE (policy assistant for Poland, 1966–1969, RFE director, 1988–1991) and academic research in the history of FEC, offered invaluable advice and support along the way, eventually kindly agreeing to comment on this manuscript. I could not wish for a better finale to the tedious process of piecing together the ACEN-FEC story.

Last but not least, I would like to thank the Kościuszko Foundation, the Polish-American Fulbright Commission, the Foundation for Polish Science, the University of Gdańsk and the Visegrad Fund for their support which made my extensive archival queries possible.

1 "For Europe Whole and Free" – ACEN Within the Organizational Framework

After the conclusion of World War II, many East Central European political exiles escaping Communist persecution found asylum in Western Europe and in the United States. In America, their presence was noticeable mostly in New York and Washington. The choice was not accidental for they wanted to continue their struggles against Soviet domination seeking help from both the United States and the United Nations. Although the exiles were quick to organize themselves into national committees or councils clustered around former prime ministers, diplomats, members of parliaments, and political party leaders their organizations were often marred by conflict. As they strove to retain their political integrity, hoping to return home one day, they found it difficult to reconcile with former political opponents. On the other hand, the legitimacy given to them before, or right after World War II, by the people in their respective countries gave them the sense of a mission to represent "the silenced peoples" in the free world. The Americans recognized them as exiled political elites of the states subjugated by the Soviets – representatives of the so-called captive nations.

The ACEN was an umbrella organization for particular groups of post-World War II émigrés – the anti-communist political exiles from East Central Europe who arrived in the U.S. in the second half of the 1940s and sought American support for their political agenda related to their homelands. Former members of post-Yalta parliaments (1945–1948), former diplomats, as well as pre-war party leaders with a clear majority of agrarians settled in the U.S. with the intention of continuing their political activities in the face of Soviet domination in East Central Europe. This group was as diverse as the pre-war and wartime experiences of their respective nations. The common features of political leaders in exile included, inter alia: high status in the country of origin (based on public office, political or professional positions, economic independence), shared initial beliefs that their exile would be temporary, a desire to continue their national political activities from abroad.[1]

As they realized that their return home was not imminent, their engagement took two paths: planning for the post-liberation period (a future federation, regional cooperation, integration with the West, etc.) or focusing on current polit-

1 Elizabeth K. Valkanier, "Eastern Europe in Exile," *Annals of the American Academy of Political and Social Science* 317 (May 1958), 146–152. See also: Mazurkiewicz, "Unwilling Immigrants ...," 159–171.

https://doi.org/10.1515/9783110661002-005

ical events (through public commentaries and publications, intelligence reports, policy recommendations) striving to keep East Central Europe on the agenda of international relations. The latter prevailed. Already by the early 1950s, the East Central European exiles gravitated toward an umbrella organization (United National Committees and Councils in Exile) attempting to strengthen their lobbying power. This was a forerunner to the establishment of the ACEN. From 1951 to 1954 the exiles negotiated among themselves and with their hosts (the FEC) the framework for cooperation.[2]

1.1 Assembly of Captive European Nations

The official inauguration of ACEN operations took place on 20 September 1954 in New York. During its first meeting the members "representing the peoples" of Albania, Bulgaria, Czechoslovakia, Estonia, Hungary, Latvia, Lithuania, Poland and Romania "determined to uphold, serve, and further the rightful aspirations to freedom, national independence, and social justice" adopted its aims and principles. Pledging cooperation based on the principles of equality and solidarity, all members agreed to work towards the liberation of "all captive nations of Central and Eastern Europe" until the "restoration of national independence and of the right to determine freely, through democratic processes the political, social, and economic forms of governments" would occur in their homelands. In the Charter, the exile assembly declared it would "confine itself to the advocacy of the basic democratic principles" and its actions were to be limited to "studies and recommendations, refraining from any commitments which only their respective peoples, through their freely elected governments will have the authority to assume."[3]

The ACEN's agreed agenda included cooperation with the United Nations which included lobbying for legitimate (that is, non-communist) representation of the captive peoples, "effective and universal implementation of the purposes and principles of the United Nations Charter," as well as providing "all available information concerning conditions in our respective countries that in any way

2 Mazurkiewicz, "'Join, or Die'", 5–43.

3 For the full text of the Charter of ACEN, see: Annex. ACEN Doc. No. 49 (Gen.) unanimously adopted in the 17th meeting of the Plenary Assembly on September 28, 1955, and, subsequently, amended in the 42nd meeting of the Plenary Assembly, on November 30, 1956, as well as in the 57th meeting of the Plenary Assembly, on September 23, 1958; Charter and Rules of Procedure of the Assembly of Captive European Nations, 1955, IHRC, ACEN, b. 1, f. 2; Charter and Rules of Procedure of the Assembly of Captive European Nations (ACEN: London, 1962).

run counter to the aims and principles of the United Nations." Similar statements were related to the Council of Europe and the European Movement, with the additional aim of "preparing the way for the integration of these nations to a United Europe, following their liberation." The ACEN also wished to attract attention to the data it would aggregate on "Communist rule, policies, tactics, and strategy," and garner support for its agenda of governments as well as private institutions, political, social, religious, cultural, and professional organizations and individuals of the free world.

In addition to the operations in the free world, the ACEN had two more arenas of active concern: one focused on their captive compatriots, the other on fellow political exiles and Cold War refugees in general. The first area of activity included both contemporary efforts at "sustaining their morals and of strengthening their will to resist and oppose communist dictatorship and alien control and dominations" as well as preparations for the future "democratic reconstruction" of their homelands by preserving cultural, and political heritage. In terms of operations, those regarding émigré unity and co-operation were key to laying "the solid foundation for future co-operation" in liberated Europe. The ACEN also pledged a joint effort to assist Cold War "democratic refugees." All ACEN members professed their commitment to the following: "[A]dherence to the principle of government of the people, by the people, and for the people; and to the principle of the rule of law, with full respect for human rights and fundamental freedoms, are and shall remain basic qualifications for all Members."[4] These aims united the political exiles under the umbrella of the ACEN, which they all hoped would give their combined voices more power to "promote the common rights and interest" of peoples "now enslaved under alien domination, and unable to speak for themselves."[5]

In its formal structure the organization of the ACEN bore a resemblance to the United Nations. It comprised a Plenary Assembly, Secretariat and working committees.[6] An elaborate formal structure was designed to present the Assembly of Captive European Nations as a true, democratic representative of East Central European nations.

The ACEN's membership consisted of three forms. The first, essential to the assembly's *raison d'être*, comprised national delegations formed by political exiles from nine "captive nations." Nine national councils, or committees, estab-

4 ACEN Charter.

5 ACEN Charter. Mazurkiewicz, "Assembly of Captive European Nations ...," in: *Anti-Communist Minorities* ..., 167–185.

6 Originally there were six working committees: Political, Social, Cultural, Economic, Legal, and Information.

lished in exile, were headquartered in the United States,[7] and retained full membership rights, which meant one vote per national delegation. Each national delegation to the ACEN consisted of 16 members selected by national committees/councils.

Exiles from the six "Yalta countries" were considered for support by the American sponsors of the ACEN. In addition to these, representatives of three committees formed by exiles from the Baltic States (Estonia, Latvia and Lithuania) were also included in the ACEN membership. Although the Kremlin turned them into Soviet republics, the U.S. government never recognized their annexation.[8] No other Communist-dominated countries, nor peoples in Europe (neither Yugoslavia, The German Democratic Republic, nor any other Soviet republics) were represented in the ACEN.

In a 1953 letter to C.D. Jackson (the psychological warfare expert), George F. Kennan, a diplomat and a mastermind behind establishment of the FEC, explained his reasoning behind the preferential treatment of some anti-communist exile groups in the context of American foreign policy. With regard to the Ukraine he wrote that the American policy towards the "minorities" within the Soviet Union should be treated with the utmost caution. Advocating any changes in the status quo was "against nature and logic."

> While anti-Soviet feeling is probably sharper in the Ukraine and other minority areas than it is in the area populated by the Great Russians, I know of no adequate evidence that there is any extensive aspiration for independence in the Soviet Ukraine proper, and I think there is very good reason to doubt that an independent Ukraine would be a feasible and practical proposition, even though that desire might be present. For us to sponsor it would inevitably place us in a position of opposition to the dominant political force in the entire traditional Russian area, namely the Great Russian people themselves. It would confront the latter with the necessity of rallying around the Soviet Government or facing the breakup of the traditional Russian state.
>
> The establishment and maintenance of an independent Ukraine could be carried through only by the use of force. The Ukrainians themselves would not have sufficient power for this purpose and we would find ourselves hooked to an awkward and impossible position as the guarantors of Ukrainian independence against the stronger and more powerful Great Russians – a task for which I feel that our own resources would surely be inadequate and which would certainly not be worth the sacrifices involved.
>
> As for the minorities outside the old 1938 borders, I would simply say the following. We are safe, I think, in standing for the independence of Estonia and Latvia, although we should make it clear that we are not in a position to win or defend that independence for them by force of arms. What I mean to say is simply that the position of the U.S. Govern-

7 Mazurkiewicz, "Decisive Factors ...," 149–167.

8 Mazurkiewicz, *Uchodźcy* ..., 320.

> ment should consistently be one in favor of the independence of these peoples, on the grounds that they demonstrated earlier their capacity to meet the responsibilities of independence. About the Lithuanians I am more doubtful, and think that should be the subject of a special study. [9]

Kennan did not have much sympathy for Slovak aspirations either, as – just like the Ukrainians – "they have much charm and much passion, but little political substance." Slovakia would "hardly be a viable entity economically, and her independence like that of Ukraine would certainly have to be defended by force of arms by some outside power."[10] Not surprisingly, the American concepts for the future of the region envisioned a unified Czechoslovak state. For Kennan, the key countries in the region (deserving of American support) were the Germans, Russians, Poles and Czechs. For the rest, he favored some form of a "Danubian Federation grouped around Vienna."[11]

In a letter cited above, Kennan, the leading architect of the early American Cold War programs, wrote to Eisenhower's chief aide: "I am extremely skeptical about the wisdom of getting ourselves hooked to the ambitions of noisy, immature, and extremist exile figures who announce themselves as 'national' leaders of various linguistic groups in eastern Europe, and whose stock in trade is to attempt the U.S. Government to a line of policy that will favor their ambitions."[12]

The letter sent a year before ACEN was established helps us to understand the American reasoning behind choosing the ACEN nine. As I have explained elsewhere, the American understanding was that the countries that were independent in 1939 were to be included in the "East European" exile support programs (that is, taken care of by the Free Europe Committee), while the larger and older Ukrainian or Russian anti-Communist political diaspora were considered for programs designed for the USSR (like AMCOMLIB and Radio Liberty).

While the ACEN members cooperating with the FEC accepted the principle of not pushing for the inclusion of Ukraine into their programs, they did occasionally cooperate with the Ukrainian Congress of America and invited representatives of the Ukrainian political diaspora to their conferences, and public events. At times, friction was hard to avoid, since the Ukrainians objected to their "guest" status. On one occasion the news broke that the Ukrainians had walked out of the ACEN conference in protest at the map displayed in the meeting hall

9 George F. Kennan (The Institute for Advanced Study, Princeton NJ) to C.D. Jackson, 15 IX 1953, C.D. Jackson Records, b. 4, f. Kennan, George.

10 Ibid.

11 Ibid.

12 Ibid.

which featured captive nations without indicating Ukraine. True, in most materials distributed to the media, the East Central European exiles did not list Ukraine, or the Byelorussian, or Moldavian Soviet Socialist Republics. The exception made for the Balts confirmed the Assembly's composition being one that was compatible with U.S. foreign policy.

A separate problem was that of Yugoslavia. Following Tito's expulsion from Cominform, for two years the Americans working with the political exiles from this country were clearly confused as to what their relations should be. In 1949, when FEC was created, Croat, Serbian and Slovene peasant party leaders were supported, the king in exile was consulted, and the process of creating the Yugoslav freedom committee and radio broadcasts publicly announced.[13] Eventually, by 1951, the FEC internal memoranda confirm that the creation of a Yugoslav committee was "prevented" due to the peculiar position of Yugoslavia on the international stage and the nationalistic agendas of various political groups in exile. This does not mean that the financial support for select Yugoslav exiles was terminated. Even the king – Peter II Karadziordzieviċ – received "heavy subsidies," as indicated in a letter from McCargar to Leich, albeit not through FEC.[14] Although, in early planning for the creation of the ACEN, the multinational assembly included delegates of the national associations of Yugoslavia, because of the FEC's insistence, on 20 September 1954 the ACEN inaugurated its activities with only nine nations represented. The select support for chosen nationals, and the emergence of the East Central European programs tailored to suit American policy goals should not be surprising. After all, as John F. Leich indicated: "the Free Europe Committee did not represent Eastern Europe, it represented the U.S. policy."[15]

Finally, the East Germans were also not listed among the "captives" and were not included in the concept of East Central Europe formulated by both the exile political organizations and the FEC. While it would be incorrect to ig-

13 The Yugoslav committees and exile political organizations (Croat, Serbian, Slovene) routinely appeared in correspondence, at the public meetings and initially (in the early 1950s) closely cooperated with other ECE exiles. When in 1952 the multinational political organization of exiles was established – United National Councils and Committees in Exile the Yugoslavs were members. It was upon the urging of the Free Europe Committee that once UNCEE became the ACEN founded by the U.S. Government). It was at that point the Yugoslavs were excluded. The ACEN delegates tried to protest and lobbied for their inclusion – to no avail. The organization UNCEE – consisting of ten delegations – ceased its activities within a year due to insufficient funding. See Mazurkiewicz, "'Join, or Die'".

14 James McCargar to John F. Leich, 15 I 1989, Leich Papers; Leich to McCargar, 29 I 1989, ibid.; Mazurkiewicz, *Uchodźcy* ..., 267–357.

15 Leich, interview with the Author, Canaan, CT, 6 VII 2009.

nore the German Democratic Republic when describing captive East Central Europe, American policy in Germany constituted a separate policy field for the U.S. government. Also, political emigration streams from the German Democratic Republic overwhelmingly led to the Federal Republic of Germany, where conditions for political operations were quite a different phenomenon.[16] While there was no discussion about including any German émigrés in the organization, in the opinions expressed by the political exiles united in the Assembly of Captive European Nations, Germany's unification constituted one of the key European problems for the émigrés that they believed had to be resolved in conjunction with a general European settlement that would provide for the elimination of Soviet domination of their homelands.

In need of American political and financial support, the East Central European exiles agreed to work within the framework established by the U.S. government with the help of private organizations and individuals. Hence, the full membership in the ACEN included the following émigré entities:

- The National Committee for Free Albania (from 1957: The Free Albania Committee)
- The Bulgarian National Committee
- The Council of Free Czechoslovakia (from 1967: The Committee for The Free Czechoslovakia)
- The Committees for Free Estonia, Latvia and Lithuania
- The Hungarian National Council (from 1958: Hungarian Committee)
- The Romanian National Committee.[17]

Since no single delegation was formed by the Poles, the Polish delegation to the ACEN included two nominating entities: the Polish Council of National Unity in the U.S. (in close connection with the Polish exiles in London) and the Polish National Democratic Committee representing the political group of Stanisław Mikołajczyk (who decided to return to Poland after Yalta, only to escape again in 1947 following rigged elections) and Karol Popiel (who left Poland in 1946).[18]

16 Bethany Hicks, "Germany," in: *East Central European Migrations* ..., 142–146.

17 For a description of national councils and committees see: *The Inauguration of Organized* ...; Mazurkiewicz, *Uchodźcy* ... .

18 During the first session, each group nominated eight delegates with Korboński (Polish Political Council; Polish Council of National Unity, PCNU) and Popiel (PNDC) co-chairing the Polish representation in ACEN, sharing one vote. With the creation of the Polish Council of National Unity in London (1954), Korboński organized its American chapter (chaired by Otton Pehr). By 1955 most of the original members of the PNDC (Mikołajczyk) delegation left for the Korboński group. These were: Stanisław Bańczyk, Stanisław Wójcik, Władysław Zaremba, Bolesław

In addition to the committees/councils formed on a national basis, the ACEN also included an associative category of membership. Thus delegates of five international political organizations became members of the ACEN, sending delegates who did not have the right to vote. Among the party internationals who sent their delegations to the ACEN were: the International Peasant Union (IPU), Socialist Union of Central Eastern Europe (SUCEE), Christian Democratic Union of Central Europe (CDUCE), Liberal Democratic Union of Central Eastern Europe (LDUCEE), and the International Center of Free Trade Unionists in Exile (ICFTUE). In some cases, the same exiles were members of both the national council and the party international, alternating between delegations.

There was also a third type of membership in the ACEN, namely, consultative members. In the Assembly's Charter these were defined as international organizations formed by exiles from Eastern Europe, "for the purpose of defending the rights or voicing the grievances of specific sections or groups of our enslaved people." Among the organizations admitted to the ACEN for consultations were: the Central and Eastern European Federation of Christian Trade Unions (New York), Council of Baltic Women (Washington, New York), Council of European Women in Exile (New York), Council of Free Youth of Central and Eastern Europe (Paris), Humanitas (a union of representatives of the former Red Cross Societies from the "captive nations," with a seat in New York), International Free Academy of Science and Letters (Paris), and Women for Freedom of Europe (New York). Their participation in discussions was limited. They also did not have the right to vote. They did enjoy consultative status in committees established by the ACEN, but, their role was really little more than observer.

Throughout its existence within the framework of the American support extended via FEC (1954–1972) the ACEN maintained membership of national delegations limited to nine captive nations and five party internationals. The ACEN's headquarters were located at 29 W 57th street in New York – an elegant building two blocks from Central Park. Despite the most prestigious address, the

---

Biega, Gadomski and Stanisław Olszewski. Therefore, out of the original members of the PNDC delegations only Karol Popiel and Konrad Sieniewicz remained. Both kept seats in the ACEN but as representatives of the CDUCE, and not on behalf of PNDC as a sign of protest. Mikołajczyk also played a role as a President of IPU. From the third session, the five seats allotted to the PNDC delegates became vacant and remained so until the eighteenth. Even with the passing of Mikołajczyk and migration to Europe by Popiel, as the PNDC ceased its operations, the Polish delegation to the ACEN (chaired by Korboński) was still restricted to 11 seats. In the written publications and official lists of delegates (see table), the PNDC is not included, except for the first session. See: tables in the Appendix section. For a detailed description of the Polish delegation to the ACEN, see: Mazurkiewicz, "The Schism within the Polish Delegation ...," 73–110.

offices on the ninth floor were rather small and "the office furniture was purchased second hand."[19]

In its formal structure the ACEN consisted of an Assembly, the General Committee, and Secretariat. The work of the Assembly was carried out in the form of Plenary Meetings and in special committees. ACEN's Plenary Meetings took place in the rented hall at the Carnegie Endowment International Center (Carnegie International Center) located at the corner of First Avenue (UN Plaza) and East Forty-sixth street (at number 345). This was not a coincidence, for the ACEN wished to be perceived as an alternative to the communist representation of East Central European nations in the free world – a "little UN" – as the "New York Times" referred to it at one point.[20] In 1956, the ACEN received some funds to organize the Captive Nations Center across from the UN Building. The money was not enough to open the actual center, but the façade of the rented building was used to display political posters directly opposite from the UN headquarters. Together with the Carnegie International Center, located just around the corner, these locations where the ACEN delegates met offered prestige and the opportunity to be noticed by the UN representatives, diplomats, journalists as well as any potential visitors and tourists.[21]

In the years 1954 to 1972, the ACEN held 18 sessions. The ACEN's Plenary Meetings were organized in concurrence with the UN sessions and therefore they began in September. The ACEN's first session encompassed the years 1954 (September) to 1955 (August). Consequently, session 18 indicates the year beginning in September 1971, although by 1972 a different entity, ACEN, Inc., was already established to continue the work of the assembly without the FEC's support or control. In the period analyzed in this book, there were also four extraordinary Plenary Meetings held by the ACEN in 1956 to 1958, three in relation to the aftermath of the Hungarian Revolution, and one in response to the workers' rebellion in Poland in 1956. Special sessions of the ACEN were also organized in France in relation to the works of the Consultative Assembly of the Council of Europe.[22]

At the height of ACEN activities (late 1950s), when all 16 delegate seats were occupied, the Plenary Meetings included 144 delegates from national councils/committees (16 delegates from each), as well as about 25 delegates of the party internationals (each sent 4 to 6 delegates, with the number varying over the years). Adding observers from the associate organizations, I assume that

19 Gadomski, *Zgromadzenie Europejskich* ..., 22.
20 "The 'Little U.N'," *The New York Times*, 21 IX 1961, 34.
21 Mazurkiewicz, "'The Little U.N.' ..., 227–245.
22 Gadomski, *Zgromadzenie Europejskich* ..., 18–28.

the number of ACEN members at any given Plenary Session could be as high as 200 people. However, when reading the reports of these meetings it becomes obvious that at least some of the plenaries were even bigger due to invited guests from friendly associations, politicians, local authorities and leaders, FEC staff, as well as national, regional and ethnic press representatives. On other occasions, the plenary sessions were much smaller, as some delegates resided abroad and sent in authorizations for proxies. It all depended on the urgency and importance of issues at stake. With time, the overall number of ACEN members decreased.

At the beginning of each regular session the ACEN constituted a General Committee in which each national member organization was represented by one delegate. Decisions in the General Committee were taken by a two-thirds majority, each national delegation having one vote. The General Committee (operating in continuous session, in periods of recess acting on behalf of the Assembly) oversaw proposing the date for the convening of the Assembly, assured the implementation of resolutions adopted, coordinated the work of the committees, and submitted proposals to the Assembly. The General Committee (GC) meetings were attended by nine representatives of national organizations plus secretary general, as well as five delegates representing party internationals: 15 people in all. The frequency of GC meetings depended on the urgency of the issues to be discussed. During ACEN's third session, the GC met 66 times, and organized 11 plenary sessions in New York, five plenary sessions in Europe (in connection with the second session organized in Strasbourg).[23]

According to ACEN's Charter, the post of ACEN's chairman was to be held in rotation, in alphabetical order. However, with the concurrence of all GC members, the first four sessions of the ACEN were chaired by Vilis Māsēns (1902–1964). He was a former member of the Latvian Foreign Service (London, Kaunas and Paris), in charge of relations with the U.S. at the Ministry of Foreign Affairs in Riga and also served as director of the Baltic division and member of the Latvian delegation to the League of Nations. Māsēns gained the trust of all the delegates and oversaw the process of ACEN's maturation.[24] His deputy was the Bulgarian peasant party leader Georgi M. Dimitrov (1903–1972), widely recognized by his nickname “Gemeto” in order to distinguish him from the Bulgarian Com-

---

23 ACEN, Third Session Nov. 1956–Sept. 1957, Organization, Reports, New York: ACEN Publication, 1957, 17–19.

24 Vilis Māsēns, Biographical Notes, September 1955, IHRC, ACEN, b. 23, f. 1; Dr. Vilis Māsēns, an Exile Leader; Latvian Chairman in Group of Captive Nations Dies, *The New York Times*, 16 VII 1964; *Słownik biograficzny Europy Środkowo-Wschodniej XX wieku* (Warsaw: ISP PAN-Rytm, 2004), 803.

munist Party leader.[25] The leader of the Bulgarian agrarians, and a victim of persecution by both Fascists and Communists, Dimitrov was the most prominent and dominant character on the Bulgarian committee, as well as playing an important role within the peasant international (IPU).

Tab. 1: ACEN Leadership, 1954–1972

session	YEARS	CHAIRMAN Gen. Committee	VICE CHAIRMAN General Committee	SECRETARY GENERAL	DEPUTY SEC. GEN.
1	1954–55	Māsēns	Dimitrov	Coste	Kotta
2	1955–56	Māsēns	Dimitrov	Coste	Kotta
3	1956–57	Māsēns	Dimitrov	Coste	Kotta
4	1957–58	Māsēns	Dimitrov	Coste	Kotta
5	1958–59	Korboński	Kővágó	Coste	Kotta
6	1959–60	Zenkl	Sidzikauskas	Coste	Kotta
7	1960–61	Sidzikauskas	Korboński	Coste	Gaspar
8	1961–62	Nagy Ferenc	Gërmenji	Coste	Gaspar
9	1962–63	Dimitrov	Kütt	Coste	Gaspar
10	1963–64	Kütt	Nagy Ferenc	Coste	Gaspar
11	1964–65	Gërmenji	Lettrich	Coste	Gaspar
12	1965–66	Sidzikauskas	Korboński/Lettrich	Gaspar	n/a
13	1966–67	Korboński	Kütt	Gadomski	n/a
14	1967–68	Dimitrov	Gërmenji	Gadomski	n/a
15	1968–69	Lettrich	Bērziņš	Gadomski	n/a
16	1969–70	Bērziņš	Gërmenji	Gadomski	n/a
17	1970–71	Gërmenji	Kovács	Gadomski	n/a
18	1971–72	Korboński	Sidzikauskas	Gadomski	n/a

25 Mazurkiewicz, *Uchodźcy* ..., 305; *Słownik biograficzny* ..., 254.

Beginning with the election of Stefan Korboński,[26] the post of the chairman was held by representatives of all associated nations but not following any particular pattern (Table 1. ACEN Leadership).

Except for the politicians mentioned above, among the ACEN chairmen were three Hungarians; Ferenc Nagy (1903 – 1979), former prime minister of Hungary 1946 – 1947;[27] Imre Kovács (1913 – 1980) peasant party politician,[28] and József Kővágó (1913 – 1996) former mayor of Budapest from 1945 to 1947, and again during the 1956 Revolution.[29] Among the chairmen from the Baltic countries were Vaclovas Sidzikauskas (1893 – 1973), Lithuanian envoy to Switzerland, Germany, Austria and Great Britain in the interwar period; Aleksander Kütt (1900 – 1968) Estonian economist, and expert on foreign trade[30]; Alfrēds [Jēkabs] Bērziņš (1899 – 1977), a Latvian politician, and minister in the government formed after the Ulmanis coup of 1934.[31] On behalf of the joint Czech and Slovak delegation was the former mayor of Prague, and cabinet minister Petr Zenkl (1884 – 1975)[32] and lawyer and politician from Bratislava, Jozef Lettrich (1905 – 1969), who was one of the leaders of the Slovak national uprising in 1944.[33] The Albanian delegate Vasil Gërmenji (1908 – 1988) who held the post of the chairman, and prior to his exile had been a teacher, was a nephew of a famous Albanian independence leader (Themistokli Gërmenji). Most of these people were at some point prisoners of either the Bolsheviks, Soviets, Nazis (including internment in concentration camps), or by both totalitarian regimes alternating in seizing control of their respective homelands. All the names of ACEN chairmen, except for Kütt and

26 In addition to his three terms as chairman, and twice as vice chairman, Korboński also took on the duties as substitute chairman in 1955 and in 1958. His election in September 1958 was controversial, as the Polish (PCNU's) position on the ACEN's policy toward Germany and the PCNU's attitude towards the Western economic assistance to the Gomułka regime in Poland put his group at odds especially with the Bulgarian and Romanian delegations. Mazurkiewicz, "Relacje pomiędzy Zgromadzeniem Europejskich Narodów Ujarzmionych a Komitetem Wolnej Europy na tle polityki amerykańskiej 1950 – 1960," *Pamięć i Sprawiedliwość* 1 (21) 2013: 213 – 244.

27 *Słownik biograficzny* ..., 883.

28 Tibor Frank, "Imre Kovács and Cold War Émigré Politics in the United States (1947 – 1980)," in: *Inauguration of Organized* ...., 309 – 322; *Słownik biograficzny* ..., 646.

29 *Słownik biograficzny* ..., 646; Wolfgang Saxon, "Joseph Kovago, 83, Hungarian Freedom Fighter," *The New York Times*, 14 XII 1996, 52.

30 Aleksander Kütt [1900 – 1968, obituary], *ACEN News* 138 (January-February 1969): 24 – 25.

31 *Słownik biograficzny* ..., 102; Should not be confused with Alfrēds [Jānis] Bērziņš (1920 – 2011).

32 *Słownik biograficzny* ..., 1424 – 1425; Cf. Nekola.

33 *Słownik biograficzny* ..., 716 – 717; Jozef Lettrich [1905 – 1969, obituary], *ACEN News* 144 (January-February 1970): 30 – 31; "Jozef Lettrich, 64, Slovak Foe Of Nazis and Communists, Dies," *The New York Times*, 2 XII 1969, 55.

Gërmenji can be found in the *Biographical Dictionary of Central and Eastern Europe in the Twentieth Century*, which confirms the importance of the roles they played in their lands before their exile.[34]

While the rotation of the chairmanship did occur, some of the exile leaders clearly dominated the work of the Assembly, with Māsēns serving four terms, Korboński three, and Sidzikauskas, Dimitrov and Gërmenji each elected twice. It was not just their prominence though. At times, traveling distance, health condition, or additional occupation with political, social or professional activities interfered with the choices of chairmen.

The daily business of the ACEN was carried out by the Secretariat. Until 1965 it was run by a former Romanian diplomat, Brutus Coste (1910–1984).[35] In the interwar years, Coste served at the Romanian legations in Paris, London, Washington and Lisbon. To assist him there was, for a decade, the post of deputy secretary general, which during the first six sessions was held by Nuci Kotta (1921–1965),[36] the son of the last prime minister of independent Albania (Kcço Kotta), who was replaced in 1960 by a Hungarian diplomat Edmund Gaspar (1915–2001).[37]

It is important to note that it was not only the ACEN leadership that consisted of prominent politicians and experienced diplomats. Based on the complete lists of the members of each national, and international delegation published as appendices to this volume, a few key observations about the profile of the ACEN can be made.

Among the 409 names of delegates who worked within the ACEN between 1954 to 1972,[38] the reader can find at least 94 former members of parliaments, including an astonishing number of 37 former members of cabinets, including four former prime ministers, speakers of parliaments, and party leaders (across the political spectrum). Within the delegates to the ACEN there were religious leaders of various denominations, professionals of a variety of occupations in-

---

34 While I am using the Polish language (original edition), there are editions in English as well. See: *Biographical Dictionary of Central and Eastern Europe in the Twentieth Century*, ed. Wojciech Roszkowski, Jan Kofman (Abingdon OX-New York: Routledge, 2015).

35 "Brutus Coste" [obituary], *The New York Times*, 5 IX 1984, B8.

36 Dr. Nuci Kotta Dies. Albanian Political Leader and Writer [October 1965], IHRC, ACEN, b. 23, f. 10; "Dr. Nuci Kotta, 44, An Albanian Exile," *The New York Times*, 23 VII 1965, 29.

37 Curriculum vitae of Dr. Edmund Gaspar, HIA, RFE/RL CF: A, b. 204, f. 13.

38 Between 1954 to 1972 there were: 51 Albanians, 22 Bulgarians, 48 Czechs and Slovaks, 37 Estonians, 44 Hungarians, 44 Latvians, 30 Lithuanians, 40 Poles, 28 Romanians. In sum, 344 exiles took part on behalf of national committees/councils. The party internationals delegated 80 people, among whom 15 overlapped with the national delegations. The breakdown was: CDU – 21, LDU – 15, IPU – 22, ICFTUE – 15, SUCEE – 7.

cluding over 70 delegates holding a doctoral (or higher) degree. Former diplomats (numbering over 35) and lawyers (over 43) constituted the largest professional group, but in the descriptions provided by the ACEN there were also public service officers, former town mayors, military officers as well as journalists and editors, agronomists, engineers, teachers, students, statisticians, writers, and theologists, etc. Among the overwhelmingly male representation there were also five women listed as delegates, and a few more (not indicated in the tables) who stepped in as substitutes, alternate members, or experts.

Taking into consideration the substitutions occurring during the sessions (death, migration, and illness), invited exile experts, and hired staff, it can be estimated that the total number of people involved in the work of the ACEN between 1954 and 1972 did not exceed 450 people. In addition to these calculations, however, there were 193 exiles involved in the work at ACEN representations abroad and at least 38 of them were also listed as ACEN delegates (either on behalf of the national or international party delegations). All in all, 560 can be confirmed as the least number of exiles involved in the work of the ACEN, although estimates go as high as 600 people worldwide in the years 1954 to 1972.

Further interpretation of the information aggregated in the tables at the end of this book allows for observations regarding the stability and viability of delegations. Some delegations were characterized by a large turnover in delegates. While Bulgarians and Romanians maintained a rather stable group (over 20), over 40 Czechs and Slovaks, Hungarians and Latvians served as delegates from 1954 to 1972. The difference was not only based on the size of the political diaspora (people available to serve as delegates) but also on the political changes in the composition of a given committee. In the case of the Albanian delegation there were 51 delegates over the 18 sessions of the ACEN, which is a testimony to the accidental choices of candidates serving only one term. In the case of party internationals, the largest number of delegates to the ACEN was provided by the CDUCE and IPU. Both organizations nominated their delegates for all 18 sessions of the ACEN.

Representing the internationals was a way for the nations not represented in ACEN to join its activities (for example, Vladko Maček, the Croat peasant party leader, or Miha Krek, a Slovenian Christian Democrat, and a cabinet minister both in his homeland and in exile).[39] At times, representing an international party organization intensified squabbles within national exile milieus. This was particularly evident in the case of the Poles. Stanisław Mikołajczyk was

---

39 *Słownik biograficzny ...*, 657–658; 764–765.

the chairman of the peasant union (IPU), which he used to maintain his position within ACEN. Mikołajczyk's associate, Karol Popiel, was a delegate to the ACEN on behalf of the CDUCE (of which he was the vice chairman).[40] The Polish exiles who boycotted the national delegation therefore used the internationals to maintain their connection with the ACEN and garner attention for their agenda.

It can be assumed that the most active members of the Assembly were the exiles who sat on the ACEN General Committee as chairmen of the national delegations and served in the working committees. Another indicator of individuals' roles within the Assembly could be their participation in ACEN delegations to prominent politicians (for example, meeting John F. Dulles,[41] members of the U.S. Congress, etc.), in foreign travels (like the Latin American tour of 1956, or the world tour of 1959). Based on the available sources, the core leadership of the ACEN is indicated in bold in the tables published in the appendices. Some key ACEN leaders' work was terminated by premature death, illness, or migration.

Leaving the ACEN was also connected with decisions to apply for American citizenship. As a general rule, rigorously observed, especially in the early years, the ACEN excluded from its ranks delegates who adopted American citizenship. While commonly deprived of home citizenship by the communist regimes, exiles' naturalization was interpreted by their peers as a loss of legitimacy to represent captive compatriots.[42] Of course, there were exceptions, and within a decade it became almost impossible to continue to work for the ACEN and make a living while remaining stateless and registered as a "foreign agent."[43] Only the key (and incidentally also the oldest) leaders, like Korboński, maintained their status until their death. However, even in his case, his wife took American citizenship to stabilize the family's economic position in exile.[44]

---

40 CDUCE was founded on 26 VII 1950 in New York. Goddeeris, "Exiles' Strategies ....," 386–387; Kosicki, "Christian Democracy ...," 225–226. On Sieniewicz see: Ziętara, *Anders, Korboński, Sieniewicz* ..., 30–155.

41 Memorandum of Conversation, Department of State, Washington, 9 I 1956, *Foreign Relations of the United States (FRUS) 1955–1957, vol. XXV: Eastern Europe*, (Washington: GPO, 1990), doc. 44., 109–114, history.state.gov/historicaldocuments/frus1955–57v25/d44, accessed 16 IX 2019. Present at the meeting with the Secretary of State, Jacob Beam (EUR) and Francis B. Stevens (EUR/EE) were delegates of all nine countries represented in ACEN: Māsēns (Latvia, ACEN Chairman), Dimitrov (Bulgaria, Vice Chairman), Hasan Dosti (Albania), Juraj Slávik (Czechoslovakia), Vahter (Estonia), Gyöorgy [George] Bakách-Bessenyey (Hungary), Sidzikauskas (Lithuania), Korboński (Poland), Vişoianu (Romania), Coste (Secretary Gen., Romania).

42 Mazurkiewicz, "Unwilling Immigrants ...," 159–171.

43 Mazurkiewicz, *Uchodźcy* ..., 122, 133–134.

44 Interview with Zofia Korbońska, Washington D.C., 6 XI 2007.

Up until the severe budgetary cuts of 1965, the ACEN secretariat included some paid staff who were not restricted in the same way as the political delegates. Paul Vajda was responsible for relations with the press, while Joseph Czako was in charge of UN Affairs, and Feliks Gadomski for social and economic affairs. This meant that the latter edited *Survey of Developments in the Captive Countries*, served as a secretary of the Plenary Meeting, was the liaison with the CACEED, as well as with ACEN member national councils and committees. He was also tasked with daily press reviews and writing memoranda and papers as needed. Political affairs were the domain of Algirdas Landsbergis, preceded by Miroslav V. Fic. What it meant in practice (as of 1965) was, for example, writing for and editing "ACEN News", being writer and editor of memoranda and other papers, serving as liaison with working committees, writing monthly and annual ACEN reports, monitoring correspondence related to ACEN publications and speaking engagements and reviews of the Congressional Record.[45] Dr. Miron Butariu took care of overall administration, while Svetlana Bachvarova was in charge of ACEN documentation. During the third session (1956–1957), which I consider the peak of the ACEN's organizational power, the Secretariat hired six typists and secretaries, and two technicians who operated the duplicating and mimeographing machines.[46]

The committees established within the ACEN and constituted at the beginning of each session included: Political, Economic, Social, Legal, Cultural and Public Relations – from the second session this was called the Information Committee. The Political Committee dealt with contemporary issues such as analysis of Western policy toward captive nations, coexistence, European integration, and international treaties. The Economic Committee worked on issues related to trading with the Soviets, or colonial exploitation by the USSR of the countries in East Central Europe. Members of the Social Committee dealt with forced labor, deportations, religious persecution and other forms of violations of human rights perpetrated by the Communists. Related to this was the work of the Legal Committee, which worked on describing and explaining Soviet violations of international covenants, as well as protecting the rights of the refugees.

All ACEN working documents adopted special annotations as to the origin of the proposal (P) for Political committee, (L) for Legal and so on. Upon approval, the results of their work were distributed as memoranda, appeals, pamphlets and other forms of publications. In the early years of the Assembly's activities

45 Distribution of tasks among members of ACEN Staff at New York Headquarters, Twelfth Session (1965–66), 30 IX 1965, ZNiO, Gadomski Papers, 123/02.
46 ACEN, Third Session, Nov. 1956 – Sept. 1957 ..., 22–23.

these committees nominated chairmen, vice chairmen and secretaries, as well as hired exile experts who were not members of ACEN delegations. Although nominally all committees existed from 1955 to 1972, the height of the work carried out in these bodies took place during the second to seventh sessions. By the early 1960s their activity was limited to two or three members, and then the financial cuts affecting the ACEN from its twelfth session effectively re-routed their work to the members of the General Committee. Officially, these were not phased out, but already from 1963 (the tenth session) the number of committees was limited to three: Political-Legal Committee (P-L), Cultural-Information (C-I), Economic and Social (E-S). Due to decreasing membership in the ACEN, some exiles served on more than one committee.

Among the organizations with a consultative status to the committees of the ACEN, most were invited to work with the Social, Legal and Cultural committees. The Council of European Women in Exile, founded in New York in 1953, included representatives from all the countries represented in the ACEN as well as from Yugoslavia, and considered itself "spokesman for the silenced sisters behind the Iron Curtain," and nominated its representatives to Legal, Cultural and Social committees.[47] The Central European Federation of Christian Trade Unions was invited to join the work of the ACEN within the Social, Legal and Economic committees. While the issue of forced labor was a factor encouraging cooperation, the Federation demanded that ACEN make it an associate member as it was authorized by the International Federation of Christian Workers and Refugees to "act on behalf of all exiled Christian Trade Unionists from the captive countries."[48] Such a status had, however, already been granted to the International Center of Free Trade Unionists in Exile (ICFTUE).

The ACEN's cooperation with "Humanitas," whose membership overlapped with some of the ACEN's leadership (Nicolae George Caranfil, Sidzikauskas, Hasan Dosti, Nikola Balabanov, Raoul V. Bossy, Aksel Mei, et al.)[49] in its contacts with ACEN's committees focused on the issue of refugees. The International Free Academy of Sciences and Letters was affiliated to the Cultural Committee as of

---

47 Gunhild Brakas (President) to Brutus Coste (Secretary General), 27 V 1959, IHRC, b. 44, f. 4. ACEN provided the following address: Council of European Women in Exile, 127 East 90th Street, NY 24, NY.

48 Anton Babnik (Secretary General) to Vilis Māsēns, 16 IX 1957, IHRC, b. 44, f. 2. Central and Eastern European Federation of Christian Trade Unions, 471 Park Avenue, New York 22, NY.

49 N. [Nicolae] G. [George] Caranfil (President), J. Papanek (Secretary General), Copy of July 14th, 1955 Humanitas' appeal to the three heads of Western Governments at Geneva Conference, 21 VII 1955, IHRC, ACEN, b. 44, f. 5. ACEN provided the following address for Humanitas, 18 East 60th Street New York 19, NY.

July 1957. Since the seat of the Academy was in Paris, the organization decided to appoint its American-based delegate to represent it at ACEN. The chosen delegate was Raoul Bossy, who was already a member of the ACEN.[50] The cooperation with Women for Freedom of Europe, Inc. also lapsed with ACEN's business. ACEN offered to share its office space with an organization that was a member of a larger entity – the general Federation of Women's Clubs. The ACEN's offer was taken up by the CDUCE.[51] As observers, delegates of these organizations had no right to vote, and no right to participate in discussions, and their advice was heard by individual committees, and it can be assumed that this was largely symbolic. The ACEN archive contains a fair number of letters with invitations, copies of reports exchanged between the independently operating organizations, yet there is a very limited account of the associations' members taking part in meetings of social and cultural committees to which they were admitted for consultation purposes in 1956.[52] In terms of participation in ACEN meetings, there are very few traces of consultative members' activities. For example, only three people participated in the Strasbourg meetings. In April 1958, Dr. Marijan Struna, Valtcho Vanguelov, and Jaroslav Vrzala represented Council of Free Youth of Central and Eastern Europe,[53] and in October 1961, the very same people were present during a special session in Paris. They were joined by Istvan Lajti, who came on behalf of the International Free Academy of Sciences and Letters. None of these delegates, sometimes listed as experts, are listed in the tables at the end of this book.

More importantly for its political operations, the ACEN established its regional outposts outside of the United States. ACEN representations in the free world included:

---

50 Istvan Lajti (secretary general) to Vaclovas Sidzikauskas (acting chairman), 8 VII 1957, IHRC, ACEN, b. 44, f. 6. By early 1960s the Academy was able to open its American Branch – care of the Polish Institute of Arts and Sciences (PIASA), New York. Oskar Halecki was the Chairman, with Raoul Bossy the Vice chairman. Among the members one finds many prominent members of the ACEN; Adolph Procházka, Sidzikauskas, Gadomski. See: Minutes of the meeting of the International Free Academy of Sciences and Letters, American Branch, held on March 16, 1962 at the PIASA (NYC), 12 IV 1962, IHRC, b. 44, f. 6.

51 Brutus Coste to Mrs. Robert P. Patterson, 15 IV 1959, IHRC, ACEN, b. 44, f. 7.

52 Vilis Māsēns to Elija Druva, 26 III 1956, IHRC, ACEN, b. 44, f. 1; Elija Druva (President) to Dr. George Dimitrov (Chairman), 5 III 1963, IHRC, b. 44, f. 1. By 1966, the ACEN decided not to list this organization among the signatories of the Captive Nations Week manifesto. Sidzikauskas to Mall Jurma, 15 VI 1966, ibid. Council of Baltic Women: 198 Sixth Avenue, Brooklyn 17, NY.

53 Strasbourg meetings delegate lists published in Sessions 1–9. Council of Free Youth of Central and Eastern Europe, 82 Avenue Marceau, Paris (8e), France.

- Delegations – consisting of a minimum of three national delegations, each of which would send at least two delegates. The delegations could establish offices (a paid director, and a small staff). Their chairmen, elected from national delegations, served in rotation.
- Representations – consisting of a minimum of three national member organizations, each of which would send at least one representative.
- Correspondents. The name was connected with their role at "ACEN News". In fact, they were local/regional liaisons.

The tasks of the regional representatives were similar to those of the ACEN: to approach local authorities and institutions, answer public statements, issue press comments, send letters, and memoranda, contact media to raise awareness and enlist support. A complete list of ACEN's offices and delegates abroad is included in the appendices. In the case of foreign representatives, a few names stand out in the ACEN archival collection as particularly active. These were Edmund Rehak – representing the Czechoslovak delegation while running the ACEN Office in Paris; Pál Auer – possibly the ACEN's key political liaison in Paris; as were Gustav Hennyey in Bonn and Aleksander Warma in Stockholm[54]; in addition, Zygmunt Zawadowski produced "ACEN News" in Arabic from his post in Beirut (Lebanon), while Edmund Gaspar efficiently established ACEN networks across Latin America. Among them there were people who maintained their own connections with Americans and West Europeans which lay outside the framework in which they were subject to the organizational control of the ACEN, or even of the FEC.[55]

The table with ACEN representatives outside of the U.S., although not flawless,[56] indicates locations on five continents where an ACEN presence was marked by the establishing of an office, delegation, or just by the selection of

54 Aleksander Warma [Obituary], *ACEN News* 150 (March-April 1971): 32.

55 Thomas W. Braden to C.D. Jackson, 6 VIII 1953, DDEL, C.D. Jackson Records (1953–54), b. 2, f.: de Auer, Paul. For example, Pál Auer (here called: Pál de Auer) – the head of the Paris ACEN office, who took part in The Hague Congress, had political contacts not only in France, but in other European countries, relying equally often on contacts with Hungarians residing in the West. On the other hand, judging from the collection of C.D. Jackson, Auer kept lively correspondence with American diplomats, the detailed and reporting nature of which is reminiscent of intelligence reports.

56 Both published and archival lists of delegates (IHRC, ACEN, b. 44) are filled with mistakes. Dates to not match; inactive representatives are listed. The spelling of their last names is questionable but difficult to verify. The table included in the annex section of this book constitutes the first effort of mapping ACEN delegations, which requires further verification. Due to large degree of uncertainty, no dates of service to ACEN were listed.

representatives or correspondents. In the case of the last category of correspondents, they were not of East Central European origin. An examination of ACEN representations abroad clearly shows that the focus of the organization was on Europe: that is where most of its offices (and funds) were directed. This is also where the delegations were most numerous, representing almost all ACEN member organizations as well as party internationals. Of course, the number of ACEN representatives worldwide was conditioned on the number of political exiles in a given region, as well as the old diasporic networks which facilitated resources as well as audiences transmitting the ACEN's messages.

The ACEN's daily activities focused on monitoring the international situation and offering its interpretation of these in the context of the fate of the "captive nations." This book discusses some of the most important of these activities in the context of American Cold War policy. The ACEN's ambition was to serve as an alternative form of representation of their nations, or at least as an international lobby trying to influence policies affecting their homelands. ACEN political activities throughout the period of the FEC's support (1954–1972) took on different forms – from meetings with party leaders, or members of parliaments to issuing press releases for the American and foreign press.[57] Other forms of activities included issuing memoranda and appeals to heads of governments. During critical moments, the ACEN sent out telegrams, to which American and foreign leaders at times replied. Sporadically, the ACEN organized rallies at the UN Plaza, in front of the so-called ACEN House in New York. What is also evident from examining the IHRC archival collection is the vast correspondence with members of the U.S. congress, numbering in all, over 800 letters. Most of them resemble an educational effort, offering an advanced course on Eastern Europe's history and the current geopolitical state of affairs.

The exiles were received by the officials at the U.S. State Department. The highlight of ACEN's prominence was a meeting of its delegates with the U.S. Secretary of State. The entire General Committee of the ACEN met with John F. Dulles for 45 minutes on 9 January 1956.[58] During the meeting, the ACEN delegates presented its views on the tactics of the "Peaceful Liberation" promised by President Eisenhower, on trade with the Eastern Bloc, countering Soviet efforts to lure back the émigrés, and shared their opinions on "national communism." Dulles took the time to explain American policy interests and shared insider information on talks with the Russians, openly stating that the increased anxiety of the Soviets caused by the unrest throughout the satellite area was to America's advant-

57 Thus far I have collected 643 press releases issued by ACEN from 1954 to 1972.

58 Memorandum of a Conversation, 9 I 1956, *FRUS 1955–1957*..., doc. 44.

age.[59] In his brief history of the ACEN published forty years later, Gadomski assessed that the premature passing of "ACEN's greatest friend" in the U.S. administration on 24 May 1959 constituted

> a great loss to the ACEN, to the establishment of which he had greatly contributed and to whose great support ACEN often owed its position almost immediately achieved in the American politics and in the international relations [...]. The death of Dulles closed the period of firm support of the American administration for ACEN.[60]

Delegates of the Assembly were then received by the Acting Secretary of State on 21 July 1959, three years after meeting with Dulles, and waited for the next high-profile meeting for two more years.[61] The Democratic administration that took over in early 1961 picked up the émigré Assembly meeting pattern. Getting to know them, the Department of State prepared talking points for the Under Secretary who met with the ACEN delegates on 6 June 1961. The ACEN was introduced to him as an organization sponsored by the FEC, the major activities of which included "issuance of resolutions and other public statements" and "representations to U.S. and other officials" for the purpose of "expressing ACEN views and urging action in the interest of freedom for the East European countries."[62] The talking points included praise for the exile Assembly's role in spreading awareness of the actual situation concerning foreign domination: "ACEN is particularly suited to work effectively in this educations effort, as it has been in the past."[63]

The exiles realized that the meetings at the highest level at the Department of State were being used by the American government not so much for the sake of elevating the exiles' morale, but as a trump card in confrontation with Mos-

---

59 The meeting took place half a year before the Poznań riots, and less than 10 months before the Hungarian Revolution. The exact words of the report were: "The Secretary believed that the Soviets were faced with considerable problems throughout the satellite area. Unrest in some of the countries was greater than in others but the entire picture seems to cause them anxiety. It was certainly to our advantage to see that anxiety increase. In the Secretary's view the situation was not hopeless. What happens behind the Iron Curtain sometimes happens unexpectedly. The basic situation indicates that certain changes may be in the making. He, of course, could not set a timetable or a date for what may likely occur." ibid.

60 Gadomski, *Zgromadzenie Europejskich ...*, 37.

61 Memorandum of Conversation [with nine ACEN delegates]: Expressions of views by Executive Committee of ACEN, 27 VI 1961, Simpson Collection, 760.00/6 – 2761.

62 Kohler (EUR) to Under Secretary, Memorandum: Visit by Delegation Representing ACEN, 2 V 1961, Simpson Collection, 760.00/5 – 261.

63 Foy D. Kohler to Under Secretary, Memorandum: Visit by Delegation representing ACEN, Talking Points, tab. A, 24 VI 1961, Simpson Collection, 760.00/6 – 2461.

cow. Such was the case early in the 1965 as the war in Vietnam was unfolding, when after meeting the Deputy Under Secretary for Political Affairs, Alexis Johnson (Dean Rusk's right handman), Korboński noted it demonstrated that the U.S. could renew the case against imposed and undemocratic governments in East Central Europe.[64]

The ACEN was vulnerable to fluctuations in American Cold War policies, and the Assembly was clearly politically dependent on the State Department. However, the American government kept its distance in both guidelines and control of exile activities. For these it relied on the FEC. This does not mean that the State Department avoided any contact with the ACEN, as its delegates obtained "periodic hearings" in the form of meeting senior officers of the European Office, and employees of the East European desks. Often, the Department of State officers (EUR/EE) would take the time to explain a U.S. position on a given matter, like the inviation to Nikita Khrushchev to visit the U.S. in 1959,[65] or to explain why delegates from Yugoslavia were not to be admitted to ACEN.[66] However, most of the meetings at Foggy Bottom were essentially reduced to the presentation of the Assembly's views.[67] Copies of these memoranda written by the Department of State staff as well as some of the many ACEN-prepared materials (appeals, addresses, adopted resolutions, etc.) were distributed among Departmental offices as well sent to U.S. diplomatic missions abroad. On many occasions, the Department asked U.S. diplomatic posts to assist and report on the

---

64 Stefan Korboński to Jan Starzewski (London), 19 XII 1965, HIA, Korboński Papers, b. 11, f. 4.

65 Memorandum of Conversation [with Korboński, Király and Slávik]: Views of the ACEN on Khrushchev's Forthcoming Visit to the U.S., 19 VIII 1959, Simpson Collection, 033.6111/8 – 1959.

66 When in 1960, ACEN's Chairman (Petr Zenkl) inquired about the possible admission of Yugoslavia to ACEN at the State Department, Harold C. Vedeler responded that the term "captive nation" referred solely to describe a nation dominated by the Soviets. Yugoslav membership in ACEN would "obscure the nature of the ACEN and confuse the conception and public posture of the organization." Memorandum of Conversation: Proposed Admission of Yugoslav Émigré Representatives into ACEN, 2 IX 1960, Simpson Collection, 760.00/9 – 260.

67 Memorandum of Conversation [with Bolesław Wierzbiański]: ACEN Favors Cultural Exchange Between U.S. and the Soviet Bloc, 18 I 1956, Simpson Collection, 511.60/1 – 1856; Memorandum of Conversation [with 14 representatives of ACEN]: Views of the ACEN on the East European question in any East-West meeting, 19 II 1958, Simpson Collection, 760.00/2 – 1958; Memorandum of Conversation [with four ACEN delegates]: Representations of the ACEN on the Berlin Crisis, 17 III 1959, Simpson Collection, 760.00/3 – 1759; Memorandum of Conversation [with Zenkl, Korboński, Māsēns]: ACEN Position Concerning Inclusion of Eastern European Question in Forthcoming Summit Meeting, 5 II 1960, Simpson Collection, 760.00/2 – 560; Memorandum of Conversation [with Zenkl, Dimitrov, Korboński, Māsēns, Nagy]: ACEN Interest in Consideration of Eastern European Question at 15th UNGA, 15 IX 1960, Simpson Collection, 760.00/9 – 1560.

ACEN delegations traveling to Europe, Latin America, Asia, or the Middle East. Usually, the instruction contained a statement informing the world of the nature of Soviet imperialism – the purpose of the ACEN tour – and was consonant with the objectives of the U.S. government.[68]

Reports on ACEN delegations' visits to Washington sporadically ended with a State Department commentary on exile views. For example, in January 1958 Vilis Māsēns met with Frederick W. Jandrey, Deputy Assistant Secretary of State for European Affairs, and invited him to attend the ACEN exhibit showcasing the "40-year record of communist imperialism." The Department considered it inadvisable to be represented at the exhibit. As evidenced in the response to Māsēns' inquiry about the possibility of ACEN delegates traveling to certain countries in the Far East, the State Department was sympathetic, but it wished to avoid any official connection or involvement with ACEN projects.[69] This does not mean, however, a lack of attention to this initiative on the part of the U.S. government. The CIA suggested actions to maximize the occasion, and Allen Dulles, the Director of the CIA, and the brother of the Secretary of State, offered help with obtaining the widest publicity by the time the exhibit reached Chicago in the summer of 1958.[70] However, all ACEN-related projects contain references to the Free Europe Committee. When the exiles attempted to forego the FEC and obtain support from the administration without the Committee's approval, their efforts were not only in vain, but resulted in a vengeful reaction from the FEC leadership.[71]

In general, the reception of ACEN delegates by the officials at the State Department (mostly by EUR and EUR/EE staff) must be considered a courtesy ex-

---

68 Department of State Instruction (CW-2894): Tour of Leaders of the ACEN, to: American Embassy Ankara, American Consulate General Istanbul, American Embassy, Nicosia, American Embassy, Rome, 29 X 1961, Simpson Collection, 0 – 32-Assembly of Captive European Nations/9 – 2961.

69 Thomas F. Hoctor (EUR/EE), Memorandum of Conversation: Visit by Mr. Vilis Māsēns, Chairman, ACEN, 14 I 1958, Simpson Collection, 760.00/1 – 858 [original stamp on the copy obtained from Simpson]; Frederick W. Jandrey (EUR) to Vilis Māsēns, 17 I 1958, Simpson Collection, 760.00/1 – 1758.

70 Allen Dulles wrote a response to Charles Kersten's letter of 29 July 1958. Kersten advised the DCI of the opening of the exhibit of ACEN in Chicago, on August 5, by saying: "The interesting suggestions contained in your letter of July 29 were passed along promptly to the appropriate people, and I hope, as you do, that the exhibit in Chicago will obtain the widest publicity." Chief, International Organizations Division, Memorandum for DCI: Letter for DCI's signature, 5 VIII 1958, National Archives College Park (NARA II), CREST, CIA-RDP80R01731R000500530 001 – 2, rel. 7 V 2002; Allen W. Dulles (DCI) to Charles J. Kersten, 11 VIII 1958, ibid.

71 Mazurkiewicz, *Uchodźcy ...*, 295.

tended to the exiles by the U.S. government. A similar courtesy was extended to the representatives of the national delegations. However, in the latter case the American patience with exile infighting ran out rather fast. In an interview years later, Thomas Braden (of the CIA) said:

> Thomas Braden (B): "The problem was with the refugees. It got to be just horrendous, they were eating up everybody's time. They were high level people. Like former prime ministers ...
> Sig Mickelson (M): ... and coming in and sitting in the waiting rooms in the Foggy Bottom.
> B: Oh, Jesus – yes, eating up everybody's time and everybody regarded it ... you know ... Allen [Dulles] saw no point in seeing this guy again even if he had been the prime minister of Czechoslovakia – you know what I mean?
> M: Exactly.
> B: Because here wasn't anything you could do for them.
> M: So, they wanted something to keep them busy ....
> B: And they also wanted to pay them – don't forget.
> M: Exactly.
> B: Because foreign former prime ministers were broke, dead broke and there had to be some way of keeping them in a blue suit. I always figured that this was what it was all about.
> M: I guess you are right but didn't [Frank] Wisner also have a deep interest in whatever intelligence he could get?
> B: Oh, absolutely.
> M: One little thing too, they wanted to have cadres available to go back into their homelands in case the Russian ...
> B: Yup. This was all true – but what happened after all was that the intelligence that they were giving us was just nothing but gossip. [...] You know they just gossiped among themselves – they postulated things and then bored Allen [Dulles] with it for two hours with it. After a while the info they got was not much good. And yet they insisted on giving them the time to give it to you.[72]

The ACEN offered a more stable platform for maintaining contact with political exiles from East Central Europe. Yet, fearing that access granted to the ACEN might set a dangerous precedent, its official delegates were kept at arm's length by the White House. When requesting a meeting with the President, for example, they were rejected on the grounds that it might "stimulate requests for similar meetings by other organizations concerned with the Eastern European area

72 Sound recordings of interviews with Ray Cline, Jan[e] Lester, and John Dunning on 6 V 1982, HIA, Sig Mickelson Papers, Sound recording, Hoover ID: 82074 a 0003878, begin: 13:55 – Tomas W. Braden (Director of Intelligence Op[eratio]ns division of the CIA, 1951–1954, with resp. for RFE liaison. For rephrased citation see: Scott Lucas, *Freedom's War* ..., 148; Johnson, *Radio Free Europe* ..., 12.

with the expectation that they would be granted the same privilege."[73] While the ACEN's request was refused in a more polite way, undoubtedly their access to the American government was of a special character. Communication lines were opened (and regulated) by contacts facilitated by the FEC. Whenever a response by the U.S. government to ACEN appeals, actions, or offers to advise occurred, it is indicated in the following chapters.

One way to reconstruct a detailed account of the ACEN activities is to examine "ACEN News". Initially, "ACEN News" bore a subheading: "A monthly review of the activities of the Assembly of Captive European Nations." In the first issue it stated:

> The aim of the monthly news review is to acquaint our readers with the activities of ACEN. The news review is not meant to replace the bulletins, press releases, and other publications of this organization. But we feel that it will serve a good purpose if we present ACEN activities in this form, as those interested in certain details of our activities will then be able to ask for pertinent material.[74]

It soon changed to bi-monthly. The cost of producing a single issue (in 1957) was between $ 2,600 and $ 2,800.[75] The cost of printing "ACEN News" by 1960 was $ 17,040, the single highest amount among the exile periodicals supported by the FEC.[76] The last issue of this journal (no. 153) was published for November-December 1971. For a brief period, the journal was published in Spanish as *Novedades de la ANCE.*

In 1956, "ACEN News" changed its graphic layout and from an organizational bulletin began to look more like a professional journal featuring op-eds, political commentaries, photographs of ACEN events in addition to regular accounts of its many activities. By September 1957, its mailing list included 7,383 addresses in the U.S. alone. The print run of the journal was 10,000.[77] By the late 1950s, the ACEN's mailing list included, among the Free Europe Committee: Ralph Walter 40 copies, 12 copies Free Europe Press, certain individuals, RFE national desk chiefs (Bulgarian, Czechoslovak, Hungarian, Polish, Romanian), var-

---

73 John A. Calhoun (Director, Executive Secretariat) to Brig. Gen. A. J. Goodpaster (The White House), Memorandum: Request by ACEN for Meeting with the President, 13 IV 1960, Simpson Collection, 760.00/4–1360.

74 *ACEN News* 1/1 (1 IV 1955): 1.

75 Cost of the April-May issue 1957. Press Officer to Secretary General, re: ACEN News for April–May 1957, (6 VI 1957?) IHRC, ACEN, b. 154, f. 6.

76 Exhibit VIII: Exile Periodical Publications attached to: Reorientation of Exile Organizations, 1 IV 1960, DDEL, C.D. Jackson Papers, b. 53, f.: FEC 1960 (2).

77 Paul Vajda (ACEN Press Officer) to Cloyce K. Huston, 11 XI 1957, IHRC, ACEN, b. 3, f. 3.

ious individuals of East Central European ancestry in Australia, Spain, Portugal, Brazil, Germany, Mexico, Argentina, France, Italy, Uruguay, Chile, Denmark, Sweden (from 10 to 25 copies) and Great Britain (50 copies for Antoni Dargas), 150 copies for U.S. Information Agency (USIA) in Washington.[78] All mailings were done by the Midtown Letter Service Co., Inc. Still, by the mid-1960s the FEC criticized the editors for having the periodical carry too much information in an unattractive form, "such as the Congressional Record." According to the new guidelines, "ACEN News" should serve two purposes – one to inform, second to "help mold opinion in matters relating to ultimate goal of freedom and independence of all the captive nations."[79] The ACEN changed the graphic format but did not apply all the recommendations. Today, various issues of "ACEN News", published uninterrupted from 1955 to 1971, are held by at least 169 libraries worldwide.[80]

The ACEN also published records of its sessions, including Strasbourg special sessions and Latin American seminars, special brochures and pamphlet series. These publications can be divided into two blocks: documenting ACEN activities, and educating western audiences (commonly distributed for free). Naturally, ACEN activities (like political meetings, public conferences) also carried educational content, which in fact epitomized their lobbying/propaganda efforts. In the first months of ACEN operations (January to May 1955) 14, 487 pieces of mail went through its offices, including 12,910 publications (books, brochures, copies of "ACEN News"). In April 1955 alone, the ACEN received 743 letters. General information about the ACEN (like its Charter and Rules) appeared in English, but also in French (1955), Spanish (1956) and German (1960),[81] while records of the first nine ACEN sessions appeared only in English. Initially the ACEN also published mimeographed reports of debates (1955 – 1957), but this was discontinued rather early.[82] The records of the ACEN special sessions held in Strasbourg

78 Betty Campbell to Mr. Goodstadt, re: ACEN mailing list, 6 X 1959, IHRC, ACEN, b. 154, f. 6.
79 Fields Associates, Report and Recommendations on ACEN News, 14 X 1964, IHRC, ACEN, b. 154, f. 7.
80 Estimate based on the WorldCat.org.
81 The name of the organization was translated into Assemblée des Nations Captives d'Europe, Asamblea de Naciones Europeas Cautivas, Assemblée der Versklavten Europäischer Nationen. In 1955 the English version of ACEN activities in English was published in 7,000 copies and distributed worldwide. ACEN Program of Activities for the year beginning on July 1, 1955, 1 VI 1955, IHRC, ACEN, b. 1, f. 7.
82 Official Reports of Debates, 13 volumes covering 13 – 44 Plenary Meetings of ACEN, in the period from April 14, 1955 to June 28, 1957.

were published both in English and in French.[83] The selection of languages was of course determined by the purpose of each publication.

A *Survey of Recent Developments in Nine Captive Countries* intended as an English-language reference publication was initiated during the first session and lasted until the budgetary cuts made it impossible to continue by the mid-1960s.[84] As the exiles were growing increasingly out of touch with the "recent developments" in their home countries, another reference-style publication was initiated entitled: *Facts on Captive Nations*. The English original was published in 1960, followed by editions in Spanish, French, and Arabic in 1961.[85]

ACEN's political lobbying effort is visible in publications containing its appeals "to the Free World" (1954),[86] evaluations of Soviet intentions before Geneva (1955),[87] or on Western policy options in 1963.[88] There were, however, publications that resulted from close cooperation with the FEC, like participation in the campaign to present Soviet expansionism as a form of "new colonialism."[89] In addition to French, German and Spanish, the ACEN bulletins were published in Finnish, Swedish and Arabic. Not all publications were translated and distributed around the world, and some targeted specific audiences. This trend is especially visible in the Spanish language publications, which is described in chapter seven. Among some of the most influential ACEN publications, there were six volumes of *Hungary Under Soviet Rule* (prepared in association with the AFCN).[90]

---

83 See ACEN publications (1955–1959) numbered 9, 10, 17, 18, 21, 23, 24, 28 and 19, and printed under similar title: *Assemblée des Nations Captives d'Europe* followed by either *Session Spéciale a Strasbourg*, or with a number (up until Cinquiéme Session, 1959).

84 Early volumes (1953–1955 and 1956–1957) were translated into French as *Etude sur la Situation Actuelle dans les Neuf Pays Asservis* (mimeographed versions).

85 *Facts on the Captive Countries* (New York: ACEN, 1960), 24 pp. Translated to Spanish as: *Datos Relativos a las Naciones Cautivas; Realités des Pays Captifs.*

86 ACEN, *Appeal to the Nations of the Free World* (New York: ACEN, 1954): 1–8; available also in French and Spanish.

87 ACEN, *Soviet Objectives at the Geneva Conferences* (New York: ACEN, 1955), 1–28; also in Spanish.

88 ACEN, *The Western Choice in East-Central Europe* (New York: ACEN, 1963), 1–8; also as *Le Choix a Faire par L'Occident en Europe Centrale et Orientale* (Paris, 1963); *Die Alternativlosung des Western in Mittlosteuropa*, (Bonn, 1963); *L'Alternativa Occidentale Nell'Europa Centro-Orientale* (Rome, 1963).

89 ACEN, *The New Colonialism. Four colored maps* (New York: ACEN, 1960), 1–20; also as *El Nuevo Colonialismo* (Buenos Aires, 1961).

90 *Hungary Under Soviet Rule* was published in six volumes: I (April-August 1957), II (September 1957–August 1958); III (Revolution to August 1959); IV (August 1959–August 1960); V (1959–1961); VI (1961–1962).

Copies of these can still be found in multiple collections, including the United Nations library.

In addition to publications, the ACEN also organized exhibits. The most successful of these was the photo exhibit "Soviet Empire 1917–1958," initiated by Petr Zenkl. Its opening took place on 20 January 1958 at Grand Central Station in New York (with Senator Jacob Javits present). On 21 March 1958 it was displayed in Washington Union Station (with George Meany [AFL-CIO]). Then it toured other cities in the United States, followed by Europe (in Strasbourg it was opened by president of the Advisory Assembly, Fernand Dehousse), in Stockholm, Paris and Rome. Then the exhibit made it to Australia and Asia. In 1959 it was printed as a photo album.[91] Furthermore, the ACEN ran the Speakers' Bureau offering guest speakers to social, trade, or ethnic organizations, often sharing the cost of travel with the organizers.

In 1964, which marked ACEN's tenth anniversary, the Assembly decided to issue commemorative medals to be presented to its most ardent and loyal supporters. The bronze medal was designed by a Polish sculptor, Nina Wierzbicka. It came with a diploma awarded to select political and civic leaders. "In 1964 and 1965 presentation of these medals was ACEN's main activity [...]. All in all four hundred medals were presented," wrote Gadomski.[92] These were given to the politicians, including incumbent senators and representatives, press and TV personae in the U.S. and abroad.

While the ACEN does not mark the first effort by various East Central European diaspora members to unite, it clearly stands out as the most elaborate, broadest in scope, impactful and exceptional under the long-term funding provided by the Americans. However, this does not mean that cooperation within this framework was smooth. The turbulent history of the interwar years in North-Eastern, Central and South-Eastern Europe prompted deep cleavages in mutual relations between the Hungarians and Romanians, Poles and Czechs, Czechs and Slovaks, Lithuanians and Poles, Ukrainians and Poles, the peoples of Yugoslavia and Bulgarians, etc. There were also traditional disagreements engraved in the mentality of the exiled politicians. Furthermore, almost all the national groups had internal frictions, dating to pre-war times, making any compromises among the national delegations harder to achieve. The exiles were haunted by the ghosts of war-torn Europe, and accusations of collaboration with either Nazis or Soviets were not uncommon.[93]

---

91 *Soviet Empire, 1917–1958—a pictorial exhibit* (photographic album), ACEN Publication no. 31 (New York: ACEN, 1959), IHRC, ACEN, b. 139, f. 4.

92 Gadomski, *Zgromadzenie Europejskich* ..., 47.

93 Mazurkiewicz, *Uchodźcy* ..., 142.

It is not only the combination of nations, languages, religions, cultures and the complicated history of mutual relations, but also a cluster of personalities, prominent "has beens", whose temperament often proved more important than their political views. Additionally, there were also Communist agents in the U.S. whose only task was to discredit the exiles. This led to accusations, suspicion and a general feeling of the looming threat of Communist penetration. These fears were mostly contained behind closed-door discussions. The single most contentious point was the ACEN's joint position on rearmament and on scenarios for the reunification of Germany. At times, ACEN was at odds not only with U.S. policy, but its internal operations were marred by conflict, too. Shain calls this, in the title of his book, *Politics of schism*. Claiming legitimacy – understood as remaining true to an old electorate – became the schism.

The schism, however, helped preserve political identity in exile. It became an inseparable part of the exile identity even though the conditions in the country of settlement favored unity, joint actions, and common lobbying efforts. While the claim for legitimacy derived from the pre-departure period made political compromises – with the host government, or with fellow exiles – less likely (thus hampering the lobbying efforts), loyalty to the *ancien régime* becoming no longer relevant due to the withering away of the old socio-political order. In such a desperate set of circumstances, the most serious problem remained the lack of real power of the exiles. Without outside support – from financial, through logistical to facilitating access to media, organizations and individual politicians – the ACEN's activities were doomed in the long term.

One thing that must be emphasized at this point is that the members of the ACEN were seasoned politicians, diplomats, or people from intellectual and professional elites. Despite their differences they understood all too well both the symbolic and political value of the ACEN – the organization that enabled them to maintain their prestige and high-level political access in exile. The public outbursts of fits of anger, newspaper publications criticizing the Assembly and internal bickering rather prevalent within the national delegations did not dominate the public discourse of the ACEN. Despite serious conflicts, threats of leaving the Assembly, offenses taken and insults not forgotten, the American press record of the Assembly seems to be almost impeccable. The sizzling pieces evidencing conflicts are to be found mostly in the ethnic and émigré press. The few cases where internal squabbles in the ACEN (not within the individual, national organizations) got out were related to three issues; ideological differences (attitudes toward post-Stalinist regimes in East Central Europe), financial problems (especially after the drastic 1965 budget cuts), and the issue of the future of Germany.

No matter how important inter-ethnic cooperation in exile was for the national delegations in order to exercise any influence, no matter how closely similar political outlooks (liberal, Christian democratic, socialist or agrarian) drew different nationals together, some of the cleavages could not be bridged. Of all the ACEN's national delegations, the Poles most consequently and staunchly resisted any cooperation with Germans and never sent a representative to the organization's Bonn office, whereas Bulgarian and Romanian delegations believed that a unified, strong Germany advanced European security. To Poles, any ambivalence on the future of the Oder-Neisse border was treated as a major insult and lethal threat to further cooperation. On the other hand, when the Polish representation decided it was ready to support American plans to send economic aid to Poland (after the "Polish October" of 1956[94]) and begin some cultural exchanges – Bulgarian and Romanian delegations were outraged. Most commonly, the lines of ideological division among the different nationalities of the ACEN, reflecting the changing tides of American Cold War policies, separated the Poles – supported by the representatives of the Baltic republics and Hungarians – from the Bulgarian, Romanian and Czechoslovak delegations. However, when faced with the Soviet invasion of Czechoslovakia, which also involved Polish troops, in 1968, ACEN's members organized a powerful demonstration of Polish-Czechoslovak solidarity jointly celebrating the fiftieth anniversary of Czechoslovakia's birth and the fiftieth anniversary of Poland's rebirth, a celebration presided over by a Lithuanian statesman, Vaclovas Sidzikauskas.

It would be wrong to assume that the only unifying force behind the ACEN was American money. By the end of 1972, with the Free Europe Committee's support gone, and only a few senior exiles given stipends, the ACEN kept on working, albeit in a changed form. Nothing was more powerful in uniting Eastern European émigrés than the lethal Soviet threat to the very existence of their beloved homelands.

It must be explicitly stated that the émigré political organs did not promote the restoration of any "old order." Their ultimate goal, using their own words, was "the restoration of genuine self-determination and sovereignty to their subjugated nations," through "free elections and withdrawal of Soviet troops." As for the future form of government in these countries, "it should be determined

94 The "Polish October" began on 19 X 1956 with 8th Polish United Workers Party Plenum and Khrushchev's sudden arrival to Warsaw. On 24 October 1956 Władysław Gomułka – the new party leader, whom Soviets reluctantly decided to accept, addressed crowds in Warsaw promising liberalization, which proved to be only a temporary relaxation of oppression. Symbolically, the "Polish October" marks the end of Stalinism in Poland.

by the peoples themselves in genuinely free elections, which is their undeniable right."

The exiles' reasoning may also have been going along with Feliks Gross' thesis of 1950, namely that "[d]emocratic exiles would like to see Eastern Europe free from both German and Russian influence and domination." They "realized that there is a broader loyalty than a nation, and that nations in Eastern Europe can survive, economically and politically, only in a general framework of a broader federal system."[95] Regardless of the differences and internal squabbles, the ACEN's members tirelessly advanced the cause of East Central Europe's liberation, striving to retain it on the agenda of international relations. In this arena, there was only one power willing to offer them much needed political and financial support – the United States.

1.2 The Free Europe Committee

By the time ACEN was officially inaugurated on 20 September 1954, the FEC had already been functioning for five years, having successfully transferred itself from under the auspices of Democratic to Republican administrations. President Eisenhower developed his original program for waging the "war of words." With the help of one of his top political advisors, C.D. Jackson,[96] the President authorized a policy of "New Look."[97] "Psychological warfare," which George F. Kennan officially referred to as "political warfare,"[98] was entering a new phase, referred to as "psychological activities" – an integral part of "the main body of diplomatic, economic and military measures by which the U.S. sought to achieve its national objectives."[99]

Already in January 1953, Eisenhower appointed William H. Jackson (former Deputy Director of the CIA) to chair the President's Committee on International Information Activities. The Committee was established to "survey and evaluate

---

95 Feliks Gross, "Political Emigration from Iron Curtain Countries," *Annals of the American Academy of Political and Social Science* 271: Moscow's European Satellites (September 1950), 175–184.

96 John Allen Stern, *C. D. Jackson. Cold War Propagandist for Democracy and Globalism* (Lanham: University Press of America Inc., 2012), xii–xiii.

97 Mazurkiewicz, *Uchodźcy* ..., 39, 81–82.

98 Ibid., 35.

99 Report to the President by the President's Committee on International Information Activities, 30 VI 1953, *FRUS, 1952–1954, National Security Affairs*, Vol. II, part 2 (Washington: GPO, 1984), doc. 370, 1796–1868. https://history.state.gov/historicaldocuments/frus1952-54v02p2/d370, accessed 10 X 2019.

the Government's information and related policies and activities with particular reference to international relations and the national security."[100] The committee presented a report to the President in June 1953, which was then turned over to the National Security Council (NSC) for study.[101] It contained a section devoted to "Operations Against the Soviet System" (part II, chapter 4) within which, among other programs like American broadcasters (the Voice of America or Radio in American Sector), there was a section devoted to the National Committee for a Free Europe. From the report, the incoming administration learned that the Committee was "created by the CIA in 1949 with the following purposes":

1. to create an institution in which the émigrés from the satellite nations could find employment which would utilize their skills and, at the same time, document for the world at large the actions of the satellite governments and Soviet Russia;
2. to utilize the political figures of such emigrations as rallying points and as symbols of unified opposition to communism in this country and abroad;
3. to relieve the Department of State of the need to deal with émigré political leaders whom they could not endorse as "Governments in Exile" at a time when the United States officially recognized the satellite governments; and
4. generally to "aid the non-fascist, non-communist leaders in their peaceful efforts to prepare the way toward the restoration in Eastern Europe of the social, political, and religious liberties, in which they and we believe.[102]

100 The Jackson Committee: William H. Jackson, a managing partner in the investment firm J.H. Whitney and Company, DD/CIA, Robert Cutler, C.D. Jackson, Roger Kyes, Sigurd Larmon, Gordon Gray, Barklie McKee Henry, and John C. Hughes. Abbott Washburn served as Executive Secretary of the Committee and was assisted by a deputy, Robert Blum. The Committee's staff and secretariat consisted of about 25 people drawn from the Department of State, Department of Defense, CIA, Mutual Security Agency, and the Office of Defense Mobilization. See: U.S. President's Committee on International Information Activities (Jackson Committee) Records, 1950–1953, Finding aid: https://www.eisenhowerlibrary.gov/sites/default/files/finding-aids/pdf/us-presidents-committee-on-international-information-activities.pdf, accessed 10 X 2019.

101 Annex E: Report of the CIA on the implementation of the recommendation of the Jackson Committee Report (list B), in: OCB, Progress Report to the NSC on implementation of recommendations of the Jackson Committee Report (NSC action no. 866), 30 IX 1953; "Implementation of Jackson Committee Recommendations on Radio Free Europe and Radio Liberty," 30 IX 1953, History and Public Policy Program Digital Archive, Obtained and contributed to CWIHP by A. Ross Johnson. Cited in his book Radio Free Europe and Radio Liberty. CIA mandatory declassification review document number C01441053 (released in march 2009), henceforth: Wilson Center, CWIHP, Ross Johnson collection, http://digitalarchive.wilsoncenter.org/document/114475, accessed: 12 V 2020.

102 Report to the President by the President's Committee on International ..., 1831–1832.

In the archival collection of Arch Puddington – author of a seminal work on Radio Free Europe – there is an unsigned memorandum from early 1954 that offers one possible way of looking at the Free Europe Committee, as it was construed at the time. "Free Europe is not a foreign office; it does not make, or even participate in the making of the foreign policy if the United States. It is not a debating society; its aim is not to arrive at eternal verities. Its policy follows that of the Government of the United States." Its functions as described in this document were propaganda aimed at the eventual overthrow of certain communist regimes (RFE), with two objectives of strategic importance: to persuade the peoples it addressed to contribute as little as possible to the Soviet war potential in manpower and material resources, and to keep those peoples in such a state of discontent with the communist regimes under which they lived that their countries lying between the Soviet frontier and western Europe should constitute an insecure rather than a secure communications zone in the event of Soviet troop movements across them.[103]

The American national interest must remain at the center of attention when analyzing the FEC's relations with East Central European exiles. "We are not neighbors," wrote Lewis Galantière, author of numerous policy papers at FEC, in February 1956: [104]

> Our economic interest is in their prosperity as a whole, allied to the prosperity of Europe as a whole; it does not lie in bilateral trade. Our immediate strategic interest is that they shall contribute as little as possible in resources and manpower to the Soviet military potential and that their opposition to Soviet hegemony shall continue to make these lands and insecure zone of communications in the event of Soviet troop movement west and south. Our long-term stake appears to rest upon the principle that the U.S. cannot afford to see any

---

103 Memorandum, 12 II 1954, HIA, Puddington Papers, b. 31, f. 8. This memorandum, albeit not verified by author (representing the FEC), in the context of political problems between Slovaks, Czechs and in relation to Germany. Puddington, 73–81.

104 Lewis Galantière, author of multiple policy papers, Political Counsel to FEC President, author of a proposal for a widely discussed FEC Policy Handbook: The Captive Nations of Central and Eastern Europe and the Four-Power Conference [third draft], 22 VI 1955, attachment to Lewis Galantière to Bernard Yarrow, 30 VI 1955, HIA, RFE/RL CF: A, b. 191, f. 5; John F. Leich to Bernard Yarrow, Memorandum: Policy Handbook by Lewis Galantière, 23 X 1956, HIA, RFE/RL CF: A, b. 191, f. 5; Huston to Yarrow, Comment on Draft Text for Policy Handbook, 23 X 1956, ibid.; Acker to Yarrow, Memorandum: FEER's mission as described therein, 23 X 1956, ibid.; Frances Hyland to Yarrow, Memorandum: Mr. Galantière's Policy Paper, 24 X 1956, ibid.; Earl L. Packer to Yarrow, Comments on FEC Policy Handbook, 23 X 1956, ibid. It is important to note that the dates of these memoranda indicate the beginning of the Hungarian Revolution and hence all the political assessment were subject to rapid and complete reevaluation in the aftermath of the dramatic events.

> single power – yesterday Germany, today the USSR – dominant on the European continent. [...] thus, it would appear to be in the interest of the three leaders of the Western Coalition that the captive nations shall be withdrawn from Soviet hegemony and their independence restored. Ideally, that restoration would take place, not in a balance-of-power system much as Britain sought for three centuries to maintain, but within the framework of a European federation or confederation.[105]

These documents sum up the thinking behind the operations of the Free Europe Committee. Envisioned as a political warfare tool by George Kennan, and using the assets available to the Americans in the form of exiles willing to cooperate to liberate their homelands. The Committee was first and foremost created to serve the American security interests. The other reasons, like finding a way to assist the political exiles and refugees (humanitarian), "maintaining a spirit of friendship for the American people among numerous central and eastern European political leaders now living in exile, particularly in the United States" (domestic information programs) et al., played a secondary role. The FEC was "obliged by its mandate to maintain friendly relations with, and to lend moderate material support to, political exiles whose good will is deemed useful to our country's interest."[106]

With the election of Eisenhower came the (faulty) promise of liberation of the captive nations. To explain what it meant in practical terms for the FEC, Galantière quoted John Foster Dulles' Chicago speech (29 November 1954): "Liberation normally comes from within. But it is more apt to come from within if hope is constantly sustained from without."[107] This can be applied to explain the FEC mission during the first term of Eisenhower's presidency, as by the end of 1956, in the aftermath of the Hungarian Revolution,[108] the FEC's tactics had to be adjusted so as not to stir up exaggerated expectations. However, it was the tactics, not the ultimate goal, that had to be re-defined to underscore the evolutionary

---

105 Lewis Galantière to Shepardson, Egan, Walker, Yarrow, Attachment, Draft dated 29 February 1956: The U.S. Stake in Central and Eastern Europe, 2 III 1956, HIA, RFE/RL CF: A, f. 191, b. 1.
106 Memorandum, 12 II 1954 ...
107 The Captive Nations of Central and Eastern Europe and the Four-Power Conference [third draft], 22 VI 1955, attachment to Lewis Galantière to Bernard Yarrow, 30 VI 1955, HIA, RFE/RL CF: A, b. 191, f. 5.
108 Memorandum: [Secret] Proposed Interim Guidance for FEC, 16 XI 1956. Obtained and contributed to CWIHP by A. Ross Johnson. Cited in his book, Radio Free Europe and Radio Liberty, CIA mandatory declassification review document number MORI 1426199, 1426201; http://digitalarchive.wilsoncenter.org/document/114746.

character of changes leading to democratization and self-determination in East Central Europe.[109] This strategic objective remained steady.

The ACEN's establishment was presented in the report of the FEC President as a result of a series of coordinated exile actions to bring pressure in connection with the UN Economic and Social Council (ECOSOC) meetings in the fall of 1954. Twenty-four exiles congregated in a Steering Committee and prepared reports on issues relevant to ECOSC debates that were then distributed to the UN delegations. "After intense debate, during which the evidence submitted by the exiles was extensively utilized, ECOSOC overwhelmingly condemned forced labor and recommended that further studies be made on the subject by the Secretariat and International Labor Office."[110] The UN's condemning of Communist forced labor practices was considered a great success, worthy of continuation. The FEC's Division of Exile Relations invited the heads of national councils and committees, who appointed coordinators to establish a permanent framework.

The best evidence of the Free Europe Committee's decision to create the ACEN is found in Lewis Galantière's draft of the FEC's policy of August 1954.[111] It indicates that during the talks within the FEC, and with the sponsors, it was decided not only to continue support for the exiles ("caretaker job"), but "to continue to try to unify national councils so that their existence would be known to all governments and peoples in the west" and "work hard with national councils if only to set good political climate." Interestingly, Galantière wrote that "it would be preferable to deal with delegates of national councils who have formed themselves into groups than to have direct relations with national councils, which would be reserved for special purposes. Sponsors pointed out that the FEC would have complete support for their decisions if successful participation could be arranged," and they wanted to see the price tag by 15 September 1954.[112]

Works on reports related to East Central European cases of forced labor, deportations, religious persecution, Soviet aggression, the status of women, forcible repatriation, genocide, the violation of peace treaties, and the abrogation of

109 The State Department approves with "comments and recommendations," 15 November 1956, CIA/IOD draft of revised guidelines for the Free Europe Committee (FEC) with handwritten revisions [presumably by a State official]. Memorandum for [redacted], subject: "Proposed Interim Policy Guidance for Free Europe Committee, Draft," 16 XI 1956, Wilson Center, CWIHP, Ross Johnson collection, http://digitalarchive.wilsoncenter.org/document/114746, accessed 12 V 2020.
110 FEC President Report 1954, 18–19.
111 Statement by Mr. Galantière, Policy, Priorities, Plans and Program, 29 VIII 1954, HIA, RFE/RL CF: A, b. 191, f. 5.
112 Ibid.

trade union rights in captive Europe carried out by the exiles throughout the summer of 1954 were coordinated by the FEC's Frederick T. Merrill.[113] Whitney H. Shepardson, the President of FEC, believed that the creation of the ACEN, which adopted a series of resolutions urging UN action, had "brought real influence to bear on UN decisions and proved to be an encouragement to the captive peoples in that it dramatically demonstrated that their cause is supported by their compatriots abroad."[114]

The process of the emergence of the ACEN must, however, be interpreted in the context of exile activities carried out independently from the FEC. Already by 1952 there were two separate multi-national assemblies in the U.S. created independently of the FEC, but by the same exiles who later founded ACEN. The Central and East European Conference (with many representatives of councils and committees in exile) and Central and East European Committee (with strong links to Peasant International, IPU). While overcoming this divide was not easy, in August 1954 the East Central European exiles established the United National Committees and Councils in Exile (UNCCE). Ten national delegations were represented in it (the ACEN nine, plus Yugoslav), the President of the united committees/councils was Vilis Māsēns.[115] While the UNCEE hoped to obtain support from the FEC, it emerged beyond its control. Faced with such a development, the Americans stepped up its effort to re-organize its relations with exile committees and councils and well as exert control over united exile delegations.

The exiles received financial, logistical, but also political and organizational assistance, which was essential for the development of their political activities. The FEC was also glad:

> We have succeeded to date because we have deliberately made efforts to keep behind the scenes, merely guiding them as tactfully and indirectly as possible. As a result, the exile

113 For earlier publications on the ACEN's origins, and a general overview of ACEN activities see Anna Mazurkiewicz, "'Join, or Die'—The Road to Cooperation among East European Exiled Political Leaders in the United States, 1949–1954," *Polish American Studies* 69, no. 2 (2012): 5–43; Mazurkiewicz, "Assembly of the Captive European Nations: 'The Voice of the Silenced Peoples'" in: *Anti-Communist Minorities* ..., 167–185. John F. Leich called him "the real organizer of ACEN," who "did the organizational legwork from our office on West 57th street, and when the organization was born, he brought in Jim McCargar to as liaison between the NCFE and ACEN. They met in an apartment across the street over the Steinway Piano agency." John F. Leich, e-mails of: 7 II 2008, 25 IV 2008, 14 X 2007.

114 Annual Report of the President of Free Europe Committee Inc., to the Directors and members of the Committee (FEC President's Report for the Year 1954), HSTL, Papers od Charles Hulten, b. 22, f.: RFE (3), 19–20.

115 Mazurkiewicz, *Uchodźcy* ..., 400–401.

> attitude toward FEC is more favorable than at any other time in recent history and we grope towards 'the climate' of understanding and cooperation that is DER's function to achieve. [...] Our own formula of starting ACEN off by inviting councils and committees to appoint coordinators and delegations [was] a formula which prevented UNCCE from taking it over.[116]

"Please, Oh, please don't let us tamper with the new-born ACEN baby at this juncture," Merril implored Galantière in January 1955.

In the 1963 internal review memorandum one other interpretation of the ACEN's origin was provided. The author (most likely from the CIA) stated that the initial reason behind supporting the ACEN was to give advice:

> The impetus for setting up ACEN came from within FEC and from within the East European exile community. The original idea, as it was developed by the first Director of RFE, Bob [Robert] Lang, was to have a body of eminent exile advisors to FEC who would both give RFE advice on broadcasting policy and also serve to absorb and deflect criticism of RFE/FEC from hostile exiles, Germans, U.S. congressmen etc. The establishment of ACEN was not requested or urged on FEC by either the EC (Executive Committee) [CIA] or the Advisory Board [Department of State]. By the time the organization actually came into being in 1954, however, the notion that it would be useful for RFE had been abandoned and it was set up under the Division of Exile Relations. It was still assumed that it might act as an advisory body to FEC.[117]

Ten years earlier, before the ACEN's establishment, a similar statement regarding the role of the exiles was included in the William H. Jackson Report of 1953, stating that the original plan to use the national committees and councils for broadcasts over RFE was rejected because of "rivalries of émigré politics." It also stated, however, that the exile political organizations could be useful to FEC in propaganda activities.[118]

As the ACEN came into being in 1954, Shepardson, the President of FEC explained the Committee's ultimate goal:

---

116 Frederick T. Merrill to Lewis Galantière, Memorandum, 3 I 1955, HIA, RFE/RL CF: A, b. 198, f. 5.

117 [CIA], Memorandum for the Record: The Assembly of Captive European Nations, 1 VII 1963, DDEL, C.D. Jackson Papers, b. 53, f.: FEC Budget 1963 (1). This memorandum constituted part of the CIA review of the FEC-sponsored Latin American activities conducted in June and July 1963.

118 William H. Jackson (Chairman) et al., Report to the President by the President's Committee on International Information Activities (top secret) [Washington,] June 30, 1953, Eisenhower Library, White House Office records, "Project 'Clean Up,'" *FRUS, 1952–1954, Vol. II, Part 2: National Security Affairs* (Washington: GPO 1984), doc. 368, https://history.state.gov/historicaldocuments/frus1952-54v02p2/d370, 1833.

> Incorporated in the State of New York in 1949, Free Europe Committee is a membership association of American citizens who believe that the peoples behind the Iron Curtain – in Albania, Bulgaria, Czechoslovakia, Estonia, Hungary, Latvia, Lithuania, Poland, Romania – are being held captive against their will by the agents of Soviet Russia who, for the time being, rule over them. The mission of FEC is therefore to work for freedom of these peoples in order that they may one day be able to erect democratic institutions of their own choosing and join with the other peoples of Europe in establishing a peaceful, fraternal and co-operative European community.[119]

In 1954 both the FEC (as non-radio programs) and RFE were perceived by the American government as "powerful propaganda and psychological political instruments":

> The purpose of FEC was to provide a means of supporting and utilizing prominent political exiles from communist-dominated countries without recognizing these groups as Governments in Exile and to avoid complications for the Department which maintained diplomatic relations with the Communist Governments of the countries from which they fled. The two major functions performed by FEC are (1) support and utilization of émigré groups as symbols of resistance and (2) broadcasts to the peoples of Eastern Europe through RFE.[120]

Moreover, the work of the FEC was not solely focused on reaching people in East Central Europe but, as Shepardson put it, the Committee was a "political warfare operation engaged in a struggle against Soviet Russian colonialism behind the Iron Curtain and communist influence this side of the curtain."[121] While the FEC operations were to be carried out on both sides of the Cold War divide, its declared, ultimate goal was a free and independent East Central Europe. In his conclusion to the report for 1955, Shepardson quoted President Eisenhower (30 December 1955): "The peaceful liberation of the captive nations has been, is, and until success is achieved, will continue to be, a major goal of United States, foreign policy."[122]

The FEC operated in between multiple government branches and agencies, with political guidelines being influenced by the Department of State, and budget provided by the funds coming from the CIA. The President of the Free Europe

---

119 FEC President's Report for the Year 1954, 1.

120 Attachment: Briefing Notes to: Memorandum from the Deputy Operations Coordinator in the Office of the Under Secretary of State (Hulick) to the Under Secretary of State (Hoover), 23 VIII 1954, *FRUS, The Intelligence Community 1950–55. Organization of U.S. Intelligence* (Washington: GPO, 2007), doc. 188, 521–522, https://history.state.gov/historicaldocuments/frus1950-55Intel/d188, accessed 10 X 2019.

121 FEC President's Report for the Year 1954, 2.

122 FEC President's Report for the Year 1955, 26.

Committee had to take into consideration opinions of both the Department of State (consulted during multiple meetings at the State and through unofficial contacts, and often referred to as an "Advisory Board"), as well as the CIA, referred to as "Friends," "The South," "Sponsors," or mentioned as the "Executive Committee" (EC).[123] Most of the FEC budget came from the CIA (two thirds to three fourths of its money).[124]

Ostensibly, however, the Committee was a private organization sponsored by the Crusade for Freedom. In October 1961, it estimated that 2.5 million dollars were provided to the FEC by the CIA.[125] Smaller sums were obtained by private donations and through the fund-raising campaigns organized by the Crusade for Freedom.[126] All in all, as established by Kádár-Lynn, between 1949 and 1971 the FEC spent 357 million dollars, 86% of which came from the CIA. In total, 76 million were spent on non-radio activities.[127] The annual budgets of the FEC were about 15 to 17 million dollars.[128] Within these, in 1960, roughly 67% of resources went to RFE, 23% to non-radio programs, and 10% to cover the cost of general administration.[129]

To illustrate the dominating role of the radio broadcasters it is sufficient to cite the statistic that from May 1949 to June 1971 Radio Free Europe broadcast to five countries in East Central Europe, and received 248.9 million dollars.[130] FEC

---

123 This should not be confused with the FEC Board of Directors' Executive Committee.

124 Attachment: Briefing Notes to: Memorandum ..., 23 VIII 1954, *FRUS, The Intelligence Community 1950–55* ..., doc. 188.

125 John Richardson Memorandum: The Free Europe Committee. A Description and a Proposal, 27 X 1961, attachment to: John C. Hughes to Allen W. Dulles, 27 X 1961, DDEL, C.D. Jackson Papers, b. 53, f.: FEC, 1961 (1).

126 Mazurkiewicz, *Uchodźcy* ..., 213, 259–265.

127 Kádár Lynn, *At War while at Peace* ..., 26–29. See chapter 3: Analysis of Free Europe Inc.. Receipts and Expenditures, 22 in: Comptroller General of the United States, Report to the Committee on Foreign Relations, U.S. Senate: "U.S. Government Monies Provided to Radio Free Europe And Radio Liberty," 25 V 1972, U.S. Government Accountability Office (GAO), B-173239, https://www.gao.gov/assets/210/204192.pdf, accessed 14 VII 2020.

128 FEC Budgets for the following years were for 1957: 16,470 th., 1958: 15,620 th., 1959: 15,580 th., 1960: 15,160 th., 1961: 15,570 th., 1962: 14,950 th., 1963: 16,450 th. FEC Expenditures (in millions of dollars), Summary, 9 IX 1963, DDEL, C.D. Jackson Papers, b. 53, f.: FEC Budget 1963 (1).

129 This sum excludes $160,000 of discontinued expenditures on the Mid-European Law Project and the International Institute of labor research. FEC Annual Expenditures, FY 1959–1960 Estimate, attached to: Reorientation of Exile Organizations, 1 IV 1960, DDEL, C.D. Jackson Papers, b. 53, f.: FEC 1960 (2).

130 At roughly the same time Radio Liberty, broadcasting to the Soviet Union, received (between January 1951 – June 1971) 158.8 million dollars from the CIA and no private donations at all. Kádár Lynn, *At War while at Peace* ..., 26–29; Johnson, *Radio Free Europe* ..., 217.

programs relating to exile organizations amounted to about 30 million dollars (including payments of stipends to individual exiles). According to the Comptroller General of the U.S., the total cost of supporting the national councils was $ 2,665,000, and of exile relations program (exile political organization division) $ 19,438,000.[131]

Some of the non-radio operations coordinated by the FEC, financed from the funds obtained from the CIA, were conducted in the U.S. As such they breached the National Security Act (1947) on the grounds of which the Agency was established. It prohibited the CIA from running domestic operations, unless these had a foreign target.[132] In the case of the ACEN, the operations were conducted by foreign nationals, who were registered as such under the provisions of the Foreign Agents Registration Act, assuming "certain responsibilities and objectives within the U.S. that are a legitimate and important part of our activities," as Robert E. McDonald wrote to the FEC President. He divided these into five categories: the FEC as a channel for information; a way to maintain the American people's interest in East Central Europe; maintaining and supporting RFE so that it could remain clearly "sponsored by the American people"; combating subversion by counteracting regime propaganda with facts; exerting influence on increasing the flow of "East European visits"; assist with the preparation of "basic materials about Eastern Europe."[133]

Richardson, who was the President at the time, in his memoir published over 40 years later, wrote: "In hindsight, I now regard as wrong the concealed use of taxpayer money for exile activities and to 'cover' those of Radio Free Europe Fund, both intended to influence American public opinion. They were, it is now clear to me, a covert infringement by the federal government on the free market of ideas on which the health of our democratic system depends."[134]

In 1961 the CIA decided it wanted to review the FEC's external operations regarding security, funding, its viability with the FEC's mission as publicly understood, the efficiency of management-administration, and in terms of operational returns.[135] Based on a questionnaire provided for the purpose, the FEC President

131 "U.S. Government Monies Provided to Radio Free Europe And Radio Liberty," 15–16.

132 Collins, "The Free Europe Committee ...," 122.

133 Robert E. McDonald to John Richardson, Jr., Bernard Yarrow, John Page, Memorandum: The responsibilities and objectives of the Free Europe Committee in the United States, 12 XI 1963, HIA, RFE/RF CF: A, b. 192, f. 1.

134 John Richardson, *A New Vision for America* (New York: Ruder Finn Press: 2006), 93.

135 The Executive Committee to The President (FEC), Memorandum: External Free Europe Committee Operations, 20 XI 1961, HIA, RFE/RL CF: FEC. INC, b. 1999, f.: Policy, External Operations 1961–1962.

collected reports on various areas of the Committee's operations, like free world operations, or Communist Bloc operations. The set also included a report on exile political operations, which discussed the ACEN (listed as one of the "external assets"), nine national committees and four internationals.[136]

With regards to the first area entitled: "cover – security – founding" the report stated that there was "fairly general public knowledge that FEC funds ACEN and the National Committees, although public statements are limited to generalities such as 'supports,' 'assists,' or 'works with.' Some degree of financial support would logically be implied by FEC's declared interest in exiles." The ACEN received no extra income above the FEC's support, except for "a few personal or member contributions of little consequence." Payments to the ACEN were made by checks, on a monthly allotment basis. Virtually all FEC employees and active members of the exile groups knew about the FEC's funding of ACEN activities. Furthermore, the questionnaire asked: Who is aware of the FEC–EC relationship? "The relationship is generally assumed, among members of the external organizations and (at least in general terms) among a large part of the exile community, not based on specific knowledge but from references in the press over the years plus guesswork."[137] When reviewing FEC operations, the CIA wanted to know if the link to FEC could still be concealed, and whether the supported organizations were vulnerable to right-wing attack. To the question on public visibility included in section two, "What do the organizations look like to the American public?" – the report on exile political organizations responded: "All appear to be what they are."

John Richardson was the eighth President of the FEC.[138] The President was responsible for the overall, daily operations of the FEC. The administration also consisted of vice presidents responsible for FEC divisions (Radio Free Europe, Free Europe Press, Exile Relations), a secretary and a treasurer. There were also heads of projects and sponsored initiatives such as the the Mid-European Studies Center, Mid-European Law Project, the East European Accessions List, the Free Europe Citizens Service (incorporated to Exile Relations in January

136 CDUCE was not listed. Exile Political Organizations, attachment to: The President (FEC) to The Executive Committee, Survey of FEC External Operations, 1 II 1962, HIA, RFE/RL CF: FEC., Inc, b. 1999, f.: Policy, External Operations 1961–1962.

137 Ibid.

138 Allen Dulles (1949), DeWitt C. Poole (1949–1951), C.D. Jackson (1951–1952), rear admiral USN ret. H.B. Miller (1952–1953), Whitney Shepardson (1953–1956), gen. Willis D. Crittenberger (1957–1958), Archibald Alexander (1959–1961), John Richardson (1961–1967), William P. Durkee (1968-). Mazurkiewicz, *Uchodźcy* ..., 200.

1956), Free Europe University in Exile, and regional office directors, etc.[139] An important role was played by counselors for political, international labor and other matters. Opinions expressed by these high-powered intellectuals often collided, especially given the fact that the FEC President had his own counselors in New York, while the RFE Director in Munich often relied on his own political advisors. Regarding the ACEN, the name of Lewis Galantière often comes up, as he authored political papers that involved tasks or areas of interest to be forwarded to the exile Assembly.[140] Galantière was nominated an advisor for policy and plans to the directors of RFE and FEP on 5 May 1954. On 1 August 1956, he became counselor-advisor to the FEC President in New York.[141] During an evaluation in 1962, his role seemed quite important: "[I]t is obvious that his experience and skill in political analysis and policy development can be invaluable to this [Policy] Division and should be available to it as frequently as possible."[142]

Control over FEC operations was exercised by the Board of Directors (which included people recommended or connected to the Department of State) and Executive Committee (CIA).[143] Policy guidelines were set by the organization's President in collaboration with the FEC's Board of Director's Executive Committee.[144] The system was not as efficient as the sponsors hoped. Already by 1954, the internal review of operations found that,

> [w]hile FEC and RFE are supposed to function within the framework of official U.S. policy and under policy guidance from the Department [of State], they have been gradually assuming a degree of independence of operation, which has created a control problem. Decisions involving matters of policy consequence are frequently taken by FEC and RFE without reference to the Department through the Agency [CIA]. This is a matter of real concern which the Department and the Agency are currently attempting to resolve.[145]

---

139 For a detailed description of the structure, as well as changes to it, see: Mazurkiewicz, *Uchodźcy* ..., 227.

140 Lurie, *Galantière* ..., 165–187.

141 Mazurkiewicz, *Uchodźcy* ..., 201–202.

142 Richard C. Rowson, Summary Report and Recommendations: Free Europe Committee, Policy Division, based on consultations in New York, Munich, Berlin, Vienna, Brussels and London, July 16–August 17, 1962, 23 VIII 1962, HIA, RFE/RL CF: A, b. 191, f. 7.

143 Mazurkiewicz, *Uchodźcy* ..., 188–189. See also: List of Members of the FEC Board, 1949–1954, ibid, 190–197. Relationship between FEC and CIA see: ibid., 203–216.

144 John F. Leich, Letter to the author, 14 X 2007.

145 Attachment: Briefing Notes to: Memorandum ..., 23 VIII 1954, *FRUS, The Intelligence Community 1950–55*, doc. 188, 521–522.

From 1951 the FEC's headquarters were located at 110 West 57th street in New York. Six years later it moved to 2 Park Avenue, and it was this address that became a synonym for American control over exile activities.

The initial name of the department within the FEC that dealt with the exiles was the National Councils Division (since April 1950). From 1952 until 1955 it was called the Division of Exile Relations (DER). From 1956 onwards it was called Free Europe Exile Relations (FEER).[146] By 1959, within the Free Europe's structure, the Exile Relations were bundled together with the publications program (FEP – Free Europe Press).[147] The new entity: Free Europe Organizations and Publications (FEOP) consumed about 23% of the FEC's overall budget in 1960.[148] Within this division, a third (34%) of a budget was allotted to the exile programs.[149] It was within this fund that the ACEN budget was located.

The FEC's exile division financed the national committees, "meritorious exiles," international organizations (inter alia consultative members of ACEN), and the ACEN itself. According to Gadomski, Bernard Yarrow's office was responsible for the ACEN's budget negotiations. In his book he says the budget was about 350 thousand dollars.[150] In 1957, which should be considered the financial peak year, the ACEN budget was 332,947 dollars.[151] In the following years it was lower, although by absorbing some of the activities previously paid for through the national councils/committees, the ACEN's budgets slightly increased from 252,540 dollars (in 1958) to 275,000 dollars (in 1959), and to 291,065 dollars (in 1960).[152] In the 1960s, the ACEN budget did not exceed 200 thousand dollars. In 1961 it was 195,260 dollars, and in 1962 it was 198,656 dollars. The ACEN never truly recovered from the major budgetary cuts of 1965, and by 1967 its budget

---

146 Richard J. Condon (European Director) to Department and Section Heads, 20 I 1956, HIA, RFE/RLCF: FEC Historical File, b. 1700, f.: FEC Exile Rel div 1953–1958.

147 Archibald Alexander to Staff Free Europe, 2 VI 1959, HIA, RFE/RL CF: A, b. 189, f. 1.

148 Charles J. McNeill (Assistant European Director, RFE) forwarding announcement by Archibald S. Alexander to Staff, FEC, 15 VI 1959, HIA, RFE/RL CF: Historical File, b. 1700, f.: FEOP 1959–1960.

149 Within the 23% for FEOP (or 3 542 000$) there was 1,384,000 (or 34%) for Exile Political Organizations. FEOP Expenditures, 1 IV 1960, attached to: Reorientation of Exile Organizations, 1 IV 1960, DDEL, C.D. Jackson Papers, b. 53, f.: FEC 1960 (2).

150 Gadomski, *Zgromadzenie Europejskich* ..., 22.

151 [CIA], Memorandum for the Record: The Assembly ..., 1 VII 1963.

152 Comparative Summary of FEER-FEP (FEOP) Expenditures, Fiscal Years 1958–1959; 1959–1960: 1960–1961, and Comparative Statement "Exile" Expenditures, attachment to: Theodore Augustine (FEC) to C.D. Jackson, 28 IV 1960, DDEL, C.D. Jackson Papers, b. 53, f.: FEC, 1960 (2).

was roughly 107,844 dollars.[153] These numbers exclude some additional project-based allotments, but the median number to measure the scale of operations that can be used is around 250 thousand dollars, which is equivalent to about 1.8 million dollars today.[154]

The ACEN's budget included an array of its activities: 24 % to the secretariat in NY; and single digit percentage points for allowances, office rental, social security payments, ACEN House, office expenses, publications, manifestations and travel. In the fiscal year of 1959, the salaries of the ACEN staff were: secretary general 6,847 dollars per year, his deputy 6,460 dollars, press officer 6,000 dollars, political affairs officer 6,160 dollars. Economic social cultural officer 5,920 dollars, UN affairs officer 4,050 dollars, administrative officer 5,440 dollars, documentation officer 5,100 dollars; librarians, typists, secretaries, receptionist, mimeo operator, steno-secretary received from 3,500 to 4,320 dollars.[155] Salaries for the ACEN's paid staff were deemed "modest, lower than those paid to the American employees."[156]

By 1959, the ACEN's budget for the first time included "delegates" (offices abroad) which amounted to 14 % of the overall budget. Overseas operations added up to 28 %. All in all, in the early 1960s the ACEN's operations abroad amounted to a mighty 42 %.[157] The same year the FEC proposed an overall budget cut by 1,290 thousand dollars, which was to affect the ACEN as well in fiscal year 1961 to 1962.[158] At this time, the ACEN's estimated expenditures for 1960 to 1961

---

153 [CIA], Memorandum for the Record: The Assembly ..., 1 VII 1963; Comparison of Expenditures, Fiscal Years 1963 – 1965, 10 II 1964, DDEL, C.D. Jackson Papers, b. 52, f.: FEC, 1964; FEOP Budget Proposal FY 1961 – 1962, Feb. 1961, HIA, RFE/RL CF: Historical File, b. 1700, f. FEOP: 1959 – 1962.

154 Lawrence H. Officer and Samuel H. Williamson, "Purchasing Power of Money in the United States from 1774 to 2008," MeasuringWorth, 2009. URL http://www.measuringworth.com/ppowerus/. The value of a dollar is determined using the Consumer Price Index from December of the previous year.

155 Exhibit VI Present Staff Members of Exile Organizations, ACEN, attached to: Free Europe Organizations and Publications, Reorientation of Exile Organizations, 1 IV 1960, HIA, RFE/RL CF: A, b. 197, f. 8

156 Gadomski, *Zgromadzenie Europejskich* ..., 22.

157 Exhibit V: Comparative Costs, 1 IV 1960, attached to: Reorientation of Exile Organizations, 1 IV 1960, DDEL, C.D. Jackson Papers, b. 53, f.: FEC 1960 (2). These numbers are adjusted in the memo of April 1. ACEN Budget 1959 – 1960 – new position comes in Delegates – added to the budget. Total sum for NY office expenses: 186,850; for overseas operations 88,150, the new for delegates 43,200.

158 Memorandum to: Executive Committee of Free Europe Committee Board in Connection with its 20 January meeting, 18 I 1961, DDEL, C.D. Jackson Papers, B. 53, f.: FEC 1961 (3).

were 242,080 dollars, while the FEC proposal reduced it by 46,820 dollars. For the "meritorious exiles," the cuts were even more drastic, reduced by 12,868 dollars from 92,868 dollars.[159]

As mentioned previously, except for the money allotted to the ACEN, its members – the national representative bodies – were also receiving financial support. However, they were not treated equally by the American sponsors. For example, in 1961, of the nine national projects (councils and committees), the biggest financial support was given to the Hungarians, Poles and Balts (treated as one representative body in the FEC's budget). This disparity can be, at least partially, attributed to the development of the Latin American programs. The Hungarian part of it, carried out mostly outside of the ACEN's structures, is not described in the chapter that follows and awaits a detailed study.

From the outset, in the mid-1940s, some of the exiles who arrived in the U.S. were supported with a stipend, a monthly payment which in most cases was about 300 dollars. By today's purchasing power that is about 2,300 dollars. Based on the 1960 FEC's budget (reorientation of exile support) the discrepancies among the individual leaders can be clearly observed. A list of exiles supported individually regarding ACEN activities and prepared in 1960, contains information on individual salaries paid per annum to then supported national councils' members. Only a few of the listed leaders (predominantly Romanians) received 3,360 dollars per year (300 dollars per month). The majority of exiled leaders received a payment of 4,800 dollars (400 dollars per month; by today's value almost 3,000 dollars). Some, like Stefan Korboński, Bolesław Biega and Pál Auer received as much as 6,000 dollars a year (today 43,600 dollars), so a salary then equal to the median annual American household income.

The "meritorious exiles" were people whom FEC considered top personnel with whom consultative meetings were held. What they had in common was education, experience, and an open mind (also to American suggestions). On 25 March 1960, Bernard Yarrow suggested top personnel for the ACEN's future program development:[160]

---

159 Based on: ibid; Comparative Statement of "Exile" expenditures for the fiscal years 1959–60–61, attached to: Theodore Augustine to C.D. Jackson, 28 IV 1960, DDEL, C.D. Jackson Papers, b. 53, f.: FEC 1960 (2).

160 Exhibit Y: Top personnel for ACEN suggested by Bernard Yarrow (for information purposes), 25 III 1960, attachment to: Reorientation of Exile Organizations, 1 IV 1960, DDEL, C.D. Jackson Papers, b. 53, f.: FEC 1960 (2).

Tab. 2: Top personnel for ACEN suggested by Bernard Yarrow, 1960

Secretariat		
Māsēns	Secretary General	USA
Coste	Deputy	USA
Korboński	Political Advisor	USA
Board (General Committee)		
None [TBA]	Albanian	Europe
Grueff*	Bulgarian	USA
Duchacek*	Czechoslovak	USA
Maim	Estonian	USA
Msgr. Varga	Hungarian	USA
Kerno*	Latvian	USA
Razkauskas*	Lithuanian	USA
Raczyński	Polish	Europe
Bossy	Romanian	USA
Representatives		
Kotta	Albanian	USA
Gavrilov*	Bulgarian	USA
Lettrich	Czechoslovak	USA
None [TBA]	Estonian	Europe
Auer	Hungarian	Europe
Kővágó	Hungarian	USA
None [TBA]	Latvian	Europe
Sidzikauskas	Lithuanian	USA
Morawski	Polish	Europe
Mikołajczyk	Polish	USA
None [TBA]	Romanian	Europe

* Persons not identified, not listed as members of ACEN (see appendices)

In the earlier version of a document related to the FEC reorganization plan, there was a list dividing the exiles of the ACEN into three categories:

a) With whom to discuss the readjustment of council support. It included: Rexhep Krasniqi, Dimitrov, Zenkl, Béla Varga, Vişoianu, Sidzikauskas, Ādolfs Bļodnieks (Latvian), Aleksander Kütt (Estonian).
b) With whom to discuss the selection of principal ACEN representatives: Krasniqi, Nicola Pentchev (Bulgarian), Lettrich, Ferdinand Peroutka, Béla Varga, Korboński, Mikołajczyk, Vişoianu, Coste, Sidzikauskas, Māsēns, Kütt.
c) Who would be desirable ACEN representatives: Lettrich, Bolesław Soumar (Czechoslovakia), Béla Varga, Béla Király, Kővágó, Auer, Korboński, Mi-

kołajczyk, Biega, Sidzikauskas, Antanas Trimakas (Lithuania) Vilis Māsēns, Auguste Abbakuks (Latvia), Kütt, Raimond Kolk (Estonia).[161]

The FEC picked favorites. In this regard the role of the people in charge of exile relations was instrumental.

Since 1954, the heads of individual departments within the FEC were called vice presidents. The man in charge of the exile relations was Bernard Yarrow.[162] Within Yarrow's realm there were a number of FEC officers whose tasks included working with the ACEN. The first man in charge of ACEN-related matters was Frederick T. Merrill, who was borrowed from the State Department by the FEC for the purpose of establishing the ACEN.[163] He was replaced by McCargar in January 1955, serving as an Assistant Director of Exile Relations[164] until his departure to Europe in April 1956. His post was then taken by Earl L. Packer,[165] followed by John F. Leich (from February 1957). Yarrow became Senior Vice President in 1957. Subsequently, the people who were in charge of exile relations at the FEC were: Joseph W. Brinkley (Director, as of 1 November 1963, who moved to Munich); Albert D. Kappel (1963–1964, his Vice Director was Jan Stransky), then Mucio F. Delgado (1965–1966, his right hand was William L. Healy, Jr.), followed by Richard Flanagan (1966–1968), and then Anne Campanaro, who took on the job of director in July 1968. During the FEC's reorganization in 1956, the European branch of exile programs was established in Paris, with units in Munich and Vienna. At this time the European operations were run by James McCargar.[166]

---

161 Archibald S. Alexander to EC, FEC Board of Directors, FEOP reorientation of Exile support, 27 I 1960, DDEL, C.D. Jackson Papers, B. 53, f.: FEC 1960 (3).

162 Bernard Yarrow (1899–1973) was born in Russia, immigrated to the United States in 1922. By 1942 he was recruited by the OSS and sent to London where he served as a liaison with exile governments of Czechoslovakia, Poland, and almost intimately with that of Yugoslavia. Richard Harris Smith, *OSS: The Secret History of America's First Central Intelligence Agency* (Guildford, CT: Lyons Press 2005), 145; Mazurkiewicz, *Uchodźcy* ..., 217, footnote 147.

163 Mazurkiewicz, *Uchodźcy* ..., 402. By 1957 he became the director of the East-West staff.

164 Bernard Yarrow to FEC, Memorandum, 23 V 1955, HIA, RFE/RL CF: A, b. 235, f. 21.

165 Packer was a former diplomat with assignments including posts in Russia (notably in 1917), Latvia and Hungary, a Deputy Chief of the State Department's Division concerned with Soviet Affairs (1925–1936). He was also affiliated with Brookings Institution. *The Soviet Union: Yesterday, Today, Tomorrow. A Report on A Colloquy of American Long-Timers in Moscow*, ed. Foy D. Kohler, Mose L. Harvey (Coral Gables, FL: Center for Advanced International Studies, University of Miami, 1975), xx.

166 McCargar was also in chargé of monitoring cooperation with exiles in France, England, Holland, Italy and Spain. "Policy and Personalities" – remarks of James McCargar at the International Conference: "Hungary and the World, 1956: The New Archival Evidence" (Budapest,

The FEC Exile relations director's office administered the affairs of the Division, including the preparation of budget, control of expenditures, reporting on activities, communications, and personnel matters. There were also specific units within the Division dedicated to areas of activities conducted via national organizations (councils and committees), international organizations (international political organizations, trade union, church and other international groups), special activities, mass activities (student, youth and Free Europe Citizen Service), and European operations (headquartered in Paris, with officers in Vienna, Munich and Düsseldorf). The ACEN's matters were dealt with within the Special Activities.[167]

The representatives of national committees/councils who joined forces with the ACEN hoped that they would have influence over FEC policymaking, as well as over the broadcasts. Within the first year of its existence, the exiles asked the FEC to grant them a consultative voice in determining over-all policy on propaganda to East Central Europe.[168] The ACEN's reasoning was that political propaganda divorced from political action was meaningless and ineffective: "To be effective political propaganda must have as its source an organized body with a clear political purpose, able and willing to assume political responsibility for the views and news it transmits." ACEN considered itself to be just that. Yet the highly effective radio service, while attributed to the exiles, gave the ACEN no voice in determination of policy.[169]

John F. Leich (Assistant Director of the Exile Relations Division of the FEC from 1950 to 1960) commented: "I can only recall Bob's [Robert Lang] outbursts against 'those f*** Polish politicians who want to tell me how to run RFE!'"[170] Initially envisioned as an advisory body, the ACEN was never close to assuming the role of political responsibility for broadcasts. Repeatedly RFE's policy regarding political leaders in exile stated that their access to radio was to be limited to asking them to broadcast

> whenever such broadcasts would be productive from a propaganda point of view [...] Such broadcasts shall not be used for the propagation of partisan viewpoints, not shall they exaggerate the importance or weight of exile activities, nor are they in any way to be taken as

26–29 IX 1996), Ralph Walter Papers; Gadomski to Stanisław [Olszewski?], 24 VI 1956, Jadwiga Gadomska Files; Yarrow to Māsēns, 9 III 1956, IHRC, ACEN, b. 3, f. 3.

167 FEER Mission and Organization, 23 X 1957, HIA, RFE/RL CF: A, b. 198, f. 5.

168 ACEN Program of Activities for the year beginning on July 1, 1955; 1 VI 1955, 1–16.

169 Chairman and Sec. General of ACEN [Sidzikauskas and Korboński] to Bernard Yarrow (Senior Vice President, FEC), Memorandum: Relations between ACEN and RFE, 2 XI 1960, HIA, Coste Papers, b. 39, f. 2.

170 John F. Leich, e-mail, 5 IX 2009.

> signifying control by the national councils of the programs or policy of the individual Broadcasting Departments.[171]

The ACEN's ability to ability to shape, or influence FEC's policies was also limited. When plans were made for the establishment of the Policy and Planning Group at the FEC in the early 1960s,[172] proposals to invite the exiles, or to employ one of the political exiles to handle exile relations were rejected:[173]

> As to exile politicians, while their views have always been heard with respect, and while in the last analysis their wishes for their people are the same as ours, their political [underscored in the original] objectives are not the same as those of the U.S. Government. It is no more than the plain truth to say that they have been increasingly out of sympathy with U.S. policy towards their homelands since the abandonment of the short-lived Dulles "liberation" doctrine in 1953. Today, there is not, to my knowledge, a single member of the ACEN General Committee who approves the current East European policy of the U.S. Government, and there are some who are bitterly offended by it.[174]

Ralph Walter in charge of exile relations, soon to take over RFE, wrote that "[t]he FEC is an American institution with primary responsibility to serve the best interests of the United States. Ultimate responsibility for policy decisions rests with Americans and can scarcely be otherwise." Therefore, he believed that the exiles deserved due respect, and their advice was to be sought after, but "policy decision must remain essentially the provide of Americans without ties to nations of East Europe."[175]

Unfortunately for the exiles, there was no room for them on another advisory body that the FEC created in 1959: the West European Advisory Committee (WEAC) – a group consisted of leading Western personalities.[176] The matters re-

---

171 C. Rodney Smith (RFE Director) to Policy Director, Directors of Broadcasting Departments, Director of RFE-New York Office, Chiefs of New York Desks, Memorandum: Policy on Broadcasting by the Exile Leaders, 15 VI 1962, HIA, RFE/RL CF: H, b. 1751, f. Exile Leaders 1962; Radio Free Europe Policy, 10 II 1954, HIA, Puddington Papers, b. 31, f. 8.

172 To advise, draft basic policy, study current intelligence, coordinate propaganda lines, initiate research studies, evaluate, and maintain contacts with outside experts.

173 Lewis Galantière to Richardson, Memorandum: Notes on a Policy and Planning Group, 8 V 1961, HIA, RFE/RL CF: A, b. 191, f. 7.

174 Lewis Galantière to Richardson, Memorandum, 11 V 1961, ibid.

175 Ralph E. Walter to Yarrow, 15 V 1961, ibid.

176 Chairman and Secretary General of ACEN [Sidzikauskas and Korboński] to Bernard Yarrow (Senior Vice President, FEC), Memorandum: Relations between ACEN and RFE, 2 XI 1960, HIA, Coste Papers, b. 39, f. 2. Ross Johnson established that the WEAC resulted from «Council of Europe's review of RFE's 1956 Hungarian broadcasts and the resulting suggestion to increase focus on European issues and involve more Eruopeans in RFE broadcasting. [...] Adverse publicity

lated to the European captive nations were to be discussed with European leaders without representatives of these Europeans who were most interested. The ACEN's prestige and ability to have an impact on FEC policy obviously suffered. It continued to exercise some influence through its studies, publications, and political activities, proposals for projects prepared independently of but approved by FEC, but it was not a part of the policy-making process at the FEC.

It must be emphasized that the ACEN was not envisioned as a mere propaganda tool: "Sponsors think main issue and one they will have to sell is point that has been made that the national council relationship is to be one of developing climate rather than one of strict political warfare."[177] Among the tasks originally assigned to the exile relations division, the FEC President listed maintaining close cooperation with political and professional organizations established in the U.S. and in the free world by "men and women who held positions of public trust in pre-Communist Eastern Europe."[178] The goals of such collaboration were:

- Symbolic; "to keep alive the hope of the captive peoples, as well as to maintain their negative attitude towards the regimes in power, by demonstrating and dramatizing the achievement of exile groups and individuals in gaining the understanding and support of the Free World for the cause of Eastern European freedom."
- Propaganda; "to bring home the lesson of their experience to the peoples of the Free World who may be threatened by Communist aggression of wavering before Soviet enticement and sophistry."[179]

Clearly, the exile operations of the FEC stand out from broadcasting, as their target audiences were located outside of the Soviet-controlled part of Europe. Having the exiles on their side gave the American's psychological activities legitimacy. They were carried on behalf of the people who vouched for these with their prestige, the legacy of their pre-Communist careers, and by sharing their knowledge, networks and political talents. In relation to RFE, by the end of 1954, a confidential FEC memorandum stated explicitly that "[i]t is agreed that ACEN activ-

---

about RFE in the wake of the Hungrian Revolution led the U.S. government and FEC to revisit the idea of European committee of advisors.» Johnson, *Radio Free Europe ...*, 124, n. 140.

177 Ibid. Consequently, by the end of August 1954, the decision was made to disband the nine-strong research panel, and the FEC President stated that "consideration will be given as to how UNCCE can forward project in NY." Statement by Mr. Shepardson, Federation Project, 30 VIII 1954, HIA, RFE/RL CF: A, b. 191, f. 5.

178 FEC President's Report for the Year 1954, 18.

179 Ibid.

ities will be the special object of RFE and Free Europe Press' interest to a degree consonant with the exploitable memorial ACEN provided and the adaptability of that material to the programs and campaigns of those political warfare divisions."[180]

> The reinstated purpose of exile activities in the U.S., when sponsored or stimulated by FEC, is to further the political warfare objectives of FEC in the countries of its interest behind the Iron Curtain, to support the aims of the Government of the U.S. in the "uncommitted areas" of the world, and to contribute to the understanding and interest of the American people in the situation of the captive peoples and implant in them the conviction that it is in the American interest that those peoples be free.[181]

Exiles united within ACEN were much more useful in this regard than the individual committees/councils since the latter had "no audience except their own people at home or abroad. Their audience at home is limited by the availability of media beyond their control and the results have been meager." Similarly, the party internationals found sympathetic audiences among their ideological counterparts.[182]

In this regard it was up to the FEER to get information about target groups, obtain guidance and evaluation (select and guide "exile instrumentalities"), maintain contact with them, learn about their own purposes and potential, evaluate in terms of FEER targets, provide information and guidance, and furnish the funds.[183] John F. Leich, Assistant Director of the Exile Relations Division of the FEC from 1950 to 1960, assessed that the

> FEER does not 'extend support' but actually realizes projects through exile political national and international organizations and creates opportunities for these organizations to give expression to the ideas [...] FEER does not 'provide opportunities for creative work' but makes possible the publication and distribution of such work when its nature is in consonance with our objectives. We not only 'counteract Communist influence by contributing to the welfare of the incapacitated' but, more importantly, nurture the national sentiments of the masses of refugees through FECS, conserving thereby in the refugee community a positive asset for the U.S. policy.[184]

---

180 Memorandum of Agreement on Exile Activities in the United States sponsored or stimulated by FEC (Confidential), 20 XII 1954, HIA, RFE/RL CF: A, b. 188, f. 6.

181 Ibid.

182 Ed McHale to Huston, Henderson, Leich, Bull Memorandum, 10 II 1958, HIA, RFE/RL CF: A, b. 200, f. 6.

183 "Challenge and Opportunity for FEER in 1958", 7 III 1958, ibid.

184 John F. Leich to Bernard Yarrow, Memorandum: Policy Handbook by Lewis Galantière, 23 X 1956, HIA, RFE/RL CF: A, b. 191, f. 5

The proactive role of the FEC was also evident on the level of control. When responding to the CIA inquiry, the FEC listed its means of control used in relation with exile organizations:

> Continuous liaison, attendance at meetings of the organizations, and conferences with their leaders are the chief responsibility and occupation of the Division Director and Deputy. Discreet control is made possible by the financial dependence of all groups on FEC; their work and the validity of their staffing and expenditures is under constant observation and subject to periodic reviews. [185]

This included an annual review made as preliminary to budget requests, and adjustments in support payments were made accordingly. It also listed management and administrative supervision by responsible FEC staff, regular audits, review and study of the periodic reports submitted by exile organizations, as well as "continuous liaison with all groups to discuss their plans and programs."[186] As mentioned above, the Assembly was chaired by one of their own. This made the exiles feel autonomous from their sponsor,[187] while the sponsors obtained a useful instrument in reaching West Europeans. Arnold Beichman, RFE advisor on labor unions, cited Richardson in one of his articles that the FEC did not interfere in the ACEN's internal affairs, which included the selection of its leaders. John Leich commented that it was "a diplomatic lie, an inept one."[188]

> One-time projects provided the greatest degree of control because they can concentrate FEER support and the organization's activity [...] when FEER provides continuing support for an organization it is really supporting all of the organization's interests, even those of secondary value to FEER's program. Supporting organizations, with considerable "political overhead" regularly is explained as a gesture of supporting because of great symbolic value, their continuing visibility and impact on important target audience.[189]

185 Exile Political Organizations, attachment to: The President (FEC) to The Executive Committee, Survey of FEC External Operations, 1 II 1962, HIA, RFE/RL CF: FEC. INC, b. 1999, f.: Policy, External Operations 1961–62.

186 Ibid.

187 Korboński, Odpowiedź na oświadczenie p. Kazimierza Bagińskiego z dnia 24 marca 1956 roku [Response to Kazimierz Bagiński Statement of 24 March 1956], 26 VIII 1956, HIA, Korboński Papers, b. 8, f. 7.

188 John F. Leich to A. Ross Johnson, cc: Mazurkiewicz, e-mail, 9 II 2008; Arnold Beichman, The story of Radio Free Europe, *National Review* 36/21 (2 XI 1984): 29.

189 Proposed FEER Program, attachment to: Memorandum: FEER Paper Entitled "Challenge and Opportunity for FEER in 1958", 7 III 1958, HIA, RFE/RL CF: A, b. 200, f. 6.

The programs for the exiles were prepared in cooperation with the exiles who submitted their proposals along with budget figures. These were subject to FEER examination and subsequently the FEC's approval on an annual basis.[190] Interestingly, Ralph Walter (in charge of ACEN matters at the FEC's exile relations from October 1958 to May 1961) said that he never saw the actual guidelines to for transmittal to the ACEN.

> It was all pioneering work. We had no precedent to rely on. We learned on the job. We did write guidelines for RFE, but I do not remember policy guidance prepared specifically for ACEN. We were in touch and talked a lot about their activities. They submitted reports, budget proposals. We tried to convince them to focus on the activities and not on feuds, but I do not remember seeing the actual guidelines.[191]

Leich confirmed that he also spent a lot of time with the exiles, having regular meetings with them at least once a week. He was invited to special meetings, which were usually held in a friendly atmosphere. "It was a practical and productive approach – they presented their case and we gave them money for it. No long-term planning. We worked almost on daily basis."[192]

Thus, the Division of Exile Relations, dealing with this particular group of exiled politicians, worked mostly via "pep-talks." For example, Bernard Yarrow held a meeting with the exiles describing the need to use "all our assets to influence underdeveloped country delegations to the General Assembly [ONZ]." He laid out a plan for a display of all of the exile groups, committee by committee, "en masse." The FEC comment was, "[y]ou can imagine that the exiles are quite excited at the opportunity to get into the act."[193] Indeed it is in this context – cooperation to achieve a common goal – that the FEC-ACEN relationship must be interpreted.

Sometimes it is very difficult to decide where a given project idea originated from. The overlap of interest is evident, for example, in the case of so-called Soviet colonialism. In the very first issue of the "ACEN News", the exiles listed Soviet colonization as one of the issues under consideration by its Political Committee.[194] Two months later, a policy paper partially related to the same theme

---

190 Robert W. Minton (Director FE Press-Exile Relations) to Coste, 6 VII 1959, IHRC, ACEN, b. 3, f. 4; Brutus Coste to Ralph Walter, Memorandum, 13 VI 1960, IHRC, ACEN, b. 3, f. 5.

191 Telephone interview with Ralph Walter (audio recording), 5 X 2007.

192 Interview with John Leich, 9 VI 1996, 114 min., HU OSA 305: Fekete Doboz Alapítvány Video Archive (Fekete Doboz).

193 Robert W. Minton (Vice President, FEC) to John F. Leich, 3 III 1961, HIA, RFE/RL CF: A, b. 198, f. 1.

194 "Activities of ACEN Committees," *ACEN News* 1 (1 IV 1955): 4.

was circulated among the FEC leadership.[195] By 1957, the FEC had at its disposal about fifty pages of material on Soviet colonialism. "Presumably this was prepared for the use of USIA. Provides valuable background for current FEER discussions."[196] The issue was included in the FEER mission in 1957 and in subsequent years.[197] The FEC President's Annual Report of 1960 said: "[W]e have contributed to a wider understanding of Soviet policy and action with regard to uncommitted nations by publishing and distributing, at the General Assembly, copies of a pamphlet describing 'New Colonialism.'"[198] In the next sections of the report, however, it stated that the FEOP provided research assistance to the ACEN through the publication of the ACEN booklet on the new colonialism.[199] The ACEN protested vehemently that the authorship of the brochure be accredited to the FEC and the FEC had to apologize. To add prestige to the group of exiles who formed the ACEN, members of its General Committee were invited to meetings with officers at the State Department before their foreign travels, with regard to upcoming UN or Council of Europe meetings.[200]

The Division of Exile Relations submitted weekly report of its activities. The ACEN had to submit its reports, which remind one of grant settlements. Sometimes, the reports did not match the agreed projects. Brinkley, who was responsible for sending monthly allotment letters, in 1962 in a letter reminding the exiles of the procedures emphasized that "in planning future events FEC should be consulted and its approval obtained, at least in principle, before any preliminary steps are taken or the matter is submitted to the ACEN General Committee for approval."[201] By August however, it was obvious that this was not the case. When reviewing the monthly statement of "Receipts, Expenditures and Unex-

---

195 The Captive Nations of Central and Eastern Europe and the Four-Power Conference [third draft], 22 VI 1955, attachment to Lewis Galantière to Bernard Yarrow, 30 VI 1955, HIA, RFE/RL CF: A, b. 191, f.5.

196 Memorandum by E. Acker [no date, after 14 May 1957], RFE/RL CF: A, b. 198, f. 5.

197 FEER Mission and Organization, 23 X 1957, HIA, RFE/RL CF: A, b. 198, f. 5; Leich, FEER Policies for the Current Year, 24 II 1958, HIA, RFE/RL CF: A, b. 200, f. 6. Memorandum: FEER Paper Entitled "Challenge and Opportunity for FEER in 1958", 7 III 1958, HIA, RFE/RL CF: A, b. 200, f. 6. Review and redirection of FEOP, 11 XI 1959, DDEL, C.D. Jackson Papers, B. 53, f.: FEC 1960 (3).

198 See page 2: Archibald A. Alexander (President, FEC), 11th Annual Report 1960 (FEC, Inc. NY), IHRC, ACEN, b. 3, f. 1.

199 See page 16, ibid.

200 Weekly report of DER Activities (strictly confidential), 25 II 1955, NARA II, RG 59, EUR/EE, Records Relating to the Baltic States, 1940–1961, lot 71D158, b. 2, f. B-801– General Political Affairs – External; Weekly report of DER Activities (strictly confidential), 25 II 1955, NARA II, RG 59, EUR/EE, Records Relating to the Baltic States, 1940–1961, lot 71D158, b. 2, f. B-801– General Political Affairs – External.

201 J.W. Brinkley to Brutus Coste, 1 II 1962, HIA, RFE/RL CF: A, b. 145, f. 7.

pected Funds" from the ACEN related to the money allotted for Latin American representations, the FEC found out that the funds were not used for the said purpose. The FEC had to remind the ACEN that "allotted money for this purpose represents a policy decision on the part of the FEC."[202]

The frequent contacts between the FEC and ACEN Secretariat and General Committee and ACEN's dependence on funds provided by the FEC provoked situations in which the FEC intervened in personnel choices[203] and often got caught in personal squabbles within the ACEN. On the other hand, the top FEC representatives, like the President of the Committee, were present at least at the ACEN plenary meetings every so often, sharing their positive impressions with the ACEN leadership and thus elevating their morale. Archibald Alexander said he was impressed by the "quality of people attending the meeting" and by "intelligent and devoted discussion on points that came up."[204] The Presidents complimented the ACEN on their achievements, and media reports on ACEN's successes, which provided content for RFE broadcasts.[205]

The ACEN was also useful to the FEC when an intervention was needed to correct American media reports on controversial issues, like East Central European refugees awaiting immigrant visas in European camps,[206] or to confront Soviet-implanted fake news. In such cases as well as in many others, the FEC supplied the ACEN with information, statistics on refugee situation, clippings from the communist press, communist radio monitoring, and news of contemporary developments behind the Iron Curtain. Most of these materials originated from the RFE research departments. On most occasions, these were forwarded to

---

202 Horace E. Henderson (FEC) to Ferenc Nagy (Chairman ACEN), 15 VIII 1962, Ibid.

203 Weekly report of DER Activities (strictly confidential), 25 II 1955, NARA II, RG 59, EUR/EE, Records Relating to the Baltic States, 1940–1961, b. 2, f. B-801– General Political Affairs – External.

204 Archibald S. Alexander (President FEC) to Stefan Korboński, Brutus Coste, 10 VII 1959, IHRC, ACEN, b. 3, f. 4.

205 Archibald S. Alexander (President FEC) to Stefan Korboński, 24 VII 1959, IHRC, ACEN, b. 3, f. 4.

206 One example was an NBC TV program on the American unwillingness to admit to the U.S. some of the East European refugees in camps in Italy and Yugoslavia. Upon encouragement by the FEC director of Public Relations (Henry P. McNulty), the ACEN contacted the station to "make whatever demarche necessary to NBC either to correct this program or to suggest that they run another program about the ACEN," which the exiles did within a week. Henry P. McNulty (FEC, Director of PR) to Brutus Coste (Sec. Gen. ACEN), 11 III 1960, IHRC, ACEN, b. 3, f. 5; See also: Henry P. McNulty thank you letter to Brutus Coste of 22 III 1960, ibid.

the ACEN with a suggestion to possibly use this information in their informal meetings, for preparation of publications, as well as to pass them to Duca, who would use it in his contacts, also with the American press, etc.[207] Quite often these suggestions were realized, and thus the ACEN played the role of a clearing house for incoming news, but it also gave them credibility. The FEC also wished to use the ACEN to promote its operations in the émigré press.[208]

The FEC would also ask the ACEN to prepare statements with clear guidelines as to the purpose, for example, of the Soviet press announcing a possible "formation of a defense union of peace-loving European people, to guarantee their security," the last attempt to neutralize Germany, before its admission to NATO, and the formation of the Warsaw Pact. The FEC asked for a statement that should

> follow semantic lines and clarify the meaning of a few words as follows: 'peace' means submission, 'peace-loving' refers to people who are unable or unwilling to resist the Kremlin's enslavement, 'aggressor' is anyone who is willing to fight for his country, 'warmonger' is anyone who resists enslavement by the Kremlin, whether on principle or out of straight patriotism.[209]

This memorandum prepared by FEC PR specialist (Frank C. Wright, Jr.) was found among the ACEN papers. The statement on the "European Security" was issued in December in direct relation to the conference Moscow which gathered representatives of communist governments from East Central Europe. It did not follow the editorial line suggested by the FEC, but the aim of it was clearly the same, and the exiles issued their original protest,[210] thus helping to advance the agenda of their sponsor.

Interestingly, the American committee adhered strictly to a policy of non-support and discouragement of demonstrations and picketing.[211]One exception

207 Henry P. McNulty (FEC, Director of PR) to Brutus Coste (Sec. Gen. ACEN), 24 III 1960, ibid; Ralph Walter (Program Officer) to Petr Zenkl (ACEN Chairman), 4 V 1960, IHRC, ACEN, b. 3, f. 5; Ralph Walter to Brutus Coste, Memorandum, 16 V 1960, IHRC, ACEN, b. 3, f. 5.

208 J.W. Brinkley to E. Gaspar, 4 X 1961, IHRC, ACEN, b. 3, f. 6.

209 Frank C. Wright, Jr. to B. Yarrow, F. Merrill, Memorandum: Opportunity for ACE[N], 18 XI 1954, IHRC, ACEN, b. 3, f. 2.

210 The Moscow Conference on "European Security." Declaration adopted in the Extraordinary Plenary Meeting, on December 3, 1954, ACEN Doc. No. 18 (Gen.), ACEN, First Session ..., part 1, 47.

211 Mucio F. Delgado to T. N. Hunsbedt, Memorandum: Advisory Committee Meeting – August 13, 1958, 14 VIII 1958, RFE/RL CF: A, b. 200, f. 6.

in the case of the ACEN was the activity related to the ACEN House at the UN Plaza. James McCargar remembered:

> We eventually got a building right across from the United Nations, where we put up all the flags of the Soviet-occupied nations. You have no idea how easy it is to do a demonstration in New York if you know how to do it. We'd get 5,000 people out there screaming in front of the UN for liberty and the right cause.[212]

These were, however, mostly organized by ACEN's friends (mostly ethnic organizations, and individual national committees/councils). The Assembly's activities were limited to speeches, flag raising ceremonies and posters covering the entire façade of the rented garage.[213] The exiles were aware of American propaganda needs, the political framework in which they had to operate, and the compromises they had to make were at times difficult. But the alternatives for their political engagement were few. And so were the available resources.

By 1958, the FEC's plans envisioned that the "great and real value of ACEN" would be bolstered particularly with respect to its task vis a vis the United Nations and the Council of Europe. In addition to its regular sessions both in the U.S. and abroad, the ACEN – the FEER memorandum stated – would be assisted in taking an active part in the campaign on the fortieth anniversary of the Bolshevik revolution and in expanding its activities in Latin America and the Afro-Asian area.[214] The last part requires additional explanation.

Obviously, the ACEN (and its member national councils/committees) was just one of many "instruments" employed to globally counter Communist influences. In close cooperation with the ACEN, often overlapping the functions played in both, were the programs by the Christian Democrats (mostly in Latin America), socialist international (mostly in Europe), or peasant international (mostly in Asia). In July 1960, the FEC established a special division for coordinating its global operations: The Free World Operations Division of Free Europe Committee, Inc. (FWOD).

Why were exiles considered "one of the great assets available to the Free World"? Dan Jacobs of the FWOD explained:

---

212 Charles Stuart Kennedy interview with Jamer McCargar, 18 IV 1995, Association for Diplomatic Studies and Training (ADST), Foreign Affairs Oral History Project accessed online: https://www.adst.org/OH%20TOCs/McCargar,%20James.toc.pdf.

213 Mazurkiewicz, "'The Little U.N.' ..."

214 FEER program and budget for the fiscal year 1958, RFE/RL CF: A, b. 200, f. 6.

- There is a shortage of dedicated people, politically aware of the nature of communism, available to do the kind of work that must be done in the places it must be done
- The political exile is both willing and able to take up residence in a new country – he is already uprooted and his motive for leaving his own country and resettling is known and not suspect
- Most exiles have or can acquire some profession or means of livelihood that enables them to become a part of the community and nation in which they settled
- They can establish contact with the large numbers of earlier émigrés from their own or neighboring nations who have already made contact within the country.
- Through these contacts assistance to local political leaders/groups (help and organizational know-how in training political and ideological cadres)- developing grass-roots organization.[215]

As George Truitt (head of the FWOD) summed up, the Soviets had been training cadres for expansion into developing areas since the revolution. By mid-1950 they had attained the economic ability to back-up a sustained political effort in Latin America, Asia and Africa. While Western powers were dispensing large-scale economic aid before the Bloc did, they were behind in exercising the political effectiveness of such aid. Truitt wrote: "[P]olitical potential of technical personnel overseas is limited due to resentment of the European colonial history in Asia and Africa, and the controversial American business and military record in Latin America."[216] In the meantime, the Soviets used economic, cultural and historical animosities to advance their agenda and presented their achievements (industrialization, nationalization, reforms pledging social equality, claiming progress of the post-Stalinist era, and technological superiority evidenced by the successful launching of Sputnik in 1957, etc.).[217] Hence, the uncommitted areas became another battlefield of the Cold War.

The mission of the FEER was adjusted accordingly. The general line remained the same: "[T]o exert influence among and through exile individuals and organizations in line with FEC policies and contributing to U.S. (and coun-

215 Dan Jacobs, Memorandum on Political Warfare in the Free World, 2 V 1962, HIA, RFE/RL CF: A, b. 200, f. 3.

216 George A. Truitt to John Richardson, Jr., Operations in the Uncommitted Areas, 19 III 1962, HIA, RFE/RL CF: A, b. 200, f. 3.

217 Leich, FEER Policies for the Current Year, 24 II 1958, HIA, RFE/RL CF: A, b. 200, f. 6.

tering Communist) political warfare operations." While the FEC's primary concern was for the captive peoples, "the captive people do not usually constitute a target group which is accessible to any significant degree to the exiles through whom FEER operates. As a general rule, therefore, most FEER operations must have free world groups as their primary or direct targets."[218] As interpreted in 1958, the mission of FEER was to secure political action on behalf of the peoples of the captive nations. One of the ways to accomplish it was

> the complex activity of influencing governmental decisions in Free World countries through the mouths and pen of Eastern Europeans who by reasons of background, ability, or 'legitimacy' can command the necessary medium of attention in the respective foreign office, embassy, or UN delegation, and cause his opinions, statements, or suggestions to be considered seriously.[219]

This idea was not new at FEC/FEER. The ACEN had already established itself at the doorstep of the UN and the Council of Europe, had its delegations in the countries of the free world, and a network of representatives largely established in 1956 after the Poznań workers' rebellion, and which were significantly expanded in the course of the global mobilization effort on behalf of the Hungarians in the aftermath of the Soviet assault.[220] The FEC also noted that the "Suez crisis last October opened up the entire area of independent formerly colonial countries to greater U.S. influence."[221]

The explanation of ACEN's peculiar role, activities coordinated by FEER and not FWOD, is found in the earlier memorandum of 1958:

> The ACEN or the national organizations are not to concern themselves with the general political or social movement in any given country, not should they become involved in unofficial or officieux anti-Soviet organizations unless they are clearly an emanation and responsibility of the local regime. This means that the ACEN should:
> a) Consolidate and re-enforce its traditional good relations with its traditionally good friends in the Philippine, Peruvian, Belgian, Dutch, etc. governments;
> b) follow up and cultivate relations established with other Latin American and European governments;

---

218 Proposed FEER Program, attachment to: Memorandum: FEER Paper Entitled "Challenge and opportunity for FEER in 1958," 7 III 1958, HIA RFE/RL CF: A, b. 200, f. 6.

219 A Policy for FEER, 10 II 1958, HIA RFE/RL CF: A, b. 200, f. 6.

220 Ed McHale to Huston, Henderson, Leich, Bull Memorandum, 10 II 1958, HIA, RFE/RL CF: A, b. 200, f. 6.

221 Huston to Yarrow, Memorandum, 12 VI 1957, with attachments: E. Acker: Suggested shift of emphasis for national councils and committees (fiscal year 1958), [no date], and a Memorandum by E. Acker [no date, after 14 May 1957], RFE/RL CF: A, b. 198, f. 5.

> c) expand and develop relations with Asiatic governments through personal contact, correspondence and publications;
>
> Two centers offer themselves naturally for ACEN activity, the organs of the UN in New York and the Council of Europe in Strasbourg. ACEN's concern of countries with the principal western powers, hence its headquarters in United states, its delegations in the UK, Germany and France, representatives in Italy, Spain, Japan, Argentina, Mexico and Brazil. But the countries of lesser accessibility and visible power must also not be neglected. Hence the ACEN tour of Latin America in the fall of 1956, and the projected visit to the chief Asiatic capitals in the summer and fall of 1958.[222]

In 1958, a program called "Operation South"[223] – as one document in Korboński's collection named it – was initiated. Its aim was to mobilize the exiles for anti-Communist propaganda activities. ACEN programs were to be expanded with increased funding allocated to the new programs developed in the uncommitted nations. The idea was to locate exiles already living in these countries and turn them into ACEN regional delegates. They were to receive funds and printed materials for distribution with the aim of influencing both the public and governments, as well as via personal contacts, local diaspora networks – under the auspices, guidance and control of the ACEN.[224] FEER's political targets were governments, foreign offices, diplomatic missions (including international organizations, like the UN, NATO, SEATO, Baghdad Pact, Organization of American States, Council of Europe), political parties in non-communist countries, international political associations. The aim of these operations was common: "to secure political action on behalf of the captive nations."[225] According to the report submitted to the CIA in 1962, the operations in uncommitted nations aimed at "preventing the formation of dangerous popular fronts and exposing Communist front movement and their propaganda."[226]

George Truitt of FWOD elaborated further:

> The unique advantages of exiles as 'ideological guerillas' are their political experience and their career mobility. They are effective as anti-communist inductors, for they can speak

---

222 Leich, Policy of FEER, 10 II 1958, HIA, RFE/RL CF: A, b. 200, f. 6.

223 Operation South, [no date], HIA, Korboński Papers, b. 11, f. 2. Note added on the margin: [G]eo A. Truitt?

224 Horace E. Henderson to Bernard J. Yarrow, Memorandum: Uncommitted Area Influence Program, 26 VIII 1958, HIA, RFE/RL CF: A, b. 208, f. 2.

225 Leich, Program Outline for FY 1959 – political targets, 18 II 1958, HIA, RFE/RL CF: A, b. 200, f. 6; earlier version of the document 13 II 1958.

226 Exile Political Organizations, attachment to: The President (FEC) to The Executive Committee, Survey of FEC External Operations, 1 II 1962, HIA, RFE/RL CF: FEC. INC, b. 1999, f.: Policy, External Operations 1961–1962.

> from personal experience. They are accepted because they have useful practical skills to contribute, and they can do so by resettling and entering the mainstream of the national life of the host country.[227]

Truitt believed the exiles were motivated, experienced in anti-Communist action, spoke the languages, and had experience and ethnic contacts in uncommitted areas.[228] The dispersed character of exiles could had been "a liability with regard to possible political pressure for liberation of their homeland, but at the same time dispersal of exiles is a remarkable asset for the purpose of FWOD." As such, "living in all four corners of the world" – Truitt wrote – they were "welcome implementers of U.S. political assistance to non-communist elements in the uncommitted areas."[229]

Before the Democratic administration took over in January 1961, the ACEN received a boost from the FEC to intensify its activities in Latin America. Of course, this was related directly to the success of the Cuban Revolution which affected American foreign policy towards the continent ever since. Within the FEC itself, a special fund for Spanish language training was introduced.[230] There was also a larger political context behind it. "Unaligned countries are sensitive to foreign political interference". The FWOD memo stated –

> the Communists achieve their goals via local Communists. The West has no such ideology to export except the doctrine of self-government of nations thus the only absolute common bond among Western and unaligned democrats is their anti-communism. It is a negation of a doctrine – not really effective in building 'antibodies to communist infection.'[231]

The FEC's staff realized that the solution worked out by the Western allies thus far – to intervene (the U.S. in Cuba in 1961) or leave (the French in Indochina in 1954) – were not effective. Early lessons of the 1960s (before the Cuban Missile Crisis, and before second Indochina War) gave U.S. psychological warfare planners food for thought.

After Robert Kennedy's trip to the Far East in the early 1962, Truitt believed that the world saw the U.S. as imperialists, but not the Soviet Union. Hence, the need to expand "front organizations" (non-government, non-American personnel), and political refugees from Communism (and not just from East Central Eu-

227 GAT [George A. Truitt], Ideological Guerillas, 26 IV 1962, HIA, RFE/RL CF: A, b. 200, f. 3.
228 G.A. Truitt (FWO Director) to John Richardson, Jr., Operations in the Uncommitted Areas, 19 III 1962, ibid.
229 FWOD, Quarterly planning report, October-December 1961, 26 II 1962, ibid.
230 Truitt to Augustine, Memorandum: Spanish language lessons for FWO staff, 31 I 1962, ibid.
231 FWOD, Quarterly planning report, October-December 1961, 26 II 1962, ibid.

rope) were a great human asset. The grand plan for keeping the Communists out was to "help to build native leaders capable of leading their countries toward economic development and social progress while maintaining democratic system consistent with self-determination,"[232] via "locating among non-communists those with greatest potential to attain power resting on a broad support of electorate."[233] When planning their activities, the FWOD's staff realized the inherent dangers involved in these sensitive projects. Intimate contacts with local politicians often entailed "risky and unsolicited requests for electoral funds, representing parties abroad, taking sides in internal conflicts." It was all the more troubling that the FEC could not act in absolute secrecy, as "top security would deprive it of its greatest asset: the exiles."[234]

An internal FEC memorandum, likely prepared by Lewis Galantière, organized American "Points for Influencing Foreign Peoples". It represents at least one way of thinking about the role that was assigned to the FEC:[235]

> There are activities in which non-Americans can serve U.S. better than Americans can. Enemy's chief advantage is that he uses organizing techniques which U.S. does not – at least overtly – use; he creates and finances front organizations in which he does not appear. We need to do the same. In countries where political parties have no ideology, but merely defend material interests, the enemy trains political-ideological cadres for work inside or outside the parties. This is an important mode of action which we should adopt. For both purposes, use should be made of exiles or refugees locally resident, who originate in countries where they learned what communism really means, how communists go about seizing power, and what the results are for workers, peasants, intellectuals, students – not only for the churches or the properties class. Still other exiles now in the U.S. or in western Europe are available who would be welcomed in target countries because they possess professional or technical skills which they could contribute. Such exiles could create nuclei of anti-communism, and, to some extent, anti-Americanism. It is not certain to what extent even skilled Cuban exiles would be an asset. But East European exiles known to the FEC and organizations associated with it, are already engaged in this work to a limited extent. Some of the themes these "ideological guerillas" could sell are: self-determination, Sino-Soviet conflict, soviet exploitation of the satellite peoples etc. Note that Americans cannot organize or lead demonstrations or other forms of mass agitation, they cannot put questions to communist public speakers that, moreover, while the masses want what Americans have, they do not want the American way of life preached to them. Only the elites can be offered descriptions of American institutions *for possible adaptation* to local traditions and conditions. [Emphasis in original]

---

232 GAT [George A. Truitt], Ideological Guerillas, 26 IV 1962, ibid.

233 FWOD, Quarterly planning report, October-December 1961, 26 II 1962, ibid.

234 Ibid.

235 LG [Lewis Galantière], Points for Influencing Foreign Peoples, 27 IV 1962, HIA, RFE/RL CF: A, b. 200, f. 3.

By 1962, there was an obvious shift of ACEN's activities towards the "developing nations." The political exiles were encouraged to travel in the developing nations, speaking, debating, utilizing psychological warfare techniques to challenge communist propaganda and describing what the Communists were doing in their own countries. "By taking the hard Cold War line they help give balance to public opinion in countries that might otherwise gravitate toward the other extreme – thus making the middle ground position more tenable and visible."[236] The exiles were also used to start a program, openly, with FEC assistance, which enlisted the participation of people native to the country, and with time it assumed a more or less autonomous character.[237] In the case of the ACEN, for example, the exiles were encouraged to initiate the establishment of local Friends of Captive Nations organizations, as well as coordinate its activities with its associate and consultative partners, the international political social and professional organizations.[238] In a subtle form, the delegates of the Assembly also sought to bring attention of foreign elites to the captive nations problem by varied means spanning from "taking a foreign minister to lunch," through organizing public meetings with the participation of local politicians, to reaching out to the media via press conferences, and inspiring articles.[239]

By 1962 FWOD was replaced by the International Development Foundation (IDF). Within the next two years (1962–1964) there was a transition period during which the FEC withdrew from these operations, claiming that by 1967 it "no longer maintained any operations in Latin America, Asia or Africa."[240] The last statement can be questioned, at least in the context of ACEN's delegates and representatives, some of whom remained active (and were supported) until the early 1970s. While the FWOD had at least 12 affiliated international organizations, the ACEN was not listed among them. Some of the exile Assembly projects mirrored those of the FWOD.[241]

236 Dan Jacobs, Memorandum on Political Warfare in the Free World, 2 V 1962, ibid.
237 Ibid.
238 Leich, Policy of FEER, 10 II 1958, HIA, RFE/RL CF: A, b. 200, f. 6.
239 FWOD, Quarterly planning report, October-December 1961, 26 II 1962, HIA, RFE/RL CF: A, b. 200, f. 3.
240 JLD [John Dunning], History of Free World Operations Division of Free Europe Committee, Inc. and International Development Foundation, 27 II 1967, HIA, RFE/RL CF: A, b. 200, f. 1.
241 FWOD, Quarterly planning report, October-December 1961, 26 II 1962, HIA, RFE/RL CF: A, b. 200, f. 3.

Re-orientation towards uncommitted nations in concurrence with the decolonization processes was not in line with the ACEN's own priorities. For the united exiles, the prime area for their operations, other than maintaining U.S. support for their cause, was Western Europe.[242] The ACEN openly requested that the FEC take this into consideration, as well as objecting to being treated as one of the FEC's instruments. While submitting their plan for activities for 1961, the Assembly's President (Sidzikauskas) and Secretary General (Coste) emphasized that their understanding of the relationship between the ACEN and FEC was one of partnership. The ACEN represented the captive nations in the free world, its financial dependence on the FEC was unavoidable, for the lack of any other sources of support; but the Assembly was not one of the branches of the FEC as stated in the FEC's Annual Report for 1960.[243] ACEN's Secretary General considered such statement "a moral assassination of ACEN." According to Coste, a fundamental principle at stake was whether the ACEN was "a genuine voice of the aspirations of nine nations of East Central Europe or a branch of an American organization and a mouthpiece of American propaganda." The FEC Annual Report depicted the ACEN as a branch of the FEC by the very fact of reporting on its activities instead of leaving this task to the exiles themselves. "It represents us as a front or a mouthpiece by stating repeatedly that whatever we said or wrote, whatever we undertook in and outside the UN was prepared with the help of FEC which, as you know, is just not true," wrote Coste to McNulty.[244]

Coste represented the annoyed exiles, but the clash foretold of a much bigger problem. Reorganization of exile relations was looming. One of the ardent supporters of efficient reorganization of the ACEN in early 1960, Ralph E. Walter, decided that it was better to wait, however, because the Soviet leader had picked up colonization as the topic of his propaganda. "We may be moving into a situation where our exiles can – if only very temporarily – have a greater impact than has been the case for many months," wrote Walter in the aftermath of Khrushchev's trip to South East Asia. "The colonialism issue should be used to the maximum (the ACEN pamphlet and maps will be of great value), plus a meeting in Europe before the Summit [in Paris]."[245] His proposal was received favorably at the FEC. Yet, when ACEN welcomed the Soviet leader in October 1960 with

242 Remarks of Mr. Stefan Korboński, 25 V 1962 to [H. Henderson?], HIA, Korboński Papers, b. 11, f. 2.

243 Sidzikauskas, Coste to John Richardson [no date, 1961?], HIA, Korboński Papers, b. 11, f. 3.

244 Brutus Coste to Henry P. McNulty (FEC), 17 V 1961, IHRC, ACEN, b. 3, f. 6.

245 Ralph E. Walter to Robert Minton, Memorandum, 18 III 1960, HIA. RFE/RL CF: A, b. 198, f. 1.

a huge poster protesting against the leader of the then-largest colonial empire, and displaying it across the UN building in New York – they were censored.[246]

Entering the new decade of the 1960s, Cord Meyer (chief of CIA's International Organizations Division, since 1962: Covert Action Staff) argued with C.D. Jackson as to how to deal with the exiles. Since both were men of temper, they sent each other letters of apologies after an explosive meeting they had had in the presence of Allen Dulles. Jackson took the time to explain "in less passionate words" that

> [o]ne of the basic reasons for FEC/RFE's success and continued impact is the "troublesome" element of emotional dedication, more or less shared by all the members of the organization. In the case of the Americans, this emotional dedication is tempered by a more objective intellectual approach than the exiles are capable of. The exiles see things pretty much in black or white; the Americans are able to appreciate the shifting tones of grey. [...] While it is possible for you and your boss, depending on your estimates of the international situation at any given moment, to turn the FEC/RFE spigot on and off as far as the Americans are concerned without precipitating a dangerous internal problem, the exiles need more than this to keep them functioning happily – in this case the synonym for 'effectively.' In other words, a psychological approach is very much needed toward these people engaged in psychological warfare. I don't believe that in all history any men marched to successful battle chanting 'don't rock the boat.' And yet that seems to be today's operative slogan.[247]

Jackson further wrote that the operative slogan could no longer be "hope" in the face of the events of October to November 1956, as the word "took a terrible beating, a beating from which it has not yet recovered."

Although the Jackson–Cord Meyer exchange was mostly related to RFE, the division of exile relations had identified the same problem two years earlier when revising its mission and tasks: "FEER's work, even in the cold and formal field of strictly diplomatic contacts, must also take into consideration the feelings, opinions – even the psychoses – of those through whom work on behalf of liberation is desired."[248] John F. Leich of the FEC, who worked with the exile groups for over a decade, wrote: "A political exile is a *sui generis* condition, with its attendant frustrations, problems and discouragements. In the absence of an electoral mandate, the political exile can only emphasize his differences with

---

246 Mazurkiewicz, "The Relationship Between the Assembly ...," 422–423; Mazurkiewicz, "'The Little U.N.' ..."

247 C.D. Jackson to Cord Meyer, 12 I 1960, DDEL, C.D. Jackson papers, b. 53, f.: FEC, 1960 (3); C. Meyer, Jr to C.D. Jackson, 25 I 1960, ibid.

248 Ed McHale to Huston, Henderson, Leich, Bull Memorandum, 10 II 1958, HIA, RFE/RL CF: A, b. 200, f. 6.

fellow exiles; and he begins to see victory in terms of favors or concessions he has extracted from the protecting power."[249]

The ACEN struggled for its independence, which was directly linked to the legitimacy of its representations in the free world. Its criticism of U.S. policy, and divergence in political assessments that had increased almost since the ACEN's founding (in the aftermath of the Geneva Conference, 1955),[250] naturally resulted in disagreements, tensions, and eventually conflicts (as Dean Rusk announced a policy of differentiation in 1964). As the ACEN was not a monolith, its relations with the FEC were often marred by internal differences, often of pivotal political significance to one or another national group. One good example was the ACEN's position on the Western response to the Khrushchev Thaw. The financial dependence of ACEN on the FEC limited the exiles' autonomy. On the other hand, it was also the reason the exiles maintained cooperation within the ACEN, since the FEC continued to limit resources allotted to individual national committees/councils. There were multiple ways in which the exiles could have caused a change of position in the FEC. One was to act in concert and when necessary to disregard the FEC's guidelines, or to spend money in ways not approved by the FEC. The other way was to protest dramatically to the White House, find and address political allies in the U.S. and abroad, as well as to seek ethnic and outside support, or part ways. The ACEN did it all.

1.3 American Friends of Captive Nations

Generally, as a rule imposed by the Free Europe Committee, the ACEN was to refrain from partisan politics. The following offers a typical answer sent by the ACEN's officials in response to any given American request for political support: "I would like to call your attention to the fact that our Assembly is an international organization of nine national and five international exile groups and not an organization of American citizens. As such, it can in no way be involved in matters which pertain to the domestic affairs of the U.S. or any other free nations."[251] This is almost a direct quote from the FEC's letter to the ACEN. But influencing domestic affairs in terms of gathering support to include Eastern Europe in the American foreign policy agenda was exactly what ACEN was

249 Leich, "Great Expectations ...," 183–196.

250 B. Yarrow to DER staff, Memorandum: DER Post-Geneva Appraisal, 23 VIII 1955, with attachment: Statement of DER post-Geneva appraisal for use in Exile Relations of 22 VIII 1955, HIA, RFE/RL CF: A, b. 198, f. 5.

251 Brutus Coste to Polly A.Yarnall, 12 II 1963, IHRC, ACEN, b. 15, f. 5.

concerned with. What is more, it is exactly this occurrence that allowed the CIA's funding. The CIA made use of a provision that exile organizations (not composed of American citizens) that orchestrated efforts to stimulate support for their homelands technically belonged to the area of foreign relations. As such, the exiles had to register under the provisions of the Foreign Agents Registration Act and repeatedly apply for renewal of their permission to remain in the U.S.[252] Their operations on the American domestic political scene were severely limited.

But the Assembly was surrounded by friendly ethnic, labor (including AFL–CIO), and anti-Communist American organizations. The ACEN maintained contact with the Polish American Congress, American Hungarian Federation, American Bulgarian League, Albanian American Literary Society, American-Latvian Association, Czechoslovak National Council of America, League and Union of American-Romanian Societies, Baltic Women's Council, Estonian National Committee in the USA, American-Lithuanian Council, Estonian Evangelic-Lutheran Conference, as well as other religious, social and cultural associations.[253] ACEN representatives were often invited to the meetings organized by these organizations as well as by groups that attempted to form larger, multi-national entities, for example by the National Confederation of American Ethnic Groups (Washington).[254] The ACEN office received a large amount of invitations as well as requests for copies of their publications, specific articles and reports from ethnic, national associations, journalists, and private citizens.[255] The ACEN staff tried to answer every piece of correspondence and distributed as many of its materials as it could. However, running a broad information campaign was not the ACEN's *raison d'être*, especially not among those already convinced.

On 30 November 1955, the ACEN organized a meeting of East Central European ethnic and national groups in New York. Among those present were delegates of organizations of nine nations represented by the ACEN.[256] Evidently, the

---

252 Mazurkiewicz, *Uchodźcy*, 122, 133–34, 215–16.

253 See relevant correspondence at: IHRC, ACEN, b. 116, f. 9.

254 It was an umbrella organization of over a hundred smaller associations representing 40 different ethnic groups. What they had in common was their anti-communism. Paul M. Deac to Vilis Māsēns, 17 IV 1956, IHRC, ACEN, b. 116, f. 9. ACEN did not pursue any closer cooperation with this group. CACEED leaders felt that it received undeserved attention. See the exchange between Vratislav Busek and John Richardson; John Richardson (FEC) to Vratislav Busek (chairman, executive committee, CACEED), 19 VI 1962, IIIA, RFE/RL CF: A, b. 163, f. 4; V. Busek to Richardson and Yarrow, 14 VI 1962, ibid.

255 See: IHRC, ACEN, b. 5, f. 10.

256 Special Conference of the General Committee ACEN and Representatives of American-National Groups, New York, 30 XI 1955, IHRC, ACEN, b. 116, f. 9.

ACEN was searching for an American base for their political operations. It is useful here to provide a detailed explanation in this regard in relation to two organizations particularly engaged in supporting ACEN activities: the Conference of Americans of Central and Eastern European Descent (CACEED) and the American Friends of Captive Nations (AFCN). Their origins are closely intertwined – both were established concurrently as the outcome of talks with members of the ACEN, at its own headquarters.[257]

The organizational framework for CACEED consisting of "U.S. citizens nationality groups from behind the Iron Curtain" was developed by Ignatius Nurkiewicz of the Polish American Congress, while Christopher Emmet took on the task of organizing the friends of captive nations; "leading American citizens who could issue policy statements."[258] Based on the guidelines worked out during the meeting that took place in ACEN's headquarters, on 28 January 1956 Nurkiewicz prepared a draft of CACEED constitution for consultations.[259] Similarly to the exiles united in the ACEN, politically engaged ethnics, from the same nine countries, wanted to cooperate across various national lines to coordinate and strengthen their voice. Estimating the number of Americans of Central Eastern European descent at ten million, the anti-Communist ethnic political leaders wished to exercise more effective influence on U.S. politics regarding their ancestral homelands.[260] Over the next decade, their goals remained the same including: coordination of the efforts of American citizens of East and Central European descent to defend "the American way of life against Communist infiltration and subversion"; to "liberate the captive nations and restore their national self-determination, national independence and their basic human rights"; and organize the support of American public opinion for these causes.[261]

The name of the organization was chosen based on Nurkiewicz's suggestion, rejecting the Romanian American National Committee's idea of calling it the Association of American Organizations for the Liberation of Captive Nations. There-

---

257 ACEN Sec. Gen. (Coste) to Earl Packer (FEC), Memorandum: CACEED, 26 VII 1956, HIA, RFE/RL CF: A, b. 163, f. 4; Minutes of the CADEED meeting, ACEN Offices, 18 XII 1957, IHRC, ACEN, b. 120, f. 7.

258 AFCN, Minutes of Meeting, 28 I 1956, IHRC, ACEN, b. 111, f. 5.

259 Ibid.

260 Ignatius Nurkiewicz (Vice President, Polish American Congress) to the Participants of the meeting on January 28, 1956, 14 II 1956, HIA, RFE/RL CF: A, b. 163, f. 4. A copy of this letter is available at: IHRC, ACEN, b. 116, f. 5.

261 Feliks Gadomski, CACEED, Summary of the Minutes of the Meeting Held on February 18, 1956 at 29 W 57th Street, New York City, 18 II 1956, IHRC, ACEN, b. 116, f. 5. See also: HIA, RFE/RL CF: A, b. 163, f. 4; Feliks Gadomski, "Conference of Americans of Central and Eastern European Affairs," *ACEN News* 124 (July-August 1966): 9–10.

fore, the focus was left on the American scope of its activities. The principal leader of the CACEED was Msgr. Jonas Balkūnas (of the Lithuanian Parish of the Roman Catholic Church) who presided over the initial meetings and coordinated overall activities as CACEED's President for many years thereafter. Each of the national representations had five delegates in the Conference, with one vote per group.[262] The early plans of activities included engaging émigré East Central European intellectuals (organization of exhibits, assistance in translation, publication and promotion of their works), the promotion of unity among CACEED members, extending assistance to refugees, inducing escapees, informing Americans (government, congress, press) on the fate of the captive nations, and rallying for moral and financial support for the causes for which it stood.[263]

The talks described above did not escape the attention of the FEC. Its evaluation prepared in March 1956 stressed the enthusiasm of the Balts, the intention to cooperate closely with the ACEN, and the absence of representatives of the Ukrainian diaspora.[264] The Ukrainian Congress Committee of America, Inc. (led by Dmytro Halychyn) was listed as a member of CACEED but was mentioned by FEC ten days later.[265] CACEED was free from limitations imposed by FEC on ACEN in terms of membership. In July, the FEC inquired of ACEN whether its new partner organization already had a letterhead listing all its member organizations, and the Assembly's Secretary General responded that CACEED was in the process of being established. By that time the ACEN had already selected its liaison with the Conference of ethnics – Feliks Gadomski.[266] Gadomski participated in the meetings of CACEED and kept its members abreast of the ACEN's activities. Though the cooperation was not free from controversies, the ACEN's chairman

262 CACEED member organizations: Albanian American Literary Society, American Bulgarian League, Czechoslovak National Council of America, Estonian National Committee in the USA, American Hungarian Federation, American Latvian Association, American Lithuanian Council, Polish American Congress, Romanian American National Committee, Ukrainian Congress Committee of America. On organizational developments see: Vladas Barciauskas (secr. CACEED), Msr. J. Balkunas (president CACEED), [Invitation to nominate delegates to the Plenary Meeting], 28 VIII 1956, IHRC, ACEN, b. 120, f. 7; Summary of the Minutes of the Preparatory Meeting of the CACEED, 26 VI 1956, ibid.; [Nurkiewicz], CACEED, Third Draft, ibid.; Feliks Gadomski to Sec. Gen. ACEN (Coste), Memorandum: CACEED, 26 VII 1956, ibid.

263 Activity of the CACEED, proposal by Vladas Barciauskas, [no date, 1956], IHRC, ACEN, b. 120, f. 17.

264 John Frazer, Jr. to Miss Hayland, Memorandum: Extra Item for Weekly Report, 1 III 1956, HIA, RFE/RL CF: A, b. 163, f. 4.

265 List of National Group Delegates of the CACEED, Attachment to the note of 12 III 1956, HIA, RFE/RL CF: A, b. 163, f. 4.

266 ACEN Sec. Gen. (Coste) to Earl Packer (FEC), Memorandum, CACEED, 26 VII 1956, HIA, RFE/RL CF: A, b. 163, f. 4; E.L.P. [Packer], Memo, 4 VI 1956, ibid.

and secretary general were considered honorary guests at CACEED meetings and vice-versa.[267]

From the FEC reports written in May 1956, we learn that the Committee monitored the process of CACEED's birth with interest, but also that "the Fund" (FEC's sponsors, namely the CIA) were not sure whether this organization was in fact separate from AFCN.[268] While there were no FEC officers present at the above meetings, the FEC archives contain consecutive drafts of CACEED's constitution.[269] According to the FEC sources, CACEED was inaugurated on 25 May 1956 in New York Town Hall. Reporting on these developments, John Frazer, Jr. of the FEC noted that "the Fund" played no role in these developments. Moreover, he recorded that the "Czechoslovaks" were worried that the Free Europe Exile Relations would attempt to meddle in CACEED's affairs.[270] Its members, however, selected 28 January 1956 as the official date for CACEED's foundation,[271] an event likely to separate itself from AFCN which was being created at the same time. While the establishment of CACEED was mostly a spontaneous act on the part of some of the anti-Communist East Central European ethnics to assist the work of the exiles, the establishment of the American Friends of Captive Nations presents a much more complex issue.

A proposal to establish what was then referred to as the National Association of the Friends of the ACEN was made in mid-January 1956. It occurred during a formative meeting between the ACEN and the organizers of CACEED and proceeded in direct concurrence with the process of establishing the Conference of the ethnics. The idea was to create a country-wide "American" organization to complement the efforts of the representation of East Central European ethnics. The AFCN would engage prominent Americans and have chapters in multiple cities, which would closely cooperate with CACEED.[272] In the case of the AFCN, its

267 Minutes of the CACEED meeting at ACEN offices, 18 XIII 1957, IHRC, ACEN, b. 120, f. 17; Minutes of the Plenary Meeting of CACEED held at the Estonian House, 22 XII 1956, IHRC, ACEN, b. 120 f. 7; Sigmund J. Sluszka (CACEED Secretary), Report: Meeting of Saturday, Feb. 9, 1957, ACEN offices, 9 II 1957, IHRC, ACEN, b. 120, f. 17

268 John Frazer, Jr. to Miss Hayland, Weekly Report – CACEED, 19 IV 1956, HIA, RFE/RL CF: A, b. 163, f. 4.

269 See: Second and Third Draft, CACEED, as well as letter by Gadomski 26 VII 1956 in: HIA, RFE/RL CF: A, b. 163, f. 4.

270 John Frazer Jr. to Miss Hayland, Weekly Report – CACEED, 3 V 1956, HIA, RFE/RL CF: A, b. 163, f. 4.

271 Feliks Gadomski, "Conference of Americans of Central and Eastern European Affairs," *ACEN News* 124 (July – August 1966): 9–10.

272 Meeting of Representatives of Organizations formed by Americans of Central-Eastern European Descent with delegates of the ACEN, 14 I 1956, IHRC, ACEN, b. 116, f. 9.

links with intelligence and direct connection with psychological operations should not be dismissed lightly mostly because of the man who chaired this organization.

Christopher Emmet (1900 – 1974) had been involved in many crucial initiatives related to building anti-Communist fronts. Educated in the U.S. (including studies at Harvard), but also in Germany (as a child born to a wealthy family temporarily living in Germany, and later as a student at Freiburg), he was involved in numerous initiatives for the advancement of a variety of causes related to foreign policy issues. The common denominator for these were his anti-Nazi and anti-Communist views.[273] Some of the organizations he joined or founded resemble front organizations, other were prestigious institutes with established traditions. Emmet was a member of board of trustees at the Freedom House, Executive Vice President of the American Council on Germany, a member of boards of directors of the Common Cause, Inc., the International Rescue Committee, as well as a member Council of Foreign Relations. While he used to introduce himself as the host of a radio program, the Foreign Affairs Round Table on the WEVD station in New York, the above-mentioned activism, combined with high-level political connections, evidently stand out against – as one author noted – Emmet's lack of previously held posts either in the government, diplomacy, and the absence of a distinguishable career in either business or academia.[274]

Emmet's introduction by ACEN read: "Chairman of the AFCN and staunch ally of the Soviet-subjugated peoples of Central and Eastern Europe." The ACEN paid attention to his earlier encounters with East Central Europe as:

> His fight against tyranny dates back to 1943 when he worked with the Polish government in exile after the revelation of the Soviet murders of [Henryk] Ehrlich and [Victor] Alter. In 1945 he became chairman of the Committee Against Mass Expulsions. In cooperation with various Polish organizations he protested the partition of Poland along the so-called Curzon

273 In 1938 he became the Secretary of the Volunteer Christian Committee to Boycott Nazi Germany. During World War II he was the Chairman of the Committee to Aid Britain by Reciprocal Trade, and a member of the executive committee of the Committee to Defend America by Aiding the Allies, Vice President of France Forever, publicly warning about the danger posed by the Soviet Russia in 1943. After the war he co-organized Committee against Mass Expulsions (Chairman) and Committee for a Just Peace with Italy. Emmet served on the Committee for a Fair Trial for Draža Mihailovich (Treasurer), American Council on NATO. He was a member of the executive committee of the American Friends of Vietnam as well as vice chairman of the Emergency Committee for U.N. Action on Hungary. Mazurkiewicz, *Uchodźcy*, 94 – 95.

274 Anne Zetsche, "The Quest for Atlanticism: German-American Elite Networking, the Atlantik-Brücke and the American Council on Germany, 1952 – 1974," Doctoral Thesis, Northumbria University, Newcastle UK, 2016, http://nrl.northumbria.ac.uk/31606/, accessed 21 III 2020, 51 – 59.

line before the Yalta Conference. He is one of the signers of the Polish American Congress in Buffalo.[275]

The last piece of information seems particularly intriguing in the context of this chapter. However, the published report of the National Convention of the Polish American Congress does not include Emmet's name.[276] For the sake of describing his role in regard to the ACEN, it is sufficient to mention that Emmet seemed to have had been involved in all major developments related to building anti-Communist fronts since World War II. "Wherever freedom was threatened, Mr. Emmet became the champion of the oppressed."[277] His involvement in these organizations related to the Cold War political warfare of global scope: American Friends of Vietnam, American Committee for Cultural Freedom, Committee of One Million, Aid Refugee Chinese Intellectuals, and the Citizens' Committee for a Free Cuba. Stephen Dorril wrote that Emmet was a "classic example of those who ran the British Intelligence fronts before and during World War II and who, having proven themselves faithful and competent, went on to run the CIA/MI6 fronts of the Cold War."[278] A thorough analysis of the Emmet papers at Hoover Institution Archives brought no further revelations in this regard. In the opinion of the British historian, the AFCN was "domestic front group for the CIA sponsored coordinating body for exile groups, the ACEN."[279] There is some scanty circumstantial evidence to add to this argument in the pages that follow, yet the fascinating story of Emmet's many engagements still awaits its historian.

Emmet was among the participants of the first meeting between the ACEN and CACEED during which an idea was discussed to establish some form of national association to assist the work of the ACEN.[280] Two weeks later, on 28 January 1956, and upon his insistence, it was decided to establish a separate "American" organization which became the AFCN. His argument was that consultations with all CACEED members would be time-consuming, especially

275 Mr. Christopher Emmet [bio note], [no date, ca. 1959], IHRC, ACEN, b. 116, f. 2.

276 *Protokół Kongresu Polonii Amerykańskiej odbytego w dniach 28, 29, 30 maja 1944 roku w Memorial Auditorium w mieście Buffalo*, New York, ed. Zygmunt Stefanowicz (Chicago: Drukiem "Narodu Polskiego," 1944).

277 Regarding his participation in the campaign demanding a fair trial for Draža Mihailović, protesting the show trial of Cardinal József Mindszenty and Archbishop Aloysius Stepniac. Mr. Christopher Emmet, [no date, likely 1959], IHRC, ACEN, b. 116, f. 2.

278 Stephen Dorril, *MI6: Inside the Covert World of Her Majesty' s Secret Intelligence Service*, (New York: Free Press, 2000), 436.

279 Ibid.

280 Meeting of Representatives of Organizations formed by Americans of Central-Eastern European Descent with delegates of the ACEN, 14 I 1956, IHRC, ACEN, b. 116, f. 9.

given that their decisions should be unanimous. The urgency of reaching the American media prompted Emmet to say that the efficiency of acting alone would allow the AFCN to organize media campaign within two months.[281] Therefore, through increased efficiency, greater freedom of action was secured to the AFCN which soon became a one-man show since most of the prominent people listed on its letterhead appeared, if they ever did, only during special events.

The American Friends of Captive Nations offered a much more efficient way to reach the broader audiences and exercise more meaningful impact. The AFCN (1955–1971) was an organization that referred to itself as: "a liaison between the ACEN and the American public and various anti-Communist organizations." In its public appeal of March 1956, it listed its raison d'être as follows:

> Because the members of the ACEN are not American citizens, and because ACEN cannot carry on educational work among the American people, much of their fine material and information goes to waste. The Crusade for Freedom and its affiliate RFE, have rendered great service in encouraging and spreading the message of these leaders behind the Iron Curtain, but RFE is prevented by its charter from engaging in educational political activity in this country. We, therefore, have decided to form an organization to be called the AFCN. [...]
>
> Our organization will not compete with or duplicate the work of the nationality groups or any other anti-Communist organization, but it can help them to be more effective on this vital liberation issue, by providing leadership and centralized information which they can disseminate to their members, and by acting as a clearing house for campaigns of political education which may be jointly carried out.
>
> Most of this information will be supplied by the ACEN, whose leaders not only have unique experience in analyzing reports of conditions in their home countries, but who have unique sources of information through the underground resistance movements and through their ability to appraise the background and reliability of refugees who escape.[282]

The operations of the AFCN gain importance when the list of names used on its letterhead is considered.[283] Yet, the AFCN should best be described as a one-man

---

281 AFCN, Minutes of Meeting, 28 I 1956, IHRC, ACEN, b. 111, f. 5; Emmet to Māsēns, 15 VI 1956, IHRC, ACEN, b. 116, f. 4.

282 Outline of Purpose of American Friends of Captive Nations, 1955. Draft. Prepared as an attachment to ask people to sign in March 1956, IHRC, ACEN, b. 116, f. 1.

283 Listed as members are the following: Rev. Msgr. Jonas Balkunas (CACEED), Jay Lovestone (U.S. labor activist), Claire Boothe Luce (conservative congresswoman, U.S. ambassador, privately – wife of publisher of *Time* and *Life* magazines), Francis J. Wazeter (prominent Polish-American leader in New York) and others. The roster included members of the U.S. House of Representatives, republicans: Alvin M. Bentley (from Michigan), Walter H. Judd (from Minnesota), Charles J. Kersten (representing Wisconsin in 1947–1955), as well as democrats: Thaddeus M. Machrowicz (representative from Michigan), and Eugene J. McCarthy (representative from Minnesota). The Executive Committee included: Moshe Decter (at the time an author specializing in

show, as Emmet was an extraordinary man, or a "super committee boy," who officially affiliated himself with the New York radio station.[284]

Emmet was extraordinarily effective in rallying political and civic support for the ACEN's goals in the U.S. For example, on 25 May 1956, the AFCN organized a rally called "Peace Through Freedom" in New York's Town Hall. Gadomski recalled the exiles organized the rally with the help of the AFCN. The flyer prepared for the event listed American Friends as organizers, while the ACEN was listed as one of 19 co-sponsors, including all member organizations of CACEED.[285] Among the prominent guests was the Polish general Władysław Anders (former commander of the Polish Armed Forces in the West during World War II, and a political exile from London, who at the time was paying a visit to the U.S.).[286] The event speakers included Senator William F. Knowland, General William J. Donovan (former chief of the OSS, by then with the International Rescue Committee, IRC), and representative Harrison Williams. The event was chaired by Angier Biddle Duke (President of the IRC). The gathered audience listened to the texts of letters received from Eisenhower, Nixon, and senators and representatives, including John F. Kennedy.[287] The meeting concluded with the adopting of a resolution representative of the ACEN's goals, an event widely covered by opinion-leading U.S. newspapers.[288]

---

research on Jews in the Soviet Union, soon to be a managing editor of the *New Leader*), Angier Biddle Duke (at the time with the IRC), John Richardson, Jr. (by 1956 – former employee of Sullivan and Cromwell, expressing interest in captive nations, involved with IRC, introduced to Emmet by Leo Cherne of the IRC), Mrs. Kermit Roosevelt (Belle Willard Roosevelt, Theodore's daughter-in-law), Merlyn Pitzele (labor editor and advisor to presidential candidates).

284 Mazurkiewicz, *Uchodźcy* ..., 94–95.

285 Gadomski, *Zgromadzenie Europejskich* ..., 28; American Friends of the Captive Nations, Liberation Rally. Town Hall [flyer], 25 V 1956, IHRC, ACEN, b. 116, f. 4.

286 Anders' visit to the U.S. included visits to the White House (meeting president Eisenhower) and Department of State on 3 May 1956. Cf.: Feliks Gadomski to Józef Lipski, 14 V 1956, Józef Piłsudski Institute of America (IJP), Subject Archive, b. 114, f. 24: ACEN; Lipski to Gadomski, 22 IV 1956, ibid.

287 Messages were received also from mayor of New York Robert F. Wagner, congressmen Alvin M. Bentley and Attorney General J. K. Javits – both friends of ACEN in the U.S. congress for years to come. Liberation Rally, ACEN News 15–17 (June-August 1956): 41–45; See photos of this meeting: HIA, Christopher Emmet Papers, Photographs, 1941–1968, Envelope D.

288 President Voices Free World Hope, *The New York Times*, 26 V 1956; Freedom's Day, New York Journal American, 25 V 1956; Knowland Opposes Plan to Invite Russians Here, *New York Herald Tribune*, 26 V 1956, IHRC, ACEN, b. 116, f. 1.

In 1966 Emmet wrote in the "ACEN News" that in organizing the AFCN,

> we sought and obtained a broad spectrum of support from liberal, middle-of-the-road, and moderately conservative anti-Communists [...] to supplement the splendid work of the ACEN one of the key fields where they could not operate-namely, in the area of trying to directly influence Congress and the Administration to adopt a more active policy to foster freedom in East-Central Europe, by using all available economic, political and public information pressures and inducements.[289]

In Emmet's view, the three organizations were to avoid any competition when seeking publicity or fundraising. Moreover, these efforts should be coordinated. The role of CACEED was to advise and open communication channels with diasporic and anti-Communist groups (for disseminating information and obtaining support).[290] The ACEN was supposed to provide him with content for the "public education campaign." Since 1956 was an electoral year in the United States, Emmet was thinking about addressing both party platform committees, as well as individual candidates running for seats in the U.S. Congress. He believed that the upcoming presidential elections constituted a great occasion for the renewal of American commitment to liberating the captive nations.[291] The ACEN was delighted by the emergence of the two organizations because the exiles believed their actions depended to a large extent on American support – both governmental and popular. Both CACEED and the AFCN were presented with the ACEN's views with the expectation that they would be useful in their contacts with the candidates of both political parties. They indeed were.[292]

In the summer of 1956, the ACEN's GC decided it would attempt to coordinate efforts of all the national groups it represented to promote among the respective ethnic organizations only one, identical demand with which to approach the Platform Committees of both Republican and Democratic Parties. The demand was for the "liberation of the countries behind the Iron Curtain

---

289 Christopher Emmet, "American Friends of the Captive Nations and the Struggle for Freedom," *ACEN News* 124 (July-August 1966): 4–8.

290 Rough Outline of Joint Program suggested by Christopher Emmet t Harvard Club Dinner, 14 VI 1956, IHRC, ACEN, b. 116, f. 1. A copy of this document is available here: HIA, RFE/RL CF: A, b. 163, f. 4.

291 Project of Mass Meeting to be held in New York, 25 May 1956, 2 IV 1956, IJP, Subject Archive, b. 114, f. 24: ACEN.

292 AFCN, Platform Plank on Peaceful Liberation to be submitted to the Republican Platform Committee at San Francisco, [no date, 1956], IHRC, ACEN, b. 120, f. 17; CACEED, Press Release of August 9, [1956]: Conference Proposes Plank for Democratic Platform, ibid.; Draft Message from the AFCN to Republican (and Democratic) Candidates for Congress and the Senate, [no date, 1956], HIA, Emmet Papers, b. 50, f. Republican Platform 1956, Captive Nations.

by means of free and unfettered elections under international supervision as one of the aims of U.S. foreign policy." A member of the Polish delegation to the ACEN (Bolesław Biega) noted: "[I]t was clearly understood that this action is to be undertaken by the Americans [underscored in the original version] and the ACEN political groups will limit their participation to the role of initiator."[293] Biega's memorandum states that the idea had been implemented and that the appropriate declarations sent. Even the President of the Polish American Congress (Charles Rozmarek) thanked the ACEN for the opportunity to address the program committees of both American political parties.[294] Similar mobilization took place in 1964. On 19 August 1964, the AFCN sent Proposals for the Democratic Platform submitted by the American Friends of Captive Nations. An identical letter was addressed to the Republican Party.[295] Just like Emmet, the FEC also tried to reach both parties with their plank proposals. In 1960, a statement distributed by McNulty (via C.D. Jackson to the Republicans, and Alexander to the Democrats) contained a basic statement that the Soviet domination of East Central Europe was the main source of international tension and an obstacle to genuine peace between East and West.[296]

The ACEN maintained its agency and used the network of "friends" to influence American domestic politics. There were demonstrations, pickets, the coordination and dissemination of press releases, and joint appeals to the UN, etc.[297] The AFCN's appeal of 5 May 1958 regarding Hungary, was signed by 40 prominent Americans members from both political parties, and both houses

293 Bolesław Biega, Memorandum, 6 VIII 1956, HIA, RFE/RL CF: A, b. 156, f. 3. In the case of Poles, assistance was obtained from Charles Rozmarek of the Polish American Congress.
294 Charles Rozmarek to Vilis Māsēns, 30 VIII 1956, IHRC, ACEN, b. 120, f. 17.
295 AFCN, Proposals for the Democratic Platform submitted by the AFCN, 19 VIII 1964, HIA, Emmet, b. 29, f: Democratic Party Platform 1964-Captive Nations Plank; AFCN, Proposed Plank on Peaceful Liberation for the Democratic Party Platform by Congressman Thomas J. Dodd, on behalf of the AFCN [no date, 1956], ibid.; Proposals for the Republican Platform submitted by the American Friends of the Captive Nations, 9 VII 1964, attached to: Christopher Emmet, Memorandum: Members and Friends of the AFCN, 27 VII 1964, HIA, Emmet Papers, b. 50, f.: Republican Party US/San Francisco 1964.
296 Henry P. McNulty to C.D. Jackson, 1 VII 1960, DDEL, C.D. Jackson Papers, b. 53, f.: FEC, 1960 (1). C.D. Jackson's secretary confirmed that her boss was "passing it along to some Republican friends." Marie McCrum to Henry P. McNulty, 6 VII 1960, ibid.
297 John Balkunas (President CACEED), Memorandum to the Hon. Henry Cabot Lodge (U.S. Delegate to the UN), 6 IX 1957, IHRC, ACEN, b. 120, f. 17.; CACEED, Mass demonstration [of Unity with the Hungarian People], November 10 [1956], IHRC, ACEN, b. 120, f. 17; AFCN, Basic Aims and Immediate Objectives, June 1957, HIA, Emmet Papers, b. 5, f.: AFCN Aims. See also: Emmet Papers, b. 26, f: CACEED.

of U.S. Congress.[298] Refuting the Communist attack on the publication *Hungary Under Soviet Rule* published jointly by the ACEN, Hungarian Committee and the AFCN, these organizations were publicly supported by former Secretary of State, Adolf A. Berle, Jr., one of the founding members and director serving on the FEC board, who was on the editorial committee of this publication.[299] Emmet was not shy to address the Secretary of State (Christian A. Herter) during the conference in Geneva and compliment him on his conduct there while "wholeheartedly" supporting the proposals already submitted to him by the ACEN.[300] The three organizations issued joint statements during the Captive Nations Week.[301]

The three organizations complemented each other's work, with a degree of interdependence, sharing the anti-Communist agenda. As such it fell within the purview of the activities coordinated (unofficially) by the FEC. Obviously, as an American, Emmet did not have to abide by the FEC rules restricting the political operations of exiles. However, he did maintain contact with the FEC officers and kept them informed of his plans involving the ACEN.[302] Based on the correspondence found in the corporate files of the Free Europe Committee, the FEC was not behind the establishment of the AFCN. If any agency of the U.S. government was involved, this must have been decided above the heads of the FEC's personnel. What was the relationship between the two organizations instrumental in helping the ACEN reach the American people and Free Europe?

Already in April 1956, Frank C. Wright, Jr., responsible for public affairs at FEC since 1950, was worried that the association with the AFCN could prove "dangerous." In his opinion, despite its professed non-partisan character, Emmet's group could and would not escape party politics, on both state and federal levels. Wright already sensed trouble in many letters addressed to Emmet by Polish, Hungarian and Czech ethnics. Indeed, Wright's worries could be arranged in two categories: keeping the ACEN (and indirectly also the FEC) away from party

298 Christopher Emmet, Statement on the Summit Conference, 5 V 1958, AFCN, Open Society Archives, Budapest, Claire de Hédervàry Collection: United Nations Special Committee Documents on the Problem of Hungary in 1956, thereafter: Hédervàry Collection, 37–249–1–4.pdf; Press Release: Hungary and the Summit Conference, 7 May 1958, ibid.

299 AFCN, News Release: Communist Attack on Hungary Report Refuted, 22 X [1958], OSA, Hédervàry Collection, 34–211–1–3.pdf.

300 Christopher Emmet (AFCN) to Christian Herter (U.S. Sec. of State), 21 V 1959, Simpson Collection, 760.00/5–2159.

301 Christopher Emmet (AFCN), Vasil Gërmenji (ACEN), Msgr. John Balkunas (CADEED), Captive Week Manifesto 1965, *ACEN News* 118 (July – August 1965): 1.

302 Christopher Emmet to Stefan Korboński, letter marked private and confidential 5 X 1966 [cc: John Richardson], HIA, RFE/RL CF: A, b. 230, f. 9.

politics, and controlling the ACEN, which was understood as *quid pro quo* for the support the Assembly received.[303]

The Division of Exile Relations was also worried. Edward McHale wrote to Yarrow that he had some "grave misgivings" regarding the creation of such organization. Both McHale and McCargar tried to dissuade Emmet from realizing his plan. Even the early lists of Americans supporting the AFCN was considered "powerhouse," while Emmet's design was deemed "a source of potential trouble." Similarly to Wright, McHale worried that because of the AFCN the ACEN could become financially independent of the FEC. Furthermore, the AFCN would be exposed to pressures from ethnics from areas beyond the FEC's purview like Ukrainians, Georgians, etc. McHale did not support the request by Emmet that either C.D. Jackson or Adolf A. Berle take part in the May 1956 "Peace Through Freedom" meeting described above. He realized he could not stop the formation of the AFCN, or interfere with the meetings it organized, but he also rejected the notion that the FEC could join in. He thought it would be not effective as the FEC would not be able to control it.[304]

A few days later, Earl Packer reported on the meeting that took place between Emmet and FEC officers working with exile political organizations (Packer, Huston and Leich). Emmet again asked for endorsement of the AFCN and declared its non-partisan character. He also said that, together with Raphael Malsin (AFCN Treasurer, son of Lena Malsin, Lithuanian immigrant and founder of the clothing chain Lane Bryant) they were ready to underwrite the total cost of organization of the May 1956 meeting. Packer wondered what was in it for them. Emmet said his aim was to present the case of the captive nations to the American people, and thus support both the ACEN and the FEC. Huston asked to be kept informed but did not declare any support.[305]

But the FEC did cooperate with the AFCN. Just a year later Emmet thanked Yarrow for 1,200 dollars the FEC spent on purchasing copies of the AFCN-published report *Hungary Under Soviet Rule*, and for assistance with its distribution. The report was prepared in cooperation with the ACEN and Hungarian Committee. Another 200 dollars was spent by the FEC on copyright for translations of the said report.[306] As mentioned above, Berle not only supported the publication by the AFCN but also went on record to defend it against attacks by the Communists to discredit it.

---

303 Frank C. Wright to Bernard Yarrow, Memorandum, Friends of ACEN, 16 IV 1956, HIA, RFE/RL CF: A, b. 143, f. 1.

304 Edward McHale to Yarrow, Memorandum: AFCN, 5 IV 1956, HIA, RFE/RL CF: A, b. 143, f.1.

305 [Packer], Memorandum, 19 IV 1956, ibid,

306 Ch. Emmet to B. Yarrow, 4 XI 1957, ibid.

Regarding CACEED, the FEC was also cautious. Considered as a likely channel for the ACEN to attempt to influence U.S. politics beyond the FEC's control, the organization of ethnics contained one more worrisome element; the representation of the Ukrainians,[307] which broadened the scope the sponsors envisioned for the FEC (and therefore also for the ACEN – as described earlier). The FEC also did not wish to support an organization consisting of American citizens. Consequently, when Balkunas officially asked FEC for shared office space with the ACEN, he was denied on the grounds that the CACEED was not an exile organization but an American one.[308] However, the early consultations, and founding meetings took place at the ACEN offices. Moreover, multiple joint events sponsored by the FEC via ACEN were in fact a way to support CACEED as well.

While these were indirect ways of supporting the two key friends of the ACEN, obviously the FEC was interested and involved in advancing the cause which they shared. Throughout its history, the ACEN proudly and publicly cited cooperation with both organizations. The ACEN did not refrain from trying to influence American opinion makers, ethnic groups, or even the general public. However, within the limits imposed by the FEC, and with American friends – the ethnics as well as anti-Communist Americans – by its side, the ACEN members' energy and focus was directed at the international arena where it hoped to build pressure on the Soviets to release its grip on East Central Europe. Hence, the ACEN's history was tightly connected with American global political warfare.

307 E. L. Packer to Yarrow, 12 IX 1956, HIA, RFE/RL CF: A, b. 163, f. 4.

308 CACEED used Lithuanian Information Center at 233 Broadway in New York.

2 "Voice of the Silenced Peoples" – ACEN and the Council of Europe

The first area of the free world to be looked at in the context of ACEN (exile) – FEC (state-private American) cooperation is Western Europe.[1] First, this was the area where most of the East Central Europeans displaced by World War II resided, which included a great number of political exiles – in Paris, London, Rome, etc. Second, strategic U.S. interests involved strengthening the Western alliance – economically (through the Marshall Plan begun in 1948), militarily (NATO was created in 1949), and culturally (establishment of the Congress for Cultural Freedom in 1950). One way to achieve its aims was to support European integration. Richard Aldrich assessed that the United States was the most enthusiastic federalist force in post-war Europe and that in the early 1950s the promotion of European integration was the CIA's biggest operation in Western Europe.[2] The American Committee for a United Europe alone spent about 60 million dollars on supporting various groups promoting European unity from 1948 to 1960.[3] Third, many of the FEC's leaders were ardent supporters of federalism, encouraged and supported exile programs and studies on regional federation (e.g. the Danubian Inquiry, Mid-European Studies Center, and expert studies), envisioning in a distant future East Central Europe's eventual integration with the West.[4] Finally, the federalist movement among the exiled political leaders in the West was especially vibrant in 1940 to 1943 and then again after 1949.[5]

1 This chapter is an updated and revised edition of my earlier (French-language) publication: "Dans l'orbite du CELU. Les sessions extraordinaires de l'Assemblée des nations captives d'Europe (ACEN), à Strasbourg," in: *Les exilés polonais en France et la réorganisation pacifique de l'Europe (1940–1989)*, ed. Antoine Marès, Wojciech Prażuch and Inga Kawka (Peter Lang: Frankfurt am Main 2017), 88–118.

2 Richard Aldrich, *The Hidden Hand. Britain, America and Cold War Secret Intelligence* (London: Gerald Duckworth & Co. Ltd., 2006), 343–344. See also: Sallie Pisani, *The CIA and the Marshall Plan* (Lawrence: University Press of Kansas, 1991), 82; Tim Weiner, *Legacy of Ashes. The History of the CIA* (New York-London-Toronto-Sydney-Auckland: Doubleday, 2007), 28–29.

3 Aldrich, 348–349, 354–357, 365–366; Andrew Defty, *Britain, America and Anti-Communist: The Information Research Department* (Oxfordshire: Routlege 2004), 192–193. Cf.: Aldrich, "OSS, CIA and European Unity: The American Committee on United Europe, 1948–60," *Diplomacy & Statecraft* 8/1 (1997), 184–227.

4 Mazurkiewicz, *Uchodźcy*, 245–249, 365–366; Implementation of NCFE's Federation Policy. A Joint Paper, 24 VIII 1953, HIA, RFE/RL CF: A, b. 191, f. 5; *Europe: Nine panel Studies by Experts from Central and Eastern European Studies. An Examination of the Post-Liberation Problem of the Position of Central and Eastern European Nations in a Free European Community*, New York: Free

https://doi.org/10.1515/9783110661002-006

Already in May 1948, 21 representatives of Central and Eastern Europe were present as observers at the Hague Congress, among them Stanisław Mikołajczyk, Grigore Gafencu, Hubert Ripka, Georgi M. Dimitrov, and Pál Auer.[6] Representatives of two émigré national committees, which were able to put together a unified representation, joined the Executive Committee of the European Movement established in October 1948 – they included a Hungarian (Pál Auer) and a Bulgarian (Georgi M. Dimitrov).[7]

In the summer of 1949, encouraged by Joseph Retinger (a Polish émigré, Secretary General of the European Movement), the list of the Movement's commissions was expanded by adding a Committee on Central and Eastern European Countries.[8] It was chaired by the future British Prime Minister, Harold Macmillan – at that time a Conservative Member of Parliament. The Commission was established for the sake of preparing a plan of future integration of both parts of the European continent. Exiles from Bulgaria, Czechoslovakia, Hungary, Poland, Romania and Yugoslavia were represented in it, including future prominent leaders of the ACEN (e. g. Pál Auer, Nikola Balabanov, Georgi Dimitrov, Virgil Veniamin, Grigore Gafencu, Adolph Procházka, Štefan Osuský, Edward Raczyński, Jerzy [George] Zdziechowski, George B. Bessenyei, Hubert Ripka, August Rei, and Ion Ratiu).[9] The overlapping leadership led some scholars to confuse the two organizations – the Committee with the ACEN.[10]Among the prominent

Europe Committee, 1954; Whitney Shepardson (FEC President) to Štefan Osuský, 5 XI 1954, HIA, Osuský Papers, b. 80, f. 2.

5 Józef Łaptos, *Europa marzycieli ...*; Sławomir Łukasiewicz, *Trzecia Europa. Polska myśl federalistyczna w Stanach Zjednoczonych, 1940–1971* (Warsaw-Lublin: IPN, 2010), 83.

6 J. Pomian, *Józef Retinger. Życie i pamiętniki pioniera jedności europejskiej* (Warsaw: Pavo, 1994 (reprint of 1972 edition), 218; Józef Łaptos, "Projekty organizacji państw Europy Środkowo-Wschodniej (1942–1950). Analiza porównawcza," *Prace Komisji Środkowoeuropejskiej PAU* 3 (1995), 119–21.

7 Józef Łaptos, *Europa marzycieli ...*, 196.

8 The Committee was chaired by Harold Macmillan (he resigned upon joining the British government), rapporteur: Edward Beddington Behrens (who became the chair of the Committee until his resignation in 1952). Jan Pomian was the Secretary of the Committee. Andrzej Pieczewski, "Komisja do Spraw Europy Środkowej i Wschodniej Ruchu Europejskiego (1949–1973) – głos emigracji w sprawie europejskiego zjednoczenia," *Studia Polityczne ISP PAN* 21 (2008); Aldrich, *The Hidden Hand ...*,364. Complete list of Committee members is available in the 1950 brochure. See: Karol Popiel/PNDC Papers, PIASA, b. 9, f. 42; Central and Eastern European Commission, European Movement, Origins and Activities, (St. Clements Press, Ltd.: London, Oct. 1951), Columbia University Libraries (CUL), Bakhmeteff Archive, Ferenc Nagy Papers, b. 65, f.: Subject Files: Organizations: CEEC.

9 Łukasiewicz, "Projekty federalistyczne ...," 75; Łukasiewicz, *Trzecia Europa*, 94, ft. 247.

10 Aldrich, *The Hidden Hand ...*, 348–49, 364.

West Europeans represented were: Julien Amery (British Conservative politician), Clement Davies (Welsh leader of the Liberal Party), two former prime ministers of France, Paul Reynaud (center-right), and Paul Ramadier (socialist), Ernest Pezet (French Christian Democrat), Arthur Greenwood (British Labour politician) and Koos Vorrink (Dutch socialist).[11]

The creation of the Commission inspired Richard Condon (RFE European director) and William E. Griffith (his political advisor) to rethink their relations with exiles.[12] The Americans realized that the formula adopted in London effectively combined national and transnational symbolism. Furthermore, it was "discretely but completely" controlled by the British, at almost no cost and no harm to their political interests. At some point, the Americans even considered merging the U.S.-based East Central European national committees and councils with the Commission.[13] This idea never materialized, but in the meantime, by 1954 the ACEN was established in New York with much broader scope, and membership restricted to East Central European exiles who were not American citizens. Thus far, the United States managed its West European political programs without utilizing the political potential of the exiles. While the East Central European exiles were not essential to achieving American goals in the capitals of Europe, the creation of the ACEN proved to be useful in one important political venue where the U.S. voice was apparently absent, the Council of Europe.[14]

Founded in May 1949 by ten West European countries, the Council proclaimed its mission to protect democracy, individual freedom, political liberty, the rule of law and to promote European unity by fostering cooperation on legal, cultural and social issues.[15] The countries of East Central Europe were

---

11 Handbook, Political Émigrés, [1954?], NARA II, RG 59, EUR/EEA, Records Relating to Poland, the Baltic States and Czechoslovakia 1951–1960, b.1, f.: PBC–Moscow's European Satellites; Virgil Veniamin to FEC President, Translation of report from Mr. Veniamin, Meeting of Commission for Central and Eastern Europe, London, 10 XII 1962, HIA, RFE/RL CF: A, b. 185, f. 11; Defty, *Britain, America and* ..., 192–93; Łukasiewicz, *Trzecia Europa* ..., 94; Łaptos, *Europa marzycieli* ..., 197.

12 W.E. Griffith, R. J. Condon, Memorandum (draft), 1 XI 1952, Dwight D. Eisenhower Library (DDEL), C.D. Jackson (CDJ) Papers, b. 57, f.: Griffith. W.E. (2).

13 Defty, 192–193.

14 The United States was granted observer status on 7 December 1995. See: Resolution (95) 37, Council of Europe, Committee of Ministers, https://www.coe.int/en/web/portal/united-states, accessed: 9 X 2019.

15 Statue of the Council of Europe, London 5 V 1949, Council of Europe: European Treaty Series 1, https://rm.coe.int/1680306052 accessed 20 III 2020. By the 1980s, the number of members was already expanded to 23, and currently features 47 member states: https://www.coe.int/en/web/about-us/our-member-states, accessed 20 III 2020.

not to be admitted to the Council of Europe, due to the undemocratic character of the communist regimes. The exiled leaders tried to be officially recognized as representatives of their respective captive nations to the Council of Europe but failed. The rather symbolic gesture of leaving empty chairs to underscore the distress caused by Soviet domination of East Central European nations did not quite serve the exiles' ambitions.[16] However, the democratically oriented exiles in the West did find a way to mark their presence in Strasbourg. It was made possible via the Committee on Non-Represented Nations established by the Council of Europe's Consultative (today known as Parliamentary) Assembly. This committee was given the task of looking after the interests of East Central Europe in the course of the European integration process. Beginning on 15 May 1951 this watchdog's function was to be performed in consultation with the political exile organizations, although it wasn't until May 1955 that the Committee assumed a permanent character.[17]

From day one of the ACEN's activities, the exiles considered future integration of East Central Europe with the West. "Security and prosperity for Western Europe can come only through reunification of all Europe," the exiles wrote in a telegram sent to the Council of Europe's Consultative Assembly on 21 September 1954.[18] During its very first session, the ACEN members stated their readiness to cooperate with Council of Europe and inquired about the most appropriate method.

Through its contacts within the framework of the Council of Europe, the ACEN tried to assure that in the future East and Central Europe would be granted its place among the members of the Council of Europe and the European community. Of course, this would only be possible once governments there were elected by the free will of the people, respected the rule of law, Human Rights, and basic freedoms. In the meantime, the exiles sought to ensure implementation of the Consultative Assembly's resolutions of 28 August 1950 and 23 September 1954.[19] The first of these resolutions (Doc. 127) established the "Special Committee to watch over the Interests of European nations not represented on the Council of Europe." It carried a provision allowing it to request the advice of ex-

16 Łaptos, "Projekty organizacji państw ...," 119 – 121.

17 Łaptos, *Europa marzycieli* ..., 199; Pomian, op. cit., 219.

18 Telegram received from the ACEN meeting in New York on 21st September 1954, Council of Europe, Consultative Assembly. Special Committee to Watch over the Interests of European Nations not Represented in the Council of Europe, Third Session, 24 IX 1954, https://rm.coe.int/090000168079adc0, accessed 20 III 2020.

19 European Integration and membership in the Council of Europe. Resolution adopted in the 11th Plenary Meeting, on Dec. 19, 1954. ACEN Doc. No. 20 (Pol.), in: ACEN, *First Session*, 54 – 55.

perts belonging to the "nations which are precluded from participating in the work of the Council of Europe nevertheless form and integral part of Europe."[20] The second provided for the Assembly Committees to invite "representatives from national committees set up by refugees from the subject nations of Central and Eastern Europe [in the final version, substituted by: "nations still subjected to an authoritarian regime"] to be heard on specific subjects at meetings of the committees."[21] Obviously, the exiled political leaders united in ACEN wished to be invited to cooperate at least in the capacity of regional experts.

2.1 ACEN Sessions in France at Strasbourg

The idea of organizing the ACEN's special sessions in Europe formally came from the exiles. Before turning to the Americans for support, the ACEN's chairman, Vilis Māsēns, first secured an appropriate invitation from the Committee on Non-Represented Nations.[22] Soon thereafter the President of the FEC (Shepardson) received the ACEN's proposal for a series of special plenary sessions to be organized in Strasburg in concurrence with the proceedings of the Council of Europe's Consultative Assembly.[23] The previous (both official and private) networks established by East Central European diplomats, politicians and other elites in the West became crucial in establishing the ACEN's entry to the Council of Europe.

The Free Europe Committee liked the idea which conveniently complemented other American programs in Europe. The ACEN proposed that each national council/committee should delegate eight representatives, including at least one from the United States. Party internationals were to send two delegates each, not more than 80 people in all. Without providing any budgetary details, the ACEN suggested that the first session should take place in May 1955. In order to lay the groundwork for it, Māsēns asked for funds to travel to London, Paris

---

20 Council of Europe Consultative Assembly, Ordinary Session 1950, 28 VIII 1950, Doc. 127: Resolution for the Creation of a Special Committee to watch over the Interests of European nations not represented on the Council of Europe, https://rm.coe.int/0900001680974b55, accessed 20 III 2020.

21 Council of Europe Consultative Assembly, Sixth Ordinary Session, 23 IX 1954, Participation of European non-Member States in certain of the Council's Activities, Doc. 276: 1031–1034 https://rm.coe.int/0900001680695f4c, accessed 20 III 2020.

22 ACEN, Program of Activities for the year beginning on July 1, 1955, 1 VI 1955, 1–16, Immigration History Research Center (IHRC), ACEN, b. 3, f. 2.

23 Māsēns to Shepardson, 5 I 1955, IHRC, ACEN, b. 3, f. 2; Shepardson to Māsēns, 7 I 1955, ibid.

and Germany. With the approaching talks in Geneva, the American partners – both the FEC as well as the American ambassador in Paris (C. Douglas Dillon) – supported the idea.[24] The U.S. Department of State voiced no objections. John Foster Dulles asked the American Consul in Strasburg for a detailed report on the ACEN meeting, including the European reactions to the exile Assembly. The Secretary of State expected about 40 participants, some of whom he believed were to remain as observers to the Consultative Assembly's deliberations.[25] Because of the changes in the Council of Europe schedule, the ACEN's first session in Strasbourg took place on 1 to 4 July 1955, right before the Consultative Assembly's meeting (5–9 July). This moved the ACEN's special session even closer to the Big Four meeting in Switzerland (18–23 July 1955).

The session, which took place on the eve of the Geneva conference, in the opinion of refugees, was to demonstrate their solidarity with the Council of Europe, voice support for its efforts to unite Europe, and underline the fact that refugees and their peoples ware part of it.[26] Among the guest speakers addressing the ACEN delegates were the following: Karl Wistrand – a Swedish senator and Chairman of the Committee on Non-Represented Nations in the Council of Europe; Frans J. Goedhart – a journalist, former Dutch parliamentarian and Vice Chairman of this Commission, as well as the Chairman of the Central and East European Committee in the European Movement – Charles Jean de la Vallée Poussin; and Edward Beddington Behrens, Honorary Chairman of this committee. Special greetings were sent, via the U.S. diplomatic post, to the participants by the U.S. Secretary of State – John Foster Dulles.[27]

In total, from 1955 to 1958, four special sessions were organized by the ACEN in Strasbourg in concurrence with the sessions of the Council of Europe's Consultative Assembly.[28] The recorded attendance at these was as follows:[29]

24 ACEN, Program of Activities for ....; Māsēns to Shepardson, 26 I 1955, IHRC, ACEN, b. 3, f. 2; Dillon to Secretary of State (Dulles), Telegram 5172, 25 V 1955, Christopher Simpson Collection, 760.00/5–2555.

25 Dulles [J.F.] to American Consulate Strasbourg, instruction A-49: Proposed ACEN Meeting in Strasbourg, 3 VI 1955, Simpson Collection, 760.00/6–355. The document indicates that it was discussed on 8 March and 11 May 1955.

26 "ACEN Rally at Strasbourg, July 1–4 1955," *ACEN News* 1/4–5 (July–August 1955): 1.

27 [J.F.] Dulles to Am. Embassy Strasbourg, Telegram no. 28, 26 IV 1957, Simpson Collection.

28 Gadomski, *Zgromadzenie Europejskich* ..., 24, 27, 33.

29 The complete records of these sessions – resolutions, speeches by ACEN members and invited guests, debates, meetings of its members with the delegates to the Council of Europe Consultative Assembly in Strasburg were printed in the ACEN reports (1955–1961), with excerpts published in the *ACEN News*.

Dates:	Exile delegates:
1–4 July 1955	44 (U.S.)
12–15 April 1956	60 (U.S. and Europe)
26–30 April 1957	72 (U.S. and Europe)
25–29 April 1958	"Not fewer"

In 1955, in Strasbourg the ACEN delegates discussed the future integration, the upcoming meeting in Geneva, current political events behind the Iron Curtain, the situation of refugees, the preservation of cultural heritage and the upbringing of young people in the conditions of emigration. In the following years, these were almost permanent sections. Among the important topics discussed at the second session (12–17 April 1956) was "Soviet imperialism" instead of "Geneva"; at the third (26–30 April 1957), the intensification of repression behind the Iron Curtain, and the European Charter of Human Rights; and at the fourth (25–29 April 1958), "Soviet colonialism." The discernible shift toward emphasizing Soviet colonial domination of East Central Europe mirrored American psychological warfare planning.[30]

Given the federalist origins of many of the ACEN members who became interested in organizing the Assembly's sessions in Europe, it may come as a surprise to learn that European integration was not the issue dominating discussions held by the exiles gathered in Strasbourg. It invariably appeared on the agenda of the European ACEN sessions, but no detailed plans for reunification of the continent were drafted. It was consistent with the principles of ACEN members who believed that detailed models of integration should be developed in a democratic framework by their free and sovereign compatriots, meaning after their liberation.[31] The most urgent task was not to let Europeans forget about the true aspirations of the "captives", and to prevent the acquiescence of the status quo of the division of Europe into two blocs.

Obviously, the work on the ACEN sessions in Europe was not a linear process. In the face of the dramatic events in Hungary in 1956, and the West's inability to act, the exiles were pondering their role and mission. Looking back at the late 1950s forty years later, Feliks Gadomski wrote: "confrontation of facts with the then recent statements of the American political leaders that the liberation of enslaved nations was one of the main goals of their actions led to dejection and

30 Mary Ann Heiss, Exposing "Red Colonialism": U.S. Propaganda at the United Nations, 1953–1963, *Journal of Cold War Studies*, 17/3 (Summer 2015), 82–115.
31 Pauli Heikkilä, *Estonians for Europe* ..., 168–169.

doubt in the ranks of ACEN. To discharge these moods, the FEC initiated the organization of the third and next session in Strasbourg."[32]

The initiative intended to make amends, however, led to the first major ACEN success on the European forum. The ACEN's presence and activities in Strasbourg were recognized by the Consultative Assembly in the form of a Special Resolution adopted in May 1957. The resolution acknowledged the importance of the reports (particularly on Hungary), presented by the ACEN and instructed the Committee on Non-Represented Nations to follow the ACEN's activities and to inform the Consultative Assembly about them.[33] The same Committee also established the position of rapporteur for the ACEN, and selected Jakob Altmaier, a German socialist parliamentarian, to fill it.[34] In February 1958, Altmaier presented a report on the ACEN on the basis of which the Committee decided to maintain contacts with it for the sake of information exchange. Furthermore, the cultural and social committees were instructed to pay attention to ACEN's activities as well.[35] According to James McCargar (representative of FEER in Paris) it was due to Wistrand's lobbying that the Council of Europe agreed to one of its committees' establishing a relationship with the ACEN.[36] Elated by the success of 1957, the ACEN planned to take part in the next sessions of the Council of Europe Consultative Assembly in the fall of 1957, "as suggested by Wistrand and Goedhart."

Calling for financial support to FEC, the exiles estimated the cost of participation in the meeting at 6,000 dollars.[37]

---

32 Gadomski, *Zgromadzenie Europejskich ...*, 32.

33 Assemblée Consultative du Conseil de L'Europe, Doc. 679: Proposition de Dierective relative á l'Assemblée des Nations Captives d'Europe présentée par M. Wistrand et plusieurs de ses collégues [Heckscher, Pezet, Kirk, Goedhart, de Gou], 4 V 1957, Committee on Non-Represented Nations, 10th sitting, 4 V 1957, Directive # 109 (1957).

34 ACEN's assesment was that because of the meetings in Berlin, The Commission formed within the Consultative Assembly took on the ACEN's initiative and on the 5 of August adopted a resolution calling for the reconvening of the 11th session of the UN with the aim to consider a report of the special committee on Hungary. ACEN, *Third Session November 1956-September 1957, Organization, Resolutions, Reports* (New York: ACEN Publication no. 16, 1957), 25.

35 Consultative Assembly Council of Europe, Report on the Assembly of Captive European Nations by M. Altmaier, Doc. 787, 14 II 1958, adopted on 3 V 1958 as Order no. 122, https://rm.coe.int/0900001680975a32, accessed 20 III 2020.

36 James McCargar, "Ferenc Nagy: Smallholder or statesman?" in: *Nagy Ferenc miniszterelnök : visszaemlékezések, tanulmányok, cikkek*, ed. István Csicsery-Rónay (Budapest: Occidental Press, 1995), 154–155.

37 Coste to Leich, 26 IX 1957, IHRC, ACEN, b. 3, f. 3.

Meanwhile, the CIA's International Operations Division staff prepared an evaluation of the ACEN's sessions in Strasbourg. To a large extent, it was based on the reports of the American consul and contained references to the previous two sessions.[38] The Americans believed that many ACEN members were "overly optimistic" about the chances of extorting the USSR to withdraw from Central and Eastern Europe as well as of their impending return home. However, the exiles were guilty of overestimating the Soviet weakness and the strength of Western pressure. According to this source, by mid-1956, the ACEN delegates were convinced that the USSR was facing a serious crisis and that immediate pressure was needed to take advantage of this weakness. The American consul assessed that the anti-communism of the ACEN delegates sometimes compromised their objectivity. When assessing the attitude of the Council of Europe to the ACEN, the report acknowledged the general atmosphere of sympathy and moral support for the exiles. These were, however, combined with the conviction that little could be offered to help them. The conclusion of the report was that the ACEN garnered publicity in the European press, which was considered a valid achievement.[39]

Before the 1958 ACEN special session in Strasbourg, the Assembly's delegate (Korboński) met with Foy Kohler, Deputy Assistant Secretary of State for European Affairs (EUR) and J.T. Kendrick (Department of State, EUR/EE). During the meeting they agreed on a general strategy of fostering evolutionary changes and maintaining internal pressures on the communist regime. At the same time, they also concurred as to the need to keep the matter of captive nations on the agenda of international meetings. In the program for the upcoming ACEN session in Strasbourg presented by Korboński, Kohler noted the Soviet colonialism issue. The chief of the European office at the State Department said that this was of particular interest to him and that he wished it to be expanded.[40] Copies of the memorandum were sent to U.S. diplomatic missions in Strasbourg, Munich, Paris, Bonn, Warsaw, Prague, Budapest, Moscow, Bucharest, to the USIA, and to the recipients in the State Department. In April 1958, John Foster Dulles sent Māsēns expressions of support despite negative recommendation from his advisors. Department of State memorandum for Dulles issued before meeting the ACEN delegation in regard to the extraordinary session in Stras-

38 Memorandum for Chief IO/1, subject: ACEN and the Rumanian National Committee, 18 IV 1957, NARA II, CREST, CIA-RDP78-02771R000200060001-0.

39 Ibid.

40 Department of State (J.T. Kendrick), Memorandum of Conversation, Special Session of ACEN in Strasbourg, 16 IV 1958, Simpson Collection, 760.00/4–1658.

bourg said: "Should the Secretary of State take a stand, he would be sailing between Scylla (liberation) and Charybdis (stupidity)."[41]

The fourth special session of the ACEN took place in April 1958. It was considered a success by the ACEN delegates who paid a visit to the Department of State in June. Korboński and Māsēns were convinced that the ACEN influenced the wording of a resolution of the Political Commission of the Council of Europe relating to the division of Germany. Before the exiles' intervention, the document failed to mention the larger issue of a continent split in half, namely the fate of East Central Europe. Korboński told Kohler that the successful session in France boosted the exiles' morale. Albert W. Sherer, the author of the memorandum (Department of State, EUR/EE), could not help but add that it must have boosted the morale of the U.S.-based ACEN members as well.[42] What they did not know at the time was that the fourth session was to become the ACEN's last in Strasbourg.

In the following years, the ACEN representatives were present at the meetings of the Council of Europe Consultative Assembly as observers, trying to direct the attention of the participants towards their own agenda. The ACEN members consistently reported to the FEC on their travels to Strasburg, which often included meetings with political leaders outside of France.[43] Given the fact that these trips were paid for by the Free Europe Committee, this was not surprising. What may be considered a surprise is the FEC's decision to underwrite one more ACEN meeting in France in 1961, this time in Paris. The reason why this could be seen as astounding is that by 1959 the Free Europe Committee had clearly developed a better plan for working with key European politicians in the form of the West European Advisory Committee (WEAC) – a body of prominent European leaders who agreed to advise the FEC on matters relating to East-West relations in Europe. Seemingly, the exiles were sidelined in the American effort to reach West European elites.

It would be very difficult to overlook the list of the "Founding Fathers" of European Unity who agreed to put their names on the list of WEAC members, like Robert Schuman (former Prime Minister of France, 1947–1948, Minister of Foreign Affairs until 1953, author of the plan to promote European economic

---

41 ACEN to Secretary Of State (Dulles), 18 III 1958, Simpson Collection ; J.N. Greene to Elbrick (via S/S), 26 IV 1958, Simpson Collection; John F. Dulles, to AmConsul Strasbourg, 28 IV 1958, Simpson Collection, 760.00/4–2858.

42 Department of State (Albert W. Sherer), Memorandum of conversation, 6 VI 1958, Simpson Collection, 760.00/6–658. Present at the meeting: Māsēns, Korboński, Foy Kohler (EUR), Sherer (EUR/EE).

43 Edmund Gaspar (Deputy Sec. Gen. ACEN) to J. Richardson (FEC President), 6 XI 1961, IHRC, ACEN, b. 3, f. 6. See attached report by Coste on the ACEN session in Paris of 26 X 1961.

unity, which resulted in the establishment of the European Coal and Steel Community in 1952, the first Chairman of the Common Assembly (of the Common Market), at the head of the European Movement (1955–1961). In addition to Schuman, the Americans enlisted the support of Paul van Zeeland, the former Prime Minister and Minister of Foreign Affairs of Belgium; João Pinto da Costa Leite (Lumbales), Speaker of the upper chamber of the Portuguese Parliament; Randolfo Pacciardi, a former Deputy Prime Minister of Italy (1947–1948) and Defense Minister; Paulo A.V. Cunha, Foreign Minister of Portugal in the 1950s; and André François-Poncet, High Commissioner and then French Ambassador to Germany.[44] Among them were also two prominent (and ACEN-friendly) members of the Committee on Non-Represented Nations: Dr. Karl Wistrand (Chairman of the Committee) and Frans J. Goedhart (Vice Chairman). The latter became the Secretary General of WEAC. The first meeting of the WEAC took place between 20 and 21 May 1959 in Paris.[45]

During the second WEAC meeting in Munich in the fall of that year, two key leaders of the Free Europe Committee were present: FEC President, Archibald Alexander and John C. Hughes (former U.S. ambassador to NATO and Director of the FEC Board of Directors).[46] While it was declared at this meeting that the struggle to maintain peace in the world would not mean abandoning basic principles, i.e. the freedom to choose the form of government in Central and Eastern Europe, one seeks in vain for the names of the political representatives of these countries in exile. The meeting in London that followed (27–28 May 1960) was no different,[47] except for the fact that the ACEN's exuberant protests were heard and the exile Assembly leaders were invited to attend one part of the meeting. During the WEAC meeting in London, ACEN was therefore represented by the organization's chairman (Petr Zenkl) and vice chairman (Vaclovas Sidzikauskas).[48]

---

44 Henrik L.N. de Kauffmann (Rector of the University of Bonn), Werner Richter (German professor), Alastair Buchan (Director of the International Institute for Strategic Studies), Birger Kildal (Journalist, in the 1950s associated with "Morgenbladet"), Dr. Franz-Joseph Schoeningh (Publisher of "Die Süddeutsche Zeitung," died 1960), Samuel Watson (British trade union leader). The FEC Annual Report of 1960 also mentions Oskar Helmer, Austria's Minister of Interior in 1949–1959 and announces the participation of representatives from Switzerland and Denmark. At least some of the people from this list related to the Americans already on other levels.
45 "Free Europe Committee" a la presse après la creation du Comite Consultatif de'Europe Occidentale, Texte du Communique, 22 V 1959, IHRC, ACEN, b. 3, f. 1; RFE, Special Press Release, 25 V 1960, ibid.
46 Free Europe Committee, Press Release, 31 X 1959, IHRC, ACEN, b. 3, f. 1.
47 RFE, Special Press Release, 25 V 1960, ibid.
48 Free Europe Committee, 11th Annual Report, 1960, ibid.

In the press release issued on this occasion, the objectives and tasks of the WEAC were characterized. These included, among others: advising the FEC on effective ways of providing information on opinions and living conditions in the West, and vice versa to the West about the conditions behind the Iron Curtain; and keeping the awareness and cultural heritage that linked both these areas alive. In public communications from the WEAC meetings (in Paris, Munich, London), it was reported that their participants demanded that the countries of Central and Eastern Europe be allowed to make their own political decisions. At the same time, the problem of Soviet domination over this region was to be raised in all diplomatic and political negotiations with the Soviet Union.[49] While the agenda clearly focused on the grand design of "Europe Whole and Free," pragmatically thinking, the East Central European exiles were no longer as useful.

In October 1961, the last big ACEN-organized event took place in France. Rather than being called a special session, it was referred to as a Conference. The participants of the meeting appealed to the free world for help for the captives, who "belonged to Europe."[50] The exile Assembly also petitioned the Council of Europe and the European Movement to provide for, and establish, a framework for their cooperation as equal partners.[51] Although these freely formulated and expressed opinions are an example of ACEN's autonomous activities, once again, the direct American influence on some of the political postulates can be highlighted.

Since the FEC worked with West Europeans via WEAC, why was ACEN's Congress endorsed by the American sponsors? The Kennedy administration (represented by Dean Rusk) sent the ACEN greetings and good wishes for a successful meeting.[52] An early explanation is found in the C.D. Jackson files. In an effort to assist the government in deterring Soviet action in Berlin, the FEC submitted pro-

49 Special Release: International Group Urges Self-Determination for Captive Nations, [date approx. 28 V 1960], ibid.; Free Europe Committee, Press Release, 31 X 1959, ibid.; RFE, Special Press Release, 25 V 1960, ibid.

50 Appeal to Europe and to the Free World. Declaration Adopted in the Fourth Plenary Meeting of the Fifth Special Session in Paris, 20 X 1961, ACEN RES/PA 277 (VIII) Sp. S.V., in: ACEN, Eight Session, September 1961 – Sept. 1962, Resolutions, Reports, Organization (New York, 1962), 179–182.

51 The Captive Nations and European Integration. Resolution Adopted in the Fifth Plenary Meeting of the Fifth Special Session in Paris, 20 X 1961 ..., 182–184; The Participation of the Captive Countries in the European Movement, Resolution adopted in the Fifth Plenary Meeting of the Fifth Special Session in Paris, 20 X 1961 ..., 184.

52 Rusk to AmEmbassy Paris, 19 X 1961, Simpson Collection, 760.00/10–1961; Rusk to AmEmbassy Paris, 17 X 1961, ibid. The final recipient was F. Nagy, ACEN Chairman.

posals of multiple actions, which included one to "hold a session of the ACEN with an urgent atmosphere, in Europe in September."[53] The conference did not take place in September, but two months after the Berlin Wall was erected. While the tension in Berlin was great, the exiles' usefulness was in the past. Therefore an additional explanation is due here.

On 1 September 1961, the USSR abrogated the moratorium on nuclear testing (of 31 October 1958),[54] so the Americans sought to include protests against nuclear testing in the text of the ACEN resolution. Already two years earlier, at the Consultative Assembly's session in April 1959, ACEN had added to it a protest against Soviet nuclear tests. On 18 October 1961, the President of the FEC sent the ACEN representative the prepared text of a similar resolution, and in fact the document was adopted. A comparison of the two texts shows that the text sent by Richardson had been expanded and changed, but its basic meaning and message remained the same.[55] Had the question of Soviet nuclear tests raised by the ACEN before 1959 also been the result of American inspiration? Even if it had been, it should be noted that this protest was in line with the views of the members of the exile assembly. However, not all of the FEC proposals corresponded with the views of the members of the ACEN.

2.2 Cacophony

By the early 1960s, programs using refugee organizations in the FEC were increasingly reoriented towards non-European areas. In 1961, the ACEN officially protested against such a policy by writing to the President of the FEC that Central European refugees could not focus on combating communism in non-aligned countries. It was Europe that constituted "the main arena on which they wanted to and should act."[56]

---

53 Free Europe Committee and the Berlin Crisis, 3 VII 1961, attached to: John Richardson (President of FEC) to Dean Rusk (Secretary of State), 3 VII 1961, DDEL, C.D. Jackson Papers, b. 53, f.: FEC, 1961 (2).

54 Op-Ed, "The Russians Broke 1958–61 Test Moratorium," *The New York Times*, 19 I 1986, sec. 4, 22.

55 John Richardson to Brutus Coste (Paris), (Night Letter) 18 X 1961, IHRC, ACEN, b. 95, f. 5. Soviet Nuclear Explosions, Resolution adopted in the Fifth Plenary Meeting of the Fifth Special Session in Paris, 20 X 1961, ACEN RES/PA 280 (VIII), SP. S.V., in: ACEN, Eight Session, September 1961–Sept. 1962, Resolutions, Reports, Organization (New York, 1962), 184–185.

56 Sidzikauskas, Coste to John Richardson, [no date], HIA, Korboński Papers, b. 11, f. 3.

When submitting the ACEN's proposed program of activities for 1961 to the FEC, the exiles emphasized that from the apex of support at the turn of 1956 and 1957, the ACEN experienced consecutive budget cuts, and relations with the Americans ceased to resemble a partnership. While they were asking for an approval of their new, higher budget, the exiles protested their marginalization demanding that their delegates be included in the works of the WEAC.

Yet, from the American vantage point, the usefulness of the ACEN was diminishing. Although the FEC's financial support for the ACEN was continued for the next decade, individual projects and positions were eliminated. The successful sessions in Strasbourg were also cancelled, ostensibly "for financial reasons." The ACEN tried to look for other opportunities to support its own operations in Europe. Thanks to General Hennyey, 20,000 dollars was offered by the German politicians to organize ACEN's Plenary meeting in Bonn, provided that the Polish and Czechoslovak delegations, even as observers, would participate in it. This was fiercely rejected by the Polish delegation to ACEN – a position reinforced by support received from the exile leaders in London.[57] This was also part of a much larger conflict within the ACEN relating to the Assembly's position towards Germany. Fearing Germany's rise, mostly in the context of possible solution leading to re-unification without prior multilateral agreement on an all-European solution which would include recognition of the post-World War II Polish-German border, the Poles objected to participation in any ACEN representations in Germany. The issue was further complicated by the fact that communist propaganda exploited any trace of Polish exile's link to Germany to discredit their operations as "fascist."[58] In 1963, Korboński expressed his fears in a letter to Jan Starzewski in charge of foreign affairs at the Polish exile political center in London: "German expellees from the East would wish to stand in one line with the East Central European exiles to demonstrate solidarity and unity of aims based on the doctrine of self-determination." The leader of the Polish delegation to ACEN considered it potentially harmful to Polish interests.[59] The tensions regarding cooperation with Germans were so high, that even the ACEN's bestowing of medals of appreciation for supporting the "captive nations cause" upon ten

57 This proposal related to ACEN's understanding that the German Committee on Foreign Affairs in Bundestag as well as German Ministry of Foreign Affairs plan to establish Captive Nations Day. Stefan Korboński to Jan Starzewski (London, EZN Foreign Affairs Dept.), 25 II 1963, HIA, Korboński Papers, b. 11, f. 6; Jan Starzewski to S. Korboński, 11 III 1963, ibid.; Jan Starzewski to Stefan Korboński, 13 II 1964, HIA, Korboński Papers, b. 11, f. 4.

58 Paweł Machcewicz, *Poland's war on Radio Free Europe, 1950–1989* (Washington D.C.: Woodrow Wilson Press, Stanford CA: Stanford University Press, 2014).

59 Stefan Korboński to Jan Starzewski (London), 28 II 1963, HIA, Korboński Papers, b. 11, f. 6.

German parliamentarians saw the ACEN award (a diploma of appreciation of support with a wooden stand featuring nine captive nations' flags) boycotted by the Poles.[60]

The last European conferences relating to the activities of the Council of Europe were organized by ACEN in 1962 and 1963. The FEC office in Europe tried to dissuade New York from supporting the ACEN colloquiums in France, warning that the upcoming ACEN meeting in Strasbourg and subsequent travels would be a "nonproductive flop, if not counter-productive."[61] John H. Page advised the FEC President against this, using the following arguments:

> European ACEN groups resent non-consultation and will therefore help less enthusiastically. Also genuinely feel it is very inappropriate both in timing and form. Not one topflight European politician will appear. Very few if any will receive later delegations. Strong feeling this very bad timing in world politics for captive nations plea. Recognize problem of complete cancelation. Would travel to Europe limited to key people for consultation with European ACEN representative and personal friends in various governments be an acceptable substitute? Overall, would not say proposed plan would be strongly counter-productive but it could be. But at very best it will amount to very little. If possible, would strongly urge compromise suggested above.[62]

Despite the unfavorable attitude, the meeting took place on 5 to 7 May 1963. The urgings of the exiles were not innovative. The Assembly cited arguments already mentioned in the past: the necessity to contact Western European leaders, maintain cooperation with exiles in Europe, project coordination, maintaining the representative character of the organization, but also, oddly-sounding, the need to "fight the belief, which was the surest way to discredit ACEN, that ACEN is an American instrument of the Cold War." The FEC's Albert Kappel granted the exiles an additional 13,816 dollars necessary for the organization of the conference, but he asked for more media-savvy resolutions and adding Munich and Copenhagen to the list of cities that ACEN representatives were going to visit at the end of the meeting. Wishing ACEN lots of success, the direc-

---

60 The case relating to Karl Theodor Freiherr von und zu Guttenberg (West German politician, 1921–1972) was a particular trouble spot, since commemorative ACEN medals given to Wenzel Jaksch, President of the Federation of Expellees already caused outrage among the Poles represented in the ACEN. Stefan Korboński to Adam Ciołkosz (London), 8 X 1964, HIA, Korboński Papers, b. 11, f. 4; S. Korboński to Jan Starzewski, 7 I 1966, HIA, Korboński Papers, b. 11, f. 4; S. Korboński to Adam Ciołkosz, 4 VI 1965, ibid.; Jan Nowak-Jeziorański to S. Korboński, 17 XII 1965, ibid.

61 Telegram, 24 IV, [1963], HIA, RFE/RL CF: A, b. 199, f. 2: FEOP, Exile org. in Europe 1961–1963.

62 Page to Richardson, Teletype, re: ACEN Meeting 1963, 22 IV 1963, HIA, RFE/RL CF: A, b. 199, f. 2.

tor of the Division for Exile Relations wrote that "the future of ACEN depended largely on the future of ACEN in Europe."[63]

Unfortunately for the ACEN, this meeting in Strasburg became a forum of yet another display of anti-German sentiment of the Poles. Adam Ciołkosz evidently lost his temper, calling on the West German government to formally recognize the Oder-Neisse border, accusing the Federal Republic of Germany of tolerating anti-Polish revisionists and criticizing the idea of giving the Bundeswehr access to nuclear weapons.[64] Referring to an article in "Der Spiegel," he demanded that in the case of military conflict, Poland would not be treated as a war zone but as an ally of the West.[65] His agenda was unilateral, and clearly represented Polish interests, but it had nothing to do with the spirit of unity among the nine delegations. The Poles were confronted by Bulgarians and Hungarians, and cooperation within the ACEN seemed on the brink of collapse.[66] Ciołkosz's emotional speech, assisted by fist banging, ended with his (and Korboński's) fiery exit from the room. Obviously, it upset those present. The incident was also reported in the French press.[67] The Strasbourg meeting ended with elevated levels of distress within the ACEN and without any spectacular success to cover up the divisions. It also proved to be the last of its kind.

The FEC had clearly-defined guidelines relating to the Polish-German relations, in particular on avoiding discussions on the border issue.[68] These were, however, used by Radio Free Europe, while some of the ACEN delegates, not for the first time, had little concern for political limits imposed by the Committee. In September 1963, Gadomski gave the following warning to his colleague: "Should ACEN maintain its position of negating and sabotaging U.S. policy it shall come to an end."[69] In the same month, Delgado recommended the FEC's

---

63 Chairman and Secretary General ACEN to FEC President, 28 III 1963, IHRC, ACEN, b. 95, f. 6; Kappel to Dimitrov, 3 IV 1963, ibid.; Kappel to Coste, 15 IV 1963, ibid.; "Colloquy Strasbourg, 5–7 V 1963," *ACEN News* 97–99 (May-July 1963): 4–5.

64 Marc Trachtenberg, *A Constructed Peace. The making of the European Settlement, 1945–1963* (New Jersey: Princeton University Press 1999), 233, 281.

65 Stanek, *Stefan Korboński (1901–1989)...*, 260.

66 According to Polish sources, following this incident and fearing Polish exit from the ACEN, the FEC delegation (Richardson, Arthur Page, Mucio Delgado, John F. Leich) visited with Polish exiles in London, and subsequently was able to tone down the conflict. Ziętara, "Emigracyjne lata Stefana Korbońskiego" *in:* Ziętara, *Anders, Korboński, Sieniewicz ...*, 353–354.

67 Feliks Gadomski to Stefan Korboński, 17 V 1963, HIA, Korboński Papers, b. 11, f. 6.

68 Mazurkiewicz, Die "Stimme Freies Polen" aus München. Radio Free Europe, die amerikanische Deutchlandpolitik und die deutsch-polnischen Beziehungen, *Inter Finitimos. Jahrbuch zur deutsch-polnischen Beziehungsgeschichte* 6 (2008): 146–170.

69 Feliks Gadomski to Stefan Korboński, 7 VIII 1963, HIA, Korboński Papers, b. 11, f. 6.

President (Richardson) against supporting the ACEN's representatives attending the NATO meeting in Ankara. The reasons given by the FEC European Director are worthy of attention:

> In principle, worthy senior exiles should always be present in the corridors of international political conferences and meetings for lobbying and other representational purposes. In actual practice, the question must be asked: 'Who can help us more than hurt us?' With German nervousness evident in NATO talks in Washington this week, their pique at ACEN's position at Strasbourg last spring, and Bonn's doubts about the future negotiations with the Soviet Union, I must say I would be foolish to encourage any Polish exile to represent the ACEN point of view at any international meeting where the West Germans are present. Certain Poles are stupid enough to demand ouster of the West Germans from NATO! Obviously, you can't exclude the Poles alone. The Balts, though in impressive numbers, are largely ineffective. That left some useful Hungarians and one or two Romanians, Bulgarians, and Czechs and Slovaks.[70]

The final European showdown between the ACEN and FEC was related not to the Council of Europe, NATO, nor ACEN-inspired conferences, trips or meetings. The falling off of cooperation between the Assembly and its guardian occurred when the ACEN decided to boycott the conference of the Commission for Central and Eastern Europe in Brussels which was organized with the assistance of FEC. The thematic conference of the European Movement prepared by the Commission was supposed to be concerned with the extension of East-West relations based on economics, politics and culture. Preparations for it began in September 1962 and included several preparatory meetings. The FEC incurred a third of the meeting's organizational costs (4,000 pounds). Among hundred participants, forty East Central European refugees were to be invited. Irritated by the fact that during the organization of the meeting, the "old" exiles were omitted, as well as by the granting of the ACEN observer status and not membership of the Commission, the exile Assembly decided to boycott the conference.[71] The biggest fear among the exiles underlying the boycott was the impression that the conference was a step on the road to appeasement, that is, to acknowledging the permanent division of Europe.[72] The position taken by the European FEC representatives did not help alleviate the situation. In its opinion, the meeting of the Commission

70 Mucio T. Delgado to Richardson, 20 VIII 1963, HIA, RFE/RL CF: A, b. 145, f. 3.

71 Delgado explained the role of Vişoianu and Nagy in his letter sent to Richardson, answering the questions posed by Kappel. Kappel to Delgado, 27 XII 1963, HIA, RFE/RL CF: A, b. 185, f. 1; Delgado to Richardson, 30 XII 1963, ibid.

72 Kajetan Morawski to Foreign Department, Executive of National Unity (London), 15 I 1964 (forwarded to Korboński 7 II 1964), HIA, Korboński Papers, b. 11, f. 4.

was not supposed to be a meeting of refugees, but members of the European Movement.[73]

In John Leich's assessment, U.S. policy was aimed at "younger" refugees who tried to take advantage of the unavoidable trend of increasing West-East relations with the aim of stepping up the pressure to liberalize Eastern European economies, expand personal freedoms and strengthen European unity. Meanwhile, the ACEN accused the organizers of pursuing the economic interests of Great Britain.[74] The FEC headquarters in New York had to react.

Consequently, FEC's President Richardson addressed a long letter to Delgado, the FEC representative in London in which he explained the action plan.[75] In order to avoid an open split, destructive to all involved, Richardson suggested "skillfully directing the exiles" towards constructive resolution. The problem at stake was larger than just exile ambitions, for the real issue was buried in the attitudes East Central Europeans in the West had towards opening to the East. The FEC's President did not realistically expect a common position among the various generations of exiles from the region. Moreover, he found advantages in the staunch position of the post-war émigrés. Their criticism could be useful in balancing excessive optimism, he wrote, constituting an important warning highlighting the threats of the tricky strategy involving dealings with the Communists. It was necessary to convince hardline refugees that the West's "march to the East" was a fact, and that they should warn the West against lurking traps and not turn back the trend of change. The best idea he found was to allow senior exiles to develop studies on trade, cultural exchanges and other politically-related issues for Western education. The others had to be persuaded to avoid the schism.[76] Such an argument was not convincing for Leich. He believed that by disturbing the actions of young and mostly leftist refugees, and labeling them as British tools, the ACEN was becoming unpopular in Western Europe, and as such it had to be considered as "basically dangerous."[77]

73 Leich to Kappel, 30 XII 1963, HIA, RFE/RL CF: A, b. 185, f. 1.

74 V. Veniamin to President FEC, Translation of report from Mr. Veniamin, Meeting of Commission for Central and Eastern Europe, London, 10 XII 1962, HIA, RFE/RL CF: A, b. 185, f. 1; Delgado to Richardson, WEOD Information Item, L-18: Central and Eastern European Commission Spring Conference Planning, 16 I 1963, HIA, RFE/RL CF: A, b. 185, f. 1. Memorandum for the Files, [no date, archived by FEOP on 30 I 1963], ibid.

75 Richardson to Delgado, 18 II 1963, ibid.

76 Delgado to Richardson, 5 III 1963, ibid.; [Leich] Memorandum for the Record: CEEC Conference, 1 XI 1963, ibid.

77 Leich to Kappel, 30 XII 1963, ibid.

In early January, the Secretary General and the Chairman of the ACEN sent instructions to their members asking for them to refrain from participating in the Brussels conference. Those who nevertheless wanted to take part in it were asked to protest the arbitrary selection of East Central European refugees and speak against the unconditional offer of economic assistance and political cooperation with the East. These elements were recognized by ACEN as an indication of Western acquiescence of the status quo, that is, the Soviet domination in Central and Eastern Europe. ACEN also called for orchestrated protests to the European Movement. Exile Assembly's Secretary General (Brutus Coste) decided to go to Europe to see to this protest being implemented.[78] Not surprisingly, the FEC decided not to cover Coste's travel expenses,[79] limiting the Romanian's ability to tour European exile centers and organize the boycott. Eventually, the two ACEN members represented in Brussels were Pál Auer (representing the "old" exiles but at odds with the instruction sent by the ACEN from New York) and Ion Ratiu, who was classified as a "young" exile.

Regardless of the ACEN protests, the Brussels conference was a success that was comparable to the one held in London in 1952, as one of the young exiles who did take part wrote.[80] Edward Raczyński, representing the Polish government-in-exile, spoke with great eloquence endorsing the position of the European Movement, as Vallée-Poussin and Beddington-Behrens emphasized that the cultural and economic exchange with the East aimed at strengthening captive peoples until the time they would be ready to decide their own fate.[81] An ambassador of the Polish government-in-exile heard rumors that the evident change of heart that took place during the conference and allowed for abandonment of the appeasing trend was caused by the ACEN's protest. He also observed that the ACEN's irritation and some of the documents circulated in the lobbies caused friction with the European Movement.[82] Korboński refuted these allegations and explained ACEN's position at the Department of State which was, according to his account, received with understanding.[83]

78 Coste to Dargas and Rehak, 2 I 1964, HIA, RFE/RL CF: A, b. 185, f. 2; Kütt, Telegram sent to ACEN representatives, 3 I 1964, ibid.

79 Richardson to Delgado, 7 I 1964, ibid.

80 Ion Ratiu to "Dear Pepa," 12 I 1964, ibid.

81 Cf. Marian Wolański, Thomas Lane, *Poland and European Integration. The Ideas and Movements of Polish Exiles in the West, 1939–91* (London: Palgrave Macmillan, 2009).

82 Kajetan Morawski to Foreign Department, Executive of National Unity (London), 15 I 1964 (forwarded to Korboński 7 II 1964), HIA, Korboński Papers, b. 11, f. 4.

83 Stefan Korboński to Jan Starzewski, 16 II 1964, ibid.

Evidently, though, the ACEN was losing its position in Europe.[84] In 1964, Mucio Delgado observed that responsible politicians in Europe recognized that refugees were hopelessly out of touch, yet their stories remained relevant as long as there was no freedom in East Central Europe. Delgado acknowledged that the ACEN had ceased to be a "politically useful instrument" in Europe. "Even its once-useful symbolism has turned into a relic of the past."[85]

The FEC recognized the ACEN protest as premature, as well as evoking the bitterness of those refugees who prepared the conference and who took part in it. Worse, the ACEN boycott and criticism of the organizers gave birth to two misconceptions: that Eastern Europeans were ungrateful for the work of the European Movement on their behalf, and that the refugees were divided into pro-European and pro-American groups. This action undoubtedly contributed to the loss of friends by ACEN. "However, the goal of the conference has been achieved", wrote Leich, "the matter was publicized, and Western Europe publicly associated itself with the Eastern European refugees."[86]

When in 1966 the Chairman of the ACEN submitted to the State Department a report of yet another European meeting, to which he was invited as an observer by the Committee on Non-Represented Nations, he maintained the same position. The ACEN leadership believed that intensifying contacts with the East should be implemented after the liberation, and not in cooperation with the communist regimes which offered no reciprocity. It is not surprising then that the ACEN refused to participate in "technical" committees established in Europe to which representatives from behind the Iron Curtain were invited.[87]

Looking at the decade-long ACEN presence among European institutions, it may be noticed that that these were not actions aiming at voicing support for European integration, but rather were focused on building support for American policy, including contesting ideas of European neutrality, reminding the West about "enslavement" of half of the continent, and about American leadership in a global confrontation against communism. The ACEN had never been an or-

---

84 Delgado to Richardson, 21 I 1964, HIA, RFE/RL CF: A, b. 185, f. 2.

85 Leich to Kappel, 22 I 1964, ibid.; Leich, Conversation with Sir Edward Beddington-Behrens, 17 I 1964.

86 [Delgado], WEOD Report, Memorandum # 36, 23 I 1964, HIA, RFE/RL CF: A, b. 185, f. 2. See the report attached to: Leich to Kappel, 15 I 1964, Report by Leich, 21 I 1964: European Movement Conference on East Europe, ibid.

87 Memorandum of Conversation: Report of ACEN Participation in the Council of Europe Meeting, 8 VI 1966, Simpson Collection. Present at the meeting: Sidzikauskas (ACEN) and of the Department of State: Raymond E. Lisle (Director, EUR/EE), Robert McKisson (Deputy Director, EUR/EE), Alton L. Jenkens (Baltic desk EUR/EE).

ganization whose raison d'être was to work for a future all-European federation, but rather for the restoration of freedom in its Eastern part. An important part of its activities in Europe also involved spreading the idea that historically, culturally, socially, economically and, given its pre-war traditions, also politically – the nine captive nations belonged with the West.

In the wake of the Brezhnev doctrine, following the Warsaw Pact invasion of Czechoslovakia in 1968, the ACEN recognized the much-feared silent acceptance by the West of the Soviet domination in Eastern Europe. Not willing to give up, in 1969 the Assembly organized teams of its delegates, assisted by chairs of the ACEN delegations in Europe, to address the governments (ministers of foreign affairs, members of parliaments and prominent politicians). The Europe-based ACEN members helped to schedule meetings in London (Antoni Dargas, Polish), Paris (Edmund Rehak, Czech), Rome (Ragip Frashëri, Albanian), Bonn (Walter Banaitis, Lithuanian), and in Copenhagen (August Koern, Estonian). As 1969 marked the Council of Europe's twentieth anniversary, the ACEN delegates also stopped in Strasbourg to attend a special banquet and chat with the parliamentarians there.

The ACEN network, combined with multiple webs of exile connections was still quite wide, and its members still enjoyed personal high-level contacts, but except for expressions of sympathy, no real political support was obtained. Feliks Gadomski, the ACEN's Secretary wrote: "Our visit to Europe was a moral success, confirming the ACEN's role as a spokesman for the captive nations and their right to freedom and independence. At the same time, we could see clearly that Europe, safe under the American atomic umbrella, was not prone to undertake any action that would shake the existing status quo."[88]

88 Gadomski, *Zgromadzenie Europejskich ...*, 56–58.

3 "Free Elections and Withdrawal of Soviet Troops" – ACEN and the Communist Regimes

The first session of ACEN which began in September 1954 was filled with initiatives suggesting that the Assembly wished to engage in direct confrontation with the Communists in the international arena – challenging its representations, operations and propaganda with facts and counteractions.[1] "The New York Times" reported on 21 September 1954 that during the ACEN's first meeting they sent a protest to the UN General Assembly against seating two communist delegations (Czechoslovak and Polish) and usurpation by the Soviet Union of the sovereign rights of Estonia, Latvia and Lithuania.[2] The paper underscored that the ACEN was organized "precisely along the lines of the United Nations" and its understanding of ACEN's role did not change until early 1960s when it referred to the ACEN as the little UN. Initially, the ACEN hoped it could use the UN to challenge the Soviets with the help of the countries of the free world. Within two years these high expectations were put to a rough test.

The year 1956 did not start successfully for the ACEN. Its members were deeply disappointed by the succeeding events beginning with the Big Powers' meeting in Geneva (18–23 July 1955), UN approval to accept the representation of communist Hungary, Romania, Bulgaria and Albania (14 December 1955), to the invitation to the Soviet leader Nikita Khrushchev (First Secretary of the CPSU) and Nikolai Bulganin (Soviet Prime Minister) to visit the European capitals, and Józef Cyrankiewicz (Polish Prime Minister) to Paris. These made the ACEN members loudly demand a clear definition of Western governments' policy towards enslaved countries.

The meeting of John Foster Dulles with Josip Broz Tito in Brioni (6–8 November 1955), and then Khrushchev's presentation at the XX Congress of the CPSU gave an impression among Western commentators that in the bloc of USSR-dominated countries there was a chance to change the nature of their relationship with Moscow. The ACEN strongly rejected such an interpretation of political events. Although the refugees were satisfied that the case of the subjugated people was again the focus of attention of the free world, from December 1955 to

1 See resolutions adopted during the first session of ACEN. ACEN, First Session ..., 31–60.

2 Kathleen McLaughlin, "Exiles Challenge 2 in U.N. Red Bloc. New Organization Protests Against Seating of Czech and Polish Delegations," *The New York Times*, 21 IX 1954, 11.

https://doi.org/10.1515/9783110661002-007

June 1956 it invariably considered unrealistic any solutions based on "deceptive concepts such as 'national communism.'"[3]

During the debate on the ACEN forum that took place on 13 June, László Bartok (Hungarian) proposed using the content of Khrushchev's paper to remind the world that it was Stalin who created the People's Democracies under Moscow's control. Vratislav Busek, the Czech member, declared that in his opinion the only way to shed this yoke was self-liberation. It would be possible if the United States government declared that in the case of USSR intervention against acts of self-liberation, they would also be willing to intervene. Dimitar Petkov (Bulgarian) stated that self-liberation was unrealistic, and liberation could only come from outside. Stefan Korboński spoke in a similar tone, emphasizing that the Poles had repeatedly tried to free themselves from a foreign yoke by their own efforts, and another attempt would be suicidal. "You cannot fight with stones against tanks," said the head of the Polish delegation on 13 June 1956, at the ACEN forum.[4]

On 28 June 1956 workers of the Poznań Metal Works, joined by thousands of protesters from other industrial plants came out on the streets demanding "bread and freedom." Discontent with food shortages, an increase in work quotas, poor work conditions and management, and incorrect calculations of the payroll tax were coupled with the workers' irritation over a fiasco of talks their delegation had had in Warsaw two days earlier. The communist authorities decided to use force against the strikers. The force was significant, as two armored divisions (360 tanks) and two infantry divisions (10,000 troops) were used to terrorize the city over the next two days. 650 people were injured, and 58 were killed with the youngest victim being only 13 years old.[5]

In the aftermath of the Poznań workers' rebellion the exiles undertook a major mobilization of all the resources within their reach hoping that the revolt would help them strengthen their case. The next month was remarkably intense, as the exiles began to check the validity of the declarations submitted to them

3 ACEN, László Bartok (Political Committee) Draft Report on the Concept of National Communism, 20 V 1956, IHRC, ACEN, b. 62, f. 5. See ACEN's position reported in a journal edited by Pavel Tigrid: "ACEN rejects liberalization in East Central Europe," *Central European Newsletter* 1/2 (7–8 July 1956) HIA, RFE/RL CF: A, b. 257, f. 5.

4 ACEN, László Bartok (Political Committee) Draft Report on the Concept of National Communism, 20 V 1956, IHRC, ACEN, b. 62, f. 5; Summary of the Minutes of the 128th Meeting of the General Committee, 13 VI 1956, ibid.; Summary of the Minutes of the 129th Meeting of the General Committee, 13 VI 1956, ibid.

5 For general overview of events, see: Agnieszka Łuczak, Poznań, June'56, IPN website: June56.ipn.gov.pl; John P.C. Matthews, *Tinderbox: East-Central Europe in the spring, summer, and early fall of 1956* (Tucson, AZ: Fenestra Books, 2003).

earlier. The ACEN employed all available tools and used all communication channels it had to the U.S. Congress and government and activated its own representatives in Europe. They were asked to organize meetings with the leaders of the countries in which they were staying, with friendly journalists, politicians and trade unionists.

The description of the ACEN's activities with regard to the "Polish June" requires an explanation of the degree of the FEC's involvement, as many of its initiatives were either inspired or substantially supported by Committee members. The Free Europe Exile Relations Department (FEER), which was then managed by Bernard Yarrow, almost immediately began coordinating activities with the ACEN, especially with the Polish delegation. Triggered by information coming from Poznań, the FEC examined various areas of potential activity. These included:

- intensive contacts of the exiles with the media (including those initiated and facilitated by the FEC);
- telegrams sent to heads of Western countries by the ACEN and by two groups of Polish political refugees representing the Polish Council of National Unity (Adam Ciołkosz) and the Polish National Democratic Committee (Stanisław Mikołajczyk), independently of each other;
- coordinated action on the UN forum that was to lead the matter to the Security Council;
- mobilization of the refugees in various parts of the world to engage the governments of these countries in criticizing the USSR;
- activities in the United States (1956 was the presidential election year) they were to draw the attention of the Americans to another brutally suppressed protest of workers behind the Iron Curtain, as a testimony to the attitude of the Soviet leaders, despite the secret Khrushchev report.[6]

Each of these areas requires additional commentary.

News about the workers' rebellion in Poznań sparked press interest. The ACEN members not only willingly responded to American journalists' calls to comment on events behind the Iron Curtain, but also organized press conferences themselves. Already on 29 June 1956, the ACEN sent out press releases to the editors of the leading titles, in which they interpreted the workers' rebellion in Poznań as an obvious negation of the progress of liberalization and improvement of living conditions behind the Iron Curtain.

---

6 FEER Action in progress on Poznań Events, 29 VI 1956, HIA, RFE/RL CF: A, b. 257, f. 6; Amended with a short report of 30 VI 1956: Additional FEER Actions (Poznań Uprising), 30 VI 1956, ibid.

Paying homage to the "heroic victims" who "without any encouragement from abroad gave voice to the subjugated millions," the ACEN demanded that the western states set a single policy that would lead to the liberation of Poland and the countries of Central and Eastern Europe; "We hope that the free world will not limit itself to expressions of compassion, as in 1953." ACEN hoped for international action: condemnation of the regime, the initiation of an investigation into the Soviet "aggression, domination and colonial exploitation," which according to the ACEN were the basis for all crimes committed against the enslaved nations. The press release also emphasized that Poznań was a clear signal for workers in Western countries that "Moscow puppets are violent aggressors who use the working class," "an enemy of workers all over the world," and every country using Soviet economic assistance or trading with the USSR had to understand that the products it receives were "torn from the mouths of starving workers" behind the Iron Curtain.[7] The content of this communication combined the ACEN's political program with the FEC's propaganda needs. And on the same day, a Hungarian, Béla Fabian, organized a picket at the headquaters the Soviet delegation to the UN in New York, which was covered by the American press.[8] The Free Europe Committee actively supported these activities by facilitating meetings with journalists and diligently collecting newspaper clippings indicating the growing interest of the American press.[9]

3.1 ACEN Reaches Out to the UN

According to the belief that the ACEN was an alternative to the Communist representation of Central and Eastern European nations in the free world, the first political steps taken in response to the workers' rebellion in Poznań were directed to the UN Security Council. At this time, it was headed by E. Ronald Walker, an Australian. Already on 29 June, the ACEN Chairman (Latvian, Vilis Māsēns)

---

7 ACEN Statement on the Events in Poznan, 29 VI 1956 in: ACEN Second Session ..., 148; ACEN Press release no. 142, HIA, RFE/RL CF: A, b. 257, f. 6.

8 Actions by exile organizations and individuals in connection with the Poznań Uprising [no date, document filed by 19 VII 1956], RFE/RL CF: A, b. 257, f. 5; Mary Hornaday, "Polish Exiles Ask West to Intervene," *Christian Science Monitor,* 30 VI 1956; "Seek UN Intervention to Halt Poznan Terror," *New York Journal-American,* 30 VI 1956; "Exiles to Appeal to UN on Poles," *The New York Times* 30 VI 1956; "An Inquiry on Poland Urged by Exile Leaders," *New York Herald Tribune,* 30 VI 1956 – all available as press clippings at HIA, RFE/RL CF: A, b. 257, f. 6.

9 FEER Action in progress on Poznań Events, 29 VI 1956, HIA, RFE/RL CF: A, b. 257, f. 6; Additional FEER Actions (Poznan Uprising), 30 VI 1956, ibid.

appealed to him for immediate action to stop the bloodshed, condemn the Polish communist regime for its crimes, and start an investigation into Soviet aggression, domination and colonial exploitation that had led to the crisis caused by the revolt of Poznań workers.[10] A copy of the telegram sent to Walker was forwarded to all non-Communist delegations at the UN.

The same day, 29 June, the ACEN sent almost identical telegrams to President Dwight D. Eisenhower, UK Prime Minister Anthony Eden and the Prime Minister of France, Guy Mollet, informing them of the contents of the telegram addressed to Walker and asking for instructions for national delegations at the United Nations regarding appropriate steps to bring Poland to the forum of the UN Security Council. If no action were taken there, the ACEN would call for an international conference that would remove the causes of tensions and violence in Central and Eastern Europe by restoring subjugated independence through the right to choose their own form of government.[11] At that time, Dag Hammarskjöld, the UN Secretary-General, was in Warsaw at the invitation of Adam Rapacki (Minister of Foreign Affairs of the Polish People's Republic).[12] The ACEN members swiftly addressed a request in response to this, asking that he use his stay in Poland to conduct an investigation into the bloodshed.[13] It did not happen.[14]

On the last day of June, 1956, the ACEN sent telegrams to all members of the UN Security Council, focusing on non-communist and non-permanent representatives of the following countries: Cuba, Belgium, Iran and Peru.[15] It appealed for support in the UN to the presidents of Brazil, Colombia, Cuba, Ecuador, Guate-

---

10 ACEN Telegram sent to the President of the UN Security Council, HIA, RFE/RL CF: A, b. 257, f. 6.

11 Māsēns to Eisenhower, Eden, Mollet, 29 VI 1956, HIA, RFE/RL Cf.: A, b. 257, f. 6. CF.: Ziętara, *Emigracja wobec Października* ...., 102–103.

12 Polish Film Chronicle, "Nasi goście. Sekretarz ONZ w Warszawie," 3 VII 1956, PKF 28/56, http://www.repozytorium.fn.org.pl/?q=en/node/10158, accessed 10 IV 2020.

13 ACEN, Press Release no. 143, ACEN takes action in connection with the Poznan riot, 30 VI 1956, HIA, RFE/RL CF: A, b. 257, f. 6.

14 Igor Lukes, Karel Sieber, "Pies, który nie szczekał: Czechosłowacja a wydarzenia w Polsce w 1956 r." in: *Polski Październik 1956 w polityce światowej*, ed. Jan Rowiński (Warsaw: PISM 2006), 155.

15 The non-permanent members of the UN Security Council in 1955 were: Belgium, Brazil, Iran, New Zealand, Peru, Turkey. In 1956: Australia, Belgium, Cuba, Iran, Peru, Yugoslavia. In 1957: Australia, Colombia, Cuba, Iraq, Philippines, Sweden. During these years a geographical allocation of seats was changed and therefore some of these states were represented for only one year.

mala and Panama, as well as Pope Pius XII (2 July 1956), who were all also asked to take action on the UN forum.[16]

The ACEN's drawing attention to minor players on the international arena, largely dependent on the United States, was dictated by the desire to bring Poland's situation to the UN Security Council, regardless of the position of the superpowers. While the Americans remained the spokespersons for the refugees, they did not intend to lead in the initiative of a direct confrontation with the USSR in the Security Council. In their contacts with the British and the French, representatives of the ACEN encountered reluctance to offer any support which was explained using legal references. Representatives of these countries cited article 2, para. 7 of the Charter of the United Nations stating that the UN was not authorized to interfere in matters that "are essentially within the domestic jurisdiction of any state or shall require the Members to submit such matters to settlement under the present Charter."[17] Peter E. Ramsbotham, a member of the British delegation to the UN, explained to the exiles that the delegation of his country at the UN would not accept the ACEN delegates, even unofficially, because it had to abide by the UN Charter. According to the British, the ACEN telegram raised issues that were not within the scope of the UN Security Council. At the same time, Ramsbotham did not rule out the possibility of exiles establishing contacts with the British Embassy in Washington.[18] The French reaction was rather similar. They wanted to transfer the dialogue with exiles regarding the reaction to the rebellion of workers in Poznań into the area of foreign relations of their own country, avoiding involvement in the UN forum.[19]

The ACEN fully understood the importance of American leadership in this area and hence it tried to arrange a meeting with Henry Cabot Lodge, Jr., the American ambassador to the United Nations. The advisor on political affairs and security matters in the United States mission to the UN, James W. Pratt, suggested to the ACEN that they should first look for a legal way to explain why the Polish case based on article 2, paragraph 7 of the Charter of the United Nations

16 Steps undertaken by ACEN in connection with the Poznań Uprisings (29 June 1956 – 6 July 1956), ACEN, IHRC, b. 158, f. 8.

17 Charter of the United Nations, Chapter I, http://www.un.org/en/sections/un-charter/chapter-i/index.html, accessed 12 III 2020.

18 Joseph Czako, Memo on the refusal of the British Mission to receive ACEN delegates, 3 VII 1956, IHRC, ACEN, b. 158, f. 8.

19 Louis de Guiringaud – the Acting Permanent Representative of France to the UN. On 3 July 1956, during his meeting with the ACEN delegates, promised them to consult with the French Ministry of Foreign Affairs. Brutus Coste to Zbigniew Stypułkowski-PCNU London (copy to: Auer in Paris), 10 VII 1956, HIA, RFE/RL CF: A, b. 257, f. 6.

was not applicable. Pratt reminded exiles of the position taken by the U.S. government with regard to Guatemala: in May 1954, the CIA had conducted a covert intervention by psychological intimidation and a small paramilitary force which overthrew the democratically elected government of Jacobo Arbenz.[20] When the issue was brought to the UN, in June 1954, the Security Council (including the U.S.) called for "immediate termination of any action likely to cause bloodshed," at the same time requesting "all Members of the UN to abstain, in the spirit of the Charter, from rendering assistance to any such action."[21] In Pratt's opinion it closed off the way of raising the Polish question in the same forum. If the ACEN found a way to bypass this obstacle then he was ready to talk.[22] This memorandum explains the presence of Guatemala in the official memorandum issued by the ACEN on 9 July.

Before the ACEN was ready with its memorandum, George Dimitrov (Vice President of the ACEN, leader of the Bulgarian delegation, and Vice Chairman of the IPU) paid a visit to the State Department. The meeting that took place only two days after the House of Representatives adopted a resolution on Poznań that was a clear manifestation of the interests of the American government.[23] Dimitrov asked that the United States take up the Poznań case in the UN Security Council.[24] At that time, ACEN researched the issue of how to link the brutally suppressed workers' protest with the violation of the provisions of the United Nations Charter.

On 5 July 1956, Zygmunt Nagórski Sr. presented his solution binding events in Poznań with the threat to international peace. Judging from the content of this study, it became the basis for the ACEN memorandum issued on 9 July 1956. Nagórski stated that the answer was found in article 34 (in Chapter VI: Pacific Settlement of Disputes): "The Security Council may investigate any dispute, or any situation which might lead to international friction or give rise to a dispute, in order to determine whether the continuance of the dispute or situation is likely to endanger the maintenance of international peace and security."[25] In Poznań,

---

20 Michael Grow, *U.S. Presidents and Latin American Interventions. Pursuing Regime Change in the Cold War* (Lawrence, KS: University Press of Kansas, 2008), 1–27.

21 Resolution 104 (S/3237), 20 VI 1954, adopted unanimously at the 675th meeting (in response to a cablegram of 19 VI 1954 from Minister for External Relations of Guatemala), UN Digital Library, digitallibrary.un.org/record/112077, accessed 16 VII 2020.

22 J. Czako, Memo, 5 VII 1956, IHRC, ACEN, b. 158, f. 8.

23 Ziętara, *Emigracja wobec Października. Postawy polskich środowisk emigracyjnych wobec liberalizacji w PRL w latach 1955–1957* (Warsaw: LTW, 2001), 109–110.

24 J. Czako, Pro domo, 5 VII 1956, IHRC, ACEN, b. 158, f. 8.

25 UN Charter, http://www.un.org/en/sections/un-charter/chapter-vi/index.html, accessed 16 VII 2020.

there was a violation of the Universal Declaration of Human Rights adopted by the United Nations (and therefore, despite the abstaining vote, also binding on the USSR). Furthermore, the rebellion of Poles was a direct response to armed intervention and the de facto occupation of Poland. Nagórski argued that this was not the only manifestation of opposition to the USSR in Poland, as well as in other countries of the region. The Polish delegate equaled this with breaking international arrangements. In January 1947, in the presence of the Soviet army, falsified elections took place in Poland, which was a direct violation of Yalta (and thus the international character of Soviet obligations).[26]

Indeed, in the text of the 9 July ACEN memorandum sent to the governments of the free world and to the press, events in Poland were recognized as "a threat to international peace and security." In fact, all the arguments prepared by Nagórski were included in it, supplemented with two paragraphs that concerned ... Guatemala and Algeria. In the first of these countries, the Americans supported the military coup in 1954, in the second the French led a colonial war. The ACEN explained that "the situation in Central and Eastern Europe is different from the events in Guatemala because the crisis of 1954 did not threaten world peace – it was only limited to this country. There were no foreign troops in this country. The insurgents in Guatemala did not have commanders from another country. There was no danger that this movement would spread to other countries." Today we know that the nature of American intervention was not as innocent as the ACEN exiles set it out. With regard to Algeria, their efforts to dispel criticism of the communist adversaries were even more risky: "As for Algeria, the international community recognized it as an integral part of France, which, in turn, never recognized in any international treaty that Algeria was the object of international relations. There was no international conference to deal with this country's problem, with the consent of France."[27]

The ACEN's members had to be aware that such an explanation would not bring a decision on the UN Security Council's investigation into Poznań any closer. It is evidenced in the text of the memorandum itself. The exiles stated that should it result only in a debate in the UN Security Council which would spell out the real reasons of the Polish crisis ("constant interference of the USSR and armed occupation of the country under the pretext of maintaining the supply lines to Germany"), it would still be in the interest of the free world. A hand-

26 Zygmunt Nagórski, Sr.'s contribution, 5 VII 1956, IHRC, ACEN, b. 158, f. 8.

27 ACEN, The events in Poland as a threat to international peace and security, 9 VII 1956, HIA, RFE/RL CF: A, b. 257, f. 6.

written note on the copy of the memorandum found in the ACEN files indicates that it was handed over to Cabot Lodge in person.[28]

The ACEN attempted to reach the delegations of non-Communist members of the UN Security Council, but smaller countries avoided taking responsibility for the appeal that was doomed to failure. The ACEN delegation headed by Māsēnes, met with Dr. Tingfu F. Tsiang, the Permanent Representative of China at the UN, on 2 July 1956. The assurance of Tsiang's support for ACEN was obtained, provided that some other member of the UN Security Council (meaning the U.S.) would bring the rebellion in Poznań to the agenda.[29] On 11 July 1956, George Dimitrov and Adam Ciołkosz were to meet Victor A. Belaúnde, Peru's representative on the UN Security Council. It turned out that the meeting was set up with the permanent representative of Peru at the United Nations.[30] Due to the confusion, it did not take place. On 9 July, Ciołkosz and Coste met with Jayme de Barros, deputy representative of Brazil at the UN, asking for support. They heard that since there was little chance that any action would be taken, and given that Brazil had diplomatic relations with Warsaw, that country would not take the initiative: at most it would support it, *after* the introduction by another country (U.S.).[31] The Australians behaved similarly. At a meeting with Michael J. Wilson, the Secretary of the Australian permanent mission to the UN (acting on behalf of Walker), Ciołkosz and Coste heard that Australia had always followed the UK in the recognition of governments. Since representatives of the Polish People's Republic sat at the UN, they could diagnose that it was their internal affair.[32] Only the Cuban representative (Emilio Núñez Portuondo) promised ACEN that he would pressure his own government to take action aimed at introducing Poznań to the UN Security Council.[33] According to Coste, since the previous meeting with Portuondo on 9 July, the Cuban delegate had asked his government thrice to bring the Poznań case to the UN Security Council but received no answer. Portuondo, who served the Batista regime in Cuba and by 1960 became an exile himself, held prominent positions in the UN, including the President of the UN Security Council in September 1956. In the opinion of ACEN delegates (Ciołkosz and Coste), Portuondo

28 Ibid. Delivered in person to Cabot Lodge on 10 July 1956 – see: IHRC, ACEN, b. 158, f. 8. See also ACEN press release no. 142, Statement on the Events in Poznan, 29 VI 1956, HIA, RFE/RL CF: A, b. 257, f. 6.

29 Czako, Pro domo, 5 VII 1956, IHRC, ACEN, b. 158, f. 8.

30 Coste, ACEN Memorandum on July 11 meeting with Belaúnde, 16 VII 1956, ibid.

31 Coste, Memorandum on July 9 meeting with De Barros, 16 VII 1956, ibid.

32 Coste, Memorandum on July 13 meeting with Wilson, 16 VII 1956, ibid.

33 Coste, Memorandum on July 12 meeting with Portuondo, 16 VII 1956, ibid.

was the spokesperson for their cause.[34] Despite his service to non-democratic regime, the ACEN recognized him as a "great friend."[35]

However, the ACEN's exiled politicians were well aware of where the key to their success lay. On 9 July 1956, Dimitrov met with Francis B. Stevens, the head of the Office for Eastern Europe at the State Department. The meeting was also attended by the counselor and the second secretary of the British Embassy.[36] The next day, Ciołkosz and Coste were received by Cabot Lodge, who was already familiar with the content of the ACEN memorandum. Lodge asked whether, given the likelihood of a Soviet veto on proposals to investigate Poznań revolt, the impact of such initiative behind the Iron Curtain would be positive. Ciołkosz assured him that regardless of the result, the very attempt of a Western state at the UN would have a constructive effect on Poland, and on the region. Although the Poznań case was legally complex, Lodge was convinced of its importance and promised to send the Department of State a recommendation in line with ACEN's intentions.[37]

Brutus Coste kept ACEN representatives in London and Paris updated on the ACEN's efforts in New York. His letters were not optimistic. After all, the ACEN consisted of seasoned politicians and careful observers of the international relations. The Secretary General of the ACEN evaluated the significance of the letters that ACEN sent to representatives of the free world (non-communist) members of the UN. "In Washington, we heard that the matter was being considered, but we should not expect action," said Coste. He continued: "[O]ur chances are slim. However, we should keep on pressing."[38] Clearly, the exiles were determined to provoke discussion on the international arena and through it exert political pressure on the USSR. Even if there was no chance to implement their plan of peaceful liberation (via free elections and withdrawal of the Soviet troops). As the UN seemed an unlikely forum to undertake a concrete action at least there was a potential for weakening the Soviet urge to pose as a champion of peace. Poznań proved to be a valid asset for waging the political warfare.

---

34 Coste, Memorandum on July 9 meeting with Portuondo, 16 VII 1956, ibid.

35 Gadomski, *Zgromadzenie* ..., 26.

36 Actions by exile organizations and individuals in connection with the Poznan Uprisings [no date, received for the files 19 VII 1956], RFE/RL CF: A 257, f. 5.

37 Coste, Memorandum on July 10 meeting with Lodge, 16 VII 1956, IHRC, ACEN, b. 158, f. 8. Korboński believed that the White House was not in favor of such action. See: Ziętara, *Emigracja wobec Października* ..., 112.

38 Coste to Stypułkowski (PCNU, Londyn), Auer (Paris), 10 VII 1956, HIA, RFE/RL CF: A, b. 257, f. 6.

3.2 American Support for ACEN's Agenda

The earliest voice of support for the Polish workers came from the United States. It was released as fast as the ACEN's appeals. The State Department issued a statement regarding Poznań on 29 June 1956 blaming USSR for the massacre and emphasizing the need to fulfill the promise of the possibility to choose a political system, which was one of the objectives of the American policy towards Central and Eastern Europe.[39] Within a few days, the American Congress also reacted. Its members not only took up the debate on Poznań (3–5 July 1956), but also passed a resolution calling on the U.S. President to bring the situation in Poland to the UN. Regarding the ACEN's activities, it should be emphasized that the representatives and senators known personally to the refugees willingly published speeches, appeals, articles prepared by ACEN in transcripts from the sessions of the American Congress.[40]

The Free Europe Committee did not leave the ACEN without help. Thanks to its commitment, the ACEN's activities had been strengthened. It should be remembered that the persons responsible for overseeing the activities of FEC sat on the advisory bodies of the President, and were in constant contact with the State Department and American intelligence agencies. Cooperation with refugees meant that FEC also played a consultative role for the aforementioned government institutions.[41]

On 29 June 1956, the FEC "arranged" a statement by Averell Harriman, which helped to publicize the rebellion of Polish workers. Harriman – a colleague of Roosevelt and Truman, a former U.S. ambassador in Moscow, a member of the Commission established in Yalta for the Polish Provisional Government, and the Governor of New York in 1956 – recognized Poznań as a milestone on the road to freedom and placed it next to workers' rebellions in the GDR and Czecho-

---

39 Jakub Tyszkiewicz, *Rozbijanie monolitu. Polityka Stanów Zjednoczonych wobec Polski 1945–1988* (Warsaw: PWN, 2015), 101; Machcewicz, *Emigracja w polityce międzynarodowej ...*, 143.

40 Senators: Paul H. Douglas (IL), introduced address by Petr Zenkl, Roman L. Hruska (NE) – ACEN statement "The events in Poland as threat to international peace and security." Paul H. Douglas, "Soviet Imperialism," 11 VI 1956, Cong. Rec., 84th Cong., 2nd Sess., *Cong. Rec.* 102, A4619; Roman L. Hruska, "Assembly of Captive European Nations," 26 VII 1956, Cong. Rec., 84th Cong., 2nd Sess., *Cong. Rec.* 102, A5956–5957. Thomas J. Dodd – representative from Connecticut introduced ACEN as "an articulate and effective foe of communism representing free elements in exile" and included "ACEN statement on the events ...". Thomas J. Dodd, "The Poznan Situation," 25 VII 1956, Cong. Rec., 84th Cong., 2nd Sess., *Cong. Rec.* 102, A 6273. See also: Actions by exile organizations and individuals in connection with the Poznan Uprisings [date before 19 VII 1956], RFE/RL CF: A, b. 257, f. 5.

41 FEER Action in Progress on Poznań Events, 29 VI 1956, HIA, RFE/RL CF: A, b. 257, f. 6.

slovakia, but also next to the rebellion in the Soviet labor camps of Vorkuta and Karaganda in 1953. The original statement combining admiration for the historical heroism of Poles with the opinion that the free world did not call for imprudent acts of heroism, as well as the sentence professing that changes in countries dominated by Communists will not happen "in one night" were removed from the first version of the speech. Harriman, on the other hand, said that he "understood the desperation of the workers" and "condemned the despots," which drew the attention of the media, but deprived the text of its political significance.[42]

Public statements of sympathy and compassion for Poles "contemporary heroes of the struggle for freedom" were excellent material for broadcasts of Voice of America and RWE.[43] They encouraged and sustained hope behind the Iron Curtain and created a climate favorable to the political action taken by ACEN. Direct support for the exiles was expressed by Cloyce K. Huston (Deputy Director of Free Europe Organizations and Publications), during the solemn Freedom Day celebration that took place at the Statue of Liberty on 1 July 1956.

> Speaking on behalf of FEC paying tribute to heroes who brought freedom to our shores and have preserved it to this day [mentioned earlier in the speech: Rochambeau, Lafayette, Kosciuszko and Pulaski] I also pay tribute to those who are here today leading the struggle for liberty and independence the live heroes now among us, the fighters of the present who pause here in the midst of battle for fresh inspiration and rededication today's warriors of freedom.[...] Warriors of freedom, on this day of freedom, at this special shrine of freedom, we of FEC salute you.[44]

Referring to the activities of political exiles as "freedom fighters with whom we are happily linked as friends and allies," Huston recognized the exile organizations combined under ACEN's umbrella as an effective instrument of political warfare and called for not ignoring changes taking place in the captive countries. "The New York Times" reported number of participants: 1,500 at the base of the Statue of Liberty as well as the presence of William A. Crawford (Deputy Director

---

42 Statement by Governor Averell Harriman on workers uprising in Poznan, Poland, 29 VI 1956, RFE/RL CF: A, b. 257, f. 6.

43 Actions by exile organizations and individuals in connection with the Poznan Uprising [no date, registered by 19 VII 1956], RFE/RL CF: A, b. 257, f. 5.

44 Cloyce K. Huston, Salute to the warriors of freedom, address on behalf of FEC, 1 VII 1956, RFE/RL CF: A, b. 257, f. 6. Stefan Korboński of ACEN spoke at the same event.

of Office of Eastern European Affairs at the Department of State) who "espoused the use of peaceful means to bring the political change."[45]

A few days later Whitney Shepardson, the president of the FEC, paying homage to the victims of Poznań and expressing his condolences to the families of the victims, declared that the Committee would use its resources to ensure that the trials of these "innocent workers" are fair and public, and those who "participated in the workers' struggle to improve their living conditions will be acquitted."[46] Obviously, the FEC intended to use Poznań in order to keep the attention of the free world focused on the fate of the inhabitants of the subjugated countries, thereby strengthening the anti-communist sentiments in the world. To this end, the Committee also undertook wide-ranging activities to create coordinated pressure on its partners, which soon embraced three continents.[47]

These activities corresponded with the FEC guidelines adopted in August. The goal of the FEC's activities was to "use outstanding and properly selected exiles in Third World countries, including South America, to explain the character of Soviet colonialism and share witnesses' reports about the techniques used by the USSR to maintain control over their countries."[48]

One cannot forget, however, that acting in the name of subjugated compatriots, in cooperation with the Americans, the ACEN members pursued their own political goals. Using their interest in Poznań, they tried to reach the members of the governments and parliaments of the free world in order to exert political pressure on the USSR. According to the ACEN, the constant emphasis on the temporary character of Soviet domination in Central and Eastern Europe was necessary to prevent the international community from acknowledging the status quo. With the means of financial and political support from FEC, ACEN activated its representatives in Europe. On 2 July, the Chairman of the ACEN (Māsēns) sent a request to Zbigniew Stypułkowski (London) and Pál Auer (Paris) to organize local representative offices and approach relevant foreign ministers. Both were

45 "Poznan Saluted on Freedom Day," *The New York Times*, 2 VII 1956, 12. For the text of the speeches see: Freedom Day, ACEN News 15–17 (June-August 1956): 37–41.

46 Free Europe Committee, Inc., Press Release, 5 VII 1956, HIA, RFE/RL CF: A, b. 257, f. 6.

47 Actions by exile organizations and individuals in connection with the Poznan Uprisings [no date, registered by 19 VII 1956], RFE/RL CF: A, b. 257, f. 5; Supplement to Chronology of Actions by Exile Organizations and Individuals in Connection with the Poznan Uprisings, 30 VII 1956, HIA, RFE/RL CF: A, b. 257, f. 6; FEER Action in progress on Poznań Events, 29 VI 1956, ibid. ; Additional FEER Actions (Poznan Uprising), 30 VI 1956, HIA, RFE/RL CF: A, ibid.

48 CIA FOIA, Agreed Policy Governing Free Europe Committee Operations, 7 VIII 1956, https://www.cia.gov/library/readingroom/docs/DOC_0001409009.pdf, accessed: 17 X 2019.

asked to make sure that ACEN's appeals (telegrams and statements) addressed to the Prime Ministers of both states had been taken into account. The ACEN delegates carried out similar activities in Washington themselves.[49]

On 12 July 1956, the ACEN delegation in London, consisting of representatives of Poland, Czechoslovakia and Bulgaria, appealed for admission to the Foreign Office. The British ordered the exiles to wait, as Stypułkowski supposed, pondering what exactly the ACEN itself was.[50] Eventually, almost two weeks later, the ACEN delegation headed by Jerzy Zdziechowski, accompanied by Václav Holub and Nikola Dolapchiev, went to the Foreign Office for a meeting with Henry A. F. "Harry" Hohler, the head of the Northern Department. For Zdziechowski, who reported on this meeting, it was clear that Hohler "accepted us only as eminent foreigners. It was obvious that he did not want to see us as representatives of our countries, or as the ACEN delegation." The British diplomat, who was soon to take up a post in Rome, categorically told the ACEN delegates that he did not share their views and did not intend to support their demands expressed in the telegram addressed to Eden and in the ACEN statement of 9 July 1956. While leaving, Zdziechowski told Hohler that the attitude of the Western powers to the events in Poland would have a negative impact on the confidence of the captive nations to the policy of the West. In the commentary addressed to Māsēns, he signaled failure, but also that ACEN's activities in Europe required a significant intensification.[51]

Auer was luckier. He managed to get to the Quai d'Orsay meeting a week earlier. The exiles were received by Maurice Faure, Secretary of State in the Ministry of Foreign Affairs in the rank of Minister, Jean Laloy (Minister Plenipotentiary for European Affairs) and Director of Faure's Cabinet. The conclusions of this meeting, which Auer included in a letter to Māsēns, were rather dismal. "Despite the goodwill shown to us, it is clear that the liberation of our nations will not be possible for a long time and we have no solution other than political. [...] The situation in Central and Eastern Europe may change through the actions of internal forces," wrote Auer, directing ACEN's chairman's attention to the Budapest events of 27 June 1956 organized by young dissidents (mostly intellectuals and professionals) gathered in the Petőfi Circle. "The role of exiles was to ensure that the west would not hinder this process and that the captive nations would not be discouraged by the Western countries." There was such a danger,

49 Vilis Māsēns (chairman ACEN) to Zbigniew Stypułkowski (PCNU London), 2 VII 1956, HIA, RFE/RL CF: A, b. 257, f. 6.

50 Stypułkowski to Māsēns, 19 VII 1956, IHRC, ACEN, b. 158, f. 8.

51 Zdziechowski to Mon cher President (Māsēns), 26 VII 1956, HIA, RFE/RL CF: A, b. 257, f. 6.

according to Auer, lurking in talks about the future of Germany without referring to the problem of Central and Eastern Europe as a whole.

After his meeting with Faure, the Hungarian exile bitterly concluded that, despite his sympathy, France ostensibly does not want to interfere in the internal affairs of other countries, while in the meantime "they are less loyal [to this rule] in Algeria!"[52] A week later, however, he added that in conversations on the Quai d'Orsay he obtained unofficial information that the French government postponed the arrival of Cyrankiewicz originally planned for September. This also encompassed negotiations regarding agreements on cultural cooperation.[53] It was a small consolation. Despite sympathy and understanding for the ACEN's demands, France was not ready to join the effort in the United Nations as "Poznań remained an internal matter of Poland."[54] Consequently, the interest in the rebellion of Polish workers could soon fade. Neither the ACEN, nor the FEC wanted to see it happen. Both Americans and the exiles wanted to "keep Poznań alive."[55] The occasion for this was the announcement of court trials that could have continued the repression of Polish workers.

3.3 Poznań Trials

Not knowing what position the Polish regime would take against the rebels, the ACEN was preparing to carry out world-class action in defense of the persecuted workers. On 11 July 1956 a meeting of representatives of several American anti-communist, ethnic and political exile organizations took place in New York.[56]

---

52 Auer to Māsēns, 20 VII 1956, ibid.

53 Auer to Māsēns, 27 VII 1956, ibid.

54 Packer to Yarrow, Huston, Memorandum, 24 VII 1956, ibid.; Auer to Māsēns, 20 VII 1956, ibid.

55 Steps undertaken by the ACEN in connection with the Poznan Uprising (Sequel to note dated July 11, 1956), 26 VII 1956, ibid.; CKH (Huston), Memorandum: actions by Exile Organizations and Individuals in Connection with the Poznan Uprisings, to Shants and McCargar, 3 VIII 1956, HIA, RFE/RL CF: A, b. 257, f. 5.

56 Minutes of Conference held by representatives of various liberal, labor and anti-Communist organizations interested in protecting the workers of Poznan, 11 VII 1956, New York, IHRC, ACEN, b. 158, f. 8. Among the representatives of various organizations there were: American Committee for Cultural Freedom, American Friends of Captive Nations, American Veterans Committee, ACEN, Jewish Labor Committee, Lithuanian American Council, PCNU, Radio Liberty, Socialist Party, Ukrainian Congress Committee. Last minute cancellations included: International Rescue Committee, Polish American Congress. The meeting took place at Samuel Tappen's of the American Veterans Committee office.

The gathering was evidently organized by Christopher Emmet, Chairman of the AFCN, who also presided over the conference. Participants of the meeting tried to coordinate their actions as some organizations have already declared their involvement in this case. Among the organizations listed there were lawyers' associations in the Hague,[57] the Congress for Cultural Freedom in Paris, the International Center of Free Trade Unionists (ICFTU), the International League for Human Rights, and even the ACEN itself. The Americans present at the meeting mainly postulated engagement of American workers in various forms of protest in defense of Poles. Representatives of the ACEN reminded those gathered about their meeting with Cabot Lodge and repeated the call to bring Poznań to the UN Security Council. It was agreed that the Workers Defense League would endeavor to create an initiative similar to that of the Committee for the Fair Trial of Draža Mihailović. Interestingly, Emmet served as treasurer of the said committee in 1946. In addition, upon the insistence of the Poles, the assembled organizations agreed to appeal to John Foster Dulles and to Henry Cabot Lodge, to prepare a press conference and also to submit a motion for a resolution to the U.S. Congress. Two days later, the FEC received a message that the Poznań trials would actually take place and that prosecution would include 285 workers.[58] The ACEN's July meeting with partner organizations led to the establishment of the Legal Commission for Poznań Trials in New York, which included the above-mentioned organizations.

The Assembly also decided, against its already established routine, to address the Polish Prime Minister directly. The excuse to act was a unique one. Three members of the ACEN: Béla Fabian (Hungarian), Jerzy Ptakowsky (Pole), and Vaclovas Sidzikauskas (Lithuanian) were all former fellow prisoners with Cyrankiewicz in Auschwitz. They decided to write to the Polish Prime Minister in the following manner:

> Mr. Cyrankiewicz,
> The tragic events that took place in Poznan, prompt us to appeal to you, who 12 years ago, shared our sufferings in the Nazi concentration camp of Auschwitz. May be that your left arm still bears the tattooed number by which the SS marked the prisoners of Auschwitz. [...] From the concentration camps you, Mr. Cyrankiewicz, returned to Warsaw to seek on the side of the Communists the better world for which so many had died. What happened to this better world? The workers of Poznań, to whom the Communist regime does not give

57 Already on 6 July 1956 ACEN thanked A. J. M. Van Dal of the International Commission of Jurists (Hague) for calling on Warsaw government to admit foreign observers to the workers' trials. Actions by exile organizations and individuals in connection with the Poznan Uprisings [no date, document reg. 19 VII 1956], HIA, RFE/RL CF: A 257, f. 5.

58 Konrad Kellen to Yarrow, Memorandum, 13 VII 1956, HIA, RFE/RL CF: A, b. 257, f. 6.

> enough bread, sent a delegation to Warsaw. Humbly and modestly – as had been the custom in Auschwitz – they protested against the reduction of their pay, asking for wages on which they would not have to face starvation. Poland, Mr. Cyrankiewicz, had been at all times, a veritable land of milk and honey. Bread had never been a luxury. Not even under the Czars or under Nazi occupation. Your answer to the workers' appeal was that your henchmen arrested the members of the delegation. This caused the strike that broke out in Poznań. And you should know, that the right to strike is the most elementary of every worker in a free country. However, in your country, as in all countries under Communist domination, strikes are considered rebellious and "anti-democratic" and are punishable by shooting or hanging. We do not know the number of the victims of the Poznań strike, 42 or 400? 1,000 or 2,000? The only thing we know is that people had to die because they had dared to demand bread and freedom. [...] To awaken your conscience is the very purpose of our telegram. [...] Mr. Cyrankiewicz! Stop shedding the blood of the heroic Polish workers [...] We appeal, not for clemency but for justice and human rights![59]

The letter was signed with the names and Auschwitz prisoner numbers. While not listing the Assembly as the sender, the letter clearly indicates the return address, which was the ACEN offices. This initiative what was reported to the U.S. Congress as "an ideological bomb for Poland," following a title added to this story by the "New York Herald Tribune."[60] Another telegram was also sent to Cyrankiewicz by Vratislav Busek (Czech) who met the Pole in Mauthausen (following the former's surviving a death march from Auschwitz) and now demanded of the former fellow prisoner an immediate stop the bloodshed of the Polish workers.[61] This appeal, sent little more than a week later, did not get as much publicity.

A separate ACEN correspondence was addressed to the members of the special Committee on Non-Represented Nations at the Council of Europe's Consultative Assembly.[62] Following the ACEN's appeal, Fernand Dehousse, the Chair-

59 Béla Fabian, Jerzy Ptakowsky, Vaclovas Sidzikauskas, Telegram [copy] to Joseph Cyrankiewicz (overt, released to the press), 9 VII 1956, HIA, RFE/CF: A, b. 257, f. 5 and IHRC, ACEN, b. 158, f. 8; ACEN Actions by exile organizations and individuals in connection with the Poznan Uprisings [no date, reg. 19 VII 1956], RFE/RL CF: A, b. 257, f. 5.

60 Hon. Abraham J. Multer (NY), 16 VII 1956, An Ideological Bomb for Poland, Cong. Rec.– Appendix, 6 VIII 1956, A6218. See also: Herbert A. Philbrick, "An Ideological Bomb for Poland," *New York Herald Tribune*, 15 VII 1956.

61 Vratislav Busek to Josef Szyrankiewicz [Cyrankiewicz], Copy of a Telegram, 18 VII 1956, IHRC, ACEN, b. 158, f. 8.

62 Steps undertaken by ACEN in connection with the Poznan Uprising (Sequel to note dated July 11, 1956), 26 VII 1956, RFE/RL CF: A 257:6 and HIA, RFE/RL CF: A, b. 257, f. 6; The Poznan Trials, Address Made by Dr. Stefan Osuský, Chairman of the Czechoslovak delegation at the meeting of the ACEN held September 27, 1956, IHRC, ACEN, b. 89, f. 3 and HIA, RFE/RL CF: A, b. 257, f. 5.

man of the Consultative Assembly, sent a request to Cyrankiewicz to admit a delegation of observers to the trials of workers accused of participating in the revolution. He received a response only after he repeated the message to the Polish Prime Minister on 18 September 1956.[63] The request was refused on the grounds that the trials would be public and "cannot have the character of an international spectacle which would be prejudicial to the dignity of our courts and would cast doubt on their impartiality and competence."[64]

The Operations Coordinating Board, a body established by President Eisenhower in 1953 to oversee covert operations, reviewed the actions of the American government taken with regards to Poznań at its meeting on 18 July 1956. Jacob Beam summed up the information campaign addressed to both the USIA and press. At the initiative of the United States (and with the help of Canadians), the revolt of the people of Poznań was discussed on 14 July 1956 at the North Atlantic Council meeting. Lodge had found a way to mention this in a recent speech in the UN. The American delegation at ECOSOC received instructions to mention the rebellion at the earliest opportunity.[65] Franklin A. Mewshaw (Public Affairs Officer, Department of State) told ACEN that the U.S. representative at ECOSOC raised the question of Poznań on 19 July 1956 during a meeting in Geneva. It did not draw any significant attention from the media.[66]

Beam complained that other governments were none too willing to help distribute materials about Poznań, but he hoped that this would change when the trials started.[67] The following comment was added to this note: "July 19, the Department instructed 15 posts in Europe, the Western Hemisphere and the Middle East to raise the issue of Poznań with the respective governments" on the

---

63 Telegram addressed by Mr. Dehousse to Mr. Cyrankiewicz, 7 IX 1956, Council of Europe, Consultative Assembly, Special Committee to Watch Over the Interests of European Nations not Represented in the Council of Europe, 4th Session, Poznań Riots, https://rm.coe.int/09000016807a4bb7, accessed 20 II 2020. See the exchange of messages that followed, ibid.

64 Cyrankiewicz [signed by Antoni Mrugalski] to the President of the [Consultative] Assembly [Dehousse], 20 IX 1956, ibid., https://rm.coe.int/090000168079b063, accessed 20 II 2020; Gadomski, *Zgromadzenie Europejskich ...*, 28–29.

65 Notes on a Meeting of the Operations Coordinating Board (OCB), Washington, 18 VII 1956, *FRUS 1955–1957*, Vol. XXV, 221–222, doc. 81, https://history.state.gov/historicaldocuments/frus1955-57v25/d81, accessed 20 II 2020.

66 ACEN was promised a copy of the statement. J. Czako, Memo, 25 VII 1956, IHRC, ACEN, b. 158, f. 8; Supplement to Chronology of Actions by Exile Organizations and Individuals in Connection with the Poznan Uprisings, 30 VII 1956, HIA, RFE/RL CF: A, b. 257, f. 6.

67 Notes on a Meeting of the OCB, 18 VII 1956, ibid.

grounds that the Polish government's reaction to the riots might be "tempered" by "Free World interest."[68]

Two days before the start of the trials, political refugees received substantial support from their biggest ally in the U.S. government, John Foster Dulles. On 25 September 1956, the Secretary of State suggested to President Eisenhower that a statement regarding the announced trials be issued: "An appropriate statement by you early this week could not only serve this purpose but would also provide the Polish people with timely evidence that they have not been forgotten and that the importance and significance of the Poznań riots have not been overlooked."[69] This memo serves as a proof how high the ACEN pressure reached:

> It might also be mentioned that the Assembly of Captive European Nations has just sent a telegram to you, as well as to the Vice President, Mr. Stevenson, and to me in the hope of obtaining appropriate statements on the Poznań trials which could be read at the Assembly's meeting scheduled for Thursday. Mr. Stevenson's reply is now being prepared. I believe it would be preferable, from the point of view of domestic as well as of foreign affairs, if you could issue the enclosed statement as early as possible.

The president annotated the memo "approved, DE."[70] Once again however, support for ACEN's cause was related to U.S. political interests in the domestic arena: building support for the administration in office.

President Eisenhower expressed his concern about the workers' fate in a statement issued on 26 September 1956. In a statement, apart from referring to trials, the American President acknowledged one fact as obvious:

> There can be no permanent solution of the situation in Poland until the Polish people are given an opportunity to elect a Government of their own choosing. The basic problem in Poland is not what particular type of economic or social system shall prevail; that is something the Polish people can and should decide for themselves. What is essential is that they be given the opportunity to do so in free and unfettered elections.[71]

---

68 Ibid.

69 Memorandum from the Secretary of State to the President, 25 IX 1956, *FRUS 1955–1957*, Vol. XXV, doc. 90, 247–248, https://history.state.gov/historicaldocuments/frus1955-57v25/d90, accessed 12 IV 2020.

70 Ibid.

71 Statement by the President Regarding Trials Following the Poznan Riots in Poland, 26 IX 1956, *Public Papers of the Presidents of the United States. Dwight D. Eisenhower, 1956, Containing the Public Messages, Speeches, and Statements of the President, January 1 to December 21, 1956* (Washington, GPO: 1958), doc. 215, 805.

It should be added, however, that a few days earlier the draft of President Eisenhower's statement, "as suggested by friends," found itself in the FEC's offices.[72]

On 27 September 1956, the ACEN inaugurated its extraordinary plenary session, which was scheduled to begin concurrently with the opening of the Poznań trials. The representatives of the captive nations gathered at the Carnegie International Center with the following aims: to undermine the right of the "vassal" government to judge patriotic Poles; to confirm the right of the subjugated people to fight for freedom; and to appeal to the free nations to use the Poznań trials to bring the matter to the UN forum. The trials were to serve as profound evidence of inhuman conditions prevailing in the countries enslaved by the USSR.[73]

The setup of this meeting must have been pretty dramatic. Besides flags of the captive nations at half mast, the exile participants and invited guests could see an enlarged photo of a "Polish Joanne d'Arc," who marched in front of the Polish flag stained with blood. Blood that was attributed to a 12-year old boy, a victim of a gun fire used against the protesters in Poznań. The proceedings opened – in accordance with the ACEN's routine – with an invocation delivered by Fr. W. Arthur Rojek from New York. Dimitrov, who spoke first, presented the current activities of ACEN in the matter of Poznań and regretted that the UN Security Council did not take up the issue of the Polish rebellion. In his opinion, the situation in the captive countries was more serious than the Suez crisis.[74]

Then the chairman of the meeting, Štefan Osuský, took the stand to discuss Poznań to deny the claims that the trend of liberalization which would radiate in the Soviet orbit was born in Moscow (as a result of Khrushchev's speech). He then read President Eisenhower's appeal which was emphasized by red pencil in the version of the speech preserved in the archives of the FEC. Next to take the floor was William Fitelson – a member of both the AFCN, and the Legal Commission for Poznań Trials sponsored by the Workers Defense League. Fitelson described their efforts to send lawyers-observers to Poznań. Acting on their behalf, he did not receive a clear refusal from Warsaw but rather an indirect suggestion

72 See earlier versions of the text: Text of President Eisenhower Statement on Poznan Trials, 26 IX 1956, IHRC, ACEN, b. 89, f. 3 as well as HIA, RFE/RL CF: A, b. 257, f. 5.

73 Dimitrov (Acting Chairman ACEN), Coste (Sec. Gen.), Telegram 25 IX 1956 sent out to senators, congressmen, businessmen, labor leaders, prominent Americans connected with FEC. The first telegram was addressed to John F. Finerty, Chairman Legal Commission for the Poznan Trials. See Telegram and distribution list: IHRC, ACEN, b. 89, f. 3 as well as here: HIA, RFE/RL CF: A, b. 257, f. 5. The responses received voicing support for ACEN came from: James G. Fulton; Thaddeus M. Machrowicz, William F. Knowland, Daniel J. Flood, Thomas J. Dodd, Robert F. Wagner (Mayor of New York), Presidential candidate – Adlai Stevenson, and John F. Dulles.

74 ACEN Press release no. 155: "ACEN Extraordinary Plenary Meeting protests Poznan <trials>", 27 IX 1956, RFE/RL CF: A, 257, f. 5 and also at IHRC, ACEN, b. 89, f. 3.

that "humanitarian organizations" should rather go to Cyprus or Kenya. Fitelson was clearly moved and did not intend to give up. The next step for these organizations was to set up a commission of inquiry, analyze the evidence and publish a "white book" prepared by lawyers and scientists.[75]

Among the prominent guests who addressed the ACEN on this occasion there was Leo Cherne, the Chairman of the International Rescue Committee in charge of the resettlement program for refugees (1946–1986). Cherne recognized the Poznań trials as part of a larger Communist crime made worse by the fact that neither the names and faces of the defendants were known, nor were the judges, or even those who stood behind them. He charismatically called for the organization of protests against unfair trials and for the restoration of the human face of the "individuality of the mind, heart and soul" to the enslaved countries.[76] Cherne ended his appeal the way which resembled the fiery speeches of the Crusade of Freedom, and which was rewarded with thunderous applause:

> This room should be filled to its last corner. The telegrams should be multiplied ten thousand fold. Statesmen and men who guide opinion in all the civilized countries should today have been under such a moral requirement that they could not please the pressure of other obligations because, in fact, there is no obligation other than the plight of a human being unjustly destroyed. This is the crime (Applause) This is your vision. This is the purpose of this extraordinary Plenary Session of the Assembly. May your work increase. May your energy multiply. May your adherents grow without number. May you bring back the human faith to the country you were compelled to leave (Applause).[77]

The next person to address the audience was Bolesław Wierzbiański, Vice President of PCNU in America. Already on 9 September 1956, and in an alarmist tone, he had informed colleagues from the ACEN that the number of victims and people arrested in Poznań was many times higher than the West knew about. The information, he claimed, came from the eyewitnesses of the rebellion – refugees from Poland – who had fought for "freedom, bread and Soviets' withdrawal." The numbers provided by Wierzbiański were exaggerated.[78] On 27 September

---

75 Ibid.

76 Address of Mr. Leo Cherne, Chairman of the International Rescue Committee at the Extraordinary Plenary Meeting held in NYC on the opening day of the Poznan trials, 27 IX 1956, IHRC, ACEN, b. 89, f. 3 and also HIA, RFE/RL CF: A, b. 257, f. 5.

77 Ibid.

78 Statement on the Poznan trials, 9 IX 1956, by Bolesław Wierzbiański, Vice President of the Polish Council of National Unity in America, on behalf of the Polish delegation to the ACEN, IHRC, ACEN, b. 89, f. 3. According to the results of the IPN investigation there were 58 people dead, including 50 civilians, 4 soldiers, 1 policeman, 3 secret police officers. There were

1956 he spoke both as the rapporteur of the ACEN's political commission, and as a member of the Polish delegation at the ACEN. On behalf of the latter he read out the statement on Poznań. It denied the legitimacy of the Soviet-imposed court to try the workers. In the opinion of the PCNU the indictment should be introduced to put "Communist governments and their Soviet masters" on trial. The statement ended with an appeal to bring the matter to the attention of the UN, because Poznań was a drastic violation of the United Nations Charter and increased the threat to world peace.[79]

The Plenary Session concluded with a unanimous adoption of a declaration. It stated that the show trials were the Communists' way of diverting the attention of the free world from the actual reasons why workers went out into the streets. While appealing to the UN, the ACEN proclaimed that "only the restoration of freedom and independence to the nations currently ruled by the Communists can remove the actual reasons that led the inhabitants of Poznań to revolt." It was unequivocally stated that ACEN paid tribute to the rebels, admired and proclaimed solidarity with the "freedom fighters" who remained in prisons.[80]

All in all, during the ACEN session, a dozen or so members of member organizations spoke.[81] Among them was Charles Peyer, Chairman of the Labor Committee (on behalf of the Hungarian National Council), who said "Poznań's riots were not anti-revolutionary and did not explode as a result of foreign incitement. The workers simply had enough of starving and began to demonstrate in the streets, which, according to their Communist rulers, belonged [only] to them."[82]

This detailed description of an ACEN special session serves as an example of the mood, the rhetoric employed and the profile of speakers. However, talking and reinforcing shared opinions was not the ACEN's main activity. Following the meeting, telegrams were sent to the American President, the Vice President,

---

573 wounded, including 523 civilians, 15 secret police officers, 7 policemen and 28 soldiers. Karolina Bittner, Ofiary Poznańskiego Czerwca 1956, IPN, https://czerwiec56.ipn.gov.pl/c56/ofiary-i-represje/9167,Ofiary-Poznanskiego-Czerwca-1956.html, accessed: 16 II 2020.

79 Draft presented by the Polish delegation, 25 IX 1956, IHRC, ACEN, b. 89, f. 3.

80 Declaration introduced at the 34th meeting of plenary assembly on Sept. 27, 1956, ACEN Doc. No 76, (Gen.), IHRC, ACEN, 89/3; HIA, RFE/RL CF: A, b. 257, f. 5.

81 Speaking on behalf of the ACEN there were: Anastas Trimakas (Lithuania), Adolf Prohazka (CDUCE), Vaclav Majer (Czechoslovakia), Leonhard Vahter (Estonia), Charles Peyer (Hungary), Ferenc Durugy (LDU), Onufrijs Rancas (Latvia), Boris Nojarov (Bulgaria), Mihai Rautu (Romania), George [Georgi] Petkov (SUCEE), Hasan Dosti (Albania), Jani Dilo (IPU) and Bolesław Biega (Poland).

82 Address of Mr. Charles Peyer, Chairman of the Hungarian National Council's Committee on Labor, 27 IX 1956, IHRC, ACEN, b. 89, f. 3.

the Secretary of State, as well as to U.S. senators and representatives, both governor and mayor of New York, the president of the AFL-CIO, Chinese (Taiwan) and Cuban delegates to the UN, the Free Europe Committee and to the media.[83] Upon receiving replies, the ACEN immediately issued its own press release. All of the prominent politicians who responded to the ACEN or issued their greetings on the occasion of the Plenary Assembly meeting were promptly listed in it. Among them were: John Foster Dulles, Adlai Stevenson (the Democratic Presidential nominee), and William Knowland (U.S. Senator), and Robert F. Wagner (Mayor of New York). The U.S. Secretary of State wrote: "It is the firm conviction of this government that America's conscience will not be at peace until all the enslaved peoples enjoy full freedom and have governments of their own choice."[84] Support for the ACEN was also expressed by a Polish-born American Representative from Michigan – Thaddeus M. Machrowicz. His response was reported by all the national desks of the RFE.[85]Among the supporters was also Portuondo, at the time the president of the UN Security Council. As before, he "was sympathetic to, and agreed with, the aims of the ACEN meeting."[86] A day after the trials opened in Poland, "The New York Times" reported ACEN's "staging a vigorous denunciation of the Warsaw regime," protesting the persecution of those indicted as a result of riots in Poznań.[87]

Meanwhile, some ACEN representatives talked about the revolt and processes of Poznań workers in Latin America. The purpose of the journey carried out on behalf of the ACEN by Korboński, Māsēns and Constantin Vişoianu, on 18 September to 17 October 1956, was urging the governments of these countries to support demands that the United Nations adopt a resolution requiring the USSR to withdraw Soviet troops and allow free elections under international control. Such actions were not aimed at obstinate pursuit in an unrealistic direction, but to apply constant pressure on the USSR through the forum, which was an important element of the Cold War's propaganda confrontation. The month spent in South America resulted in meetings at the highest level. ACEN delegates met

---

83 George M. Dimitrov (Acting Chairman), Brutus Coste (Secr. Gen.), Telegram, 24 IX 1956, IHRC, ACEN, b.7, f. 2.

84 Vajda to Silde, Szilagyi, Telegram, 27 IX 1956, IHRC, ACEN, b. 7, f. 2.

85 Newsroom to All Radio Desks, Munich, 27 IX 1956, HIA, RFE/RL CF: A, b. 257, f. 5. Other members of Congress (both chambers) expressing support for the ACEN: James G. Fulton, Douglas, Stuart Symington, Karl E. Mundt, James E. Murray, Irving McNeil Ives, Edith S. Green, George D. Aiken, J.F. Kennedy, Joseph W. Martin, Jr. and Flood.

86 Vajda to Silde, Szilagyi, Telegram, 27 IX 1956, IHRC, ACEN, b. 7, f. 2.

87 "Warsaw Assailed by Red Bloc Exiles," *The New York Times*, 28 IX 1956, 3.

with presidents, ministers, parliamentarians and journalists. The ACEN received pledges of support for its cause in the UN in Argentina, Chile and Cuba.[88]

The Poznań Trials ended in early October without a major violation of Human Rights. Still, before Gomułka's assent to power which marked the Polish "Thaw," in the light of Cyrankiewicz's vulgar threats towards the protesters made earlier in the year, the trials can be described as being of a relatively mild character.[89] Warsaw even allowed three, carefully selected, foreign observers in the courtroom. The Polish Communists outwitted the exile-inspired elaborate international campaign before it could unfold its banners. Without the victims of the show trials, there was little that mobilized activists could do.

Were the Poznań trials carried out in a way that departed from the Stalinist standards as a result of the free world's public interest and political pressure on Poland? Was it a signal of a will to continue the post-Stalinist "Thaw"? One thing remains rather certain, that the ACEN did its best to mobilize international and private actors to exert pressure on Warsaw. Despite success, the CEN's call for action in the UN did not become the focus of discussions.

The Free Europe Committee recognized that the trials were carried out with a significant dose of "fairness and frankness." However, these adjectives did not apply to the communist media. Hence the FEC came up with an idea of comparing what was happening in the courtroom and what the Communists reported in the state media.[90] ACEN's Vice Chairman (Dimitrov) wrote in his mid-year report that the members of the exile Assembly did not lose hope that the UN General Assembly would take up the case of East Central European nations on its agenda.[91]

In a letter to the press that the "The New York Times" published on 29 July 1956, the ACEN reminded readers of this opinion-forming daily about what it did in the international arena. According to exiles, the West should introduce a policy of liberation to announce to the world that the enslavement of 100 million people in Central and Eastern Europe was one of the main reasons for international tensions and was invariably a threat to international peace and security. In addition, the ACEN demanded that the problem of the liberation of enslaved nations be introduced to the program of every international conference with the participation of the USSR, while the solution to this problem was to become a

88 Korboński, *W imieniu Polski* ..., 278–333. Peru and Brazil declared support earlier.

89 Jan Nowak-Jeziorański, *Wojna w eterze* (Kraków: Znak, 2005), 252–254.

90 Konrad Kellen to W.J. Convery Egan, 11 X 1956, HIA, RFE/RL CF: A, b. 257, f. 7.

91 Report of the Vice Chairman, Dr. George M. Dimitrov on the activities of the ACEN since its last Plenary Assembly in New York, June 23, 1956 to Sept. 27, 1956, presented to the plenary assembly on Sept. 27, 1956, IHRC, ACEN, b. 89, f. 3.

condition for any further talks or agreements with the USSR. In accordance with the adopted tactics, the ACEN also strove to draw the UN's attention to the fact that communist regimes were established in violation of the principle of the law of self-determination and against the United Nations Charter, breaking the fundamental rights and freedoms contained therein. UN action was therefore called for to restore freedom and independence in Central and Eastern Europe through free and unfettered elections carried out under international control. It was an important voice because it represented the common position of East Central Europeans, who, if it were not for the Soviet Communists, would surely play important roles in the politics of their respective countries.[92]

Already in July 1956, the staff study for the NSC assessed that the ACEN had garnered the attention of both American and foreign media and politicians and had become "by far" the most effective tool for East Central European political refugees to exert influence and demonstrate their position towards public opinion on both sides of the Iron Curtain:

> Since 1945 none of the organized political émigré groups from the Eastern European countries have been recognized by any of the Free World countries as governments-in-exile. The passage of time, the proliferation of exile organizations, and the diverse voices raised to claim to represent the views of the peoples behind the Iron Curtain, have tended to discourage Eastern European political leaders and to diminish the effectiveness of their émigré organizations. In recognition of this trend, the exile leaders joined forces in 1954 to create the Assembly of Captive European Nations (ACEN) in order to provide a unified and cohesive forum for their national voices. Through periodic deliberations and actions in this forum, the exiles have been able to attract more serious attention of the U.S. and foreign press and of the Free World statesmen, and thus the ACEN has become to date the most effective device of the Eastern European political exiles to exercise influence on and expound their views before public opinion outside and within the Iron Curtain.[93]

92 ACEN Letter of 19 VII 1956 to *The New York Times* signed by all members of the General Committee was published on 29 VII 1956. Hasan Dosti (Albania), George M. Dimitrov (Bulgaria), Petr Zenkl (Czechoslovakia), Leonhard Vahter (Latvia), George B. Bessenyei (Hungary), Vilis Māsēns (Latvia), Vaclovas Sidzikauskas (Lithuania), Stefan Korboński (Poland), Constantin Vişoianu (Romania), "To Free Captive Nations. Policy with Goal of Restoring Freedom and Independence Urged," *The New York Times*, 29 VII 1956, HIA, RFE/RL CF: A, b. 257, f. 6.

93 See section: "Significance of Eastern European Political Exiles and Their Organizations" in: NSC Staff Study, U.S. Policy toward the Soviet Satellites in Eastern Europe, Annex to NSC 5608, 6 VII 1956, *FRUS, 1955–1957*, Vol. XXV, 205–206. https://history.state.gov/historicaldocuments/frus1955-57v25/d76, accessed 20 II 2020.

Thus, the expectations of the American psychological warfare planners who saw the ACEN as "promising organization" a few months earlier, were met.[94]

It can be assumed that both partner organizations – the FEC and ACEN – planned to continue their Poznań-related programs. As it turned out, within a month, the elaborate mechanism for political and information/propaganda action served as the basis for action at the UN during the Hungarian Revolution.

94 Operations Coordinating Board to the NSC, Progress Report on NSC 174, United States Policy toward the Soviet Satellites in Eastern Europe, 29 II 1956 (The report covers: 1 V 1954 – 29 II 1956), ibid., 123 – 124. https://history.state.gov/historicaldocuments/frus1955-57v25/d49, accessed 20 II 2020.

4 The "Little U.N." – ACEN and the United Nations

The ACEN's organizational design, its location in New York, the coordination of its sessions with those of the UN, and its self-presentation as an alternative to the UN delegates appointed by Moscow-controlled regimes naturally prompted it to focus its attention and direct its operations to the United Nations. As non-Americans, speaking on behalf of their captive nations, the exiles advanced both their agenda (peaceful liberation of their homelands) as well as American anti-Communist goals in the world international arena.

There were at least three ways in which the ACEN influenced the delegates at the United Nations. First, there were personal meetings, talks, letters, and some times: close cooperation. The ACEN members obtained permits to enter the UN Headquarters and often hosted delegates of China (Taiwan), Korea (South), the Philippines, and Vietnam (South) during the ACEN Plenary Sessions. Second, from 1956 to 1963 the ACEN (FEC) rented a small warehouse opposite the United Nations headquarters in Manhattan. While its ambitious plan to move its own seat to the renovated "captive nations center" never materialized, the ACEN organized demonstrations and picket lines in front of it. Most importantly however, the façade of the building was used as a huge billboard (19 x 24 ft).[1] Third, the exile Assembly prepared reports, collected and published studies, analysis and records of the events behind the Iron Curtain – most notably a series of six volumes of *Hungary Under Soviet Rule.*

Already during its first session the ACEN issued an "Appeal to the Free Nations Represented in the Ninth General Assembly of the United Nations" addressed to the UN. This was the first document issued by the ACEN addressed to a concrete international body.[2] It contained a three-point program for liberation, spelled out in the improved version of the document released in December as "Appeal to the Nations of the Free World."[3] The three points were: withdraw recognition of the so-called governments imposed on the East Central European nations by the USSR; recognize that the captive nations were deprived of legal authorities and administer free elections under UN supervision; the UN must rec-

1 Mazurkiewicz, "The 'Little U.N.' ...," 235.

2 Appeal to the Free Nations Represented in the Ninth General Assembly of the United Nations. Adopted at the Second Plenary Meeting, September 20, 1954, ACEN Doc. No. 2 (Pol.).

3 Appeal to the Nations of the Free World. Adopted in the 12th Plenary Meeting, on Dec. 20, 1954, ACEN Doc. No. 24 (Gen.), in: ACEN, *First Session*, 57–59.

https://doi.org/10.1515/9783110661002-008

ognize any country that would try to disrupt the process of establishing conditions for free and unfettered elections in the region as a danger to international peace and security (in short: an aggressor).

The first major protest orchestrated by the ACEN related to the presence of the delegation of the communist governments of Poland and Czechoslovakia at the UN. The ACEN protested on the grounds that the UN delegates represented illegal regimes, which only guarded the interests of the USSR.[4] It was followed by a similar protest concerning usurpation of the sovereign rights of the Baltic states by the USSR. The ACEN postulated that only legitimate diplomatic representatives and national representations of these countries could appear in their name.[5] Given the fact that both declarations were presented on the same day that the ACEN, the General Committee and the committees were established, it must be acknowledged that cooperation between refugees predated the ACEN's creation and with demonstrable results.[6] The following day, documents regarding current issues discussed at the UN were adopted by the ACEN's Plenary.[7]

The next protest that garnered much media attention was related to the so-called package deal – an agreement of 14 December 1955 that provided for the admission to the UN of the Communist-controlled countries of Albania, Bulgaria, Hungary and Romania. Delegates from these countries submitted their applications in the UN Security Council and to the 9th session of the UN General Assembly in September 1954. The ACEN acted promptly submitting their documents. The exiles recalled examples from the previous sessions when UN condemned the same communist governments for violations of Human Rights and basic freedoms.[8] The ACEN's argumentation was based on the UN Charter and warned the organization that "the admission of these four governments without the support and trust of these nations would run contrary to UN purposes, and destroy its moral and political prestige." Moreover, the exiled politicians argued it would bring no practical gain. Rather than improving the living conditions in these countries, it would assure their rulers that their cynical attitude was the right

4 Joint Czechoslovak-Polish Declaration Concerning the Illegitimacy of the Czechoslovak and Polish Delegations to the United Nations. Approved in the Second Plenary Meeting, on Sept. 20, 1954, ACEN Doc. No. 3 (Pol.)

5 Joint Declaration of Protest made by the Delegations of Estonia, Latvia, and Lithuania. Approved in the 2nd Plenary Meeting on Sept. 20, 1954, ACEN Doc. 4 (Pol.), ACEN, First Session, 34.

6 Mazurkiewicz, "Join, or Die ..."

7 Draft Code of Offences Against the Peace and Security of Mankind. Resolution adopted in the 4th Plenary Meeting, on Sept. 21, 1954, ACEN Doc. No. 5 (Gen.), in: ACEN, First Session, 34–35.

8 ACEN, First Session, 36–37.

one – thus granting them authority and sanctioning the communist regime.[9] The ACEN's protests against seating of the representatives of the "Communist puppet regimes" were reported by the U.S. press.[10]

Although fruitless, it allowed the ACEN to establish its name and contacts in the UN. Efforts to obtain support for bringing the workers' protests in Poznań to the attention of the UN Security Council allowed the ACEN to build a solid network of professional contacts, as well as awareness and empathy towards the captive nations. By August 1956, the ACEN had acquired friends in the UN that it could address directly and could count on them to present exile-prepared memoranda. This was a lobbying power that the FEC had wanted to see all along.

Along with other world powers, the Soviet Union considered the UN a forum for presenting its own views and a tool to pursue its own political goals. It occupied a strategic, permanent seat in the Security Council, which of course came with a power of veto. Other countries with a permanent seat in the UN Security Council – the United States, the United Kingdom, France and China (Taiwan) had to consider the fact that every measure calculated to limit Soviet domination in Central and Eastern Europe would be doomed. Moreover, France and Great Britain were particularly vulnerable to a propaganda counterattack given their colonial entanglements. The ACEN members believed that despite these obstacles, the UN Security Council's taking up the case of captive nations in Central and Eastern Europe would be of paramount importance in exerting political pressure on Moscow.

4.1 ACEN's Action in the UN during the Hungarian Revolution

On 23 October 1956, peaceful demonstrations of students and workers in Budapest, which were an expression of protest against Soviet domination over Hun-

9 Request for Admission to the United Nations Membership of the Satellite Governments of the So-Called People's Republics of Bulgaria, Hungary, Romania and Albania. Resolution Adopted in the 6th Plenary Meeting on Oct. 22, 1954, ACEN Doc. No. 3 (Pol.), in: ACEN, First Session, 36–38.

10 "The New York Times" published two letters sent on behalf of the ACEN. General Committee of the ACEN (Dosti, Dimitrov, Slávik, Vahter, Bessenyey, Māsēns, Sidzikauskas, Korboński, Vişoianu), "Puppet Regimes in U.N. Membership for Soviet-Controlled Nations Called Charter Violation," *The New York Times*, 23 XI 1955, 22; Vaclovas Sidzikauskas, "Fate of Baltic States. Their Place as Nations Despite Present Plight Affirmed," *The New York Times*, 26 XII 1955, 18.

gary (16 demands) and display of solidarity with Poles,[11] turned into a brutal confrontation with the security forces (AVH) after the demonstrators tried to take over the radio station. The next morning, Soviet tanks entered the Hungarian capital, and street fighting lasted four days. The Hungarian Prime Minister (András Hegedüs) was replaced by Imre Nagy,[12] while János Kádár became the head of the Hungarian Workers' Party instead of Ernő Gerő.

Then, on 25 October 1956, in a radio address, Prime Minister Nagy announced plans for developing of a program of reforms "in the socialist spirit," as well as his entering into negotiations with the USSR on the nature of mutual relations, and the withdrawal of troops stationed in Hungary. At the same time, he called on compatriots to "stop fighting and restore order, peace and normal-

---

11 Nikita Khrushchev paid an unexpected visit to Warsaw on 19 to 20 October 1956 to look into the prospects of Władysław Gomułka's assuming the post of the First Secretary of the Polish United Workers Party (PUWP, acronym in Polish: PZPR) and introducing reforms. Bullying the recently rehabilitated Polish Communist leader with the military threat of Soviet troops (stationed in Poland) moving towards Warsaw, Khrushchev left Poland with the assurances of no dramatic shifts in policies to be taken by Gomułka and that People's Poland would not question its membership in the Warsaw Pact. On 21 October 1956 Gomułka became the first secretary of the PUWP and two days later addressed a cheering crowd in Warsaw. His flexibility, ability to present his program as socialist reform and to exploit public support, as well as the Chinese Communist pressure on Khrushchev not to intervene in Poland (October visit to Moscow) saved Gomułka from Imre Nagy's fate. On 1 November 1956, Gomulka and Cyrankiewicz met Khrushchev and Anastas Mikoyan (the USSR's Deputy Chairman of the Council of Ministers) at a remote airfield near in the border zone. At the time, the Polish Communist leader supported the idea of Soviet troops staying in Hungary. Gomułka, secure in his post of party leader watched as the Hungarian Revolution unfolded. With the second Soviet intervention, he publicly condemned it and attempted to speak in defense of Nagy on several occasions. Andrzej Werblan, "Październik 1956 roku – legendy a rzeczywistość," in: *Polski Październik 1956 w polityce światowej*, ed. Jan Rowiński (Warsaw: PISM, 2006), 13–40; Janos Tischler, " Polski Październik a Węgry," ibid., 109–144.

12 Imre Nagy (1896–1958) joined the Communists in 1918, in 1920 became member of both the Hungarian and Russian Communist Parties. From 1930 to 1944 in USSR. Upon his return to Hungary Nagy became the Minister of Agriculture of the Provisional Government, 1947–1949 – he was the Speaker of the Parliament, head of the Agrarian Department of the Hungarian Communist Party, member of Political Committee of the party, but fell out of party leadership over collectivization. Returned a year later as Minister of Food, and in 1952 Minister for Farm Deliveries, then Deputy Prime Minister. From July 1953 to April 1955 he was the Prime Minister of Hungary and attempted to introduce reforms in the spirit of the post-Stalinist "thaw." Estranged from Mátyás Rákosi – the First Secretary of the Hungarian Working People's Party, 1948–1956, Nagy was removed from power, reappeared in October 1956 when asked to head the government. Imre Nagy Memorial House, http://www.nagyimreemlekhaz.hu/en/imre-nagy.html, accessed: 30 IV 2020.

ity [...]."[13] On 1 November, Nagy announced that Hungary was leaving the Warsaw Pact to become a neutral country. The very same day he sent an appeal to the UN General Assembly requesting help with upholding this decision and general assistance for the country in the face of Soviet presence. It was at this point that the "case of Hungary became a UN matter."[14] Nagy's appeal was registered in New York at 10:26 am on the same day. Four hours later, a UN Plenary session began during which the debate was held on the Suez crisis.[15]

On 29 October 1956 Israel attacked Egypt. On 30 October, the British and the French initiative to intervene in Suez was vetoed by U.S. Regardless, the two European powers deployed their troops to Suez and began bombing Egypt. On 1 November 1956, the UN was discussing the Middle East. France and Great Britain tried to divert the discussion in the UN into supporting Hungarian neutrality, while the U.S. joined the USSR in condemning the Suez invasion by the European allies. Already on 27 October, UK and France suggested that the UN discuss the situation in Hungary which was included in the agenda for the next day. So, the discussions continued the following day without adopting any resolutions.[16] In the meantime, Imre Nagy recalled the head of the Hungarian delegation to the UN (and a Soviet agent) but the credentials of the new appointee were not approved.[17] In the first days of November, Imre Nagy appealed to Dag Hammarskjöld for help but received no response. The UN Secretary-General did not take part in the UN Security Council meetings regarding Hungary (on 2 and 3 No-

---

13 Imre Nagy, "Przedstawię wszechstronny program reformy. Przemówienie radiowe 25 października 1956," in: *Wielkie Mowy Historii 3* (Warsaw: Polityka-Spółdzielnia Pracy, 2006), 303.
14 Korboński, *W imieniu Polski* ..., 361.
15 ACEN's take: "Suez, Captive Nations and International Law," *ACEN News* 15–17 (June-August 1956): 3–4.
16 "Hungarian Revolution. The Situation in Hungary: Chronological review of events in Hungary and in the United Nations," *ACEN News* 18–20 (September–November 1956): 2–3.
17 The case was referred to the Credentials Committee which by 21 II 1957 recommended to take no decision regarding the credentials of the Hungarian representatives. "This decision had only moral results, since according to Clause 29 of the Rules of Procedure, the de facto recognition of the delegation made it possible for it to participate fully in the Assembly until the final decision should be made regarding its credentials." Barnabas Racz, *Hungary and the United Nations 1956–1962: A Legal and Political Analysis* (Budapest: UN Association of Hungary, 2007), 5–6, http://www.menszt.hu/data/file/racz_barnabas.pdf, accessed: 20 III 2020; ACEN Deplores Approval of Hungarian Credentials in the United Nations, ACEN Press release no. 495, 6 VI 1963, IHRC, ACEN, b. 103, f. 3; Christopher Emmet (AFCN) to Secretary of State (Dean Rusk), Under Secretary of State Averell Harriman, 14 V 1963, ibid. Copies of the Emmet protest were sent to 13 U.S. senators and 11 representatives, as well as to the FEC offices (Albert Kappel).

vember 1956).[18] During the UN Security Council meetings of 3 November, upon an American initiative, the Council considered a call for the withdrawal of Soviet troops from Hungary. The ACEN account of the discussions is very telling: "upon assurance of the Soviet delegate that negotiations for the withdrawal of Soviet troops have been initiated and, upon the proposal of the Yugoslav delegate, no vote is taken [on the draft resolution proposed by the U.S.]."[19]

In the meantime, Kádár disappeared from Budapest to appear two days later (4 November 1956) in Debrecen as head of the pro-Soviet Hungarian government. On the same day, Soviet troops entered Budapest. Nagy sought refuge in the Yugoslav Embassy, from where he pleaded for help from the free world and to the Soviets to stop their aggression and withdraw.[20] On 4 November 1956 the UN called the First Emergency Special Session of the General Assembly to discuss the Suez crisis. The same day however, Henry Cabot Lodge, Jr., American ambassador to the UN, put forth a resolution regarding situation in Hungary during a meeting of the UN Security Council. Not surprisingly it was met with a Soviet veto. Arkady Sobolev, the Soviet ambassador to the UN, must have been mindful of the UN action in the face of Communist invasion on the Korean peninsula in June 1950 and was not likely to boycott any of the meetings of the Security Council. Thus, because of the Soviet veto power, this body was effectively paralyzed. However, as Soviet tanks were rolling into the streets of Budapest, the UN Security Council decided (10:1, Soviets against) to call a Second UN Emergency Special Session based on the "uniting for peace" resolution. It was originally introduced by Dean Acheson on 3 November 1950, to end the deadlock in the Security Council. Its provisions gave the UN General Assembly the power to act in the case that the Security Council failed to exercise its primary responsibility for the maintenance of international peace and security.[21] On 4 November 1956 it was used to put the U.S. draft resolution in the Hungarian case to a vote by the UN General Assembly. It was consequently approved (50 for, with 15 abstentions) with only 8 votes against – all coming from the Soviet bloc representatives. Thus, the path

---

18 Béla K. Király, "The United Nations Organization and the Hungarian Revolution," in: *The Ideas of the Hungarian Revolution, Suppressed and Victorious, 1956–1999*, ed. Lee W. Congdon, Béla K. Király (Highland Lakes, NJ: Social Science Monographs, Boulder CO; New York: dist. Columbia Univ. Press, 2002), 142–165.

19 United States of America: Revised draft resolution, Document S/3730/Rev.1, 4XI 1956, UN Digital Library, https://digitallibrary.un.org/record/539673, accessed: 20 III 2020; "Hungarian Revolution. The Situation in Hungary ...," 5.

20 "Hungarian Revolution. The Situation in Hungary ...," 5–12.

21 Christian Tomuschat, Introductory note to: Uniting for Peace. General Assembly resolution 377 (V), New York, 3 November 1950, UN Audiovisual Library of International Law, https://legal.un.org/avl/ha/ufp/ufp.html, accessed 20 IV 2020.

for UN action in the case of Hungary was opened. On 7 November 1956, the UN General Assembly established its first ever UN Emergency Force, within a week the first troops arrived in Cairo. The UN attention was dominated by the situation in the Suez Canal.

The American and NATO's response to the Hungarian Revolution has already been described in great detail – both in the area of foreign policy[22] as well as in regard to the political warfare – including the role of the Free Europe Committee and its operations behind the Iron Curtain. Among these, most scholarly attention was devoted to the role of RFE in the Hungarian Revolution. Many important books were also were written on the subject by historical witnesses.[23] To date, the most comprehensive and richly sourced analysis of RFE's role in Hungary was published by A. Ross Johnson.[24] Thus far limited attention was given to the ACEN's activities relating to the Revolution.[25]

The FEER, a division within the FEC responsible for working with exile political organizations, noted that a) "the national committees and councils supported by FEER are by and large out of touch with events and sentiment in their homelands;" b) that they are "either unknown or disdained in their homelands;" and that "the bases upon which the various national councils and committees were formed are not in sufficiently close relation to the political, econom-

---

22 Among the works by Hungarian scholars available in English there aforementioned edited volume: *The Hungarian Revolution and War for Independence ...*, contains chapters by historians: Csaba Békés on American, French and British responses (494–512), Gusztáv Kecskés on the NATO response (112–141), as well as Gyula Borbándi who discussed the role of the Hungarian exiles (672–695). See also: László Borhi, *Hungary in the Cold War, 1945–1956. Between the United States and the Soviet Union* (New York, Budapest: CEU Press), 269–307.

23 Cord Meyer, *Facing Reality: From World Federation to the CIA* (New York: Harper and Row, 1980); Charles Gati, *Failed Illusions: Moscow, Washington, Budapest and the 1956 Hungarian Revolt* (Stanford, CA: Stanford University Press, 2006); Richard H. Cummings, *Cold War Radio. The Dangerous History of American Broadcasting in Europe, 1950–1989* (Jefferson, North Carolina, London: McFarland & Company, Inc. Publishers, 2009).

24 See chapter: "Two Octobers" in: Ross Johnson, *Radio Free Europe ...*, 79–130. See also: A. Ross Johnson, "To the Barricades: Did Radio Free Europe Inflame the Hungarian Revolutionaries of 1956? Exploring One of the Cold War's Most Stubborn Myths," *Hoover Digest* no. 4 (2007). For readers interested in the complete broadcasts, please consult the database (in Hungarian) based on transcribed archive RFE and Radio Kossuth programs aired between 22 X and 13 XI 1956, www.tit.oszk.hu/szer.

25 Partial analysis of ACEN's activities related to the aftermath of the Hungarian Revolution was published by Józef Łaptos. However, his work focuses on exile activities in Europe and does not discuss ACEN activities in the UN forum. Józef Łaptos, *Europa marzycieli ...*, 289–303.

ic and social facts of life in the captive nations today."[26] Yet the ACEN, while "suffering from similar atrophy,"[27] was "particularly well-adapted to the business of influencing and bringing about UN action," provided it would be improved by the addition of more recent representative émigrés.[28] The shock caused by the brutal Soviet invasion of Hungary raised the ACEN's activism to an unprecedented level. Within a year, the ACEN activities described above with regard to the Poznań riots faded, the exile effort being multiplied many-fold. The ACEN's voice on Hungary was the loudest of all of its action campaigns. It was also the longest lasting.

The experience gathered during the Poznań campaign served the ACEN well. On day one, that is 24 October 1956, the exile Assembly was ready for action in the UN. It already had friends within the Security Council – the Chinese (Taiwan, until 1971), and potentially supporters coming from the ranks of non-permanent members. At this time, the UN Security Council consisted of five permanent members (the U.S., Great Britain, France, the Republic of China and the USSR) as well as six (ten, since 1965) non-permanent members. Because of the two-year term in the latter case, during the period under analyis representatives of particular interest to the ACEN were coming from Peru (1955–1956), Belgium (1955–1956), Iran (1955–1956), Australia (1956–1957), Cuba (1956–1957), and Yugoslavia (1956). The list of potential allies in the Security Council changed over the next two years to include Iraq (1957–1958), Colombia (1957–1958), the Philippines (1957); and Sweden (1957–1958). Among these, delegates from Peru, Cuba and the Philippines should be considered sympathetic to the ACEN's goals before 24 October 1956. The following pages offer a look at the Hungarian case in the UN as seen and influenced by the ACEN.

Already on 24 October 1956, the ACEN General Committee had issued an appeal to the free world referring both to events in Poland and Hungary. In a letter addressed to world leaders and the press, the ACEN called for active involvement and "support of the heroic struggle for freedom and independence" and the "use of all possible means to prevent armed Soviet intervention."[29] A similar request was made in a telegram sent to non-Communist heads of governments and their delegates in the UN Security Council (Chairman, Bernard Cornut-Gentille), as

---

26 FEC Memorandum: Recasting of FEER activities and organizations, 5 XII 1956, HIA, RFE/RL CF: A, b. 198, f. 5.

27 Ibid.

28 Draft: Memorandum: Reorientation of Exile Activities in the Light of Developments in Central and Eastern Europe, 5 XII 1956, HIA, RFE/RL CF: A, b. 198, f. 5.

29 "Steps undertaken by ACEN, Message to Free World," *ACEN News* 18–20 (September-November 1956): 26–27.

well as to the UN Secretary-General (Dag Hammarskjöld), Secretary of State (John Foster Dulles) and the President of the Consultative Assembly of the Council of Europe (Fernand Dehousse). The ACEN called for an immediate convocation of the Security Council to consider "the very grave situation created by the political intervention of the Soviet Union backed by the threat to use force in the internal affairs of Poland and by the brutal intervention of Soviet armed forces in Hungary for the purpose of thwarting the struggle and crushing the will of the Polish and Hungarian peoples to regain their freedom."[30] The case was referred to the Special Committee to watch over the Interests of European Nations not represented in the Council of Europe.[31]

According to the exile Assembly, Soviet interventions constituted a violation of the UN Charter, the right to self-determination, the basis of world peace, and the commitments undertaken by the USSR, and required strong intervention to put an end to the political and military intervention of the USSR in the affairs of other countries. Interestingly, before the second Soviet assault on the Hungarians (4 November 1956), Poland and Hungary were paired in most of the ACEN's appeals.[32]

Naturally, all available information was immediately forwarded to the ACEN's offices worldwide.[33] Brutus Coste invited representatives of opinion-leading American journals, New York-based dailies, and television and radio stations to attend the ACEN press conferences.[34] On 26 October 1956, the Information Committee of the ACEN, with the Hungarian National Council, organized a picket in front of the building hosting the seat of the Soviet delegation to the UN, while

---

30 Vilis Māsēns, Telegram sent to the Chairman of the Security Council of the United Nations [Bernard Cornut-Gentille], 24 X 1956, IHRC, ACEN, b. 102, f. 3; Minutes of Proceedings, Council of Europe, Consultative Assembly, 8th Ordinary Session (2nd part), 25 X 1956, https://rm.coe.int/09000016807a23af, accessed 20 II 2020.

31 Cf.: Resolution (56) 18, Expression of feelings of solidarity with the Hungarian nation, 42nd Meeting of the Ministers' Deputies, Strasbourg, 6 XI 1956, https://rm.coe.int/090000168091d593 accessed 20 II 2020; Draft Resolution adopted by the Special Committee on 16 XI 1956 for submission to the Sending Committee, Consultative Assembly, Council of Europe, 17 XI 1956, https://rm.coe.int/090000168079b04f, accessed 20 II 2020; Gadomski, *Zgromadzenie Europejskich ...*, 31.

32 Andrzej Werblan, "Październik 1956 roku – legendy a rzeczywistość," in: *Polski Październik 1956 w polityce światowej*, ed. Jan Rowiński (Warsaw: PISM, 2006), 13–40.

33 Sample: Māsēns to Kallay and Czartoryski (Rio de Janeiro), Telegram, 25 X 1956, IHRC, ACEN, b. 7, f. 2.

34 Brutus Coste, Telegram, 25 X 1950, ibid.

delegations of the ACEN representatives met with the American, Belgian, Chinese and Peruvian UN Missions.[35]

The ACEN kept on pushing Hammarskjöld, using stronger language than before, urging him to finally pay attention to the "terrible plight of our peoples under the most brutal colonial yoke the world has known." The exiles hoped that the concurrent events in Poland and Hungary (20 – 24 October 1956) would help to focus the UN's attention on East Central Europe:

> After openly intervening and using the threat of force to determine the course of internal events in Poland, Soviet armed forces are now engaged in open warfare against the people of Hungary who have risen to regain freedom and independence. Stop. We pray that the sacrifice of the Hungarian people awaken[s] the conscience of the United Nations and determine them to face the ugly realities of the world we live in. Stop. Continued preoccupation with areas of the world in which evolution is toward progress and freedom, while ignoring the subhuman conditions prevailing in Soviet controlled area will deprive the United Nations of any moral strength and thus jeopardize the cause of freedom the world. Over.[36]

The exiles hoped for American support in their pleas addressed to the UN. Given the tumultuous events of the late fall of 1956 – the Hungarian Revolution, the Polish October, the Soviet invasion of Hungary and the Suez crisis – Eisenhower's bid for reelection as well as congressional elections are easily overlooked. However, it must be underscored that as the dramatic events of October and November 1956 unfolded, the presidential campaign in the United States dominated the news. The elections in the U.S. took place on 6 November 1956. Aware of this context, the ACEN tried to exploit the opportunity to add more pressure on the Eisenhower's administration.

Three days after the first telegram was sent to all heads of governments represented in the UN Security Council (23 October 1956), the ACEN again sent a message to President Eisenhower, but also to his Democratic rival in the upcoming presidential election – Adlai E. Stevenson (who became U.S. Ambassador to the UN in 1961). In the telegram addressed to the Stevenson-Kefauver Campaign Committee the exiles subtly suggested that the nations "in need of help in their heroic struggle for liberty and worldwide condemnation of brutal Soviet aggression and massacre of Hungarian people" were also the nations that were "tied to United States, not only in their ideals of liberty and democracy, but also in com-

35 "Steps of the ACEN in regards to situation of Poland and Hungary," 24 X 1956 – 29 X 1956 (part 1), IHRC, ACEN, b. 102, f. 3.

36 Māsēns and Coste to Dag Hammarskjöld, Telegram, 25 X 1956, IHRC, ACEN, b. 7, f. 2.

mon ancestry."[37] Thus a reference to the East Central European ethnic voting bloc was made.[38]

The message sent to the incumbent President was unlike earlier communications. Obviously colored by emotions, and faced with initial UN inactivity, the ACEN suggested legal grounds for confronting the Soviets. According to the exiles, the Paris Treaty of 1947 stated that the Soviets were supposed to withdraw their troops once the Austrian treaty had been implemented; in addition, the Warsaw Pact of 1955 claimed to be of a defensive character – not to threaten the Poles or wage a war against Hungarians. The military intervention in internal affairs and "naked aggression" constituted a flagrant violation of article 2, paragraph 4, of the UN Charter. "Assembly is well aware that you are now in midst of important political campaign but it does not doubt that you and the American people will act to meet this issue of tremendous importance to the cause of freedom everywhere."[39] Four days later, CACEED, the ACEN's ally representing the ethnics, addressed the U.S. Secretary of State asking for a meeting to present their views on "tragic events in Hungary and inflammatory situation in Poland."[40]

The ACEN asked for help from other organizations as well. Among these were naturally all member organizations, like the SUCEE in London which was

---

37 Vilis Māsēns (ACEN Chairman) to Adlai E. Stevenson (Stevenson-Kefauver Campaign Committee), Telegram, 26 X 1956, ibid.

38 While not impressive by sheer numbers (about 28 million ethnics, including about 6 million Americans of Polish ancestry), these voters were mostly concentrated in 17 strategic states in the north-east and around the Great Lakes. As the elections of 1952 (and earlier in 1946) made clear, it was possible to swing their votes away from the traditionally democratic slate. Robert Szymczak, "Hopes and Promises: Arthur Bliss Lane, the Republican Party, and the Slavic-American Vote, 1952," *Polish American Studies* 45/1 (Spring 1988): 12–28.

39 Māsēns to Eishenower, Telegram, 26 X 1956, IHRC, ACEN, b. 7, f. 2. Copies of Māsēns telegrams addressed to the U.S. President and Secretary of State were directed to Fisher Howe, Director of the Executive Secretariat at the Department of State. The Simpson Collection contains numerous copies of these, including the telegram discussed above. Māsēns telegram to the Secretary of State (John Foster Dulles), 24 X 1956, Simpson Collection, 764.00/10 – 2756; Māsēns telegram to the President (White House), 26 X 1956, Simpson Collection, 764.00/10 – 2756.

40 Msgr. John Balkunas (CACEED Chairman) to John F. Dulles (U.S. Secretary of State), 30 X 1956, IHRC, ACEN, b. 7, f. 2. In the following years CACEED continued to support ACEN's actions aiming at the UN, with the able assistance of Christopher Emmet. Vaclovas Sidzikauskas (ACEN), Christopher Emmet (AFCN), Msgr. John Balkunas (CACEED), Telegram to Ambassador Wadsworth: UN Delegations Asked to Thwart or Boycott Hungarian Quisling's Speech in UN, ACEN Press Release no. 371, 29 IX 1960, IHRC, ACEN, b. 102, f. 2. Most interestingly the response from James J. Wadsworth on the official letterhead, addressed to Vaclovas Sidzikauskas, was sent from a New York address Two Park Avenue. Ibid.

asked to appeal to socialist governments and parties across Europe, as well as the American trade unions, or the Red Cross that was urged to send medical relief to Hungary.[41] By 27 October 1956, the ACEN received support from the Liberal International (the international federation of liberal parties, founded in 1947), but also from the governments of Iraq, and Argentina, as well as receiving news about the Council of Europe's appeal to European governments to take action at the UN.[42] Also on the same day, members of the ACEN delegation in France (Gafencu, Morawski, Auer) met with Minister Jacques Roux, director of the office (cabinet) of the Ministry of Foreign Affairs (of Christian Pineau). In the light of the information provided in the "ACEN News" in the following days, the Assembly received several other communications evidencing interest, support or sympathy for their efforts (Cuba, Brazil, Spain). The ACEN was in touch by sending appeals or thanking for support with representatives of: Peru, Austria, Venezuela, Guatemala, Cuba, Chile, Dominican Republic, Uruguay, Nicaragua, Greece, Vietnam, Australia, Haiti, Ecuador, Laos and the United Kingdom (Pierson Dixon).[43]

On 28 October 1956, Iraq's prime minister (Nuri as-Sa'id), responded to the ACEN's cable of 25 October 1956, saying, "[w]e sympathize with your cause. Instructions have been sent to our delegation United Nations to raise the case at General Assembly Meetings."[44] This was followed by an immediate response that the ACEN received from the President of Peru – Manuel Prado, who informed the exiles that their message had been transmitted to the Peruvian Permanent Delegation at the UN.[45]

41 Māsēns to Vilem Bernard (London), Telegram, 26 X 1956, IHRC, ACEN, b. 7, f. 2; Māsēns to George Meany, 26 X 1956, ibid.; Māsēns to American National Red Cross, 26 X 1956, ibid.

42 On 26–27 October 1956, the Council of Europe Advisory Assembly adopted two resolutions on the interference of the Soviets in the internal affairs of the Central European countries, and on the unification of Germany, which was reported by Wistrand, Chairman of the special commission. "Steps of the ACEN in reagrds to situation of Poland and Hungary," 24 X 1956–29 X 1956 (part 1), IHRC, ACEN, b. 102, f. 3; John H. MacCallum Scott (Secretary General, Liberal International) to Vilis Masens, Teletype, RCA Communications, 26 X 1956 London, IHRC, ACEN, b. 102, f. 3.

43 Steps undertaken by ACEN (24 X 1956–28 XI 1956), *ACEN News* 18–20 (September-November 1956): 26–41; Pierson Dixon (UK Delegation to the UN) to Vilis Māsēns, Note, 30 X 1956, IHRC, ACEN, b. 102, f. 3.

44 Nuri Assaid (Prime Minister of Iraq) to Vilis Māsēns, Teletype, RCA Communications (IQ476 Baghdad), 28 X 1956, ibid.

45 Manuel Prado (President of Peru) to Vilis Māsēns (Chairman ACEN), Telegram (NA121 Lima), 25 X 1956, ibid.

On 30 October 1956, the ACEN delegation met with Souza Gomes, the General Secretary of the Brazilian Ministry of Foreign Affairs. The following day, the exiles met with Ulysses Guimaraes, President of the Brazilian Lower House of Parliament. On 31 October 1956, the ACEN's representatives (Korboński, Gyöorgy [George] Bakách-Bessenyey, Māsēns) met with Robert Murphy (the Deputy Under Secretary of State) in Washington, reiterating earlier appeals to the governments of the United States, Great Britain and France.[46] The sheer fact of the exiles being received at this intense time implies that their opinions were at least noted, if not considered in the course of further actions in the UN.

On 31 October 1956, the ACEN distributed a memorandum (and distributed parts of it as a telegram) which was used as the basis for a joint initiative in the UN Security Council. It consisted of ACEN measures suggested by the ACEN that the UN could take with regard to Hungary, reduced to three points: the immediate withdrawal of Soviet forces from Hungary, free elections, and establishment of UN commission to watch and report the observance of these measures.[47] On 1 November 1956, the Cuban delegate to the UN, Nunez Portuondo, supported by Peru (UN: Victor Belaunde), called upon the Security Council to adopt a resolution calling for the removal of Soviet troops, confirmation of the rights of Hungarians to select their government, and the creation of a UN Commission to oversee its implementation. The sole fact that this call was almost identical to the ACEN's telegram of 31 October 1956 would probably not suffice to argue that the UN Security Council it considered the ACEN-prepared document during the 752nd meeting. However, according to the ACEN account, the Cuban delegate himself told the ACEN's Secretary General that he had spoken by phone that very morning with the president of Cuba who instructed him to espouse the ACEN's proposals. "It is obvious," wrote the ACEN secretary, "that the Peruvian delegate had similar instructions." A letter from President Manuel de Prado of Peru, confirming the receipt of the telegram of 31 October 1956, as well as having sent supplementary instructions to the Delegation "for action in favor of effective Hungarian freedom" appears to confirm the ACEN's claims.[48] Although Peru's voice was particularly important because of its seat in the UN Security Council (1955–1956) and Iraq's because of its delegation incoming for the 1957 to 1958

46 Steps undertaken by ACEN (24 X 1956–28 XI 1956) ..., 30.

47 Māsēns, Telegram sent to the heads of governments of Turkey, Ireland, Thailand, Norway, Denmark, Netherlands, Ecuador, Iran, Brazil, Italy, Philippines, Spain, Argentina, 31 X 1956, IHRC, ACEN, b. 102, f. 3.

48 "Ampliando instrucciones nuestra delegacion ONU en favor efectiva libertad Hungria trasmitole contendio su cablegrama." Manuel Prado (President of Peru) to Vilis Māsēns, Telegram (NA250, Lima), 1 XI 1956, IHRC, ACEN, b. 102, f. 4.

term, it may be mentioned that similar instructions related to raising the Hungarian issue were also sent by delegates of other countries represented in the General Assembly. Among the delegates some, like Juan José Carabajal Victorica, Chairman of the delegation of Uruguay during the UN 11th session, were considered ACEN's friends.[49]

The one UN delegation that the ACEN could rely on which was not subject to rotation on the UN Security Council was Republic of China (Taiwan). On 1 November 1956, the exiles met with Yu-Chi Hsueh (Minister Plenipotentiary, Deputy Permanent Representative of China to the UN) and K.W. Yu (Minister Plenipotentiary in charge of information and press). Both men had just arrived from Taipei to work at the UN and wanted to establish "close contact with the ACEN and its member organizations." While they sought information on conditions in the Soviet enslaved European countries, thus the exiles hoped that they would take up their cause in the UN. According to Brutus Coste, the new delegates promised to take the matter up with Tingfu F. Tsiang (Representative of Republic of China at the UN), whom the ACEN already considered friendly to their cause and who frequented ACEN-organized events. Coste thought "since the visitors have only recently arrived from Taipei, their allusions to a greater Chinese initiative in the UN may be reflecting the thinking in the Chinese ministry of foreign affairs."[50]

As stated above, on 4 November 1956, as Soviet tanks were rolling into the streets of Budapest, the UN General Assembly adopted a resolution. It called upon the USSR to desist its military intervention, withdraw its troops, and allow observers to travel to Hungary. It affirmed the rights of Hungarians to self-determination, pleaded for humanitarian assistance to Hungarians, and requested the UN Secretary-General to investigate the Hungarian case. [51] As the USSR bluntly ignored these provisions and "violent repression of by the Soviet forces of the Hungarian people to achieve freedom and independence continued," the UN General Assembly adopted another resolution on 9 November 1956.[52] While shorter, it was more direct. The USSR should withdraw its forces immediately, and free elections under the auspices of the UN were to be held "as soon as law and order have been restored." It also underscored the plan

49 Steps undertaken by ACEN (24 X 1956 – 28 XI 1956) ..., 32.Carabajal Victorica had previously proved most helpful during ACEN visit to Montevideo in September 1956.

50 Brutus Coste, Visitors from the Chinese Mission to the UN, New York, 2 X 1956 IHRC, ACEN, b. 99, f. 15.

51 Resolution 1004 (ES-II), 564th Plenary Meeting, UN General Assembly, 4 XI 1956, http://www.un.org/en/ga/search/view_doc.asp?symbol=A/RES/1004(ES-II), accessed, 30 IV 1956.

52 Resolution 1005 (ES-II), 571st Plenary Meeting, UN General Assembly, 9 XI 1956, http://www.un.org/en/ga/search/view_doc.asp?symbol=A/RES/1005(ES-II), accessed, 30 IV 1956.

to investigate the situation caused by foreign intervention in Hungary and report its findings to the General Assembly. [53]

These resolutions contained every point that the ACEN wished to achieve – in short: a call for the USSR to withdraw its troops, and for there to be free elections.[54] Yet, the exiles had no illusions regarding either Soviet compliance with the resolutions, or the looming failure to effectuate concrete action on behalf of the Hungarian people by the United Nations. On 10 November 1956, the fighting in Hungary ceased. The Revolution was crushed. The free world did not intervene. No foreign observers were allowed in. The UN General Assembly was unable to implement its resolutions.

Two days later, the ACEN inaugurated its third session at the Carnegie International Center in New York. Opening the meeting, Vilis Māsēns did not hide his grave disappointment at UN inaction in the face of "popular eruption against Soviet colonialism and Communist tyranny." Among the guests present at the opening session were Nunez Portuondo and General Willis Crittenberger (the FEC president). The latter said to the gathered audience that the role of the ACEN in this critical situation might prove to be of immeasurable significance."[55]

During the ACEN's Plenary Meeting on 13 November 1956, Bolesław Wierzbiański, Polish delegate to the ACEN, summarized the meaning of the Hungarian Revolution to the exile operations in the free world:

> First, it shows that the theory of self-liberation is of no practical value. Secondly, it proves the absolute catastrophe of Soviet efforts in Central and Eastern Europe. Thirdly, it showed the world and the captive peoples that in the present state of affairs, people fighting for freedom will get verbal rather than practical help from the West in their efforts. [...] Fourthly, the Hungarian Revolution, the Polish struggle and the perseverance of all our peoples has given the UN its first opportunity to call formally for the withdrawal of Soviet forces from our countries, and to accept the principle of free elections under international control. This represents a political gain of great importance to us, although very dearly paid for with Hungarian blood, and to a certain extent, by the blood of hundreds of Poznan workers. Fifthly, in our efforts to arouse government and the United Nations, we had on our side the unconditional support of public opinion of the whole free world.[56]

53 Ibid.

54 The Question of Hungary before the United Nations, United Nations, Dept. of Public Information, Press Release, GA/1546, 6 IX 1957, IHRC, ACEN, b. 101, f. 8.

55 "ACEN Plenary Meetings, Third Session Opens in New York," *ACEN News* 18–20 (September–November 1956): 44.

56 Speech by Bolesław Wierzbiański, member of the Polish Delegation to the ACEN, Plenary Meeting, New York, 13 XI 1956, IHRC, ACEN, b. 41, f. 2.

While mindful of the previous experience with the West's inability to act on behalf of the freedom fighters in East Central Europe (reminding the participants of the ACEN's Plenary Meeting of the Warsaw Uprising of 1944),[57] the exiles wished to continue their fight and not to let the world forget about Hungary. Some ACEN delegates suggested that in the case that the Soviets did not comply, international forces were to be established to oversee the process of their troops' withdrawal as well as to secure the conditions for free elections. The "pseudo-government" (Kádár's) established in Hungary was to be denied international recognition, which included its representatives being expelled from the UN.[58]

However, the Assembly's goal was to establish a broader case by forming a link between the Hungarian Revolution and the case of peace and security in the entire region of East Central Europe. For the period 24 October through 3 December 1956 there were over a hundred and twenty initiatives undertaken by the ACEN – communications (telegrams, letters), meetings and appeals, etc. At one time, the same message was sent out in English, French and Spanish to 68 heads of state (7–8 November 1956) asking for continued pressure to be applied on the USSR to comply with the UN General Assembly resolutions of 4 and 9 November.[59]

This unprecedented scale of operations of a two-year old ACEN was not entirely in vain. The United Nations could not let the issue of Hungary go away. From 26 October to 23 December 1956, the ACEN received scores of letters of support and sympathy from members of governments from around the world. Counting all the pieces of correspondence together with meetings with representatives in the U.S., in the UN, or in these countries (by ACEN delegates), the scale of the ACEN's activities within the last two months of 1956 becomes evident. Nineteen communications were received from countries of Western Europe, 11 from representatives of East-Central Asia and Australia, 4 from the Middle East and the Horn of Africa, 11 from the Caribbean, 6 from North America, 17 from Latin America and 5 from the UN officers and staff.[60] For a group of exiles operating from a small office in New York, the feedback indicative of the support garnered is impressive. For the ACEN, however, its turn to the Third World countries was tactical. Their activities were political – developed to obtain support for their cause in

57 Adam Ciołkosz, Speech at 37th Plenary Session ACEN, 13 XI 1956, RFE/RL CF: A, b. 161, f. 6; Korboński, *W imieniu Polski ...*, 360.

58 "ACEN Plenary Meetings, Third Session Opens in New York," *ACEN News* 18–20 (September–November 1956): 42–49.

59 Vilis Māsēns, ACEN Telegram to Chairmen of 68 UN Delegations, 25 I 1957, ACEN, 3rd Session, Organization, Resolutions, Reports (New York: ACEN, 1957), 67.

60 See: IHRC, ACEN, b. 102, f. 3–4.

the UN. For their sponsors, this effort helped to solidify and expand the anti-Communist alliance.

Interestingly, James J. Wadsworth (Deputy U.S. Representative to the UN) in his 28 November 1956 communication to the ACEN said: "I am bringing your communication to the attention of officials of the Department of State." If the ACEN was primarily supported by the FEC as a propaganda tool, its political opinions were thereby seemingly transmitted back, to influence the U.S. government. Yet, it must be remembered that the FEC coordinated its political warfare programs with the Department of State and therefore the nature of contacts with representatives of the U.S. administration must not be confused with "influence" but rather as a sort of partnership.

By mid-November, two slight changes occurred in the ACEN's actions. Fewer mentions regarding Poland were included in its communications and more attention was directed towards working with governments sympathetic to the ACEN's agenda (withdrawal of Soviet troops and free elections) than to the United Nations itself. Throughout November the ACEN continued to seek support for its updated idea on how to force the Soviets to leave Hungary. Still, UN delegates attending the 11th session in New York were the easiest way for the exiles to get access to the representatives of the governments of the free world. The original design for the exile Assembly to open its sessions concurrently to the United Nations General Assembly paid off.

In a memorandum sent on 16 November 1956 to the Chiefs of the UN Delegations of the non-Communist participants in the UN's 11th session, the ACEN called for the employment of the provisions of the UN Charter.[61] According to the exiles, faced with Soviet non-compliance with the resolutions of 4 and 9 November, the UN should act in accordance with its founding document. First, representatives of Kádár's Hungary should not be allowed to participate in the sessions. Second, Kádár's government should not be granted recognition. Third, it should be assumed that the situation in Hungary was no longer to be considered solely under the provisions of article 34 of the Charter, that is, to investigate the dispute of situation likely to endanger international peace and security (mentioned during the UN Security Council meeting of 27 October 1956). It was high time to consider it an act of aggression in accordance with article 39 and thus pave a way to "make recommendations or decide what measures shall be taken in accordance with Articles 41 and 42."[62] Article 41 speaks of punishment

61 ACEN Memorandum: "Soviet Aggression Against Hungary," 16 XI 1956, *ACEN News* 18–20 (September-November 1956): 38–39.

62 See: UN Charter, http://www.un.org/en/sections/un-charter/chapter-vii/index.html, accessed: 1 V 2020.

measures short of the use of force, like economic sanctions. Should the measures provided for in Article 41 be inadequate, Article 42 envisioned "action by air, sea, or land forces as may be necessary to maintain or restore international peace and security."

As the USSR did not comply with the calls of the UN General Assembly to withdraw its army from Hungary, and furthermore, it kept preventing the UN from investigating inside the country, the ACEN believed that the General Assembly should recommend joint action based on articles 41, 42, and 6 of the Charter. Article 6 threatens expulsion from the UN, as follows: "A Member of the UN which has persistently violated the Principles contained in the Charter may be expelled from the Organization by the General Assembly upon recommendation of the Security Council."[63] For the ACEN, using these articles meant the UN Secretary-General calling emergency forces to keep order in Hungary until free elections were organized. As always, the ACEN stressed that it was necessary to bring to attention of the 11th UN session participants the situation in all nine captive nations. The memorandum concluded with a repeated call for the withdrawal of Soviet troops from the region, and confirmation of the rights of the peoples to free and unfettered elections under international supervision. Seventy-four copies of the ACEN's memorandum were distributed among the UN delegates.[64] In a series of telegrams, the exiles thanked all governments and their delegations who supported the three-point plan previously distributed by the ACEN.[65]

On the last day of November 1956, the ACEN adopted a resolution, followed by an appeal to all free nations and their delegates to the UN. It called for the establishment of factual evidence that the Soviet Union had refused to comply with UN General Assembly's resolutions. It also called for the motion to unseat the "illegitimate representatives" and to declare the Soviet Union guilty of violations of the UN Charter. Finally, the ACEN asked for an extension of the discussion to other captive nations and thus to exert pressure to end colonial rule in East Central Europe.[66]

By mid-December hopes among the ACEN members were fueled by the communiqué issued by the North Atlantic Council. The NATO ministers of foreign affairs meeting in Paris acknowledged that "the peoples of Eastern Europe have the right to choose their own governments freely, unaffected by external pressure

---

63 Ibid.

64 Memorandum for the Record, B.E. Lethbridge, 18 XI 1956, IHRC, ACEN, b. 102, f. 1.

65 See: IHRC, ACEN, b. 7, f. 2–3.

66 Recent developments in the captive European countries and the free world. Resolution adopted in the 40th Plenary Meeting, 30 XI 1956 (ACEN Doc. 84), in: ACEN, Third Session November 1956–September 1957; Organization, Resolutions, Reports (New York: ACEN 1957), 47–53.

and the use or threat of force, and to decide for themselves the political and social order they prefer."[67] On 12 December 1956, the United Nations General Assembly voted on a resolution submitted by twenty countries. The Assembly duly declared,

> [t]hat by using armed force against the Hungarian people, the Government of the Union of Soviet Socialist Republics is violating the political independence of Hungary; 2. Condemns the violation of the Charter of the United Nations by the Government of the Union of Soviet Socialist Republics in depriving Hungary of its liberty and independence and the Hungarian people of the exercise of their fundamental rights; 3. Reiterates its call upon the Government of the Union of Soviet Socialist Republics to desist forthwith from any form of intervention in the internal affairs of Hungary; 4. Calls upon the Government of the Union of Soviet Socialist Republics to make immediate arrangements for the withdrawal, under United Nations observation, of its armed forces from Hungary and to permit the re-establishment of the political independence of Hungary; 5. Requests the Secretary-General to take any initiative that he deems helpful in relation to the Hungarian problem, in conformity with the principles of the Charter and the resolutions of the General Assembly.[68]

Once again, the UN adopted a resolution almost identical to the ACEN's own program.

4.2 "The free world made a major error"

On 10 January 1957, the UN General Assembly voted to establish a Special Commission on Hungary to investigate and submit a comprehensive report on the 1956 Hungarian Revolution.[69] It was sometimes referred to as the "Committee of Five," after the number of countries represented in it: Australia, Ceylon, Denmark (Alsing Andersen – Chairman of the Committee), Tunisia and Uruguay. The Secretary-General appointed W. M. Jordan as Principal Secretary of the Committee and Povl Bang-Jensen as Deputy Secretary.[70] The tasks of the commission included: monitoring of the situation in Hungary, examination of witnesses, col-

---

67 Final Communiqué, North Atlantic Council, Paris, 11–14 XII 1956, NATO Online Library, https://www.nato.int/docu/comm/49-95/c561214a.htm, accessed: 15 IV 2020.

68 Resolution 1131 (XI), UN General Assembly, 618th Plenary Meeting, 12 XII 1956, http://www.un.org/en/ga/search/view_doc.asp?symbol=A/RES/1131(XI), accessed: 30 IV 2020.

69 Resolution 1132 (XI) UN General Assembly; 636th Plenary Meeting, 10 I 1957, https://undocs.org/en/A/RES/1132(XI)

70 UN Report of the Special Committee on the Problem of Hungary, General Assembly Official Records, 11th Session, New York 1957, Hungarian Electronic Library, http://mek.oszk.hu/01200/01274/01274.pdf, 15 IV 2020.

lecting evidence and reporting to the United Nations General Assembly. The ACEN reaction was cautious: "We endorse the proposal to establish special committee of Assembly [...] [b]ut we must warn against any attempt to use such intervention as a substitute for effective action or as an excuse to further defer long overdue enforcement efforts."[71] The UN Special Committee on the Problem of Hungary inaugurated its meetings on 17 January 1957. The Chairman of the UN General Assembly was to oversee the work of this Commission. During the 11th UN session this was Prince Wan Waithayakon (of Thailand), during the 12th session it was Sir Leslie Munro of New Zealand.

In the early spring of 1957, the ACEN's voice was greatly strengthened by the arrival in the U.S. of Hungarian political and military leaders forced into exile. Anna Kéthly, Minister of State in the Hungarian Government of Imre Nagy; Major-General Béla Király, Military Commander of the City of Budapest and Commander-in-Chief of the National Guard during the Hungarian Revolution; and József Kővágó, Mayor of Budapest during the years 1945 to 1947 and again during the days from 31 October to 4 November 1956. Their impact stretches far beyond the scope of this book, but their activities influenced the work of the Hungarian Committee – a member of the ACEN. Király and Kővágó became members of the Hungarian delegation to the ACEN. [72] Most importantly, their accounts were taken into consideration by the UN Special Committee on the Problem of Hungary.

An internal ACEN memorandum of 2 April 1957 summarized the position of most of the exiles:

> The recent lack of proper reaction to the Hungarian uprising (protests and declaration cannot be substituted for reactions) has again proved that the Western World is unwilling to take any concrete political action aimed at liberation of the countries behind the Iron Curtain. The ease with which the U.S. created a doctrine for safeguarding the Middle East against communism in spite of the great risk involved, emphasize even more clearly its reluctance in becoming involved in the affairs of Central and Eastern Europe.[73]

---

71 "U.N. General Assembly delegates approached on Hungarian Question," ACEN Press Release no. 194, 10 I 1957, IHRC, ACEN, b. 102, f. 5.

72 Katalin Kádár Lynn, "The Hungarian National Council/Hungarian National Committee; Magyar Nemzeti Bizottmány/ Bizottság 1947–1972," in: *The Inauguration of Organized* ..., 237–308.

73 Memorandum of the Polish delegation (Bolesław Biega, Stefan Kaczorowski, Stefan Korboński, Bolesław Łaszewski, Michał Mościcki, Niebieszczański, Jerzy Panciewicz, Otton Pehr, Bolesław Rodowicz, Bolesław Wierzbiański, Stanisław Wójcik) to ACEN General Committee, 2 IV 1957, HIA, Korboński Papers, b. 13, f. 4.

What was left for the ACEN to do? Gadomski wrote that in order to elevate the exiles' spirits the third session in Strasbourg was underwritten by the FEC. During the ACEN's session in Europe, Māsēns said:

> We are grateful to the free nations, including those which are not members of the Council of Europe, for their sympathy, humanitarian aid, and indignation that they manifested when faced with the Hungarian tragedy. We cannot remain quiet on what is deeply buried in our hearts- our grave disappointment. Reinstating freedom in East Central Europe is not a humanitarian issue, it is a political problem, which cannot be resolved by moral condemnation of the aggressor.[74]

In October 1957, the Committee on Non-Represented Nations (Consultative Assembly of the Council of Europe) debated the UN Report on Hungary.[75] The debates were dominated by voices (i.a. by Goedehardt and Wistrand) sympathetic to the ACEN's position. Godehardt even connected the Hungarian case to the fate of the region of East Central Europe at which point his speech was interrupted on the grounds that the debate was not related to East-West relations.[76] No political action followed.

Throughout the next year, the ACEN mobilized its field offices. Special instructions were issued on 17 June 1957 for the ACEN delegations in Argentina, Brazil, England, France, Germany, Uruguay, representative in Japan, correspondents in Mexico and Chile. New York headquarters instructed them to: set up a small delegation for the purpose of making representation to request urgent convocation of UN General Assembly, give support to public actions organized by Hungarians in which a variety of ethnic groups should participate, and coordinate the activities of those various groups. The ACEN also continued to issue pleas to UN members, condemning wars of aggression waged by the USSR, call for an immediate cease fire, call for a halt to more troops, and calls for the immediate withdrawal of those present. It also called for the formation of a UN truce commission, an emergency UN force, non-recognition of any new government formed in Hungary, the acknowledgement of the right of the Hungarians to a form a government resulting from free elections, and the employment collective measures based on articles 41 and 42.

---

74 Vilis Māsēns, Speech, 26 IV 1957, Strasbourg, ACEN's Fourth special session, IHRC, ACEN, b. 94, f. 3.

75 Draft Report on the report of the UN Special Committee on recent events in Hungary, Consultative Assembly, Committee on Non-Represented Nations. Strasburg 30 VII 1957, OSA, Hédervâry Collection, 10–39–9–6.pdf.

76 Council of Europe, Consultative Assembly, 9th ordinary Session (2nd part), official report, 19th sitting, 23 X 1957, AS (9) CR 19, 13–42–7–2.pdf.

The final Report of the Special Committee on the Problem of Hungary was adopted by its members on 7 June 1957, released in July 1957, and subsequently published in 30 thousand copies. It drew from transcripts of witness hearings (111 refugees, of whom 81 names were confidential),[77] non-governmental organizations (submitting memoranda and documents), émigré organizations, media coverage, and correspondence between the UN and the Hungarian government. The UN report concluded that 1956 was an "instinctive national uprising" suppressed by an act of Soviet external military aggression. The USSR deprived Hungary of its political independence, violated human rights, and had imposed a new government by means of military assault. The report further mentioned mass deportations, and Soviet violations of the Geneva Convention and the Paris Peace Treaty.[78] Thus the report both condemned the Soviet Union as well as encouraging the UN to continue its actions on behalf of the Hungarians.

The ACEN received a draft of the summary of the report before its official release. In its telegram sent to Andersen, the ACEN's Acting Chairman expressed "sincere admiration for the thoroughness and objectivity of the report." Sidzikauskas hoped that the conclusions of the report would be useful for establishing of an international order based on truth and moral law.[79] On 14 September 1957 a Resolution (1133/XI) was passed at the UN to enforce the Report's recommendations, including the continued monitoring of developments in Hungary. [80] In 1958, Leslie Munro became Special Representative on the Question of Hungary – essentially, a rapporteur. Neither he, nor any of the members of the UN Commission were allowed to visit Hungary.[81]

On 17 June 1958, Hungarian radio reported that the previous day Imre Nagy and General Pál Maléter had been executed one day after their sentencing. Following the former's secret trial and execution, the UN Committee issued a statement of protest, and a second, supplementary report on post-revolutionary retaliations, human rights violations, and political trials, approved by UN General

77 Thirty-five in the UN headquarters in New York, 21 in Europe (Geneva), 16 in Rome, 30 in Vienna, 9 in London, and then some again in Geneva. Report text, 11.

78 UN, Report of the Special Committee on the problem of Hungary, General Assembly, Official Records: Eleventh Session, Supplement No. 18 (A/3592), New York 1957, 244–247, Hungarian Electronic Library, http://mek.oszk.hu/01200/01274/01274.pdf, accessed: 15 IV 2020. See: ACEN, Statement on the occasion of the publication of the Report ..., 21 VI 1957, IHRC, ACEN, b. 102, f. 8.

79 Sidzikauskas to Alsing Andersen, 21 VI 1957, OSA, Hédervåry Collection, 32–204–3–2.pdf.

80 Resolution adopted by the General Assembly, 11th session, 677th Plenary Meeting, 14 IX 1957, A/RES/1133 (XI), OSA, Hédervåry Collection, 12–41–17–2.pdf.

81 U.N. Failure in the Hungarian Question, *Neue Zürcher Zeitung*, 11 VII 1959, OSA Hédervåry Collection, 50–431–1–1.pdf.

Assembly Resolution 1312/XIII on 13 December 1958. Thereafter, the Committee ceased to function, and the UN's Special Representative, Sir Leslie Munro, and his advisor, Claire de Hédervåry, contributed to keeping the Hungarian question on the UN's agenda, where it remained until 1962.[82] However, already by July 1959 Munro publicly announced the complete failure of his mission. The single outcome of the Committee's efforts was the report. All in all, from November 1956 to December 1958 the UN adopted 18 resolutions regarding Hungary.[83] It is thanks to Claire de Hédervåry[84] that the documentation relating to the works of the UN Special Committee on Hungary was saved, despite the ordinance that it be destroyed three years after the conclusion of its works.[85] The collection includes the ACEN's press release of 1960 reporting the commemoration of the fourth anniversary of the Hungarian Revolution. In the presence of the UN delegates from China (Taiwan), Philippines, and Australia the ACEN Chairman (Sidzikauskas) said: "Today it is widely admitted that the free world made a major error in the handling of the 1956 events in Hungary."[86]

4.3 "Hungary Under Soviet Rule"

The fall 1956 issue of "ACEN News" carried a meticulously prepared list of dramatic events in Hungary from 23 October to 30 November 1956, juxtaposed with the activities undertaken at that time by the United Nations. But it must have been obvious by then that the UN's response had been belated and inadequate. Before the year's end the ACEN had already pointed out that international atten-

82 Munro submitted his final report on 25 IX 1962.

83 Korboński, *W imieniu Polski ...*, 363–364.

84 Claire de Hédervåry was the Economic Affairs Officer at the Middle East section of the Technical Assistance administration for developing countries. In January 1957, she volunteered to work for the Secretariat of the Special Committee on the Problem of Hungary, eventually becoming the advisor to the Special Envoy appointed by UN Secretary-General. In 1956–1962 she collected extensive documentation related to the Hungarian case in the UN. Claire de Hédervåry's Biography, http://w3.osaarchivum.org/index.php?option=com_content&view=article&id=1656:hedervary-bio&catid=84&Itemid=1517, accessed 5 VI 2018.

85 The UN Special Committee Documents on the Problem of Hungary in 1956 (1956–1962), known as the Hédervåry Collection after its donor, were donated the Hungarian National Széchényi Library's Manuscript Department. Over three thousand documents from this collection were scanned and are available at the Open Society Archives in Budapest. See: Hédervåry Collection, http://hdl.handle.net/10891/osa:693f36ae-56a5-4564-89ee-0bc7b20eb414, accessed 1 V 2020.

86 ACEN Plenary Commemorated Hungarian Revolution. U.N. Delegates Guest Speakers, ACEN Press Release no. 373, 24 X 1960, IHRC, ACEN, OSA, Hédervåry Collection, 37–254–1–11.pdf.

tion was focused on providing help to the victims rather than actions aimed at reducing the threat. The list of events in Hungary, as described in the text, was based on the materials of the Free Europe Committee ("The Revolt in Hungary") which was based on Hungarian broadcasts (Budapest Radio and provincial radios) and on reliable press coverage.[87] In addition to reprinting FEC materials, the ACEN looked for any sources of credible information. While the Hungarian National Committee had some informal (and confidential sources), the information published by the ACEN was largely based on the reports received via FEC's Citizens' Service operations in Europe. This is evidenced by a collection of almost daily teletypes by the Chief of FECS operations in Vienna (Hungarian Emergency Operations) sent to Bernard Yarrow, found in the ACEN archives.[88] There were also other sources that the ACEN used – the RFE's Research and Information Department, press releases, and Free Europe's Press. Obviously, the exiles searched for non-FEC related sources as well, and relied on UN materials as primary sources.[89]

The ACEN was not the source of news on Hungary during and after the Revolution. It was, however, an excellent analytical unit which placed the Revolution in the political context and greatly expanded pool of useful information that was sought after by the media, by members of congress, academics, and other interested members of the public. This became the ACEN's main mission, to collect, process, analyze, publish and distribute information on the Revolution and its repercussions. By the end of 1958, in the eyes of one American journalist, "the best source of truth about what is still going on in Hungary is a study just completed by the AFCN and ACEN – for the use of the UN delegates. It is largely drawn from Communist documents but is supplemented from information smuggled out of Hungary and from letters sent directly from Budapest."[90]

The ACEN's single greatest contribution to the Hungarian case in the free world was the preparation of the six volumes entitled *Hungary Under Soviet Rule*. The volumes (1957–1962) contain a detailed record of the situation in Hungary before, during and after the Revolution, including information on the Western response to the international crisis. This publication was prepared by the

87 "Hungarian Revolution. The Situation in Hungary (Chronological review of events in Hungary and in the United Nations)," *ACEN News* 18–20 (September-November 1956): 2–22.
88 Bauer to Yarrow, Teletype, FECS Service Reports 3–32 (31 X 1956–28 XI 1956), 1 XI 1956, IHRC, ACEN, b. 101, f. 8.
89 See: IHRC, ACEN, b. 101, f. 8: Documentary File; Claire de Hédervány to László Varga (FEC), 7 XII 1960, OSA, Hédervány Collection, 2–13–1–23.pdf.
90 Roscoe Drummond, "Stand on Hungary Terror Faced by the U.N. Assembly," *New York Herald Tribune*, 12 XI, 1958, press clipping at OSA, Hédervány Collection, 53–55–15–6.pdf.

ACEN in cooperation with the AFCN, the Hungarian Freedom Fighters Federation, the Hungarian National Council, and the National Representation of Free Hungary. The editorial committee included a former diplomat, Adolf A. Berle, Jr., the Chairman of the International Rescue Committee, Leo Cherne; diplomat and politician, and wife of Henry Luce, the publisher of magazines such as "Time" and "Life," Clare Boothe Luce, and the political commentator Reinhold Niebuhr.[91] Clearly, this was not just the ACEN's project but one prepared under the FEC's oversight. The FEC also paid for its publication: 6,000 dollars for 10,000 copies (1957) to 3,000 dollars for 3,000 copies (1960). The series also appeared in other languages, often in an abbreviated form.[92]

The impact of the series went beyond serving as background material (speeches, communications received and sent by UN members).[93] The volumes were also included in the UN's collections and were listed in the Review of Communications Received which was distributed to all delegates to the UN General Assembly.[94] Obviously, not just the *Hungary Under Soviet Rule* volumes were sent to the UN.

The Héderváry collection, although mostly related to 1957 to 1958, allows for a further examination of the ACEN's attempts to influence the UN as an entity, and not only through its individual members. A January 1959 list of U.S.-based organizations interested in the Hungarian case found in the Héderváry collection included:

- Hungarian Committee (Mgr. Béla Varga) – "this organization is similar to a government in exile"
- ACEN (Stefan Korboński) – "nine national committees of countries under Soviet rule and thus represents also the Hungarian Committee"

91 The complete set of *Hungary under Soviet Rule* is available at the IHRC, at OSA as well as numerous libraries worldwide. Vol. 1: *A Survey of Developments since the Report of United Nations Special Committee*, New York 1957, HU OSA, 398 – 0 – 1 – 10147; Vol. II: A Survey of Developments from September 1957 to August 1958, 1958, HU OSA 398 – 0 – 1 – 10149; Vol. III: A Survey of Developments from the Revolution to August 1959, 1959, HU OSA 398 – 0 – 1 – 10151; Vol. IV: A Survey of Developments from August 1959 to August 1960, 1960, HU OSA 398 – 0 – 1 – 10153; Vol. V: Fifth Anniversary Issue 1956 – 1961 with Appendix Containing the United Nations Resolutions on Hungary, 1961, HU OSA 398-0-1-10155.

92 For example: ACEN, AFCN, Hungarian National Council, *La cas non-résolu de la Hongrie occupée par les Soviets: la Hongrie sous la domination soviétique, 1953 – 1963* (Paris: ACEN, 1964).

93 Coste to Minton, 28 VII 1960, IHRC, ACEN, b. 3, f. 5.

94 Christopher Emmet (AFCN), Stefan Korboński (ACEN) to Dag Hammarskjöld (UN Sec. Gen.), 29 IX 1958 and William M. Jordan (Sec. Comm. on the Problem of Hungary) to Ch. Emmet, 1 X 1958, OSA, Hédervváry Collection, 33 – 209 – 2 – 14.pdf.

- AFCN (Christopher Emmet) – "this organization acts as liaison between the ACEN and the American Government. It has a small staff"
- Emergency Committee for United Nations Action on Hungary (A. Biddle Duke) – "non-partisan organization [...] formed to exert moral pressure on the U.S. government for the withdrawal of credentials of the Hungarian delegation to the 13th session"
- American-Hungarian Federation (George Hajdu) – "most of them second generation, considered a middle of the road organization"
- Committee for Hungarian Liberation, Inc. (Gyula Kovács) – "sponsors organizations throughout the U.S. Has somewhat rightist tendencies, not very influential"
- Federation of Hungarian University Students in North America (Istvan Szent-Miklosy) – "helps former freedom fighters who were students to continue their studies"
- Federation of Hungarian Former Political Prisoners (Béla Fabian) – "political prisoners since the first world war"
- Federation of Hungarian Freedom Fighters (Béla Király); World Federation of Hungarian Political Prisoners ([Ferenc] Vidovics).[95]

Out of these organizations only three did not consist of Hungarians, but all three had one thing in common – they were all somehow connected to the FEC. Based on the annotations made on the envelopes it can be assumed that the communications addressed to Hammarskjöld were forwarded to Secretary William Jordan (UK). The paper mountain resulting from the many initiatives, appeals, letters and meetings kept on rising, solidifying the general sympathy for the victims, but with no practical results. By 1958, the ACEN's activity in the UN was most disheartening. Two dramatic events of the summer 1958 served as final blows to the belief that any action could be effectuated by the UN that would change Soviet behavior.

The first one resulted from continued Communist prosecution of revolutionaries. On 18 June 1958, the ACEN held an extraordinary public meeting in New York to protest the murders of Imre Nagy (prime minister), gen. Pál Maleter, Miklós Gimesz (Defense Minister) and also of József Szilágyi (before 1949 in charge of police forces). The ACEN sounded alarms on secret trials (including Maleter's) in December 1957, in March 1958, so months before Moscow announced the trial and execution of the Hungarian revolutionaries, begging the UN authorities to "exert all your influence to prevent the judicial murder."[96] Faced with the executions, the exile Assembly issued another resolution calling the attention of the

95 Principal Organizations Interested in the Question of Hungary Located in the United States, 21 I 1959, OSA Hédervári Collection, 34–214–1–1.pdf.

96 Māsēns sent telegrams to Leslie Munro (President of the 12th General Assembly) and to Dag Hammarskjöld (Un Secretary-General). Action Taken by the ACEN with regard to the trial of gen. Maleter and associates, 13 XII 1957, IHRC, ACEN, b. 102, f. 8; ACEN Press Release no. 236, ACEN Appeals to Hammarskjöld intercede in Moscow behalf Hungary, 24 III 1958, ibid.

heads of free governments and of the UN to "the latest example of Soviet treachery."[97] In its appeal addressed to Hammarskjöld to stop murders in Hungary, the ACEN called Kádár's regime "a local organ of Soviet colonial administration."[98] What was left for the ACEN was to demand expulsion of both the USSR and Hungary from the UN, which was effectively reduced to attempting to revoke the credentials of the Hungarian UN delegation. The Department of State inquired whether the ACEN "had taken any soundings in New York to see what the chances of success would be if a move were undertaken to reject Hungarian credentials."[99] Five months later, in November 1958, during another meeting the exiles tried to convince Foy D. Kohler that even if unsuccessful, such a vote in the UN would have a favorable effect in Hungary and in the region, at best the proposal would receive "at least the support of all the major Western powers."[100] The Kádár regime was able to secure credentials for its delegation by June 1963.

The other one resulted from the UN's lack of consideration for the safety of the Hungarian refugees who testified before the members of the Special Committee on Hungary in Geneva and Vienna in the spring of 1957. Povl Bang-Jensen, Danish Deputy Secretary of the Committee, strove to protect their identity fearing that if forwarded to the UN Secretariat the anonymity of the witnesses would be compromised, which could have grave consequences for their relatives still in Hungary. In order to protect the identity of the Hungarian refugee witnesses, Bang-Jensen initially hid the list.[101] For defying orders on the handling of secret documents, Hammarskjöld suspended him. The ACEN did not hesitate to side with Bang-Jensen, as the witnesses had been assured at the time of their interviews that their names would not be disclosed. The exile Assembly sent a letter to the members of the Special Committee, with copies distributed to all free delegations in the UN. Christopher Emmet mobilized his network and addressed a

---

97 Vilis Māsēns to John F. Dulles, 24 VI 1958, Simpson Collection, 754.00/6 – 2458. Four days earlier ACEN delegation (Māsēns and László Bartok) had a meeting at the State Department (Murphy) during which the resolution was presented in person. Department of State, Memorandum of Conversation: Call of ACEN Delegation concerning Nagy Execution, 24 VI 1958, Simpson Collection, 764.00/6-2458.

98 Sidzikauskas to Hammarskjöld, Telegram, 3 VII 1957, IHRC, ACEN, b. 102, f. 8.

99 Department of State, Memorandum of Conversation: Call of ACEN Delegation concerning Nagy Execution, 24 VI 1958, Simpson Collection, 764.00/6 – 2458.

100 ACEN was represented by: Stefan Korboński (outgoing ACEN Chairman), Jozsef Kővágó (incoming ACEN Chairman) and Vaclovas Sidzikauskas. Department of State, Memorandum of Conversation, 13 XI 1958, Simpson Collection, 760.00/11 – 1358.

101 Incident of an Official of the Hungarian Committee, *Neue Zurcher Zeitung*, 12 XII 1957, OSA Hédervāry 45 – 374 – 2 – 1.pdf.

telegram to the UN Secretary-General as well as to U.S. senators and representatives, press and opinion leaders with many taking a sympathetic stand.[102]

Following a decision of the Special Committee established by Hammarskjöld to investigate the case, Bang-Jensen burned all copies of it (24 January 1958), so that the Soviets could not get hold of it.[103] This was not an imaginary threat since at the time Anatoly Dobrynin was the Under Secretary of Political and Security Council Affairs at the UN. The burning of the lists on 24 January 1958 was considered a victory by the ACEN, but it proved to be a very bitter one.

By March 1958, Bang-Jensen faced further disciplinary procedures. The ACEN's Secretary General, Brutus Coste, acting on behalf of the International League for the Rights of Man, appealed to the Abolhassan Hatami (Secretary, Joint Disciplinary Committee UN) to reinstate Bang-Jensen to his position with no loss of salary.[104] Nevertheless, Bang-Jensen was fired in early July 1958. On 27 July 1958, the ACEN released a statement concerning the Bang-Jensen case with the aim that justice would be done to the Deputy Secretary of the Special Committee who – the exiles ascertained – "was acting in good faith to protect the witnesses and their relatives in Hungary." The ACEN endorsed the position taken earlier by the International League for the Rights of Man, citing the higher moral obligation and hoped that its publicly voiced opinion would be useful to see that the Bang-Jensen case be reviewed and he would be reinstated.[105] This proved not to be the case. As his case was fading away, on 26 November 1959, the ACEN was shocked by the news of the violent death of Bang-Jensen. He had died from a gunshot wound, which was pronounced as suicide. The exiles seriously doubted this account,[106] and so did some of the journalists[107] and the writers examining this case.[108] The ACEN, and most of all its Hungarian members, had lost a devoted friend and freedom fighter.

---

102 ACEN Memorandum: ACEN and the Bang-Jensen Case, 3 II 1958, IHRC, ACEN, b. 103, f. 5.

103 Ibid.; Settlement of the Bang-Jensen Affair, *Neue Zurcher Zeitung*, 26 I 1958, OSA, Hédervàry Collection, 46 – 388 – 2 – 1.pdf.

104 Bang-Jensen's Prudence, *Irodalmi Ujsag* (Literary Gazette, Hungarian Writers' Association Abroad, London), 1 VII 1958, OSA, Hédervàry Collection, 49 – 413 – 2 – 1.pdf.

105 "ACEN on Bang-Jensen case," *ACEN News* 40 – 41 (July – August 1958): 27.

106 Korboński, *W imieniu Polski* ..., 365 – 66; Király, 159.

107 Bang-Jensen left a wife and their five children (4 to 16 years old). See photo published by: *Milwaukee Sentinel*, 25 I 1960, part 1, page 5; K. L. Billingsley, "An Unsolved 'Suicide,'" *The Spectator*, 18 XI 1989, 14 – 15, http://archive.spectator.co.uk/page/18th-november-1989/14, accessed 16 XI 2013.

108 Bang-Jensen left a hand-written suicide note but many facts did not match. There was a strange annotation to "6 A" possibly indicating an address of one of the interview sites. The note said "I underestimated the forces I stood up against." Moreover, Bang-Jensen was missing

As the ACEN commemorated the fourth anniversary of the Revolution, on 23 October 1960, after the American and Hungarian hymns were played in the Carnegie International Center in New York, the ACEN's Chairman said:

> Today, it is widely admitted that the Free World made a serious error on how to deal with events in Hungary in 1956 ... For the UN Hungary was the key test that so far it has failed. Some people with good intentions tried to explain this failure by insinuating that further UN actions in Hungary would provoke worse persecution by the Communists. There is no better answer to such a explanation of silence than the statement of facts that took place in Hungary. As the attention of the world was focused on Hungary by the UN – through debates and resolutions – the Communist repression was temporarily loosened. Conversely, as soon as the General Assembly dissolved without making decisions about Hungary, the pressure of the Communists on Hungarians increased. This statement is true in the case of the execution of Prime Minister Nagy and General Maléter in 1958, as well as in relation to the intensity of compulsory collectivization in 1959 and 1960.[109]

This constituted a serious accusation against the free world, finding it guilty of worsening the situation in Hungary by its failure to act. At the same time, it was also a clear indicator of faith in the institutional potential of the UN to effectuate change in the divided, Cold War world, and expressed by the leader of a group of nearly 160 exiles from East Central Europe.

Throughout the 1960s, the ACEN continued its mission of informing Western audiences of what was going on behind the Iron Curtain by publishing "ACEN News" but also, for example, the *Survey of the Recent Developments in Nine Captive Countries*. Political, economic, legal and social analysis were in demand by the press and political leaders, and more and more so by academics and students.[110] But of the 238 press releases distributed by the ACEN after the suppression of the Hungarian Revolution (between January 1957 and June 1972), fifty-two discussed matters solely related to Hungary or the UN.[111] No other issue was repeatedly brought to the public attention by the exile Assembly as often.

---

for 48 hours prior to his death, and yet he still held the 5 dollars with which he left the house. He was supposed to be in touch with likely defectors ... so, the speculation continued. DeWitt Copp, Marshall Peck, *Betrayal at the UN. The Story of Paul Bang-Jensen* (New York: The Devin-Adair Company, 1961); Julius Epstein, "The Bang-Jensen Tragedy. A Review based on the Official Records," *American Opinion. An Informal Review* 3/5 (May 1960).

109 Vaclovas Sidzikauskas (ACEN Chairman), ACEN Press Release no. 374, Plenary Commemorates Hungarian Revolution. U.N. Delegates Quest Speakers, 24 October 1960, IHRC, ACEN, b. 135, f. 8.

110 Survey of the Recent Developments in Nine Captive Countries from October 1959 to March 1960, 1961, HU OSA 398 – 0 – 1 – 10145.

111 ACEN Press releases, IHRC, ACEN, b. 135, f. 6 – 8.

4.4 "Soviet Colonialism"

The Hungarian question remained on the UN agenda for the next six years.[112] In the words of Gusztáv Kecskés, "[t]he Revolution was primarily an ideological issue for the West. It offered ammunition for propaganda warfare, an outstanding frontline in the Cold War and in the race to extend the control of the Third World."[113] Considering the ACEN's shift to programs directed to Latin America and Asia, this statement requires examination in the context of exiles' political activities.

For example, among the guests present at the celebrations of the fourth anniversary of the Hungarian Revolution held during the ACEN's Plenary Meeting in New York were Dr. Tingfu F. Tsiang, Ambassador, and the Chairman of the Delegation of the Republic Of China (Taiwan) to the UN General Assembly; the Hon. Ramon Bagatsing, Member of the Delegation of the Philippines to the UN General Assembly, member of the Philippine parliament, the Chairman of the Council of the Asian Peoples' Anti-Communist League; and the Hon. William C. Wentworth, member of Australian parliament and of the Australian Delegation to the UN General Assembly.

In the presence of the esteemed guests the ACEN Chairman said:

> Since Khrushchev had the audacity to pose in the UN as the chairman of anti-colonialism and to demand freedom for all remaining Western colonies, the most vital interest of the free nations militates against a mere glossing over of the Hungarian issue in the World Organization this year. We hope that in this session of the General Assembly the Hungarian question will be discussed in all its implications, even extending it to the entire East Central European area. The General Assembly can still take up the resolutions which it bravely passed in 1956–1957, and impose economic and political sanctions for their defiance.[114]

---

112 Throughout and beyond, the Hungarian case was continuously monitored by the ACEN. The Sixth Anniversary of the Hungarian Revolution. Declaration unanimously adopted in the 101st Meeting of the Plenary Assembly (9th Session) in New York on 23 October 1962, ACEN Release, 24 X 1962, IHRC, ACEN, b. 103, f. 3; The Question of Hungary before the United Nations, Declaration unanimously adopted in the 105th (Extraordinary) Meeting of the Plenary Assembly (9th session), in New York on 23 January 1963, 23 I 1963, ibid. ; ACEN for Hungary Debate in UN, ACEN Press Release no. 388, 6 III 1961, IHRC, ACEN, b. 102, f. 2; Vaclovas Sidzikauskas (Chairman, ACEN), Msgr. Béla Varga (Chairman, Hungarian Delegation) to Adlai Stevenson (U.S. Ambassador to UN), 9 III 1961, ibid.; Sidzikauskas to Stevenson, 21 IV 1961, ibid. See also Stevenson's replies of 14 III 1961 and 1 V 1961, ibid.

113 Gusztáv Kecskés, "The North Atlantic Treaty Organization and the Hungarian Revolution of 1956," in: *The Ideas of the Hungarian Revolution* ..., 132.

114 ACEN Plenary Commemorated Hungarian Revolution. U.N. Delegates Guest Speakers, ACEN Press Release no. 373, 24 X 1960, OSA, Héderváry Collection, 37–254–1–11.pdf.

The FEC was very interested in the ACEN advancing the idea that Communists were the largest colonial empire to emerge in the twentieth century and to have expanded after World War II. Yet, when it came to the message that the ACEN was spreading regarding future action on behalf of Hungary, the FEC was probably not as content, given the fact that American policy was changing. Therefore, rather than focusing on the inability of the free world to act on behalf of the Hungarians, the FEC skillfully directed exile attention to a broader issue: the UN becoming a battleground for the hearts and minds of the non-aligned, developing countries and regions of the world yet to be integrated into the two opposing alliances by the dominant powers.[115]

Presenting the Soviets as imperialists was not a new concept for the ACEN. Already in 1955, an appeal was sent by the ACEN to the signatories of the Bandung Declaration (1955) and non-European member countries of the UN – from Turkey to Japan – to the heads of 25 states. In October 1956, the ACEN addressed the Bandung signatories with a plea: "We count on your support in this case of flagrant imperialist intervention, which is intended to assure Soviet colonial domination over its possessions."[116] And even as one of the leaders of the exile Assembly, disheartened by the inability to act in the Hungarian case, called the UN the "Organization of Bickering Nations," he acknowledged the fact that it might have also been the captives' last hope, given the increasing number of new members shedding their colonial bondage.[117]

In January 1958, a working group was called in the State Department to discuss possible ways to counter Soviet propaganda on Western colonialism. Among the proposals put forth to "overcome the difficulties of attaching the colonialism label to the Communists" the first place in the list of eight was occupied by the idea of utilizing the conference of Captive European Nations "including trips of its representatives to far East, to focus attention on 40 years of Communist imperialism."[118] The preliminary report of the working group stated that colonialism was only one of many charges that the Soviets brought against the

---

115 Mary Ann Heiss, "Exposing 'Red Colonialism.' U.S. Propaganda at the United Nations, 1953–1963," *Journal of Cold War Studies* 17/3 (Summer 2015): 82–115.

116 Vilis Māsēns (ACEN Chairman) to UN delegates of Liberia, Ethiopia, India, Egypt, Saudi Arabia, Jordan, Lebanon, Iraq, Syria, Turkey, Iran, Afghanistan, Pakistan, Burma, Laos, Cambodia, Philippines, Japan, Ceylon, Indonesia, Thailand, Nepal, Libya, Sudan, Nepal, South Vietnam, 24 X 1956, IHRC, ACEN, b. 7, f. 2; ACEN Reminds Bandung Declaration Signatories of Soviet Intervention in Poland and Hungary, ACEN press release, 25 X 1956, IHRC, ACEN, b. 102, f. 3.

117 Korboński, *W imieniu Polski* ..., 363, 366.

118 Andrew H. Berding (P) to Mr. Murphy (G), Memorandum: Countering Soviet Charges of Western Colonialism, 21 I 1958, NARA II, RG 59, Bureau of Public Affairs, Subject Files on the Policy Plan and Guidance Staff 1946–1962, b. 41, f. Anti-Communist Working Group Jan. '58.

West. And while "it was doubtful" whether "the label of 'colonialism' can successfully be pinned to the Soviets" because of the "psychological and historical barriers to Afro-Asian recognition of communist expansion as 'colonialism'" – the working group acknowledged that this was one of the ways to overcome anti-West charges, especially in the UN General Assembly. It suggested an immediate study to prepare for the recurrence of this effort and how to overcome it during the next general Assembly. Moreover, the group consulted with USIA to utilize three themes closely related: red colonialism, decolonization in progress, as well as the "Hungarian revolt," taking note that thus far only the Hungarian case had achieved considerable impact.[119]

The same file in the Department of State contains a complete set of ACEN-prepared materials on "Soviet Colonialism." The forty-page report consisted of political, military, economic, social and cultural aspects of Soviet domination.[120] The report was prepared for the ACEN conference in Strasburg (25–29 IV 1958) and delivered to Foy Kohler of the Bureau of European affairs by Stefan Korboński. During their meeting, Kohler inquired if the ACEN would have the opportunity "for additional work on the colonialism theme." The Vice Chairman of the Assembly responded that the exiles were planning a conference solely devoted to the topic of colonialism.[121] Such a conference with the participation of peoples from within the Soviet Union did not materialize. Based on the findings included in its report, during its fourth Special Session in Strasbourg, the ACEN adopted a Declaration on Soviet Colonialism defined as "Moscow's imperialistic conquest and economic exploitation of foreign countries" which was limited to the nine countries who were members of the Assembly.[122] In 1959, the ACEN published

119 Preliminary Report of Working Group on Countering Anti-West Charges Arising from Communist-Inspired Conferences, 18 III 1958, NARA II, RG 59, Bureau of Public Affairs, Subject Files on the Policy Plan and Guidance Staff 1946–1962, b. 41, f. Anti-Communist Working Group Jan. '58.

120 Soviet Colonialism. Report introduced by Vaclovas Sidzikauskas in the 3rd Meeting of the 4th Special Session of ACEN at Strasbourg, 26 IV 1958, NARA II, RG 59, Bureau of Public Affairs, Subject Files on the Policy Plan and Guidance Staff 1946–1962, b. 41, f. Anti-Communist Working Group Jan. '58.

121 Foy D. Kohler (EUR) to Andrew H. Berding (P), Memorandum: Conference on Colonialism, 17 IV 1958, NARA II, RG 59, Bureau of Public Affairs, Subject Files on the Policy Plan and Guidance Staff 1946–1962, b. 41, f. Anti-Communist Working Group Jan. '58.

122 Soviet Colonialism, Tentative Draft Declaration introduced in the 3rd Meeting of the 4th Special Session of the ACEN Plenary Assembly, Strasbourg, 26 IV 1958, NARA II, RG 59, Bureau of Public Affairs, Subject Files on the Policy Plan and Guidance Staff 1946–1962, b. 41, f. Anti-Communist Working Group Jan. '58; Soviet Colonialism Declaration (unanimously adopted during the course of the Strasbourg Session), ACEN News 38–39 (May-June 1958): 16–18.

a map depicting old and new colonialism since 1939.[123] When reprinted by the U.S. press it carried the interpretation in line with expectations, as "Russian imperialism shown in maps." Maps were prepared by the ACEN "showing how much of the world has fallen under Communist domination, largely thru Russian power, or intrigue. In contrast it shows the many areas which formerly were colonies of western powers and now are free or about to become so."[124]

In 1960, the ACEN published a brochure, "A few facts on the new colonialism,"[125] which (judging by numerous requests received by the Assembly by December 1960) became very popular. Among the institutions requesting the booklet there were universities, government agencies, public libraries and think tanks like RAND Corporation.[126] By the end of October 1960, the U.S. press carried at least 115 articles mentioning this publication.[127] Also, the FEC leaders considered it one of the ACEN's best projects, although not failing to notice that it was "written largely by FEOP." Writing on behalf of the Free Europe Organizations and Publications Department Robert Minton noticed that the exiles' contacts at the UN were "excellent."[128] The New Colonialism brochure, sent to the American and foreign media, stimulated great interest and thus added to the generally unfavorable reception of Khrushchev who returned to the U.S. a year after his rather successful visit of 1959.[129] The context for the 15th Session of the UN was thus set, and the session was particularly memorable for several reasons.

1960 was recognized as "the year of Africa," since in just one year seventeen African nations gained independence. This obviously had significant consequences for the balance of power in the UN. Furthermore, in 1960, Nikita Khrushchev, the Chairman of the Council of Ministers of the USSR came to New York as a self-nominated delegate to the UN.

The 15th Session of the UN became a turning point for the exiles' realization of their role vis-à-vis the UN. As mentioned in chapter one, in order to advance its goals, from 1956 to 1963 the Assembly rented a small warehouse opposite the United Nations in Manhattan. The façade of the building was used as a huge bill-

---

123 ACEN, Map: Decline of the old and expansion of the new colonialism since 1939 (ACEN: New York, 1959).

124 The Grim Story of Red Imperialism, as Told in Maps, Chicago Daily Tribune, 27 II 1960, A8.

125 ACEN, *A few facts on the new colonialism* (ACEN: New York, 1960), pp. 30.

126 ACEN's Secretary General to LaVerne Baldwin, Memorandum, 1 XII 1960, IHRC, ACEN, b. 3, f. 5.

127 See: Burrelle's Press Clipping Bureau for the ACEN Records, IHRC, ACEN, Scrapbooks.

128 Robert W. Minton to C. D. Jackson, Two Years of FEOP, 16 III 1961, DDEL, C.D. Jackson Papers, B. 53, f.: FEC 1961 (2).

129 Peter Carlson, *K Blows Top: A Cold War Comic interlude starring Nikita Khrushchev, America's most unlikely tourist* (New York: Public Affairs, 2010).

board clearly visible from all UN office windows facing Manhattan. Up until this time, the most common message displayed there was a one sentence demand: free elections and withdrawal of Soviet troops, signed by "the peoples" of the nine captive nations represented by the ACEN.[130] In the two years following the Hungarian Revolution, the ACEN displayed a number of posters related to its aftermath,[131] as well as to contemporary events, which garnered the ACEN a lot of publicity. The case of Hungary was used to expose Soviet duplicity. A sample message said: "Free Nations: don't let the UN-Convicted Soviet Aggressors, who have enslaved our countries, pose as champions of national freedom."[132] On the occasion of the issuing of the second Captive Nations Proclamation (1960), the ACEN presented a poster depicting Khrushchev riding in a sedan chair carried by the nine captive European nations. The description below the image was a quote from Khrushchev's February speech in Indonesia: "We feel bound by close ties to the colonial peoples."[133] Perceiving the USSR as the world's largest colonial empire, the ACEN wanted to ridicule Soviet efforts in the UN General Assembly to pose as a champion of the anti-colonial struggle. Calling on all free world delegations, the ACEN representatives sent out over a hundred communications and personally addressed sixty delegations, including the new members of the UN, and distributed "The New Colonialism." By the end of October 1960, one hundred fifteen articles that contained a reference to the "New Colonialism" were clipped by Burrelle's Press Clipping Bureau for the ACEN's records.[134]

However, on the day of Khrushchev's arrival, the ACEN sedan chair poster had been covered with a plain, white sheet.[135] The exiles were stunned by this

---

130 *ACEN News* 117 (January 1965): 4; *ACEN News* 111–113 (Jul.-Sept.1964): 4; *ACEN News* 102 (October 1963): 5; *ACEN News* 89–90 (Aug.-Sept.): 5; *ACEN News* 79 (Oct. 1961): 6; *ACEN News* 57 (Dec. 1959): 15; *ACEN News* 55 (Oct. 1959): 8; *ACEN News* 52–54 (Jul.-Sept. 1959): 6; "Poster Warns Free Nations," *The New York Times*, 8 XI 1957, 5.

131 Khrushchev in military uniform saying, "I freed Hungary. I will 'liberate' all nations" and quotations such as "We will bury you"; Quote of November 1956, in: William Taubman, *Krushchev: The Man and His Era* (New York, London: W.W. Norton & Company: 2003), 427. As the 13th U.N. session, opened on September 16, 1958, the ACEN was ready to begin its next campaign against "Kádár's usurpers" seated in the UN.

132 http://korbonski.ipn.gov.pl/portal/kor/1116/8545/Polityk_na_emigracji.html

133 *ACEN News* 64/66 (July–September 1960): 6.

134 Korboński, *W imieniu Polski ...*, 609–613: F. Hailey, "Exiles Assembly to Meet Near UN," *The New York Times*, 16 September 1960; R. Dole, E. Salveson, " 'Greeters' set for K.", *New York Mirror*, 17 September 1960, in: Scrapbooks, IHRC, ACEN, b. 164. The *New York Herald Tribune* and *New York Mirror* cited the data contained in the ACEN rapport on Soviet colonialism.

135 "What Khrushchev Won't See", *New York Herald Tribune*, 23 September 1960, in: IHRC, ACEN, b. 164, Scrapbooks.

obvious case of censorship. In "ACEN News", the organization explained it as an "embargo imposed by the authorities."[136] The covering of the ACEN poster in order not to aggravate the Soviet leader was not just a sign of the American authorities administering the UN Plaza attempting to ratchet down the tensions. Permission to stage a protest scheduled in front of the ACEN House was also withdrawn.[137]

The incident relating to Americans censor ship of the ACEN's direct assault on the Soviet leader can be explained by looking at the record of this exile umbrella organization and the role assigned to it by the FEC. On the forum of the United Nations, the American-supported exiles were supposed to help form an anti-Soviet alliance by exposing the true nature and methods of Communist domination of their nations. What the ACEN was not supposed to become was an organization targeting the communist regimes directly. None of its appeals were addressed directly to the Soviet, or Soviet-controlled, governments.[138] None of its UN actions included direct calls addressed to the Communist delegates, but called on free nations to act. Since all the ACEN operations were public, as was its association with the FEC, the Americans could not risk their relationship with Moscow to be harmed by the East Central European exiles. What they hoped for was that the ACEN would be useful in strengthening the anti-Communist alliance in the free world.

On 23 September 1960, Khrushchev submitted a letter requesting the inclusion of an additional item in the agenda of the 15th UN session: a draft declaration on the granting of independence to colonial countries and peoples (A/4502). This initiative was countered by a second draft submitted on 28 November 1960 by Cambodia on behalf of 26 Asian and African countries (eventually sponsored by 43 delegations). The latter was adopted verbatim by the UN General Assembly.[139] In the meantime, the impact of the Soviet leader posing as a champion of freedom to the colonial people was potentially harmful to the American interests.

On 12 October 1960, Lorenzo Sumulong – the Philippines' UN delegate (a country considered one of the ACEN's friends in the UN), suggested that the USSR was to be blamed for colonization itself. He conditioned support for the

---

136 *ACEN News* 67 (October 1960): 8.

137 Mazurkiewicz, The Relationship Between the Assembly ...," in: *The Inauguration of Organized* ..., 397–437.

138 See: except for the letter to Cyrankiewicz of 1956 referenced in the previous chapter.

139 The Declaration was adopetd on 14 December 1960. Selected preparatory documents, UN, Codification Division, Office of Legal Affairs, https://legal.un.org/avl/ha/dicc/dicc.html, accessed: 26 X 2016.

"Declaration on the Granting of Independence to Colonial Counties and Peoples" on including recognition of East Central Europe as among the regions subjugated to foreign domination and exploitation. He said:

> It is our view that the declaration proposed by the Soviet Union should cover the inalienable right to independence not only of the peoples and territories which yet remain under the rule of Western colonial Powers, but also of the peoples of Eastern Europe and elsewhere which have been deprived of the free exercise of their civil and political rights and which have been swallowed up, so to speak, by the Soviet Union.[140]

Khrushchev could not control his anger. His irrational behavior during the 902nd Plenary meeting of the UN General Assembly became legendary.[141] In his memoirs Korboński observed: "By taking off his shoe, Khrushchev showed his Achilles heel [i.e. Soviet domination of East Central Europe] but no one tried to get him there."[142]

Less than two weeks later, on 24 October 1960, the ACEN held a special session during which prominent guests voiced support for the captives. Among them were the Chinese (Taiwanese) delegate to the UN, Tingfu F. Tsiang, a member of the Philippines' delegation, Ramon Bagatsing, whose fellow delegate – Lorenzo Sumulong – had so enraged Khrushchev, and William C. Wentworth of the Australian delegation.[143] During this special session, the ACEN adopted a resolution addressed to the 15th UN session calling for the withdrawal of the accreditation given to the Hungarian regime's representatives and – as usual – demanding that the issue of free elections in East Central Europe and Soviet troop withdrawal be included in the text of the "Declaration."[144]

The Soviet colonialism message was continuously promoted by the ACEN. By November 1960, a new poster was unveiled on ACEN House. This time Khrushchev was a jailer who commanded the captives to "Shout: down with imperialism!" while the other prison cell doors (British, French, and Belgian) were wide open. The subheading read: "U.N. open all the doors."[145] Speaking at a lun-

---

140 UN General Assembly, 15th Session, Official Records, 902nd Plenary Meeting, 12 X 1960, 682, UN Digital Library, https://digitallibrary.un.org/record/679180?ln=en, accessed 1 V 2020. See: Carlson, *K Blows Top*, 292–295; Taubman, *Khrushchev*, 475.

141 *ACEN News* 68 (November 1960) 2–5; Carlson, *K Blows Top*, 286–290.

142 Korboński, *W imieniu Polski* ..., 614.

143 *ACEN News* 68 (November 1960) 2–5. Victor Jaanimets, the Estonian sailor who defected from the *Baltika*, made his first public statement in the ACEN. J. G. Rogers, "Baltika Defector Asks Stronger Action by West", *New York Herald Tribune*, 25 October 1960. The ACEN Scrapbook collection contains 75 press articles on the case published from October 25 to 29.

144 *ACEN News* 68 (November 1960): 2–5.

145 Ibid., 6.

cheon given in his honor by the ACEN, William Wentworth – member of the Australian delegation to UN General Assembly – said that the exiles should establish a special information and analysis center on the highest level "for the guidance of the delegates."[146]

A week before the Declaration on the Granting of Independence to Colonial Countries and Peoples was adopted by the UN General Assembly, a meeting between ACEN delegates (Korboński, Zenkl and Dimitrov) and U.S. politicians was held at the State Department. Richard H. Davis and Arthur I. Wortzel (EUR) politely listened to exile proposals on how to include the East Central European countries in the text of the Declaration calling for the right for self-determination for them as well. Davis stated that while the U.S. was not content with the wording of the declaration, but its authors did not wish to discuss any changes. However, once adopted, the U.S. would likely consider it applicable to this region as well. In the meantime, Davis was grateful to the ACEN for its educational efforts on the UN forum.[147] The Declaration was adopted by the UN on 14 XII 1960 by a vote of 89 delegations, none against, but with 9 abstentions, including the Americans.[148]

In the ACEN report to the FEC, Sidzikauskas summarized the exiles' activities in the UN during the 15th session.[149] "In connection with the colonialism issue, ACEN already carried out a comprehensive program of contact making with the European, Latin American and Afro-Asian delegations." Sidzikauskas informed Yarrow that this effort was to continue during second part of the 15th session with a "special emphasis on developing contacts with delegations from Afro-Asian nations." In particular, the ACEN plan for UN action included pressing for early action on the question of Hungary, supporting the efforts of the Afro-Asian Council ("with which we have been in close relations" wrote the ACEN Chairman) on the question of Tibet, "exposing the hypocrisy of the Romanian Communist proposal on regional peaceful coexistence," as well as to

---

146 Joseph Zullo, "Urges Center to Analyze Red U.N. Goals," *Chicago Daily Tribune*, 3 XI 1960, S19.

147 Department of State, Memorandum of Conversation, Interest of ACEN in UNGA Debate on Colonialism, 7 XII 1960, Simpson Archive, 760.00/12–760.

148 Declaration on the Granting of Independence to Colonial Countries and Peoples, New York, 14 XII 1960, https://www.un.org/ga/search/view_doc.asp?symbol=A/RES/1514(XV), accessed 26 III 2019; Abstaining: Portugal, Spain, Union of South Africa, United Kingdom, U.S., Australia, Belgium, Dominican Republic, and France. UN, General Assembly, 15th Session. Official Records, 947th Plenary Meeting, 14 XII 1960, Agenda item 87: Declaration on the granting ..., 1274, https://legal.un.org/avl/pdf/ha/dicc/A%20PV%20947.pdf, accessed 12 III 2019.

149 Chairman of the ACEN (Sidzikauskas) to B. Yarrow, Memorandum: ACEN Action in Connection with the United Nations, 10 III 1961, IHRC, ACEN, b.1, f. 6.

"build up support for a future resolution against soviet colonialism." This agenda matched American goals in the UN.

In order to bring these plans to fruition, the ACEN envisioned using the same strategies as in the 1950s. One way to foster contacts with the UN delegates was to organize receptions at the Carnegie International Center for about 200 to 250 people (to be paid for by the FEC to the amount of about 800 dollars). The other way was to obtain access to the UN delegates lounge. Four or five ACEN members needed appropriate "yellow" passes to access it,[150] preferably as the UN delegates emerged from the meetings. According to the ACEN, the best hours were: 12–1:30, 2:30–3:30, 5:30–7:00.

"If the Hungarian question remains on the agenda," wrote Sidzikauskas, "special appointments with various delegations at their offices should be arranged." However, in the light of past experience, the ACEN realized that only a fraction of the delegations responded to such appointments during the session for the mere purpose of establishing contact. "There has to be a precise peg, and it has to be an issue on the agenda of the UN with which we can rightly be concerned." Coordination of contacts and visits was to be reported to Gadomski (Vice Secretary of the ACEN). Māsēns and Gadomski were supposed to work out a plan for approaching the 45 Afro-Asian delegations by dividing their members among the nine ACEN national member organizations "with due consideration for the language problem." In the spring of 1961, the ACEN also planned to undertake a special effort to contact African and Asian journalists in New York. In this regard, again, it turned to the FEC for assistance in securing a list of journalists specially accredited to this session (which was not published by the UN Secretariat).

In November 1961, Joseph W. Brinkley of FEC asked Edmund Gaspar to look into racial discrimination in South Africa. As surprising as this may sound three years before the adoption of the Civil Rights Act by the Americans themselves, the FEC was able to make an argument linking apartheid with the ACEN goals. "It was suggested to us, through our contacts with the UN," wrote Brinkley, "that it would be reasonable for ACEN to make a public statement with copies for all UN members against racial discrimination in South Africa and for self-determination for all nations."[151] This suggestion was a result of the speech on apartheid of a South African representative in the UN, and the statement of a member of the American delegation to the UN, Francis T.P. Plimpton, that followed shortly thereafter. "ACEN coming out with such a view may influence woo-

---

150 Yellow pass (D) – equal to minister counselor, or UN staff (S).
151 J.W. Brinkley (FEC) to E. Gaspar (ACEN), 3 XI 1961, IHRC, ACEN, b. 3, f. 6.

ing African and Asian countries to the East Europe self-determination cause. I think you would like to discuss this with the members of the general committee – I would like to hear your views on this topic." Again, the FEC wanted to use the ACEN to help strengthen and legitimize its voice in the UN. While the ACEN did not comply with this one, the exiles addressed the new African members in the UN,[152] cooperated with the anti-Communist networks in Asia, and engaged its resources and talents in Latin America. In each of these forums, the Hungarian Revolution served as evidence of the nature of Soviet domination over East Central Europe.

152 Dr. V.K. Kyaruzi (Permanent Representative of Tanganyika to the UN) to Ferenc Nagy (Chairman ACEN), 29 XII 1961, IHRC, ACEN, b. 89, f. 7.

5 “Captive Nations” – ACEN and the U.S. Congress

By the 1950s, the term “captive nations [...] suffused American understanding of the Eastern bloc and its inhabitants.”[1] As early as 1953, the Secretary of State was using it in official statements.[2] In its 1954 edition, the *New York Times Index* included an entry: “European Nations, Assembly of Captive,” which directly referred to the activities of the ACEN. A year later, “captive nations” was indexed for the first time in the post-war history of the paper. One of the first books with “captive nations” was Josef Korbel’s monograph published in Canada in 1955.[3] The author, diplomat and political scientist, was a political refugee from Czechoslovakia (1948), who nowadays is mostly recognized as the father of Madeleine Albright.

In the index to the “Congressional Record,” the term “captive nations” appeared for the first time in the first half of 1956 with regard to the riots in Poznań.[4] Two years later, it was listed in debates in the House of Representatives calling for celebrations of the “captive nations days.”[5] In July 1959, the U.S. Congress decided to designate the third week of that month a Captive Nations Week and obliged the U.S. President to issue an appropriate Proclamation.

When searching the HeinOnline database containing digital versions of the Congressional Record with the key words “captive nations” and “Captive Nations Week” (chronological scope: 1947–1989) about 4,000 hits are reported. However, when organized by date, it turns out that the 1950s do not mark the most inten-

---

1 Carruthers, *Cold War Captives*, 5.

2 “Captive Peoples,” Department of State Press Release no. 93 (18 II 1953), no. 344 (30 VI 1953), Princeton University Library (PUL), John F. Dulles Papers, b. 68, f. 1953; J.F. Dulles, The Goal of Our Foreign Policy, Department of State, 29 XI 1954, J.F. Dulles Papers, b. 79, f.: 1954.

3 Josef Korbel, *The Captive Nations*, Behind the headlines, v. 15, no. 5 (Toronto: Canadian Institute of International Affairs, 1955). See also: Daniel, Hawthorne, *The ordeal of the Captive Nations* (Garden City, N. Y.: Doubleday, 1958); P. C. Beezley, *The captive nations handbook* (Seattle: Captive Nations Council, 1966); Bernadine Bailey [ABN endorsed], *The captive nations, our first line of defense* (Chicago: Chas. Hallberg, 1969); Patrick Brogan, *The Captive Nations: Eastern Europe, 1945–1990* (New York: Avon Books, 1990).

4 The first remark was published in the Annex (A 5656), see: “Events in Poland as Threat to Peace.” I checked the index beginning with vol. 93, part 14 (3 I 1947–19 XII 1947, 80th Congress, 1st Session). See: “Captive European Nations” in: *Congressional Record*, 84th Congress, 2nd Session, Index 102/12, 3 I 1956–27 VII 1956 (Ann Arbor, Michigan: University Microfilms International, n.d.), 2569, accessed University of Minnesota, Minneapolis, MI6.

5 Captive Nations’ Days, Remarks in the House: observe (12989), *Cong. Rec.*, 85th Cong., 2nd Sess., Index 104/16, 7 I 1958–24 VIII 1958.

https://doi.org/10.1515/9783110661002-009

sive use of this term but rather 1961 to 1968, followed by another apex in 1977 to 1980. This may serve as partial evidence of the vitality and impact of the captive nations discourse in the U.S. Congress.

Chart 1: Mentions of the "captive nations" and "Captive Nations Week" (CNW) in the Congressional Record, 1956–1989

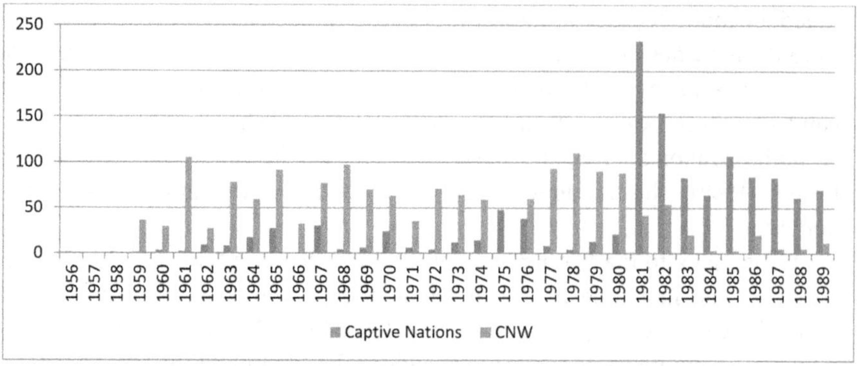

What does this mean in regard to the ACEN activities? Were the exiles responsible for at least a part of the "captive" content of the debates in Congress? Did the members of U.S. Congress pay any attention to the activities and publications of the ACEN? Did the exiled political leaders from East Central Europe, often former members of parliaments themselves, obtain any access, or any allies in the U.S. Congress? After all, American lawmakers should have been attuned to their constituencies which included ethnic groups from East Central Europe, especially since these tended to be concentrated in strategic states. Winning their votes might have included supporting the case promoted by the ACEN. On the other hand, the exiled politicians took into serious consideration the fact that Congress could exert specific pressure on the U.S. government (budget, foreign affairs and special committees, confirmation of nominations and approval of treaties by the Senate, controlling functions within checks and balances.)[6]

Another set of questions on exile lobbying potential can therefore be formulated.[7] Was the ACEN treated with respect as reliable source of information and

6 See chapter: "Congress and Foreign Policy," in: John J. Harrigan, *Politics and the American Future* (New York: Random House, 1987), 420.
7 Mazurkiewicz, "East European Lobby in the U.S. during the Cold War," in: *Our Past and Present in the Shadow of the Cold War: The Legacy and re-emergence of a conflict between the United*

opinions? What documents or materials prepared by the ACEN were included in the transcripts of the congress's meetings? What issues were most often addressed by the ACEN? Were any concrete steps taken by Congressmen based on the initiatives of the ACEN? Did the problems suggested by the ACEN only bring to the forum of the Congress representatives of districts and states with a significant percentage of inhabitants with Eastern European roots? Could it be said that the ACEN found greater support among members of one of the American parties? Can people introducing the ACEN's materials to the transcripts be characterized as "radical anti-Communists" (similar to, for example, Joseph McCarthy)?

5.1 ACEN on the Floor of Congress

The answers to the above questions are based on a detailed analysis of the "Congressional Record" in the period of the ACEN's highest popularity and most stable financial situation, 1955 to 1965. At that time, members of the American congress most often referred to the studies and meetings with members of the ACEN in 1963. Throughout the existence of the ACEN and ACEN, Inc. (1954–1989) the "golden" period of this organization should be considered 1961 to 1966, when its opinion was referred to during the meetings of Congress from 14 to 23 times a year. This number does not include statements and materials from ACEN members who were mentioned in Congress due to activities carried out under the banner of other ethnic organizations, or through individual writings or political actions.

Among the materials submitted to the members of the Congress were memoranda regarding current political problems on the international arena, placing East Central Europe in this context and emphasizing its importance in planning peaceful and long-term solutions for Europe.[8] Additionally, letters sent by the

States and Russia, ed. Anna Péczeli, Zsolt Pálmai (Budapest: Antall József Knowledge Centre, 2017), 80–91.

8 Alvin M. Bentley, "Resolutions of UN General Assembly in Regard to Hungary," 7 II 1957, 85th Cong., 1st Sess., *Cong. Rec.* 103, 1778; Daniel J. Flood, "Berlin and the Balance of Power," 3 III 1959, 86th Cong., 1st Sess., *Cong. Rec.* 105, A1686; "The Western Stake in the Spirit of Resistance of the Captive Nations," 86th Cong., 2nd Sess., *Cong. Rec.* 106, A2064; Paul H. Douglas, "The Captive Nations and the Freedom of Europe," 3 V 1961, 87th Cong., 1st Sess., *Cong. Rec.* 107, A3038; Thomas J. Dodd, "The Western Choice in East-Central Europe," 1 V 1963, 88th Cong., 1st Sess., *Cong. Rec.* 109, 7547; Paul J. Krebs, "The road to Freedom in East-Central Europe," 30 III 1965, 89th Cong., 1st Sess., *Cong. Rec.* 111, A 1522.

ACEN to individual members of Congress or published in the press were added to the "Congressional Record" (most commonly reprinted in the appendices). Members of the U.S. Congress also invoked personal meetings with members of the ACEN, speeches delivered at the forum of this organization, as well as cited the awards received from exile Assembly.[9]

In the years 1955 to 1965, the ACEN was more than three times more likely to be referred to the House of Representatives than in the Senate (75% of mentions). However, the disproportion between the representatives of the Democratic Party (controlling the government from 1961) and the Republicans was small (52% – D, 48% – R). Yet, when examining who referred to the ACEN most often, one finds that Republicans were more likely to mention the exile Assembly, on average more than twice during their term. Among them there were (in the order of number of mentions): Edward J. Derwinski (HR-R, IL), Kenneth B. Keating (S-R, NY), Alvin M. Bentley (HR-R, MI), Jacob K. Javits (S-R, NY), Albert H. Bosch (HR-R, NY), Edna F. Kelly (HR-R, NY), Seymour Halpern (HR-R, NY), Usher L. Burdick (HR-R, ND). Among the Democrats, who commonly referenced the exile Assembly there were: Thomas J. Dodd (S-D, CT) and Paul H. Douglas (S-D, IL). Quantitative data for the decade being analyzed shows, however, that the member of the U.S. Congress who referred to the ACEN the most was a democratic representative of Pennsylvania – Daniel J. Flood.

Flood served in the U.S. Congress 1945–1980, with the exception of two terms (1946–1948 and 1952–1954) when he lost elections as the Democrats lost the support of East Central European ethnic groups.[10] His congressional district encompassed the coal mining towns like Scranton, Nanticoke, Wilkes-Barre, attracting migrants from Wales and Ireland, but later also from Poland and Uk-

9 See: Jacob K. Javits, "Visit of Vice President Nixon to Moscow – Captive Nations Week," 23 VII 1959, 86th Cong., 1st Sess., *Cong. Rec.* 105, 14063; John W. McCormack, "Francis E. Walter Honored by ACEN," 17 IV 1961, 87th Cong., 1st Sess., *Cong. Rec.* 107, 6026; James A. Burke, "Speaker John W. McCormack Receives Award for Efforts in Behalf of Captive Nations," 87th Cong., 2nd Sess., *Cong. Rec.* 108, 14388; Harold C. Ostertag, "Senator Keating Honored by the Assembly of Captive European Nations," 29 VII 1963, 88th Cong., 1st Sess., *Cong. Rec.* 109, 13624; W.J. Bryan Dorn, "Hon. John S. Monagan Addresses ACEN," 18 VII 1963, 88th Cong., 1st Sess., Cong. Rec. 109, 12997; Steven B. Derounian, "Voting Record of Hon. Steven B. Derounian," 3 X 1964, 88th Cong., 2nd Sess., *Cong. Rec.* 110, 24183; Ralph W. Yarborough, "Captive Nations Week," 10 VIII 1965, 89th Cong., 1st Sess., Cong. Rec. 111, 19849.

10 Robert D. Ubriaco, Jr., "Bread and Butter Politics or Foreign Policy Concerns? Class versus Ethnicity in the Midwestern Polish American Community during the 1946 Congressional Elections," *Polish American Studies* 51/2 (Autumn 1994): 5–32; Szymczak, "Hopes and Promises...," 12–28.

raine.[11] Both facts could have influenced his activities on the House floor. As shown in the chart below, most of the references to the ACEN came from representatives of the states with a significant percentage of residents with East Central and East European ancestry.

Chart 2: Representatives and Senators mentioning the ACEN in U.S. Congress by state, 1955–1965

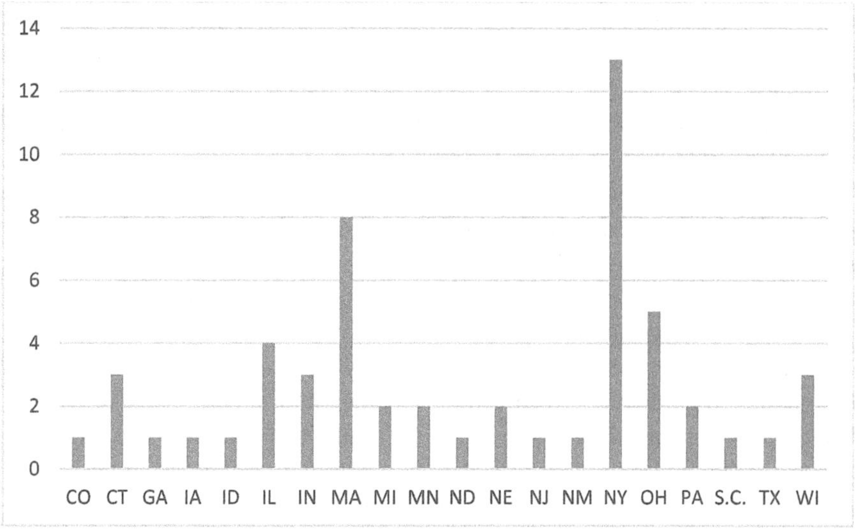

In the case of New York, both the representatives and senators were much more likely than representatives of other states to refer to the ACEN in their speeches. This could be attributed to the fact that the headquarters of the ACEN was in New York and most of the meetings and public campaigns organized by the exiles took place in that city.

Obviously, the ACEN's influence on the Hill cannot be judged by the "Congressional Record" alone. The ACEN archives contain copies of correspondence exchanged between the ACEN's General Committee and members of both houses of the U.S. Congress. For the period from 25 September 1954 to 21 September

---

11 Flood, Daniel John, (1903–1994), Biographical Directory of the United States Congress, https://bioguideretro.congress.gov/Home/MemberDetails?memIndex=F000209 (accessed 23 IV 2020); Richard D. Lyons, "Daniel Flood, 90, Who Quit Congress in Disgrace, Is Dead (Obituaries)," *The New York Times*, 29 V 1994.

1972, I examined 465 letters.[12] The ACEN closely monitored debates in the U.S. Congress related to East Central Europe and swiftly reacted to individual speeches with praise, invitations to address the exile Assembly, or – faced with new developments in the international arena – with calls for more decisive action and pressure on the U.S. government. While this was mostly one-way communication with the exiles distributing their materials, it was not fruitless. Among its incoming mail, the ACEN received from members of the U.S. Congress requests for its reports, or thank-you notes confirming that the ACEN information materials were placed in the "Congressional Record" with appropriate clippings attached. In the long-term perspective, providing information and building awareness, not letting the Congress forget about the fate and aspirations of people behind the Iron Curtain was as important as were small gains in the form of ACEN-stimulated discussions on the Hill.

There were few initiatives taken by the members of Congress that could be directly linked to the ACEN appeals. For example, representative Michael A. Feighan (Democrat from Ohio) said that he was encouraged by the ACEN appeals to support the effort to set up a special commission for Soviet aggression in Hungary.[13] This was soon after the Select Committee to Investigate the Incorporation of Lithuania, Latvia, and Estonia into the USSR, since 1954 known as Select Committee on Communist Aggression, concluded its work and released its findings. During a series of public hearings, the Committee collected, and then published a series of reports including over three hundred witness accounts. The FEC was instrumental in assisting the members of the Congress with contacts with the exiles, as well as broadcasting parts of the reports behind the Iron Curtain.[14]

The Committee of which Feighan had been a member since 1954, was chaired by Charles J. Kersten, U.S. Representative from Wisconsin 1947–1949 and 1951–1955.[15] Kersten was one of the most active politicians in the Congress to lobby for active measures (from psychological warfare to organization of the

---

12 See: IHRC, ACEN, b. 111, f. 1–6.

13 Michael A. Feighan, "Address by Michael A. Feighan before International Freedom Rally, New York, 30 XII 1956," 3 I 1957, 85th Cong., 1st Sess., *Cong. Rec.* 103, 51.

14 The Kersten Commission included materials related to the following countries: Albania, Armenia, Belarus, Bulgaria, Czechoslovakia, Estonia, Georgia, Lithuania, Latvia, Poland, Romania, Ukraine, Hungary. Mazurkiewicz, *Uchodźcy* ..., 414–415.

15 The original commission established on 27 July1953 consisted of the following members of the U.S. Congress: Fred E. Busbey (R-IL), Alvin M. Bentley (R-MI), Edward J. Bonin (R-PA), Ray J. Madden (D-IN), Thaddeus M. Machrowicz (D-MI), Thomas J. Dodd (D-CT). Under a new name the commission was expanded on 4 March 1954 by adding Patrick J. Hillings (R-CA), and Michael A. Feighan (D-OH). It concluded its work by the end of 1954.

exile armies) to challenge Communist rule in East Central Europe.[16] In 1953, Kersten visited the headquarters of RFE, as did his many colleagues from the Hill, being favorably impressed by its operations.[17] In 1955–1956 he served as a consultant on psychological warfare to Nelson Rockefeller (who had replaced C.D. Jackson as Eisenhower's advisor for psychological strategy).[18] In 1958, the former Congressman advised the Director of Central Intelligence (Allen Dulles) of opening of the ACEN exhibit in Chicago (5 August 1958) suggesting action to be taken in order to "maximize the occasion." Upon consultations with Cord Meyer [IOD], the director of the CIA responded saying that the "interesting suggestions were passed along promptly to the appropriate people."[19]

At its earlier showing in New York, Senator Javits called the exhibit "impressive" as he delivered a speech at its opening, published in the "Congressional Record." The U.S. Senator related one of the sections of the ACEN's exhibit called "Indivisibility of Freedom" to "the essence of the message that our country has to give to the Free Word and to the Soviet Union to paraphrase Abraham Lincoln, it is that this world cannot permanently endure half slave and half free."[20]

Another way of examining the ACEN's contact with the U.S. Congress is to look at the meetings held in Washington. Among the ACEN delegates to visit the Capitol most commonly were chairmen of the Assembly and one or two accompanying members of the General Committee. Among the announced topics for the meetings there were: general information about the ACEN; exile views on western policies; and presentations of memoranda prepared before summits, international conferences, or in the face of major policy shifts. Altogether, between 1 February 1955 and 5 April 1963, I counted 175 meetings with the members of Congress.[21] Usually, the ACEN asked for meetings with the speakers, majority and minority leaders, as well as chairmen of the Committee on Foreign Relations (Senate) and Committee on Foreign Affairs (House). Searching for ACEN allies on the Hill one must consider continuity of such contacts. Between 1955 and 1965 more than three meetings were held with Homer E. Capehart (S-R, IN), Paul H.

---

16 Mazurkiewicz, *Uchodźcy*, 407–434.

17 Journal, Office of Legislative Counsel, 13 XI 1953, CIA, CREST, CIA-RDP91–00682R0002000 90024–8, released 24 VI 2002. For additional context related to this visit, anti-RFE campaign in West Germany and in the U.S., see: Johnson, *Radio Free Europe ...*, 70.

18 Osgood, *Total Cold War ...* ,82–84.

19 Allen W. Dulles to Charles J. Kersten, 11 VIII 1958 (in response to letter of July 28, 1958), CIA, CREST, CIA-RDP80R01731R000500530001–2, released 7 V 2002.

20 Address by Sen. Javits at the opening ceremony of pictorial exhibit by ACEN, 23 I 1958, 85th Cong., 2nd Sess., *Cong. Rec.* 104, 823.

21 See: IHRC, ACEN, b. 111, f. 5–6.

Douglas, Jacob K. Javits, Walter H. Judd, Kenneth B. Keating, John F. Kennedy (S-D, MA), Thaddeus M. Machrowicz (HR-D, MI), Joseph W. Martin, Jr. (minority leader, former Republican Speaker of the House, MA), and John W. McCormack (majority leader, Democratic Speaker of the House since 1962, MA).

On 7 February 1957, nineteen members of Congress signed a letter to President Eisenhower urging the U.S. to request a United Nations inquiry into Soviet intervention in Eastern Europe. All were Democrats, among them: Eugene J. McCarthy, John D. Dingell and Henry S. Reuss.[22] According to Reuss, who replaced Kersten in the seat of Wisconsin's 5th district representative in the U.S. Congress, this letter was edited after the meeting with representatives of the ACEN.[23] Also Alvin M. Bentley (representative from Michigan), mentioned the ACEN as the source of both information and inspiration for implementing the UN resolution on Hungary.[24] Ultimately, it did not achieve the intended result during the then already closing 11th session of the UN.

In July 1959, Daniel J. Flood spoke on the House floor demanding that Soviets fulfill wartime obligations regarding free and unfettered elections, and that these should become a condition for any future summit conference.[25] In 1961, together with organizations of Americans of Central and East European descent, the ACEN became involved in supporting the initiative of Flood to establish a special committee for captive nations in the congress.[26] The Representative from Pennsylvania tried to bring this idea to fruition for two years, encompassing two terms of the lower house of the American Congress (1961–1965). In 1963, John S. Monagan, a member of the Foreign Affairs Committee of the House of Representatives, tried to prove that it was not necessary to appoint a special

---

22 The communication was signed by Representatives: Charles A. Boyle (D-IL), Frank M. Coffin (D-ME), John D. Dingell (D-MI), Harlan Hagen (D-CA), Eugene McCarthy (D-MN), Henry S. Reuss (D-WI), Peter W. Rodino (D-NJ), Frank Thompson, Jr. (D-NJ), Stewart L. Udall (D-AZ), George M. Rhodes (D-PA), Thomas Ludlow Ashley (D-OH), Edith Green (D-OR), Hugh J. Addonizio (D-NJ), Barratt O'Hara (D-Il), James Roosevelt (D-CA), George S. McGovern (D-SD), Charles A. Vanik (D-OH), Torbert H. Macdonald (D-MA), and B. F. Sik [Bernice Frederic Sisk] (D-CA). "19 Congressmen Urge President Press for Inquiry in UN, *ACEN News* 21–24 (December 1956–March 1957): 43.

23 Henry S. Reuss, "United States Policy Toward Eastern Europe: A Lost Opportunity," 5 III 1957, 85th Cong., 1st Sess., *Cong. Rec.* 103, 3176.

24 Alvin M. Bentley, "Resolutions of UN General Assembly ...

25 Daniel J. Flood, "The pitfalls of Disengagement," 29 IV 1959, 86th Cong., 1st Sess., *Cong. Rec.* 105, A3554; Flood, "Free Elections in East Central Europe should be made a condition for any Future Summit Conference," 26 VIII 1959, 86th Cong., 1st Sess., *Cong. Rec.* 105, A7409; Popular Support for House Resolution 211 establishing Special Committee on Captive Nations," 10 V 1961, 87th Cong., 1st Sess., *Cong. Rec.* 107, 7738.

26 Daniel J. Flood, "Popular Support for House Resolution 211 establishing Special Committee on Captive Nations," 10 V 1961, 87th Cong., 1st Sess., *Cong. Rec.* 107, 7738.

committee as proposed by Flood. He argued his position that the captive nations had already been raised by the commission he was a member of. He referred to a letter from George M. Dimitrov, the Chairman of the ACEN, which was to make his claim credible.[27]

On 26 July 1961, the ACEN sent a telegram to John F. Kennedy in which the exiles criticized the President's speech regarding Germany for the lack of any mention of East Central Europe. This criticism was noted and repeated (also with the full content of the telegram) by several deputies who openly expressed their support for the position of refugees.[28] Edward J. Derwiński stated: "It would be my thought that our Government should explore the possibility of raising in the coming session of the UN the question of Soviet control of the satellite countries of East Central Europe."[29]

In 1962, Frank T. Bow appealed to the House to pay attention to the ACEN's specific proposal that the U.S. should launch an offensive directed at diplomatic representatives of the Soviet satellite regimes in the United States.[30] In 1963, members of the congress actively supported the ACEN's efforts to block the publication of the UNESCO brochure containing "cheap Soviet propaganda," as the exiles called it. The six-page publication contained false information on the Baltic States' voluntary accession to the USSR in the 1940s, and unreal descriptions of the racial and political equality allegedly prevailing in the Soviet Union.[31] It was at this time, that Senator Dodd described the exile Assembly in the most flattering terms: "Of all refugee political organizations in this country the ACEN is unquestionably the best known and most effective."[32]

---

27 John S. Monagan, "The Committee on Foreign Affairs Continues Its Interest in the Captive Nations," 28 III 1963, 88th Cong., 1st Sess., *Cong. Rec.* 109, 4927.

28 Silvio O. Conte, "Berlin and the Captive Nation," 1 VIII 1961, 87th Cong., 1st Sess., *Cong. Rec.* 107, A5905; John D. Dingell, "Text of Telegram Sent by the ACEN to President John F. Kennedy on July 26, 1961," 8 VIII 1961, 87th Cong., 1st Sess., *Cong. Rec.* 107, A 6182.

29 Edward J. Derwiński, "Telegram to the President from the Assembly of Captive European Nations," 31 VII 1961, 87th Cong., 1st Sess., *Cong. Rec.* 107, A5877.

30 Frank T. Bow, "Captive Nations Week" [debate], 2 VI 1962, 87th Cong., 2nd Sess., *Cong. Rec.* 108, 12610.

31 Frank F. Church, "Subcommittee on International Organizations Affairs Investigation of Actions by UN," 4 II 1963, 88th Cong., 1st Sess., *Cong. Rec.* 109, 2310; Clement Zablocki, [debate], 14 II 1963, 88th Cong., 1st Sess., *Cong. Rec.* 109, 2242; Harold R. Gross, "Aiding the Enemy," 18 II 1963, 88th Cong., 1st Sess., *Cong. Rec.* 109, A758.

32 Thomas J. Dodd, "The Western Choice in East Central Europe," 1 V 1963, 88th Cong., 1st Sess., *Cong. Rec.* 109, 7547.

Referring to the ACEN's memorandum on the Denial of Human Rights in East Central Europe, representative Roman Pucinski of Illinois stated: "The ACEN, a highly respected organization of victims of both Nazi and Communist aggression and who have gallant records of service to the cause of freedom and dignity, has prepared a most impressive analysis of the situation that now exists in the captive nations of Europe." Pucinski wished the UN would investigate the violations cited in this "historic document," "which should serve as a guide-post for those who throughout the world are concerned about retaining freedom and dignity for men."[33]

Comments on the ACEN's reception in the U.S. Congress should start with the statement that the organization, in most citations, was considered a reliable source of information. In 1957, Senator Hubert Humphrey, a Democrat from Minnesota who served as U.S. Vice President from 1965 to 1969, characterized the ACEN as follows:

> One of the outstanding organizations which I have been privileged to know and to work with in trying to build world peace based upon justice and freedom. [...] It was my privilege during my service as delegate to UN [1956–1957], to speak to ACEN, and to work with them on occasion respective problems which are very close to the hearts of the delegates, one of which is the Hungarian question.[34]

Republican Alvin M. Bentley (Representative from Michigan), who attended the ACEN-organized meeting on 28 June 1957 alongside Christopher Emmet (AFCN), introduced the latter's speech to the Congressional Record with the following comment on the ACEN's effectiveness:

> You lifted the cause of your captive countries out of the obscurity and confusion of divided refugee groups into an institution which had played an increasingly important role in the war between freedom and communism, [...] given us the benefit of your special knowledge in statements with dignity, in clarity, in English, which has clarified the thinking of the American people and people of Western Europe.[35]

---

33 Roman Pucinski, "The 15th Anniversary of the Adoption of the Universal Declaration on Human Rights shows continued denial of freedom behind Iron Curtain," 10 XII 1963, 88th Cong., 1st Sess., *Cong. Rec.* 109, 23983–5.

34 [Hubert] Humphrey, Assembly of Captive European Nations, 22 I 1957, 85th Cong., 1st Sess., *Cong. Rec.* 103, 811.

35 Alvin M. Bentley, "Talk to Plenary Meeting of the Assembly of Captive European Nations, Friday, June 28, 1957, on the Anniversary of the Poznań Uprising and on the UN Representation on Hungary by Christopher Emmet, Chairman of the American Friends of Captive Nations," 18 VII 1957, 85th Cong., 1st Sess., *Cong. Rec.* 103, A5786.

In 1963, Senator Thomas J. Dodd said: "ACEN is undoubtedly the best known and the most effective of all political refugee organizations in this country."[36] Senator Kenneth B. Keating echoed: "It has been my privilege and honor to address the ACEN and to have had rather close ties with those dedicated men who are trying to preserve the free governments in exile, as one may say. They are performing a great service."[37] With relative ease, more examples of very flattering opinions and expressions of support for the ACEN's speeches and initiatives could be found.[38]

It can be stated that the ACEN was perceived, at least by some congressmen, as a representation of "captives." Some members of Congress even demanded that the ACEN should act more energetically as an ethnic lobby, which of course it was not. In the fall of 1961, John H. Ray (a Republican from New York) introduced an article from the "New York Daily News" to the "Congressional Record," the author of which demanded that the "ACEN, get to work, get to work right away."[39] It should be mentioned, however, that during the decade analyzed here, the cases of citing ACEN materials by staunch anti-Communists in the congress were rather sporadic. For them, this organization was not radical enough.[40]

---

36 Thomas J. Dodd, "The Western Choice in East-Central Europe," 1 V 1963, 88th Cong., 1st Sess., *Cong. Rec.* 109, 7547.

37 Kenneth B. Keating, "Thoughtful Comments from the ACEN," 17 VIII 1959, 86th Cong., 1st Sess., *Cong. Rec.* 105, 13677, 15934.

38 See: Thomas J. Dodd, "The Poznan Situation," 25 VII 1956, 84th Cong., 2nd Sess., *Cong. Rec.* 102, A6273; Alvin M. Bentley, "One hundred and ninth anniversary of Hungarian Independence," 85th Cong., 1st Sess., *Cong. Rec.* 103, 2860; Kenneth B. Keating, "Kozlov's Visit and the Captive Nations," 86th Cong., 1st Sess., *Cong. Rec.*105, 13677; Edward Derwinski, "Telegram to the president from the Assembly of Captive European Nations," 31 VII 1961, 87th Cong., 1st Sess., *Cong. Rec.* 107, A5877; [Clement] Zablocki, [debate], 7 III 1962, 87th Cong., 2nd Sess., *Cong. Rec.* 108, 3574; Carl T. Curtis, "Tribute to a Noble Peoples – Latvian Independence Day, November 18," 18 XI 1963, 88th Cong., 1st Sess., *Cong. Rec.* 109, 2107; Roman Pucinski, "The 15th Anniversary of the Adoption of the Universal Declaration of Human Right shows continued denial of freedom behind Iron Curtain," 10 XII 1963, 88th Cong., 1st Sess., *Cong. Rec.* 109, 23983; Roman L. Hruska, "The Assembly of Captive European Nations – Address by Senator Hruska," 31 VII 1964, 88th Cong., 2nd Sess., *Cong. Rec.* 110, 17510.

39 John H. Ray, "Sure, Talk Colonialism," 5 IX 1961, 87th Cong., 1st Sess., *Cong. Rec.* 107, A6955. See similar appeal: Olivier P. Bolton, "The Role of Captive Nations Groups in the U.S. Foreign Policy in 1964," 1 I 1964, 88th Cong., 2nd Sess., *Cong. Rec.* 110, 1674.

40 Usher L. Burdick, "Sudeten Germans Need for Peaceful Policy of Liberation for Peoples of Czechoslovakia," 11 III 1958, 85th Cong., 2nd Sess., *Cong. Rec.* 104, 4051; Albert H. Bosch, "A New Czech Exile Newspaper Understands and Fights Communism," 2 VI 1960, 86th Cong., 2nd Sess., *Cong. Rec.* 106, 11775.

While this analysis has been narrowed down to 1955 to 1965 and includes only a few of the most representative examples of the ACEN's reception by the members of the U.S. Congress, it can be assumed that the exile Assembly was considered a credible and desirable source of information. At the same time, it was also a way to endorse senators' and representatives' records and strengthen their political base among their constituencies. Association with the ACEN was useful for their publicity and the exiles knew and exploited it by honoring the members of the Congress with dinners, awards, invitations to events organized mostly, but not exclusively, in New York. There are few obvious examples where one congressman introduces information about his colleague's recognition by the ACEN, likely to save him from producing the impression of boasting and self-promotion.[41] Other individual motivations prompted U.S. representatives and senators to cooperate with the ACEN. Sometimes it was their own ethnic background (Derwinski, Hruska, Pucinski, et al.), or the concern for ethnic voters in their own districts.

In sum, the ACEN's best allies on Capitol Hill with whom the exiles cooperated, who were in direct contact with the exiles, and whose concrete actions were recognized by the exiles were: representatives Daniel J. Flood (D-PA) and Walter H. Judd (R-MN), and senators: Thomas J. Dodd (D-CT), Paul H. Douglas (D-IL), Jacob K. Javits (R-NY). It can therefore be assumed that this alliance was political and not sentimental. It should be considered quite relevant that at least some of the names of the ACEN's friends in Congress were also listed by Tom Braden (chief of CIA's International Organization Division 1950–1954, before Meyer) as being on "friendly terms" with him and his deputy. Among them there were, inter alia: Representatives Walter H. Judd, Jacob K. Javits and Senator Paul H. Douglas.[42]

At the time when the ACEN was operating under the aegis of the FEC (1954–1972), the "captive nations" discourse in the U.S. was not dominated by the exile Assembly, but rather by the Captive Nations Week-related materials. This must be attributed mostly to the hundreds of mentions of proclamations announced by state or municipal authorities, which were later published in the "Congressional Record" at the request of congressmen from relevant districts. The ACEN devoted a significant effort to popularizing the event through its publications and events,

---

41 Harold C. Ostertag, "Sen. Keating Honored by ACEN," 29 VII 1963, 88th Cong., 1st Sess., *Cong. Rec.* 109, 13624; W.J. Bryan Dorn, "Hon. John S. Monagan Addresses ACEN," 18 VII 1963, 88th Cong., 2nd Sess., *Cong. Rec.* 109, 12997.

42 IOD Chief, Memorandum for DCI, subject: Congressional Contacts, 15 XII 1953, CIA/CREST CIA-RDP58–00597 A000200030012–6, released 25 VIII 2000.

and via its political channels in the U.S. and abroad. However, it did not take part in the preparation of the text of the original resolution and had little to do with the organization of non-ethnic regional commemorations of Captive Nations Week across the United States. The Resolution's significance, including its influence on the popularization of the issues of restoring freedom in the countries behind the Iron Curtain, as well as long-term effects, make it necessary to devote a separate section to this initiative.[43]

5.2 Captive Nations Week

While there were earlier initiatives to publicly commemorate the fate of the captives in the U.S. (as early as 1955),[44] it can be said that the 1959 Captive Nations Week Proclamation resulted from the lobbying efforts of a Georgetown Professor, Lev. E. Dobriansky (1918–2008). Dobriansky, the son of Ukrainian immigrants, was President of the Ukrainian Congress Committee of America (UCCA) from 1949 to 1954, and again from 1962 to 1983. In 1959 he initiated the establishment of, and subsequently chaired, the National Captive Nations Committee (NCNC). This American organization, which attracted partnerships with a number of smaller ones, listed among its members university professors and administrators, leaders of trade unions, representatives of church organizations, industry, press and publishing houses, in addition to representatives of numerous ethnic groups. Among its honorary members one finds 17 American senators and 65 representatives. The NCNC's seat was in Washington. Its activities, supported by donations, focused on informing the public opinion about the events behind the Iron Curtain.[45] Dobriansky was so renowned for his commitment to the captive nations that he was sometimes called "Mr. Captive Nations."[46]

The difference between the NCNC and ACEN was substantial; according to its charter, the ACEN members could not be U.S. citizens. Moreover, in practice this

---

43 The following chapter is based on Author's earlier publication: Mazurkiewicz, "'Narody ujarzmione'" – lobby polityczne czy projekt propagandowy?" *Studia Historica Gedanensia* 5 (Gdańsk: Wydawnictwo UG, 2014): 354–392. It has been re-written and updated.

44 S. Res. 127, 84th Congress, 1st session, 11 VII 1955, J.F. Dulles Papers, b. 90, f. 1955 re: "Captive Peoples."

45 Captive Nations Week, 3 VIII 1961, 87th Cong., 1st Sess., *Cong. Rec.* 107, 14617.

46 Lee Edwards, "Remembering 'Mr. Captive Nations' Lev Dobriansky," *Human Events Online*, 14 II 2008, https://web.archive.org/web/20080318120055/http://www.humanevents.com/article.php?id=25023, accessed: 12 III 2020. See: Leo [Lev] Dobriansky, Introduction in: Roman Smal-Stocki, *The Captive Nations: Nationalism of the Non-Russian Nations in the Soviet Union* (New York: Bookman Associates, 1960).

organization was part of the public-private organization that formed the arm of U.S. government propaganda (FEC). Among the members of the FEC-sponsored ACEN there were no representatives of Yugoslavia, Ukraine, or Belarus. Meanwhile, unhampered by such restrictions, Dobriansky, among the "captive nations," in addition to the ACEN nine, listed not only Ukraine and "White Ruthenia," but also Armenia, Azerbaijan, Georgia, Turkestan, East Germany, "mainland China," North Korea, North Vietnam, and Tibet. Obviously, citing the nations that were Soviet Republics was especially anathema to Soviet leaders. Asian "captives" made the agenda global – counting the People's Republic of China as an enemy. At the same time, mentioning ephemeral republics like Idel-Ural or Cossackia (Ukrainian Hetmanate), estranged even some East Central European exiles. Furthermore, Dobriansky's list of the captive *peoples* – in contrast to the ACEN concept of 1939 independent *states* – did not, however, list the one national group that had suffered under Communist oppression the longest: the Russians. The ACEN's secretary interpreted the expanded list of nations as a result of "Dobriansky's drive to partition Russia." "His text was adopted as an anti-Soviet demonstration without paying attention to the fact that United States policy did not intend to partition Russia."[47] The text proposed by Dobriansky was problematic to the editors at Radio Liberty broadcasting to various parts of the USSR who wished to adhere to the policy of non-predetermination regarding future political systems or boundaries in the territory of the USSR.[48]

All in all, the interpretation of the "captives" proposed by Dobriansky diluted political exiles from East Central Europe into a wider, anti-Communist environment, but at the same time it placed the United States in the position as defender of freedom throughout the world.

On 6 and 8 July 1959, the United States Congress received a resolution proposed by senators Paul Douglas (D-IL), Jacob K. Javits (R-NY), signed by 17 senators, as well as the majority leader in the House (John W. McCormack, soon to become the speaker). The joint resolution was approved by both Houses on 17 July 1959. In it, Congress authorized and requested that the President of the United States issue a Proclamation designating the third week in July 1959 Captive Nations Week, and to issue a similar proclamation each year "until such

47 Gadomski, *Zgromadzenie Europejskich* ..., 39.

48 These were to be decided based on self-determination principle, following their liberation. By 1960 the RL editors wished either to ignore the resolution, or to cover it briefly focusing attention on the U.S. public opinion without identifying "Soviet national groups" enumerated as captive nations. Radio Liberty, Policy Position Statement "Captive Nations," [1960], CIA, C06768235, released 29 X 2019. Copy of the document received from A. Ross Johnson.

time as freedom and independence shall have been achieved for all the captive nations of the world."[49]

The Joint Resolution said that the United States, as a country of immigrants, had both the "understanding and sympathy for the aspirations of peoples everywhere." Congress, by adopting this resolution, voiced concern about "Communist imperialism" that made "a mockery of the idea of peaceful coexistence between nations." What is more, the "imperialistic and aggressive policies of Russian communism" were dated back to 1918, a novelty in the Cold War captive nations discourse. Notably, the Congressional resolution said it was "vital to the national security of the United States that the desire for liberty and independence on the part of the peoples of these conquered nations should be steadfastly kept alive."[50] The doctrine of global involvement, which was not specified at the time, thus entered into the books of American law as Public Law 86–90.

Interestingly, few contemporaries saw the long-term potential inscribed in the original document. In an article published in the opinion-making "Foreign Affairs" in 1981, Charles Mc. C. Mathias, Jr. acknowledged Dobriansky's authorship ("adopted by Congress verbatim from a draft submitted by Professor Lev Dobriansky") as well as the effectiveness of the ACEN's lobbying power ("strongly promoted by"). At the same time, he doubted that the members of the Congress realized that they were contributing to a major international commitment (major foreign policy enactment). Quoting a well-known contemporary political commentator, he compared the above resolution to announcing the celebration of "national hot-dog month." Mathias wrote that the congressmen treated the project routinely, hoping to meet the expectations of Americans whose ancestral lands fell under the Soviet yoke. Matthias assessed that Congress had not "moved" in the sense of having taken an autonomous policy initiative based on debate and deliberation. "Congress had, in fact, *been* moved by interest groups whose goal, although desirable, was practically unattainable." According to Mathias, the one entity to take the resolution with all seriousness was, in fact, the Soviet government.[51]

According to his biographer, the Soviet leader said the resolution stank "like a fresh horse shit, and nothing smelled worse than that," to which Nixon supposedly replied that the "Chairman was mistaken. There was something that

---

49 Joint Resolution Providing for the designation of the third week of July as "Captive Nations Week," 86th Cong., 1st Sess., S.J. Res. 111 (Public Law 86–90), 22 VI 1959, IHRC, ACEN, b. 142, f. 9.
50 Public Law 86–90, ibid.
51 Charles Mc. C. Mathias Jr., "Ethnic Groups and Foreign Policy," *Foreign Affairs* 59/5 (1981): 975–998.

smelled worse and that was pig shit."[52] This marked an intense beginning of the visit of Vice President Richard M. Nixon to Moscow. After this rough start, Nixon felt that he should explain to Khrushchev the circumstances of issuing a proclamation, which was basically equivalent to apologizing for the actions of Congress: "[A]ctions of this type cannot, as far as their timing is concerned, be controlled even by the President, because when Congress moves, that is its prerogative. Neither the President nor I would have deliberately chosen to have a resolution of this type passed just before we were to visit the USSR."[53]

Adopted unanimously, the Proclamation spelled out a pledge of support, offering an answer to the exiles' lobbying efforts. It proclaimed that the desire for individual and religious liberty and independence by the captives constituted a "powerful deterrent to war and one of the best hopes for a just and lasting peace." Furthermore, it found it was "fitting that we clearly manifest to such peoples through appropriate and official means the historic fact that the people of the United States share with them their aspirations for the recovery of their freedom and independence."[54] This text sounded like unwavering support for the exiles' cause. This should not be surprising, since the adopted resolution was based on the literal text presented by Dobriansky and was not even sent to the Senate Foreign Relations Committee for consultation. Analyzing this somewhat peculiar resolution in the late 1970s, Stephen Garret assumed that no one in Congress wanted to be put on record as a person who opposed freedom for captive nations.[55]

The ACEN, privy to the earlier efforts to bring the captives to the forefront of American attention, joined the initiative to observe Captive Nations Week almost immediately following Paul H. Douglas's speech. On 22 June 1959, Douglas submitted a motion for a resolution to the U.S. Senate. The exiled political leaders had no doubts that publicizing and building support around this initiative was in line with their mission. The ACEN's Chairman hoped that the unanimous adoption of the resolution by Congress in early July was a way to foster political action. Speaking on behalf of the ACEN, Korboński wanted to believe that the Americans provided the exiles with political capital of vital importance and offered them a chance of promoting a policy other than peaceful coexistence, trade and cultural exchange. On behalf of the ACEN he thanked the initiators of the

52 Taubman, *Khrushchev ...*, 417.

53 Mathias Jr., "Ethnic Groups ...," 975–998.

54 Public Law 86–90.

55 Stephen A. Garrett, "Eastern European Ethnic Groups and American Foreign Policy," *Political Science Quarterly* 93/2 (Summer 1978): 301–323, 316.

resolution for "an expression of continuing interest and solidarity with the captives," shown at the time when the USSR wished to solidify the status quo and when the West wished to adopt "a realistic course."[56]

Already on 8 July 1959, thus so nine days before President Eisenhower issued Proclamation no. 3303: "Captive Nations Week, 1959" as requested by the Congress, the exiles were getting ready to publicize it. The ACEN joined its resources and manpower with the American Friends of Captive Nations (AFCN) as well as the Conference of Americans of Central-Eastern European Descent (CACEED) and established the Committee for the National Observance of Captive Nations Week. The absence of the NCNC should be noted. Five hundred information packages were prepared and then sent to churches of various denominations with a request for further publicity, during both the organized commemorations and masses said for the "captives." Publishers and journalists of the opinion-leading journals received a further few hundred sets. Together with the AFCN and CACEED – both representing the American people rather than foreign and former political leaders – the ACEN planned to address radio and TV stations, producers of film chronicles. Using its own connections, the Assembly members were to approach the Voice of America and RFE, while individual councils and committees were given the task to reach out to the ethnic press. All interested groups strove to make the headlines on 19 July 1959, the day marking the inauguration of Captive Nations Week.[57]

On 9 July 1959, Senator Douglas expressed his gratitude to ACEN for its support of his initiative and asked for further assistance since, in his opinion, "the American government does not seem to be adequately concerned."[58] On 17 July 1959 his office sent a telegram to the ACEN headquarters informing the exiles that he had "assurance captive nations proclamation will be issued by the President late this afternoon. Will wire you as soon as announced."[59] Following the announcement, the ACEN, CACEED and AFCN planned to issue a joint declaration, send letters to the American authorities (both state and regional), lay flower wreaths at the Tomb of the Unknown Soldier as well as at John Foster Dulles' grave. Some other initiatives included meetings on the Hill as well as in Phila-

---

56 "Address by Stefan Korboński at ceremony honoring Sen. Paul H. Douglas, Sen. Jacob K. Javits, and rep. John W. McCormack, Washington D.C. 22 VII 1959" in: Jacob K. Javits, "Visit of Vice President Nixon to Moscow ..."

57 ACEN's Secretary General to ACEN's General Committee, Memorandum, 8 VII 1959, IHRC, ACEN, b. 142, f. 9: Captive Nations Week.

58 Paul H. Douglas to Stefan Korboński (ACEN Chairman), ACEN, Telegram, 9 VII 1959, ibid.

59 Mary Nolan (Executive Secretary to Senator Paul H. Douglas) to Brutus Coste (ACEN Sec. General), Telegram, 17 VII 1959, ibid.

delphia, and a ceremonial mass in the St. Patrick's Cathedral in New York celebrated by cardinal Spellman.[60] Using the façade of the ACEN House, the exiles prepared a special poster that was displayed across from the UN Headquarters in Manhattan.[61]

The ACEN's archival collection contains eight boxes with information on preparations, publicity campaigns, and various forms of commemorations organized in connection with the Captive Nations Week. Among these are multiple copies of declarations of support from the members of the U.S. Congress, as well as state and municipal leaders who sent the ACEN copies of their own Captive Nations Proclamations and other evidence of commemorations organized throughout the country. Through its worldwide network of regional offices, delegates and correspondents, ACEN's campaigns also reached Europe, Latin America and Australia.[62]

Politically, the exiles considered the Presidential Proclamation issued a week before Nixon's departure for his Moscow trip (23 July – 2 August 1959), a tremendous boost for their activities.[63] The executive Proclamation designating of the third week in July as Captive Nations Week was not as flamboyant as the Congressional one, though. In short, the President observed that "many nations throughout the world have been made captive by the imperialistic and aggressive policies of Soviet communism"; and that "the peoples of the Soviet-dominated nations have been deprived of their national independence and their individual liberties." Eisenhower did not list any countries in particular. The general message contained in the Proclamation explained why Americans should commemorate the captives. Eisenhower said that "the citizens of the United States are linked by bonds of family and principle to those who love freedom and justice on every continent," and "it is appropriate and proper to manifest to the peoples of the captive nations the support of the Government and the people of the United States of America for their just aspirations for freedom and national independence." All in all, the Presidential text was vague and bore no promises of

60 Committee for the National Observance of Captive Nations Week, Memorandum re: Captive Nations Week, 15 VII 1959, IHRC, ACEN, b.142, f. 9; Christopher Emmet (AFCN), Msgr. John Balkunas (CACEED), Stefan Korboński (ACEN) to Robert F. Wagner (Mayor, New York), Telegram, 16 VII 1959, ibid.

61 On the ACEN House: Mazurkiewicz, "The Little U.N...." Gadomski further explained that ACEN strove to promote it, also by organizing the Annual CNW Award Dinner – a banquet organized at the National Press Club in Washington which attracted about 200 guests, including members of Congress, diplomats, press. Gadomski, *Zgromadzenie Europejskich ...*, 39 – 40.

62 See for example: IHRC, ACEN, b. 142, f: 9 to b. 150, f. 4.

63 *ACEN News* 52/54 (July–September 1959) 13; Taubman, *Khrushchev*, 416 – 419.

any political engagement. The only encouragement for action is to be found in the following sentence: "I invite the people of the United States of America to observe such week with appropriate ceremonies and activities, and I urge them to study the plight of the Soviet-dominated nations and to recommit themselves to the support of the just aspirations of the peoples of those captive nations."[64]

Despite this, the exiles considered the Captive Nations Week Proclamation a "milestone," "an act of historical significance."

> Never before have the rights of these nations to live in freedom under governments and institutions of their choosing been given a more authoritative support. And never before have the tyrants of the Kremlin been forced to a more open confession of the precariousness of their hold on the once free nations they are keeping in bondage at the very time when they are masquerading the world over as champions of the emancipation of colonial peoples.[65]

The exiles' convictions were seemingly reinforced by President Eisenhower himself. When asked about Khrushchev's furious response to the news about Captive Nations Week during a press conference on 29 July, the President said that there could be no true peace until all nations were able to decide their fate themselves.[66] Some of the press comments admitted that the timing of the Captive Nations Week Proclamation coinciding with Nixon's visit was unfortunate, but the media nevertheless supported Eisenhower by openly voicing support for the captives' aspirations for freedom.[67] "The Harrisburg (Pennsylvania) Patriot" commented that "resolution accomplished what the State Department has never succeeded in doing – it got Eastern Europe on the agenda for the high-level U.S.-Russian talks. Moreover, it was Soviet Premier Khrushchev who brought it up during the Nixon visit."[68] It appeared then that the Central and East European exile agenda would continue to receive unwavering American support.

What the ACEN did not know in July 1959 was that the same day it received a copy of the Captive Nations Proclamation of 17 July from Under Secretary of State

---

64 Proclamation 3303: Captive Nations Week, 1959, 17 VII 1959, in: Code of Federal Regulations (CFR), Title 3: The President, 1959–1963 Compilation (Washington: U.S. Government Printing Office, 1964), 41. Also; https://www.presidency.ucsb.edu/documents/proclamation-3303-captive-nations-week-1959, accessed 26 XII 2018.

65 Ibid., 1.

66 Ibid.

67 "Crossfire in Moscow," *Christian Science Monitor*, 25 VII 1959; "Gesture to Captive Nations," *Toledo Blade*, VII July 1959; "Spark of Freedom Still Burns," *Erie (Pennsylvania) News*, 1 VIII 1959, in: IHRC, ACEN, Scrapbooks, b. 162.

68 "The Captive Nations," *Harrisburg (Pennsylvania) Patriot*, 29 VIII 1959, in: IHRC, ACEN, Scrapbooks, b. 162.

Douglas Dillon (21 July 1959), Khrushchev had accepted the invitation to visit the United States. So while during the ceremony, Dillon said the United States would never acknowledge Soviet domination of East Central Europe,[69] the administration by mistake, or not, was opening a way for the first ever visit of a Soviet leader to the U.S.[70] From today's perspective, it is already clear that U.S. policy had been heading towards "peaceful coexistence" at least since 1956 and that nobody responsible for its shape in 1959, including President Eisenhower, took seriously the possibility of "liberating" countries behind the Iron Curtain.[71]

Maybe the Proclamation was not about the "captives" after all. Careful rereading of the original text unveils the essential source of danger to world peace, namely Russian imperialism; it also included themes reminiscent of the "Four Freedoms Speech". Adding to it phrases from the text related to the ideas of American greatness, democratic tradition prevailing despite diversity, global interdependence in the struggle for peace in which the United States stands out as "a citadel of human freedom" – a beacon of hope for the captives around the world and a leader in bringing about their liberation.[72] This interpretation fits John Fousek's thesis that the post-World War II American policy shift to one of global engagement was built on a triad of factors, namely the American conviction of the country's national greatness, feelings of global responsibility, and anti-communism. In his opinion, the Manichean vision of the world, which was based on anti-communism, made it possible to put the new ideological construct (that is, American "nationalist globalism") in motion.[73] Even if it was not the case in 1959, the fact that every single American president issued the Captive Nations Week Proclamation every single year from then on prompts one to ponder.[74]

Legal analysis of the Proclamation published in 1960 in the "American Journal of International Law," shows that it was not consistent with U.S. obligations

---

69 *ACEN News* 52/54 (July–September 1959): 9.

70 Mazurkiewicz, "The Relationship Between the Assembly ...," 397–427.

71 See: Robert J. McMahon, "U.S. national security policy from Eisenhower to Kennedy" in: *The Cambridge History of the Cold War*, vol. 1: *Origins*, ed. Malvyn P. Leffler, Odd Arne Westad (Cambridge: Cambridge University Press, 2011), 293–297.

72 Public Law 86–90: approved July 17, 1959, Joint resolution [S. J.Res. 111] providing for the designation of the third week of July as "Captive Nations Week," 86th Congress, 1959–1960, http://www.gpo.gov/fdsys/pkg/STATUTE-73/pdf/STATUTE-73-Pg212.pdf , accessed 20 VI 2019.

73 John Fousek, *To Lead The Free World: American Nationalism & The Cultural Roots of the Cold war* (Chapel Hill: The University of North Carolina Press, 2000), 2.

74 Since 1959, Captive Nations Week has been proclaimed every year. See: Donald J. Trump, Proclamation on Captive Nations Week, 17 VII 2020, https://www.whitehouse.gov/presidential-actions/proclamation-captive-nations-week-2020/, accessed: 21 VII 2020.

in the light of international law. The legal dilemma was provoked by the examination of the provisions of the United Nations Charter as well as the American declarations regarding the conduct of international relations on the basis of peaceful coexistence and respect for territorial integrity. Under the presidential U.S. proclamation, the United States became involved in "subversive intervention." Quincy Wright, the author of this study, asked: how is international law to protect new countries in Africa and Asia from a Communist sabotage if it cannot protect the Communist countries from sabotage conducted by Western democracies? Wright quoted "ACEN News" when describing the harsh reaction of the Iron Curtain regimes to the American proclamation and stated that the Captive Nations Week was a mistake. "The United States recognized the Soviet Union and the countries of Eastern Europe, the so-called satellite countries. It is difficult to understand what is the purpose of the presidential Proclamation of the Captive Nations Week if it is not to encourage and stimulate the rebellion of the inhabitants against the governments that the U.S. has recognized."[75]

Eisenhower was very reluctant and reserved in issuing the consecutive Proclamation (1960), which was almost identical in wording.[76] The texts of proclamations issued by the democrats who took over the administration in 1960 were rather insignificant. John F. Kennedy in 1961–1963 highlighted the historical relationship of Americans with various regions of the world and attachment to the values and ideals that in the President's opinion were the common heritage of humanity (such as freedom and the right to self-determination).[77] The 1963 proclamation was repeated (literally) by Kennedy's successor Lyndon B. Johnson, in subsequent years introducing only cosmetic corrections to the text.[78]

---

75 Quincy Wright, Subversive Intervention, *American Journal of International Law* 54/3 (1960): 521–534.

76 Eisenhower, Proclamation 3357: Captive Nations Week, 1960, 18 VII 1960, https://www.presidency.ucsb.edu/documents/proclamation-3357-captive-nations-week-1960, accessed: 12 IV 2020.

77 John F. Kennedy (JFK), Proclamation 3419: Captive Nations Week (CNW), 1961, 14 VII 1961, in: CFR, Title 3: The President, 1959–1963 Compilation (Washington: U.S. Government Printing Office, 1964), 129; JFK, Proclamation 3482: CNW, 1962,13 VII 1962, in: ibid. , 209. JFK, Proclamation 3543: CNW, 1963, 5 VII 1963, in: ibid., 294.

78 Lyndon B. Johnson (LBJ), Proclamation 3594: CNW, 1964, 18 VI 1964, *The American Presidency ...*, http://www.presidency.ucsb.edu/ws/?pid=75207, accessed 12 IV 2013; LBJ, Proclamation 3661: CNW, 1965, 2 VII 1965, *The American Presidency ...*, http://www.presidency.ucsb.edu/ws/?pid=75271 , accessed 12 IV 2013; LBJ, Proclamation 3732: CNW, 1966, 8 VII 1966, in: CFR, 1966 Compilation, Title 3: The President (Washington: U.S. Government Printing Office, 1967), 61; LBJ, Proclamation 3793, CNW, 1967, in: CFR, 1967 Compilation, Title 3: The President (Washington: GPO, 1968), 65; LBJ, Proclamation 3857, CNW, 1968, CFR, 1967 Compilation, Title 3: The President (Washington: GPO, 1969), 54.

In the first five years after announcing the proclamation by Eisenhower, it seemed that its formula was already exhausted. In view of changes in policy towards satellite countries ("building bridges"), President Johnson did not attach much importance to it. Duplicated texts also aroused less and less interest to the growing disappointment of refugees.

At first glance, the Captive Nations Week Proclamation of 17 July 1959 seems to have been the single, greatest achievement of the exile lobby. In fact, however, no political actions followed the letter. Worse, for the exiles, in the fall of 1959 Nikita Khrushchev arrived in the U.S. where he received courteous treatment.[79] Individual members of the U.S. Congress maintained interest by introducing ACEN texts to the Congressional Record, met with ACEN delegations, attended their meetings, but little political action resulted from this, except for a consensus that these countries must be free, that their citizens wanted democracy and an alliance with the U.S. In this regard, the ACEN should be credited for its contribution.

79 Carlson, *K Blows Top.*

6 "Asian People's Freedom Day" – ACEN and the APACL

The origin of Asian People's Freedom Day dates to the Korean War. The war that started with Kim Il-sung's aggression on the Republic of Korea, triggering the UN military involvement,[1] ended with twenty countries involved.[2] It ended in a negotiated ceasefire after prolonged negotiations, which were stalemated many times, over the issue of the prisoners of war. The armistice talks suffered a major setback in early January 1952 when the U.S. introduced the concept of voluntary repatriation of prisoners of war (POWs). According to the Geneva Convention Relative to the Treatment of Prisoners of War of 12 August 1949, the prisoners were supposed to be repatriated to their homelands.[3] However nearly two thirds of the captured Chinese soldiers who had served in the Kuomintang before 1949 defied communism and wished to go to Taiwan or remain in South Korea.[4]

President Truman and Secretary of State Dean Acheson considered both the moral dilemma and the possible propaganda gain. The President kept relating the situation in Korea to the end of World War II in Europe saying that the Soviets had broken every agreement from Teheran to Potsdam, subjugated Poland, Romania, Czechoslovakia, Hungary, Estonia, Latvia and Lithuania, and turned three million World War II POWs into slave labor. Acheson stressed that voluntary repatriation would also gain U.S. public and political support and it was consistent with American morality and psychological warfare against communist tyranny.[5] Reading between the lines, the initiative not to repatriate POWs to communist states should be interpreted in the light of American experience with the forcible repatriation of Soviet POWs at the end of World War II, as well as in the

1 Made possible by temporary Soviet boycott of the UN Security Council protesting Taipei and not Beijing represented there.

2 Waldemar Dziak, *Korea, pokój czy wojna* (Warsaw: Świat Książki, 2003), 120; Peter Lowe, 286. Arnold A. Offner, *Another Such Victory. President Truman and the Cold War 1945–1953* (Stanford University Press, 2002), 422.

3 The U.S. signed but at the time the war in Korea began it had not yet ratified the Geneva Convention of 1949. The North Koreans announced they would abide by the Convention's stipulations. Walter G. Hermes, *Truce Tent and Fighting Front* (Washington D.C.: Center of Military History, U.S. Army 1992), 135.

4 Offner, 409–412.

5 Ibid, 410–423.

https://doi.org/10.1515/9783110661002-010

context of the post-war uses of anti-communist escapees, and defectors as described in the U.S. Escapee Program introduced in 1952.[6]

Both sides of the Korean War used the POWs to their psychological advantage. The North Koreans practiced impressment of the South Korean POWs, agents from the North penetrated the UN-administered POW camps and stirred discontent. It was aggravated by the fact that the conditions inside the camps were poor. Koreans from both parts of the divided country were subjected to intense pressures, which led to riots and violent conflicts within the camps.[7] As the Americans realized that many of the captured Communists (among the Chinese "volunteers") were former soldiers serving under Chiang Kai-shek, disaffected and ready to refuse repatriation, they began planning for their non-repatriation. General Robert A. McClure, Army Chief of Psychological Warfare, suggested that the repatriation should include the option to go to Taiwan.[8] The Communists objected, citing the Geneva conventions. By May 1952, the issue of repatriation became the single most important roadblock to end the conflict.[9]

Judging by his public speeches, President Truman's desire to gain a psychological Cold War Victory at home and abroad was based on the "captivity myth." The President said: "we will not buy an armistice by turning over human beings for slaughter or slavery," and on an other occasion in May: "[W]e won't buy an armistice by trafficking in human slavery."[10] The enslavement included both the body and the minds of the "captive people." In the public discourse, the situation of the Korean POWs included the dichotomy – free will (yearning for freedom) and brainwashing (effect of enslavement). Mindful of a possible blowback should any of the UN captured personnel not wish to be repatriated, by February 1953, the U.S. government worked out a plan for an "intensified propaganda campaign designed to sponsor worldwide revulsion against the established Communist techniques of indoctrination and forced confession." It included provisions for "preparing the world, and particularly the U.S. public" for likely return of "effectively indoctrinated UN captured personnel" as well as a possible refusal to be repatriated by some captives who were to be presented as victims of "brain-washing."[11]

---

6 Mazurkiewicz, *Uchodźcy,* 112–113, 435–444; Alexey Antoshin, USSR, in: Mazurkiewicz (ed.), *East Central European Migrations ...*, 333–335; Tromly, 36–37.

7 On the most notable case of the Koje-do POW camp see: Hermes, 233–262.

8 Ibid, 136, 233.

9 Offner, 411.

10 Ibid, 411–412.

11 Untitled Document 86566, date: before 17 II 1953, CIA, CREST, CIA-RDP80–01065A0006001 00004–7, released: 27 IX 1999.

The early months of 1953 brought a change: with Stalin's death in March 1953 and a new administration in Washington willing to maintain Truman's firm position on repatriation, the Soviet and Chinese leaders agreed to settle the conflict even at the price of making concessions on the prisoner issue.[12] The final armistice was signed on 27 July 1953.[13] It was followed by Operation Big Switch (August 1953 – December 1954) – the exchange of 75,823 Communist POWs (70,183 North Korean and 5,640 Chinese) for 12,773 UN POWs (including 7,862 South Koreans and 3,597 Americans).[14]

As anticipated, there were former prisoners who refused repatriation. Among the 22,604 Communist non-repatriates were 14,704 Chinese.[15] They were turned over to the Neutral Nations Repatriation Commission, consisting of delegates from Sweden, Switzerland, Czechoslovakia, Poland, and India, and ultimately released as civilians. But there were also non-repatriates on the other side. All in all, 359 UN troops refused to return home.[16] This part of the story got somehow omitted from the textbooks, but did produce a lot of media attention at the time. The majority of the UN non-repatriates were South Koreans (335) but there were also 23 Americans and one British soldier who declined to return home, and chose life in China instead.[17] Their televised interviews condemning the "McCarthyism, Mccarranism,[18] and KKKism" were a significant blow to the story of the

12 James G. Hershberg, transl. Vladislav Zubok, "Russian Documents on the Korean War, 1950–53. Introduction," *Cold War International History Project Bulletin* 14/15 (Winter/Spring 2003–2004): 372; Lowe, 277–278.

13 See the text of the Armistice Agreement in: Hermes, 516–532. For Article III: Arrangements relating to Prisoners of War, see: 527–531. The armistice was signed by gen. Nam Il representing Korean People's Army and Chinese People's Volunteers and Lt. William K. Harrison, Jr. (UN Command Delegation). It was approved by North Korean leader (Kim Il-sung) and as well as Chinese commander Peng Dehuai [The-huai] (listed as Chinese People's Volunteers, by 1954 China's Defense Minister) and by gen. Mark W. Clark (Commander-in Chief UN Command). Note the telling absence of the South Korean delegate. Interestingly, on 18 June 1953 Syngman Rhee suddenly released more than 25,000 North Korean POWs without notifying Washington. Hershberg, 372.

14 Appendix B: Prisoners of War, in: Hermes, 514. Operation Big Switch followed the Little Switch (April 1953) which included repatriation of 7,354 POWs among whom there were 6,670 Communists (5,640 North Koreans).

15 Appendix B-2: Nonrepatriates, in: Hermes, 515.

16 Offner, 419–420.

17 Appendix B-2: Nonrepatriates, in: Hermes, 515; Carruthers, 217–220.

18 The Internal Security Act (Subversive Activities Control Act, McCarran Act) 1950 that required the registration of Communist organizations with the United States Attorney General and established the Subversive Activities Control Board to investigate persons suspected of engaging in subversive activities or otherwise promoting the establishment of a "totalitarian dictatorship," Fascist or Communist. Members of these groups could not become citizens, and in some

22,000 whose decisions (although not free from coercion) were regarded as the one major moral victory of the Korean war.[19] After the initial sympathy (the view that obviously they must have been brainwashed) there was a wave of hatred directed towards the American non-returnees (they were branded traitors who had denounced their colleagues and were afraid to return and "face the music," spies, boys in love with Chinese girls, and even homosexuals).[20]

The greater the tension evoked by the 23 Americans unwilling to return, the greater the need was to promote the story of the 22,000. Non-repatriation became a case for commemoration, an occasion to celebrate freedom among the representatives of the captives – first in Asia, and then among the exiles from behind the Iron Curtain as well. A symbolic date was selected:

> On January 23, 1953, 22,000 anti-communist Chinese and Korean prisoners of war in the custody of the United Nations forces refused to return to the Chinese mainland and to the northern part of Korea. They rejected totalitarian communism which had forced them to fight against the Republic of Korea and the United Nations forces. They decided to go to the free territory of their respective countries in order to serve the cause of freedom for their peoples.[21]

In fact, the date the ACEN cited was wrongly referred, since it was 23 January 1954 that some 14,000 Chinese defectors arrived in Taiwan. In the following years this mistake was not repeated.[22]

---

cases were prevented from entering or leaving the country. Citizen-members could be denaturalized in five years. U.S. Code, Title 50: War and National Defense, chapter 23: Internal Security, https://uscode.house.gov/view.xhtml?path=/prelim@title50/chapter23&edition=prelim, accessed: 20 III 2020.

19 Carruthers, 174–216. See: B.J. Bernstein, The struggle over the Korean armistice: prisoners of repatriation, in: Bruce Cummings (ed.) *Child of Conflict: the Korean-American Relationship, 1943–1953* (Seattle: University of Washington Press, 1983).

20 Carruthers, 176–177, 228.

21 Editorial, "The Sixth Anniversary of Freedom Day," *ACEN News* 58 (January 1960): 3.

22 ACEN Observes Asian People's Freedom Day," *ACEN News* 150 (March-April 1971):29–30. In 1971 the event was attended and addressed by Ambassador Liu Chieh (Permanent Representative of the Republic of China to the UN), Dr. Jin Chul Soh (Counsellor to the Office of the Permanent Observer of the Republic of Korea to the UN) et al. A year earlier the Asian speakers attending ACEN's observances of the 16th anniversary included: Chun-Ming Chang (Deputy Permanent Representative of the Republic of China to the UN), Nguyen Huu Chi (Permanent Observer of the Republic of Vietnam to the UN), Chul Nam (Deputy Permanent Representative of the Republic of Korea to the UN). "Asian People's Freedom Day," ACEN News 145 (March-April 1970): 18–21. In 1969: "ACEN Observes Asian People's Freedom Day," *ACEN News* 139 (March-April 1969): 22–23. Chun-Ming Chang (Deputy Permanent Representative of the Republic of China to the UN), Yong

From the late 1950s it has been celebrated by the ACEN, always around 23 January, but under changing names. In the early ACEN documents one finds it celebrated as Chinese and Korean Freedom Day,[23] or Anti-Communist Freedom Day.[24] In 1964, in ACEN internal notes, the January celebrations were called Asian Freedom Day,[25] and by the end of the decade it was called Asian People's Freedom Day.[26]

In order to present the ACEN's initial engagement with this project, it is crucial to explain the nature of the East Central European Assembly's contacts with the Asian Peoples Anti-Communist League (APACL).

The APACL was founded on 15 June 1954 in Jinhae (often spelled, including by the U.S. Navy, Chinhae),[27] the wartime capital city of Republic of Korea. The founders of the League were: Chiang Kai-shek (Republic of China, on Taiwan), Elpidio Quirino (Philippines), Syngman Rhee (Republic of Korea), as well as representatives of Vietnam, Thailand, Okinawa (later as Ryukyu), Hong Kong,

---

Shik Kim (Permanent Observer of the Republic of Korea to UN), Nguyen Huu Chi (Permanent Observer of the Republic of Vietnam to the UN) but also congressman Lester L. Wolff (D-NY).

23 ACEN Press Release 344, 22 I 1960, IHRC, ACEN, b. 135, f. 8

24 ACEN announced it wished to associate the captive European nations with the commemorations taking place in Taiwan, Saigon, Seoul, and other Asian countries, at the initiative of the APACL. It wished to stress solidarity and common determination in anti-communist fight. Often these ceremonies included guest representatives of Asian countries. For example, in 1969 Yong Shik Kim (Ambassador, ROK Permanent Observer to the UN) accepted an invitation to speak to ACEN 15th anniversary of the Anti-Communist Freedom Day. Brutus Coste to Tingfu F. Tsiang, 8 I 1960, IHRC, ACEN, b. 99, f. 15; Yong Shik Kim (Ambassador, ROK Permanent Observer to the UN) to Lettrich (ACEN), 6 I 1969, IHRC, ACEN, b. 108, f. 19.

25 Deputy Sec. Gen (ACEN) to Sec. Gen. (ACEN), Memorandum, 20 I 1964, IHRC, ACEN, b. 89, f. 7; David L. Hackett (Special Assistant to Mr. Kennedy) to Vasil Gërmenji (ACEN), 31 XII 1964, ibid.

26 ACEN Press Release 624, ACEN observes Asian people's Freedom Day, 26 I 1970, ZNiO, Gadomski Papers, 120/02, f. 2: Dokumentacja dot. działalności ACEN; ACEN Press Release 637, ACEN observes Asian People's Freedom Day, 25 I 1971, ibid. ; Gadomski to Wolff Lester I.(HR) list, 30 I 1968, IHRC, ACEN, b. 7, f. 2; "Asian People's Freedom Day" *Daily News*, 23 I 1964, IHRC, ACEN: Scrapbooks.

27 A Brief History of the Asian Peoples' Anti-Communist League," 5 III 1956, Wilson Center, History and Public Policy Program Digital Archive, B-392–008, Documents Related to the Asian Anti-Communist League Conference, Papers Related to Treaty-Making and International Conferences, Syngman Rhee Institute, Yonsei University (Wilson Center, APACL), http://digitalarchive.wilsoncenter.org/document/118348, accessed 12 V 2020; "Constitution of the Asian Peoples' Anti-Communist League, Republic of China," 31 VII 1954, Wilson Center, APACL, http://digitalarchive.wilsoncenter.org/document/118335, accessed 12 V 2020; "Proposals for the Establishment of an Anti-Communist Union of the Peoples of Asia" June 1954, Wilson Center, APACL, http://digitalarchive.wilsoncenter.org/document/118343, accessed 12 V 2020.

Macao. APACL opened its China chapter in Taipei on 1 July 1954.[28] The central office (secretariat) was established in Saigon in 1957. By 1960, the organization had eight more members (Australia, Burma, Iraq, Malaya, Pakistan, Philippines, Singapore, Turkey). In the early 1960s the Chairman of the APACL was Ku Cheng-kang of Taiwan, while the Secretary General was from Thailand (Plang Phloy-phrom), soon replaced by Tran Tam his deputy from Vietnam.[29] In 1967, the APACL was integrated into the World Anti-Communist League as its regional division.[30]

As noted by Victor Hsu, the APACL was a "political initiative spearheaded and brought to fruition by the leaders of the Asian anti-Communist regimes with little involvement from the United States," founded "with the intention of

28 The Asian People's Anti-Communist League, 1957–1964, HIA, RFE/RL CF: A, b. 145, f. 2.

29 Ku Cheng-kang: Former Minister of the Interior of Taiwan (1950), prominent member of the Kuomintang, under Chiang Kai-shek: Head of the National Defense Council (1940–1947), Minister of Social Affairs (1940–1948), Director of the Political and Party Affairs of Kuomintang (1949–1950); Minister of Interior (1950), member of Central Reform Committee of Kuomintang. The Asian People's Anti-Communist League, 27 V 1960, ibid.

30 In 1966 the memberships of the APACL had increased to 27, in Asia, Australia, and Africa. At its 12th Conference in Seoul on 3 November 1966, a 15-member committee was formed to discuss the expansion of this organization. The committee eventually decided to set up a new anti-Communist organization, including the APACL, regional organizations, and an international anti-Communist organization. On 7 November 1966, the delegates adopted the "Charter of the World Anti-Communist League" at the plenary session. It also resolved that the Republic of China Chapter was in charge of organizing the first General Conference. The Charter of the World Anti-Communist League (WACL), with 8 chapters and 32 articles, came into effect on 1 April 1967. It stated that the WACL should immediately set up its regional organizations in six regions: Asia (now known as Asian Pacific League for Freedom and Democracy), Middle East (now known as Middle East Solidarity Council), Africa (now known as the African Organization for Freedom and Democracy), and Europe (now known as the European Council for World Freedom), North America (now known as the North American Federation for Freedom and Democracy), and Latin America (now known as the Federation of Latin American Democratic Organization). The organization in the Asian region was the main force to push for the mission of the World League. To adjust to the worldwide political changes and to strive for recruiting more people to join the fight for freedom and democracy, the WACL held its 22nd General Conference in Brussels on 23 VII 1990, and the delegates resolved that this organization should be renamed as the "World League for Freedom and Democracy" (WLFD). This resolution came into effect on 1 January 1991. See: http://www.wlfdroc.org.tw/, accessed 12 V 2020. See also: Pierre Abramovici, "The World Anti-Communist League: Origins, Structures and Activities," in: *Transnational Anti-Communism ...*, 113–127. Nota bene: in this general survey the author provides incorrect information about the ACEN (sponsorship, members, and standing). Ibid, 121.

rallying anti-Communist Asian states to contribute equally to their own collective security by strengthening military, economic and cultural ties."[31]

The principles of this organization unanimously adopted at Jinhae stated:

> Ours is the call to all free peoples everywhere to join with us in repealing the Godless Communists, and in beginning the erection of a world system that will assure our children and our children's children that aggressors can never again steal into their lands and their homes. We are wholly convinced aggressive totalitarianism can be stopped, rolled back, and eventually eradicated. This we must do, because the world can never endure half slave and half free. It must be one or the other, and our choice lies unalterably on the side of freedom.[32]

The phrase used in the last sentence is reminiscent of the slogans promoted by both the FEC and the ACEN (established in the same year as the APACL). Yet, scholars note that the APACL branches were in "symbiotic relation" with respective national governments, including financing its operations.[33] This may imply lesser U.S. state-private networks' involvement in its operations. Moreover, it should be emphasized that there was a separate organization created in the United States called the Committee for Free Asia (CFA) which could be considered a project similar to the NCFE. However, as explained by W.H. Jackson, Chairman of the Committee on International Information, there were some crucial differences between the two:

> Although the Committee for Free Asia differs from NCFE [FEC] in that its activities are directed primarily to the free countries of Asia rather than behind the Iron Curtain, in its work in these countries CFA operates on the concept that a private organization, particularly in Asia, can accomplish results which an official agency by its very nature cannot. It presupposes that the more it obscures its American label the more effective it will be. It seeks to foster among Asian peoples a sense of their importance as individuals, to develop in Asia a community of interest in resisting communism, and to encourage and promote native lead-

31 Victor Hsu, "Pacific Destinies. The Asian People's Anti-Communist League (1953–1962) and the Anti-Communist struggle in Asia Pacific," Dissertation , MA/MSc in International and World History, Columbia University (New York) and London School of Economics, 22 IV 2016, 4–5.
32 "Principles of the Organization of Asian Peoples' Anti-Communist League," Chinhae, 17 VI 1954, Wilson Center, APACL, http://digitalarchive.wilsoncenter.org/document/118333, accessed 12 V 2020.
33 Torben Gülstorff, "Warming Up a Cooling War: An Introductory Guide on the CIAS and Other Globally Operating Anti-Communist Networks at the Beginning of the Cold War Decade of Détente," *Cold War International History Project, Working Paper* 75 (Washington: CWIHP, 2015), 7, https://www.wilsoncenter.org/sites/default/files/cwihp_working_paper_75_warming_up_a_cooling_war_0.pdf, accessed 21 IX 2019; Hsu, 8.

> ership of activities which will strengthen freedom. In working toward these objectives CFA encourages individuals and groups to act in their own right as Asians, in Asian self-interest, for Asian objectives.[34]

This Committee – just like the FEC – organized broadcasts in May 1951, in three Chinese dialects and English (Radio Free Asia, RFA). The Jackson Committee Report of 1953 (proposing major reorganization of the CIA) stated that

> [s]urveys revealed that on the Chinese mainland the audience was restricted to government officials and others specifically authorized to listen to short-wave broadcasts. Because of this situation, RFA concentrated on the overseas Chinese audience in Southeast Asia. This audience was not thought to justify the expense of the program and it was recently decided to discontinue RFA entirely.[35]

Indeed, the RFA was discontinued in 1953.[36] Therefore, although founded by its members and established outside of the American state-private networks, the APACL was the natural partner to American information programs.

However, there were some drawbacks. The hawkish and McCarthyite sound of APACL's early press releases caught the attention of the radical anti-Communist Russian groups first.[37] In the report of the 1955 Manila conference (and then in 1957) one finds greetings "from Free Russians," these being members of the Anti-Bolshevik Bloc of Nations (ABN), or the National Labor Alliance of Russian Solidarists, NTS (Narodno-trudovoi soiuz)[38] – with whom the Free Europe Committee deliberately did not wish to maintain contact.

The first of the above-mentioned organizations established in 1943 consisted of exiled representatives of non-Russian peoples whose program included the overthrow of the communist regime, and the establishment of sovereign national

---

34 Jackson (Chairman) et al., Report to the President by the President's Committee on International Information

35 Ibid.

36 The original RFA is not directly linked to the Radio Free Asia which began broadcasting in 1996 with U.S. government's official support. Richard H. Cummings, *Radio Free Europe's "Crusade for Freedom": Rallying Americans behind Cold War Broadcasting, 1950–1960* (Jefferson NC, London: McFarland & Company, 2010), 48–52, 90, 98.

37 Asian Peoples' Anti-Communist Conference, Press Release No. 4, 17 VI 1954, Wilson Center, APACL, http://digitalarchive.wilsoncenter.org/document/118314, accessed 12 V 2020.

38 "Asian Peoples' Anti-Communist League Third Annual Conference: Speeches and Reports" 27 III 1957, Wilson Center, APACL, http://digitalarchive.wilsoncenter.org/document/118361, accessed 12 V 2020; "Materials from the Asian Peoples' Anti-Communist League Conference, Manila" 9 III 1955, Ibid, http://digitalarchive.wilsoncenter.org/document/118346, accessed 12 V 2020.

states on the basis of ethnographic principles.[39] Dominated by Ukrainians, the ABN remained an anathema to the Russians in exile. Already in 1949, Yaroslav Stetsko (leader of the Organization of Ukrainian Nationalists, Bandera Faction) and a president of the ABN, wished to establish cooperation with the FEC.[40] Citing the geographical focus on the nine nations, the FEC repeatedly declined.[41] "The functions and funds of the National Committee for a Free Europe, Inc., are limited and restricted to certain specific operations, to which we feel we must confine ourselves at the present time" – this was the ambiguous response by Frederic Dolbeare, Vice President of the FEC.[42] In 1957 Ralph E. Walter noted: "The ABN is altogether a sticky business."[43] Three years later in his internal memorandum, John F. Leich was even more straightforward:

> The ABN is led by Slovak separatists, Hungarian Arrow-Crossists, Croatian Ustashi elements, extreme Ukrainian nationalists, and the like, many of whom are veterans of SS units assimilated into the German armed forces toward the end of World War II. The Bulgarian National Front is led by the remnants of the Tsankov government, a puppet regime established by the Nazis in Vienna after the Bulgarian surrender in 1944. We customarily do not acknowledge correspondence form these groups, since they tend to make use of any acknowledgement as an FEC endorsement of their aims.[44]

Because of the separatist and right-wing character, as well as the wartime record of some of the ABN members, the FEC was adamant about not wishing to associate itself with either the Bloc, or its American Friends – an organization established in the U.S.[45] While ABN included representatives of Bulgarians, Estonians,

39 Mazurkiewicz, *Uchodźcy*, 294–295; Anti-Bolshevist Bloc of Nations – basic data sent by the Common Council for American Unity (Yaroslav J. Chyz), February 1951, HIA, RFE/RL CF: A, b. 144, f. 6.
40 Yaroslav Stetz[s]ko (Munich) to Joseph C. Grew (New York), 26 VIII 1949, HIA, RFE/RL CF: A, b. 144, f. 6. He also appealed to generals Eisenhower and Lucius D. Clay inquiring about possible inclusion in the Crusade for Freedom programs, to no avail. Stetz[s]ko to gen. Dwight D. Eisenhower (President of Columbia University), 15 IX 1950, Ibid; Stetz[s]ko to Lucius D. Clay, 27 XII 1950, ibid.
41 William E. Griffith (Assistant to the President) to Yaroslav Stetz[s]ko (President ABN), 10 X 1950, HIA, RFE/RL CF: A, b. 144, f. 6.
42 Frederic R. Dolbeare to Yaroslav Stetz[s]ko, 2 II 1951, HIA, RFE/RL CF: A, b. 144, f. 6.
43 REW [Ralph Walter] to CKH [Cloyce Huston], 31 VIII 1957, HIA, RFE/RL CF: A, b. 142, f. 18.
44 Leich to Huston, 29 II 1960, ibid.
45 Spas T. Raikin (Secretary General, American Friends of the Anti-Bolshevik Bloc of Nations, Inc.) to Archibald S. Alexander (FEC President), 24 VIII 1959, HIA, RFE/RL CF: A, b. 142, f. 18.

Hungarians, Lithuanians, Romanians and Slovaks, ACEN and ABN membership did not overlap.[46]

The NTS was one of the organizations established by the Russians in exile. A thorough and detailed survey of the anti-Soviet Russian political organizations prepared by Benjamin Tromly characterizes the tangled web of Russian émigré organizations among which the NTS (or "Solidarists") became "the most important client of the U.S. power."[47] Right-radical, fascist influenced – as Tromly characterized the NTS – this organization, along with other Russian émigré groups (the Whites, socialists and Vlasovites) was never a part of the Free Europe Committee system.[48] Since the Russian projects, like American Committee for the Liberation of the Peoples of Russia (AMCOMLIB), constituted a separate area of American psychological warfare projects, the ACEN was not exposed to direct contacts, or requests for cooperation from these groups.

While the FEC did not wish to be associated with either ABN or NTS, and – to the best of my knowledge – neither did the ACEN, the exile assembly's listing alongside ABN and NTS in the Asian anti-Communist league materials, caused some concern. Regardless, the cooperation with the APACL continued throughout the ACEN's existence.

6.1 ACEN and APACL

The initial contact between the two organizations dates to a letter sent by Ku Cheng-kang, the President of the Board of Directors of the APACL, addressed to the ACEN's secretariat "hoping for your close cooperation so that we may see the early crush of our common enemy – Communist Imperialism." The ACEN's Chairman responded by suggesting exchange of publications and thus working contact was established with Taipei.[49] In this form, the contacts between

46 The one ACEN member who appears in the ABN materials before 1954 is Alfreds Berzins. In 1951 Stetsko referred to the former Latvian minister as ABN's representative in the U.S. Stetz[s]ko to Lucius D. Clay, 25 I 1951, HIA, RFE/RL CF: A, b. 144, f. 6.

47 Tromly, 40–46.

48 On one occasion, Alexander Kerensky (prime minister of Russia July-November 1917) was invited to sign the "Philadelphia Declaration of Aims and Principles of Liberation of the Central and Eastern European Peoples" (Philadelphia, 11 II 1951). Mazurkiewicz, "'Join, or Die'...," 22. On AMCOMLIB, see: Johnson, 26–36; Tromly, 153–158.

49 Ku Cheng-kang to ACEN Secretariat, 17 X 1955, IHRC, ACEN, b. 117, f. 7; Māsēns to Cheng-kang, 21 XII 1955, ibid. , Cheng-kang to Māsēns, 9 I 1956, ibid.

the two organizations were courteous but limited to sharing information about their respective activities.

In August 1956, the Ambassador of the Republic of China (Taiwan) in Manila sent a private letter to Christopher Emmet. The letter was transferred to the ACEN most likely by Emmet himself.

> There is now in the Philippines an organization known as the Philippine-Chinese Anti-Communist League. It was formed by respected leaders of the Chinese community. It has 72 branches in various parts of the country. They are manned by people willing and able to devote time and money to fighting communism.
>
> A nationwide convention of the League is scheduled to meet in Manila on September 27, 1956. The convention is composed of representatives from the 72 branches. Its specific purpose is to map up a comprehensive program to combat Communist propaganda and infiltration in the light of the "New Look" of Moscow and Peiping [Beijing].
>
> I take the liberty od addressing this letter to you to enlist your support of this endeavor. I would like to obtain as many messages of encouragement as possible from anti-Communist organizations and leaders in the U.S. Such messages will be of incalculable value in focusing public attention on the forthcoming convention. They can be forwarded to the convention through me. Knowing of your deep and abiding interest and concern in the defense and preservation of the free way of life, I am sure you will not fail me.[50]

At this time, the ACEN sought support in the UN in the aftermath of the Poznań workers' protest in Poland. Taiwan's seat in the Security Council, together with some other Asian delegates in the UN (like Lorenzo Sumulong), gave the ACEN access to this forum on the grounds of their shared anti-communist and pro-American outlook. Continuing tensions in South-East Asia (the communist threat in the context of recent Korean and First War Indochina War, 1946–1954) almost naturally brought the two anti-communist organizations closer. Already in September, the ACEN's secretary addressed the APACL congratulating them on the publication "All Roads Lead to Freedom."[51] On the eve of the Soviet aggression in Hungary, Paul Vajda thanked the APACL for another publication received noting: "it helps in our common fight against totalitarianism."[52]

In the aftermath of the Hungarian Revolution, the contacts between these two organizations intensified. From exchanging publications, the cooperation between the ACEN and APACL expanded to organizing events in support of

---

50 Chen Chin-Mai (Ambassador, Republic of Manila) to Christopher Emmet (New York), 9 VIII 1956, IHRC, ACEN, b. 124, f. 19.

51 Nuci Kotta (Deputy Sec. Gen.) to APACL (Taipei), 14 IX 1956, IHRC, ACEN, b. 7, f. 2.

52 Pál [Paul] Vajda to Ku Cheng-Kang (Pres. Board of Directors, APACL, Taipei), 22 X 1956, IHRC, ACEN, b. 7, f. 2.

their respective causes. For example, Ku Cheng-kang informed the ACEN that a special Committee of Civic Organizations of Republic of China in Support of Struggle for Freedom Behind the Iron Curtain was established in Taiwan. Himself a Chairman, Ku Cheng-kang explained that the aim of the Committee was to raise funds for the "heroic freedom-fighters of Hungary." Fifty thousand dollars had already been forwarded to Dr. Tingfu F. Tsiang (UN) "for the relief of Hungarian refugees," on top of government's donation of food.[53] Also in February 1957 the APACL informed the Hungarian exiles affiliated with the ACEN (Hungarian National Council) of a 3,000 people strong rally that took place in Taipei pledging support to the Hungarian people in their struggle for national independence.[54]

Since the members of the APACL were not exiles, and conducted their operations from the countries threatened, but not dominated, by the Communists, their activities must be interpreted in the context of the activities of their respective governments. Their support for the ACEN case in the UN has already been described in Chapter Four. Each of these governments wished to advance their agenda for one "using the APACL, Taiwan pushed the case of the illegitimacy of the communist regime in mainland China at every opportunity."[55]

The ACEN also maintained close relations with Tran Tam, the Vietnamese Secretary General of APACL. Veteran of the anti-Japanese, anti-French, and then anti-Communist struggle (1942–1949), he regularly appeared at the ACEN's meetings, as well as served as a host during ACEN delegations' visits to Asia.[56] FEC's Bernard Yarrow, who considered Tran Tam a "stalwart fighter in the cause of freedom of the Asian people," gave in to a Hungarian (Király's) request to organize Tran Tam's visit to RFE in Munich in 1962. "We had a talk with Mr. Tam asking him to bring before the League in a very effective way the self-determination issue of our captive nations and he has already undertaken several overt steps to bring it to the fore at their congresses and overall activities" – wrote Yarrow.[57] Clearly, the FEC wished to advance its own agenda in – yet another – foreign forum.

53 Ku Cheng-kang (President Board of Directors, APACL) to Māsēns (ACEN), 15 II 1957, IHRC, ACEN, b. 117, f. 7.

54 Kádár Lynn, "The Hungarian National Council ...," 286.

55 Abramovici, 118.

56 Korboński, *W imieniu Polski* ..., 437; Ferenc Nagy to Bernard Yarrow, 10 IX 1962, HIA, RFE/RL CF: A b. 145, f. 2.

57 Yarrow to C. Rodney Smith (Director RFE), 11 X 1962, HIA, RFE/RL CF: A, b. 145, f. 2, as well as b. 344, f. 12. Tran Tam, the author of several books on Sino-Soviet aggression, Communist subversion in Asia, member of International Association of Jurists (on its behalf he was an observer at UN session), was also a professor of international law at the University of Geneva (teaching there 3 months a year). Király to Yarrow, 10 X 1962, HIA, RFE/RL CF: A, b. 145, f. 2. By October

By the 1960s, the ACEN significantly increased their efforts to observe the Asian People's Freedom Day introduced by the APACL. The cooperation initiated in 1956 led to the ACEN delegates taking part in the APACL conferences in Manila (Sidzikauskas in 1961, and Coste in 1965). In 1965, while listed as "observer," the ACEN was included as one of the supporters of the appeal addressed to the 20th Session of the UN General Assembly opposing the plan to admit communist China to the United Nations. The list also featured ABN, NTS, and Dobriansky's NCNC.[58]

Obviously, such cooperation was not developed without FEC's knowledge. The ACEN delegates submitted reports of their visits to events organized by the APACL.[59] The FEC cautiously monitored this association – also based on its publications. In 1960, the FEC considered APACL as mostly representing Nationalist Chinese rather than the interests of all Asian people, with the language of their publications being "very aggressive toward communism." The Free Europe Committee obviously noticed the ACEN greetings addressed to the Chinese chapter of APACL on the occasion of Freedom Day, alongside ABN being described as "a rightist (Banderist) [sic!] Russian émigré group."[60]

In 1962, the CIA gave the following instruction to the President of the Free Europe Committee: "Our colleagues [Department of State] inform us that it is U.S. policy not to participate in the APACL meeting as a government and that attendance and/or support by private organizations and individuals is discour-

1963 Király wrote that Tran Tam "cased him a considerable disappointment." Király to Yarrow, 4 X 1963, HIA, RFE/RL CF: A, b. 344, f. 12.

58 Coste applications for visas (Chinese, Japanese, Korean and Philippine), 6 VIII 1965, IHRC, ACEN, b. 23, f. 8. The 11th Annual Conference of the Asian People's Anti-Communist League which met in Manila, the Philippines, in September 7–12, 1965, addresses this appeal to the 20th Session of the UN General Assembly, Display Ad, *New York Times*, 25 X 1965, 10, available at CIA, CREST, CIA-RDP73-00475R000101390001-3, released 6 I 2014.

59 Report by Vaclovas Sidzikauskas to Bernard Yarrow (5 VI 1961) on the Lithuanian's participation in the 7th APACL Conference in Manila (2–5 V 1961), HIA, RFE/RL CF: A, b. 145, f. 2; copy at: IHRC, ACEN, b. 3, f. 6; Vasil Gërmenji, Vice chairman and delegate of the ACEN on the First Conference of the WACL, 25–29 September 1967, Taipei, 20 X 1967, HIA, RFE/RL CF: A, b. 363, f. 6; Committee for a Free Estonia, Information about the Anti-Communist Conference in Saigon, Vietnam, 27 III 1957, and Radio Broadcasts From Formosa to Siberia, 6 III 1957, HIA, RFE/RL CF: A, b. 145, f. 2; A. Blodnieks (Committee for a Free Latvia) to E.L. Packer (FEC), 27 III 1957, ibid.; Kütt's information that Ku Cheng Kang (President of APACL) was in the U.S., 24 IV 1957; Sidzikauskas (teletext) from Saigon, [report on the 9th APACL session], 8 XI 1963, ibid.

60 To any Ukrainian member of the ABN such expression was an oxymoron. Yet, as late as 1960s, Soviet Union and Russia was still used interchangeably. The Asian People's Anti-Communist League, 27 V 1960, HIA, RFE/RL CF: A, b. 145, f. 2.

aged."[61] The note was sent in relation to the APACL meeting in Seoul (10–16 May 1962) to which not only the ACEN and Béla Király but also U.S. senators (Dodd, Hiram Fong, Karl E. Mundt and William J. Fulbright) were supposedly going to be invited by the APACL. The document contains a handwritten note of 26 April 1962 indicating that both the ACEN and Király were "advised and have sent regrets. EC informed." This was an extraordinary APACL conference called in response to the crisis in Laos, whose neutrality, was covertly violated by all major parties involved, namely Vietnam, the USSR and the U.S. During a meeting, Tran Tam criticized both the decision of 1961 as "out-of-date, backward, and narrow-minded policy of the big powers," and the international arbitration process in Laos that followed. In his opinion it "had doomed" Laos to follow the fate of Korea and Vietnam.[62] Tran Tam's career in Vietnam was also doomed. He was replaced soon thereafter and was not present at the APACL session in Tokyo (1–6 X 1962). In 1962 he broke with the Ngo Dinh Diem regime and chose exile in Geneva.[63]

The following year, in response to the request for guidance coming from FEC's European staff, John H. Page said bluntly about exiles' participation in the APACL meetings:

> It's a legitimate, O.K. organization, but is far right and as a result generally considered not too effective. I would be against spending any of our own money to send someone to their meetings or to contribute to any of their activities. However, if a given person is desperately anxious to go to one of their meeting and is willing to spend his own money, or they are willing to put up the money, I see no real objection.[64]

Yet the ACEN obviously maintained contact with the APACL, and voiced support for some of its public campaigns. Although the ACEN included representatives of nine nations, in its support for the APACL it listed the enslaved people of China, North Korea, North Vietnam and Tibet "as an excellent example of this close interdependence between freedom fighters in Europe and Asia, is the impact of the Hungarian Revolution of 1956 which spread panic among the Communist over-

---

61 The Executive Committee (FEC) to the President (FEC), Memorandum" Asian Peoples Anti-Communist League (APACL), 11 IV 1962, HIA, RFE/RL CF: A, b. 199, f. 2.
62 Citation after: Hsu, 50.
63 Leich to Richardson, 8 II 1965, HIA, RFE/RL CF: A, b. 344, f. 12; John Richardson to Mucio F. Delgado, 11 II 1963, ibid. Tran Tam contacted FEC at least a few times asking for support, also of his anti-Communist publications – to no avail. In one of responses Delgado suggested going via ACEN to inquire whether APACL had resources to assist their former Secretary-General. Mucio F. Delgado (Director for Europe) to John Richardson (FEC President), 18 II 1963, ibid.
64 John H. Page to Mucio F. Delgado (London), 12 IX 1963, HIA, RFE/RL CF: A, b. 145, f. 2; Delgado/Leich to Richardson, 4 IX 1963, ibid.

lords in Asia."[65] The ACEN members traveled to the APACL meetings, in which they took part as observers. These organizations' leaders hosted individual members of the ACEN during their visits to South East Asia. The ACEN delegates shared their accounts of these trips not only with the Assembly but also with the FEC.

Upon his return from the Tenth APACL meeting in Taipei (23–27 November 1964), Vasil Gërmenji provided the chief of exile relations at the FEC with a detailed account of the meeting attended by 140 delegates from 50 countries in Africa, Asia, Europe and the Americas.[66] Among the ACEN-affiliated observers were Pál Auer and Arvo Horm from Europe, and Gërmenji from the ACEN's headquarters in New York. "As far as Eastern and Central Europe is concerned, the League seems to be under the strong extremist influence of the ABN." Gërmenji went on to say: "Asians who are very favorable to the freedom and independence of the actual Communist-ruled countries, are not very much concerned about the background and past political activities of the participants, provided they are anti-Communists." The ACEN observer assessed that the organization of the meeting could have cost as much as a quarter of a million dollars and was largely paid for by Taiwan, with some money coming from South Korea and the Philippines. The FEC's Kappel (of exile relations) praised the Gërmenji report saying, "it provides one of the best insights into the conduct of the [APACL] Annual Conference and allied activities."[67] Of particular interest to the FEC was the information that Dobriansky (NCNC) proposed to organize a conference in the U.S., implying cooperation with the ACEN. In the talks with the President of the APACL, the ACEN delegate voiced concern regarding cooperating with "extremists and former collaborators with the Nazi occupators [occupants]" as well as the ostensibly partisan (i.e. Republican) character of Dobriansky's organization. This proposal never materialized.

The Albanian representative of the ACEN thus characterized the Assembly's position in relation to the APACL:

> The League considers ACEN as the only other working effectively organization. In my conversation with Generalissimo Tchang Koi Chek [Chiang Kai-shek], I was agreeably surprised

---

65 Ferenc Nagy (Rapporteur), The Ninth Anniversary of Freedom Day. Draft Declaration introduced at the Extraordinary (105th) Meeting of the Plenary Assembly on Wed., Jan. 23, 1963, ACEN Doc. 336 (IX) Gen., 14 I 1963, IHRC, ACEN, b. 89, f. 7.

66 Vasil Gërmenji to Albert D. Kappel, Memorandum: APACL, 16 XII 1964, HIA, RFE/RL CF: A, b. 145, f. 2. Copy of this document also in HIA, RFE/RL CF: A, b. 205, f. 4.

67 Albert D. Kappel to Richardson, Yarrow, Page, Memorandum, 23 XII 1964, HIA, RFE/RL CF: A, b. 205, f. 4.

> to listen to him make a very good appraisal of our organization. A broad publicity was given to the ACEN by the Chinese [Taiwanese] Press, and I had the feeling that this was somehow an embarrassment for the organizers of the Conference. The ACEN award to the APACL, and the medals given to premier [Chia-kan] Yen and to Ku Cheng-kang [President of APACL], were widely published in the pres. I lectured on Albania, and many interviews about ACEN and Albania appeared in the press.[68]

Among the resolutions adopted at the meeting was a document prepared by the ABN calling for the liberation of Slovaks, Serbs, Croats, Slovenes, etc., which was opposed only by Gërmenji, Auer and Vladimir Poremskii (of the NTS). While it is rather obvious why a Russian would oppose it, given the multi-national character of the state, in the case of the ACEN, the position of its delegates clearly mirrored the U.S.'s political line. At the time, national separatism was an anathema to U.S. policy in East Central Europe. Representing the exile assembly, Gërmenji believed that:

> Contact and cooperation of ACEN with APACL should be continued and increased. An effort has to be done in order to correct some of the extremist tendencies actually prevailing. This can be done by actively participating in all the meetings, and by explaining with insista[e] nce, the dangers of such corrections, which make easy the counterattacks of the communist regimes. Another point to make is advocating true democracy, and this is difficult to make when you have amidst you 'compromised persons or organizations.'[69]

According to Karl Reyman, a political analyst for RFE, originally from Czechoslovakia, whom Puddington called "in effect political director of the New York [RFE] bureau," the Gërmenji report became a major point on the agenda of the staff meeting.[70] Reyman noted Gërmenji's "uneasiness with the grip the ABN and Dobriansky have on the 'East European' segment of APACL thinking and activities."[71]

In 1967, an ACEN delegate attended the first WACL conference in Taipei. A copy of Gërmenji's report to the ACEN's General Committee was forwarded

68 Vasil Gërmenji to Albert D. Kappel, Memorandum: APACL, 16 XII 1964, HIA, RFE/RL CF: A, b. 145, f. 2.

69 Ibid.

70 Puddington, xiv, also as "key member of policy staff", 147–148, and "chief policy aide during invasion [1968] period, 150. See also: James F. Brown, *Radio Free Europe: An Insider's View* (Washington D.C.: Vellum/New Academia Publishing, 2013), 94.

71 Karl Reyman memo for "Dick" rerouted to John Dunning, 30 XII 1964, HIA, RFE/RL CF: A, b. 145, f. 2.

to the FEC.[72] A comment stapled to his report, most likely prepared by the outgoing president of the FEC for the incoming president, read: "You might be interested in the attached delegate's eye-view of the WACL, successor to the APACL, but still financed largely by (or through?) the Taipei and Seoul governments. Our ACEN friends have managed to have a delegate at every annual meeting, with all expenses paid by the League."[73]

The ACEN archives do not contain detailed reports of these meetings and trips, so confirming the ACEN's presence at all of the APACL meetings was not possible. However, what can be confirmed is that the ACEN was not a member of either the APACL or WACL. The Asians were evidently upset that the ACEN refused to apply for membership in the WACL at the time of its inauguration, citing the need to consult the Assembly's General Committee.[74] Gërmenji had doubts but not related to the ideological or political content of the meeting but instead worried that "because of many unknown international organizations among whom ACEN would have been submerged and because of the lack of seriousness of some applications, had I had the freedom to apply, I would have withheld it, in order to report and discuss it again in the [ACEN] General Committee."[75]

Among those present in Taipei in 1967, Gërmenji pointed to Dobriansky's NCNC (which declared the will to join before the subsequent meeting in Saigon) as the American ally of the WACL, and the European Freedom Council, which he called "a subsidiary to ABN" – which applied for membership in the WACL and thus aspired to represent it in Europe. The APACL became a regional organization, alongside the South American Division of the WACL which was formed during the meeting in Taipei. Gërmenji explained that the ACEN has been "associat-

---

72 Report of Mr. Vasil Gërmenji, Vice-Chairman and Delegate of the ACEN on the First Conference of the World Anti-Communist League, 25–29 September 1967, Taipei, Taiwan, HIA, RFE/RL CF: A, b. 363, f. 6.

73 Note: Item X: APACL/WACL by "JR [John Richardson, FEC President 1961–1967] note to WPD [William P. Durkee, FEC President taking over in 1968], 9 XI 1967," attached to Gërmenji's Report on the First Conference of the WACL, 1967.

74 Ibid. Gërmenji also attended the third WACL Conference held on 3–5 December 1969 in Bangkok, Thailand – as an observer. Upon initiative of Parviz Kazemi (Senator from Iran) and Honorary Chairman Ku Cheng-kang, he was invited to deliver closing remarks at the conference. "Third Conference of WACL," ACEN News 145 (March-April 1970): 22–23.

75 Organizations represented in Taipei: ABN, Asian Christian Anti-Communist Association, Asian Lay-Christian Association, ACEN, Christian Anti-Communist Crusade, Cardinal Mindszenty Foundation, European Freedom Council, Free Pacific Association, International Conference on Political Warfare of the Soviets, Inter-American Confederation of Continental Defense, International Young Christian Workers, World Buddhist Sangha Council, World Youth Crusade for Freedom.

ed with APACL from the very beginning and had fruitful and steady cooperation." Until all members represented in the ACEN General Committee discussed it, the Assembly wished to maintain its status as an observer.

The FEC had every reason to be worried by this association. It included the organizations, like the ABN, or Ukrainian-led NCNC, with whom the Committee refrained from maintaining contact with. The FEC had no financial or personal leverage over its operations. Yet it tolerated the ACEN's contacts with the APACL and underwrote some of the travel expenses for trips that included meetings with the leaders of the League. The FEC received detailed information about the anti-Communist league operations which may have justified the expenses but would probably not suffice to risk public association with right-wing organizations and regimes sponsoring it. It is possible that the reason and the value that the FEC saw in these contacts was the opportunity to add a global flavor to its own operations. While not joining, and not formally associating itself with the league through the ACEN, it gained yet another venue to advance its world agenda. On the basis of numerous FEC memoranda one can state that from 1957 to 1965 the Committee sought to reach audiences in Asia, Africa and Latin America, by means of its exile partners. Thus, the global American public diplomacy agenda was supported by authentic voices, with a little help from the "friends." The ACEN's role, however, seemed to have been bringing the idea of the global nature of anti-Communist struggle home to the U.S.

6.2 Freedom Day

Obviously, the ideas of publicly celebrating freedom in America in contrast with Communist-imposed "captivity" were multiple and varied, vastly surpassing the public-state network, or the FEC programs. Within the FEC-organized realm, public demonstrations of joint representations of the East Central European exiles' devotion to freedom preceded the establishment of the ACEN, like the public signings of the Declaration of Liberation in Philadelphia (1951) and in Williamsburg (1952).[76] The exiles were also involved in celebrations of the first "Freedom Day" proclaimed on the 1 July 1954, the seventieth anniversary of the gift of the Statue of Liberty.

While Freedom Day was an occasion to express the importance of French-American bonds, as well as U.S. immigration history, its symbolic value also included using the Statue of Liberty as a symbol of freedoms that was being de-

76 Mazurkiewicz, *Uchodźcy*, 367–371, 378–380.

stroyed. In order to proclaim a worldwide Freedom Day, the FEC found it useful to suggest the presence of those who had temporarily lost their freedoms and found refuge in the U.S. Such a suggestion was made by Frederick T. Merrill, who at this time was involved in negotiations leading to the establishment of the ACEN.[77] Merrill hoped he could count on 200 exiles to attend. While the exact number of exiles present on 1 July 1954 is impossible to verify, the exile national councils were represented at the ceremony.

In a document called the "Declaration of Freedom" read by a representative of the Hungarian National Council, the following definition of liberty appeared: "[F]reedom of every individual from domestic tyranny and exploitation; of every nation from imposed foreign rule; of mankind from the hazards or war, conquest and economic crisis, achieved by the free associations of nations."[78] With the ACEN structure in place, the FEC invited the exiles to attend the New York Freedom Day celebrations in years to come.[79] In 1960, the ceremonies of Freedom Day were held in conjunction with the renaming of Bedlow Island to Liberty Island, and the dedication of the island itself to becoming a museum of immigration. Henry P. McNulty encouraged the ACEN and its member organizations to attend, as well as to "secure a large participation by their respective countrymen [...] in national costumes whenever possible."[80] The ACEN understood that it was the FEC that was responsible for the organization of the event. In 1962, the celebrations were moved to Philadelphia,[81] where by 1963 it had became a Freedom Week event sponsored by the city of Philadelphia in association with the Free Europe Committee. The last indication of the ACEN's partaking in this initiative bears the date 30 June 1965. This was the twelfth Annual observance of the World

77 Merrill to Betts, FEC Inc. Memorandum: Subject of Liberty Ceremonies, July 1, 16 VI 1954, IHRC, ACEN, b. 141, f. 3. See: Mazurkiewicz, "Join, or die ..."

78 Final draft (24 VI 1954): Declaration of Freedom at the Statue of Liberty, 1 VII 1954, IHRC, ACEN, b. 141, f. 3; Press clipping: "Freedom Day Marked at Statue of Liberty, Given by France to America 70 years ago," ibid.

79 Bernard Yarrow (Vice President, FEC) to Dr. Vilis Māsēns (Chairman, ACEN), 25 V 1955, IHRC, ACEN, b. 141, f. 3; "ACEN Statement on Freedom Day," *ACEN News* 4–5 (July-August 1955): 24–26; "U.S. Denies Dulles Softened Views. [Andrew H.] Berding Rejects Khrushchev Statement That Secretary Wavered on Policies," *New York Times*, 2 VII 1959, 4. See also chapter: 3.2.

80 ACEN Secretariat to ACEN Member Organizations, Memorandum, 14 VI 1960, IHRC, ACEN, b. 141, f. 3.

81 ACEN Secretariat to Members and Observers of General Committee, Chairmen of National Organizations, Memorandum, 15 VI 1962, ibid.

Freedom Day.[82] The ACEN was a featured guest at these events but was not involved in their organization.

Beginning in 1960, the ACEN devoted a significant amount of time and energy to contributing to the celebrations of Asian People's Freedom Day. The common publicity line throughout the next decade was that the ACEN mobilized its resources to "commemorate the Freedom Day in honor of the 22,000 Chinese prisoners of war in Korea who chose freedom."

In 1960, the ACEN celebrated the Chinese and Korean Freedom Day in the presence of Tingfu F. Tsiang and Ben C. Limb of (South) Korea. The ACEN habitually refrained from calling the Republic of Korea – "South Korea." In his speech Petr Zenkl – the ACEN's Chairman – emphasized strong bonds between captive Europe and captive Asia:

> The love of liberty and the spirit of resistance of the Communist-subjugated peoples throughout the world is, perhaps, the most neglected force in today's global struggle between democracy and communism. It remains our great task to make the Free World aware that the road to victory and to a genuine peace lies in a dynamic policy based on a true alliance with our captive peoples, and not in the reliance upon the promises of dictators, in the espousal of delusive hopes or catering to fear.[83]

Clearly, the ACEN wished to strengthen its own voice by allying with Asian anti-Communists.

Much effort went into the preparations for the seventh "global commemoration" of the Freedom Day planned for 23 January 1961. Trying to assure the broadest and most effective commemoration did not mean that the ACEN worked with the APACL on the details of the program, or that it should be considered a joint endeavor. The ACEN would routinely send a message to APACL expressing support and invite a number of Asian leaders available in the U.S. to be guest speakers at public meetings organized in New York. In January 1962 there were prominent Chinese, Korean, Filipino and Vietnamese guests – mostly ambassadors. The ACEN was also planning to invite representatives of the Cuban democratic opposition to "underscore worldwide solidarity of all those who struggle for freedom and the global character of this struggle ACEN and APACL."[84] Realizing the

82 Brochure: World Freedom Day, 1 VII 1963; FEC, Inc. Press Release (for Sunday, June 27) June 1965, IHRC, ACEN, b.141, f. 5.

83 ACEN Press Release, ACEN Commemorates Chinese and Korean Freedom Day, 22 I 1960, IHRC, ACEN, b. 141, f. 3.

84 ACEN Memorandum, 6 I 1961, IHRC, ACEN, b. 89 f. 7. Contacts were established and the president of the Cuban Revolutionary Council delegated Dr. Andres Valdespino (of New York) to at-

plan to "tighten the bonds of unity between all victims of communism, and particularly between captive Europe and captive Asia", the ACEN's Chairman (Sidzikauskas) sent greetings to the President of the Republic of China (Chiang Kai-shek) and Prime Minister of the Republic of Korea (Chang Myon).[85] This gesture was repeated the following year and met with gratitude by the recipients, including the president of South Korea, who replaced Syngman Rhee.[86] This signaled continuity since in the 1950s the ACEN also maintained courteous contact with Rhee.[87] In response to birthday wishes sent to him by the ACEN, the leader of South Korea wrote:

> I am sure that by association in the United States they [your countrymen] find some comfort and also replenish their determination to free their soil from the heel of the aggressor. We must convince our powerful friends that there must be no further retreats – and more – that the hour has come to topple the Soviet regime from its position of authority in lands that should be free. The people of America are slowly but surely gaining the realization that their own liberty is in dire peril and as much as war is dreaded it must be faced as the lesser evil.[88]

Regardless of doubts concerning Rhee's poor reputation, the anti-Communist front on the international stage was mounting.[89] In the late 1950s and early 1960s, the ACEN maintained relatively regular contact with both the Chinese and Philippine UN missions.

---

tend the celebrations. Dr. Jose Miro Cardona (President, Cuban Revolutionary Council) to Edmund Gaspar (ACEN Secretary), 16 I 1962, ibid.

85 Vaclovas Sidzikauskas (ACEN Chairman) to Chiang Kai-shek (President of the Republic of China, Taipei, Taiwan), Telegram, 23 I 1961; Vaclovas Sidzikauskas (Chairman, ACEN) to Dr. Chang (Prime Minister of Republic of Korea, Seoul, Korea), Telegram, 23 I 1961, IHRC, ACEN, b. 89, f. 7.

86 Yun Posun (President of the Republic of Korea, 1960–1962) cited in: Soo Young Lee (Republic of Korea, Ambassador) to Ferenc Nagy (ACEN Chairman), letter, 26 I 1962, IHRC, ACEN, b. 89, f. 7.

87 You Chan Yang (Korean Ambassador) to Vilis Māsēns, 15 III 1957, IHRC, ACEN, b. 108, f. 9; Petr Zenkl to Syngman Rhee, Telegram, 24 III 1960, IHRC, ACEN, b. 108, f. 19; Nam Ki Lee (Third secretary, Korean Embassy) to ACEN, 7 VIII 1959, ibid. ; Korboński to Nam Ki Lee, 13 VIII 1959, ibid. ; Villis Māsēns (Chairman ACEN) to Dr. You Chan Yang, 11 III 1957, IHRC, ACEN, b. 108, f. 9.

88 Syngman Rhee to Dr. Dimitrov, 21 IV 1955, IHRC, ACEN, b. 108, f. 9. Birthday wishes signed by Dimitrov were sent 31 III 1955, ibid. Response letter: 25 V 1955, ibid.

89 While South Korea was not a full member of the UN until 1991 it did participate in the General Assembly as an observer since 1948.

The ambassador of the Republic of China (Tingfu F. Tsiang and then Yu Chi Hsueh) attended ACEN meetings,[90] as well as assisted in an exchange of letters with Chiang Kai-shek.[91]

In 1962 Tsiang forwarded the following words on behalf of the Chinese president:

> The government and the people of China are deeply touched by the fact that the ACEN convened on 23 January this year [1962] an extraordinary plenary meeting to commemorate the Eight Freedom Day. This action on the part of the Assembly further demonstrates the strong bond between the free peoples of the world in their common struggle against the tyranny of international communism.[...]
>
> While being constantly on the alert for an opportunity to extend our helping hands to our own people on the mainland, we are also keenly concerned over the fate of millions of people still under the yoke of Soviet imperialism in Europe. We fully share your conviction that the free nations and the free peoples in the world should pursue a more positive and dynamic policy in seeking the liberation of the captive peoples in Europe as well as in Asia.[92]

With such words of solidarity and high-level contacts established in Asia, the ACEN mission of global outreach with its agenda seemed to have been accomplished.

In May 1961, the APACL's 7th conference in Manila adopted a resolution on the expansion of the freedom movement by urging all democratic nations all over the free world to designate January 23 of each year as Freedom Day, as well as the third week in July as Captive Nations Week for worldwide collective action in support of captive people's struggle for freedom.[93] A united front for collective information campaign of a global scope was established.

---

90 Liu Chieh (Republic of China Permanent Representative to the UN) to dr. George M. Dimitrov (ACEN Chairman), 14 I 1963, IHRC, ACEN, b. 89, f. 7. Jaginto G. Bork (Permanent Representative of the Philippines to the UN) to dr. George M. Dimitrov (ACEN Chairman), 18 I 1963, IHRC, ACEN, ibid. Vilis Māsēns (ACEN Chairman), Brutus Coste (ACEN Sec. General), Telegram to Tingfu F. Tsiang (Ambassador, Permanent Rep. of China, UN), 10 X 1957, IHRC, ACEN, b. 99, f. 15; Tingfu F. Tsiang to Vilis Māsēns, Brutus Coste, Telegram, 14 X 1957, ibid; Tingfu F. Tsiang to Stefan Korboński (ACEN Chairman), 23 I 1959, ibid.

91 A copy of the letter: Chiang Kai-shek (President, Republic of China, Taiwan) to ACEN, 21 IX 1960, IHRC, ACEN, b. 99, f. 15.

92 Tingfu F. Tsiang (Permanent Representative of China to the UN) to Ferenc Nagy (ACEN Chairman), 16 II 1962, IHRC, ACEN, b. 89, f. 7.

93 Ku Cheng-kang, Committee of Civic Organizations of Republic of China in Support of Struggle for Freedom behind the Iron Curtain (Taipei), 16 XII 1963, IHRC, ACEN, b. 89, f. 7.

The following year, in his commemorative speech, the ACEN's Chairman (Ferenc Nagy) answered the question that must have been puzzling many Americans observing the ACEN's devotion to Asian Peoples' Freedom Day: "Why is the Chinese and Korean prisoners' choice of freedom of such great importance? The answer is, because it demonstrated with irrefutable clarity on whose side the oppressed Chinese and Koreans stand when they are given a free choice. As we all remember, the Hungarian people expressed the same truth in their Revolution of 1956."[94] When one considers the fact that approximately two hundred thousand Hungarians fled the country after the Soviet invasion, and that the said prisoners (mostly Chinese) were resettled to Taiwan, this argument seems to be a bit blown out of proportion both in scale and the nature of exile. His speech, however, went beyond slogans.

Nagy said that the loyalty of the oppressed peoples of Asia and Europe to the cause of the free world was one of the most important political and strategic Western assets in the global struggle. "Yet paradoxically, the importance of these assets is too easily forgotten in the Free World." There was an inclination in the West to believe that the resistance spirit of the captive peoples presented more dangers than opportunities, Nagy continued: "[H]ence a desire of some western policy planners to see the captive people more content, more resigned to their fate" – less anti-Communist, less pro-Western, less desirous of liberty. This way they hoped that the regimes would have less fear of revolt, would employ less harsh measures and would be more eager to liberalize their rule. The former prime minister of Hungary warned that this was a false assumption.[95]

> The minute the captive peoples will grow content with Communist rule, the strategic position of the Free World will become infinitely worse; the instant the captive peoples will resign to their fate, there will be less security for the West and also less freedom for the captives themselves. ... It seems to us indeed that while Europe is the place where the forces of freedom could in the coming years suffer decisive defeats, it is in Asia, China to be exact, where they could win at the earliest time important victories.[96]

So, as the ACEN's Chairman was criticizing the liberalizing trends in U.S. foreign policy, he was strongly endorsing firmer engagement in Asia. While it would be

---

94 Address by Ferenc Nagy, Chairman of the ACEN on the Eighth Anniversary of Freedom Day, ACEN Extraordinary (96th) meeting of the Plenary Assembly, New York, 23 I 1962, IHRC, ACEN, b. 89, f. 7.

95 Ibid.

96 Aleksander Kütt (Estonia), Rapporteur, The Eight Anniversary of Freedom Day. Draft Declaration introduced at the (96th) Extraordinary Meeting of the Plenary Assembly, held in New York City, on 23 January 1962 – adopted as: ACEN Freedom Day Declaration, 3 I 1962, ibid.

two-and-a-half years before the Gulf of Tonkin resolution, this growing involvement and PR campaign must be seen in the light of the growing American entanglement in Vietnam. While it begun under Truman, and was continued by Eisenhower (mainly in the form of assistance to the French), it was during the Kennedy administration that American presence was further expanded.

Speaking on behalf of the ACEN, its Chairman highlighted the "global character of the struggle between forces of liberty and tyranny" and the futility of efforts to solve the Cold War tensions as separate issues, "be it Berlin, or Laos." In the same speech Nagy was able to make an argument that the Anti-Communist Freedom Day was also "a most effective rebuttal of the tendencies in the non-Communist would to lend undeserved prestige to the Red Chinese regime by admitting it into the UN." He then called for the captive people to "hold it their duty to warn the countries of Africa and Asia, especially the newly independent ones, against their tendency to disregard the Soviet brand of colonialism, whose maintenance and expansion threatens their own security and their very existence as independent nations." This was all in line with U.S. foreign policy of the time. But that would change in the coming decade.

Using the 23 January celebrations, joined by the Chinese, Korean and Cuban (exile) representatives, the ACEN's Chairman sent a letter to President Kennedy.

> We respectfully express our conviction that the present doctrinal strife and the popular ferment in the Soviet empire present the West with a new opportunity to reactivate the issue of the captive countries. We therefore trust that your recent call, Mr. President, on the UN to debate colonialism in full and apply the principle of free choice and the practice of free plebiscites in every part of the globe will soon be followed by concrete American initiatives. [...] And we assure you, Mr. President, of the solidarity of the captive European peoples with the cause of the Free World as long as the Free World actively supports their inalienable right to self-determination.[97]

Given the fact that "Soviet colonialism" was one of the FEC's most avidly supported initiatives this appeal neatly combines the agendas of both the exiles and their American mentors. How was it related to U.S. policy? It seems as if it offered additional legitimacy for more decisive actions in Asia. By the end of 1962, U.S.-Soviet relations entered a new phase in the aftermath of the Cuban Missile crisis. The globalist notion was soon dropped, but the expressions of solidarity between the captive Europeans and Asians continued.

When commemorating the ninth anniversary of the 22,000 refugees reaching Taiwan, the ACEN sounded a more belligerent note than before:

---

97 Ferenc Nagy (ACEN Chairman) to Hon. John F. Kennedy (U.S. President), 23 I 1962, IHRC, ACEN, b. 89, f. 7.

> We are here to declare the determination of our captive nations of East-Central Europe to make all necessary sacrifices in order to recover their freedom and national independence, as well as their human dignity, because as Woodrow Wilson said 'freedom is more precious than peace.' For us, all those who are fighting for the sacred, inalienable human rights, no matter in which part of the globe they may be, are soldiers on one and the same front, defensing the same ideal: the front of liberty.

The ACEN quoted Patrick Henry ("Give me liberty, or give me death") as well as Abraham Lincoln and Benjamin Franklin.[98] The same month, the ACEN recognized the book by Dalai Lama, *My Land and My People*, to remind its audiences of Tibetan resistance.[99] What was not discussed was U.S. involvement in the 1956 to 1957 uprising that was eventually crushed by 1959 and ended with Dalai Lama's escape to India.[100] Obviously, Asian People's Freedom Day was a vehicle to rally support for anti-Communist struggles on this continent. As the events of 1963 unfolding in Vietnam proved, the policies and leaders chosen by Americans for support in the region made further engagement there unavoidable.

In October 1963 Sidzikauskas traveled to Saigon and met with Ngo Dinh Diem, before traveling to Taiwan to meet with Chiang Kai-shek. Ostensibly, the reason for his journey was the ninth APACL conference that took place in Saigon. This was not the first time the ACEN representatives were present at the APACL conference, as Sidzikauskas travelled in 1961 to a conference in Manila. The conference of 1963 in Saigon adopted a resolution on expanding the liberation movement behind the Iron Curtain and against the Soviet intrigue of "peaceful coexistence." It stated that "this freedom day movement aiming at tearing down the Iron Curtain has now become a global collective effort.[101] In order to expand the international impact of the commemorative activities for the tenth anniversary of Freedom Day the APACL's China chapter invited the NCNC, ACEN, and the Exiled People's Committee in West Germany to come to Taipei.

---

98 Dr. George M. Dimitrov (Chairman, ACEN), Opening remarks: 105th (Extraordinary) Meeting of the Plenary Assembly in Commemoration of the 9th Anniversary of Freedom Day, 23 I 1963, IHRC, ACEN, b. 89, f. 7; Chiang Chun (Secretary General to the President of the Republic of China) to George M. Dimitrov, 23 II 1963 (Taipei), ibid.

99 Dr. Jozef Lettrich (Czechoslovakia, member of the Gen. Comm., chairman of the Information Committee), Statement on the ACEN Book Citation for January 1963, ibid.

100 Kenneth Conboy, James Morrison, *The CIA's Secret War in Tibet* (Lawrence: Kansas: University of Kansas Press, 2002).

101 Ku Cheng-kang, (Chairman Committee of Civic Organizations of Republic of China in Support of Struggle for Freedom behind the Iron Curtain, Taipei), Letter of 16 XII 1963, with attachment, a 4-page brochure: "Note on the Celebration of the 10th anniversary of Freedom Day and the Expanded movement in support of captive people to regain their freedom." IHRC, ACEN, b. 89, f. 7.

The details of Sidzikauskas' meetings with Diem and Chiang Kai-shek were not available in the examined archival collections. General appreciation for the opportunity was sent to the President of the APACL who fostered this meeting at the time of the Lithuanian's participation in the League's conference in Saigon.[102] These meetings were preceded by a Ferenc Nagy's trip to Tokyo in October 1962, and to Taiwan where he also met with Chiang. This was followed up by Aleksander Kütt going to Taiwan in January 1964 (for the Freedom Day celebrations), from where he also visited Quemoy – the site of Chinese Communist assault in 1958.[103]

For the ACEN, contacts with the leaders who were willing to strengthen its voice in the UN were precious, as the exile Assembly's mission was to lobby the free world to keep applying pressure on the Soviet Union. The United Nations was thus an important forum for that.

Judging by the accounts of earlier meetings – for example during the ACEN's world tour of 1959[104] – the meetings were likely of little political substance other than supporting the case of captive nations in the UN. Their aim, as seen by the FEC, which paid for the travel, was mostly purely "white" anti-Communist propaganda, as opposed to grey (unattributed), or black ("fake news").[105]

The cover of this book features a photograph depicting Saigon's city hall decorated by a banner saying: "Welcome the ACEN Delegation. Discussion of [anti-] Communist refugees of East Central Europe." The photo was taken on 26 February 1959. A detailed account of this day given by Stefan Korboński seems to support the above thesis. While taken aback by the Diem portraits saturating the city landscape, the ACEN delegate described the meeting attended by 3,000 people. Chaperoned by Tran Tam (Secretary General of the APACL) the Pole was told that

102 Sidzikauskas to Ku Cheng-kang, 18 XII 1963, HIA, RFE/RL CF: A, b. 145, f. 2.

103 Gadomski, *Zgromadzenie Europejskich* ..., 44–45; Sidzikauskas to Ku Cheng-kang, 18 XII 1963, HIA, RFE/RL CF: A, b. 145, f. 2.

104 The ACEN Delegation included: Korboński, Kővágó, Māsēns. The representatives visited Japan, Korea, Taiwan, Philippines, Australia, Singapore, Malaya, reaching Vietnam on 24 February 1959. In the Philippines, the exiles were received as official guests of the City of Manila, and special public session of the Municipal Board of Manila was held to which they were invited and greeted with a standing ovation. They met with the country's president (Carlos P. Garcia), secretary for foreign affairs as well as the mayor of the city. Each of them assured ACEN of their support for the captive nations cause in the UN. From Vietnam they continued on to visit India, Pakistan, Turkey, Greece, Italy. Detailed account of this trip is provided in: Korboński, *W imieniu Polski* ..., 377–498; ACEN Delegation Tour in Far East and Europe, *ACEN News* 46–47 (January-February 1959): 17–19; ACEN Delegation Tour in Far East and Europe, *ACEN News* 48 (March 1959): 15–17.

105 Mazurkiewicz, *Uchodźcy* ..., 32.

interest was so great because the Vietnamese wanted to hear about one white-skinned nation being colonized by another white-skinned nation. According to Tran Tam – most listeners were Saigon intellectuals and students. Korboński spent most of the two-and-a-half hour-long meeting discussing the Polish case during World War II and immediately thereafter finishing with the topic of fraudulent elections. The audience interrupted his speech a number of times voicing their understanding and relating the Polish story to their own encounters with communism.[106] Solidarity was in the air, and the meeting (and the ACEN tour of the region) definitely served the aims of the APACL.

With regards to the ACEN's political agenda, the exiles mentioned meetings with members of Vietnamese parliament and government including Secretary of State for Foreign Affairs (Vu Van Mau), State Secretary of at the Presidency, and the Minister of Information who sponsored a dinner in honor of the ACEN delegation.[107]

In 1964, the tenth annual observance of Asian Peoples Freedom Day in the United States was different both in its character and the guest list. Neither the Filipino, Vietnamese nor Chinese delegates could make it.[108] Only the Korean representatives confirmed their intention to come (Woonsang Choi, counselor, representing the permanent observer of the Republic of Korea to the UN).[109] Present and vocal at the celebrations on 23 January 1964, however, were Peter H. Dominick, a U.S. Senator from Colorado, Adolf A. Berle Jr. (listed as former U.S. ambassador to Brazil, though his previous role in the FEC was not mentioned), and representative Robert Taft, Jr. of Ohio. The list of speakers included Stefan Korboński, Władysław Michalak (ICFTUE, Chairman of the delegation, former President of the Federation of Christian Trade Unions in Poland) and Vaclav Majer (Czechoslovakia). The paper presented during the meeting by George

106 Korboński, *W imieniu Polski*, 438–440.

107 The exiles met with refugees from North Vietnam and members of the Cultural Freedom Association and Victims of Communism organization. "ACEN Delegation Tour in Far East and Europe," *ACEN News* 48 (March 1959): 17.

108 Jacinto Castel Borja (Ambassador Extraordinary and Plenipotentiary, Permanent Representative of the Philippines to the UN) to Aleksander Kütt (Chairman, ACEN), 3 I 1964, IHRC, ACEN, b. 89, f. 7; Tran Ngo Thach [Tran Van Dinh] (Charge d'Affaires, Permanent Observer of the Republic of Vietnam to the UN) to Aleksander Kütt (Chairman, ACEN), 15 I 1964, ibid; Helen Liu (Secretary, Permanent Mission of the Republic of China to the UN), to Aleksander Kütt, 15 I 1964, ibid. In the latter case, Chun-Ming Chang – minister plenipotentiary representing permanent rep. of the RoC to the UN did come.

109 Edmund Gaspar (Deputy Sec. General) to Dr. Woonsang Choi (Counselor, Permanent Mission of the Republic of Korea to the UN), 14 I 1964, IHRC, ACEN, b. 89, f. 7.

[Georgi] Petkov dealt mostly with East Central Europe.[110] An appropriate declaration regarding Freedom Day was also presented by Sidzikauskas.[111]

If the absence of the Chinese ambassador Liu Chieh (Permanent Representative of China to the UN) was an indication of a crisis in its cooperation with the ACEN, it must have been a temporary one, because in 1965 both he and the ambassador Nguyen Phu Duc (Permanent Observer of Vietnam to the UN) joined the ACEN in commemorating the eleventh anniversary of Chinese refugees reaching Taiwan. The list of American politicians was much shorter. The U.S. was represented by Arthur G. McDowell, Executive Secretary of the Council Against Communist Aggression, and former congressman Walter H. Judd, a great friend of the ACEN and participant at the 11th APACL session in Manila (1965) representing American Afro-Asian Educational Exchange.[112] The permanent representative of the Republic of China to the UN addressed the ACEN-organized commemorations of Asian People's Freedom Day repeatedly until its seventeenth Anniversary.[113]

The Free Europe Committee "fully supported" these initiatives, which included seeking the participation of American Ambassador Arthur J. Goldberg (the Permanent representative of the U.S. to the UN) in the ACEN-organized twelfth Anniversary of the founding of the Anti-Communist Freedom Day.[114] On the oc-

110 Denial of the Rights and Freedoms of the Working People in East-Central Europe.

111 Provisional Agenda of the 112th (extraordinary) meeting of the Plenary Assembly. Carnegie [International] Center Auditorium of Foreign Policy Association, NYC, 23 I 1964, IHRC, ACEN, b. 89, f. 7.

112 ACEN Invitation to the extraordinary Plenary Meeting on Jan. 23, 1965 in commemoration of Freedom Day, 18 I 1965, IHRC, ACEN, b. 89, f. 7; Arthur G. McDowell to Brutus Coste (ACEN), 8 II 1965, ibid. "I hope to write an editorial for our *Union Journal*, inspired by that meeting on the 23rd. You may not remember that it was our Union Convention in 1953 at which Chris Emmet broke and apparently prevented the scandal of the appointment of Kristina [V. K. Krishna] Menon as the UN head of the prisoner examination board in Korea. We were the only organization at the moment that would dare publicly say and wire Eisenhower our flat declaration that Kristina [Krishna] Menon was a Communist and a Soviet stooge, of necessity[y]. A.G.M [McDowell]."

113 Vaclovas Sidzikauskas (Chairman ACEN) to Liu Chieh (Republic of Korea, Ambassador to UN), 28 XII 1965, IHRC, ACEN, b. 99, f. 15. He did come, see: thank you message: Sidzikauskas to Chieh, 24 I 1966, ibid. ; Feliks Gadomski (Acting Sec. General) to Liu Chieh (Ambassador Extraordinary and Plenipotentiary, Permanent Representative to UN, Permanent Mission of China to UN), 30 I 1968, IHRC, ACEN, b. 5, f. 3.

114 Mucio F. Delgado (Director, Exile Political organization Division) to Ms. Garaventa, 14 I 1966, HIA, RFE/RL CF: A, b. 145, f. 3. In 1966 the ACEN guests – all permanent representatives of Asian nations to the UN – included: Liu Chieh (Republic of China), Yong-Shik Kim (Republic of Korea), Nguyen Duy Lien (South Vietnam).

casion, the Chinese delegate said: "[T]hat your assembly should hold this special meeting year after year is, as you have so well said 'a clear demonstration of the solidarity of the peoples of Europe and Asia in the struggle for freedom and justice in the world.'"[115] In October 1971 the United Nations General Assembly, against the wishes of the United States, voted in favor of admitting Communist China to the UN, which included granting it a seat on the Security Council. The ACEN lost an ally in the UN, but at this point in the organization's history it was just another nail in the coffin. The holiday, now called World Freedom Day is still celebrated in Taiwan and in South Korea (on 23 January).

Commemorating Asian Peoples' Freedom Day was part of a larger plan by the ACEN to rally Asian support for its cause in the UN, to maintain East Central Europe on the agenda of international relations at a time when the world's attention was moving to South-East Asia. Joining their cause with the global agenda was thus a pragmatic solution. It was also in line with the FEC's propaganda planning, which in the 1960s – the decade of decolonization – included Asia, Africa, but also, in the post-Cuban Revolution era, Latin America.

115 C.M. [Chun-Ming] Chang (Permanent mission of the Rep. of China to the UN) to Alfrēds Berzins (Chairman ACEN), 4 II 1970, IHRC, ACEN, b. 99, f. 15.

7 "Naciones Cautivas Europeas" – ACEN in Latin America

The ACEN's activities in Latin America fall under the category of complex U.S. relations with the countries of the region and the fading of the wartime alliance. In Asia ACEN cooperated with local anti-Communists. In Africa, it had almost no local contacts except ephemeral plans for an office in Egypt, and a one-man (Zygmunt Zawadowski) – led effort in Lebanon. By contrast, south of the Rio Grande the exile Assembly had at its disposal both East Central European ethnic communities and post-World-War Two exile networks. It enabled the ACEN to establish regional offices and carry out a variety of programs. The prime reason for the ACEN's engagement with Latin American countries was to seek their support at the UN, evident from the correspondence with its local representatives and accounts of meetings with political leaders held between 1956 and 1965.

For the Free Europe Committee, the mission was to disenchant Latin American progressives and oppositionists from "toying with communism."[1] Truitt, in his 1962 report, wrote: "Drawing on its special assets acquired in operations to Eastern Europe, in the years 1957–1959 FEC launched a number of exploratory programs designed to add trained East European exiles to the western order of battle in the uncommitted areas."[2] In fact, the FEC had developed a Latin American pamphlet project, in cooperation with Latin American exiles, at least two years earlier. By 1956, the FEC was advancing its anti-Soviet colonialism agenda by distributing Spanish-language pamphlets with the help of the ICFTUE (most importantly under Sacha Volman),[3] and reaching out to the Inter-American Regional Organization of Workers (one of five regional organizations of the ICFTU).[4]

---

1 Edward McHale to Bernard Yarrow, FEC Memorandum: Latin American Pamphlet Project, 18 V 1955, HIA, RFE/RL CF: A, b. 274, f.: FEC Inc. LA Pamphlet Project 1956.

2 G.A. Truitt to John Richardson, Jr., Operations in the Uncommitted Areas, 19 III 1962, HIA, RFE/RL CF: A, b. 200, f. 3.

3 See HIA, RFE/RL CF: A, b. 274, f.: FEC Inc. LA Pamphlet Project 1956 and the following folder for 1957–1958.

4 Inter-American Regional Organization of Workers (ORIT) – International Center of Free Trade Unionists in Exile Agreement, HIA, RFE/RL CF: A, b. 274, f: FEC Inc. LA Pamphlet Project 1957–58. It included all free unions of North, Central and South America and Caribbean totaling in 25 million members, 15 in U.S. and Canada along. Its headquarters were in Mexico. There were no American or Canadian full-time officers. More on ICFTU and ORIT in: Robert J. Alexander, *International Labor Organizations and Organized labor in Latin America and the Caribbean. A History* (Santa Barbara, CA-Denver, CO-Oxford, England: Praeger, ABC Clio, 2009), 147–150.

https://doi.org/10.1515/9783110661002-011

The U.S. realized that the Soviets were winning support from the peoples in Latin America because they employed propaganda concepts that were hard to argue with (peace, education, workers' rights) and used seemingly harmless proxies: the World Peace Council, International Union of Students, and the World Federation of Trade Unions. The FWOD took on this example and enlisted the support of 12 affiliated international organizations ("largely private") that focused on non-controversial issues like self-determination, social progress, humanism, trade unionism, student cooperation, and freedom of the press.[5] The East Central European exiles were an excellent resource for explaining what communism meant in practice: for their homelands, about the methods of Communist subversion, to the false promises of economic and social advancement, to the hardships of daily life under communism. An additional asset was that they were not tainted by either colonial or imperial pasts in their dealings with Latin American countries.

The FWOD was originally engaged in assisting East Central European exile Christian Democrats to work with their Latin American counterparts to resist and expose Communist infiltration.[6] The link between the American program in this regard and the ACEN was established via the CDUCE. Some of its members, István Barankovics, Konrad Sieniewicz and Janusz Śleszyński, were also involved in the works of the ACEN.[7] It must be emphasized that the issue of American support for Christian Democrats in Latin America is multifaceted and much larger than the exile operations. It spans across meetings facilitated by the CDUCE, between the FEC and politicians such as Eduardo Frei Montalva (Chile) and Rafael Caldera (Venezuela),[8] to the clandestine support of the Christian democratic parties at the election time, and intelligence operations, coverage of which goes beyond the scope of this book.

In the narrower context of ACEN representations, the trend to seek support of the Christian Democrats was most in evidence in the networks and local contacts

5 FWOD, Quarterly Planning Report, October–December 1961, 26 II 1962, HIA, RFE/RL CF: A, b. 200, f. 3.

6 István Barankovics, Plan for enhancing CDUCE potential, HIA, RFE/RL CF: A, b. 161, f. 1.

7 Janusz Śleszyński (CDUCE) to John Leich (FEC), 3 V 1960, HIA, RFE/RL CF: A, b. 274, f.: FEC Latin American Program (journalism) 1959–1963. The folder contains reports of visits by the CDUCE representatives (Sieniewicz, Barankovics), and the Report on First International Congress of Working Newspapermen and First Latin American Congress of Free Press. On Śleszyński and Sieniewicz, see: Paweł Ziętara, "Strategia konia trojańskiego: aparat bezpieczeństwa PRL wobec emigracyjnego Stronnictwa Pracy," *in:* Ziętara, *Anders, Korboński, Sieniewicz ...*, 103–155.

8 Piotr H. Kosicki, "Christian Democracy's Global Cold War," in: Piotr H. Kosicki, Sławomir Łukasiewicz (eds.), *Christian Democracy Across the Iron Curtain: Europe Redefined* (Cham, Switzerland: Palgrave Macmillan, 2018), 221–255.

that the exiles built beyond the established FEC framework. For example, in Uruguay, mostly thanks to Juan (Jan) Pawłowski, and in close cooperation with Hungarian exile organizations, the ACEN secured cooperation with the Movimiento Cristiano del Uruguay Pro Defensa de la Libertad y los Derechos Humanos (MCU), as well as other anti-Communist organizations. From September to October 1961 it helped the exiles promote the pictorial exhibit on the crimes of communism, which had been touring Latin American countries since 1957.[9]

The ACEN tried to expose and counteract Soviet-planted content in the public discourse,[10] using the assistance of friendly local organizations, provided they subscribed to the same ideals and upheld democratic standards.[11] In Mexico, the ACEN representative reported interest in cooperation coming from the Union Civica International.[12] Luis Roberto Hidalgo of El Salvador was interested in the operations of Centro Latinoamericano de Informaciones Democraticas (CLID).[13] At times, their names sounded familiar, like the Brazilian Center for a Free Europe, where the Rio de Janeiro delegates often met.[14] A report on the ACEN activities submitted to the FEC in the summer of 1962 confirms that the associations, offering support to the exiles (including material assistance for propaganda campaigns) was subject to the Committee's approval.[15]

The exiles were aware that at least in some countries they could have been perceived as "rightists," "conservatives," or "reactionaries," something which they sought to avoid. Their goal was to reach young, educated intellectuals

---

9 Magdalena Broquetas San Martin, *Demócratas y nacionalistas. La reacción de las derechas en el Uruguay (1959–1966)*, Tesis de Doctorado en Historia, Facultad de Humanidades y Ciencias de la Educación, Universidad Nacional de La Plata, 2013), 84–85, avaliable: http://www.memoria.fahce.unlp.edu.ar/tesis/te.879/te.879.pdf, accessed: 18 IX 2019.

10 Among the examples ACEN members cited: Alliance of Latin American Patriots against Colonialism and Imperialism, 1957; Stalin Peace Prize by Circle of Mexican Students, 1955; and organization of initiatives such as: Latin American Conference for National Sovereignty, Economic Emancipation and Peace et al. Brutus Coste to Simon Ance, telegram 1 III 1961, IHRC, ACEN, b. 151, f. 4; Memorandum "not for distribution", 27 II 1961, IHRC, ACEN, b. 151, f. 4. This unsigned document was most likely prepared in the ACEN's office.

11 Edmund Gaspar to Jerzy Skoryna-Lipski, 10 VIII 1962, IHRC, ACEN, b. 56, f. 1.

12 Jerzy Skoryna Lipski to ACEN, NY, 21 XII 1956, ibid. See also: Gülstorff, "Warming Up a Cooling War …," 39.

13 Luis Roberto Hidalgo (El Savlador) to Edmund Gaspar, 2 IV 1965, IHRC, ACEN, b. 58, f. 8.

14 See IHRC, ACEN, b. 47, f. 10.

15 "We would appreciate your advice if the collaboration of our Representative with the abovementioned organizations [Liga de Defensa Juridica Internacional, Asociaciones Continentales Pro-Liberacion de las Naciones Cautivas] could be approved." Dep. Sec. Gen. ACEN to J.W. Brinkley, FEC, Memorandum: Activities of ACEN-representatives, 9 VIII 1962, IHRC, ACEN, b. 44, f. 13.

with their message on what they learned communism meant in practice.[16] Via films, exhibits, photos and accounts of suffering inflicted on the captive peoples of all classes, the exiles realized that the Catholic Church in Latin America was their most natural (if not their only) ally. As the ACEN representative in Mexico learned, the entire exile information campaign could not mention the supporting role of the U.S. Otherwise, trust would be lost, and the exiles would be branded as American agents.[17]

Many of the ACEN representatives closely cooperated with the Catholic clergy. The ACEN's representative in Colombia – Myk M. Tamosiunas (Lithuanian) – was a priest. On multiple occasions, the events organized by the ACEN representatives began with a "solemn mass" dedicated to the victims of communism,[18] wreath-laying ceremonies organized to commemorate important anniversaries, or Captive Nations Weeks, which often included religious leaders.[19] In this regard, the FEC avoided interfering with programs and considered them to be parts of ongoing cultural programs. Where it did have a stake was in the world of the media.

The ACEN headquarters in New York sent materials to its delegations and representatives asking that they try to distribute them locally and then report back with clippings and any available feedback. These materials ranged from current developments behind the Iron Curtain to reminders of important anniversaries related to the Communist domination of East Central Europe, as well as cultural content aimed at ethnic communities.[20] As mentioned before, the ACEN's publications and abbreviated versions of its thematic reports were translated into Spanish and distributed with the help of local representatives.[21]

---

16 The adjectives Gaspar feared being branded with were: "derechistas," "reacionarios," "conservadora". Edmund Gaspar to Rev. M. Tamosiunas (Medellin), 20 I 1964, IHRC, ACEN, b. 50, f. 1.
17 Jerzy Skoryna-Lipski (Mexico) to Edmund Gaspar, 24 V 1962, IHRC, ACEN, b. 56, f. 1.
18 Jozef Lettrich to Alfonso Mejia, 14 XI 1968, IHRC, ACEN, b. 50, f. 5; Feliks Gadomski to Alfonso Mejia, 1 XI 1968, ibid; Jerzy Skoryna Lipski to ACEN NY, 5 X 1956, IHRC, ACEN, b. 56, f. 1.
19 See: Photos of Captive Nations Week, 1966 (Buenos Aires), IHRC, ACEN, b. 46, f. 5.
20 Edmund Gaspar to Luis R. Hidalgo (El Savlador), IHRC, ACEN, b. 58, f. 8; Luis R. Hidalgo Z. to Edmund Gaspar, 18 X 1966, ibid.
21 For example, a 59-page Spanish version of *Hungary Under Soviet Rule: Hungria Bajo la Dominacion Sovietica*. Some publications were released only in Spanish *¿Que pueden Esperar los Obreros del Sistema Comunista?* (Montevideo: ACEN, 1963). A Portuguese version of the nine reports on communist takeover in the Captive Countries was published in Brazil, and in Spanish in Argentina. For a detailed list of Spanish and Portuguese language publications see list: "ACEN Publications as of October 15, 1963," in: ACEN, *Ninth Session, 1962–1963, Resolutions, Reports, Organization* (New York: ACEN, 1964), 153–155.

From 1959 to 1963 there were also programs for Latin America run by the International Federation of Free Journalists (Free News Service, FNS).[22] In this case, the link with the ACEN was established via Bolesław Wierzbiański. However, both the ACEN and FNS used similar sources of information and therefore much of the content provided to audiences in Latin America overlapped.

The Free Europe Organizations and Publications Department (FEOP) set a separate agenda for the Hungarian Committee. The FEC wanted to encourage them toward political action so as to mobilize an estimated 200,000 Hungarians living in Latin America. "Kovács and Varga are concluding a round-robin trip designed to secure the organizational base."[23] A similar plan was under construction for the Balts, as their operations also overlapped with the ACEN's.

Within a year, the list of FWOD associations encompassed a variety of programs: press (International Federation of Free Journalists of Central and Eastern Europe and Baltic and Balkan Countries/from Central and Eastern Europe, FNS, International Feature Service, academic placements (Paderewski Foundation, Kossuth Foundation, Center for International Placement), youth (Institute for International Youth Affairs, Association of Hungarian Students in North America), "ideological warfare section" (including projects like: Peace with Freedom, prepared with the assistance of Christian Democratic Union, International Center for Social Research, Committee for Self-Determination, Christian Democratic Center); education section (within it: International Advisory Council) and special projects on Berlin, atomic weapon testing, and the World Council of Churches conference in New Delhi or the Helsinki Youth Festival.[24] The ACEN's projects were not listed within these. Yet the ACEN touched all of these areas – as evidenced in the correspondence with its respective delegates.

In the ACEN engagement in Latin America three periods are easily discernible: from initial attempts at establishing exile representations in 1956 to the victory of the Cuban Revolution (1959); from the Revolution to the American intervention in the Dominican Republic (1965); and the phasing out of all operations by 1972.

The first phase should be considered mostly within the context of the ACEN's general program for the free world. It included expanding the Assembly's outreach, promoting its views, lobbying for international political pressure to force USSR to allow free elections and withdraw its military forces from East Cen-

---

22 See HIA, RFE/RL CF: A, b. 274, f. FEC Latin American Program (journalism) 1959–1963.
23 Robert W. Minton to C. D. Jackson, Two Years of FEOP, 16 III 1961, DDEL, C.D. Jackson Papers, b. 53, f.: FEC 1961 (2).
24 List of Projects July 1961-June 1962: FWOD, 1 V 1962, HIA, RFE/RL CF: A, b. 200, f. 3. The updated list of 10 X 1961 found in the same folder mentions also PEN Writers in Exile, ibid.

tral Europe. The Hungarian tragedy gave the ACEN a powerful weapon in its political warfare. From October 1956 onward, the lessons of the Hungarian Revolution had reverberated through all meetings, media releases, and commentaries expressed in its print publications and radio broadcasts.

7.1 Between Hungary and Cuba (1956–1959)

With no Soviet tanks, secret police, or workers' party members parachuted from Moscow in sight, before 1959 Soviet communism in Latin America sounded like something alien. Even though there were communist parties it was not until the victory of Cuban revolution, with Castro seeking protection from Moscow, that the Cold War reached Latin America. Yet, the Soviet Union was oceans away, it did not pose a direct threat, and the American narrative of the horrific dangers of communism was not necessarily understood as a warning against a totalitarian regime but rather as a way for America to maintain its paternalism and patterns of economic exploitation.

On 17 September 1956, Vilis Māsēns, Stefan Korboński and Constantin Vişoianu began their trip to Latin American countries (Brazil, Argentina, Uruguay, Chile and Cuba). The trip had begun after the Polish workers' rebellion in Poznań and before the Soviet intervention in Hungary. The Castro brothers, Che Guevara, Camilo Cienfuegos and other members of the Granma crew were still in Mexico, as the three displaced European leaders left for their Latin American tour. "Dispiritedness in ACEN, especially in the Polish delegation, caused by the lack of American reaction to the workers' rebellion in Poznań, was unburdened by the Free Europe Committee's initiative of a propaganda visit of the ACEN's delegation to the five Latin American countries."[25] Ostensibly, the aim of the trip was to inform the governments and societies there about the ACEN's existence, its aims, and to ask for support in the UN regarding Soviet troop withdrawal and the organization of free elections under international supervision. From the perspective of the present, it looks like a reconnaissance tour for mapping out potential means of expanding information programs.

On 8 October 1956, thus relatively late, the Acting Secretary of State signed an instruction for U.S. posts in Latin America classified as "secret" providing the complete itinerary as well as the purpose of the visit: "[T]o establish contacts

---

25 "Friendly reception everywhere. Received by four presidents, press conferences, radio and tv interviews (170 press clippings brought back to NY)." Gadomski, *Zgromadzenie Europejskich* ..., 29.

with refugees from the Iron Curtain countries." The instruction contained description of the ACEN as "the most prominent organization of refugees." It said that the missions were "to extend appropriate courtesies to Mr. Māsēns," wrongly identified as a Lithuanian (he was a Latvian), as well as to "report to the Department on the impact, effect, and coverage of his visit." According to this instruction signed by Herbert Hoover, Jr., from 12 to 20 October 1956 Māsēns was supposed to visit Chile (Santiago), Panama City, Mexico City, with Havana being his last stop.[26] "According to a controlled American source" Māsēns did not arrive in Panama as scheduled, and no one from the embassy met him there, which was dutifully reported to Washington.[27] A similar note arrived from Venezuela – no record of Māsēns' visit was reported.[28]

Without the exiles' memoirs it would be very difficult to understand what happened in early October to the Māsēns trip that put embassy staff in Latin America on alert. First, he was not alone. He headed the ACEN delegation consisting of two other representatives of the captive nations. His companions included a former Romanian Minister of Foreign Affairs (Constantin Vişoianu), and Stefan Korboński, a wartime civilian resistance leader and former Member of Parliament. The second reason that the delegation was not found paying any visits in Panama or Caracas was as simple as the fact that these places were just flight layovers. A detailed diary of the ACEN delegation's trip to Latin America was provided in Stefan Korboński's *W imieniu Polski Walczącej*. According to one of the ACEN's most prominent leaders, the goal of the trip was to inform governments and societies of South America about the ACEN and its goals, and then ask for their support in the UN by proposing a resolution demanding that the USSR withdraw its troops from the nine captive nations and thus provide convenient conditions for free elections under international supervision. Korboński provided an outline and a list of meetings with his assessment. According to his itinerary[29] the group's itinerary was as follows:

---

26 (Hoover, Acting) Department of State Instruction: Visit of Zilas Māsēns, Chairman ACEN, CA-3073, 8 X 1956, Simpson Collection, 032 MĀSĒNS, ZILAS/10–856. Herbert Hoover, Jr. was the U.S. Under Secretary of State from Oct. 1954 to Feb. 1957.

27 Duncan A.D. Mackay to Dep. Of State, Despatch no. 169, ref.: CA-3037, Visit of Zilas Māsēns, Chairman of ACEN, 16 X 1956, Simpson Collection, 032 MĀSĒNS, ZILAS/10–1656.

28 Charles M. Urruela (Second Secretary of AmEmbassy, Caracas) to Department of State, Despatch no. 290, ref.: CA-3037, 19 X 1956, Simpson Collection, 032 MĀSĒNS, ZILAS/10–1956.

29 Korboński, *W imieniu Polski* ..., 278–333. Korboński misspelled some of the names – here corrected.

Tab. 3: Latin American Tour by ACEN Delegates, 17 IX–18 X 1956

Date: 1956	city	Meetings/audiences	Impact (by Korboński)
17 IX	VENEZUELA Caracas	None, layover flight; Romanian exile couple gave delegates a ride to the airport	
19–25 IX	BRAZIL Rio de Janeiro and São Paulo (23 IX)	– Meetings (part 1): Francisco Negaro de Lima – City Major, former Minister of Justice; José Parsifal Barroso – of the Ministry of Labor; Clóvis Salgado – Minister of Education. – Press: televised interview, press conference (20–21 IX) – Lectures to the émigré communities; greetings at airport; both formal and informal parties. – Meetings (part 2): Pedro Aurélio de Góis Monteiro – General, Judge on the Military Court, ambassadors representing other Latin American nations, Juscelino Kubitschek – President of Brazil, Minister of Finance, Minister of Foreign Affairs, papal nuncio, representative of the National Bank of Brazil; President of the Confederation to Defend Latin American Continent (Penna Boto); President of the Christian Democratic Union.	Wide coverage by the Brazilian press (14–22 IX): *O Jornal, Diário de Noite, O Globo, Correio de Manhã, Jornal do Commercio, O Jornal do Rio de Janeiro, Jornal do Brasil, Diários Assciados, O Estado de S. Paulo.* – Political leaders interested in conditions behind Iron Curtain (political, social, economic, international trade) – "We are received as representatives of East European nations whose voice is being faked by official delegations" – Proposal to establish ACEN office in Brazil, with the assistance of state authorities (already established: Anti-Communist Brazilian Crusade) – Uniting émigrés from various East Central European diasporas in Brazil – President of Brazil (partially of Czech origin) – promised support for the ACEN cause.
26–30 IX	URUGUAY Montevideo	– Meetings: Uruguayan League to Fight Communism; émigrés from East Central Europe; – Formal parties; talks with ambassadors of central and south American republics;	Press coverage; *El Día, El Plata, Acción, El Bien Público, El País, La Mañana* – Support for ACEN's mission promised by diplomatic representatives and Uruguayan Minister of Foreign Affairs

Tab. 3: Latin American Tour by ACEN Delegates, 17 IX–18 X 1956 *(Continued)*

Date: 1956	city	Meetings/audiences	Impact (by Korboński)
		– Martinez Bersetsche (organizer of the Atheneum press conference); Francisco Gamarra – Minister of Foreign Affairs; Dardo Regules, former Minister of the Interior, leader of the Christian Democratic Party; Carabajal Victorica and Eduardo Jiménez de Aréchaga – university professors.	– Wreath-laying ceremony at gen. Artigas' monument in Montevideo turns into a manifestation protesting the Soviet domination of East Central Europe (30 IX)
30 IX–8 X	ARGENTINA Buenos Aires	– Émigrés from East Central Europe – formal and informal parties; – Amigos de las Naciones Unidas, Vice Minister of Foreign Affairs and of the Interior present; papal nuncio (Mario Zanin); Laureano Landaburu, Minister of Interior Affairs; President Pedro Aramburu; Vice President – adm. Isaac Rojas; – Address to temporary parliament Junta Consultiva – Chief Justice of the Supreme Court Dr. Alfredo Orgaz – Institute of International Law, members of the Bar Chamber – U.S. ambassador and his deputy, as well as French ambassador (inquiry into meeting with Aramburu and Rojas).	– Press coverage; *La Prensa, Clarín, La Razón, Noticias Gráficas, Crítica, El Mundo, El Laborista, Democracia, La Epoca, La Nacion, Freie Presse, El Pueblo, Buenos Aires Herald* – Promise to support ACEN's cause in the UN from President and Junta Consultiva – Encouragement to open ACEN chapter in Argentina – Radio interviews – Wreath-laying ceremony at gen. San Martín's monument in Buenos Aires turns into a manifestation protesting the Soviet domination of East Central Europe (7 X).
9 X–11 X	CHILE Santiago	– Carlos Ibáñez – President of Chile – Papal Nuncio – archbishop Sebastian Baggio; Cardinal Caro – Ministry of Foreign Affairs staff; Roberto L. Aldunate (Envoy to UN), – Luis Valdes Larrain Chair of the Foreign Affairs Commission – party with thirty members of parliament in attendance	Press coverage: *El Mercurio, Las Ultimas Noticias, El Debate* – Carlos Ibáñez promised support for ACEN's initiative in the UN – Members of parliament discussed how to bring the case to the UN; Chile delegation's to UN promised support

Tab. 3: Latin American Tour by ACEN Delegates, 17 IX–18 X 1956 *(Continued)*

Date: 1956	city	Meetings/audiences	Impact (by Korboński)
		– Minister of Foreign Affairs – Osvaldo Sainte-Marie Soruco – Speaker of the Parliament Julio Durán – Speaker of the Senate Fernando Alessandri – Chinese Ambassador Pao-Yu Yin (Taiwan) – Congress for the Defense of Culture (intellectuals, trade unionists, liberals) – Émigré groups, including Catholic priests.	– ACEN encouraged to open its chapter in Chile.
12 X–13 X	PERU Lima	None, layover flight; Latvian exiles –sightseeing trip. Left business cards at the Ministry of Foreign Affairs	Press coverage: *El Comercio*
13 X	PANAMA Panama City	None, layover flight – brief break at the airport	None
14 X	USA Miami, FL	None, one day layover	None
15 X–17 X	CUBA Havana	– Minister of Foreign Affairs – Gonzalo Güell – President of Cuba Fulgencio Batista and Núñez Portuondo – Cuba's delegate to the UN – Émigrés	Press coverage: *Diario de la Marina, El Mundo, Alerta, Informacion, Prensa Libre* – Cuba's non-recognition of seizure of the Baltic states, non-recognition of Warsaw government – confirmed – Support in the UN promised
18 X	USA, Miami FL to Washington D.C.	None	None

The discussions held with Latin American interlocutors described by Korboński focused on sharing information about life under the Soviet yoke, the origin and activities of the ACEN, but also a lot of time and attention was devoted to the recent rebellion in Poznań. The Polish workers' protest focused much of the attention on Poland. What struck Korboński was the great interest with which

Latin American leaders listened to his descriptions of the situation in Poznań, to accounts of communization of Eastern Europe, as well as how little possibility there seemed to be for communization of their own continent. The Communists ware so far away that they seemingly posed no threat to countries like Brazil.

Some of the people that the ACEN delegates met could hardly be called democratically oriented. Most relied on U.S. support. How did the exiles negotiate support against the communist regime from a representative of another regime (like Batista)? Korboński explained his doubts in his account of the tour. "Can a democrat by conviction and by practice ask a dictator like Batista for political support?" The positive answer in his view stemmed from the fact that support for East Central European nations' sovereignty was a steady part of Cuba's foreign policy, that had not changed under Batista. He added that on the same grounds Poles in the West would support the Warsaw (Communist) government with regard to Poland's western borders.[30]

Writing his memoir in the mid-1960s, Korboński summarized the accomplishments of the tour saying it had revitalized interest in the case of independence for captive nations in the South American states, had brought promises of support for the ACEN's actions in the UN, strengthened the relationship with émigrés from the nine captive nations, and established cooperation with local ethnic organizations. Korboński summarized the tour offering the following statistics: five countries visited, including five capitals, two in passing, meetings with four presidents, ten ministers, three speakers of the respective parliaments, tens of dignitaries, a few ambassadors from the region, three papal nuncios, over 100 members of parliaments, including delivering one address to the parliament, six press conferences, three radio interviews, and two TV shows. Korboński himself gave ten public lectures, and not only to Poles. Together they collected 117 press clippings on captive nations and their visits,[31] with all the clippings meticulously collected by the delegates.

In October 1956 the Department of State received the accounts from its foreign service offices from Montevideo, Santiago, Buenos Aires and Havana. The report of 18 October in Montevideo was created two weeks after the ACEN delegates left Uruguay. The American Ambassador (Patterson) relied on the account of the Lithuanian Minister, Kazimieras Graužinis, who admitted taking care of Māsēns, which included taking him to the foreign office, holding a press conference and giving a talk at the Montevideo Atheneum.[32] According to Graužinis,

30 Korboński, *W imieniu Polski ...*, 330.

31 Ibid., 333.

32 A young Lithuanian member (Vastakas) who worked for the state-owned telephone services "served as a figurehead for the Lithuanian legation chief – Graužinis, who did not wish to be listed." Dr. Jan K. Tarnowski to Stefan Korboński, 19 IX 1959, HIA, Korboński Papers, b. 13, f. 7.

due to "physical indisposition" Māsēns was unable to make any other official calls. The U.S. ambassador was obviously surprised that he was not aware of the ACEN's visit and blamed the media.

Graužinis pointed to "El Día," which was reported as being generous with its comment on the visit. While Patterson concluded that "the party were sympathetically received, much of the attention accorded to them in public meetings came from compatriots in exile rather than from the Uruguayan public."[33] With his foreign service dispatch, he included a memorandum prepared by Conrad Manley, the Press Officer of the U.S. Information Service (USIS). While Manley correctly named all the members of the ACEN delegation, he repeated the mistake of calling Māsēns a Lithuanian. The USIS (i.e. the overseas arm of the U.S. Information Agency) received no instructions, he wrote, but he learned about the delegation's arrival from a press clipping. He met with Korboński and Vişoianu, who explained that "their mission was one of propaganda, to call wider world attention to the plight of their countries, and to call on the governments of the countries it touched to support their case before the UN." The USIS officer described in greater detail the meetings of the ACEN delegates, including the assurance of the Foreign Minister who "advised them only that Uruguay was sympathetic and would do what it could in the UN if and when the subject of Soviet domination of their countries was debated." Manley reported that the ACEN asked the USIS that their visit be given publicity, and this was done in the form of dispatches sent to the USIA's Press Section synthetizing relevant newspaper reports. The USIS officer's report concluded with this evaluation: "On balance it appears that the visit of the group was of some value in the continuing effort to make the Uruguayan officialdom and public aware of Soviet imperialism, even though no strong official commitment was received."[34]

The report of 19 October 1956 from Santiago mentioned all three members of the ACEN delegation.[35] The reference to Stefan Korboński as Esteban may indicate that the embassy personnel relied on press reports when describing the trip. This may be confirmed by multiple references to press titles describing the ACEN's visitors. The embassy official noted that "the press coverage of their visit was quite good" mentioning Chilean opinion-leading journals description of the origins and aims of the ACEN, Korboński's account of Poznań and its

33 Jefferson Patterson (AmAmbassador, Montevideo) to Dep. Of State, Despatch no. 300: Visit of Zilis Māsēns, 18 X 1956, Simpson Collection, 032 MĀSĒNS, ZILAS/10 – 1856.

34 C. Conrad Manley to Ambassador (Patterson), Memorandum: Visit to Montevideo of Representatives of ACEN, 18 X 1956, ibid.

35 Robert Foster Corrigan (First Secretary of AmEmbassy Santiago, Chile) to Dep. Of State, Despatch no. 380: Visit of Zilis Māsēns, 19 X 1956, ibid.

aftermath. The Catholic press ("El Diario Ilustrado") in its editorial "paid high tribute and tendered a warm welcome to the deputation." The ACEN delegates informed the Chargé d'Affaires that after the meeting with the President and Minister of Foreign Affairs, alas without any formal commitments, they were sure that "Chile was sympathetic to their viewpoint."[36]

A report from the U.S. diplomatic post in Buenos Aires was the most comprehensive, and best-informed. Prepared by Willard L. Beaulac (the U.S. Ambassador to Argentina) the report opened with the information that the post received a heads-up about the ACEN's visit from Earl L. Packer, a former Foreign Service officer who by then worked for the Free Europe Committee. In his letter addressed to Beaulac, Packer described the purpose of the ACEN visit as intending "to acquaint important persons in each country visited with conditions in the captive countries and to arouse public opinion to view with sympathy the plight of the captive peoples and their aspirations to regain control of their own affairs." Interestingly, Parker also included a peculiar wish list as to whom the FEC hoped the ACEN delegates "would have an opportunity to meet." It included: the president, the foreign minister, other government officials, prominent political figures, members of the diplomatic corps, and members of the press. The Ambassador contacted the Under Secretary for Foreign Affairs (24 IX 1956) and told him about the proposed meetings: "Castiñeiras made note of the pertinent names and dates." As confirmed also by the Korboński memoirs, the delegates met President Pedro Eugenio Aramburu and were received at a special session of the Junta Consultiva Nacional, where they made a brief address and answered many questions. They also saw the Vice President and several cabinet ministers, and other important figures in the government, including Under Secretary Castiñeiras. The Ambassador obviously wished to exploit the possibility of "using this visit to direct public attention to the danger of Communist propaganda and infiltration," as he put it in his report. He acknowledged the Foreign Minister's decision not to meet the ACEN's delegates, explaining this was due to criticism coming from the communist ambassadors and ministers accredited to the Argentine government.[37] Beaulac mentioned extensive coverage in the Argentinian press.

---

36 Ibid. See also Stefan Korboński's comment: "In a professor-like manner Ibáñez gave us practical advice which we had to consider simply excellent." Korboński, *W imieniu Polski* ..., 320.
37 His decision not to meet with ACEN's delegates was explained in the next dispatch sent by the Minister-Counselor of the American Embassy (Ackerson) three days later. Argentina had diplomatic relations with Russia and all of the European communist countries, so it was "inadvisable to expose the Foreign Minister to probable protests from the diplomatic representatives in Buenos Aires of those countries." Garret G. Ackerson, Jr. (Minister-Counselor of AmEmbassy,

Overall evaluation of the significance of the visit fit well with earlier reports and the general sentiment evident in Argentina, including the "strong anti-communist tenor of recent speeches by President Aramburu, and the heavy propaganda against the Communist repatriation program of Russian and Satellite nationals." He concluded: "The Embassy believes that visits of refugees of the standing, ability, and obvious sincerity of this delegation from the ACEN serve a useful purpose and should be encouraged." The favorable opinion about the delegates was most likely influenced also by the personal meeting that took place shortly before their departure. ACEN's delegates informed the Ambassador that the Vice President hoped that the ACEN would establish an office in Buenos Aires and offered his government (provisional government) assistance in this regard. Also, the Minister of Communications said that radio facilities would be made available to the Assembly for its counter-communist work in this country. Māsēns reportedly said that he would recommend that the ACEN open an office in the Argentinian capitol but on an independent basis, "without being in any way dependent upon or beholden to the Government."[38]

The Buenos Aires embassy followed up with one more interesting report, this time related to the ACEN's continued trip to Chile. Prepared by the Minister-Counselor (Garret G. Ackerson), it contains an account of what was discussed between the ACEN and the Chilean President and Minister of Foreign Affairs. On the basis of information coming from an unidentified source, Ackerson wrote that when the ACEN requested the support of the Chilean government for "resolution and any other action which might be taken within the UN looking forward liberation of the Satellite countries from Russian domination," they had hoped that such initiative should come from the Western Hemisphere, possibly from Chile at the forthcoming General Assembly meeting of the UN. According to the report, Ibáñez suggested turning directly to the U.S. government. The ACEN delegates were then reported to have said that the U.S. was "too big, too powerful, and too much immersed in the attack on international communism," and insisted it should come from some other country in the Western Hemisphere. Both the President and the Minister were sympathetic but made no undertaking in this regard. It remained unclear whether a similar request was presented to Aramburu.[39]

Buenos Aires) to Dep. Of State, Despatch no. 483, 25 X 1956, Simpson Collection, 032 MĀSĒNS, ZILAS/10 – 2556.

38 Willard L. Beaulac to Dep. Of State, Despatch no. 465: Visit to Argentina of Delegation from ACEN, 22 X 1956, Simpson Collection, 032 MĀSĒNS, ZILAS/10 – 2256.

39 Garret G. Ackerson, Jr. (Minister-Counselor of AmEmbassy, Buenos Aires) to Dep. Of State, Despatch no. 483, 25 X 1956, Simpson Collection, 032 MĀSĒNS, ZILAS/10 – 2556. The copy

The last "report on Māsēns' visit" in response to Hoover's instruction of 8 October 1956, was sent in March 1957. The counselor of the embassy in Havana reported that "according to the Cuban Ministry of State," Māsēns visited Cuba from 16 to 19 October 1956. He met the President on the 16th and Minister of State on the following day. "He did not call on or request assistance from the Embassy." The visit was routinely reported in the local press and brought no significant public reaction. "Those officials of the Foreign Office who came in contact with him were all favorably impressed."[40]

These reports from U.S. embassies are important in trying to establish the place the ACEN held in U.S. foreign policy. Apart from its immediate goals of uplifting émigré spirits and searching for new opportunities, it seems as if the ACEN trip was not related to any urgent issue of U.S. foreign policy. Interestingly, none of the American reports mentioned the ACEN delegates meeting with Catholic Church representatives (see the Korboński itinerary above).

By the end of 1956, the ACEN had already established its delegations in Argentina, Chile, Brazil and Uruguay. Initially, all remained under the administrative control of the ACEN's Secretary General (Brutus Coste). The list was soon expanded by adding representatives and correspondents. Within four years, the ACEN network in Latin America covered the most important countries of the continent.[41]

The delegations experienced a rather rough start. Established mostly in November and December of 1956, with the immediate intention of lobbying for action regarding Hungary in the UN, they lacked space, resources and manpower (offices, money for translations, and secretaries).[42] There was a competition for primacy among the Latin American representations of the ACEN, especially be-

---

I have obtained from Christopher Simpson was redacted (case: [b][1]). I could not confirm the identity of the person who informed the U.S. Embassy in Argentina on the talks between the ACEN delegates and Chilean politicians, but the report classified as confidential is worth quoting regardless. Please note that Garret G. Ackerson had already served in Hungary, where he was about to return as charge d'affaires and remained there until 1961, hosting Cardinal Josef Mindszenty who lived in the U.S. Embassy in Budapest until 1971. Lee A. Daniels, "Garret G. Ackerson, 88, Envoy In East Europe During Cold War," *New York Times*, 16 IX 1992, D25.

40 AmEmbassy, Havana (Vinton Chapin, counselor) to the Dept. of State, ref.: CA-3037, Despatch no. 615: Visit of Zilas [original spelling] Māsēns (ACEN), 26 III 1957, Simpson Collection, 032 MĀSĒNS, ZILAS/3 – 2657.

41 Only few Latin American countries were missing: Panama, Belize, Nicaragua, Guatemala, Honduras, Bolivia, Paraguay, Guyana, French Guyana and Suriname. In the Caribbean, up to 1959, the ACEN was in touch with a Cuban delegate to the UN, Portuondo.

42 ACEN, Buenos Aires to gen. Ernesto A. Peluffo (Secretario de informaciones del estado), 15 V 1958, IHRC, ACEN, b. 45, f. 1.

Tab. 4: ACEN's Latin American delegations, 1956–1957 (Third Session of the ACEN)

	ARGENTINA Buenos Aires	CHILE Santiago	BRAZIL Rio de Janerio	*URUGUAY* Montevideo
CHAIRMAN	*Stanisław Śliwiński* **Poland**	*Henry Helfant* **Romania**	*Edward Ressel* **Romania**	*Miroslav Rasin* **Czechoslovakia**
OFFICERS	*Radu Cutzarida* **Romania** **Vice Chairman** *Evald Talvari* **Estonia, Secretary**	*Talivaldis Buss* **Latvia, Secreatry**	(ACTING DELEGATION)	*Edmund Gaspar* **Hungary** **Vice Chairman** *Jan Tarnowski* **Poland, Secretary**
DELEGATES	Bulgaria Hungary (2) Latvia (2) Lithuania (2) Poland	Bulgaria (2) Czechoslovakia Lithuania (2) Poland	Bulgaria (2) Czechoslovakia Estonia (2) Hungary Latvia Lithuania (2) Poland (2)	Bulgaria Estonia Hungary Lithuania Poland
ACEN nine nations	7 OF 9	6 OF 9	8 OF 9	6 OF 9

tween Buenos Aires (Stanisław Śliwiński) and Montevideo (Jan Tarnowski).[43] The establishment of delegations was also marred by exile infighting. The competition between Tarnowski (Polish) and Edmund Gaspar (Hungarian) in Uruguay was particularly mean-spirited.[44] Uruguay, despite its small size, deserves special attention. It was the first South American country to establish diplomatic ties with the Soviet Union. Montevideo was considered the second (after Mexico City) hub for Soviet operations on the continent.[45] Instead of Uruguay, and fearing the exile conflicts, the ACEN headquarters decided to continue with a delegation in Montevideo, but locate its office in Argentina.

The ACEN office in Buenos Aires was in charge of the preparation and distribution of Spanish-language publications to ACEN's delegates and representa-

43 Dr. Jan K. Tarnowski to Stefan Korboński, 19 IX 1959, HIA, Korboński Papers, b. 13, f. 7; Stanisław Śliwiński to Stefan Korboński, 16 X 1959, ibid.

44 Stefan Korboński to Jan K. Tarnowski, 15 XI 1959, ibid.; Tarnowski to Korboński, 9 X 1962, ibid.

45 Roberto Garcia Ferreira, "Espionaje politica: La Guerra Fria y la inteligencia political Uruguaya, 1947–64," *Revista Historia* 63–64 (enero-diciembre 2011): 15, 20.

tives. The monthly "Novedades" was published in Argentina.[46] For the Portuguese versions, the ACEN relied on Colonel Edward Ressel in Rio de Janeiro.[47] The ACEN leaders from New York sent their delegates clippings from the U.S. press, items from the FEC-published "News From Behind the Iron Curtain," asking them to translate, edit and use them in local press and specialized journals, as well as during professional meetings (like the Conference of the Inter-American Bar Association).[48] On 22 October 1957, the ACEN was able to inform its delegates overseas that in addition to its own materials, the FEC had agreed to supply its delegations abroad with Free Europe Press publications on a regular basis.[49]

In addition to asking delegates to influence politicians and opinion leaders to endorse action on behalf of Hungarians, the ACEN also asked its representatives to undertake efforts to create local associations of the Amigos de la Naciones Cautivas Europeas. These organizations, modelled after the AFCN, were supposed to engage the local leadership in the anti-communist struggle. Obtaining support from local prominent personalities (politicians, writers, journalists, entrepreneurs, artists, and other opinion makers) served as a protective shield for local ACEN representatives, acknowledging their relevance to the local issues, helping to expand exile networks, and build moral support for their activities. Via the Amigos, the ACEN obtained patrons for their public meetings, forewords to its publications, and signatures for the adopted manifestos. In short, legitimacy was gained for their presence and operations there.[50]

However, this was not the ACEN's prime interest. In a rare, angry letter emerging from the ACEN's headquarters, Edmund Gaspar explained that the Colombian representative Stany Sirutis' demand for three to four thousand dollars a year to facilitate the work of the Amigos was grossly missing the point of their establishment. They were supposed to serve as a framework for helping the ACEN and to add prestige to exile operations. "You realize that the case of the Captive Nations isn't one of prime urgency" – wrote Gaspar. What they were look-

46 [Edmund Gaspar] to Jerzy Skoryna-Lipski (Mexico), 13 VIII 1962, IHRC, ACEN, b. 56, f. 1.
47 Ed. Ressel to Kotta, 16 IV 1957, IHRC, ACEN, b. 47, f. 10.
48 Cf.: IHRC, ACEN, b. 56, f. 1.
49 Sec. Gen. ACEN [Coste] to ACEN Delegations Abroad, Memorandum: FEP Publications, 22 X 1957, IHRC, ACEN, b. 56, f. 1; Sec. Gen ACEN to General Committee, Memo: FEP Publications, 22 X 1957, IHRC, ACEN, b. 45, f. 1.
50 Gaspar to Gaete (Ecuador), 15 V 1963, IHRC, ACEN, b. 50, f. 4; Śliwiński (Argentina) to Māsēns, 2 XII 1956, IHRC, ACEN, b. 45, f. 1; Vilis Māsēns to H. Stabielski (Mexico), 2 VIII 1957, IHRC, ACEN, b. 56, f. 1; Jerzy Skoryna-Lipski (Mexico) to ACEN (translation), 21 XII 1956, ibid.; Edmund Gaspar to Albert Kappel (FEC), 16 VI 1965, IHRC, ACEN, b. 50, f. 5.

ing for was that at least once a month there would be a mention of the ACEN in the periodicals, political and sociological in scope, that articles about East and Central Europe would appear in the press, and that once a year the Captive Nations Week would be organized, including organizing the masses, visits, speeches, etc.[51] As he further explained in his letter to the ACEN representative in Venezuela, his job was to set up the Friends of Captive Nations, develop contacts with the press, radio and TV, develop and maintain relations with the country's government and the congress, and establish some youth educational programs, perhaps in cooperation with other anti-communist organizations.[52]

Then again, one must be reminded that the FEC envisioned that the exile network would lead to the establishment of local, authentic hubs of activists supportive of the cause the ACEN promoted. In other words, the ACEN's role was meant to inspire the creation of local groups and not to lead any major anti-communist offensive in the countries south of the U.S. border. The exile focus remained on young Latin American intellectuals,[53] and contemporary political elites to advance their prime goal which was clearly focused on East Central Europe.

Sometimes, the personal contacts of local ACEN representatives resulted in direct access to the members of governments. For example, Luis Gaete, representing the ACEN in Ecuador, taught Sandra, the daughter of President Carlos Julio Arosemena (1961–1963), as well as served as the Private Secretary of the President, and offered to facilitate meetings between the ACEN delegate from New York and the President.[54] This did not materialize, however, as a military junta took power in July 1963.

A rare instance of an ACEN delegate asking for the ACEN's moral support in Latin American matters took place when its delegate in El Salvador, Luis Roberto Hidalgo Zelaya, asked for the ACEN's endorsement in the Organization of American States during the conflict with Honduras in July 1969.[55] The ACEN could not be of any assistance, something which did not discourage Hidalgo, the elected member of the parliament representing Usulután district in 1970, from maintaining contacts with the ACEN headquarters.[56] When the Colombian government de-

---

51 Edmundo Gaspar to Stany Sirutis, 22 XI 1963, IHRC, ACEN, b. 50, f. 1.

52 Matei Ghica (Venezuela) to Edmund Gaspar, 27 May 1963, IHRC, ACEN, b. 58, f. 7; Gaspar to Ghica, 14 X 1962, ibid.

53 Edmund Gaspar to Rev. M. Tamosiunas (Columbia), 20 I 1964, IHRC, ACEN, b. 50, f. 1.

54 Gaete to Gaspar, 23 V 1963, IHRC, ACEN, b. 50, f. 4; Gaspar to Gaete, 3 VI 1963, IHRC, ACEN, b. 50, f. 4.

55 Luis Roberto Hidalgo to ACEN Chairman, 22 VII 1969, IHRC, ACEN, b. 58, f. 8.

56 Luis Roberto Hidalgo to Alfreds Berzins (ACEN, NY), 10 I 1970, ibid.

cided to restore, after twenty years, its relations with the USSR, Hildago decided to travel to Bogota to talk to his old friend who then held the post of Minister of Foreign Affairs (Dr. Fernando Martinez Gômez), trying to convince him not to acknowledge the Soviet annexation of the Baltic countries.[57]

The way the ACEN tried to use its network in Latin America to advance its prime goals can be demonstrated by looking at the memorandum "A Continuous Threat to International Peace and Security; The situation created by Soviet Aggression and intervention in the Internal affairs of the Countries of East Central Europe," which was adopted at the ACEN's Third Session in Strasburg. The memorandum was translated into Spanish, sent to the representatives south of Rio Grande with an instruction to form local delegations and present the memorandum to the governments there and ask that it would be placed on the agenda of the twelfth session of the UN.[58] In Argentina, the ACEN delegates, accompanied by Dr. Juan Carlos Palacios who organized the Association of Friends of ACEN there, visited Minister of Interior Carlos R.S. Alconada Aramburu and obtained his support.[59] In Brazil, the ACEN delegation met with the Minister of Foreign Affairs, who promised to forward the ACEN memorandum to the President, and the Secretary General of the Foreign Office gave favorable instructions to the Brazilian Delegation at the UN.[60]

The idea was that the UN delegates in New York would receive instructions from their respective governments.[61] To achieve that, the "ACEN Delegation is requested to set up a small group in order that, upon receipt of a telegraphic communication from the ACEN headquarters, it may call on the appropriate authorities, requesting the urgent convocation of the UN General Assembly to deal with the Report prepared by its Special Commission on Hungary."[62] When sending instructions to Mexico, Coste wrote that the delegation was "free to inform the press of the substance of our thesis and subject to agreement of the official bodies you approach, of the fact of your intervention on behalf of ACEN."[63]

---

57 Tamosiunas to Gaspar, 15 XI 1963, IHRC, ACEN, b. 50, f. 1. Colombia *de jure* pursued the policy of non-recognition of the Baltic states' forceful incorporation into the Soviet Union until the 1990s.

58 Argentina: Coste to Cutzarida, 14 VI 1957, IHRC, ACEN, b. 45, f. 1; Śliwinski to Māsēns, 6 XI 1957, IHRC, ACEN, b. 45, f. 1; Mexico: B. Coste to H. Stabielski, 17 VI 1957, IHRC, ACEN, b. 56, f. 1; Brazil: Vilis Māsēns to Ed Ressel, 9 VIII 1957, IHRC, ACEN, b. 47, f. 10.

59 Śliwinski to Māsēns, 6 XI 1957, IHRC, ACEN, b. 45, f. 1.

60 Ressel to Māsēns, 26 VIII 1957, IHRC, ACEN, b. 47, f. 10.

61 Gaspar to Jerzy Skoryna-Lipski, 13 VIII 1962, IHRC, ACEN, b. 56, f. 1.

62 Coste to Ressel (Rio de Janeiro), 17 VI 1957, IHRC, ACEN, b. 47, f. 10.

63 Coste to Stabielski, 14 VI 1957, IHRC, ACEN, b. 56, f. 1.

At times, things did not go smoothly. When the Romanian delegate, Radu Cutzarida, wrote a letter to the Argentinian delegate to the UN, Mario Amadeo, to protest his recognition of status quo in Eastern Europe, the ACEN delegation thought it was not enough. Therefore, the delegates decided to release their protest to the press in neighboring Uruguay ("El Día") signed as *nautilius*. What they did not coordinate was Cutzarida sending his letter to the Ministry of Foreign Affairs under his own name. Hence, the ACEN positioned itself as publicly critical of the government on the international stage.[64]

One other area of ACEN activities in Latin America was the organization of public demonstrations (meetings, parades, masses, pickets). In the aftermath of the Hungarian Revolution, the ACEN's early efforts to garner public attention focused on demands for international action in the UN. Dr. Béla Fabian, Chairman of the ACEN Information Committee and member of the Executive Committee of the Hungarian National Council, came up with the initiative of organizing public demonstrations on 30 June 1957 in "as many places all over the world" as possible in support of the exile demands for convocation of the UN General Assembly. The ACEN wished to engage local labor, church, civil liberties, and cultural groups in addition to the ethnics and Cold War exiles and encourage them to adopt resolutions similar to these of the AFCN.[65] Béla Fabian coordinated this, as well as following public mobilization efforts.[66] However, his activities appear to have been much broader. Their scope and relevance to the FEC programming also requires a further, thorough study. What is clear, based on the FEC reports, is that by 1963 the "Béla Fabian activities" were terminated.[67]

The ACEN delegates, representatives and correspondents submitted reports, often with political analysis of the situation in their country of settlement. Of these reports, only a few remained in the ACEN collection at IHRC. It is likely that they were useful for the FEC and its political and intelligence superiors. There is scattered evidence of information gathering, for example when Gaspar

---

64 Śliwiński (Buenos Aires) to Korboński (President PCNU), 23 VIII 1959, HIA, Korboński Papers, b. 13, f. 7.

65 Nuci Kotta (Acting Sec. Gen. ACEN) to Stabielski, 21 VI 2917, IHRC, ACEN, b. 56, f. 1; Coste to Stabielski, 19 VII 1957, ibid.; Coste to Ressel, 17 VI 1957, IHRC, ACEN, b. 47, f. 10.

66 Kotta (Acting Sec. Gen. ACEN) to Stabielski, 13 VIII 1957, IHRC, ACEN, b. 56, f. 1; Coste to Cutzarida, 17 VI 1957, IHRC, ACEN, b. 45, f. 1.

67 Evaluation of the International Development Foundation (IDF) and other FEC-sponsored Latin American Activities, attachment B to John Richardson to John C. Hughes, Ernest A. Gross, C.D. Jackson, Memorandum: FEC and Partisan Politics, 8 XI 1963, DDEL, C.D. Jackson Papers, b. 52, f.: FEC, 1963 (2); The President (FEC, Richardson) to the Executive Committee, Subject: Dr. Fabian, 22 VII 1963, C.D. Jackson Papers, b. 53, f. 1: FEC Budget, etc., 1963 (1).

was inquiring about particular people,[68] asking about a political situation,[69] about general moods of populations in a given country,[70] or – most frequently – when both the FEC and ACEN requested evidence of regional representatives' activities in the local press and radio.[71]

Members of the ACEN's General Committee asked their partners south of U.S. borders for advice on best ways of advancing lobbying efforts.[72] The early months of operations were difficult but the emotional response to Hungary and favorable feedback from the Latin Americans kept the ACEN delegates going. By 1958, however, the excitement and hope were in deficit. The delegations had mounting problems. Among them was the lack of personnel (even secretarial assistance), lack of full engagement by volunteering exiles, no office space. Even if there was an office – as in Argentina – there was no heating, or no working typewriter as in Uruguay.[73] The ACEN in New York could only apologize and promise to look for more funds, but systematic cooperation was difficult.

By 1958, the FEC reviewed its programs carried out by the ACEN. The suggested revised mission for the ACEN was to "consolidate and re-enforce its traditional good relations with its traditionally good friends in the Philippine, Peruvian, Belgian, Dutch etc. governments;" "follow up and cultivate relations established with other Latin American and European governments," and "expand and develop relations with Asiatic governments through personal contact, correspondence and publications." It meant that the ACEN's Latin American programs were gaining prominence. The internal FEC memorandum further specified the forms of the ACEN's activities: "While ACEN and the national organizations are not concerned with local free world mass political and social movement, they can gain much by coordinating their activities with those of

68 Like asking about the Honduran poet Felipe Elvir Rojas. Hidalgo (San Salvador) to Gaspar (ACEN), 18 VI 1966, b. 58, f. 8; Hidalgo (San Salvador) to Gaspar (ACEN), 13 VI 1966, ibid. The mission was accomplished. Information collected together with some signed [!] poems. See IHRC, ACEN, b. 58, f. 8.

69 Edmund Gaspar received a confidential report on the situation in Ecuador from Gaete. Para el dr. Edmundo Gaspar (Confidencial), no date, IHRC, ACEN, b. 50, f. 5.

70 Questionnaire on communist propaganda in Venezuela as "purely personal request." Edmund Gaspar to Matei Ghica (Venezuela), 21 XI 1963, IHRC, ACEN, b. 58, f. 7.

71 For example : Tamosiunas (Colombia) to Edmund Gaspar, 15 XI 1963 and 29 I 1965, IHRC, ACEN, b. 50, f. 1; Gaete (Ecuador) to Gaspar, 27 V 1965, IHRC, ACEN, b. 50, f. 5; Edward Ressel (Brazil) to Nuci Kotta, 17 VII 1957, IHRC, ACEN, b. 47, f. 10; Antonio Tagle Valdes (Chile) to Edmund Gaspar, 14 IX 1964, IHRC, ACEN, b. 49, f. 7.

72 Māsēns to Śliwiński (Buenos Aires), 27 XIII 1957, IHRC, ACEN, b. 45, f. 1.

73 See the correspondence available at IHRC, ACEN: b. 46, f. 1; b. 57, f. 9.

their associate and consultative partners, the international political social and professional organizations. This must be one of the functions of the ACEN General Committee." The American leaders of the exile activities within the FEC realized that at times, contacts with members of the regimes could be compromising in the light of the ACEN's democratic record. "There is a price for alliances," said the memo. The authors used the example of an "immensely useful tactical ally" the ACEN had in the UN Security Council (nationalist China). Therefore, the ACEN had to express solidarity with Dr. Tsiang: "ACEN must express a judicious amount of sympathy for local issues in Free World countries when the moral basis for political action on such issues corresponds to that of ACEN action."[74]

The same year, American Vice President Nixon visited a number of Latin American countries.[75] The trip made it plain that North Americans were not popular among the people of Latin America. In Lima (Peru) and in Caracas (Venezuela) the Vice President and his wife were even assaulted by demonstrators. Hearing of the attack on 27 May 1958, on behalf of the ACEN delegation in Buenos Aires its Chairman (Stanisław Śliwiński) sent Nixon a letter expressing "deepest indignation" about the "hideous outrages and attacks perpetrated in Lima and Caracas by Communists and their fellow travelers against your distinguished person":

> [T]hese events as well as some hostile incidents in Buenos Aires, Montevideo and La Paz during your excellency journey prove with clear evidence the high degree of clandestine Communist infiltration in South America, already well known to this delegation. This delegation offers fullest collaboration to U.S. government in struggle against Communist infiltration. Śliwiński declared they would be happy if the American Embassy in Argentina would forward adequate instructions to put such collaboration in practice.[76]

The Vice President responded personally two weeks later sharing his interpretation of the events: "I only hope that the end result of the incidents that occurred during our trip will be an increased awareness in both the United States and Latin America of the determination and ruthlessness of those who instigated

74 Ed McHale to Huston, Henderson, Leich, Bull Memorandum, 10 II 1958, HIA, RFE/RL CF: A, b. 200, f. 6.

75 Montevideo (28 IV); Buenos Aires (30 IV), Asuncion, Paraguay (30 IV), La Paz (5 V), Lima (7 V), Quito (9 V), Bogota (11 V), Caracas (13 V) 1958. Marvin R. Zahniser, W. Michael Weis, "A Diplomatic Pearl Harbor? Richard Nixon's Goodwill Mission to Latin America in 1958," *Diplomatic History* 13/2 (Spring 1989): 163–190.

76 Asamblea de las Naciones Cautivas Europeas, delegation en Buenos Aires to Richard Nixon (U.S. Vice President), 27 V 1958, IHRC, ACEN, b. 45, f. 1.

the riots, and a strengthening of the economic, political and cultural ties between this country and our valued friends and neighbors to the South."[77]

The good-will trip was a nightmare but also a lesson that more soft-power was needed in relations with the countries of South America. When President Eisenhower visited Brazil, Argentina, Chile and Uruguay between 23 February and 3 March 1960 there were no similar incidents.[78] The four countries he visited were the ones in which the ACEN maintained offices in.

Before John F. Kennedy's visit to Venezuela and Colombia from 16 to 17 December 1961 the FEC received a request from the CIA for information. "John Page called, meeting Reynolds, to say our inventory of sources and activity assets in Colombia and Venezuela greatly received. EC wants, as urgently as possible, all we can pull together in the way of information and estimates on the climate and possibilities of Communist action and pro-Kennedy counteraction in both countries."[79] Wether or not with the use of information from the exile associates, the visit was prepared in such a way that no incidents similar to Nixon's visit of 1958 occurred. Most importantly, the American President came to present his original plan for development in Latin America.

7.2 After Cuba, before the Dominican Republic (1960 – 1965)

With the Kennedy administration came two major developments in U.S. Latin American policy: the Alliance for Progress and the fallouts of the Cuban Bay of Pigs invasion (1961) and the Cuban Missile Crisis (1962).

The Alliance for Progress was a program of socio-economic and political reform announced publicly on 13 March 1961. The Charter of Punta del Este of August 1961 proclaimed American assistance which looked like the Marshall Plan and civil rights program combined.[80] With the economic assistance of roughly

---

77 Richard Nixon to S. Śliwiński (ACEN, Buenos Aires), 13 VI 1958, IHRC, ACEN b. 45, f. 1.

78 Instruction from the Department of State to All Diplomatic Posts in Latin America, 4 II 1960, *FRUS, 1958 – 1960, American Republics*, Vol. V (Washington: GPO, 1991), doc. 74, 275 – 278.

79 During the exchanges, Page asked "for the names of the two (?) persons you have mentioned as either arriving from or arriving in Bogota. I want quite sure what he was referring to … is it the Hungarian lecturer and his wife?" That FEC needed information is evident from the Urgent request: John Dunning to Brinkley, 5 XII [1961], HIA, RFE/RL CF: A, b.199, f. 2. There is no year given in the memo, but Kennedy visited both countries in 1961.

80 Tony Smith, *American Mission. The United States and the Worldwide Struggle for Democracy* (Princeton, Oxford: Princeton University Press, 2012): 220. Interestingly, one of the people instrumental in formulating the alliance was Adolf Berle, hence the overlap with European Council of Europe programs (Retinger mentions him, see above); Andrzej Mania, *Department of State i For-*

22.3 billion dollars, this most ambitious plan aimed at the promotion of democratic governance and economic improvement. On a continent where roughly 5 to 10 percent of the population owned 70 to 90 percent of the land this was not an easy task. Navigating between revolution and reaction, given class and race polarization, projected a dim prospect for spreading an American-style democracy. Initially, it looked as if the Christian Democrats might be the political force to rely on. Soon however, they found themselves tolerating, if not actually condoning authoritarian governments or military rule.[81] Already in June 1961, in response to the assassination of the dictator of the Dominican Republic, Rafael Trujillo, the American President said, "there are three possibilities in descending order of preference: a decent democratic regime, a continuation of the Trujillo regime, or a Castro regime. We ought to aim at the first, but we really can't renounce the second until we are sure we can avoid the third."[82]

By 1961 the USSR had also intensified its efforts to expand its activities in Latin America.[83] The Cuban Missile Crisis pushed Americans even further. In just three years American policy changed dramatically. From a muted opposition to events in the Dominican Republic and in Honduras, tolerance towards coups in Guatemala and Ecuador in 1963, to enthusiastic endorsement of the military takeover in Brazil 1964, the U.S. gradually changed its attitude. By 1965, the United States had launched a military intervention against an undertaking that called itself a "constitutional movement" in the Dominican Republic. This was now the political context in which the exiles operated in Latin America. Although there were regional variations, from 1960 to 1965, when the ACEN operations were at their most intense, the international situation was truly dynamic.

The ACEN correspondents were busy trying to organize associations of friends of captive nations, establishing access paths to intellectual and political elites, organizing events related to either Captive Nations Week, or important anniversaries (like the Hungarian Revolution), distributing ACEN-prepared materials to the local press and securing guests for radio programs. The coordination of such efforts throughout the 1960s was up to one man, Edmund Gaspar, who was elected the ACEN's Deputy Secretary General in September 1960.

In order to take up his duties in New York, Edmund Gaspar had to obtain permission to immigrate to the U.S. from Uruguay, which before the Hart-Celler

eign Service w polityce zagranicznej USA lat gorącej i zimnej wojny 1939–1989 (Kraków: Wydawnictwo Uniwersytetu Jagiellońskiego, 2019), 332–334.

81 Smith, *American Mission* ..., 224–225. See: Edmund Gaspar, *United States, Latin America: A Special relationship?* (Washington: American Enterprise Institute, 1978).

82 Smith, *American Mission* ..., 226.

83 Ferreira, "Espionaje politica ...", 14.

Act of 1965 was particularly difficult since Latin America had no established immigration quotas (only qualitative restrictions). Impatiently waiting for his visa in Montevideo he continued his duties as chairman of the ACEN's permanent delegation there. He assumed this post in October 1959, having previously served as a vice chairman. Gaspar emigrated to Uruguay with his family in 1949 as a refugee under the auspices of the IRO. Already in May 1950 he became the representative for the Hungarian National Council (HNC) in Uruguay, and later of the Hungarian Committee (April 1958).[84] Since these organizations were members of the ACEN, many of Gaspar's activities were not only reported to but also supported by the Assembly.[85] Since 1956, Gaspar had served as the Chairman of the Hungarian Red Cross Relief Committee, funded "Cultural Assistance Uruguay – Free Hungary," and organized two exhibits on the Hungarian Revolution in 1958, one in Montevideo one in Paysandu. In August 1958, he organized a visit by the Hungarian Committee's delegation and accompanied them to Chile and Peru. As editor of the Catholic anti-communist monthly "Antorcha" (in Spanish), he initiated the local ACEN bulletin, introduced texts prepared by other national delegations in the ACEN, the Assembly itself, as well as FEP to the local press. He was fluent in Spanish, French, English and German, his mother tongue being Hungarian. Prolific in writing, editing and organizing articles, studies, booklets, lectures on captive nations, Gaspar was the ACEN's great asset in the South. In 1960 he organized a campaign focused on demanding an amnesty for Hungarian political prisoners. In October 1960, he even managed to arrange the naming of

84 Edmund Gaspar was born 9 IV 1915 at Nagybecskerek (Zrenjanin), a graduate of the Cistercian Fathers' school in Budapest and held a PhD in law from the University of Budapest (1937). He spent a semester in Paris writing a thesis on the International law of radio-electricity. The academic year 1940/1941 he spent at the Hungarian Diplomatic Academy at the Hungarian Ministry of Foreign Affairs. Between October 1941 and November 1942, he served as an attaché for the press and cultural departments at the MFA. His diplomatic career (under Horthy, with the Allies from October 1944) took him to Ankara (November 1942–1944) where he worked as the secretary of the legation, but resigned when a Fascist Ferenc Szálasi took power. Gaspar returned to Budapest in March 1946 and was re-admitted to the diplomatic service. From June 1946 to April 1947 he was the assistant head of the Hungarian restitution mission in Frankfurt am Main (U.S. zone). From May 1947 to January 1948 he had a variety of assignments in the Ministry of Foreign Affairs. In January 1948, when the Communists took over the foreign affairs, he, along with 150 other deputies was purged. In October 1948, he left the country with his family. Until February 1949 they stayed in Paris, from where he applied to emigrate to Uruguay. He left for Montevideo as a refugee, under the auspices of the IRO. He held different jobs there – correspondent, secretary, treasurer, and later market researcher and financial analyst at Uruguayan firms. Curriculum vitae of Dr. Edmund Gaspar, HIA, RFE/RL CF: A, b. 204, f. 13.

85 Cloyce K. Huston to Edmund Gaspar, 24 X 1957, HIA, RFE/RL CF: A, b. 204, f. 12.

"Budapest Square" in the center of the Uruguayan capital.[86] And in 1960, during his trip to Brazil and Argentina, Sidzikauskas detoured to Montevideo to visit Gaspar shortly before his departure for the U.S. He confirmed that Gaspar was just the right person to run the ACEN's Latin American project.[87]

Becoming deputy secretary general meant that Gaspar would be responsible for meetings of the ACEN's organs and supervise all administrative work. His full-time position came with an annual salary of 6,700 dollars. Coste asked Robert Minton for help to "kindly intercede with immigration authorities to secure the required admission of Gaspar and his family to U.S. as a permanent resident."[88] A positive response came from Minton within a week. Two letters attesting to his fine character – possibly for visa purposes – came from Joseph Kővágó and Msgr. Béla Varga, Chairman of the Hungarian Committee. Both mentioned Gaspar as being indispensable to the ACEN, neither were based on personal acquaintance, but clearly based on Gaspar's CV.[89] Immigration visas for Gaspar, his wife and three daughters were then expedited smoothly and arrangements for shipping of his possessions were taken care of by the FEC. Obviously, the FEC wanted Gaspar to run the Latin American project as well. The timing of Gaspar's appointment was not coincidental. The FEC was on its way to mobilizing its resources to intensify its efforts in the free world.

Free Europe Committee's objectives of early September 1962 (a month before the Cuban Missile Crisis) contained the following tasks regarding utilization of the East Central European exiles: namely to furthering U.S. national interests in Europe, Africa, Asia and especially Latin America in highly selected high-priority propaganda and political projects in which they could offer the unique advantages of their particular skills, their superior motivation and knowledge of communism, their non-American identification, and their private, as contrasted with government, sponsorship. Practical means for pursuing this objective (as listed in annex B) included "utilization of carefully selected East Europeans who are integrated residents of South America" in venues such as schools,

86 Dr. Edmund Gaspar, 6 IX 1960, Resume, HIA, RFE/RL CF: A, b. 204, f. 12.

87 During his visit (1–3 XII 1960) ACEN's Chairman met the acting Minister of Foreign Affairs, local party leaders, newspaper editors and journalists, members of the congress (including a visit with Venacio Flores of the Christian Democratic Party), as well as U.S. Embassy staff (Ralph Collins described as Counselor, expert in ACEN-affairs), including a chat with U.S. Ambassador (Woodward) during an evening party. Vaclovas Sidzikauskas to Edmund Gaspar, 23 XI 1960, IHRC, ACEN, b. 57, f. 9; Edmund Gaspar to Brutus Coste, 4 XII 1960, ibid.

88 Coste to Robert Minton, 23 IX 1960, HIA, RFE/RL CF: A, b. 204, f. 12.

89 Joseph Kővágó, To whom it may concern, 24 IX 1960, HIA, RFE/RL, CF: A, b. 204, f. 12; Béla Varga, To Whom it may concern, 27 IX 1960, ibid.

trade unions, seminars, discussions, teaching and technical placements. Interestingly the ACEN was not listed among these. It appeared under objective no. 3: "to overtly stimulate worldwide interest in and support for the eventual freedom of East European countries and to utilize the experience of these countries as an objective example of the dangers of Soviet imperialism." Annex C of the same document mentioned RFE materials and officers providing information to the West Europeans, as well as utilizing the advice, assistance and help of leading West European politicians (WEAC). Finally, under section C, it said: "[T]he sponsorship of former leaders of East European countries organized in national committees and ACEN, and other international groupings in exile to press the strategic, moral, political and propaganda significance of the East European countries on the Free World governments."[90] For both the FEC and the ACEN, operations in Latin America were just a tactical part of a larger strategic operation.

The ACEN used the United States' interest to expand their operations as well as gain additional funding that came with it. Obviously, its operations had to be controlled. A CIA document of 1962 stated:

> We understand (based on fact sheet by Henderson) that ACEN wants to establish representations in Santiago, Lima, Bogota, Caracas and one city in Central America. As you know we are obliged to check this kind of arrangement out with our colleagues both here and abroad. We would appreciate having from you a list of nominees for these positions, with several weeks lead time before action has to be taken by the ACEN.[91]

During its ninth session, the ACEN had nine active hubs in Latin America.

Tab. 5: ACEN Latin American delegations, 1962–1963

DELEGATIONS Captive nations representatives (by origin)	REPRESENTATIVES	CORRESPONDENTS
ARGENTINA: *Latvia, Romania, Estonia, Lithuania* *BRAZIL:* *Poland, Romania* *CHILE:* *Hungary* *URUGUAY:* *Bulgaria, Poland, Lithuania (2)*	COLOMBIA: *Lithuania* MEXICO: *Poland* PERU: *Romania* VENEZUELA: *Romania*	ECUADOR: Luis Cornejo Gaete (native of Ecuador)

90 Memorandum for EC: FEC Objectives 1962, 5 IX 1962, DDEL, C.D. Jackson Papers, b. 53, f.: FEC 1962.
91 The Executive Committee [CIA] to the President (FEC), Memorandum: ACEN Representatives in Latin America, 11 IV 1962, HIA, RFE/RL CF: A, b. 199, f. 2.

On the basis of their willingness to cooperate, the ACEN's projects were expanded. The audiences the exiles desired to reach included politicians (via official meetings, usually using as an excuse presentation of ACEN memorandum or visits of ACEN delegates from New York), educators (through seminars and Spanish-language publications), members of social and cultural associations (by enrolling them into the Amigos-type of association), ethnic and immigrant communities (to mobilize their potential, offer advice, and inspire), and general public (via press, radio broadcasts, demonstrations, commemorations of the Captive Nations Week and the like).

Edmund Gaspar was so optimistic as to propose almost doubling the budget for the ACEN delegates in Latin America during the tenth ACEN's session (1963–1964).

Chart 3: Budget for ACEN Activities in Latin America 1962/63–1963/64

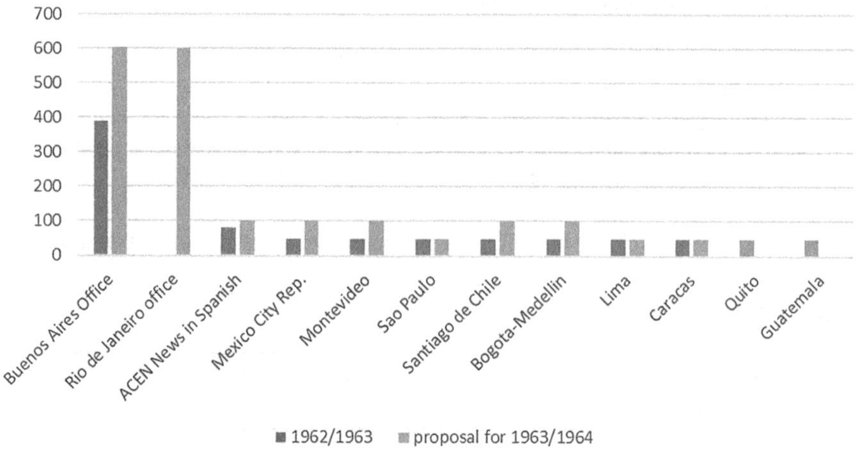

Operations in Quito and Guatemala had to be suspended because of a lack of appropriate persons to take charge of them. The chart above based on Gaspar's estimates does not include costs for proposed new projects – extra travel, extra personnel individual salaries, new brochures program or the costs of running associations of Amigos. Dreaming about expanding Latin American projects, Gaspar increased the sums from 20,064 dollars allotted by the FEC in 1962/63 to (amazingly) more than double: 54,519 dollars.[92] Based on his exchanges with Brinkley, Gaspar believed that Brinkley endorsed this proposal. He was convinced that he could ask for more support since his and Coste's 1962 trips to Latin America were successful. Both trips proved that the Latin American press and radio were receptive to the claim of self-determination of East Central European countries. The Argentinian government sponsored Captive Nations Week, Chilean and Brazilian congressmen showed keen interest in communist methods of enslavement, and ample press coverage of both visits was published in eight Latin American countries. Gaspar wrote next to his budget proposal:

> [I]t seems beyond doubt that the testimony of spokesmen of an authentically East European organization bears strength and produces more impact than that of blatantly U.S. sponsored cover-organizations. It is equally evident that the lessons Latin Americans might draw from the experience of the captive European peoples would strengthen their resistance to communist subversion and Soviet infiltration.[93]

Gaspar then gave his interpretation of why the Communists had any chance of success rallying support in Latin America:

> In view of these peoples' desire to progress from a patriarchal-authoritative agrarian pattern toward industrialization and democratic land reform, there exists a certain trend even among non-Communist Latin leaders to accept the Communist system as a short-cut in this development. The industrial progress in East-Central Europe is presented by the Communist propaganda in these countries as wonderful performance of the socialist system. The atrocities are dismissed as anomalies of Stalinism, and it is alleged that those who are responsible are being punished, etc.[94]

Gaspar understood that the exiles' program had to be tailored to counter these allegations. So while the ACEN's aim was to keep alive the claims of independence and freedom of the peoples of East Central Europe, the Hungarian put forth a proposal for innovations that would advance both.

Gaspar envisioned establishing an actual editorial board for "Novedades" ("ACEN News" in Spanish) in Buenos Aires, establishing more associations of Friends of Captive Nations (modeled on the one in Argentine). Gaspar also believed that the Latin American countries not covered by the network of ACEN delegates, representatives or correspondents should not be forsaken. His idea was to select one exile to travel between Paraguay, Bolivia, Ecuador, visiting these

---

92 [Edmund Gaspar] Memorandum and Budgetary estimate on Increased ACEN activities in Latin America, 15 I 1963, HIA, RFE/RL CF: A, b. 145, f.7.

93 Ibid.

94 Ibid.

countries at least twice a year. Finally, Gaspar also shared with the FEC the idea of organizing Latin American seminars. While exiles in the free world usually responded emotionally to their anti-communist tasks, what was needed – according to the ACEN's Deputy Secretary General – was a training seminar consisting of seven to ten topics which would include a survey of the situation in East Central Europe, an examination of communist tactics in Latin America, technical details of administrative cooperation, or methods of psychological warfare.[95] In his memorandum, Gaspar used the expressions "cadres of activists," and "congress of exile agents" – which fited the language used in the early 1960s by Galantière et al. The idea of the seminars included the participation of the ACEN's delegates from New York. The seminars were meant to attract the interest of the media at their opening and closing sessions. This last idea came to fruition in the form of two Latin American seminars organized by the ACEN, the first in Argentina (1963), followed by one in Colombia a year later.

The concrete plan for the seminars was born in January 1963, "as a consequence of a thorough reappraisal of ACEN's program of activities in Latin America." After his trip in October 1962 Gaspar wrote: "[R]ather loosely knit network of delegations of ACEN did not prove to be efficient enough to maintain alive the cause of the Captive Nations all over the continent." Traditional strongholds of ACEN representations included Buenos Aires, Montevideo, and Rio de Janeiro. There was also a working representation in Santiago de Chile for two and a half years. The ACEN's Secretary General noted a failed effort to establish one in Mexico, where "only Skoryna-Lipski has accepted the challenge to represent the ACEN in a country where official coolness peppers this task with possible troubles and risks." He continued: "Mr. Skoryna's relations remain, however, confined to the Catholic clergy and opposition quarters." Yet, as reported by Gaspar, there was a new type of ACEN representation that functioned in Quito (Ecuador). Professor Luis Cornejo Gaete, an Ecuadorian, accepted the role of ACEN correspondent and established an Ecuadorian Friends of Captive Nations. With a group of friends, he also maintained a weekly broadcast related to the Captive Nations.[96] On the other hand, as Dr. Nicolas Mara reported to Brutus Coste from Lima, Gaspar's visit allowed him to point out the importance of such trips to the field offices: "Our common cause, the fate of the Central and Eastern European Captive Nations, are by all means not forgotten by the local public opinion, but we have to admit that the issue is slowly fading."[97]

---

95 Ibid.

96 ACEN's Deputy Secretary General to ACEN's General Committee, Memorandum: Latin American Seminar Program, 6 X 1964, HIA, RFE/RL CF: A, b. 145, f.: ACEN Latin America Seminar.

97 Dr. Nicolas Mara to Brutus Coste, 18 X 1962, IHRC, ACEN, b. 56, f. 5.

In March 1963, Gaspar started looking for scholars of communism from East Central Europe, asking them to contribute to a project of lectures drawn up by the ACEN for Latin America. To all potential lecturers he addressed the same questions: Is communism a short cut for underdeveloped countries towards industrialization? What were the costs and results of the industrialization in the East Central European countries? Was forced collectivization a stimulus for agricultural productivity? Describe the delusion of higher living standards in the communist countries, scope and usefulness of the Soviet economic aid to underdeveloped countries. Explain its political strings. Some feedback he received included criticism that little attention was given to cultural or intellectual issues.[98]

Gaspar regularly informed the FEC on progress.[99] There is no doubt that the FEC did not simply give the ACEN a lump sum but first asked for the solid program proposal to examine it with other members of the staff. This included Gaspar considering suggestions such as: "perhaps subtly mold your conference material into a framework stressing the value of the individual to society and the arts,"[100] or to add another lecture "on the long-range imperialistic strategy of the Soviet Empire," which Brinkely described as "four dimensional warfare of international politics (two forward, one back)."[101]

While the tone of Brinkley-Gaspar exchanges suggests cooperation rather than passing on instructions, at times deferring final (personal and program) choices to the Hungarian, members of the ACEN committees got to work only after Brinkley gave Gaspar the OK to spend 75 dollars per lecture after reading their outlines.[102] Gaspar proposed to obtain some lecture materials from the RFE employees. However, Brinkley discouraged it;

> there are several things you should keep in mind in connection with work by the FEC personnel. I am sure you are aware that most of these gentlemen, while experts in the different fields, spend most of their time developing learned articles rather than subtle propaganda lectures. These is a difference in technique and the one does not suit your purposes at all.[103]

98 See correspondence: IHRC, ACEN, b. 152, f. 9.

99 Edmund Gaspar to Brinkley, ACEN Seminars in Latin America, 14 III 1963, IHRC, ACEN, b. 152, f. 9; Edmund Gaspar to Brinkley, 24 IV 1963, ibid. List of members of FEC approached to write texts for ACEN: Vilmos Juhasz; Sandor Kiss, Pavel Korbel, Jerzy Ptakowski, Ivanko Gabenky, Alois Rozehnal.

100 J.W. Brinkley to E. Gaspar, 15 III 1963, ibid.

101 Brinkley to Gaspar, 26 IV 1963, letter 2 (two pages), ibid.

102 Brinkley to Gaspar, 23 IV 1963, ibid.; Brinkley to Gaspar, 26 IV 1963, letter 1 (single page), ibid.

103 Brinkley to Gaspar, 26 IV 1963, letter 2 (two pages), ibid.

The real purposes of the seminars for Latin America were not covert, and – possibly even more importantly – not a subject of contention.

The second trip of the Deputy Secretary General took place in July 1963. Its purpose was to establish Latin American Friends of Captive Nations in Colombia, Peru, Ecuador, Chile, Argentina, Uruguay, Brazil, Venezuela and Mexico. Of these only Argentina, Chile, Uruguay and Ecuador "proved to be durable and still render service to the cause of Captive Nations," reported Gaspar. When re-evaluating its Latin American program, the ACEN General Committee noted that Brazilian Friends of Captive Nations was founded by office director in Rio de Janeiro, colonel Ressel. Despite, ACEN had to acknowledge failure: "After proper period of patience, monthly allowances to representations in Bogota, Lima, Caracas and São Paulo had to be suspended due to inefficiency." The ACEN representative in Santiago de Chile emigrated to the U.S. The U.S.-based exiles noted that over the past three years a trend had appeared when affiliates in Latin America felt as if their anti-communism posed a threat. They were not eager to enter a public sphere with such an agenda. "It gets harder every day to recruit new representatives for ACEN," stated an ACEN survey of its programs. "Latin America is shifting to the left," wrote Gaspar. In his opinion, presented to the ACEN General Committee Members, radical reforms in Venezuela, Peru and Chile (regimes installed by popular elections) were all congenial to Mexican and Bolivian revolutionary régimes. The ACEN's Deputy Secretary General observed: "[R]evitalized Peronism in Argentina," noting that "Uruguay was like a volcano," while "only in Brazil the leftist trend was reversed by the coup d'état of last April."[104]

The first seminar took place in Buenos Aires from 8 to 14 September 1963, with the ACEN's Deputy Secretary General selecting the participants. Out of 44 applications, 35 were selected (eight participants from Ecuador, 12 from Colombia, three from Salvador, six from Peru, two from Mexico, one from Chile, two from Uruguay, and one from Argentina). Selection criteria, as explained by Gaspar, were based on the future prospects of the Latin American presenters to become involved in future operations by the ACEN – either in the capacity of independent corresponding group or as activists of Friends of Captive Nations.[105] The discussions in Argentina focused on East Central European themes like legal systems, religion, economy (industrialization, collectivization), communist takeover, standard of living, women, culture, and Human Rights' violations. These

---

104 ACEN's Deputy Secretary General to ACEN's General Committee, Memorandum: Latin American Seminar Program, 6 X 1964, HIA, RFE/RL CF: A, b. 145, f. 5.
105 Ibid.

issues were then analyzed in an Latin American context.[106] One concern brought up by a Romanian exile in charge of the ACEN projects in Venezuela, was that the original purpose of the ACEN was being diluted: "[W]e do not want to inspire with our experience the countries in which we have come to live, and protect them from falling into the hands of the Communists at the expense of the people of our enslaved countries."[107]

The aim of the seminar, as described by Gaspar, was to give the ACEN's representatives as well as Friends of Captive Nations a scholarly survey of recent developments in the Captive Nations. The *spiritus movens* behind most of the ACEN's programs in Latin America observed, with obvious discontent, that "strangely enough, most of our East European collaborators showed little interest in this enterprise, under the false presumption that they know everything by their own experience and don't need to be indoctrinated." Gaspar considered it a mistake. In his opinion to combat propaganda factual evidence was needed, especially on the changes since the end of the Stalinist era.[108]

The proceedings of the seminar were published the same year by the ACEN in New York. Soon thereafter, via the contacts of Jerzy Skoryna-Lipski in Mexico, JUS, a local publishing house, offered to release the proceedings in Spanish.[109] This cooperation was intended to expand beyond seminar materials. Gaspar was already discussing publication of a brochure prepared by Barankovics (CDUCE) on the fate of the Catholic Church in Hungary.[110] Other publication projects included Korboński's *Warsaw in Chains*, followed by *Fighting Warsaw*. Skoryna-Lipski reported that Mexicans loved books about great love, fight and suffering, heroism and sacrifice for the homeland.[111] If so, the deal with JUS should not be surprising as it was profit-oriented. As per the ACEN-JUS agreement, book printing costs were charged to the ACEN, which was entitled to refunds on the sales price (not more than 50%). Both Korboński's books, in Spanish, were to be published in 2,000 copies at the total cost of 5,884 dollars. The ACEN asked the FEC to underwrite this project.[112] By June 1965, the ACEN was distrib-

106 *ACEN Seminars in Latin America. Lectures in the Seminar held in Buenos Aires, Argentina, September 8 – 14, 1963* (New York: ACEN, [1964?]).

107 Matei Ghica to Edmund Gaspar, Letter 1, 6 XI 1963, IHRC, ACEN, b. 58, f. 7.

108 ACEN's Deputy Secretary General to ACEN's General Committee, Memorandum: Latin American Seminar Program, 6 X 1964, HIA, RFE/RL CF: A, b. 145, f. 5.

109 Edmund Gaspar to Albert Kappel, 1 V 1963, IHRC, ACEN, b. 152, f. 9.

110 Gaspar to Kappel, 2 V 1963, ibid.

111 Jerzy Skoryna-Lipski to Edmund Gaspar, 25 V 1962, IHRC, ACEN, b. 56, f. 1.

112 Gaspar to Free Europe Committee (J.W. Healy, jr), Memorandum: Book-publication program in Latin America, 1 VI 1964, IHRC, ACEN, b. 157, f. 3

uting Korboński's book (most notably *En el nombre del Kremlin*), collecting 60% of profits.[113] Interestingly, in El Salvador this book's distribution via post was banned as "textos rojos." The ACEN's representative in the country interpreted it as an obvious sign of "the ignorance and anti-intellectual attitude of our government employees" ("incultura y antiintelectualidad de nuestros empleados de Gobierno.")[114]

JUS was not the only publisher involved. The next two books were planned to be published in Buenos Aires where Giullermo Kraft secured a publisher who would cover the cost of printing, with the ACEN being obliged to purchase a certain number of copies (up to a total of 1,000 dollars for each book). The selected books were: Leonard Kirschen: *Prisoners of Red Justice* (describing ten years of captivity of an AP correspondent in a Romanian communist prison); and Vincent Savarius' *Volunteers for the Gallows* (describing a former Hungarian Communist, Béla Szasz's show-trial, torture and conversion).

Brinkley was clear that most of the responsibility for success in Latin America rested on Gaspar's shoulders. As appreciative as he was, by May 1963 he also started to voice some concern regarding the rising costs of the operations. Gaspar's planned trips seemed too long with too many stops on the itineraries. His ideas regarding TV programs were met with the following comment: "I think most of your actions to date have been the right approach. But I have few cautions and questions to voice. Planning to TV is great but you have budget you must abide by. If you think you can afford it – go ahead."[115] This of course did not limit Gaspar. After another trip to Latin American countries in May 1964 he achieved the planned purpose – he found the place and local sponsors for another Latin American ACEN Seminar. His choice was Medellin in Colombia. Gaspar was delighted by the invitation from the rector of the University of Antioquia, who agreed to host the exile Assembly and their guests in early December. Colombia seemed very reasonable as the ACEN had a valuable asset there – the ACEN's representative, Father Tamosiunas.

Unlike Skoryna-Lipski in Mexico, or Sirutis in Bogota, the Lithuanian priest had both enough time and energy to help with organization of the seminar. In his report to Kappel, Gaspar wrote that he had already secured 23 applications from young Latin American intellectuals who wanted to attend. Among them there were student leaders, reporters (center and left), some Christian Democrats, anti-communists, as well as "anti-capitalists." The characterization of

113 Gaspar to Kappel, 16 VI 1965, IHRC, ACEN, b. 50, f. 5.
114 Luis R. Hidalgo Z. (San Salvador) to Edmund Gaspar (New York), 18 VIII 1966, IHRC, ACEN, b. 58, f. 8. See also: Luis R. Hidalgo Z. to Edmund Gaspar, 21 V 1965 and 22 V 1965, ibid.
115 Brinkley to Gaspar, 27 V 1963, IHRC, ACEN, b. 152, f. 9.

the Latin American audiences calls for some citations from Gaspar's report: they were seen to "admire the achievements of communism in Eastern Europe," "their ignorance in matters of East-Central Europe is beyond any imagination," "they are anxious to learn, and look with envy to their communist faculty-mates who are being taken in large groups to Moscow, Prague, Pekin for ideological training," "their outlooks are provincial," but "in most cases, at least in appearance, they are idealists and sympathetic to the cause of captive nations."[116] The aim of the five-day seminar was "awakening interest," possibly their joining the ranks "of those who are already working for our cause, like the student-groups in Ecuador and El Salvador." Printed material was to follow (just like after Buenos Aires seminar) which was intended for utilization in teaching courses on communism. Gaspar was writing to Kappel from Mexico where he was about to join Skoryna-Lipski in ceremonies paying homage to the captive nations in Veracruz (with the help of Archdiocese). By October 1964 Gaspar was ready with the progress report, approved after much discussion by the ACEN's General Committee on 7 October. The preparations for Medellin, Colombia were underway.[117]

The report on the seminar planned for 30 November to 4 December 1964 included plans for sessions on how East Central Europe had been overtaken by the Communists, its agriculture, industry, religion, economy, "freedom of mind," human rights under communism, as well as one on regional organizations. All sessions were to be complemented with distribution of ACEN-prepared brochures, with some translated into Spanish.[118] Among the participants, the program included local ACEN representatives like Reverend Tamosiunas ("will read text prepared by ACEN"), Csanad Toth (Colombia),[119] and ACEN-endorsed delegates from New York – Jan Stransky, János Horváth, Jan Wszelaki, as well as non-ACEN American participants (mostly university professors of East Central European descent), and local participants – and Latin Americans (academic teachers, student leaders, journalists). As of October 1964, invitations had been sent to seven participants from Ecuador, eight from Colombia, three from Salvador, three from Peru, two from Mexico, one from Chile, three from Uruguay, and one from Argentina.

---

116 Edmund Gaspar (ACEN, from Mexico) to Albert Kappel (Director Exile Organizations, FEC), 12 V 1964, HIA, RFE/RL CF: A, b. 145, f. 5.

117 Albert D. Kappel to Page, Memorandum: ACEN Seminar Project, Medellin, Colombia, 13 X 1964, ibid.

118 ACEN, Progress Report on the ACEN seminar Project in Medellin, Colombia, ibid.

119 Csanad Toth, a 1956 Hungarian exile, worked for the International Development Foundation (IDF) from 1962–1966. J. Y. Smith, "Csanad Toth, State Dept. Official, Dies," *The Washington Post*, 21 VI 1983.

According to Gaspar's report given to the ACEN General Committee, the focus of the Medellin seminar was supposed to be on economics, because "students and professors alike, regardless of their political affiliation, are boundless admirers of the economic progress achieved by communism in East Central Europe." Yet, as evidenced by the program of the Seminar, this was not really the case. The nine sessions focused on the following topics: communist takeover, agriculture, freedom of mind, industrialization, religion, economy, human rights, regional organizations, and follow-up plans.[120] Featured speakers at the seminar were Wszelaki, Stransky, Horváth, Csanad Toth, Fernand Torres de Leon (Colombian Professor of Sociology), et al.[121] Among the participants were: Colombians (16), Ecuadorians (6), Peruvians (3), Salvadorians (3), Uruguayans (3), Chilean (1), Argentinian (1), and a Mexican (1). Among the ACEN-affiliated participants were: the ACEN representative in Mexico City Jerzy Skoryna-Lipski; the ACEN correspondent in Quito – Luis Cornejo Gaete; Francisco J. Iujnevich – in charge of the Lithuanian radio program in Buenos Aires; and Wanda Siudyla – in charge of the Polish radio program in Montevideo. There were also exiles who worked on the Lithuanian hour on Radio Bolivariana in Medellin – Miss A. Laguardia and Alphonse Max from Montevideo, and Tomas Puig, from Santiago. Politically Skoryna and Puig were conservative, while the rest of the audience was described as rather leftist (non-Marxist), and much more vocal than their conservative fellow-participants.

The Medellin seminar was not a smooth, self-gratifying event. Toth's lecture was "of a strongly progressive tendency and contained sharp criticism of the Latin American ultra-conservative circles. (I had to make a statement from the chair, describing his views as not officially representing the ACEN's position)," wrote Gaspar in his report. "Bitter attacks against ruling oligarchs and the influence of 'foreign interests' supporting blood thirsty dictatorships, followed each other monotonously in the speeches of Ecuadorian, Salvadorian and Peruvian participants."

> Suspicious of the American way of democracy, critical of their own traditionalist political structures, looking with aversion towards Russia and China, the progressive-minded youth are anxious to pave a genuine Latin American way towards a modern industrialized

---

120 *ACEN Seminars in Latin America. Lectures of the Seminar Held in Medellin, Colombia, Nov. 29–Dec. 4, 1964* (New York: ACEN, [1965]).

121 Edmund Gaspar (ACEN, Dep. Sec. Gen.), The Second Seminar of ACEN in Latin America, Medellin, Nov. 29-Dec. 4, 1964: An Evaluation of its achievements and possible follow-up actions, HIA, RFE/RL CF: A, b. 145, f. 5. Invitations of Davila Torres and Amores Vasco were cancelled due to "suspected of Communist ties." Two others excused themselves. Gaspar also submitted confidential report concerning Dr. Cesar Davilla Torres.

> democracy, wiping out illiteracy, misery, and frightful sanitary conditions. They consider that those who are merely anti-Communists serve to perpetuate the rule of the exploiting classes and their U.S. allies.[122]

During the discussion on the conclusions, conservatives agreed to include the sentence: "Elimination of the present economic and social conditions would weaken the Communist Parties in Latin America."

Despite this, the FEC was delighted by the results of the meeting and offered its congratulations. In particular, the chief of exile relations (Kappel) mentioned the follow-up activities: press clippings, "Voice of Poland" (broadcast in Montevideo, Uruguay by a "few dedicated individuals with comparatively limited means"), listeners' reactions, the "apparent eagerness of some of the participants to utilize the Medellin experience for political action."[123]

As part of the follow-up, Gaspar proposed that an ACEN correspondent be established in all the countries of the Hemisphere. At the time there were five active representations of the ACEN in Latin America (Buenos Aires, Rio de Janeiro, Montevideo, Mexico City and Quito) and regular radio programs sponsored by the Assembly. By July 1964 there were six broadcasts coordinated by the ACEN and supported financially by the FEC.[124]

Tab. 6: ACEN-coordinated broadcasts in Latin America, 1964

City, ethnicity of dir. broadcaster	Staff	Radio station used	Broadcast time, day of the week	Financial endorsement per month
Montevideo, Uruguay, Lithuanian	Director: Casimiro Cibiras Verax (Lithuanian) – press attaché of the Lithuanian Legation, writer, newspaperman.	CX 50 Radio Independencia	weekly 15 minutes in Spanish	$ 30

122 Ibid.

123 Albert D. Kappel (Director, FEC/EPO) to Edmund Gaspar (Dep. Secr. General, ACEN), 26 I 1965, ibid.

124 Edmund Gaspar (Dep. Sec. ACEN) to Jan Stransky (FEC/EPO), Memorandum: ACEN Radio Broadcasts in Latin America, 23 VII 1964, IHRC, ACEN, b. 133, f. 10.

Tab. 6: ACEN-coordinated broadcasts in Latin America, 1964 *(Continued)*

City, ethnicity of dir. broadcaster	Staff	Radio station used	Broadcast time, day of the week	Financial endorsement per month
	Collaborators: Martinez Bersetche – Chairman of Uruguyan anti-totalitarian and pro-captive nations organization; Anatolius Grisonas – Charge d'Affaires of Lithuanian legation Montevideo; Rodolfo Katzenstein – Uruguayan Catholic newspaperman; Juan Carlos Gamarotta – Uruguayan lawyer, active member of the liberal (Batllista) party; The last two according to Gaspar were his closest associates.			
Polish program in Montevideo, Uruguay	Director: Stanisław Samsel – president of the Marshal Pilsudski Association (top-organization of non-communist Poles in Montevideo); Roman Tustanowski – head of the Polish veterans' organization, Wanda Siudyla, secretary, office staff, Polish ancestry.	CX58 Radio Clarin	la Voz de Polonia Libre, in Spanish weekly, Sundays 30 min.	$ 30
Lithuanian program in Buenos Aires, Argentina	Director: Ceferino Iujnevich – Lithuanian member of the ACEN-Delegation and his son – Francisco Jose Iujnevich, a university student. Wenceslao Rymaricius – musical advisor – director of Lithuanian choir; Carlos Misuinas – administrator	L.R. Radiodifusora Antartida	in Spanish, 25 minutes weekly	$ 45

Tab. 6: ACEN-coordinated broadcasts in Latin America, 1964 *(Continued)*

City, ethnicity of dir. broadcaster	Staff	Radio station used	Broadcast time, day of the week	Financial endorsement per month
Lithuanian program in Medellin, Colombia	Director: rev. Tamosiunas – ACEN representative in Colombia	Radio Sutatenza & radio Cultural Boliviana	weekly 2 broadcasts of 15 minutes each; in Spanish	$ 30
Captive Nations program in Quito, Ecuador	Director: Luis Cornejo Gaete[125] – ACEN correspondent in Ecuador, assisted by Luis Eduardo Granja Estrella – director of Radio Ecuatoriana (could be heard in Central America, Colombia and Peru, even USA [EE.UU.])[126] and members of an Ecuadorian student organization	radio station: Emisora Central	in Spanish weekly 30 min.	$ 25
Proposed Lithuanian Broadcast in Rio de Janeiro, Brazil	Director: Peter Babickas – secretary of Lithuanian delegation; helped by msgr. Ignatavitius – Lithuanian priest.	Radio Vera Cruz	weekly 15 min., in Portuguese,	$ 0

The contents of the broadcasts consisted mostly of samples of music originating from East Central Europe, news (supplied by FEC), commentaries, interviews, guests, and invited submissions by from local leaders. The programs lasted up to 30 minutes and were usually broadcast in the native language (Polish, or Lithuanian). There were also occasional broadcasts, like Radio Vanguardia in El Salvador,[127] or re-broadcasting initiatives, like using Gaete's programs over the airwaves of two major stations ("La voz de Riobamba," and "El Prado") in

125 See biographical note on Rodolfo Perez Pimentel (historian, biographer) web site: Diccionario Biographico Ecuador, http://www.diccionariobiograficoecuador.com/tomos/tomo11/c7.htm, accessed: 22 IX 2019.

126 Luis Eduardo Granja Estrella (biographical note), IHRC, ACEN, b. 133, f. 10.

127 Luis R. Hidalgo Z. (San Salvador) to Edmund Gaspar (New York), 24 VI 1965, IHRC, ACEN, b. 58, f. 8.

Ecuador's fourth largest city.[128] In order to engage his listeners, Gaete organized competitions for his listeners, asking them, for example: What do you know about the captive nations of East Central Europe and how can we help and what lessons can be derived from this "painful and tragic" experience?[129]

As was the case with the Asian anti-communist organizations supported (overtly and covertly by the U.S.), in the case of Cuban exiles, the FEC tried to put the ACEN in contact with anti-communists as well. "It is embarrassing to say this, but majority of Latin American countries ignore what you are doing in favor of these countries and democracy," wrote one anti-Castro exile leader. "Before Castro's arrival to Cuban power, almost all Cubans ignored all problems that those European countries suffered. What I want to ask you now is that if you have any pamphlets with a little of history of these countries is explained, please send them to me." This came from Rolando Castano representing Directorio Revolucionario Estudiantil de Cuba in Cali (Colombia) and was addressed to the FEC (Kappel).[130] Castano, "intelligent and energetic," (obviously ardently anti-Castro: his father was executed by the regime) but unidentified as to his political leanings by the FEC, was referred to the ACEN with a special reference to Hungarians because of "Soviet military watchdogging with its parallels to the Soviet troops in Cuba." The other idea was for Truitt, "by an entirely 'coincidental' and separate approach," to bind him into one or more youth enterprises in Colombia.[131] What is important to note is that the Cuban exile students' revolutionary movement was actually "conceived, created and funded by the Agency [CIA] in September 1960 and terminated in December 1966." It was an outgrowth of the activist student group in Cuba which fought against Batista and later against Castro. At first used for intelligence and paramilitary tasks, after the Bay of Pigs failure its "members were used through 1966 as political action agents, for publishing propaganda which was sent throughout Hemisphere, attending international student meetings at Agency direction, and producing radio programs and special propaganda campaigns."[132]

128 Gaspar to Kappel, 16 VI 1965, IHRC, ACEN, b. 50, f. 5; Gaete to Gaspar, 27 V 1965, ibid.
129 Gaete to Gaspar, 1 III 1965, ibid.
130 Rolando Castano (For Cuba's Freedom, Cali, Colombia) to Alton Kastner (Director of Public Information, FEC), 26 II 1963, HIA, RFE/RL CF: A, b. 199, f. 2.
131 John Dunning to Kappel, 1 III 1963, ibid. Handwritten note on the margin: "Dunning: ACEN have sent appropriate materials, plus are having their Bogota rep. get in touch with Castano. JWB". [Brinkley?]
132 "At present there are delegations in most Latin American countries which have maintained some contact with various agency stations over the years although the DRE is no longer very active. Student Revolutionary Directorate Created by CIA, JFK Assassination documents, CIA, HSCA segregated CIA collection, b. 42, record number 104–10106–10771, agency file number

There was an attempt to organize another Latin American Seminar in Bogota in 1966. Gaspar excitedly informed the FEC that his partners offered not only to host the seminar but also underwrite most of its costs. John Dunning discussed the idea with George Truitt, and Truitt was all in favor. It is interesting to look at his arguments: Colombia's economic and social problems were pressing, and were about to get worse before they got better, so "a word of caution and warning against over-trusting and optimistic resort to Communist ideas and Communist support would be timely." The target audience again included educators but, in concurrence with the ACEN's views, "out-and-out propaganda of an extreme sort would be self-defeating [...] doubly so because Chinese Communist propaganda has flagrantly exceeded effective limits in Colombia."[133]

Gaspar presented the idea to Mucio Delgado of FEC. The idea of the seminar in Bogota came from the Under Secretary of Education in one of the regions in Colombia (Cundinamarca). The Colombian invitation said that the travel and other expenses of professors and school directors would be paid by it. The ACEN's cost would be its four members plus translations.[134] Suddenly, in the early days of August, the Colombians changed their mind citing the unavailability of translation equipment. Gaspar asked them for a one-week postponement because he had his citizenship hearing in the U.S., but Free Europe thought the reasons for cancelation to be purely political.[135]

7.3 Divergence

The challenges to the ACEN's operations in Latin America stemmed not only from the local conditions. Dean Rusk's speech at the Eighth Meeting of the Foreign Ministers of Nations Belonging to the Organization of American States, in Punta del Este, Uruguay, infuriated the East Central European exiles. In January 1962, the American Secretary of State said that the Cold War could end "tomor-

---

80T01357 A, CIA historical review program. Release in full 11 XI 1998. Available at Mary Ferrell Foundation, https://www.maryferrell.org/showDoc.html?docId=13958#relPageId=2&tab=page, accessed: 21 XI 2018.

133 John Dunning to George Truitt, Memorandum of conversation: Proposed ACEN Seminar in Bogota (for educators of Department of Cundinamarca) August 1966, 7 VII 1966, HIA, RFE/RL CF: A, b. 145, f. 5.

134 Edmund Gaspar (ACEN) to Mucio Delgado (FEC), Memorandum, 17 II 1966, ibid.

135 Richard H. Flanagan to Mr. Kinyon (cc: Richardson, Yarrow, Dunning, Rowson), Memorandum: Latin American seminar, 8 VIII 1966, ibid.

row if Communist leaders ceased hostile activities."[136] In August 1963, Moscow signed the partial Nuclear Test Ban Treaty, followed by a grain shipment to Russia in October of that year. The ACEN almost aggressively confronted such policies. The Chairman of the ACEN wrote to Rusk after his Punta del Este speech, calling the new policy turn, "a stab in the back of the Captive Nations."[137]

On the other hand, the FEC was already concerned in 1962 with the ACEN's performance in Latin America. The projects designed by the Free Europe Committee were not being carried out as planned. Upon reviewing the financial statements of the ACEN, Horace E. Henderson of the FEC wrote to the Assembly's Chairman (Nagy) concerned that monies allotted for representation abroad, particularly the special representation in Latin America, has not been used for this purpose during the month of July. He continued "All monies allotted to ACEN must be used substantially for the purposes for which they are allotted. This is particularly true in the matter of salaries or allotments for individuals to represent ACEN in other countries because allotted money for this purpose represents a policy decision on the part of the Free Europe Committee."[138] Correspondence included in the C.D. Jackson collection at the Eisenhower Library sheds more light on when and how and why the FEC changed its programs for Latin America, including reducing East Central European exile participation in it.

The first issue under consideration was the FEC's shrinking budget. As demonstrated in the FEC memorandum prepared by John Richardson in October 1963, the annual budget for its operations was reduced by roughly 250,000 dollars, but it was two million less than they asked in their budget proposal for 1964, with an obvious signaling that reduction was to be the trend for the coming years.[139] Attached to this letter were a series of memoranda pertaining to the Latin American Programs. These resulted from an exchange with CM (Cord Meyer) who in early June 1963 brought up a series of criticisms of Latin American operations. It was followed by a thorough evaluation of these. Before the report can be presented, an explanation of organizational changes that occurred within FEC is in order.

136 Statement of January 25 [1962] in: *Department of State Bulletin* XLVI, No. 1182, 19 II 1962, 276, https://archive.org/details/departmentofstat461962unit/page/266, accessed 12 IV 2018.
137 Gadomski, *Zgromadzenie Europejskich* ..., 43–44.
138 Horace E. Henderson to Ferenc Nagy, 15 VIII 1962, HIA, RFE/RL CF: A, b. 145, f. 7.
139 John Richardson, Jr. to John C. Hughes, Ernest A. Gross and C.D. Jackson, 4 X 1963, DDEL, Jackson Papers, b. 53, f. 1: FEC Budget, etc., 1963 (1); Memorandum by the Board of Directors of FEC (Gross, Hughes, Jackson, Richardson), 19 IX 1963, ibid.

In 1960 and 1961, "in response to the rising challenge of communism in Latin America," Free Europe decided to consolidate various exile resources in the FWOD. However, in the aftermath of the Cuban Missile Crisis, its "priorities were changing" and "emphasis shifted sharply toward maximum communication with East Europe."[140] Despite this, the existing Latin American program remained with the long-term goal of "assisting development of stronger economies and democratic processes." Its form was modified to phase out East Central European exiles. Some programs were continued under the auspices of a new organization, the International Development Foundation (IDF), established in 1962. It took two years to completely transition the FEC operations from the FWOD to the IDF, with decreasing support from the FEC.[141] Finally, by June 1964, the IDF was separated from the FEC, though it hired some of its former staff. At this time, the FEC claimed it no longer maintained operations in Latin America, Asia or Africa,[142] apart from a few thousand dollars of assistance to the ACEN enabling it to maintain part-time representation in a few South American countries and in Lebanon. Programs which were not transferred to the IDF were terminated. Among the leftovers within the FEC were a "one-man self-determination project in Europe" and some programs for Hungarian exile students (created on an ad hoc basis). John H. Page, who was Vice President of Free Europe until his resignation in August 1965, became the IDF's chairman.[143]

In June and July 1963 the CIA critically evaluated the FEC Latin American programs which resulted in general reappraisal of FEC activities in Latin America and exile relations. The internal review said that the "FEC/IDF is trying to do too much in Latin America, in too many different directions at once with inadequate arrangements for planning, guiding and coordinating its operations. The EC [CIA] has exercised too little control over these activities and has failed to pro-

---

140 The reason given in the report was: "collapse of the Soviet-Cuban missile threat has deflated Communist prestige in the Western Hemisphere", JLD [John Dunning], History of Free World Operations Division ...

141 The CIA continued to channel money to the IDF through other means. See: Sol Stern, with Lee Web, Michael Ansara, Michael Wood "A Short Account of International Student Politics and the Cold War With Particular Reference to the NSA, CIA, Etc." published in *Ramparts* (March 1967), introduced to the *Congressional Record* by representative William F. Ryan (NY) under the heading: "Control of the CIA," 90th Cong., 1st Sess., *Cong. Rec.* 113 (part 5), 9 III 1967, 6153–6156.

142 JLD [John Dunning], History of Free World Operations Division of Free Europe Committee, Inc. and International Development Foundation, 27 II 1967, HIA, RFE/RL CF: A b. 200, f. 1.

143 Reasons and methods of Reorganization of FWOD to ID, see: Memorandum re: FEC Operations in the Developing Areas, 28 III 1962, HIA, RFE/RL CF: A, b. 200, f. 3.

vide as much guidance and servicing as FEC/IDF has a right to expect." Consequently, the evaluation of the FEC/IDF activities was arranged in three categories: generally sound, worth continuing and developing, and those that were reduced and/or discontinued. Most of the ACEN activities fell into the third category as "unsound." Some of the programs listed in the third category were listed as "may have promise but need to be better focused; guided and coordinated."[144] As the IDF was being separated from the FEC (and become a separate CIA project), it was supposed to focus solely on Latin America and "dilute its East European flavor." This did not mean abandoning it completely but that it should "hire people who are not necessarily of East European origin and avoid approaching every operational task form an East European exile viewpoint."[145] The CIA decided that the FEC should retain responsibility only for symbolic exile political activity directed at Latin America and support some publication efforts. "FEC's tendency to become a worldwide propaganda and political operations mechanism, which has been increasing ever since the mid 1950's should be halted and reversed," the evaluation concluded. The mid-1960s were considered as "likely to be another period of ferment in Eastern Europe," in which case the FEC "should be freed to give its best to its primary East European targets during the next few years."[146]

What remained of interest to the sponsors of the FEC in Latin American operations were programs run by the Christian Democrats to "build-up forward – looking Christian Democratic elements in Latin America as a major U.S. policy aim." In this regard the CDUCE, a member of the ACEN, was mentioned but more control and stricter guidance was to be employed. For example, "Śleszyński [an officer of the CDUCE in charge of Latin American and UN affairs[147]] should meet more regularly with the EC [CIA] case officer."[148] László Varga, another member of the ACEN, was mentioned in the CIA report in conjunction with the Committee for Self-Determination. Their activities included organization of

144 Memorandum B delivered to the FEC by a regular CIA liaison officer – a summary of a series of papers developed by the evaluation procedure. "Evaluation of the International Development Foundation (IDF) and other FEC-sponsored Latin American Activities," attachment to John Richardson to John C. Hughes, Ernest A. Gross, C.D. Jackson (board of Directors, FEC), Memorandum, 4 X 1963, DDEL, C.D. Jackson Papers, b. 53, f.: FEC Budget, 1963 (1).

145 Ibid.

146 Ibid.

147 McHale to Alexander, Memorandum: Aide Memoir [original spelling] of Luncheon at Princeton Club, September 29 1959, 30 IX 1959, HIA, RFE/RL CF: A, b. 161, f. 1.

148 Evaluation of the International Development Foundation (IDF)...

local self-determination committees in Latin America and sponsorship of radio and TV program on East Central European themes.

> Much of what it does overlaps with, and seems to some degree to be inseparable from, activity of the ACEN, since in certain cases the same people are used by both organizations. A small investment of effort in this field is desirable if it can be proved that a general target audience (not simply other émigrés and persons of East European origin) is being reached and that the propaganda is not so heavy-handed that its impact is only on those already convinced of its validity. But the effort should remain small and be under effective control.

The CIA was also concerned with the overlapping of operations and people representing the ACEN and other non-IDF organizations as well. The FEC connection was also considered "superfluous and potentially a security problem."[149]

The CIA wished to save 250,000 dollars through cuts in publication programs targeting Latin America because "with few exceptions, most of this material appears to be mediocre in quality, duplicative of various other efforts, and poorly controlled and coordinated." The Foreign News Service, which was run by Bolesław Wierzbiański (also affiliated with the ACEN) was found to have no justification to continue, as it "brought us almost nothing that can be described as concrete propaganda results [...] with a life on its own without reference to either FEC or EC objectives." The cost of FNS's operations was listed as 184,000 dollars: "Though the claims which Mr. Wierzbiański makes for the impact of FNS in Latin America appear in part to be fraudulent, they mean little even if they are accepted at face value, for practically all the newspapers which he lists as recipients of his service are already served better by other EC-supported news and feature services and field operations."[150]

Coming to the activities of the ACEN, it was described as duplicating much of what the IDF was already doing in Latin America. Therefore, "far from expanding ACEN and permitting it to inaugurate a series of operations of unprecedented (for it) scope in Latin America, FEC should be contemplating how to cut it back and phase it out." The CIA concluded:

> Over the perspective of the next four or five years, it is bound to become a wasting asset and an instrument of dubious value, both because of its tendency to operate as a rightist-oriented lobby in the United States and because of the absence of any convincing evidence that it has a capability for carrying on propaganda and political action likely to be effective with

---

149 Evaluation of the International Development Foundation (IDF)... Interestingly, the text mentions IDF having only one field representative "of its own" in Latin America – F. Bregha in Peru.
150 Ibid.

> the groups we are most interested in influencing in Latin America. Expansion plans should be limited to those which FEC and the EC agree and are in accord with basic propaganda objectives.[151]

The document described above (marked as memorandum B) was expanded by a series of papers developed by the CIA within evaluation procedures (including a detailed memorandum on the ACEN dated 1 July 1963), all subject to discussions with the FEC President and members of the FEC Board of Directors.

Memorandums C, D and E were formal responses by the FEC President, John Richardson, to the EC (CIA). In one of them (D), he explained that while the bulk of the FEC's Latin American efforts and funds were already under the IDF's supervision, one of the exceptions was the ACEN, whose Latin American operation was approximately at the 40,000 dollars level. Rejecting much of the criticism as unfair, blaming it on poor communications, Richardson wrote that in less than two years the IDF had gained a significant standing in Latin America and the U.S. among serious and significant students of Latin American affairs. It had established a reputation of being one of the few organizations aimed at affecting the heart of the Latin American problem, i.e. influencing political forces without which other forms of assistance, economic, technical, etc., would have had only a marginal effect. Among the points Richardson wished to discuss was continuance of a limited ACEN Latin American program.[152]

Attached to Richardson's memo was also the IDF's response to the evaluation. In the section related to East Central European exiles, under the heading "dilution of exile flavor," the IDF stated that its personnel consisted of 128 people, of various status regarding citizenship. The opinion of the IDF was firm: "This entire operation has been built on the motivation and talents of political exiles. To lose them would be to lose a great policy asset. In addition, it is at least initially through assimilated exiles that IDF was able to localize its operations in Latin America. This capability represents a unique asset in the technical sense."[153]

---

151 Evaluation of the International Development Foundation (IDF)...

152 The President (FEC, Richardson) to the Executive Committee [CIA], 26 VII 1963, C.D. Jackson Papers, b. 53, f. 1: FEC Budget, etc., 1963 (1).

153 IDF response to evaluation of IDF and other FEC-sponsored Latin American Activities, attached to Richardson's report to the EC, 26 VII 1963 C.D. Jackson Papers, b. 53, f. 1: FEC Budget, etc., 1963 (1).

As these discussions continued in July 1963, the ACEN was subject to a more general evaluation.[154] Regarding the ACEN's Latin American program, the larger memorandum referring to the ACEN's future, contained a rather brief mention:

> There is nothing to indicate that the ACEN activity in Latin America is having in toto or is likely to have serious impact on the groups we are trying to influence who are most susceptible to Communist or Castroite propaganda. One gets the distinct impression that most of ACEN's activity in Latin America to the extent that it has any significant impact at all – which is probably very small – results merely in bolstering the convictions and prejudices of the already convinced.[155]

Since some sentences in this report are identical to the EC (CIA) memo described earlier, as well as the recommendation that Executive Committee staff be given more control and guidance, it can be assumed this also came from the CIA. Indeed, the financial arrangements soon became a major obstacle for continuing the ACEN's operations. These resulted, however, from changes in American foreign policy.

When in 1965 American troops landed in the Dominican Republic, the ACEN Latin American program – no matter how small it now was – was doomed. Following the assassination of Trujillo in 1961, there was a brief plan to introduce reforms, which included re-distribution of the dictator's land (1.4 million acres generating one third of the country's GNP). Given that half of the Republic's population worked in agriculture, the circumstances called for land reform – had that been successful, it could have established a socioeconomic infrastructure for democracy – something envisioned in the Alliance for Progress as a *sine qua non* for stabilization in the region and the strengthening of the democratic alliance.[156] However, landed families on the island, as well as officers, wanted the spoils, while reformist President Juan Bosch (1962–1963, Dominican Revolutionary Party) effectively alienated these elites. Ousted by a military coup in September 1963, Bosch built a "constitutionalist movement" and tried to orchestrate an insurrection. American military intervention, the first in more than three decades, put an end to domestic strife.[157]

---

154 [CIA], Memorandum for the Record: The Assembly ..., 1 VII 1963.

155 Ibid.

156 Smith, 230–231.

157 Piero Gleijeses, "Hope Denied: the U.S. Defeat of the 1965 Revolt in the Dominican Republic," *Cold War International History Project, Working Paper* 72 (Washington: CWIHP, 2014), accessed: 21 IX 2019.

The repercussions of this action were reported by Gaspar, who collected feedback from the ACEN offices in Latin America.[158] He reported that all the ACEN's correspondents sent him clippings confirming the "flare-up of nationalism," the "growing influence of communism," and the distortion that the image of U.S. has suffered "as a consequence of the unfortunate events in the Dominican Republic."

Dr. László Simon, director of the Buenos Aires office, reported unequivocally negative effects: "Latin Americans are usually very sensitive toward such developments." According to his report, communist propaganda was in full swing, exploiting this chance to bash "Yankee aggressors." At the same time, he observed a complete lack of counterpropaganda in Argentina. Professor Fernand Torres Leon from Bogota reported the very negative impact the American action had had in Colombia. Protests were coming from all political sectors, and the U.S. had definitively lost its prestige. The good news was that the "weak Communist Party here cannot take full advantage of the situation to their benefit." Gossip swirled that Colombia would be next, turning even the church and oligarchs against the U.S. Torres Leon cited the press titles: "[T]he gringos want to settle the problems with their marines." To his despair, more and more students were prone to becoming "Cuba-Peking-line Marxists." Wanda Sidyla, reporting from Montevideo, wrote that even "El Día" and "El Pais" no longer supported North-American attitudes unconditionally. In Uruguay, papers like "Accion" (of the left-of center Batllista party), "EPOCA" (a pro-communist daily), "El Popular" (a daily of the Communist Party) were gaining popularity. Jerzy Skoryna-Lipski wrote from Mexico that the country's newspapers followed the government's policy of no intervention, self-determination, though generally he observed indifference, except for some protesting students.[159]

Luis Roberto Hidalgo Zelaya, reporting from San Salvador (in El Salvador), wrote that the majority of the population was sharply against the American intervention. But he also stated his private opinion that had it not been for the U.S., there would have been "a second Cuba."[160] Gaspar shared this sentiment. While careful to express his private views, as the ACEN decided to take no official stance on the invasion,[161] the Hungarian leader of the Assembly's Latin American programs believed that the people of the Dominican Republic lacked

158 Gaspar to Kappel, Memorandum: Repercussions of the Dominican Crisis in Latin America, 2 VI 1965, HIA, RFE/RL CF: A, b. 145, f. 3.

159 Ibid.

160 Luis R. Hidalgo Z. to Edmund Gaspar, 18 V 1965, IHRC, ACEN, b. 58, f. 8.

161 Gaspar to Hidalgo, 28 V 1965, ibid.

democratic structures that would allow them to resist the abuses of either the right or the left.[162]

Reading through all of the incoming reports, Gaspar summed up: "[T]here is no doubt that the Dominican events will temporarily impair our efforts in Latin America," noting that "the intervention of U.S. armed forces into the Dominican internal crisis have raised the specter of haunting analogy with the crushing of the Hungarian Revolution by the Red [Soviet] Army." Juan Bosch called Santo Domingo the "Budapest of Latin America" while liberal congressman Francisco Sanfuentes Bulnes in Chile went on the record to say that the "U.S. did not dare to go to the help of those Hungarians who, in the streets of Budapest clamored for its support." Dr. Simon in Argentina reported that the comparison reached such a level that President of Centro Hungaro – Andres Szechenyi – had to go on Radio Belgrano ("speech prepared by our office director," added Simon). In that speech he rejected allegations, recalled the principal facts of the Hungarian Revolution, and pointed to the fundamental differences between the targets and methods of the two interventions.[163]

The ACEN's (and FEC-supported) programs in Latin America possibly broadened awareness of the fate of East Central Europe under communism. They did not influence the opinions of the Latin Americans related to their domestic situation though. Moreover, the exiles could not escape being branded as right-wing. Symptomatically, Eva R. Stonek, who took on the task of running the ACEN delegation in Uruguay, reported an incident to Feliks Gadomski in late October 1966 that occurred during the meeting organized at "Plaza Budapest" in Montevideo. The event was organized to commemorate the tenth anniversary of the Hungarian Revolution, and was attended by the "ACEN's President" (most likely Edmund Gaspar[164]) who made a speech in the presence of the President of the Association of Uruguayan Friends of the Captive Nations (Maria Sara Faget) and other prominent Uruguayans. "The manifestation was disturbed by Communists who passed by on noisy motorcycles, shouting 'Fascists' through loudspeakers."[165] The historical context of the East Central European experience with fascism, before it was replaced by communism, was lost in cultural translation. What the Latin Americans learned well from the East Central European exiles, however, was what they could relate to their own experience: imperial-

162 "Los dominicanos carecen de una estructura democratica suficientemente amplia para resistir a los asaltos tanto de la derecha como de la izquierda." Gaspar to Hidalgo, 21 V 1965, ibid.

163 Edmund Gaspar to Albert Kappel, Memorandum: Repercussions of the Dominican Crisis in Latin America, 2 VI 1965, HIA, RFE/RL CF: A, b. 145, f. 3.

164 "ACEN Around the world: Gaspar's Trip," *ACEN News* 126 (Nov.-Dec. 1966): 21.

165 Eva R. Stonek (Uruguay) to Feliks Gadomski, 31 X 1966, IHRC, ACEN, b. 58, f. 3.

ism, brutal force, and a lack of respect for self-determination that put the small nations in a losing position when faced with major power. Yet, these developments did not bring the ACEN much success in the UN, and were definitely not in accordance with the American plans. Both lost their quest for support in Latin America.

Throughout the 1960s and most of the 1970s, the American domination of the region continued unchallenged until the Sandinista victory of 1979, the first communist force to come to power since Cuba.[166] However, American interests in the region were facilitated not by the success of the Alliance for Progress or winning the hearts and minds of the Latin Americans. There were nine military coups against civilian, constitutional governments just in the first five years under the Alliance for Progress.[167] Of the four countries where the ACEN had its offices, all suffered such a fate: Brazil in 1964, Argentina in 1966, and later in 1973 Chile and even Uruguay. The ACEN maintained correspondence with its regional representatives until 1971 (see table 9). After 1965 these carried little substance or hope for efficient political action.

166 Smith, *American Mission ...*, 223–232.
167 Ibid., 223.

8 “We can only buy their time ...” – Free Europe Committee and ACEN

The ACEN’s role and usefulness in American political warfare between 1954 and 1972 underwent significant changes and so did the assessment of its significance by the FEC. Throughout the 1950s, the FEC continued to praise the ACEN’s accomplishments. Complimenting the Assembly on its first year of existence, the Vice President Yarrow (head of exile relations) reported to the FEC President:

> The ACEN has successfully surmounted the organizational problems of its first fifteen months and has established itself well beyond the most optimistic expectations as a central organization for all exiles, and not merely those resident in the U.S. Its prestige not only among exiles resident in Europe, but also with Western European governments, is notable. It can provide an ideal focus of action for exile activity throughout Western Europe. [...]
>
> Both collectively and individually, the exiles have developed their effectiveness in a most gratifying way as a consequence of their training and experience in the various national councils and committees over the past few years they have gained confidence and refined their techniques, studied the tactics and objectives of the Communist regimes and otherwise improved their “professional” skills.
>
> They are a valuable, and potentially great, political warfare force. By dispatching representatives to European congresses and meetings for specific purposes and bringing their European members to the U.S. on appropriate occasions and for justifiable purposes, both the national and international organizations have generated interest and inspiration in their ranks, and at the same time evolved an effective mobility and adaptability to meet shifting challenges.
>
> Not only are they fulfilling their role as the constituent bodies of the ACEN, but they seek out and attack new situations in which their organizations or members thereof can meet every fresh Communist move. [...] As the struggle becomes more critical [...] our exile forces are prepared to move into forward positions and meet the enemy on the firing line.[1]

During the Freedom Day celebrations on 1 July 1956, Cloyce K. Huston (Deputy Director of FEOP) publicly praised the “truly gigantic achievements” of the East Central European exiles, whom he referred to as “warriors of freedom” listed alongside Rochambeau, Lafayette, Kościuszko and Pułaski. The long list of their accomplishments included the following:

1 Yarrow to Shepardson, Memorandum: DER Program of Activities for First Six Months of 1956, 21 XII 1955, HIA, RFE/RL CF: A, b. 198, f. 5.

https://doi.org/10.1515/9783110661002-012

> They have created powerful instruments of political warfare in the form of committees and councils, both national and international, with representatives in most of the capitals and strategic points of the free world;
>
> They have capped their organizational activities by the creation of a truly remarkable master instrument – the Assembly of Captive European Nations;
>
> They have written, published and distributed in a dozen languages literally hundreds of valuable books to inform the world of what happened to their countries, of the Communist techniques of power, the destruction of their nation's institutions, the sapping of its economies;
>
> By a flood of pamphlets, letters, newspaper articles, public statements, protests, and studies of all kinds, they have recited the horrors of executions, massacres, deportations, imprisonment;
>
> They have edited and published scores of newspapers and magazines devoted to the cause of freedom;
>
> They have given thousands, tens of thousands, of lectures in universities, churches, clubs, theaters and public halls of all kinds;
>
> They have challenged Communist representatives and apologists on any platform or in any forum where they could be found;
>
> They have sent representatives or delegations to conferences, congresses, and rallies all over the world, to any arena where the interests of their enslaved nations and the cause of freedom have been at stake;
>
> They have maintained close touch with the United Nations, the Council of Europe and other important international organizations;
>
> Among them are leaders who have ready access to every chancellery in the Western world, who have the ear of government leaders and statesmen of every free nation;
>
> In their conversations, wherever they go, they have constantly reminded the world of the Communist takeover of their countries, of the humiliations, degradations, and deprivations of their peoples;
>
> By every means that is humanly possible, they have sent a continuous stream of messages to their brothers behind the Iron Curtain to provide them hope and encouragement, to maintain their faith and their determination;
>
> They have faithfully and loyally interpreted the hopes and aspirations of their compatriots in the homeland;
>
> They have visited their less fortunate brothers in the refugee camps, even seeking ways to help them in matters of emigration, resettlement and employment, to maintain schools and summer camps for their children;
>
> And so on indefinitely.[2]

This speech was delivered in New York as part of an effort to counter the ideas coming from Moscow. It took place before the Hungarian Revolution, which constituted the ACEN's most wide-spread, longest-lasting single project aimed at lobbying international support for their cause. This overly positive assessment

2 Address by Cloyce K. Huston on behalf of Free Europe Committee, Freedom Day, 1 VII 1956, HIA, RFE/RL CF: A, b. 257, f. 6.

of the role of the exiles met one of the aims for which the ACEN was established – to offer legitimacy as "living instruments of national identity in exile" for American anti-communist action, by acting on behalf of the captives and using them to counter communist propaganda.

Both their ability to serve as spokesmen for their compatriots and act as a useful political warfare instrument, was established and publicly acknowledged by early 1956. McCargar, who until March 1956 served as FEC liaison to the ACEN, said in the radio program that the ACEN provided "a spearhead for the national aspirations" of the émigré groups, which were "political spokesmen organized by democratic processes and as various issues come up they arrive at their positions on such issues. They make various statements and undertake certain actions, a number of which are of great assistance to RFE and Free Europe Press, in their actual propaganda contact with the captive people."[3] The FEER was delighted that in its three years of existence the ACEN had remarkable series of political successes. In the program and budget planned for 1958, the division of exile relations wrote: "It can be safely said that the ACEN can now command serious and influential attention in some of the most important UN circles, acting as it does as the spokesman of all the captive nations."[4] The extraordinary lobbying effort undertaken by the ACEN on a global scale in the aftermath of the Hungarian Revolution was both praised and generously supported by the FEC. In the evaluation preceding budgetary decisions for 1958, the FEC had noted some "structural deficiencies," which were to be corrected. Among these, the exile relations division listed, inter alia, "excessive conservatism in outlook, a strong tendency toward exclusivity, a still inadequate activity in Europe."[5] At this time, the most important task was accomplished: "FEER's friends in the exile have brought the cause of Eastern Europe to the attention of the UN, Council of Europe, and other international bodies. Through their tireless endeavors this problem has been kept 'on the agenda' of the Free World."[6] Similarly, in the spring of 1959, the FEC was considering the reinforcement of the ACEN as the "most effective instrument at FEER disposal in the national and international

3 The World War Behind the Iron Curtain, Georgetown University Radio Forum – discussion moderated by Matthew Warren with the participation of: John A. DeChant (Vice President, Crusade for Freedom), James G. McCargar (Assistant Director of Exiled Relations, FEC), Gerald Streibel (Deputy Director of Information, RFE), transcript, 19 II 1956, IHRC, ACEN, b. 3, f. 3.

4 FEER program and budget for fiscal year 1958, HIA, RFE/RL CF: A, b. 200, f. 6.

5 Ibid.

6 Free Europe Exile Relations [given to Mr. Minton:], 28 V 1958, HIA, RFE/RL CF: A, b. 200, f. 6.

organization field for use in the representational pressure on governmental and political personalities in the Free World."[7]

Although the prime focus remained on the UN and the Council of Europe, for the 1958 budget the FEC already planned to "further bolster "the great and real value of the ACEN" by assisting the exiles in taking an active part in the campaign on the fortieth Anniversary of the Bolshevik Revolution and in expanding its activities in Latin America and the Afro-Asian area.[8] Within five years of the ACEN's existence, the FEC President was able to report to the FEC Board of Directors that the ACEN was recognized as "the chief means by which exile desires for a free Eastern Europe can be effectively expressed. As the most broadly representative exile organization, the ACEN has a force greater – and can have a force far greater – than that of the national councils to represent effectively the rightful aspirations of the East European nations in the important parts of the non-communist world."[9]

Three years later, however, when reviewing the overall FEC operations, the CIA was less optimistic about the potential and usefulness of the ACEN.

> By its very existence ACEN is a residual symbol of East European opposition to Communist domination, but there is very little to indicate that it is widely known or highly regarded in Eastern Europe itself. As a symbol, what value it has must lie primarily in the West for it represents the past as far as Eastern Europe is concerned – a past to which practically no one in Eastern Europe now has any illusions about returning.[10]

Clearly the political context in which the ACEN operated as well as its usefulness was diminished by its aging members. According to the author of this memorandum, the ACEN became an asset which could not be "maintained indefinitely":

> As a body ACEN exhibits the psychoses and contradictions that political exiles usually display as inevitable. ACEN knows that it may well be irrelevant for Eastern Europe and that its influence on U.S. and European policy makers, which has never been great, is decreasing. It has turned increasingly toward the underdeveloped world in its efforts to find something useful to do, to make an impact and justify its existence. [...] It is hard to see, however,

---

7 Huston to Yarrow, 10 III 1959, RFE/RL CF: A, b. 200, f. 6. Attachment: A New Approach to National and International Organizations, ibid.

8 FEER Program and Budget for Fiscal Year 1958, no date [1957?], HIA, RFE/RL CF: A, b. 200, f. 6.

9 Archibald S. Alexander to the Executive Committee FEC Board of Directors: Free Europe Organizations and Publications. Reorientation of Exile Support (revised version of the document), 8 II 1960, DDEL, C.D. Jackson Papers, b. 53, f.: FEC 1960 (2).

10 [CIA], Memorandum for the Record: The Assembly ..., 1 VII 1963.

how ACEN – given its background and all its limitations – can be or ever could become a propaganda instrument of real significance in Latin America.

The ACEN was also growing increasingly out of tune with U.S. politics since “developments toward liberalization in Hungary during the past year and the steadily progressing efforts of the Kádár regime to rehabilitate itself with the U.S. and other Western powers pose a great problem for the ACEN.”[11]

While reviewing the ACEN’s activities, due attention was paid to the ACEN’s effort to advance the notion of Soviet colonialism, frequently termed self-determination. Interestingly, already by 1963, the CIA had already realized that while there was indeed

something to this issue [...] but perhaps less in Latin American than in Africa or Asia, and everywhere it is an issue which cannot be exploited too unsubtly, particularly by East Europeans, without leading to disadvantageous propaganda conclusions. To equate Soviet policies in Eastern Europe with U.S. ‘domination’ in Latin America or British, French or Belgian colonialism in Africa, can rather easily lead to the notion that Western powers have been just as bad as the Communists though they have now mended their ways.

Harland Cleveland, Assistant Secretary of State for International Organizations, expressed serious doubts about the ACEN’s approach to Eastern Europe and to the underdeveloped world,” as well as the “lack of originality in keeping old issues alive.”

The divergence in policy interpretations was becoming all too apparent.

[Mr. Cleveland] ‘believed that the peoples of Eastern Europe recognize the difference between words and actions and are aware of Western policy which draws attention to their situation, but which will not resort to force... Mr. Cleveland said that it has always seemed to him that using the context of Afro-Asian colonialism is a dubious means of raising the Eastern European question; that the two are not the same and that it is a mistake to equate the classic colonialism of the 18th and 19th centuries with Soviet behavior in Eastern Europe. He said that the issue of self-determination is, however, a viable one and that we should try to make the case concerning Eastern Europe on its own merits and not by association with the issue of colonialism.’[12]

And then there was the issue with control – as the FEER’s internal document of 1958 put it:

11 Ibid.

12 Ibid. The document references State Department Memorandum of 15 IX 1961.

> Control of an exile organization means ensuring that it will act in the interest of FEC's objectives and therefore depends, in the least analysis, on the degree to which the organization shares FEC's interest in these objectives as defined in terms of targets and intentions. The financial lever can be used to limit or expand existing activities. But before new activities can be started, new interests must usually be stimulated and defined and interested and capable operators found. FEER money only buys their time; agreement on defined interests provides the only real guarantee that they will do what FEER wants them to do.[13]

By 1963, the CIA knew that the partnership with the exiles was not efficient, as the political differences were not guaranteeing voluntary cooperation: "Far from considering an expansion of ACEN [...], we should be considering how to disengage from ACEN during the next few years, how gradually to phase it back and reduce it (at most) to nothing more than a brass nameplate, a letterhead and a list of names who can sign proclamations when there is some real need for them."[14] For the CIA, the ACEN was little more than a front organization in American political warfare. The FEC was not the CIA though. Its state-private character provided support for émigré programs that were not necessarily of much tactical use (like the radio broadcasts), but rather served the needs of the public concerned with global ideological struggle.[15]

8.1 From Partnership to "Exile Front"

The new decade of FEC activities opened with an awareness that the situation in Eastern Europe had become more complex, more different country-by-country, and thus "far less susceptible to accurate analysis by exile or by professional American propagandists, [than] when it was when FEC began its operations in

13 Proposed FEER Program, attachment to: Memorandum: FEER Paper Entitled "Challenge and Opportunity for FEER in 1958", 7 III 1958, HIA, RFE/RL CF: A, b. 200, f. 6. See the later version of the same memo: "'Control' of an exile organization means ensuring that it will act in the interest of the FEC's objectives and therefore depends, ultimately, on the degree in which this organization shares the interest of FEC in achieving these goals. [...]. Only the time of exiles can be bought for the money of FEC, their commitment must result from a common interest." FEER, Challenge and Opportunity for FEER in 1958, 7 III 1958, attached to: Huston to Hunsbedt, Memorandum: Policy Group's Consideration of FEER Paper Entitled "Challenge and Opportunity for FEER in 1958", 12 III 1958, HIA, RFE/RL CF: A, b. 200, f. 6.

14 [CIA], Memorandum for the Record: The Assembly ..., 1 VII 1963.

15 In 1955 there were some 45 (by 1964 – still about 30) émigré organizations connected with FEC. Johnson, *Radio Free Europe* ..., 76.

1949–1950."[16] Pondering the changing international context of détente (a word used in the FEC questionnaire) William E. Griffith authored a study with suggestions regarding the FEC's future programs. He observed that it was highly unlikely for the East Central European exiles to return to their freed countries in the foreseeable future. Their response to the U.S. policy of "gradual evolution" was likely to be unfavorable. Griffith proposed that the FEC's political warfare operations should be drastically "de-propagandized," and "the use of political exiles should be limited to the maintenance of a minimal, inexpensive symbolic roof organization, with no dividends of a political warfare nature ('action programs' and the like) planned for, demanded, or obtained." Moreover, Griffith believed that in the changing context of "international détente," the FEC would also become "unfitted to fulfill its changing role" because of its "past 'cold war' history and identification." Rather than maintaining the "fronts" the FEC should "operate indirectly, through other organizations, as much as possible in all non-RFE activities," focusing on long-term gains generated by services like scholarships, fellowships, books, study opportunities, etc. "To use a cliché, FEC needs to be made more 'respectable,' and what was respectable during the 'cold war' period is not necessarily so during a détente."[17]

The word "détente" was used prematurely, as both Kennedy and Johnson endured heightened tensions in relations with the USSR. We now know it became a political program of Nixon's administration. However, both Democratic Presidents took steps to ease these tensions, such as installing a direct line of communication between the White House and Kremlin in the aftermath of Cuban Missile Crisis, or Johnson's meeting with Soviet Premier Alexei Kosygin in Glassboro to discuss possible limitation of strategic arms. However, even before Kennedy assumed office, the FEC realized on its own that the "instruments" at its disposal were becoming out-of-date.

As Eisenhower's second term was approaching its end, the upcoming presidential elections in the U.S. inspired the FEC to seek reform. In the summer of 1960, the thinking within the FEC was that the coming years would bring increased contacts with the communist regimes (like cultural exchanges) and that military confrontation was unlikely. The FEC's own thinking about the exiles

16 William E. Griffith (Research Associate) to Bob [Robert W. Minton, FEC], 5 I 1960, DDEL, C.D. Jackson Papers, b. 57, f.: Griffith. W.E. (1). The study was prepared in response to Minton's questionnaire. William E. Griffith, a Harvard graduate, began working for FEC in June 1950. In April 1951 arrived to Munich where he was a policy advisor at RFE until 1958. He then moved to academic career at the MIT in 1959 as a senior research associate at the Center for International Studies.

17 Ibid.

was that its programs were out of date. The case for the captive nations was losing momentum in Western Europe. In this regard, the ACEN's activities there were not a raging success, as they probably couldn't realistically be at that time.[18] In 1960, even RFE seemed to be in trouble, torn between New York and Munich, with the so-called Czech scandal, which resulted in the departure of some key personnel in Germany, under fire from American diplomats, most notably ambassador Jacob Beam in Warsaw, under constant budgetary pressures.[19]

One of Eisenhower's top political advisors in the field of international information programs, C.D. Jackson, tried to lobby for the maintenance of support of exile programs. Jackson, who was reelected to the FEC Board, and became a member of its Executive Committee in October 1960,[20] wrote to the FEC President that slight adjustments could be made in the exile political operations "without abruptly destroying the morale, prestige, and potential usefulness of these people, individually or in groups."

> However, as the Eastern European satellite countries represented the Achilles heel of the imperial Communist structure [...] to destroy the morale and to turn loose several hundred articulate, hurt, confused, and disgruntled, if not angry, exiles at this moment seems to me to be the height of folly. I would add, having listened to the over concerted attacks by the State Department and USIA on RFE that I have recently heard in Washington, that if these efforts are successful on top of my earlier remarks regarding the exiles, we will then have 'had it,' for sure. [...] Please believe me when I say that our whole effort is probably in greater jeopardy that it has ever been. The uninformed mood of the times, combined with the counsels of diplomatic expediency, are all against us. It seems to me that this is the moment to conserve and use our assets, and not the moment to toss some of them out because they appear untidy, or because their output is not of uniform effectiveness week after week.[21]

FEC President Alexander assured C.D. Jackson that there were no plans to let go of the exiles, but cuts would be made to clerical and similar staff of the national and international organizations.[22]

---

18 Ralph E. Walter to Gene [Eugene Metz, FEOP, France], ACEN Dinner and Press Conference for Council of Europe, 10 VI 1960, HIA, RFE/RL CF: A, b. 200, f. 5.

19 Aide Memoire on Free Europe Committee, 6 III 1961, DDEL, C.D. Jackson papers, b. 53, f.: FEC, 1961 (3); Richard S. Greenlee to Bernard Yarrow, Emmons Brown, Reorganization of Free Europe Committee, Inc., 28 III 1961, DDEL, C.D. Jackson Papers, b. 53, f.: FEC, 1961 (2). See also: Johnson, *Radio Free Europe* ..., 118–129.

20 Theodore Augustine to C.D. Jackson, 10 X 1960, DDEL, C.D. Jackson Papers, b. 53, f.: FEC, 1960 (1).

21 C.D. Jackson to Archibald Alexander, 4 V 1960, ibid.

22 Archibald S. Alexander to C.D. Jackson, 6 V 1960, ibid.

The reforms came to the FEC in December 1960 as a result of the U.S. President's Committee on Information Activities Abroad (The Sprague Committee) recommendations. The Committee's task was to update the original Jackson Committee report of 1953.[23] Even before the conclusions stating that RFE and RL were "slow to adapt to changes in the Soviet orbit and resulting shifts in U.S. policy," and contrary to the wishes of the Free Europe Committee's staff, which asked its sponsors for increased allotments,[24] its budged was cut by 1,290,000 dollars.[25] All programs were affected by this decision, including the FEOP, within which the national committees/councils and the ACEN were located. While the ACEN's overall budget was originally increased at the expense of national committees and councils, as well as internationals, with the intention of the Assembly taking on additional duties,[26] by the end of the year the decision was made to cut the ACEN's budget by 46,820 dollars.[27]

"FEC was on the verge of falling apart in the spring of 1961", wrote John Richardson, who became FEC President that year, in his report to the Board of Directors. According to the President, staff morale was at an all-time low, many employees were resigning on top of the elimination of 10% of FEC staff, with the exiles being "disheartened and ready to give up."[28] Faced with budgetary cuts, its personnel also needed to adjust to the new administration. The meeting with the new Secretary of State (Dean Rusk) was "not all smooth." Forty-five minutes spent with the Secretary produced the impression that he was "friendly and polite but otherwise not especially communicative." "I believe" – wrote Richardson – "we got across quite successfully the impression that we are a re-

---

23 "Sprague Committee Critical of Radio Free Europe and Radio Liberty," December, 1960, Wilson Center, CWIHP, Ross Johnson collection, https://digitalarchive.wilsoncenter.org/document/115040, accessed: 16 VII 2020; Johnson, *Radio Free Europe* ..., 127–128; Mazurkiewicz, *Uchodźcy* ..., 96–97.

24 John C. Hughes to C.D. Jackson, 16 VI 1960, DDEL, C.D. Jackson Papers, b. 53, f.: FEC, 1960 (1); EC to President (FEC), FEC Budget for 1960–61, ibid.

25 Archibald S. Alexander (FEC President) to Executive Committee of the Free Europe Committee Board in Connection with Its 20 January Review, 18 I 1961, DDEL, C.D. Jackson papers, b. 53, f.: FEC, 1961 (3).

26 Exhibit V; Comparative costs attached to: Reorientation of Exile Organizations, 1 IV 1960, DDEL, C.D. Jackson Papers, B. 53, f.: FEC 1960 (2). Appendix B: Comparative Costs, (based on 6 months, projected for 12 months), Reorientation of Exile Support (revised version of the document), 8 II 1960, DDEL, C.D. Jackson Papers, B. 53, f.: FEC 1960 (2).

27 Archibald S. Alexander (FEC President) to Executive Committee of the Free Europe Committee Board in Connection with Its 20 January Review, 18 I 1961, DDEL, C.D. Jackson papers, b. 53, f.: FEC, 1961 (3).

28 John Richardson to Executive Board of Directors, Memorandum: the effect of budgetary proposals on FEC, 5 III 1962, HIA, RFE/RL CF: A, b. 189, f. 5.

sponsible organization which can be helpful." Rusk asked for a policy paper along the lines discussed with Richardson to facilitate a "more satisfactory triangular relationship."[29] The paper preparations were initiated, with C.D. Jackson taking the lead. He worried that the Kennedy administration did not realize the importance of East Central Europe in the struggle with the Soviets.[30] The updated FEC mission statement was ready by July.[31]

Richardson wanted to convince Rusk that the FEC could be "extremely helpful toward the attainment of major long-term U.S. foreign policy objectives," as the satellite area offered a "unique opportunity for an imaginative Western policy capable of affecting directly Soviet confidence and behavior." Regarding short-term goals, the FEC mission statement of 1961 said:

> [N]othing could covey more clearly to Moscow the firm U.S. determination to defend Berlin than activities which indicate a willingness on our part to activate anti-communist attitudes in East Central Europe against the Soviet Union. FEC is in a position to convey such indications credibly since it is regarded by Moscow primarily as an (unadmitted) trouble-making agency of the U.S. government for this region.[32]

A year later, he wrote to Hughes: "[T]he persistent will to self-determination of the peoples of East Central Europe inhibits the Soviet power position in Europe and throughout the world."[33] The White House agreed.[34] However, the level of support for the FEC was still on the wane.

In March 1962, Richardson feared the consequences of further limits put on the FEC's budgets: "FEC will become strictly a declining cold war instrument." The FEC President argued against the newly reduced numbers proposed by the CIA. For the 1962 to 1963 fiscal year the exile political organizations and individual stipends were to be reduced by 36.8%. In general, all non-RFE operations that used to receive 3,766,962.98 dollars now had to manage with only 2,654,770 dollars. Richardson realized that the FEC's main asset – the RFE –

---

29 Richardson to John C. Hughes, 28 VI 1961, HIA, RFE/RL CF: A, b. 191, f. 7.

30 C.D. Jackson to John Steele (Time), 17 VI 1963, DDEL, C.D. Jackson Papers, b. 53, f.: FEC Budget 1963 (3); John L. Steele to C.D. Jackson, 5 VII 1963, ibid.

31 John Richardson (President of FEC) to Dean Rusk (Secretary of State), 3 VII 1961, DDEL, C.D. Jackson Papers, b. 53, f.: FEC, 1961 (2).

32 The Mission of the FEC, 3 VII 1961, attached to: John Richardson (President of FEC) to Dean Rusk (Secretary of State), 3 VII 1961, DDEL, C.D. Jackson Papers, b. 53, f.: FEC, 1961 (2).

33 John Richardson to Ernest A. Gross, John C. Hughes, 6 IX 1962, DDEL, C.D. Jackson Papers, b. 53, f.: FEC, 1962.

34 U. Alexis Johnson (Deputy Under Secretary) to Ernest A. Gross (Curtis, Mallet-Prevost, Colt & Mosle), 29 XII 1962, DDEL, C.D. Jackson Papers, b. 53, f.: FEC Budget 1963 (2); Free Europe Committee Objectives – 1962, 5 IX 1962, ibid.

had to be protected at all costs, but many budget items including "support to exiles and exile organizations (ACEN etc.) will have to be cut by withdrawal of support to symbolic or politically active exiles." Within the overall FEC budget proposed by EC (15,557,000 dollars for the fiscal year 1962 to 1963), funding was not endangered for programs (no longer referred to as the "instruments") including: participation in Christian Democratic movements, supporting the Alliance for Progress, information programs including pro-Western news in Spanish, enhancing East-West contacts, exchanges for students from uncommitted areas, campaigns directed to leaders of common markets to include East Central European nations.[35] Clearly, the exiles, if they were to further American interests in Europe, Africa, Asia, and especially Latin America had to take part in "selected, high-priority propaganda and political projects in which they offer unique advantages by – their particular skills, superior motivation and knowledge of communism their non-American identification and their private as contrasted with Government sponsorship." The ACEN's role was listed as capable of "overtly stimulating worldwide interest in and support for the eventual freedom of the East European countries and to utilize the experience of their countries as an objective example of the dangers of Soviet imperialism."[36]

Was the net gain from the organizations' operational activity proportionate to its cost, asked the CIA in regard to the exile programs. Richardson replied:

> Justification of political-organization activity must be measured in terms of the necessity for political symbolism and representation as well as tangible projects. However, the cost of maintaining the organizations is commensurate with the repeatedly evidenced value of their existence as spokesmen for East Europe and representatives of East European thinking in contacts with Free World leaders and organizations. In addition, periodic special projects pay handsome dividends, and it is the aim of FEC, while maintaining these groups, to extract increasing value from them through such projects.[37]

In 1963 the FEC decided to undertake yet another exile reorganization program to improve cost-efficiency. It divided the objectives of the exile programs into two sections: symbolic (maintaining hope among the captives) and operational. In the latter, two areas were mentioned: national cohesion (which meant mobiliza-

35 John Richardson to Executive Board of Directors, Memorandum: The effect of budgetary proposals on FEC, 5 III 1962, HIA, RFE/RL CF: A, b. 189, f. 5. See also attached Chart III.
36 John Richardson to Ernest A. Gross, John C. Hughes, 6 IX 1962, DDEL, C.D. Jackson Papers, b. 53, f.: FEC, 1962.
37 Exile Political Organizations, attachment to: The President (FEC) to The Executive Committee, Survey of FEC External Operations, 1 II 1962, HIA, RFE/RL CF, FEC. INC, b. 1999, f.: Policy, External Operations 1961–62.

tion for the captive nations cause in the free world) and political action against Soviet imperialism (via engaging political, economic and academic elites in political warfare). The exile political organizations' financial backing of the three areas was as follows: 10% for symbolism and national cohesion, each, and 80% toward political action against Soviet imperialism.[38]

The FEC attempted to reverse the old pattern when 80% of the money went to support symbolic functions. Within the 1963 exile reorganization plan, the political action was to target the United States, South America and Western Europe. The national councils/committees were to be further reduced in size, office space, number of publications, etc. Older exiles, or less effective ones, were to be moved to the Meritorious Exile Program, to make room for more effective action. Most of it was to be coordinated by the ACEN, which would attract the most talented exiles in the U.S. and abroad, selected on the basis of ability, prestige, effectiveness and regardless of political affiliation. The ACEN would coordinate overseas offices. Its General Committee would become more of a policy board and organize plenary meetings only if necessary. The secretary general would seek advice from the General Committee on matters of purely ACEN political concern, but would report to the FEC on political and operational matters. Working committees were to be reorganized into action groups in certain fields – economic, political cultural – with responsibility for developing reports, speeches and articles for use by ACEN dignitaries, or representatives traveling or living in different parts of the world. The ACEN would see an increase in office staff, by hired translators, writers, and public relations experts.[39]

Indeed, the budget figures that came with this proposal looked encouraging: the allotment for the ACEN would increase from 227,200 to 519,780 dollars,[40] and chairmen of the committees would receive salaries from 500 to 600 dollars. The ACEN would devote its energies to developing brochures on East Central Europe to "offset communist material, which is widely circulated," would work on positive and constructive denunciations of communism, exposing the myths surrounding its doctrine, organize speakers bureau, improve PR activities by issuing professional press releases, prepare exhibits, organize award ceremonies, establish exile-ethnic office, organize Friends of Captive Nations overseas, improve its relations with RFE, cooperate with other organizations (like APACL, or Cuban exiles), or "[m]aybe ACEN should become the Assembly of Captive Nations (CAN);

---

38 John Richardson, Jr., to Yarrow, Page, Brown, Dunning, Rowson, Kappel, Brinkley, 2 I 1963, Memorandum: Exile Reorganization (strictly confidential), RFE/RL CF: A, b. 199, f. 2.
39 Ibid.
40 Annex I to: Exile Reorganization (strictly confidential), ibid.

maybe the World Congress of Captive Nations."[41] As described in previous chapters, the ACEN did undertake a number of practical steps to enhance its activities, some of which are listed above. The FEC wished to turn the ACEN into an effective instrument at its disposal, with the exiles eventually becoming its employees.

In order to initiate the reorganization of exile political operations in 1963, the FEC management had to consult with both the CIA and ACEN. The people selected to begin the consultations from within the ACEN were: Brutus Coste (the Secretary General), Dr. Dimitrov, and Msgr. Varga; and then Dr. Gaspar was to join ("it would seem that he is highly qualified to head up the ACEN South American activities"), followed by more members of the General Committee of the ACEN.[42] There was one problem, though. The ACEN was not willing to give up its autonomy. The financial leverage used by the FEC did not turn out to be sufficient to extract the desired outcome.

8.2 ACEN's Choices versus "Vis Maior"

The story of the ACEN's falling out of the FEC's graces consists of three parts: political, financial and personal. As such, it epitomizes the relationship between the ACEN and FEC from its earliest days. The first public manifestation of differences between the ACEN and U.S. policy which resulted in curbing exile action was related to the incident of covering the ACEN-prepared poster at the time of Khrushchev's visit to the UN in 1960. The reasoning given to the exiles for limiting exile action was not to further provoke the Soviet leader's fury as he returned to the U.S. in his capacity as a delegate to the UN. Of course, there was a policy shift behind it.

By 1963, it became obvious, that the exile alliance with the FEC was coming to an end. The CIA's internal evaluation of the ACEN's actions reveals a divergence in aims:

> ACEN has always to some extent functioned as a lobby for Eastern European interests on the U.S. political scene and in respect to the United Nations. Most of its formal and most energetic activity of this sort has been directly or indirectly sanctioned by U.S. policy – especially its activities following the Hungarian Revolution. There have always been other peripheral activities by ACEN and its members which are less clearly in the basic U.S. interest. Such activities have up until now usually been quite well contained. During the past year or

41 Annex III: to: Exile Reorganization (strictly confidential), ibid.
42 Annex IV: Exile Reorganization (strictly confidential), RFE/RL CF: A, b. 199, f. 2.

> two, however, there has been increasing evidence of divergence between the exile views and interests, as expressed by ACEN and some of the exile national committees and councils, and the basic interests of the U.S. Government. This is also applicable to some extent to problems with which the U.S. becomes involved in the United Nations. ACEN found it difficult to reconcile itself to a more moderate U.S. policy on Hungary. ... On this and many other facets of relations with Eastern Europe, ACEN appears to be basically out of sympathy with the current U.S. policy of encouraging gradual loosening of ties between Moscow and the East European Satellites and capitalizing on freer U.S. – East European contacts.[43]

To make matters worse in terms of cooperation, in the fall of that year, the FEC was again faced with a political crisis prompted by the ACEN's public actions. The Assembly's Chairman and Secretary General distributed a press release protesting against the American decision to sell grain to the USSR. The exiles called the American decision a "stab in the back."[44] The crisis it created affected the FEC's relations with the CIA. The exiles sent their statement out on 11 October 1963, as the FEC staff celebrated Columbus Day. They learned about it three days later. And while, according to Richardson, the FEC usually tried to refrain from censoring or controlling the political statements issues by the exiles, it had confidence and an expectation that the organizations it supported would not publicly distribute opinions insulting to the U.S. government. Richardson stated that he took all the necessary measures to remove the people responsible for this incident, although it was a delicate task since, as he put it, the exiles treasured their autonomy. The FEC President considered the case closed until 25 October 1963. The Kennedy White House conferred with Cord Meyer (Covert Action Staff) about the statement, about which CIA had had no warning from FEC. Richardson had to explain his neglect to McGeorge Bundy (National Security Advisor) and send explanations to the CIA.[45] Meyer then had meetings with the Chairman of the Board of Directors of the FEC, John Hughes, and the Chairman of the FEC Board's Executive Committee, Ernest Gross, to try to establish how such an incident had been possible.[46]

Richardson was in a particularly vulnerable position since during the 1960 electoral campaign, but before becoming FEC President, he had been in charge

---

43 [CIA], Memorandum for the Record: The Assembly ..., 1 VII 1963.

44 Aleksander Kütt, Brutus Coste "Stab in the Back," *Chicago Tribune*, 22 X 1963, 14.

45 Richardson's letters to the CIA were sent 25, 26, 28 October. John Richardson, Jr., Memorandum: The ACEN "Stab in the back" News Release, 4 XI 1963, DDEL, C.D. Jackson Papers, b. 52, f.: FEC, 1963 (1).

46 John Richardson, Jr. to C.D. Jackson, 8 XI 1963, DDEL, C.D. Jackson Papers, b. 52, f.: FEC, 1963 (1).

of ethnic group mobilization for the Nixon-Lodge ticket (Republican).[47] Because of the ACEN-provoked crisis there was now an internal review of procedures within the FEC aimed at thwarting similar occurrences in the future. On a larger scale, the investigation aimed at preventing the FEC leadership from improper uses of its instruments for domestic political purposes.[48] This hit Richardson directly. He was charged with supporting exiles (especially the ACEN), who must have entered into alliance with the Republican National Committee from which they received content to generate accusations for the sake of weakening ethnic support for the U.S. policy of the Democratic administration. Brutus Coste – an employee of the Republican Party – was named.

Richardson fended off this charge by repeating that it was a standard rule of cooperation with the exiles for them not to criticize any current U.S. administration. They were warmed against getting involved in U.S. partisan politics. The FEC had no means of controlling all exile actions, as it could only exercise control over those it supported. In that regard, Richardson had no information to confirm whether they allied themselves with one of the parties. He refuted the claim that the ACEN criticized the Democratic administration with the FEC's permission, although he said that traditionally the FEC allowed the members of the Assembly to disagree and voice their "rational" criticism of Western and American policy. To the charge that the FEC favored the Republicans, Richardson pointed out all the Democrats within the leadership, including Executive Vice President – John Page, Bernard Yarrow (Senior Vice President), Albert Kappel – in charge of Exile Relations.[49]

There was, however, a sentiment present among some of the FEC's former staff of losing their ability to act on behalf of the captives and of alienating some of the enthusiasts of the anti-communist agenda at the FEC. Horace E. Henderson wrote to Richardson that his exile friends and former associates advised him of serious changes and budgetary reductions in 1963. The press reported a crackdown on exile activities. "You know how strongly I feel about the necessity for continuing and increasing exile activities [...] I have always believed that the exile activities are as important as the radio activities, and they could even be much more so."[50] At the time, Henderson was a Chairman of the Repub-

47 John Richardson, Jr. – Biographical Sketch, 27 I 1961, DDEL, C.D. Jackson Papers, b. 53, f.: FEC, 1961 (2).

48 John Richardson to John C. Hughes, Ernest A. Gross, C.D. Jackson, Memorandum: FEC and Partisan Politics, 8 XI 1963, DDEL, C.D. Jackson Papers, b. 52, f.: FEC, 1963 (2).

49 Ibid.

50 Horace E. Henderson (Republican Party of Virginia letterhead) to John Richardson, Jr., 25 IV 1963, HIA, RFE/RL CF: A, b. 208, f. 2.

lican Party in Virginia.[51] In September he sent the FEC President another letter criticizing both Republicans and Democrats:

> Without any partisan reference whatsoever, the tragic truth is that the policies of both the Eisenhower and the Kennedy administrations have led to the situation today, wherein the Captive Nations issue is hopeless as a national policy in the absence of organized political action. As I see it, unless effective political action is undertaken in advance of the 1964 election, the present trend towards recognition of the status quo in East Europe will become a reality. [52]

His proposal included exerting the political pressure of twenty-four million ethnics on both political parties, and not to lose hope for the freedom of the captive nations.

Even before the electoral party conventions met, the inevitable split between the Americans and Eastern European exiles took place during Johnson's first term, precisely after Dean Rusk's speech of 25 February 1964: "Why we treat different Communist countries differently."[53] The U.S. Secretary of State spoke of the need to reach more agreements with the Soviets to reduce the chance of war, the introduction of differentiation among East Central European regimes, and attempts to encourage evolutionary changes within the communist system. Having read this speech, the ACEN's Chairman, Aleksander Kütt, signed a letter prepared by secretary Brutus Coste which was very critical of the new American policy.[54] The U.S. government's response to the ACEN's public letter was to be expected. If it could not be controlled, the ACEN's autonomy was to be restricted, or its activities be phased out.

The second area of conflict between the ACEN and the FEC was related to one person – the ACEN's Secretary General – elected ten years in a row (1954–1964), who signed the "stab in the back" press release, and who signed

---

51 Unsuccessful Republican candidate for Congress from Virginia in 1956, later served as Deputy Assistant Secretary of State for International Organization Affairs during the Eisenhower Administration. He left the Republican Party in 1972 and ran unsuccessfully as an Independent for the U.S. Senate from Virginia. In the 1958 election, the Republicans lost 14 seats in the Senate and 48 seats in the House. In 1960, Nixon lost a close election for President to Massachusetts Senator John F. Kennedy (who had been reelected in 1958).

52 Horace E. Henderson (Travelers Insurance letterhead) to John Richardson, Jr., 4 IX 1963, HIA, HIA, RFE/RL CF: A, b. 208, f. 2. Henderson talked to ethnic leaders to convene National Ethnic Political Action Conference in D.C. A copy of this letter was sent to Christopher Emmet.

53 D. Rusk, "Why We Treat Different Communist Countries Differently," *Department of State Bulletin* L/1920, 16 III 1964, 390–396, https://archive.org/details/departmentofstat501964unit, accessed 20 III 2020.

54 "ACEN's Reaction to Dean Rusk's Speech," *ACEN News* 108/109 (1964): 21–22.

the letter protesting the Rusk speech. Coste had already been singled out as a troublemaker in July 1962 when he had a meeting with "a high EC official" which was interpreted as a lobbying effort "with a rightist orientation, which the ACEN is prone to engage with."[55] Yet Coste was selected by the FEC in 1963 to help transition the ACEN into a more effective instrument within the FEC programs. The man put in charge of the exile reorganization in 1963 was Albert D. Kappel. In his capacity as Director of Exile Political Organizations at the FEC, he was a key figure in the ensuing conflict between the FEC and the ACEN's Secretary General, Brutus Coste.

Already in October 1963, Kappel had informed the FEC President that, "Brutus Coste is not cooperating towards implementing FEC plans for reorganization of exile activities in the spirit of partnership that had been hoped for." The new director of exile relations was convinced that Coste's "aggressively negative attitude towards U.S., FEC and RFE policies and his action in reaction to them do not appear to be even in the best interest of ACEN."[56] The lengthy memorandum Kappel wrote in October 1963 is worthy of special attention as it explains that the FEC's methods of "control through persuasion" had "only very limited success." Moreover, his appointment seems to have marked a change in the FEC in that he was tasked with "making ACEN the 'exile front' we envisage." This was to be achieved via tacit or covert control (the General Committee of the ACEN functioning as the overt policy-making body), or via actual overt control (the GC functioning as advisory body). If not successful, the remaining alternatives were reductions in status, funds and staff, overheads and projects, and their phasing out, or transfer. This is where the actual origin of the ACEN-FEC rift can be seen to be located. The ACEN leaders would not give in to becoming the "exile front," but they did not wish to lose the FEC's support either.

As Kappel had already indicated that Coste would be difficult to work with, he envisioned ways of finding him suitable employment. He also began a search for his replacement. Coste was to be retained only if he would agree to cooperate with regard to planning, organization and administration, and a joint policy review. These operations were not kept secret from the exiles, as Kappel had already sent Coste a long letter in July 1963 listing all the troublesome areas. While there was no alternative to an FEC-led reorganization, the letter contains encouragement for imaginative, positive and newsworthy planning of new activities. Kappel asked for precise things, like reports on progress related to the pub-

55 [CIA], Memorandum for the Record: The Assembly ..., 1 VII 1963.

56 Albert D. Kappel to Richardson (copy to Yarrow, Page, McDonald), Memorandum, 15 X 1963, HIA, RFE/RL CF: A, b. 165, f. 1.

lications program (praised), and proposals for the establishment of the speakers' bureau, etc. In the margins, Kappel listed Coste's responses, which in most cases said, "never received." Whenever any were received, Kappel noted it was only because of "constant pressure [on Coste] by Brinkley." Lack of money was cited as a reason for the ACEN submitting requests for approval for every project before planning new ones. The need for savings (office, calls, travel) was used as an explanation for moving the national committee's headquarters closer to Park Avenue and 30th Street.[57] Kappel further indicated that he had approached Vişoianu asking him to prepare a memorandum of differences and agreements hoping to show that there is "a great deal of leeway for fruitful cooperation." Kappel was frank, and tried to maintain the constructive spirit, but he also included a word of caution addressed to Coste: "I feel it would be a serious mistake at this stage to, as I believe you contemplated, engage in an open 'fight.' I am not sure what you have in mind, but I feel certain that even an appeal of Mr. Richardson at this time would be counterproductive."[58] The two men could not get along.

Coste refused to cooperate with Kappel on the reorganization plan. A year later, in June 1964, the ACEN's Chairman (Kütt) received a letter from Kappel asking for a reevaluation of activities and the effectiveness of the Secretariat on an individual basis, that is, of the Secretary and his staff. According to Coste, "this was the opening shot in a policy of tireless harassment Mr. Kappel has been conducting against ACEN and its Secretary General" for the next year.[59] Coste had his own way of interpreting the FEC's initiatives. In his view, the FEC was intimidating Kütt and "preventing ACEN from expressing frankly and honestly its own views on developments in Eastern Europe and on Western policies toward the area." Coste complained that the ACEN's publications were put on a project basis (including "ACEN News"). It meant that the funds for printing were available upon approval of the texts to be printed. Coste believed that financial dependence was going to be used to control the editorial line. As an example, he cited elimination from the January 1965 issue of an article by a Democratic Senator Thomas J. Dodd – which was already typeset. Indeed, the issue does not contain an article by Dodd, but it did carry a report of President Johnson's

57 Albert D. Kappel to Brutus Coste, 24 VI 1963, HIA, RFE/RL CF: A, b. 165, f. 1. See also: Anna Mazurkiewicz, Decisive Factors in the Selection of Place of Residence within the United States by the Post-World War II Political Émigrés from East Central Europe in: *The United States Immigration Policy and Immigrants' Responses: past and present*, ed. A. Małek, D. Praszałowicz (Peter Lang Edition: Frankfurt am Main 2017), 149–167.

58 Albert D. Kappel to Brutus Coste, 24 VI 1963, HIA, RFE/RL CF: A, b. 165, f. 1.

59 [Brutus Coste], Note on FEC-ACEN relations, [no date, July 1965], HIA, Coste papers, b. 1, f. 11.

luncheon for RFE which took place on 2 December 1964.[60] The following issue of the journal was published in a changed form with a more attractive layout intended for broader audiences – another indication of the FEC's intervention.

Coste cited another intrusion when Kappel intervened in June 1965 with regards to the ACEN program for Captive Nations Week, as – in Kappel's opinion – it would counteract the FEC's efforts. Coste called it censorship of ACEN publications, and blatant interference by the FEC. More examples of conflicts related to editorial policies including materials the ACEN wanted to publish prepared by the American Security Council (a right-wing, anti-communist group), or Christopher Emmet's statement which the FEC, according to Coste, rejected on the grounds that they "interpreted Western policies in a controversial way." The ACEN's Secretary General bitterly suggested that the FEC "objects to any material which expresses the honest opinion of the ACEN and departs from the narrow FEC interpretation of the official U.S. policy on Eastern Europe."[61] Indeed, Kappel did have a problem with two reprints which represented a biased point of view,[62] as he openly shared his opinion with the ACEN's chairman few months later:

> The ACEN, of course, is free to adopt critical attitudes to Western or even to U.S. policies. However, it seems to me that this should be done at the right time, in the right place, with a clear understanding of the expected results, and in a manner, which will be respected, and which could not affect the sympathies of its friends. You will agree that the two quotes are hardly typical for the mainstream of American thinking; moreover, I very much doubt that they would even be unanimously endorsed by the ACEN General Committee. Is it then really in the interest of the ACEN to give publicity to such untypical and controversial views? What results are expected from this?[63]

The controversial issues of "ACEN News" are filled with texts and photos both by and of Coste, though. He considered Kappel's remarks a case of censorship. Kappel, in turn, believed that "ACEN News" was not attractive to general audiences – both in content and in form.

---

60 President Johnson on U.S. Policy Towards Eastern Europe at White House Luncheon for Radio Free Europe- December 2, 1964, *ACEN News* 117 (January 1965): 12.

61 [Brutus Coste], Note on FEC-ACEN relations, [no date, July 1965], HIA, Coste Papers, b. 1, f. 11.

62 He had a problem with: "the fundamentals of peace" on page 5, "the heart of the matter" on page 7. Albert D. Kappel (Director, EPO) to Aleksander Kütt (Chairman, ACEN), 18 IX 1964, HIA, RFE/RL CF: A, b. 145, f. 7.

63 Albert D. Kappel (Director EPO) to Vasil Gërmenji (Chairman, ACEN), 27 I 1965, HIA, RFE/RL CF: A, b. 145, f. 7.

The FEC's plans for reforming the ACEN also included encouraging younger exiles to join. Because of the provisions requiring delegates not to be naturalized citizens of the countries of exile, the only way to attract the young was to rewrite Chapter I Rule 5 of its Rules of Procedure, and Chapter II Article 3 of its Charter. Kappel asked Korboński to select the alternative that suited them best, and to draft the texts.[64] It seemed as if no area of the ACEN's activities remained untouched by FEC's interventions. According to Coste, in January 1965 Kappel met individually with members of the General Committee of the ACEN announcing a 40 % reduction in the Secretariat budget, at which time he hinted at a "wish of FEC to see early end to association of secretary general with ACEN."[65]

On 7 June 1965, the ACEN's chairman was informed by Kappel that the monthly FEC grant to the ACEN (all regular expenses) as of 1 July 1965 would be decreased from 16,000 to 8,000 dollars (finally settled at 9,070 dollars per month). A shocked Gërmenji called an emergency meeting of the ACEN's General Committee for 16 June. In the proposed budget there was no provision for a secretary general. The deputy secretary general's remuneration (750 dollars) was listed under secretary general. The Secretariat included: one typist, 50 dollars for mailing, and no money for a mimeograph operator.[66] This time, the ACEN was not consulted but presented with a budget.

Coste implied that some of the cuts were subject to being rescinded should the Secretary General (i. e. Coste) be removed. During the meeting of the ACEN's General Committee on 16 June 1965, the Chairman (Gërmenji) asked Coste to stand down to assure the survival of the ACEN. Coste was determined to finish his term "not contingent upon the allotment or non-allotment of funds by FEC for his salary." According to Coste, the FEC used other leaders of the ACEN to "bribe him into surrender", either by paying until the next ACEN elections, provided he did not run, or by him leaving and taking a paid vacation after the Captive Nations Week. According to Coste, the offers were made by Korboński and Gërmenji. Coste did not want to strike a deal, and decided to stand by his rights and complete his term.[67]

Coste, who had been ACEN Secretary General from the beginning, saw the basic issue at stake. Given the bridge-building policy of the Johnson administration ("tactically-motivated policy of increased contacts with the communist regimes ruled out official statement in support of the strategic objective of freedom

64 Albert D. Kappel to Stefan Korboński, 10 XII 1964, HIA, Korboński Papers, b. 12, f. 6.
65 [Brutus Coste], Note on FEC-ACEN relations, [no date, July 1965], HIA, Coste Papers, b. 1, f. 11.
66 Ibid.
67 Ibid.

and independence for the nations of East-Central Europe") the role of the ACEN was very important – existence and publication of its actions can act as a substitute for and maintain the spirit of resistance among the captives.[68] Coste believed it gave the exiles a neat form of leverage to argue that the ACEN could not become a satellite of the FEC. The FEC should be a conveyor of means, representing middle-level bureaucracy, not treating the ACEN as its own branch.

Coste, believing he had the support of powerful Republicans, felt confident enough to include a personal attack on Kappel: "The present philosophy of the officials of the FEC is best expressed in a statement repeatedly made by Mr. Kappel, a retired furniture manufacturer catapulted into expertise on Eastern Europe, that 'you (i.e., exiles or ACEN) are free to hold and express any opinion, but not on our money.'"[69] In fact, Kappel was taken out of "the RFE Fund" (successor to the Crusade for Freedom). He was a trusted employee vetted by Bernard Yarrow, supported by Richardson.[70] Assigned a concrete task, he was not an opponent to be demeaned.

The clash led to the situation that by January 1965 Coste and Kappel barely talked to each other. This paralyzed any effort to save the ACEN within the FEC. Moreover, Coste's fight with Kappel must be interpreted in the context of internal dynamics within the ACEN. In his correspondence with the Polish Council of National Unity (London), Korboński mentioned a three-hour talk he had had with Kappel during which the American said that Coste had been neglecting all the FEC's organizational and technical guidelines for years. While not denying his contacts with the FEC, he wrote that Coste had started an open war with the FEC. Already in January the Polish delegate in the General Committee of the ACEN was sure that if Coste did not resign, the ACEN's budget would be slashed in half. Kappel claimed that the reduction in budget was not going to be the first step to liquidate the ACEN, but rather a necessity to resolve a situation caused by one man's ambition and stubbornness.[71]

Korboński had no reason to side with Coste. The Polish delegation to the ACEN had been at odds with the Romanians for years. Korboński listed his grievances against Coste, including the latter's lack of respect for the Polish decision to support cultural and economic exchanges with communist Poland, and his "unconsciously [bemused] pro-German position."[72] The Pole was referring to a decision to award ACEN medals to Wenzel Jaksch and Baron Guttenberg. Neither

68 Ibid.
69 [Brutus Coste], Note on FEC-ACEN relations, [no date, July 1965], HIA, Coste Papers, b. 1, f. 11.
70 John Richardson, Jr. to Horace E. Henderson, 17 IV 1962, HIA, RFE/RL CF: A, b. 208, f. 2.
71 Stefan Korboński to Adam Ciołkosz, 11 I 1965, HIA, Korboński Papers, b. 11, f. 4.
72 Ibid.

were supported by the Polish delegation, and were publicly criticized. The infamous meeting in Europe in 1963 further agitated the conflict within the ACEN. Korboński also held against Coste his dominating style, and his disregard for consecutive chairmen. As the Polish delegation in the ACEN did not support Coste's candidacy for the Secretary General during the 1964/65 session, it was not willing to defend him against Kappel's push in 1965. Korboński concluded that “Coste will fight back, and since he has established some good connections, it can result in a crisis.”[73] The Polish delegate in the ACEN's General Committee was clearly not sympathetic to his Romanian colleague whom he saw as “aggressive towards current U.S. administration,” who “needlessly got us all involved in internal, controversial U.S. matters, supporting the right wing of the Republican Party.”[74]

Having played an important role within the ACEN while enjoying good rapport with the FEC, Korboński reported to London that the American Committee had some serious unpleasantness on its hands in Washington. He wrote that in private exchanges with the FEC, the case was presented as a simple choice: either the ACEN or Coste. In April 1965, Korboński reported to London: “[R]elations within ACEN are really bad. There is a clear pressure to get rid of Coste. He dared [the Americans] too much and the decision [regarding him] must have been made somewhere high. I think that the case will linger on up till elections and that someone else will be elected to replace him. As I wrote before, we have no reason to defend him.”[75]

However, as the General Committee of the ACEN met on 23 June 1965 to discuss the budget cuts and to decide whether the Secretary General should be fired, cooler heads prevailed. The ACEN accepted the 44 % budget cut (originally 56 %) with three votes against it (Vişoianu, Dimitrov and Lettrich). A unanimous decision was made to reinstate the salary for Coste as “no member of the [ACEN] General Committee complied with the injunction of FEC to take a specific vote against the Secretary General relieving him of his functions.”[76]

Coste issued a statement on 23 June 1965 which said:

> I can neither be pressured nor bribed into relinquishing my responsibilities before the term of my office expires [...] my continued service is not contingent upon the allotment or non-allotment by FEC of funds for my salary [...] while the reduction of the monthly allotment to

73 Ibid.

74 Stefan Korboński to Jan Starzewski, 9 VIII 1965, ibid.

75 Stefan Korboński to Adam Ciołkosz, 16 IV 1965, HIA, Korboński Papers, b. 12, f. 5.

76 [Memorandum], Supplementary note on FEC-ACEN relations, 24 VI 1965, HIA, Emmet Papers, b. 34, f.: FEC Memoranda.

> about 9,000 $ must be regarded, for the time being at least, as a fact, as a *vis maior* situation, I will deem it as my foremost duty to make every effort and use all legitimate means to secure redress.[77]

At that time, Emmet (AFCN) stepped in. Concerned that without the ACEN, the reason for the existence and activities of the AFCN would be lost, he wanted to talk Richardson into affirming in writing the following guarantees: the ACEN's independence, non-interference of the FEC (which he refers to as the RFE), including no interference with personnel, defining of the scope of the FEC's right of consultation, promising avoidance of implied financial threats in connection with all the ACEN's basic policies, and seeking restoration of at least half of the ACEN's recent budget cuts. He wanted to achieve all this with the help of his powerful friends, including senators Dodd and Douglas. In the meantime, however, he asked Coste to recognize temporary cuts, accept his salary, run for reelection, offer minimum cooperation with the FEC, and reconcile with Gërmenji.[78]

Fearing escalation of the conflict and its impact on American politics, Emmet wrote a lengthy memorandum to his personal friends within the ACEN. In early September he shared his concerns related to the likely firing (and no reelection) of Coste at the FEC's insistence.[79] For one, he saw potential danger in rising public criticism coming from Goldwater Republicans, extremist Ukrainian, and Slovak and Anti-Bolshevik Nations organizations, as "the extremist nationality groups have always criticized ACEN as a stooge of the CIA." "There were already press reports," he wrote, "thus far, inaccurate, so no harm was done." However, if Coste was dropped it would be ascribed to conflict over policy, not personalities, and to interference by the FEC with the independence of the ACEN, as a result of pressure from Washington. Emmet wanted Coste to stay on, and possibly resign later, after the continued independence of the ACEN has refuted the rumors, hence no damage would be done.

Another danger that Emmet indicated was that if the ACEN position appeared to be exclusively in support of right-wing Republicans, Democrats would no longer push the Johnson administration to keep the captive peoples in sight when dealing with satellite regimes. "Because its leaders are not U.S.

---

77 Statement of Brutus Coste before the General Committee ACEN, 23 VI 1965, HIA, RFE/RL CF: A, b. 145, f. 7.

78 CE Suggestions, attached to Supplementary note on FEC-ACEN relations, 24 VI 1965, HIA, Emmet Papers, b. 34, f.: FEC Memoranda.

79 Emmet, Memorandum to Personal Friends within ACEN about the Annual Elections in September, 2 IX 1965, HIA, Coste Papers, b. 1, f. 11.

citizens and have behaved with great dignity as guests in this country, ACEN is the only organization which has been wholly free from U.S. partisan politics, and largely free from the ideological divisions within anti-Communist ranks.” Emmet noted its usefulness in this regard. During the previous three years, the ACEN had received support from liberal anti-Communists as well, thus the ACEN “helped to prevent the almost total identification of the hard anti-Communist line exclusively with conservatives and Republicans.”[80]

Coste’s position was severely weakened on 21 September 1965, as he was not re-elected the ACEN’s secretary general, with five votes against, three for, and one abstention. Coste felt particularly betrayed by Gaspar, who had promised his support to his Romanian colleague, pledging he would not run for his post, but then did exactly that. In addition to hypocrisy and disloyalty, Coste found the letter Gaspar sent to him most offensive. In his response he was angry and upset that Gaspar had given him no warning of his intention to run before 21 September 1965, and thus “forfeited any claim to his friendship, esteem or even good will,” earning contempt or pity by “aping a gentleman.”[81] Coste did write – on the day after his defeat by Gaspar – to all foreign delegates of the ACEN with a farewell, but did not include any attack on Gaspar.[82]

In the Coste files there is a statement, most likely prepared by him, after his defeat. It starts with: “The FEC drive to tame ACEN into conformism reached its goal on September 21 as a result of pressures and inducements on the part of the main financial sponsor of the exile group, five of the nine members of the General Committee of ACEN cast their votes against Brutus Coste, Secretary General since the establishment of ACEN, in September 1954.”[83] In the statement, obviously prepared for further distribution without attributing it to Coste, the exile leader listed all the points of contention that pitted him against the FEC:

- Coste’s stand on the October 1963 “wheat deal” with Moscow;
- Coste’s refusal to assist the FEC in reducing the national councils and committees and their transferal to the ACEN (“intended to become a sort of an information bureau”);

---

80 Ibid.

81 Brutus Coste to Dr. Edmund Gaspar, 30 IX 1965, HIA, Coste Papers, b. 39, f. 2. Coste said that FEC was calling the Carnegie International Center during the meeting and that Gaspar was not an exile, since he had adopted Uruguayan citizenship. Cite from [Coste] his memo to Emmet.

82 Brutus Coste to Ragip Frashëri, Béla Padanyi-Gulyas, Edward Ressel, Zygmunt Zawadowski, Visvaldis Gusts, August Koern, Aleksander Warma, Edmund Rehak, Antoni Dragas, Gustav Hennyey, Radu Arion, 22 IX 1965, HIA, Coste Papers, b. 39, f. 3.

83 [Coste?], [Statement/Press Release?], [no date, after 21 IX 1965], HIA, Coste Papers, b. 1, f. 11.

- The Coste-inspired strong stand against the Brussels conference of the European Movement – convened to secure the endorsement of the East Central European exiles to the idea of increasing trade and granting credits to the East Central European communist regimes (January 1964). The ACEN boycotted it, while the FEC provided substantial funds;
- Coste's authorship of a memorandum that the ACEN presented to the State Department on the eve of May 1964 U.S.-Romanian negotiations and made it public in the "The New York Times," demanding political concessions in exchange for economic advantages;
- Coste's memorandum that the "ACEN is being nibbled to death" – covering the account of events from June 1964 to June 1965; and
- Coste's refusal to quit (June 1965) which made the FEC wait until September internal ACEN elections.[84]

Coste was obviously considering his role as the chief spokesmen and representative of the ACEN. He believed he had scored a small victory in the removal of a man "who conducted a 'psychological warfare' against us" (Kappel) and the placement of a "more civilized man" in charge of exile relations at FEC.[85] But it was he who became "persona non-grata with the FEC."[86] Worse for the ACEN, with or without Coste, its budget was slashed. The news of severe budget cuts led to many written protests by prominent Americans addressed to the FEC.[87] In November 1965, Korboński assessed: "I will not conceal the fact that by this unconscious [bemused] attacks on the Democratic administration and personal connections with the far right wing of the Republican Party, Coste made enemies among Democrats. [...] Our warning but not supporting him last year, was ignored, so this year we acted more decisively, others joined us, seeing that with Coste the ACEN won't achieve anything with the present administration, we stood up against him."[88]

Realizing the FEC's fears, Coste decided to publicize his fate. He had a powerful ally at his side. Emmet contacted the same three ACEN leaders asking them to supply him with evidence of the FEC's interference, including phone calls

84 [Coste?], [Statement/Press Release?], [no date, after 21 IX 1965], HIA, Coste Papers, b. 1, f. 11.
85 B. Coste to lt. gen. Charles H. Bonesteel, 30 VIII 1965, HIA, Coste Papers, b. 39, f. 2. Kappel remained with FEC in New York through 1967 working on public affairs.
86 [Coste?], [Statement/Press Release?], [no date, after 21 IX 1965], HIA, Coste Papers, b. 1, f. 11.
87 Copies of telegrams forwarded to John Richardson, Jr., 24 VI 1965, HIA, RFE/RL CF: A, b. 145, f. 7.
88 Stefan Korboński to Ryszard Krygier (Australia), 2 XI 1965, HIA, Korboński Papers, b. 12, f. 6.

from Mucio Delgado (FEC) during the ACEN meeting at Carnegie Hall on 21 September 1965, trying to secure written testimony that FEC sought to oust Coste by mobbing the ACEN leaders using financial leverage. He also asked Coste for an affidavit, or a letter with facts, quotes, and dates.[89] The document cited above giving Coste's account of events was most likely prepared in response to Emmet's request.[90]

Emmet wrote a memorandum to the FEC President in early September, but it wasn't a unilateral endorsement of Coste's position. Emmet informed Richardson of his attempts to tone down criticism directed at the FEC coming from powerful people. Emmet was clear: "[W]ithout the cooperation of the ACEN, whatever I have accomplished, either individually or though the AFCN on behalf of Eastern Europe, would have been impossible."[91] He expressed similar admiration and gratitude toward the FEC, without which the ACEN would not have been possible. "In fact, the organization of FEC is about the only imaginative U.S. organizational innovation that I know of in the cold war." His statement was balanced and intended for distribution in across the ACEN, FEC, AFCN, and with a copy intended for Coste.[92]

By the end of the year, Emmet's conciliatory tone was gone. In his meeting with Richardson he protested against the FEC's "crimes and blunders in connection with ACEN loss of Brutus Coste," warning him that should there be "any sign of shift in the substance of the ACEN line" the AFCN would be "compelled to take a public position against it and against the FEC for its responsibility in connection with any such weakening of the ACEN's position as a result of FEC's role in Coste's ouster."[93] It must be emphasized that Coste's was not the ACEN's line. Great differences existed within the ACEN, as which soon became public.

89 C.E. [Emmet] to Vişoianu, Dimitrov, Lettrich, draft letter, [no date, after September 1965], HIA, Coste Papers, b. 39, f. 2.

90 [Coste?], [Statement/Press Release?], [no date, after 21 IX 1965], HIA, Coste Papers, b. 1, f. 11.

91 Lyons, Lehrman, Judd (via David Martin). [Emmet] to John [Richardson], 3 IX 1965, ibid. Similar statement: Emmet said that had the AFCN had more money he would pick up the reduced activity and prestige of ACEN- with AFCN's largely liberal personnel. Not enough, so, tries to mediate problems of ACEN. Emmet can finance it himself, but alone, without ACEN, AFCN cannot maintain its prestige and influence. Emmet saw hope in growing American involvement in Vietnam, recent action in Dominican Republic – hoping Johnson would be tougher, Dodd and Douglas would obtain more funds for FEC. Emmet, Memorandum to Personal Friends within ACEN about the Annual Elections in September, 2 IX 1965, ibid.

92 Emmet, Memorandum, 3 IX 1965, ibid.

93 [Emmet], Meeting with Richardson, 9 XII 1965, HIA, Emmet Papers, b. 14: ACEN Memoranda.

Press activity relating to these developments – as collected by the FEC – was significant. From 14 July to 22 November 1965 at least 30 articles were published in papers, as well as some syndicated columns by Edgar Ansel Mowrer or Dumitru Danielopol, or Alexander Holmes, appearing from New York to San Diego.[94] Béla Varga of the Hungarian Committee, and a member of General Committee of the ACEN, reacted to the Coste statement which appeared in the 10 October 1965 issue of the "New York Herald Tribune" – condemning his former colleague for releasing confidential data on budget figures to the press. Arnold Beichman signed the text, and Beichman advised the FEC that the article was to appear in October. Richardson thought that the FEC "came off rather well," but the fears of Coste's not "remaining silent too long" were there. "He is a rather successful PR man for his cause [...]. Beichman is not the only one he has contacted."[95] Emmet tried to discourage the publication of Beichman's article, as he admitted in a letter to Richardson, consequently following his conviction that, the after publicity that followed the dropping of Coste he thought the real damage had already been done, and no further serious damage was in sight. His personal opinion on Richardson was that "nothing which I sign or endorse will question your motives or your honesty; though, as I wrote you, I do seriously question your judgment on more than one point connected with the recent sad events."[96]

To counter the ill feelings prompted by Coste's departure, other exiles tried to show support for the FEC. Béla Varga stated that he could attest that there was no pressure from the FEC, adding: "I have never seen the least sign of FEC's wanting to intervene in ACEN's internal affairs." [97] In the letter, the prominent Hungarian leader offered his understanding of ACEN-FEC relations:

> to the best of my knowledge, partnership relations exist between FEC and ACEN, just as between FEC and individual national committees. From this partnership logically stems the obligation that both sides should beneficently consider each other's interests. My conclusive experience over more than a decade and a half shows that FEC always sought to consider them within the limits of possibility. ACEN's former Secretary General – involuntarily refuting his own charges – demonstrates, through his budget data, FEC's generous understanding of ACEN's aims. Wisdom and the mutual obligation deriving from this partnership obliges us, too, to take into consideration FEC's standpoints.[98]

94 Press clippings on ACEN and Coste [1965], HIA, RFE/RL CF: A, b. 165, f. 1.
95 John Richardson, Jr. (president, FEC) to Chester W. Ott (acting director RFE, Munich), 13 X 1965, ibid.
96 Emmet to Richardson, 11 X 1965, ibid.
97 Press clippings on ACEN and Coste [1965], ibid.
98 Béla Varga (Hungarian Committee) to John Richardson, Jr. (FEC), 13 X 1965, ibid.

In October, Béla Varga stated that other persons, not the FEC, sought to influence him, including Emmet and David Martin. Varga disagreed with their views and arguments, as Coste had "lost his usefulness," but the Hungarian did not find it to be an intervention in internal Hungarian Committee affairs. However, the choice of words may be significant, as Varga did not write "ACEN affairs."

Fears of Coste going to the press with revelations that would hurt both the ACEN and FEC, took a surprising turn when in December 1965 the ACEN's Sidzikauskas sent a letter to the press.[99] Evidently trying to disavow his former colleague, the Lithuanian Chairman of the Assembly claimed that the General Committee of the ACEN was "under considerable pressure applied by Mr. Coste's friends to vote for him." Sidzikauskas mentioned memoranda, personal contacts, and the actions of David Martin, Emmet, senators Dodd and Douglas. Having learned about the Sidzikauskas letter, one of the three Coste allies in the General Committee, Vişoianu, "bustled into the [FEC] premises with a copy of a letter he has written to Sidzikauskas" protesting against "the misconceptions of the pro-Brutus clique."[100] Vişoianu was angry that Sidzikauskas had issued the letter on behalf of the ACEN (as its chairman) but without consulting with the General Committee, flipping over the situation as he understood it. Rather than admitting that the FEC pressured the ACEN General Committee into removing Coste (and thus trying to safeguard the ACEN's independence), Sidzikauskas claimed it was caused by the outside interference of Coste's supporters trying to induce his reelection. Vişoianu was bitter: "In the face of such misrepresentation I can only assume that, having fought the Communists for so many years, you have been unwittingly contaminated by their methods and dialectics."[101] The Romanian member of the General Committee planned to send a copy of his letter to the press as well. Mucio F. Delgado of the FEC appropriated this exchange to refer to the American context: "Goldwynism intentional."[102] Delgado dissuaded Vişoianu from escalating the conflict with the hope that the coming year would be "normal," and that it would not be filled with "bizarre times full of dislocations

99 Emmet, Memorandum to Dimitri Danielopol. Comment on Dr. Sidzikauskas Letter to Him, 21 XII 1965, ibid.

100 Mucio F. Delgado to Richardson, Dunning, Kappel, Memorandum: Aftermath of a sub-orbital storm, 17 XII 1965, ibid.

101 Constantin Vişoianu (ACEN, General Committee) to Sidzikauskas (Chairman ACEN), 16 XII 1965, ibid.

102 Mucio F. Delgado to Richardson, Dunning, Kappel, Memorandum: Aftermath of a sub-orbital storm, 17 XII 1965, ibid. "Goldwynisms" – "the mixed metaphors, grammatical blunders and word mangling" of Samuel Goldwyn. Albin Krebs, Samuel Goldwyn Dies at 91, *The New York Times*, 1 II 1974, https://www.nytimes.com/1974/02/01/archives/samuel-goldwyn-dies-at-91-samuel-goldwyn-pioneer-film-producer.html.

and crises." The mood at the FEC must have been particularly fraught, given the bizarre title of the memorandum, "aftermath of sub-orbital storm."

A limited budget caused administrative hassles, infrequent meetings, delegates leaving (by adopting citizenship, or dying), with very little hope left of stimulating interest among younger exiles. An attempt to stabilize the situation in 1966 resulted in yet another crisis. Divisions within the ACEN had existed before, but the FEC intervention – its budget cut and the removal of Coste – aggravated the differences. In 1966 the internal crisis in the ACEN involved yet another Romanian – Constantin Vişoianu.

Since the ACEN's founding there had been no chairman from Romania. Given the importance of the position held by Coste, this was tolerated. However, in September 1966 it was the Romanian delegate's turn to take over the yearly chairmanship. Yet his supporters (like Dimitrov and Lettrich) were the same exiles who fought alongside Coste and continued to object to "sacrificing our national interests in order to accommodate number two Park Avenue."[103] To prevent another feud with the FEC, a Polish, Baltic and Hungarian coalition was formed within the ACEN to elect Korboński in 1966.[104] The work of the ACEN was stabilized but would never be as well-founded and as efficient as it had been at the end of the 1950s. In the journal of the CIA's Legislative Counsel, under 1 May 1967, the following entry is found:

> I brought to the attention of A/DDP and [...] the so-called annual pilgrimage to Washington of a group from the ACEN. The papers indicated they had a list of 31 senators and 52 congressmen that they were to see on 3 and 4 May to push the Assembly's views. Cord Meyer advised later in the day that it took some doing but that this had been called off. We both agreed that this almost certainly would have caused some difficulties.[105]

The American hosts who were also the gate keepers initially opening, and later limiting, exile access to the U.S. political and media establishment, were now merely looking for the ways to disengage from exile projects. Soon the situation became one of urgency, as in 1967 the news of covert CIA support for FEC was leaked to the public. By 1972, the remaining political exiles were left to their own devices as all FEC support for ACEN was terminated.

103 Synopsis of Remarks regarding the letter of three submitted to ACEN GC meeting for deliberation, 23 I 1967, ZNiO, Gadomski Papers, 118/02/02.

104 George Dimitrov, Jozef Lettrich, Constantin Vişoianu to Stefan Korboński, 27 XI 1966, ZNiO, Gadomski Papers, 118/02/01.

105 Journal Office of Legislative Counsel, Monday, 1 May 1967, CREST: CIA-RDP70B00338R000200230046–1, Approved For Release 2004/05/12, Available also at CIA FOIA Library: https://www.cia.gov/library/readingroom/docs/CIA-RDP70B00338R000200230046-1.pdf.

9 Conclusion, or what was ACEN?

This book describes the ACEN's efforts to rally support for its cause on a truly global scale. The aims of the exiles remained clearly defined throughout the ACEN's existence. Their accomplishments, limited as they were by U.S. foreign policy, must be analyzed in the context of a symbiotic relationship with the FEC. Any attempt to assess the ACEN's impact must thus begin by answering a seemingly prosaic question: what was the ACEN? The answer depends on whom we ask.

According to the exiles, the ACEN was "a forum in which the common view and aspirations of the silenced peoples of the once free and independent nations could be forcefully voiced in the Free World." It was meant to "serve the cause of liberation of Central and Eastern European nations," be an "authoritative source of information on conditions created by the Soviet domination and Communist rule in captive nations," "a fountainhead of constructive ideas and promoter of courses of action which would enable the Free World to help the enslaved peoples to help themselves and thus further their own vital interest – to attain a world order based on freedom and justice for men and nations," "to counter the Communist propaganda, supply the Free World delegates in the UN with factual information on issues of special concern to captive nations," and "to remind the Free World of its vital stake in the cause of free Central and Eastern Europe."[1]

Individual members of the Assembly referred to it as an exile organization speaking in one voice for almost 100 million silenced peoples (Vilis Māsēns), an East Central European cooperation platform in order to be heard in the West (Feliks Gadomski), an alternative to the communist representatives in the United Nations; a legitimate representation of the Captives in the Free World (Stefan Korboński); "a kind of a parliament, regional parliament of these countries" (János Horváth); a living testimony of true aspirations of the captive peoples (Stanisław Gebhardt).[2]

1 ACEN, *First Session (Sept. 20, 1954 – Feb. 11, 1955): Organization, Resolutions, Reports, Debate*, Part I, New York, 1955, 11.

2 Māsēns, Speech, 15 III 1957, IHRC, ACEN, b. 23, f. 3. This notion was also corroborated by the FEER: "The ACEN is the authentic voice of countries either unrepresented or misrepresented in the UN." Free Europe Exile Relations [given to Mr. Minton:], 28 V 1958, HIA, RFE/RL CF: A, b. 200, f. 6. See also mentions in the U.S. press, including: Op.-Ed., "The Voice of Freedom," *The New York Times*, 1 X 1955, 18; Gadomski, *Zgromadzenie Europejskich* ...; Korboński, *W imieniu Polski* ...; Interview with János Horváth (Budapest), 29 IX 2010; Interview with Stanisław Gebhardt, Warsaw, 4 XII 2014.

https://doi.org/10.1515/9783110661002-013

The ACEN wanted to inspire, and possibly influence, U.S. foreign policy in order to bring about free elections and the withdrawal of Soviet troops from their respective homelands. Hence its leaders made frequent calls and appeals to the U.S. government, tried to reach the American public via press and scholarly/professional publications (to generate grassroots pressure), and, finally, to find allies in the U.S. Congress who would push for American non-recognition of the status quo in a divided Europe and thus maintain interest in the fate of the peoples behind the Iron Curtain; in short, a political lobby, speaking on behalf of the nine captive nations of East Central Europe.

However, the ACEN operations can be seen in a different light if we take into consideration the fact that this organization was technically a part of the FEC. As such, it was expected to be politically amenable to the line of the U.S. Department of State (which oversaw their activities), and financially supported by the Free Europe Committee which received its funds from the CIA. We therefore seem to be examining the activities of a lobby consisting of non-American citizens which in fact was an organization (even if distantly) connected to the American executive that actively worked (tried desperately) to influence the American legislature in order to advance American anti-communism for the benefit of foreign and distant "captive nations."

For the FEC, the ACEN was meant to: "further political warfare objectives of FEC in the countries of interest behind the Iron Curtain; support the aims of the U.S. government in the 'uncommitted areas'; contribute to the understanding and interest of the American people in the situation of captive nations and implant in them the conviction that it is in the American interest that those people be Free."[3] In the collections of President Eisenhower's propaganda advisor C.D. Jackson, one may find documents in which the ACEN is called "an American propaganda agency and the people in it are not free," which evolved from an organization meant to give "advice on broadcasting policy and legitimacy to FEC/RFE" to one that "helped to keep frustrated East European exiles busy." According to the communication exchanged between the FEC leadership and the CIA, by 1963 the ACEN was supposed to become "a body to which U.S. officials and leading citizens could address expressions of sympathy for Eastern Europe and assurances of eventual change."[4]

The role of the ACEN must be analyzed in the light of changing policies though. As late as 1958, John Foster Dulles proclaimed in a letter addressed to

3 Memorandum of Agreement on Exile Activities in the U.S. sponsored or stimulated by FEC, 20 XII 1954, HIA, RFE/RL CF: A, b. 191, f. 5.

4 [CIA], Memorandum for the Record: The Assembly ..., 1 VII 1963.

Māsēns, that the ACEN was a "forum, where issues relating to the situation and aspirations of the captive nations were discussed by those, who cherished ideals of freedom." Thus, the ACEN played a "useful and constructive role."[5] By 1960 the FEC wanted to maintain the ACEN in the following roles:

- as a symbol of captive peoples in the free world, to dramatize their plight, keeping alive in the free world the subject of Soviet colonialism;
- to undertake representational activities and specific projects which keep the issue of the captive peoples before world opinion, including the UN and free world governments and organizations, with emphasis on non-U.S. opinion;
- to provide the free world, particularly the policy makers and molders of public opinion, accurate information on developments in the Soviet bloc, particularly the East European countries;
- to maintain contact with principal democratic exile organizations and individuals, throughout the world;
- to provide a representative forum for exile leaders from the captive nations;
- to organize Friends of Captive Nations in European countries, along the lines of the AFCN;
- to publish an improved "ACEN News," and occasional inexpensive brochures on specific issues relating to East Central Europe; and
- to carry out ad hoc projects as the need arose.[6]

As early as 1963, the CIA overseeing the work of the FEC stated that the "ACEN functioned primarily as a propaganda organization and a lobby. Only very occasionally does its activity result in direct political action."[7] When examining the FEC's records, by the mid-1960s it indeed seems as if the ACEN was assigned particular tasks (for example attending international meetings of FEC's interest) so it operated almost like a "front organization."[8]

---

5 John F. Dulles, to AmConsul Strasbourg, 28 IV 1958, Simpson Collection, 760.00/4–2858.

6 Archibald S. Alexander to the Executive Committee FEC Board of Directors: Free Europe Organizations and Publications. Reorientation of Exile Support (revised version of the document), 8 II 1960, DDEL, C.D. Jackson Papers, B. 53, f.: FEC 1960 (2). This document was reviewed on April 1, to be discussed by FEC and EC on April 7, 1960. FEOP, Reorientation of Exile Organizations, 1 IV 1960, DDEL, C.D. Jackson Papers, b. 53, f.: FEC 1960 (2). See also: HIA, RFE/RL CF: A, b. 197, f. 8.

7 [CIA], Memorandum for the Record: The Assembly ..., 1 VII 1963.

8 For example, international gatherings having FEC Sponsorship or interest in 1965 included: Council of Europe, International Catholic Press Union, 7th World Congress, Rotary International – 5th Annual Convention, UN Economic Commission for Europe session, Inter-American Bar Association, 14 biennial Congress, UN ECOSOC session, World Association of World Federalists, etc.

In a series of interviews, former FEC employees shared their opinions on what they thought the ACEN was, and what was its major role. John F. Leich responded that the ACEN was a "shadow UN." As such, it served both as a symbol of free states that existed before the war, as well as of their unity – within national committees/councils and within the ACEN.[9] The ACEN was also a useful instrument for keeping the case of East Central Europe alive, and informing the West about its fate. It was very clever, said Leich, that the U.S. recognized the communist governments but simultaneously tried to undermine them.[10] John Richardson said that the CIA used the FEC to allocate money for anti-communist propaganda, and to maintain the morale of people behind the Iron Curtain by showing that their case was represented in the West.[11]

A letter from Zbigniew Brzeziński offers a different view. The National Security Advisor to Carter made the following assessment: "I believe the initial purpose of the ACEN was to provide political legitimacy for sustaining from outside the internal opposition to communism."[12] His is the observation that I found more reflective of the material I was able to analyze.

Based on all available accounts, it can be said that the ACEN played multiple roles. It was a forum for East Central European exiles where joint positions related to the current political developments were negotiated. The ACEN was also a political lobby pleading for support in the UN, Council of Europe, American Congress, and among political leaders in the free world. The ACEN was also a cohesive Eastern European information-education center based in New York. In addition, it was a symbolic indication of the ability of the East Central Europeans to cooperate – paving the way for post-liberation integration. Viewed from the exile organizations' perspective, the ACEN provided them with means of getting funds from the Americans in order to further exiles' goals. As for the FEC, it was one of its propaganda projects. One in which "the subject moves in the direction you desire for reasons which he believes to be his own."[13] Finally, viewed from Washington D.C., the ACEN served as means of legitimizing U.S. global involvement.

---

9 Interview with John Leich, 9 VI 1996, HU OSA, Fekete Doboz.

10 Author's interview with John Leich (by telephone), 29 X 2007.

11 Charles Stuart Kennedy interview with John Richardson Jr., 9 II 1999, Association for Diplomatic Studies and Training (ADST), Foreign Affairs Oral History Project accessed online http://www.adst.org/OH%20TOCs/Richardson,%20John%20Jr.toc.pdf; Mazurkiewicz, *Uchodźcy* ..., 32–33.

12 Zbigniew Brzeziński, e-mail to the Author, 19 IX 2007.

13 Stonor Saunders, *The Cultural Cold War* ...., 4. The citation used by the author comes from NSC Directive of 10 VII 1950.

As discussed elsewhere, the ACEN as a political lobby stood on the fringes of American foreign policymaking. Rather it resulted from it. The intersection of the American government, Congress and American public opinion (within which ethnic groups should be located) creates the context in which foreign policy is both formulated and promoted. There is no room for "foreign agents" (political exiles) in this arrangement. However, if a group gets access to the government facilitated by FEC, through its allies in Congress, and friendly, native social organizations and media outlets – it lands right in the heart of the process. The problem, however, remains in controlling this newcomer. The ACEN members were not American citizens (hence dependent on the hosts' good will). They were not financially independent (so the hosts had additional project-based leverage). Under the veil of autonomy, the FEC retained access control and acted as an agenda gatekeeper. Therefore, the impact of the ACEN cannot be interpreted separately from that of the FEC.

The Free Europe Committee also tried to evaluate the ACEN's impact and whether it worked to its advantage. In 1963 the CIA realized it did not:

> ACEN's quarterly reports list a great deal of activity whose impact is only and primarily in the United States. (It is by no means primarily rightist-oriented – much of it simply involves publicizing the Hungarian Revolution, Captive Nations Week, various East European anniversaries, etc.) Activity which many of the EC's [CIA's] other projects and sponsored activities carry on in the United States can usually be justified by the fact that it is in support of propaganda or political action activity abroad or that its actual impact is intended to be primarily of foreign target areas. With ACEN's activity we are on very slippery ground in trying to use this justification, for very little of it is publicized in Eastern Europe (nor should it be) and it is hardly necessary for ACEN to be carrying on propaganda in the United States for it to be effective (if, indeed, it is) in Latin America or Africa or India. [...] We thus find ourselves in the position of supporting a lobby which is likely to be working more and more against basic U.S. Government interests and which is prone to associate itself more and more with extremist and unrepresentative elements in American life.[14]

Such an evaluation, however, only relates to direct uses of the exile organization for American propaganda purposes. As mentioned above, the ACEN played many other roles as well. Moreover, it must be remembered that for most, if not all, exiled political leaders, the ACEN was one of the forums on which they were active. Representing national councils/committees they maintained their national, ethnic, and personal networks and the sum of these can only point to the exiles' overall impact on the East Central European case during the Cold War.

---

14 [CIA], Memorandum for the Record: The Assembly ..., 1 VII 1963.

The above-cited CIA memorandum stated that "[p]erusal of ACEN clipping files for the past two and one-half years revels large quantitative [underscored in the original] propaganda production. Quantity is not matched by quality. Relatively little of the material is placed in first-class publications with large or influential readership."[15] Even a basic examination of the U.S. press delivered enough evidence to show that while the ACEN had no ability to become a general propaganda instrument, instead serving political purposes, the articles, letters, and reports on the activities of its members were widely published in the American and foreign press.[16] In terms of its political uses, about the same time Christopher Emmet, who counted on the ACEN to continue operations of the American Friends of Captive Nations, gave his view of the importance of the exile Assembly:

> Because of the dignity and reliability of the ACEN's publications and statements, it has more influence than any other group in maintaining the sympathy in Congress for the passive resistance of the captive peoples, as against merely cultivating relations, trade and credits with the Communist governments [...] The influence of the ACEN in Congress hinges, to a considerable degree, on the personal contacts. [...]
>
> As things are now, the ACEN is the most widely known and respected group among Members of Congress which promotes the above theory, because it does so with more moderation, documentation authority than any other group.[17] The ACEN has become a symbol of unity and continuity behind American commitment to the fundamental issue of freedom of Eastern Europe. [...]

Emmet believed that almost an equal number of members of Congress from each party supported the ACEN and its position on Eastern Europe. The ACEN therefore played an important role of keeping the consensus of legitimizing anti-communist policies (in fact U.S. global engagement). When faced with a threat of exposing its links with the U.S. government in 1965, Emmet expressed his fears:

> If the activity and prestige of the ACEN declined, or if a widespread charge is made that its policies are no longer independent; and if the Administration were attacked by the Repub-

15 Ibid.

16 My survey of "The New York Times" and "Chicago Tribune" (1954–1972) encompasses 198 articles, including multiple editorials related to the Assembly or letters by signed by ACEN officers. Individual exiles published even more. Korboński alone authored over a hundred articles published in the opinion leading American newspapers. Stefan Korboński, *Listy amerykańskie, 1953–1983*, ed. Roman W. Rybicki, Bartosz Nowożycki (IPN: Warsaw, 2019).

17 Emmet, Memorandum to Personal Friends within ACEN about the Annual Elections in September, 2 IX 1965, HIA, Coste Papers, b. 1, f. 11.

> licans for muzzling the ACEN, this would inhibit many Democratic Congressmen from continuing to openly identify with ACEN's position, as they do now.[18]

While this may be considered an overstatement, Emmet's interpretation represents the mood of one of the most active political lobbyists, well-connected in Congress, with links to the American government at the time. From a distance, the view of the ACEN's significance from the people involved in working for FEC became more sensible. Leich believed that the ACEN's lasting impact rested in successfully keeping the case of East Central Europe on the agenda of international relations.[19] Ralph Walter thought that the ACEN offered a way to pressure the American allies, be it at the UN, or via distributed appeals and statements. They had – in his opinion – a negligible impact, but these actions provided useful content for domestic policy uses.[20]

Naturally, there was a price to be paid by the exiles for entering into cooperation with America's prime Cold War political organization. They had to work "hand in glove" with the Department of State, eventually endorsing U.S. foreign policy.[21] The exiles were willing to accept the limitations imposed by control mechanisms employed by the host country in exchange for the ability to continue their political operations with a degree of autonomy.[22] However, to advance their goals they sometimes ended with "immensely useful tactical allies" who had very little in common with their original ideology or ultimate ends. Such was the case when, for example, representative of the Batista regime in the UN became the chief spokesperson in the UN for the Hungarian freedom fighters.[23] As Leich framed it: "ACEN had to express a judicious amount of sympathy for local issues in Free World countries when the moral basis for political action on such issues corresponds to that of ACEN action."[24] One should add, and with American interests in mind, from which the ACEN's impact cannot be separated.

When divorced from the context of its usefulness for U.S. policy, ACEN's impact fades. In Ralph Walter's view:

---

18 Ibid.

19 Interview with John Leich, 9 VI 1996, HU OSA, Fekete Doboz.

20 Author's interview with Ralph Walter (telephone), 5 X 2007.

21 Author's interview with John Leich, Canaan, CT (U.S.), 6 VII 2009.

22 James McCargar, "Ferenc Nagy: Smallholder or statesman?" in: Nagy Ferenc miniszterlenök ..., 154; Author's interview with Zofia Korbońska, Washington, 1 XI 2007.

23 See "Portuondo "listonoszem" dla uchodźców," *Trybuna Ludu* of 10 Feb.; Exiles at the service of dictators – Trujillo (Dominican Republic), Stroessner (Paraguay), Batista (Cuba). See HIA, Korboński Papers, b. 13, f. 7.

24 Leich, Policy of FEER, 10 II 1958, HIA, RFE/RL CF: A, b. 200, f. 6.

> It will hardly be easy to determine the actual impact which ACEN activities may have had. Having had experience both working with exile political groups and with Radio Free Europe and Radio Liberty, there is no doubt in my mind that the latter were overwhelmingly more important. The lot of political exiles is rarely a happy one. And the longer those involved are forced to remain in exile, the unhappier their situation inevitably becomes. The radios, on the other hand, were a part of the daily lives of the people to whom they broadcast. They were deeply and actively involved, in a position to inform and even influence their audiences. During the lengthy period of the Cold War, exile political organizations were never able to play such a role, for many reasons. No exile or exile group associated with the ACEN would ever have considered the role of the ACEN as that of an American propaganda tool. They believed they were working in the interests of their native lands, and the best of them went about their work with dedication. As with all political exiles, there were petty quarrels and squabbles over positions of basically non-existent power. There were also some genuine disagreements on political issues.
>
> You know from the files the types of efforts in which they were engaged. Not surprisingly, a good deal of what they did, particularly in contacting representatives of governments, be they of the U.S. Government, members of UN delegations, or whatever, amounted to pushing at open doors. Or they were exercises in futility. Generally, ACEN representatives would be received politely or even with respect, but that is far from saying they were in a position to exercise serious political influence.[25]

Paul Henze, deputy RFE political advisor in the 1950s, reiterated such a point of view:

> As far as I can recall, ACEN was not taken very seriously as a contribution to the propaganda war against the East European communist regimes. It was seen more as a device to keep the emigration busy and occupied and to satisfy interested Congressmen that something was being done. During my time in RFE its activities were the subject of broadcasts, and statements by some of the participants were used; also the statements made to the ACEN by prominent American and other political figures. But everything in relation to it was regarded as marginal to the main purpose of RFE.[26]

There is no doubt that the radio played the most important and dominant role within the FEC. There is also no doubt that anyone working for the radio would focus on their role. An attempt to identify the impact areas of the ACEN produces a much bigger challenge. The areas in which ACEN's impact and legacy can be observed are:

- the preservation of national political tradition abroad;[27]

25 Ralph Walter, e-mail to the Author, 30 IX 2007. Similar views were expressed during interviews: (telephone) Ralph Walter, 5 X 2007.

26 Paul B. Henze, e-mail to the Author, 27 IX 2007.

27 Jonathan H. L'Hommedieu, "The Baltic Freedom Committees: Politics and Polices of an Exile Community" in: *The Inauguration of Organized Political Warfare* ..., 230.

- providing an intellectually stimulating safe haven for elites (opinion making printed works – distributed in the U.S., abroad and behind the Iron Curtain);[28]
- a precedent for public display of broad regional cooperation of East Central European politicians with shared aspiration for integration with the West;[29]
- as a research and information center on East Central Europe at a time where the Slavic Studies in the United States meant Russian/Soviet studies;[30] and
- weakening the communist regimes by maintaining surrogate political opposition abroad.[31]

The exiles gathered under the ACEN umbrella entered a Cold War alliance often called partnership.[32] It allowed the exiles to continue their operations from abroad, against a common enemy. In the era of American government's global engagement during the Cold War, the FEC Exile Political Operations were useful in that they provided legitimacy to the anti-communist rationale. And as part of its public diplomacy effort in the free world, it worked.

From the American point of view, it was easier to establish cooperation with exile political organizations than to phase them out and face ethnic, anti-communist public discontent. Abrupt termination of exile activities would naturally be welcomed by the communist regimes which were irritated by American support the former political leaders for almost twenty years. Keeping the ACEN alive for so long as the Assembly survived despite major political shifts may be explained as a way of deterring Soviet action, as their potential for conducting a political move could be re-activated at any time.

In a letter written in response to John F. Leich's request for a review of his article on the division of exile relations, George F. Kennan, an intellectual father of the Free Europe Committee wrote:

> I feel that much injustice has been done in sections of American opinion to those of you who took upon yourselves this difficult and often thankless task [...] Suppose the [Free Europe] Committee had never been set up at all (as we must suppose many of its critics would have liked). What would have been the results? Would there not have been, on the part of these refugees, a general sense of coldness, indifference and abandonment at the hands of

28 Collins, 127–128.

29 Author's interview with John Leich, Canaan, CT (U.S.), 6 VII 2009.

30 L'Hommedieu, 224.

31 Łaptos, Narodowy Komitet na rzecz Wolnej Europy a komitety emigracji środkowoeuropejskiej (1949–1952), in: *Studia z historii Polski XIX i XX w. ofiarowane prof. Józefowi Buszce w 50. Doktoratu*, ed. Irena Paczyńska (1990), 375.

32 Interviews with: John Leich (Canaan, CT), 15 X 2007; Ralph Walter (Berlin), 5 X 2007.

> American society? And would that not have been exploited by the Stalinist forces then predominant in the Soviet Union and in other countries? Obviously, those of you who addressed yourselves to the task of helping these people found yourselves up against the reflection of all the unsolved national and ethnic problems of eastern Europe. But did not your efforts teach many people to put these frictions into better perspective and to recognize the importance of trying to overcome them by the means of mutual understanding and compromise? And did not some of this communicate itself, at least in some degree, back into the homelands?[33]

As research on political thought in exile in the countries in East Central Europe is continuously growing, the legacy of the political exiles in the West during the Cold War should be considered in the context in which it was created: influenced by certain transpolitical, transnational and spaces. These were formed, pressed and spelled out in conditions that are multifaceted, rather than simply transmitted from the pre-Soviet traditions, or resulting from contacts with "captive" compatriots. If this was the case, then ACEN's impact will find its place alongside the American effort and will indeed reach the homelands with its original message regarding East Central Europe's place in Europe and in world affairs.

---

33 George F. Kennan (the Institute for Advanced Study, Princeton NJ, School of Historical Studies) to J. F. Leich, 19 IX 1989, John F. Leich Papers; John F. Leich to George F. Kennan, 13 IX 1989 (copy), Leich Papers; George F. Kennan (the Institute for Advanced Study, Princeton NJ, School of Historical Studies) to J. F. Leich, 19 IX 1989, Leich Papers. Leich also received comments from James McCargar. James McCargar to John F. Leich, Letter, 15 I 1989, ibid.

10 Epilogue

We now know that the CIA operated a "Mighty Wurlitzer" by supporting a plethora of organizations and projects.[1] However, the scale, duration and impact of the FEC (1949–1972) clearly makes it stand out from other psychological/political warfare projects. Although there were earlier allegations of U.S. government and even specifically CIA's support for the Radios (RFE and RL),[2] the first time that repeated effort to interest the U.S. public in the governmental support for the Free Europe Committee was in the late 1950s, when journalist Fulton Lewis, Jr. suggested a CIA link during his radio programs.[3] Lewis criticized the FEC not only for its connections to the U.S. government, but also for taking a soft-line on national communism, for directing propaganda to the free world, for deficiencies in management and control over its operations.[4] All the evidence he collected was transmitted to the FBI and to Senators James Eastman, William Jenner and Stiles Bridges.[5] No major investigation resulted from it. Ross Johnson, an author whose book was based on research in the classified CIA archives, described ways in which "the CIA protected the Radios from irresponsible outside interference." In the case of Lewis's campaign, it included the CIA's working with the White House and key senators.[6]

The next time CIA sponsorship of the FEC came up was in 1964, when the book *The Invisible Government* by David Wise and Thomas B. Ross was published, and directly linked the CIA with the FEC.[7] However, it was only in 1967

1 Hugh Wilford, *The Mighty Wurlitzer: How the CIA Played America* (Harvard University Press, London-Cambridge, MA, 2008).

2 Tromly, 127–129; Johnson, *Radio Free Europe ...*, 204.

3 See broadcasts for the period from 16 XII 1957 to 13 II 1958 available at NARA II, CREST, Transcript of Broadcast by Fulton Lewis, jr., Station WGMS, 7–7:15 pm, CIA-RDP63T00245R000100220168–1 to RDP63T00245R000100220119–5; Puddington, 118–121, 231–260; Johnson, *Radio Free Europe ...*, 126–127; Noel L. Griese, *Arthur W. Page. Publisher, Public Relations Pioneer, Patriot* (Atlanta: Anvil Publishers Inc., 2001), 385.

4 Transcript of Broadcast by Fulton Lewis, Jr., Station WGMS, 7–7:15 pm, 16 XII 1957, NARA II, CREST, CIA-RDP63T00245R000100220168–1, rel. 27 X 2004; Transcript ..., 31 XII 1957, Ibid, RDP63T00245R000100220159–1. Transcript ..., 14 I 1958, RDP63T00245R000100220150–0, rel. 27 X 2004; Transcript ..., 26 XII 1957, CIA-RDP63T00245R000100220163–6, rel. 27 X 2004.

5 Transcript of Broadcast by Fulton Lewis, jr., Station WGMS, 7–7:15 pm, 1 I 1958, NARA II, CREST, CIA-RDP63T00245R000100220159–1, rel. 27 X 2004.

6 Johnson, *Radio Free Europe ...*, 233.

7 Johnson, *Radio Free Europe ...*, 204. See also: Puddington, *Broadcasting Freedom*, ch. 12; Sig Mickelson, *America's Other Voice. The Story of Radio Free Europe and Radio Liberty* (New York: Praeger, 1983), ch. 13; Gene Sosin, *Sparks of Liberty: an insider's memoir of Radio Liberty* (Uni-

https://doi.org/10.1515/9783110661002-014

that the publication in "Ramparts" (the political and literary magazine, associated with the New Left) revealing that the CIA was sponsoring a number of cultural organizations, notably the foreign activities of the National Student Association, triggered a reaction. By the end of the 1960s, in the era of Civil Rights, student upheaval, the Vietnam War, and after the U-2 incident, the Bay of Pigs, or the Gulf of Tonkin, covertly-supported governmental operations were recognized by the public as abuses of power, and attempts to lie and deceive the public. Recently A. Ross Johnson described in detail the process of Radio Free Europe's severing of its ties with the CIA.[8] A short summary based on his analysis is in order before the situation of the exile political organizations (including the ACEN) can be explained.

Reacting to the public uproar caused by the "Ramparts" article, President Johnson called Nicholas Katzenbach (Under Secretary of State) to investigate the case. Upon receiving the report (March 1967), the President ordered its recommendations be followed, which can be abridged to including no more covert funding or support to U.S. educational, private and voluntary organizations. Johnson suggested that an alternative solution for providing support openly should be established and this became the job of the Rusk committee. In the meantime, tentative solutions like the advanced allocation of funds (by the Johnson administration), or assuming Free Europe was not a private voluntary organization (Nixon's team) allowed Free Europe Committee operations including RFE and exile programs, to continue to January 1971. Trying to suggest a solution, while critical of the CIA's role, on 21 January 1971, Senator Clifford Case delivered a speech in the U.S. Congress becoming the first official to publicly confirm CIA funding for the Free Europe Committee (and the Radio Liberty Committee). While suggesting a bill to fund the radio stations openly he disturbed a great advocate of the relaxation of tensions with the Soviet Union, and the longest-serving Chairman of the Senate Foreign Relations Committee (1959–1974), James William Fulbright.

Fulbright vehemently opposed continued support for the Radios, emphasizing the costs of operating them at the time of the greatest budgetary deficit since World War Two. (Both radios employed a total of 2,533 people at the time!) He also doubted the real impact of the radios (basing his opinion on a personal meeting with 27 Russian journalists, rather than trusting RFE reports or other sources). Furthermore, he wrote: "Since our gov't does its best to suppress the

---

versity Park, PA: The Pennsylvania University Press, 2005), ch. 9; Cord Meyer, *Facing Reality ...*, ch. 5.

8 Johnson, *Radio Free Europe ...*, 205–207, 217–218.

truth to the Congress, it is really ironic that it insists on broadcasting 'truth' to the Russians." Most importantly though, the U.S. Democratic Senator mostly remembered today for the international exchange program he founded in 1946, believed that the Free Europe Committee was an obstacle to improving relations with the East. This "relic of the Cold War" was, as he argued, meddling in the internal affairs of East Central European countries, was responsible for carrying out spy activities by the radios' personnel, and was covertly influencing American public opinion via informal contacts of the discredited personnel. Naturally, his heated arguments against the radios were readily picked up by the communist regimes.

A combination of the following factors posed a deadly threat to Free Europe. First, Clifford Case's speech and Fulbright's drive to kill the radios (the Voice of America supposedly being next on his list) both intended to influence American public opinion in favor of ceasing exile activities. Second, Congress's attempt to change the methods of financing and control which – given the diplomatic protests from the communist regimes in the East – could possibly lead to the Department of State seizing control over the content of exile programs. And last, but not least, West Germany's *Ostpolitik* threatened the operations in Munich. The future of the radios seemed murky. The combination of international and domestic pressures caused a real danger, which almost led to the closing of all Free Europe's activities, which then meant the radios. At one point, a date (23 February 1972) had even been set for ending the broadcasts, and letters laying-off staff were prepared. While all attention was devoted to the radios, making it seem as though other programs were already dead, other exile programs escaped the eye of the public debate.

Despite the Communists' efforts to discredit it, the East Central and East European lobby in the United States had tremendous leverage. Its pressures did not go unnoticed. The best example to illustrate their impact comes from a memo to President Nixon from the Director of the Office of Public Liaison at the White House, Charles Colson:

> Wholly apart from any foreign policy arguments, we will suffer politically if RFE has to discontinue operations. All of the organized Eastern European ethnic groups in this country are, as you well know, on the order of the Hungarian Freedom Fighters, very hawkish and very anti-communist. Thus far, the Polish American Congress, the various Lithuanian and Hungarian groups have been relatively calm over the China initiative, your trip to the Soviet Union and the general lessening of cold war tensions. The demise of RFE however, could well be the straw that broke the camel's back.
>
> It's all well and good for us to assume that Fulbright will be the principal target of their ire, but that is not the way it will turn out.

> Fulbright has maneuvered the publicity to make it appear that he is doing it for you – to be consistent with your present policies toward China and the Soviet Union.[9]

On 10 March 1972, Nixon sent letters to the members of Congress urging them to act in the Radios' defense, and publicly endorsed the Radios the next day– thus decisively distancing himself from Fulbright. Eventually, after two years of uncertainty and temporary funding from USIA and the State Department, in October 1973 and based on the International Broadcasting Act 1973 (PL 93–129), money was provided for 1974 and a new oversight body was formed: the Board for International Broadcasting. The Radios were saved, and to quote the former RFE director A. Ross Johnson: "the FEC and the RLC, freed of earlier émigré-related activities, now focused solely on broadcasting and research."[10] The book program was taken over directly by the CIA.[11] But what happened to the other exile organizations supported by Free Europe?

It turns out that their demise had already begun much earlier, during Eisenhower's second term. In the aftermath of the Hungarian Revolution – arguably the height of East Central European exiles' influence in the U.S.– the exile activities and information efforts were skillfully directed by the FEC towards the countries of the free world faced by a "Communist threat" (mostly developing countries in Asia and Latin America). As much as the exiles wanted to promote the case of liberating their homelands (via free elections and the withdrawal of Soviet troops) from the high point of proclaiming liberation in 1952, by 1956 American policy towards the Soviet Union was becoming increasingly disappointing to the émigré milieus. From 1958, a series of reorganization programs affected the work of the ACEN, gradually shifting support from its member committees/councils to the Assembly. By 1963, the decision was made to turn the ACEN into a limited front organization, gradually phasing it out, to which the exiles responded disapprovingly, with some entering an open confrontation with the FEC Exile Relations staff. The era of partnership, relative exile autonomy and mutual trust was coming to an end. The powerful blow to the ACEN's future came in June 1965 in the form of a cut in its budget. This is when *détente* hit the exiles – three years before Nixon was elected president, seven years before he went to China.

Feliks Gadomski, the ACEN's Secretary General, in a private letter stated:

---

9 Charles Colson to The President (Nixon), Memorandum: Financing of RFE and RL, 7 III 1972, Nixon Presidential Materials Project, White House Central Files, Subject Files, IT (International Organizations), NARA II, b. 3, f.: EX IT 9 Free Europe Inc. 1/1/71–12/31/72.

10 Johnson, *Radio Free Europe* ..., 222.

11 Reisch, 42.

> Our situation has changed greatly over the course of the last year. Neither the ACEN, nor the national committees have the position they used to have during the height of Cold War tensions. The "party internationals" literally lost all influence in the eyes of our sponsors [...] as the Communist monolith breaks, and Communist regimes grow increasingly independent from the Kremlin, the U.S. policy focuses on supporting these trends [consolidation of national communism], hoping that the next phase will be their liberalization. [...] Consequently, some people claim that the captive nations are no longer the case, and that the émigré organizations, which live by cold-war slogans and do not see the changes occurring on both sides, cease to be useful – from the American point of view. In practice it means that the funds are to be limited, including funds for ACEN. Severe budget cuts seem to be just a matter of time.[12]

It was obvious that the budgetary cuts of 1965 caused serious repercussions – exile activities were now severely limited. By the 1970s, many prominent exiles were already gone, and many younger ones had left for regular jobs. As they were struggling to support the survival of the Radios in 1971 – to which they too assigned priority and primary importance – they did worry about the fate of their FEC-supported organizations in the U.S. as well. In his July 1971 exchanges with Jan Nowak, the Director of the Polish Section of RFE, Stefan Korboński inquired: "Do you have any news regarding funds for the ACEN and the committees? The White House proposal mentions the Radios only."[13]

In November a similar inquiry was sent by General Lucius Clay (the hero of the Berlin Airlift, and the Chairman of the Free Europe Board) to National Security Advisor Henry Kissinger. Clay was not so much concerned about the demise of the ACEN but about the repercussions the withdrawal of funding might cause:

> On or before January 1, 1972, the government subsidies which have been made through Radio Free Europe to the Assembly of Captive European Nations and to the National Committees of East European exiles will be terminated. The continued existence of these organizations is therefore in jeopardy.
>
> These groups were established in the late forties and early fifties with the encouragement and assistance of the Department of State. At the request of the Department, RFE has administered the government grants to these organizations and maintained liaison with them. The government subsidy has been approximately $ 200,000 a year. Under the pending bill authorizing government support to Radio Free Europe, RFE will no longer have the authority or the funds to subsidize these groups. [footnote: A list of the organizations involved and background documentation on their origins are attached. It is my understanding that the arrangements are being made through the Department of State to provide annuities for the 55 exile political leaders who have heretofore received stipends through Free

12 Gadomski (New York) to Barbara Karwecka (The Committee of Liberal Exiles. The Liberal International (World Liberal Union), London), 31 III 1965, Jadwiga Gadomska Files.

13 Stefan Korboński to Jan Nowak, 24 VII 1971, HIA, Korboński Papers, b. 4, f. FEC/RWE 1.

Europe, Inc. The problem of the organizations described above, however, has not been resolved.] It is also doubtful if these funds could be made available within the purview of the continuing resolution.

I do not understand the State Department is supporting the continuation of this financial aid. Nor am I recommending its continuance. However, I do feel that I should advise you that there may be some "repercussions" from various ethnic groups.

These associations are valued by Polish-Americans and other ethnic groups in this country. Their modest programs of research, publications, and conferences give expression to the desires of their countrymen for freedom and independence. Their activities culminate in the Captive Nations Week, which has been proclaimed by the President of the United States annually since 1959.

For these reasons, you may wish to consider alternative means of continuing the government subsidy.[14]

NSC staff member Peter Jessup who interpreted this letter and prepared a reply, wrote to Kissinger:

> Actually, there are none [funds] in sight, unless it be émigré "angels" of a particular ethnic persuasion who may choose to keep some of these groups going. Short of having the CIA go back in this business, no way out is foreseen. They must be considered a casualty of the times.

He further noted:

> Clay notes that he understands 55 (actually 62) annuities are being arranged through the State for some of the exiles involved in these committees. This is correct and the Presidential Determination Order proposal which you approved on 28 August is almost ready for White House signature.[...] If we take care of 62 senior citizens and interim funding is found on the Hill for continuance of the Radios (even through a study commission), we will have accomplished much and be batting 2 for 3.[15]

In his reply to Clay (1 November 1971), Kissinger repeated the above arguments, skipping the baseball reference. Jessup had included another sentence in his

14 Lucius D. Clay (Chairman of the RFE Board) to Henry J. Kissinger, 7 X 1971, Nixon Presidential Materials Project, White House Central Files, Subject Files, IT (International Organizations), NARA II, b. 4, f.: GEN IT 9 Free Europe Inc. 1/1/71–12/31/72 [1 of 2].

15 Peter Jessup to Dr. Kissinger, Memorandum from Lucius D. Clay Regarding Government Subsidies Made Through Radio Free Europe, 20 X 1971, Nixon Presidential Materials Project, White House Central Files, Subject Files, IT (International Organizations), NARA II, b. 4, f.: GEN IT 9 Free Europe Inc. 1/1/71–12/31/72 [1 of 2].

draft reply which Kissinger crossed out: "I am afraid the organizational aspect to which you refer must be considered a casualty of these changing times."[16]

When, just around Christmas 1971, the exiles realized that American support for their organizations in the U.S. was about to end, they naturally protested. They did so on behalf of individual national committees, on behalf of the ACEN, by asking their friends in Congress, and former Free Europe officials to intervene on their behalf. Representative Walter H. Judd (R-MN, 1943–1963, President, American Council for World Freedom) wrote to President Nixon:

> The precipitate termination of these funds, preceding your trips to Pekin and Moscow may lead many to the conclusion that the U.S. and you personally have abandoned America's historic position of supporting the return to freedom of all captive nations and peoples. We respectfully request the immediate review and reversal of the decision to cut off funds and thus give a reaffirmation of America's historic support of all peoples behind the iron, bamboo and sugar cane curtains, and their efforts to regain their freedom.[17]

The exiles (Poles, Bulgarians, Romanians, Hungarians) in their communications emphasized the demoralizing impact in the countries behind the Iron Curtain – an obvious sign of resignation, acknowledgement of the status quo, thus giving the Communists a reason to triumph. Détente should not equal surrender. Vişoianu protested in his letter to the Special Assistant to the U.S. President (Harry Dent) arguing that the withdrawal of American support would mean the triumph of the Communists. His protest was not so much related to finances as to losing a strategic ally:

> I fear this act will be interpreted by the Romanian nation and by Romanians in exile as a political move of grave and deep significance. This help from the U.S. government has been not only a generous gesture but an act of exceptional political wisdom. [...] Elimination of this token of American interest and concern would deeply affect Romanian hopes for liberty and a better life. The loss of even this meager instrument of expression of their true feeling would be demoralizing.[18]

---

16 Henry A. Kissinger to Lucius D. Clay, 1 XI 1971, Nixon Presidential Materials Project, White House Central Files, Subject Files, IT (International Organizations), NARA II, b. 4, f.: GEN IT 9 Free Europe Inc. 1/1/71–12/31/72 [1 of 2].

17 Walter H. Judd (President) American Council for World Freedom to President Richard M. Nixon, 30 XII 1971, Nixon Presidential Materials Project, White House Central Files, Subject Files, IT (International Organizations), NARA II, b. 4, f.: GEN IT 9 Free Europe Inc. 1/1/71–12/31/72 [2 of 2]

18 Constantin Vişoianu (Chairman, Romanian National Committee) to Harry Dent (Special Assistant to the President, White House), 5 II 1972, Nixon Presidential Materials Project, White House Central Files, Subject Files, IT (International Organizations), NARA II, b. 4, f.: GEN IT 9 Free Europe Inc. 1/1/71–12/31/72 [2 of 2]

The Department of State in cooperation with the Office of Management and Budget (White House) came up with a template (or a boiler plate as one official called it) which was sent in reply to this and other letters:

> Free Europe, Inc., has informed the Department of State that recent actions in the Congress have meant that there is no longer any legal basis on which that organization can contribute financially to the ACEN or to the National Committees. Legislation now before congress provides support only for the broadcast activities of RFE and other activities have been dropped. We have no desire to see these groups dissolved and we vigorously opposed the action taken by Congress. We are aware of the valuable work they and their officers have done. Hopefully, interested individuals and organizations will be prepared to assist them to carry on their important work.[19]

Interested individuals did in fact carry on. In a letter to Nowak written in April 1972, Korboński wrote:

> Let me inform you that the ACEN will be sustained by the nine émigré organizations. We are about to move to a smaller office, but in the same building. We were able to collect couple of thousand dollars from friends and for the time being, at least for the length of my term as a chairman, the minimum for our survival is provided. Our members are truly generous, few people work for free, in short: *sursum corda!*[20]

Despite the decision to end financial support, neither the ACEN nor the national committees ceased to exist. Given the complexity of interests, ideological positions and historical animosities, it is remarkable that ACEN's members decided that the organization had to continue its existence. On 22 May 1972, the Assembly was incorporated into ACEN, Inc., and as such registered by the Justice of the Supreme Court of the state of New York with all nine Eastern European nations represented.[21]

Despite significant financial burdens, ACEN, Inc. continued its operations.[22] Its budget was so modest that not only were salaries out of the question, but desperate émigrés also decided to establish annual dues to support its modest func-

---

19 Michael B. Smith (Staff Assistant to the President) to Walter H. Judd (President, American Council for World Freedom, Washington D.C.), 16 II 1972, Nixon Presidential Materials Project, White House Central Files, Subject Files, IT (International Organizations), NARA II, b. 4, f.: GEN IT 9 Free Europe Inc. 1/1/71–12/31/72 [2 of 2]

20 Korboński to Jan Nowak, 18 IV 1972, HIA, Korboński Papers, b. 4, f. 1.

21 Certificate of Reservation, State of New York, Department of State, 28 III 1972, ZNiO, Gadomski Papers, 121/02; Certificate of Incorporation of Assembly of Captive European Nations, Inc. Pursuant to Section 402 of the Non-for-profit Corporation Law of New York, 18 IV 1972, ibid. ; By-laws of Assembly of Captive European Nations, Inc., ibid.

22 ZNiO. Gadomski Papers, 124/2002.

tions. The ACEN's Secretary General described how their office was organized at the Lithuanian Committee's quarters, later moved to the Albanian Committee limiting its office to one shared desk. The ACEN's plenary meetings took place in Estonian House on 34th St.[23] Eventually the headquarters were moved to Korboński house on Decatur St. in Washington.

Nevertheless, as an organization now independent of the American government, ACEN's delegations continued to be received in the State Department, generally invited individually for consultations, reminding one of a peculiar think tank. Also, the U.S. Congressmen did not abandon the captives, eagerly inserting their appeals and articles published by them in the American press into the Congressional Record. It was always a good way to enhance one's name with the electorate and put one's testimony of defending freedom and democracy on the record.

In 1988, John F. Leich, who from 1950 to 1960 worked in the exile division of FEC in New York, and then for five more years as a vice director of WEOD in London, decided to publish his account of working for the Free Europe Committee.[24] Looking for a good conclusion to his story, he wrote to Stefan Korboński and László Varga asking about the whereabouts of ACEN, Inc. Was the ACEN still commenting on developments in East Central Europe? If so, what did they think about changes in Eastern Bloc?[25] In response, László Varga sent Leich some material and explanations, also about his own role. With regards to ACEN, Inc. he said:

> We are still going every year to the State Department, to visit a few Congressmen and to the White House to discuss with the Director of the National Security Council and we give them our memorandum. If we feel that we have to write letters to the President or to the Secretary of State, we do it. That's all! I know it is very little, but our possibilities are very little, because we don't have as you know any financial help and we pay everything from our pockets.[26]

23 Gadomski, *Zgromadzenie Europejskich ...*, 69.
24 Leich, *Great Expectations ...*," 183–196.
25 Leich to László Varga (ACEN Chairman), 16 XII 1988, Leich Papers.
26 László Varga also stated that after Korboński's resignation in September 1984 "there was no other alternative but him assuming the Chairmanship or the ACEN would terminate." He had to take the steering wheel or the organization would have fallen apart. "I took it and I try to resign every year but nobody takes it, so I am still the 'captain of this sinking ship,' because the young generation is not interested to participate." László Varga (ACEN Chairman) to Leich, 17 IV 1989, Leich Papers.

Writing his letter on 17 April 1989, Varga added:

> Regarding the situation in Hungary: I hope that our people stepped on the road to independence, that could slow down or be stopped by the Communist regime, but they cannot turn back [...].[27]

Korboński died on 23 April 1989 – roughly two weeks after the Round Table Talks in Poland ended in the signing of an agreement based on which the first free elections (to the country's Senate) in the Communist Bloc since 1947 were to be held.[28] Béla Varga (1903–1995), having fled the country in 1947 as the youngest speaker of the Parliament, in 1990 returned to free Hungary to become the oldest in the same position.[29] The last Secretary of the ACEN, Feliks Gadomski (1898–1998) spent his final months reunited with his daughter in Warsaw.[30] At least some of the original ACEN members, the exiles of the post-World War II cohort, witnessed their homelands regain freedom. The remains of Stefan Korboński – the man who inspired me to write this book – as well as his wife, Zofia, who had helped me to understand the zeal behind their life-long devotion to the cause, were returned to Poland in 2010.[31]

Today, the ten nations represented in the ACEN (Czech Republic and Slovakia as independent states) are members of NATO. Nine joined the European Union with Albania being an official candidate for accession since 2014. Howev-

---

27 In his response, Leich urged Varga to pass his warmest regards to Msgr. Vela Varga "glad to know he was also well and active." Leich to László Varga (ACEN Chairman), 20 IV 1989, Leich Papers. His last letter to László Varga was dated 18 may 1989. This was the last piece of ACEN correspondence I was able to locate. Leich to László Varga (ACEN Chairman), 18 V 1989, Leich Papers.

28 William Lipinski (Representative of Illinois), "Stefan Korboński A True Polish Hero," 101 Cong., 1st Sess., *Cong. Rec.* 135, 27 IV 1989, 7633; Steny H. Hoyer (Representative of Maryland), "A Tribute to a Fallen Polish Leader – Stefan Korboński," ibid. , 9 V 1989, 8744. The elections were free to all contestants only to the reinstated country's Senate, while only 35% of seats the lower house (the Sejm) were opened to free ballot. Solidarity swept all available seats, except for one independent Senator. Yet, by August 1989, Warsaw saw its first non-communist prime minister since 1939.

29 "Béla Varga. Hungarian politician, 92," *The New York Times*, 15 X 1995, 41.

30 Feliks Gadomski (1898–1998): Obituary, Jadwiga Gadomska Files.

31 Stefan i Zofia Korbońscy pochowani w Świątyni Opatrzności Bożej, 3 X 2012, Dzieje.pl Portal Historyczny, https://dzieje.pl/aktualnosci/stefan-i-zofia-korbonscy-pochowani-w-swiatyni-opatrznosci-bozej, accessed: 14 VII 2018.

er, the exile Assembly's operations were never closed. ACEN, Inc.'s status with the state of New York is still listed as "Active."[32]

32 Entity name: Assembly of Captive European Nations, Inc., Initial DOS Filing Date: 24 May 1972, NYS Department of State, Division of Corporations, Entity Information, ACEN DOS ID: 330762. https://appext20.dos.ny.gov/corp_public/CORPSEARCH.SELECT_ENTITY, accessed 25 IV 2020. See also commercial services.

Appendices

ACEN Charter and Rules of Procedure (as of 1958)

CHARTER OF THE ASSEMBLY OF CAPTIVE EUROPEAN NATIONS[1]

WE DEMOCRATIC REPRESENTATIVES
OF THE PEOPLES OF ALBANIA, BULGARIA,
CZECHOSLOVAKIA, ESTONIA, HUNGARY,
LATVIA, LITHUANIA, POLAND AND ROMANIA

determined to uphold, serve, and further the rightful aspirations to freedom, national independence, and social justice of our people, now enslaved under alien domination, and unable to speak for themselves; estimating that, through our combined efforts within the Assembly of Captive European Nations, we have been able more effectively to voice and promote the common rights and interest of our peoples;

RESOLVE, to carry on our common efforts until all objectives set forth in the "Statement of Aims and Principles" adopted at the constitutive meeting of the Assembly of Captive European Nations, on September 20, 1954, shall be fully attained; and to that end, to perfect our solidarity.

Therefore, we now solemnly agree to adopt the present.

CHARTER OF THE ASSEMBLY OF CAPTIVE EUROPEAN NATIONS
Chapter I
Purposes and Principles
ARTICLE 1

The purposes of the Assembly of Captive European Nations are:

1. To work for the liberation from Communist dictatorship and Soviet domination of the captive nations of Central and Eastern Europe.
2. To affirm and sustain the right of the captive European nations to be represented in the United Nations only by their own legitimate governments, responsive to the will of the respective peoples.

---

1 ACEN Charter, ACEN Doc No. 49 (Gen.) unanimously adopted in the 17th meeting of the Plenary Assembly on September 28, 1955, and, subsequently, amended in the 42nd meeting of the Plenary Assembly, on November 30, 1956, as well as in the 57th meeting of the Plenary Assembly, on September 23, 1958.

https://doi.org/10.1515/9783110661002-015

3. To co-operate with all free nations represented in the United Nations, with the view of attaining the effective and universal implementation of the purposes and principles of the United Nations Charter.
4. To furnish the United Nations and its specialized Agencies, as well as its free member nations, with all available information concerning conditions in our respective countries that in any way run counter to the aims and principles of the United Nations.
5. To supply information and documentation to governmental and private institutions of the free world, as well as prominent personalities in the free world, making known the true situation prevailing in the captive European countries, and the indomitable struggle of our enslaved peoples for freedom, independence, social justice, and democracy.
6. To seek in every appropriate way to enlist the support and cooperation of political, social, religious, cultural, and professional organizations of the free world, whose democratic activities might be apt to further the cause of the liberation of the captive nations.
7. To make available to the free world the knowledge and experience of Communist rule, policies, tactics, and strategy, gained by the captive European nations.
8. To co-operate with the Council of Europe and the European Movement, with the aim of assuring an adequate representation of the captive European nations in those bodies, and of preparing the way for the integration of these nations to a United Europe, following their liberation.
9. To maintain contacts with the peoples behind the Iron Curtain by all available means, with the view of sustaining their morale and of strengthening their will to resist and oppose Communist dictatorship and alien control and domination, notably by providing the people with correct information on international developments, on the efforts made on their behalf by the free world, and on the activities of their own exiled spokesmen.
10. To strive to preserve and foster democratic ideals in the hearts and minds of the enslaved peoples, and to preserve and promote true values of their own spiritual, cultural, and political heritage both at home and abroad; and to promote research and studies apt to help freely elected governments in countries of Central and Eastern Europe, after liberation, in the task of democratic reconstruction.
11. To promote a spirit of understanding, unity, and co-operation among the national representations and groups in exile, and to seek to lay the solid foundations for future co-operation.
12. To provide all possible assistance to the democratic refugees from our enslaved countries, notably to endeavor to obtain that they might freely exer-

cise their chosen profession and be employed, in the countries that shelter them, on an equal footing with the nationals of these countries; to protect them against repatriation to their enslaved countries of origin, attended by any form of duress whatsoever; to safeguard their human rights, personal self-respect, and national dignity, thus encouraging them, both individually and collectively to preserve their cultural heritage and to contribute worthily to the cause of the liberation of their nations, as well as to their reconstruction following liberation.

ARTICLE 2

The Assembly of Captive European Nations and its individual members, in pursuit of the purposes set forth in Article 1, shall act in accordance with the following principles:

1. The Organization is based on the principle of equality among all nations.
2. All members, in order to secure to each the full rights and benefits resulting from membership, shall, in good faith and to the best of their ability, strive to carry out the obligations assumed under the present Charter. They likewise undertake to settle by conciliation all differences that might arise among themselves.
3. The restoration of freedom and independence to the nations represented in this Organization is the common concern of all Members. Therefore all Members pledge themselves to the fullest measure of solidarity. They shall not cease or diminish their common efforts until liberation, as stated in Article 1, p. 1, is attained for all.
4. All Members agree in the view that all men and all nations have the inalienable right to liberty; that the cause of freedom is, like that of peace itself, one and indivisible; and that the suppression of freedom in any part of the world endangers the freedom of all nations and of all men.
5. Adherence to the principle of government of the people, by the people, and for the people; and to the principle of the rule of law, with full respect for human rights and fundamental freedoms, are and shall remain basic qualifications for all Members. Members may base their own actions upon any democratic doctrine consistent with the above principles, and the Organization for its part will treat such doctrines with equal respect.
6. The sole end of the Organization is the restoration to our respective nations of national independence and of the right to determine freely, through democratic processes the political, social, and economic form of government under which they wish to live. Therefore, in regard to the international relations and status of these nations following their liberation, the Organization will confine its action to studies and recommendations, refraining from any

commitments which only their respective peoples, through their freely elected governments, will have the authority to assume. In regard to the establishment of governments responsive to the will of the people, the Organization shall confine itself to the advocacy of the basic democratic principles.

Chapter II
Membership

ARTICLE 3

1. Membership in the Assembly of Captive European Nations is confined to National Committees or Councils, which shall be represented therein by national delegations, of which there shall be no more than one for each nation represented in the original membership. Each delegation shall consist of not more than 16 delegates.
2. Each delegation shall have one vote.

ARTICLE 4

National Committees or Councils representing nations that have not been represented as participants in the establishment of the Assembly may be admitted to membership. Such admission shall be effected by the affirmative vote of two-thirds of the members of the organization.

ARTICLE 5

1. International political organizations based on major political parties or groups from the nations represented in the Assembly shall be eligible in the capacity of Associate Members.
2. Associate Members shall be represented each by a delegation of not more than six persons.
3. Such delegations of Associate Members shall participate on equal terms with those of Members in the plenary meetings and working committees of the Assembly. They shall not, however have the right to vote.

ARTICLE 6

The primary qualification for both full membership and associate membership shall entail that the political purpose, character, structure, and by-laws of the respective National Committee or Council and of such International Organizations as are described in Article 5 be wholly consistent with the purposes and principles set forth is the present Charter.

ARTICLE 7

1. International organizations formed by the exiles from Central and Eastern Europe for the purpose of defending the rights or voicing the grievances of specific sections of groups of our enslaved peoples, such as religious, professional, cultural, humanitarian, and women's or youth organizations, may be granted the status of consultative organizations.
2. Consultative organizations shall be admitted to participate in the work of certain working committees of the Assembly, but shall not have the right of vote therein. The representatives of such consultative organizations may be eligible to address plenary meetings of the Assembly on matters in which the representative organizations are particularly qualified.

Chapter III
Organs

ARTICLE 8

1. The principal organs of the Assembly of Captive European Nations are established as follows: The Plenary Assembly; the General Committee; the working committees; and the Secretariat.
2. Subsidiary organs or special agencies may be set up by the General Committee, as necessity arises, anywhere in the free world.

PLENARY ASSEMBLY

ARTICLE 9

1. The Plenary Assembly shall consist of the delegations duly appointed by the Members and Associate Members of the Organization.
2. The Plenary Assembly shall convene in ordinary session each year, during month of September, and shall remain in session for one year thereafter.
3. The Plenary Assembly may take cognizance of and discuss any issue or specific question within the scope of the present Charter, or relating to the powers or functions of the organs provided for in this Charter.
4. Decisions on all matters, with the exception of matters on which the Charter specifically provides otherwise, on matters involving principle and on administrative matters, shall be taken by the affirmative vote of an absolute majority of the member delegations. Decisions on any matter involving principle shall be taken by the affirmative vote of two-thirds of the national delegations. The determination of issues involving principle shall be made by an absolute majority vote of the member delegations. Decisions on administrative matters shall be taken by an absolute majority of the member delega-

tion present. The determination of an administrative matter shall be made by the affirmative vote of an absolute majority of the member delegations.

5. Two-thirds of the national delegations in the Assembly shall constitute a quorum.
6. The Plenary Assembly shall convene in New York, the seat of the Assembly of Captive European Nations and of the United Nations. The General Committee may, however, call the Plenary Assembly into special session in any other place in the free world.
7. The meeting of the Plenary Assembly and of Special Sessions shall be presided, in rotation, by the chairmen of national delegations or by the members of the General Committee.

GENERAL COMMITTEE

ARTICLE 10

1. At the beginning of each session, the Plenary Assembly shall constitute a General Committee, which shall remain in continuous session for one year thereafter. The members of the General Committee, one of each nation, shall be designated by the respective national member organization.
2. The General Committee shall meet upon being convened by its chairman or whenever one-third if its members so decide.
3. The General Committee shall: propose the date for convening the Assembly; prepare and submit proposals to the Assembly; assign tasks to, and coordinate the work of, the working committees; make decisions on all matters relating to membership, provided for in Article 3, 4, 5, 6, and 7 of the present Charter; elect, subject to confirmation by the Plenary Assembly, the officers of the Organization, to wit, the Chairman, the Vice-Chairman, the Secretary-General, and the Deputy Secretary-General; act in the name of the Organization during the periods between the meetings of the Plenary Assembly, adopt during such periods, and subject to approval by the Plenary Assembly, reports and resolutions on any questions or matters within the scope of the president Charter; assure the implementation of the provisions of the present Charter and of the Rules of Procedure, and interpret these provisions; establish, within the general policy laid down through resolutions of the Plenary Assembly, the policy and program of the Organization, and supervise the execution of the budget of the Organization; direct and supervise the work of the Secretariat, and, through its officers, execute the budget, and take all the steps called for in the implementation of the purposes and principles of the present Charter.
4. The Chairman of the General Committee or, in his absence, the Vice-Chairman, shall preside over the meetings of the General Committee.

5. During the intervals between the meetings of the General Committee, the Chairman of the General Committee or, in his absence, the Vice-Chairman, may act in the name of the Assembly upon urgent matters within the scope of the present Charter, and within the general policies laid down by the Plenary Assembly.
6. The Chairman of the General Committee or, in his absence, the Vice-Chairman, shall represent the Assembly of Captive European Nations, in its relations with international, governmental, and private institutions or organizations.

WORKING COMMITTEES

ARTICLE 11

1. The Plenary Assembly shall set up a Political Committee, a Social Committee, a Cultural Committee, an Economic Committee, a Legal Committee, and an Information Committee.
2. Each national delegation shall be represented in each of these Committees.
3. International political organizations admitted to be Associate Members shall likewise be represented on these Committees by one representative each; their representatives, however, shall not have the right to vote.
4. Consultative organizations shall be represented, each by one delegate, in every Committee to which they may be admitted; their delegates shall, however, have no voting rights.
5. Subjects to confirmation by the Plenary Assembly, each Working Committee shall elect its own Chairman, and Secretary.
6. The Committees shall be in permanent session. Their task is to study all matter assigned to them by the General Committee. They may, however, initiate such assignments by themselves proposing subjects appropriate in their estimation for consideration by the Assembly.

SECRETARIAT

ARTICLE 12

1. The secretariat shall comprise: one Secretary-General, one Deputy Secretary-General, and such other staff and personnel as the Organization may decide it requires.
2. The Secretary-General shall act in that capacity in all meetings of the Plenary Assembly and of the General Committee, and he shall also perform any other functions that might be entrusted to him by these organs. The Secretary-General shall make annual reports on the work of the Organizations to the General Committee. These reports shall be submitted to the Plenary Assembly.

3. Subject to instructions from the General Committee, the Secretariat shall carry out the decisions of the Plenary Assembly. It shall put into effect the decisions of the General Committee itself, and lend such technical assistance as shall be considered necessary to all organs, subsidiary organs, and special organizations of the Assembly of Captive European Nations.
4. In the performance of their duties, the Secretary-General and the members of his staff shall not seek nor receive instructions from any Member organization, or from any other authority external to the Organization. They shall not be members of any of the national or international organizations to the Assembly. They shall at all times refrain from any action that might reflect on their standing as officials of the Assembly of Captive European Nations, responsible only to the Organization.

Chapter IV
General Provisions

ARTICLE 13

Rules of procedure, to be adopted by the Plenary Assembly, shall determine the organization and procedure of the organs of the Assembly of Captive European Nations.

ARTICLE 14

The Plenary Assembly may revise or amend the present Charter. This shall be done by the affirmative vote of two-thirds of the voting Members of the Organization.

ARTICLE 15

The Assembly of Captive European Nations shall be dissolved upon the liberation of all nations represented therein.

RULES OF PROCEDURE OF THE ASSEMBLY OF CAPTIVE EUROPEAN NATIONS[2]

Chapter I

Plenary Assembly

RULE 1

(Sessions)

1. The Plenary Assembly shall meet in ordinary session each year during the month of September.
2. The date of the beginning of each new session will be determined by the General Committee at least thirty days in advance.
3. Each annual session will be numbered.

RULE 2

(Date of meetings)

1. During each session the Plenary Assembly shall meet at the dates set by the General Committee.
2. The Plenary Meetings shall be consecutively numbered, beginning with the first plenary meeting of the first session.

RULE 3

(Credentials)

1. Ten days before the beginning of each new session, each member and associate member organization, as well consultative organization, shall submit to the General Committee, acting as credentials committee, the names of its delegates.
2. The duly signed credentials of member organization shall include the name of the representative of the respective member organization in the General Committee and the name of his alternate, as well as the names of members and experts for each committee.
3. The duly signed credentials of the associate member organizations shall indicate the name of the chairman of the respective delegation, as well the name of the member, alternate and expert for each committee.
4. The duly signed credentials of the consultative organizations shall indicate the name of their representative, alternate, and expert for each committee to the work in which they were admitted to participate.

2 Rules of Procedure of the ACEN, ACEN Doc No. 50 (Gen.) unanimously adopted in the 17th meeting of the Plenary Assembly on September 28, 1955, and, subsequently, amended in the 57th meeting of the Plenary Assembly, on September 23, 1958.

RULE 4

(Validation of credentials)

1. Acting as credentials committee, the General Committee shall examine the credentials with the view of establishing that they were issued by the responsible authority of each member, associate member, or consultative organization and that they conform to the provisions of the Chapter and of the present Rules of Procedure.
2. On the basis of its findings the General Committee, shall submit in the first meeting of each annual session a report on credentials. Following the adoption of this report the provisional list of delegates becomes final for the whole session.
3. Any change in the composition of delegations during a session is subject to the procedure set forth in the preceding two paragraphs.

RULE 5

(Delegations)

1. Only nationals of the nations represented in the Organization who have not acquired another citizenship shall be designated as members in the national and international delegations. This rule shall, however, not apply to experts.
2. Once duly accredited a delegate shall not join or represent any other delegation for the duration of the respective session.

RULE 6

(Opening meetings of each session)

1. The opening meeting of each session of the Plenary Assembly shall be devoted to matters of organization.
2. The chairman of the General Committee shall preside over the opening meeting of each ordinary and special session.
3. The opening meeting of each annual session will take up matters of organization in the following order:
   a. Approval of the agenda proposed by the General Committee for the opening meeting.
   b. Report of the General Committee on credentials.
   c. Adoption of the General Agenda proposed by the General Committee for the whole session.
   d. Proposals of the General Committee for the revision or amendment of the Charter or of the Rules of Procedure.
   e. Constitution of the General Committee.
   f. Constitution of the Committees.
   g. Report on the election of officers by the General Committee.

h. Report on the election of officers by the Committees.

4. In the course of the session, the Plenary Assembly may revise the general agenda it has adopted adding, deleting, deferring, or altering its items.

Chapter II
Conduct of the Business of the Plenary Assembly

RULE 7
(President)

1. The Chairmen of national delegations or members of the General Committee preside by rotation over the ordinary meetings and special session meetings of the Assembly, with the exception of the opening meeting of each ordinary and special session. The first President will be chosen by the General Committee by lot, to be succeeded by subsequent Presidents in English alphabetical order following the name of the country of the first President.
2. The President shall not vote.

RULE 8
(Voting)

Each national delegation in the Assembly shall have one vote. The Assembly shall vote by show of hands except that a roll-call is taken at the request of any delegate.

RULE 9
(Agenda for each morning)

The first order of business in any plenary meeting or special session meeting is the adoption of the agenda for the respective meeting.

RULE 10
(Speeches)

The President shall call upon speakers in the order in which they signify their desire to speak. The President may call a speaker to order if his remarks are not relevant to the subject under discussion.

RULE 11
(Precedence)

The Chairman and the Rapporteur of a Committee may be accorded precedence for the purpose of explaining the conclusions arrived at by their Committee.

RULE 12
(Point of order)

During the discussion of any matter, a delegate may rise to a point of order which the President shall immediately decide in accordance with the rules of procedure. The ruling of the President shall stand unless overruled by a majority of the members present and voting. A delegate rising to a point of order may not speak on the substance of the matter under discussion.

RULE 13
(Time Limit on Speeches)

The Assembly may limit the time to be allowed to each speaker, and the number of times each delegate may speak on any question.

RULE 14
(Closing of List of Speakers)

During the course of a debate the President may announce the list of speakers and, with the content of the Assembly, declare the list closed.

RULE 15
(Adjournment of Debate)

During the discussion of any matter, a delegate may move the adjournment of the debate on the item under discussion.

RULE 16
(Closure of Debate)

A delegate may at any time move the closure of the debate on the item under discussion. The motion shall be put to the vote after two speakers opposing the closure have had permission to speak.

RULE 17
(Suspension or Adjournment)

During the discussion of any matter, a delegate may move the adjournment, sine die or to a fixed, of the debate on the item, or the suspension of the adjournment of the meeting. Such motions shall be immediately put to the vote without debate.

RULE 18
(Order of Procedural Motion)

The following motions shall have precedence in the following order over all other proposals or motions before the meeting:

a) A motion to suspend the meeting;
b) A motion to adjourn the meeting;
c) A motion to adjourn the debate on the item under discussion;
d) A motion for the closure of the debate on the item under discussion.

Chapter III
General Committee

RULE 19

(Officers, alternates and observers)

1. The Chairman and Vice-Chairman shall be elected at the beginning of each ordinary session for one year from among the members of the General Committee. They shall not be elected to the same office for a consecutive second term.
2. The Secretary General and the Deputy Secretary General shall be elected for one year. They may be re-elected.
3. Each national member organization shall appoint one alternate representative to the General Committee.
4. Alternates may attend all meeting of the General Committee. They are only entitled to vote or participate in the debate in the absence of the representative.
5. The Chairmen of the Committees shall participate as observers in the meetings of the General Committee whenever matters assigned for study to their respective Committees are under consideration. They shall have no right to vote and shall confine their participation in the debate to matters of direct concern to the work of their committees.
6. The General Committee may invite the participation in its meetings, as observers, of a representative of each associate member.

RULE 20

(Conduct of Business)

1. The rules provided for the conduct of business of the Plenary Assembly shall apply to the General Committee which may also establish the supplementary rules it may find necessary.
2. The General Committee shall take decisions only if two-thirds of its members are present.
3. The first order of business in each meeting of the General Committee shall be the approval of the minutes of the preceding meeting unless it is decided to postpone consideration thereof for the next meeting.

4. The meetings of the General Committee shall be numbered consecutively beginning with the first meeting of the first session of the Assembly of Captive European Nations.

RULE 21

(Public meetings)

Whenever circumstances prevent the convening of the Plenary Assembly and urgent public action on the part of the Organization is required, the General Committee may convene in public meeting. A representative of the international member organizations shall participate in such meetings on the same terms as they are taking part in the Plenary Assembly.

Chapter IV
Committees

RULE 22

(Members, alternates and experts)

1. Each national delegation may appoint not more than three members and two experts for each working committee. Only one delegate, however, shall take part in the debate and vote at any given meeting.
2. Each international delegation may appoint one member, one alternate and one expert for each committee in the work of which it was admitted to participate.
3. Alternates shall meet the qualification set forth by Rule 5, para. 1.

RULE 23

(Sub-Committee)

1. Each Committee may set up such sub-committees as it deems necessary. Each sub-committee shall elect its own officers.
2. Alternates and experts may be appointed to membership in sub-committees.

RULE 24

(Conduct of business)

The rules for the conduct of the business of the Assembly shall apply to committees and sub-committees, except that an absolute majority of the national delegations shall constitute a quorum and that decision shall be taken with a simple majority of the national delegations present.

RULE 25

(Regional Working Committees)

In accordance with article 8, paragraph 2, of the Charter, the General Committee may establish for the duration of a session or on a more temporary basis, working committees, sub-committees or groups in places other than the seat of the Organization.

Chapter V
Secretariat

RULE 26

(Organization and procedure)

1. The General Committee shall adopt, on the proposal of the Secretary-General, a Regulation of organization and procedure of the Secretariat.
2. The General Committee shall appoint on the proposal of the Secretary General members of the Secretariat staff.
3. The General Committee may establish Secretariats and/or Press Officers, or appoint correspondents in places other the seat of the Organization. Such subsidiary organs shall act in accordance with rules to be determined by the General Committee.

Chapter VI
General Provisions

RULE 27

(Guest Speakers)

The General Committee or, on its authority, the Chairman, may invite distinguished personalities from the nations of the free world to address the Plenary Assembly.

RULE 28

(Revision or amendment of the Rules of Procedure)

The present rules may be revised or amended by the Plenary Assembly voting in accordance with article 9, paragraphs 4 and 5, of the Charter.

RULE 29

(Abrogation of Rules of Procedure adopted in first session)

The present Rules of Procedure supersede the Rules of Procedure adopted in the first plenary meeting of the first session of the Assembly, on September 20, 1954, which are thereby abrogated.

ACEN Delegates (1954–1971)

The tables below include the names of ACEN delegates (nominated by the national committees/councils, and affiliate international organizations although they could not vote).[3] The number in parenthesis (1) indicates the number of a session that the person was accredited for. Letters in caps indicate membership in ACEN's committees: political – P, legal – L. "Chairman of delegation" is used to mark a person in charge of a given national committee/council or organization, which is indicative of membership in the General Committee. Members of the General Committee during the first session were also called vice chairmen of the ACEN. Please note that ACEN leadership functions were already listed in table 1.

3 I have used the original spelling of names, as well as descriptions of individuals (experience, profession, occupation) as printed by the ACEN. I have also indicated changes in these descriptions since it is useful to observe how by the ACEN's third session both the adjective "socialist" and the fact of former military service disappear, as do some of ACEN's actual members (delegates of national and international groups). The descriptions provided in the tables in appendices represent how ACEN described its members in its publications up to the 9th session. "No description" either relates to the sessions 10–18 when ACEN did not publish its reports or did not provide information. ACEN did not use uniform spelling, transliteration rules. The obvious mistakes (spelling) of names were corrected. I would like to thank Agata Domachowska, Inga Zakšauskienė, Francis Raška, Pauli Heikkilä, Beatrice Scutaru and Detelina Dineva for helping me identify the people whose names were spelled in a way that raised doubts as to their identity.

Tab. 7 ACEN Delegates by National Council/Committee, 1954 – 1972

Sources: ACEN archival collection at IHRC as well as ACEN publications (see ACEN Publications, 1954 – 1971).

Tab. 7A: ALBANIA

MEMBER ORGANIZATION:
National Committee for a Free Albania, NCFA (session 1), **Free Albania Committee** (from session 8)
ADDRESS: 119 West 57th Street, New York 19, NY

FIRST, LAST NAME of delegate to ACEN	AFFILIATION – all descriptions listed by the ACEN with session numbers	FUNCTIONS IN THE ACEN (L-Legal, P-Political, S-Social, E-Economic, I-Information, C-Cultural)	YEARS LISTED AS A DELEGATE BY ACEN
Dr. Çesk Ashta	No description by ACEN		11 – 18 (1964 – 1972)
Reshat Agaj	Member, Legitimist Party (1); agronomist (1 – 3)		1 – 3 (1954 – 1957)
Vasil Alarupi	Journalist (3)		2 – 3 (1955 – 1957)
Dr. Sotir Avrami	No description (4, 5, 6) FEC, council member: 4,200$/y. (as of 1960)		4 – 6 (1957 – 1961)
Dr. Halim Begeja	Executive Member of the NCFA (2,3)	Deputy GC (2 – 3); **GC (4);** I (2 – 3); L (1 – 3); S (1); See: LDUCEE	2 – 4 (1955 – 1958)
Isuf Begeja	Former Army Officer, journalist, independent (8,9)	See: France	5 – 18 (1958 – 1972)
Joseph Deda	No description by ACEN		13 – 18 (1966 – 1972)
Hiqmet Delvina	Lawyer; former Minister of Justice; former Vice Chairman [Speaker] of the Albanian Parliament	P (2)	1 – 3 (1954 – 1957)
Dr. Odhise Dhima	Former judge, writer, member Balli Kombëtar Organization (8);	I (8) See: France	5 – 8 (1958 – 1962)
Mexhid Dibra	No description		2 – 3 (1955 – 1957)

Tab. 7A: ALBANIA *(Continued)*

MEMBER ORGANIZATION: **National Committee for a Free Albania, NCFA** (session 1), **Free Albania Committee** (from session 8) ADDRESS: 119 West 57th Street, New York 19, NY			
FIRST, LAST NAME of delegate to ACEN	AFFILIATION – all descriptions listed by the ACEN with session numbers	FUNCTIONS IN THE ACEN (L-Legal, P-Political, S-Social, E-Economic, I-Information, C-Cultural)	YEARS LISTED AS A DELEGATE BY ACEN
Hasan Dosti	Former justice, Albanian Supreme Court (1); Former President of the Albanian Supreme Court; President of the Albanian Agrarian Party (2, 3) President of the National Committee for a Free Albania	**GC (1–3)**; Vice Chairman C (2); C (2,3); S (1–3); P (1)	1–3 (1954–1957)
Qazim Emeo	Member, Executive Committee, Balli Kombëtar Organization, former Army Officer (1); Army captain, accredited a delegate to 26th plenary meeting (2)		1–2 (1954–1956)
Reuf Fratari	Army Major; Member of NCFA (2,3)	E (2–3)	2–3 (1955–1957)
Dr. Ragip Frashëri	ACEN: Lawyer, member Monarchist Party (8,9). FEC: council member 1,800$/y. (as of 1960)	See: Italy	5–18 (1958–1972)
Dr. Athanas Gegaj	Former professor, author on history; Agrarian Balli Kombëtar-Dosti faction (9)	C, L (8,9)	5–18 (1958–1972)
Vasil Gërmenji	Executive Member of NCFA (2, 3); former Professor, journalist, member Free Albania Committee, independent (8, 9) FEC: council member 4,200$/y. (as of 1960)	ACEN Chairman (11,17); ACEN Vice Chairman (14, 16); **GC (5, 7–18);** P-L (10); I, P (8, 9); I (7); Secr.: P-L (15)	2–18 (1955–1972)
Kristo Gjeka	No description		7 (1960–1961)
Ndue Gjonmarkaj	ACEN: Member of Free Albania Committee, executive member of National Independent Bloc (8–9)		5–16 (1958–1970)

Tab. 7A: ALBANIA *(Continued)*

MEMBER ORGANIZATION: **National Committee for a Free Albania, NCFA** (session 1), **Free Albania Committee** (from session 8) ADDRESS: 119 West 57th Street, New York 19, NY			
FIRST, LAST NAME of delegate to ACEN	AFFILIATION – all descriptions listed by the ACEN with session numbers	FUNCTIONS IN THE ACEN (L-Legal, P-Political, S-Social, E-Economic, I-Information, C-Cultural)	YEARS LISTED AS A DELEGATE BY ACEN
	FEC: date of exile XI 1944, stipend: 250$/mo.; FEC: council member 3,000$/y. (as of 1960)		
George Gogh	Former Professor, journalist, executive member of Monarchist Party (8 – 9)	I (8,9)	6 – 10 (1959 – 1964)
Ismet Hoxha	Member, Executive Committee, Balli Kombëtar Organization (1); former army officer (2 – 3)	C (2)	1 – 3 (1954 – 1957)
Prof. Hysni Jenishehri	Member, Executive Committee, Balli Kombëtar Organization (1); agronomist (2 – 3)	C (2,3)	1 – 3 (1954 – 1957)
Nuci Kotta	Lawyer, Member, Executive Committee, Party of Legality (1)	ACEN Deputy Secretary (1 – 6); L (1); See: LDUCEE	1 – 6 (1954 – 1960)
Dr. Ali Klissura	ACEN: Former member of Parliament, writer, Chairman of Bali Kombëtar Organization, member of the Council of Education; President of the Free Albania Committee, independent FEC: date of exile 1944, stipend: 150$/mo., since 1 IX 1961; FEC: council member 1,800$/y. (as of 1960)	C, S, E (8,9)	5 – 10 (1958 – 1964)
Dr. Lisimak Kondi	No description		5 (1958 – 1959)
Dr. Rexhep Krasniqi	No description FEC, council member: 4,800$/y. (as of 1960)	**GC (6);** C-I (10); E-S (10)	6, 10 – 18 (1959 – 1960, 1963 – 1972)
Petro [Petraq] Ktona	Member, Agrarian Democratic Party (1); Former District Ad-	P (8,9); P-L (10)	1 – 3; 6 – 15, 18

Tab. 7A: ALBANIA *(Continued)*

MEMBER ORGANIZATION: **National Committee for a Free Albania, NCFA** (session 1), **Free Albania Committee** (from session 8) ADDRESS: 119 West 57th Street, New York 19, NY			
FIRST, LAST NAME of delegate to ACEN	AFFILIATION – all descriptions listed by the ACEN with session numbers	FUNCTIONS IN THE ACEN (L-Legal, P-Political, S-Social, E-Economic, I-Information, C-Cultural)	YEARS LISTED AS A DELEGATE BY ACEN
	ministrator (2, 3); former journalist. Agrarian Balli Kombëtar-Dosti faction (8,9)		(1954–1957, 1959–1969, 1971–1972)
Rexhep Kumbarçe	Student in political science, independent (8,9)	S (8,9); E-S (10) See: Belgium	8–14 (1961–1968)
Idriz Lamaj	No description		17 (1970–1971)
Qani Lesko	Teacher, member, Executive Committee, Balli Kombëtar Organization (1); member of NCFA (2–3)		1–3 (1954–1957)
Ragip Lohja	Former public service officer, victim of Communist persecution (10 years forced labor camp), Legalite (Monarchist) Party (8)		8 (1961–1962)
Faik Miraku	Political Scientist, member, Legitimist Party (1)		1 (1954–1955)
Hysni Muleti	No description		5 (1958–1959)
Dr. Fuat Myftija	Lawyer, executive member of Legalite (Monarchist) Party (8)	I (8)	8 (1961–62)
Zef Nekaj	No description		5 (1958–1959)
Rev. Dr. Joseph J. Oroshi	No description		9–18 (1962–1972)
Rrok Nalbani	Member, peasant Party		1 (1954–1955)
Theodor Papalilo	Former professor, executive member Balli Agrar-Dosti	P, E (8,9)	5, 8–10 1958–1959, 1961–1964)

Tab. 7A: ALBANIA *(Continued)*

MEMBER ORGANIZATION: **National Committee for a Free Albania, NCFA** (session 1), **Free Albania Committee** (from session 8) ADDRESS: 119 West 57th Street, New York 19, NY			
FIRST, LAST NAME of delegate to ACEN	AFFILIATION – all descriptions listed by the ACEN with session numbers	FUNCTIONS IN THE ACEN (L-Legal, P-Political, S-Social, E-Economic, I-Information, C-Cultural)	YEARS LISTED AS A DELEGATE BY ACEN
Nexhat Peshkepia	ACEN: Former professor, journalist, member of Free Albania Committee, Secretary General Balli Kombëtar-Agrar Dosti Faction. FEC: date of exile XI 1944, stipend: 350$/mo., since 1949; FEC: council member 4,200$/y. (as of 1960).	C, I (8,9); C-I (10)	5 – 16 (1958 – 1970)
Maliq R. Petrela	Member, Balli Kombëtar Organization (1); former district administrator (2, 3)		1 – 3 (1954 – 1957)
Mazhar Pustina	Former army officer (1), army major (2, 3)	S (2,3); E (1,2)	1 – 3 (1954 – 1957)
Sami Repishti	Student of economics (9)	E (9); E-S (10)	9 – 10; 12 – 14 (1962 – 1964; 1965 – 1968)
Lec Shllaku	No description	See: France	14 – 18 (1967 – 1972)
Myftar Spahia	No description		5 – 7 (1958 – 1961)
Loro Stajka	No description		11 – 14 (1964 – 1968)
Sali Toptani	No description		4 (1957 – 1958)
Mahmut Tsungu	Construction engineer	P (9); P-L (10)	9 – 14 (1962 – 1968)
Selandin Velaj	No description	See: LDUCEE	4 (1957 – 1958)

Tab. 7A: ALBANIA *(Continued)*

MEMBER ORGANIZATION: **National Committee for a Free Albania, NCFA** (session 1), **Free Albania Committee** (from session 8) ADDRESS: 119 West 57th Street, New York 19, NY			
FIRST, LAST NAME of delegate to ACEN	AFFILIATION – all descriptions listed by the ACEN with session numbers	FUNCTIONS IN THE ACEN (L-Legal, P-Political, S-Social, E-Economic, I-Information, C-Cultural)	YEARS LISTED AS A DELEGATE BY ACEN
[Kemal] Qemal Vokopola	Statistician (1,2)	PR/I (1) E (1)	1–2 (1954–1956)
Teki Xhindi	Former District Administrator		1–3 (1954–1957)
Tajar Zavalani	Student (1); noted Albania writer, author of "How strong is Russia" and "Historia e *Shqipërisë";* Secretary General of PEN Centre in Exile (8,9)	See: Great Britain	1, 7–12 (1954–1955, 1960–1966)
Mrs. Maria Selma Zavalani	No description	See: Great Britain	16–18 (1969–1972)

Tab. 7B: BULGARIA

MEMBER ORGANIZATION: **Bulgarian National Committee, BNC** ADDRESS: 724 Ninth Street, NW, Washington 1 D.C.; 200 West 57th Street, New York 19, NY			
FIRST, LAST NAME of delegate to ACEN	AFFILIATION – all descriptions listed by the ACEN with session numbers	FUNCTIONS IN THE ACEN (L-Legal, P-Political, S-Social, E-Economic, I-Information, C-Cultural)	YEARS LISTED AS A DELEGATE BY ACEN
Emil Antonov	ACEN: Former Member of Parliament; Member of the Executive Committee of BNC (3–9); accredited delegate to 30–34 plenary meetings (2). FEC: council member 4,200$/y. (as of 1960)	S (8,9); E (3); E-S (10)	2–18 (1955–1972)
Nikola Antonov	ACEN: former Minister Plenipotentiary, President, Democratic	P (1,2,8,9); P-L (10) Vice Chair: P (1)	1–17 (1954–1971)

Tab. 7B: BULGARIA *(Continued)*

MEMBER ORGANIZATION: **Bulgarian National Committee, BNC** ADDRESS: 724 Ninth Street, NW, Washington 1 D.C.; 200 West 57th Street, New York 19, NY			
FIRST, LAST NAME of delegate to ACEN	AFFILIATION – all descriptions listed by the ACEN with session numbers	FUNCTIONS IN THE ACEN (L-Legal, P-Political, S-Social, E-Economic, I-Information, C-Cultural)	YEARS LISTED AS A DELEGATE BY ACEN
	Party in Exile, member, Executive Committee, BNC; FEC: council member 4,200$/y. (as of 1960)		
Tsenko Barev	ACEN: Journalist; Member of the Executive Committee of BNC; FEC: council member 2,700$/y. (as of 1960); FEC: international organizations staff 2,700$/y. (as of 1960)	E (2,3) See: France	1–18 (1954–1972)
Panajot Butchvarov	Student (1); Doctor of Philosophy (Professor) (2,3)	C (2)	1–4
Dr. George M. Dimitrov	M.D., former Member of Parliament, President of the BNC; FEC: council member 4,800$/y. (as of 1960)	ACEN Chairman (9,14); ACEN Vice Chairman (1–4); **GC (1–18)**	1–18 (1954–1972)
Mrs. Gloria Dimitrova	Socialist Party Representative was accredited delegate to 16–29 plenary meetings	S (2)	2 (1955–1956)
Ms. Milka Genadieva	Journalist, Doctor of Law, expert on PR		2 (1955–1956)
Dr. Nikola Dolapchiev	ACEN: Dr. Jur. (Berlin and Bonn), former Minister Plenipotentiary, professor of Executive Committee of the Bulgarian Academy of Sciences, Member of the Executive Committee of BNC FEC: date of exile 1945, stipend: 275$/mo., since 1 IX 1961; FEC: council member 4,200$/y. (as of 1960)	C (8) L (3, 8, 9), P-L (10) See: Great Britain	2–11 (1955–1965)
Dr. Biser Kolev	Representative of the Bulgarian Socialist Party (2); M.D. (8,9)	S (3)	2–18 (1955–1972)

Tab. 7B: BULGARIA *(Continued)*

MEMBER ORGANIZATION: **Bulgarian National Committee, BNC** ADDRESS: 724 Ninth Street, NW, Washington 1 D.C.; 200 West 57th Street, New York 19, NY			
FIRST, LAST NAME of delegate to ACEN	AFFILIATION – all descriptions listed by the ACEN with session numbers	FUNCTIONS IN THE ACEN (L-Legal, P-Political, S-Social, E-Economic, I-Information, C-Cultural)	YEARS LISTED AS A DELEGATE BY ACEN
Dr. Kiril Konakchiyski	Economist; Dr. Rer. Pol [PhD in Political Science] (Innsbruck)	E (8,9); Vice Chair: E (2), E (3); E-S (10)	1–17 (1954–1971)
Eftim Krastev	ACEN: Licencié en Droit (Paris), student in international law and economics. FEC: council staff 4,680$/y. (as of 1960)	I (8); E (3)	3, 8 (1956–1957, 1961–1962)
Ivan Metev	Doctor of Arts	C (8,9)	8–9 (1961–1963)
Boris Nozharov [Nojarov]	ACEN: Chairman (2), representative (3), President (8,9) Free Trade-Unions; FEC: council member 4,200$/y. (as of 1960)	C (3); S, E (8, 9); S (2,3); C-I (10)	2–18 (1955–1972)
Leo Olivenbaum	Lawyer, expert on legal and cultural problems	C (2,3); L (3)	2–18 (1955–1972)
Dimitar K. Petkov	ACEN: Lawyer and former career diplomat, member of the Executive Committee of the Bulgarian National Committee. FEC: council member 4,200$/y. (as of 1960)	L, P (8,9); L (1–3; 6–7); Chair: P-L (10)	1–18 (1954–1972)
Dr. Georgi Petkov	former Socialist member of Parliament, professor of economics FEC: 4,200$/y. (as of 1960)	Chair: S (1); See: SUCEE	1 (1954–1955)
Iskar Shumanov	journalist (I)	Secr.: PR/I (1–3); I (6,9); Vice Chair: C-I (15); C-I (10)	1–18 (1954–1972)
Hristo Stoyanov	scientist	C, E, I (9); E-S (10)	9–13 (1962–1967)
Toma Tomov	Representative of the Bulgarian Democratic Party in Exile	S (3); E (2)	2–3, 6 (1955–1957, 1959–1960)

Tab. 7B: BULGARIA *(Continued)*

MEMBER ORGANIZATION: **Bulgarian National Committee, BNC** ADDRESS: 724 Ninth Street, NW, Washington 1 D.C.; 200 West 57th Street, New York 19, NY			
FIRST, LAST NAME of delegate to ACEN	AFFILIATION – all descriptions listed by the ACEN with session numbers	FUNCTIONS IN THE ACEN (L-Legal, P-Political, S-Social, E-Economic, I-Information, C-Cultural)	YEARS LISTED AS A DELEGATE BY ACEN
Boris Yanakiev	Theologian	C (2,3)	2 – 4 (1955 – 1958)
Vasil Yurukov	Former Minister Plenipotentiary; Vice Chairman of BNC	I (3); C (2)	2 – 4 (1955 – 1958)
Tsvetko [Zwetko] Penov	Socialist party representative		2 (1955 – 1956)

Due to discrepancies in transliteration appearing in ACEN documents, the last names of members of the Bulgarian delegations are listed using uniform rule of replacing -ff with -v (as in the case of Shumanoff – the spelling was changed to Shumanov).

Tab. 7C: CZECHOSLOVAKIA

MEMBER ORGANIZATION: **Council of Free Czechoslovakia**, since 14th session **Committee for Free Czechoslovakia** ADDRESS: 471 Park Avenue, New York 22, NY			
FIRST, LAST NAME of delegate to ACEN	AFFILIATION – all descriptions listed by the ACEN with session numbers	FUNCTIONS IN THE ACEN (L-Legal, P-Political, S-Social, E-Economic, I-Information, C-Cultural)	YEARS LISTED AS A DELEGATE BY ACEN
Vladislav Brdlík	ACEN: Professor; former Cabinet Minister FEC: date of exile 6 VIII 1948, stipend: 173$/mo., since 1 VIII 1955; FEC: meritorious exile 2,376$/y. (as of 1960)	C (3); E (2)	1 – 4 (1954 – 1958)
Mikulas Cecur	No description		7 (1960 – 1961)
Bohuslav Čermák	No description		17 (1971 – 1972)

Tab. 7C: CZECHOSLOVAKIA *(Continued)*

MEMBER ORGANIZATION: **Council of Free Czechoslovakia,** since 14th session **Committee for Free Czechoslovakia** ADDRESS: 471 Park Avenue, New York 22, NY			
FIRST, LAST NAME of delegate to ACEN	AFFILIATION – all descriptions listed by the ACEN with session numbers	FUNCTIONS IN THE ACEN (L-Legal, P-Political, S-Social, E-Economic, I-Information, C-Cultural)	YEARS LISTED AS A DELEGATE BY ACEN
Ignor Chandricky	No description		17 (1971–1972)
Dr. František Černý	former Minister Plenipotentiary	L (2, 8,9)	6, 8–10 (1959–1960, 1961–1964)
Josef Černý	ACEN: Former Cabinet minister; former Member of Parliament FEC: date of exile III 1948, stipend: 100$/mo., 1 XII 1950–21 XII 1953, 1 I 1956–30 XIII 1957, since 1 I 1959. FEC: emergency support 1,200$/y. (as of 1960)	P (8, 9); L (3,8,9); P-L (10)	1–18 (1954–1972)
Dr. Jozef Dieška	Chairman of the Freedom Party	C (2)	1 (1954–1955)
Vladislav Dzamulic	No description		6 (1959–1960)
Vasil L. Fedinec	Member, Executive Committee Council of Free Czechoslovakia (1); Chairman of the Subcarpathian Ruthenian National Council (8,9)		1, 8–16 (1954–1955, 1961–1970)
Kornel Filo	No description	See: France	5 (1958–1959)
Zdeněk (Zdenko) Formánek	Diplomat		3–4 (1956–1958)
Mikuláš Franek	Former Cabinet Minister; former Member of Parliament	E (2,3)	1–7 (1954–1961)
Jiří Görner	No description		17–18 (1970–1972)

Tab. 7C: CZECHOSLOVAKIA *(Continued)*

MEMBER ORGANIZATION: **Council of Free Czechoslovakia**, since 14th session **Committee for Free Czechoslovakia** ADDRESS: 471 Park Avenue, New York 22, NY			
FIRST, LAST NAME of delegate to ACEN	AFFILIATION – all descriptions listed by the ACEN with session numbers	FUNCTIONS IN THE ACEN (L-Legal, P-Political, S-Social, E-Economic, I-Information, C-Cultural)	YEARS LISTED AS A DELEGATE BY ACEN
Prof. Ctibor Grandtner	No description		18 (1971 – 1972)
Arnošt Heidrich	ACEN: Ambassador; former Secretary General, Ministry of Foreign Affairs. FEC: council member 4,800$/y. (as of 1960)	I (3); P (8, 9); P-L (10)	1 – 14 (1954 – 1968)
Fedor A. Hodža	ACEN: Former Member of Parliament; former Secretary General, Democratic Party of Slovakia. FEC: council member 4,200$/y. (as of 1960)	P (1,2); L (3)	1 – 15 (1954 – 1969)
Václav Holub	Former Member of Parliament	See: Great Britain	8 – 15 (1961 – 1969)
Mrs. Alica Jarošová	No description		18 (1971 – 1972)
Štefan Kočvara	Former Vice Prime Minister; former Member of Parliament	L (2,3)	3 – 4 (1956 – 1958)
Jan Kučerák	No description		17 – 18 (1970 – 1972)
Dr. Martin Kvetko	Former Slovak Commissioner for Agriculture, Member of Parliament (E);	E (8, 9); **GC (17,18);** E-S (10)	8 – 18 (1961 – 1972)
Dr. Jozef Lettrich	ACEN: Former President, Slovak National Council, former Chairman, Democratic Party Slovakia, former Member of Parliament (C, I). FEC: council member 4,200$/y. (as of 1960)	ACEN Chairman (15); ACEN Vice Chairman (11, 12); **GC (5, 8 – 14, 16)**; P (4,7); C (8, 9); I (3, 6 – 9); C-I (10)	1 – 16 (1954 – 1970)
Dr. Radomír Luža	No description	P (5)	4 – 5 (1957 – 1959)

Tab. 7C: CZECHOSLOVAKIA *(Continued)*

MEMBER ORGANIZATION: **Council of Free Czechoslovakia**, since 14th session **Committee for Free Czechoslovakia** ADDRESS: 471 Park Avenue, New York 22, NY			
FIRST, LAST NAME of delegate to ACEN	AFFILIATION – all descriptions listed by the ACEN with session numbers	FUNCTIONS IN THE ACEN (L-Legal, P-Political, S-Social, E-Economic, I-Information, C-Cultural)	YEARS LISTED AS A DELEGATE BY ACEN
Dr. Otakar Machotka	No description	C (8)	8 (1961–1962)
Václav Majer	ACEN: Former Cabinet Minister, former Member of Parliament FEC: date of exile 1940, stipend: 275$/mo., 1 II 1951–18 VII 1952, since 1 VIII 1956; FEC: meritorious exile 3,600$/y. (as of 1960)	S (2, 8, 9); E (3); Vice Chair: E-S (15); E-S (10)	1–18 (1954–1972)
Adolf Mokrý	No description		17–18 (1970–1972)
Josef [Jaromir] Nebeský	No description		17–18 (1970–1972)
Dr. Jindřich Nosek	No description		5 (1958–1959)
Štefan Osuský	ACEN: Former Cabinet Minister; Ambassador. FEC: council member 4,800$/y. (as of 1960)	**GC (1–4, 15)**	1–18 (1954–1972)
Ján Papánek	Ambassador; former Czechoslovak delegate to the United Nations	I (3); C (2); S (3, 5)	3–7 (1956–1961)
Vladimír Pavlík	No description		6–7 (1959–1961)
Ferdinand Peroutka	Former member of Parliament, journalist		1 (1954–1955)
Adolph Procházka	ACEN: Former Minister and Member of Parliament (1,2) Accredited a delegate for 16–21 Plenary Meetings (2). FEC: council member 3,600$/y. (as of 1960)	See: CDUCE	1–2 (1954–1956)

Tab. 7C: CZECHOSLOVAKIA *(Continued)*

MEMBER ORGANIZATION: **Council of Free Czechoslovakia**, since 14th session **Committee for Free Czechoslovakia** ADDRESS: 471 Park Avenue, New York 22, NY			
FIRST, LAST NAME of delegate to ACEN	AFFILIATION – all descriptions listed by the ACEN with session numbers	FUNCTIONS IN THE ACEN (L-Legal, P-Political, S-Social, E-Economic, I-Information, C-Cultural)	YEARS LISTED AS A DELEGATE BY ACEN
Ota [Otto] Rambousek	No description		17 – 18 (1970 – 1972)
Emil Ransdorf	No description		7 (1960 – 1961)
Hubert Ripka	Former Cabinet Minister; former Member of Parliament	Chair: C (2), C (3)	1 – 4 (1954 – 1958)
Ing. Antonín Roubík	No description		18 (1971 – 1972)
Alois Rozehnal	Former Member of Parliament	S (1 – 3); E (3)	1 – 3 (1954 – 1957)
Dr. Josef Šádek	No description		18 (1971 – 1972)
Mirko Sedlák	Former Member of Parliament	S (3)	2 – 4 (1955 – 1958)
Dr. Juraj Slávik	ACEN: Ambassador; former Cabinet Minister; former Member of Parliament FEC: date of exile 1948, stipend: 350$/mo., 1 XII 1950 – 18 VII 1952, since 1 V 1954; FEC: council member 4,200$/y. (as of 1960)	P (2) Chair: C (3 – 7)	1 – 7 (1954 – 1961)
Dr. Vilém Svoboda	ACEN: No description. FEC: international organizations staff 2,400$/y. (as of 1960)	See: Great Britain	16 – 18 (1969 – 1972)
Rev. Dušan Tóth	No description		17 (1970 – 1971)
Dr. Felix Uhl	No description	I (2)	6 – 7 (1959 – 1961)
Dr. Emil Vidra	No description		17 – 18 (1970 – 1972)

Tab. 7C: CZECHOSLOVAKIA *(Continued)*

MEMBER ORGANIZATION: **Council of Free Czechoslovakia**, since 14th session **Committee for Free Czechoslovakia** ADDRESS: 471 Park Avenue, New York 22, NY			
FIRST, LAST NAME of delegate to ACEN	AFFILIATION – all descriptions listed by the ACEN with session numbers	FUNCTIONS IN THE ACEN (L-Legal, P-Political, S-Social, E-Economic, I-Information, C-Cultural)	YEARS LISTED AS A DELEGATE BY ACEN
Petr Zenkl	ACEN: Former Chairman, Czechoslovak National Socialist Party, Former Vice Premier; former Member of Parliament (1–3). FEC: council member 4,800$/y. (as of 1960)	ACEN Chairman (6) **GC (6–7)**; I (2)	1–7 (1954–1961)
Jaroslav Zich	No description	E (5–7)	4–7 (1957–1961)
František Zvěřina	No description		17–18 (1970–1972)

Tab. 7D: ESTONIA

MEMBER ORGANIZATION: **Committee for a Free Estonia** ADDRESS: 270 Park Ave, New York 17 NY			
FIRST, LAST NAME of delegate to ACEN	AFFILIATION – all descriptions listed by the ACEN with session numbers	FUNCTIONS IN THE ACEN (L-Legal, P-Political, S-Social, E-Economic, I-Information, C-Cultural)	YEARS LISTED AS A DELEGATE BY ACEN
Alfred Anderson	Former Senior Vice President, Co-operative enterprise, former associate publisher of "The Baltic Times", member, Estonian World Council		1 (1954–1955)
Karl Ast	Former Member of Government and Parliament, former member, Central Committee of the Estonia Socialist Party		5, 8–11 (1958–1959; 1961–1965)
Rev. Aleksander Hinno	Dean of the First Estonian Ev. Lutheran Conference; Member, Estonian World Council		2–18 (1955–1972)

Tab. 7D: ESTONIA *(Continued)*

MEMBER ORGANIZATION: **Committee for a Free Estonia** ADDRESS: 270 Park Ave, New York 17 NY			
FIRST, LAST NAME of delegate to ACEN	AFFILIATION – all descriptions listed by the ACEN with session numbers	FUNCTIONS IN THE ACEN (L-Legal, P-Political, S-Social, E-Economic, I-Information, C-Cultural)	YEARS LISTED AS A DELEGATE BY ACEN
Ludwig-Karl Jakobsen	No description	See: Germany	5–7 (1958–1961)
Rev. Aleksander Jürisson	Administrator of the Estonian Orthodox Church		1 (1954–1955)
August Kärsna	Former lawyer, member, Estonian National Committee in the USA (1); Member, Estonian World Council (2–3); member of the Board, Association of former Members of the Estonian Agrarian Party (8,9)		1–18 (1954–1972)
Harold Kikas	Former judge, member, Estonian World Council		1–2 (1954–1956)
Johannes Klesment	Former member of Parliament; former Counselor to the Estonian President and Government; Chairman, Association of Estonian Jurists of New York	**GC 4**; secr.: P (2); I (5); Vice Chair: L (1–3); L (5)	1–6 (1954–1960)
Raimond Kolk	ACEN: Journalist, member, Committee for a Free Estonia, member of the Board, Estonian National Council in Sweden, Secretary, Estonian Socialist Party in Exile. FEC: council member 2,400$/y. (as of 1960)		6–9 (1959–1963)
Aleksander Kütt	ACEN: Former Chairman and Executive Vice President, Central Cooperative Associations, former Associate Publisher, "The Baltic Times", Member Estonian World Council (1); Chairman, Committee for a Free Estonia (2,3, 8, 9); FEC: council member 4,800$/y. (as of 1960)	ACEN Chairman (10); ACEN Vice Chairman (9, 13) **GC (6–9)** E (2–3; 7–9)	1–15 (1954–1969)

Tab. 7D: ESTONIA *(Continued)*

MEMBER ORGANIZATION: **Committee for a Free Estonia** ADDRESS: 270 Park Ave, New York 17 NY			
FIRST, LAST NAME of delegate to ACEN	AFFILIATION – all descriptions listed by the ACEN with session numbers	FUNCTIONS IN THE ACEN (L-Legal, P-Political, S-Social, E-Economic, I-Information, C-Cultural)	YEARS LISTED AS A DELEGATE BY ACEN
Heinrich Laretei	Former Cabinet Minister, former Member of Parliament, former Estonian Minister to Stockholm, Oslo and Copenhagen, Vice President, Estonian National Congress in Sweden (8,9)	See: Sweden	4–18 (1957–1972)
Miss Adelaida Lemberg	No description		18 (1971–1972)
Voldemar Ludig	Former member, Estonian Foreign Service		1 (1954–1955)
Dr. Nikolai Maim	Professor of Law, former member of Parliament; President, Estonian Political Association (1); Member, Estonian World Council (2,3) former Dean of Law Faculty, Estonian State University of Tartu (8,9)	L (2,3)	1–9 (1954–1963)
Heinrich Mark	No description		18 (1971–1972)
Aleksander Mekkart	Former member of Parliament; former Member of the Central Committee of the Estonian Socialist Party; Member, Estonian Political Association in the USA		2–5 (1955–1959)
Aksel Mei	ACEN: Former State Controller-General; former President of City Council (1,3); former President of the Nomme Town Council (8,9); Member, Committee for a Free Estonia FEC: date of exile 1944, stipend: 225$/mo., since 1 IX 1961; FEC:	C (2,3); I (3); L (2,3); S (1,2); E (2); C-I (10)	1–10 (1954–1964)

Tab. 7D: ESTONIA *(Continued)*

MEMBER ORGANIZATION: **Committee for a Free Estonia** ADDRESS: 270 Park Ave, New York 17 NY			
FIRST, LAST NAME of delegate to ACEN	AFFILIATION – all descriptions listed by the ACEN with session numbers	FUNCTIONS IN THE ACEN (L-Legal, P-Political, S-Social, E-Economic, I-Information, C-Cultural)	YEARS LISTED AS A DELEGATE BY ACEN
	council member 4,200$/y. (as of 1960)		
Johan Müller	Former minister of justice; former Attorney General; president Estonian National Committee in Canada		2 (1955–1956)
Olev Olesk	Member of the Board, the Estonian Committee in Sweden		3–4 (1956–1958)
Peeter Ollen	Former Colonel, Estonian Army; jurist		2 (1955–1956)
Rudolf Panksepp	Member, Estonian World Council	PR/I (1)	1–2 (1954–1956)
Dr. Adolf Perandi	Professor of Law; Member, Committee for a Free Estonia	P (1), Vice Chair: C (3); C (4); S (1)	1, 3–4 (1954–1955, 1956–1958)
Olev Piirsalu	Former District Secretary of the Estonian Agrarian Party (1–3); former Deputy Secretary General, Estonia Agrarian Party, President, Association of former Members of the Estonian Agrarian party, President, Estonian World Council (8,9)		3–18 (1956–1972)
Johannes Plaks	No description		16–18 (1969–1972)
Arnold Raag	No description		10–18 (1963–1972)
Ilmar Raamot	ACEN: Former Secretary General, United Framer's and Smallholders' Party; Member, Committee for a Free Estonia. FEC: council member 4,200$/y. (as of 1960)	I, P (8,9); S (1–3, 5–9); E (2–3, 8–9); Chair: C-I (15); E-S (10); C-I (10)	1–18 (1954–1972)

Tab. 7D: ESTONIA *(Continued)*

MEMBER ORGANIZATION: **Committee for a Free Estonia** ADDRESS: 270 Park Ave, New York 17 NY			
FIRST, LAST NAME of delegate to ACEN	AFFILIATION – all descriptions listed by the ACEN with session numbers	FUNCTIONS IN THE ACEN (L-Legal, P-Political, S-Social, E-Economic, I-Information, C-Cultural)	YEARS LISTED AS A DELEGATE BY ACEN
Harold Raudsepp	Editor, member, Estonian World Council		1 (1954–1955)
Elmar Reisenberg	Former Deputy Mayor of Viljandi	See: Germany	9–18 (1962–1972)
Endel Rennit	Editor, Secretary General, Estonian National Council in the U.S.A.		1 (1954–1955)
Enn Salurand	Journalist, Secretary General, Estonian National Committee in Canada		6–18 (1959–1972)
Karl Selter	Former Minister of Foreign Affairs; former Minister of Economy; former Minister to Switzerland; former Chief Delegate to the League of Nations	See: Germany	2–4 (1955–1958)
Albert Suurkivi	former Member of Parliament; Member, Estonian Political Association (2–3); former Member of Parliament, former member of Presidium, Farmer's and Smallholders' Party, member of the Board, Estonian Political Association (8–9)		2–18 (1955–1972)
Meinhard Treilmann	Former District Secretary, Estonian Socialist Labor Party		4–14 (1957–1968)
Leonhard Vahter	Lawyer, former member of Parliament, Vice President, Estonian National Committee in the USA (1); Member, Committee for a Free Estonia (2, 8–9); Vice Chairman, Estonian World Council (8,9). FEC: council member 4,200$/y. (as of 1960)	C, S, P (8, 9) **GC (1–3, 5, 10–18)** L (4, 7–9); Vice Chair: P-L (15) S (1,3); Secr.: P-L (10)	1–18 (1954–1972)

Tab. 7D: ESTONIA *(Continued)*

MEMBER ORGANIZATION: **Committee for a Free Estonia** ADDRESS: 270 Park Ave, New York 17 NY			
FIRST, LAST NAME of delegate to ACEN	AFFILIATION – all descriptions listed by the ACEN with session numbers	FUNCTIONS IN THE ACEN (L-Legal, P-Political, S-Social, E-Economic, I-Information, C-Cultural)	YEARS LISTED AS A DELEGATE BY ACEN
Eduard Vallaste	Journalist; Member, Estonian National Committee in the USA	I (3)	1–3 (1954–1957)
Dr. Juhan Vasar	Accredited as a delegate for the first eight Plenary Meetings		1 (1954–1955)
Aleksander Warma	Former Minister of Estonia to Finland, Vice Chairman, Estonian National Council in Sweden, Chairman, Estonian Liberal Democratic Union in Exile	See: Sweden	5–17 (1958–1971)

Tab. 7E: HUNGARY

MEMBER ORGANIZATION: **Hungarian National Council, HNC,** since fifth session: **Hungarian Committee HC** ADDRESS: 125 East 72 Street NY 21, NY			
FIRST, LAST NAME of delegate to ACEN	AFFILIATION – all descriptions listed by the ACEN with session numbers	FUNCTIONS IN THE ACEN (L-Legal, P-Political, S-Social, E-Economic, I-Information, C-Cultural)	YEARS LISTED AS A DELEGATE BY ACEN
Joseph Adorjan	ACEN: Former Member of Parliament, member of the Hungarian Committee FEC: date of exile 25 XI 1956, stipend: 275$/mo., since 1 VII 1958; FEC: council member 4,800$/y. (as of 1960)		5–8 (1958–1962)
Dr. László Acsay	accredited delegate for the first eight Plenary Meeting		1 (1954–1955)
Dr. Pál Auer	ACEN: Former Member of Parliament; Minister Plenipotentiary; Member, Executive Committee, HNC (2,3); former Chairman of	See: France	2–18

Tab. 7E: HUNGARY *(Continued)*

MEMBER ORGANIZATION: **Hungarian National Council, HNC**, since fifth session: **Hungarian Committee HC** ADDRESS: 125 East 72 Street NY 21, NY			
FIRST, LAST NAME of delegate to ACEN	AFFILIATION – all descriptions listed by the ACEN with session numbers	FUNCTIONS IN THE ACEN (L-Legal, P-Political, S-Social, E-Economic, I-Information, C-Cultural)	YEARS LISTED AS A DELEGATE BY ACEN
	the Foreign Affairs Committee of the Hungarian Parliament, former Hungarian Minister to France, member of the HC (8,9). FEC: council member 6,000$/y. (as of 1960)		
Györgi [George] Bakách-Bessenyey	Minister Plenipotentiary; Member, Executive Committee, HNC (2, 3)		1–4
Dr. István Barankovics	ACEN: Former Member of Parliament; Leader, Democratic People's Party; Member, Executive Committee, HNC (2,3); editor, member of the HC. FEC: council member 4,800$/y. (as of 1960)	C (2, 3, 8, 9); S (3)	2–18
Dr. László Bartok	ACEN: Minister Plenipotentiary FEC: date of exile 1947, stipend: 400$/mo., since 1 IX 1957; FEC: council member 4,800$/y. (as of 1960).	P (2, 8, 9)	2–5
Francis Chorin	Former member of the Upper House of the Hungarian Parliament, former President, Association of the Hungarian Manufacturers		1
Dr. Joseph Czako	former staff member, Hungarian Foreign Office	ACEN Secretariat staff member (3–9); S (1)	1
Dr. Tibor Eckhardt	Royal Hungarian Privy Counselor, former member of Parliament and Chief Delegate to the League of Nations	**GC (1);** P (1)	1
Joseph Emody	Agricultural expert	P (1)	1

Tab. 7E: HUNGARY *(Continued)*

MEMBER ORGANIZATION: **Hungarian National Council, HNC**, since fifth session: **Hungarian Committee HC** ADDRESS: 125 East 72 Street NY 21, NY			
FIRST, LAST NAME of delegate to ACEN	AFFILIATION – all descriptions listed by the ACEN with session numbers	FUNCTIONS IN THE ACEN (L-Legal, P-Political, S-Social, E-Economic, I-Information, C-Cultural)	YEARS LISTED AS A DELEGATE BY ACEN
Dr. Béla Fabian	Lawyer; former Member of Parliament; Member, Executive Committee HNC	Chair: I (2,3) I (4)	1 – 4
Max Fenyo	Former member of Parliament		1
Andrew Frey	Editor		1
John Gara	Lecturer	S (1)	1
Gyula Gombos	Editor-publisher	S (1)	1
Alexander Hahn	ACEN: Lawyer FEC: date of exile 1948, stipend: 500$/mo., since 1 III 1958. FEC: council staff 6,000$/y. (as of 1960)	E-S (10)	5, 10
Lajos Hajdu-Nemeth	ACEN: Former Member of Parliament, leader, Christian Democratic Union, member of the HC FEC: date of exile 1947, stipend: 275$/mo., 1 I 1952 – 28 II 1953, 2 III 1953 – 30 VI 1955, since 10 IV 1958; FEC: council member 4,800$/y. (as of 1960)	S (8)	5 – 8
Gustav Hennyey	ACEN: Former Foreign Minister. FEC: council member 5,220$/y. (as of 1960)	See: Germany	9 – 13
Gen. Alexander Homlok	Accredited delegate for the first eight Plenary Meetings		1
Pál Jonas	ACEN: Chairman of the Petofi Circle, member of the HC (P, E). FEC: council member 4,800$/y. (as of 1960)	P, E (8,9); E (5); E-S (10); P-L (10)	5 – 11
Mikós [Nicholas] Kállay	ACEN: Former Member of Parliament; Former Prime Minister;		2 – 3

Tab. 7E: HUNGARY *(Continued)*

MEMBER ORGANIZATION: **Hungarian National Council, HNC,** since fifth session: **Hungarian Committee HC** ADDRESS: 125 East 72 Street NY 21, NY			
FIRST, LAST NAME of delegate to ACEN	AFFILIATION – all descriptions listed by the ACEN with session numbers	FUNCTIONS IN THE ACEN (L-Legal, P-Political, S-Social, E-Economic, I-Information, C-Cultural)	YEARS LISTED AS A DELEGATE BY ACEN
	Member, Executive Committee, HNC. FEC: council member 4,800 $/y. (as of 1960).		
Maj.-Gen. Béla Király	ACEN: Commander of the Hungarian National Guard during the Revolution of 1956, member of the HC. FEC: council member 4,800$/y. (as of 1960)	P (5,6)	5–13
Sandor Kiss	Former Member of Parliament, Director, Hungarian Peasant Association, member of the HC	I (8, 9); C-I (10)	6–16
Imre Kovács	Writer; former Member of Parliament; Member, Executive Committee, Hungarian Peasant Association in Exile (2,3); member of the HC (8)	ACEN Vice Chairman (17); I (8)	2–8, 14–18
Joseph Kővágó	ACEN: Former Mayor of Budapest, Vice Chairman of the HC (8,9). FEC: council member 4,800$/y. (as of 1960)	ACEN Vice Chairman (5); E (8,9); E-S (10)	4–14
Msgr. Joseph Közi Horváth	Former Member of Parliament; Chairman, Christian Democratic Union; Member, Executive Committee, HNC		3
John Mike	Former Leader, Hungarian Christian Trade Unions		1
Ferenc Nagy	ACEN: Former Member of Parliament; Chairman, Smallholders' Party; former Prime Minister; Member, Executive Committee, HNC (2,3), member of the HC (8, 9). FEC: council member 4,800$/y. (as of 1960)	ACEN Chairman (8); ACEN Vice Chairman (10) P (7,8,9); P-L (10); See: IPU	2–17

Tab. 7E: HUNGARY *(Continued)*

MEMBER ORGANIZATION: **Hungarian National Council, HNC**, since fifth session: **Hungarian Committee HC** ADDRESS: 125 East 72 Street NY 21, NY			
FIRST, LAST NAME of delegate to ACEN	AFFILIATION – all descriptions listed by the ACEN with session numbers	FUNCTIONS IN THE ACEN (L-Legal, P-Political, S-Social, E-Economic, I-Information, C-Cultural)	YEARS LISTED AS A DELEGATE BY ACEN
Dr. Vince Nagy	ACEN: Former Minister of the Interior, former member of Parliament FEC: date of exile 1947, stipend: 100$/mo., since 1 IX 1957; FEC: emergency support 1,200$/y. (as of 1960).	L (1); S (1)	1
Dr. Béla Padányi-Gulyás	No description	See: Switzerland	10 – 18
Dr. Zoltan Pfeiffer	ACEN: Lawyer, former Member of Parliament; Chairman, Independence Party; Member, Executive Committee, HNC (2,3); former Under Secretary of State for Justice, Leader of the Hungarian Independence Party, member of the HC (8,9). FEC: council member 4,800$/y. (as of 1960)	I (4 – 9); L, P (8,9) L (2,3); P-L (10); C-I (10)	2 – 18
George Perenyi-Lukas	Former diplomat (3); former counsellor of the Legation; representative of HNC in Turkey, replaced by Béla Telekyi on October 18, 1956 (2)	I (3); L (3); E (2 – 4)	2 – 4
Charles Peyer	Former Cabinet Member, former Member of Parliament, President, Hungarian Social Democratic Party (1); Chairman Hungarian Social Democratic Party, member Executive Committee HNC (2).	S (1 – 2), See: ICFTUE	1 – 2
Dr. Fred Pisky Schmidt	Journalist	C (2) S (2 – 3)	2 – 3

Tab. 7E: HUNGARY *(Continued)*

MEMBER ORGANIZATION: **Hungarian National Council, HNC**, since fifth session: **Hungarian Committee HC** ADDRESS: 125 East 72 Street NY 21, NY			
FIRST, LAST NAME of delegate to ACEN	AFFILIATION – all descriptions listed by the ACEN with session numbers	FUNCTIONS IN THE ACEN (L-Legal, P-Political, S-Social, E-Economic, I-Information, C-Cultural)	YEARS LISTED AS A DELEGATE BY ACEN
Istvan Revay	ACEN: No description FEC: date of exile 1949, stipend: 275$/mo., 15 II 1952 – 30 IX 1952, since 7 XII 1959; FEC: council member 3,600$/y. (as of 1960)	C (8 – 9); S (9); Secr.: C-I (10); E-S (10)	8 – 10
Dr. László Sandor	Attorney at Law	L (1)	1
Paul Schell	Former Diplomat	C (3); P (2); I (3)	2 – 3
Pál Szabo	ACEN: Former Member of Parliament, former Under Secretary of State for Public Welfare, Member of the Hungarian Committee. FEC: council member 4,800$/y. (as of 1960)	S, E (8)	5 – 8
Béla Teleki	Agricultural expert, former member of Parliament	PR/I (1)	1
George Ulmann	former General Manager of the Hungarian General Credit Bank		2 – 3
Frenec Vali	ACEN: Professor of International Law, member of the Hungarian Committee FEC: date of exile 1956, no stipend, received HNC 50$/mo. retainer.	L (8,9)	5 – 13
Msgr. Béla Varga	ACEN: former Speaker of Parliament; President, HNC (2); Chairman of the HC (8). FEC: council member 4,800$/y. (as of 1960)	**GC (2 – 18)**	2 – 18
Dr. László Varga	Attorney at Law, former Member of Parliament (1); member of the HC (8);	L (1, 8) S (1 – 2)	4 – 8

Tab. 7E: HUNGARY *(Continued)*

MEMBER ORGANIZATION:
Hungarian National Council, HNC, since fifth session: **Hungarian Committee HC**
ADDRESS: 125 East 72 Street NY 21, NY

FIRST, LAST NAME of delegate to ACEN	AFFILIATION – all descriptions listed by the ACEN with session numbers	FUNCTIONS IN THE ACEN (L-Legal, P-Political, S-Social, E-Economic, I-Information, C-Cultural)	YEARS LISTED AS A DELEGATE BY ACEN
Frenec Vidovics	ACEN: Former Governor of Somogy County, former Member of Parliament, member of the HC FEC: date of exile 25 XI 1956, stipend: 400$/mo., since 1 VII 1958; FEC: council member 4,800$/y. (as of 1960).	C, S (8)	4–8

Tab. 7F: LATVIA

MEMBER ORGANIZATION:
Committee for a Free Latvia
ADDRESS: 270 Park Ave, New York 17 NY

FIRST, LAST NAME of delegate to ACEN	AFFILIATION – all descriptions listed by the ACEN with session numbers	FUNCTIONS IN THE ACEN (L-Legal, P-Political, S-Social, E-Economic, I-Information, C-Cultural)	YEARS LISTED AS A DELEGATE BY ACEN
Augusts Abakuks	No description	See: Great Britain	10, 12–18 (1963–64, 1965–1972)
Augusts Alksnītis	Chairman, Latvian Freedom Committee, European Center		1 (1954–1955)
Kārlis Berends	No description	See: France	11–18
Alfrēds Bērziņš	Former Cabinet Minister; former Member of Parliament (1–9); of the Committee for a Free Latvia, Vice Chairman of the Latvian World Federation, Deputy-Chairman, American Latvian Association (8–9)	ACEN Chairman (16); ACEN Vice Chairman (15); PR/I (1–3); S (1); C-I (10); **GC 13–16**	1–18

Tab. 7F: LATVIA *(Continued)*

MEMBER ORGANIZATION: **Committee for a Free Latvia** ADDRESS: 270 Park Ave, New York 17 NY			
FIRST, LAST NAME of delegate to ACEN	AFFILIATION – all descriptions listed by the ACEN with session numbers	FUNCTIONS IN THE ACEN (L-Legal, P-Political, S-Social, E-Economic, I-Information, C-Cultural)	YEARS LISTED AS A DELEGATE BY ACEN
Ādolfs Bļodnieks	ACEN: Former Prime Minister; former Member of Parliament, and Member of the Presidium of the last Parliament (1,2,8); Chairman (member, 8,9) Committee for a Free Latvia (2,8). FEC: council member 4,800$/y. (as of 1960)	S (1, 2, 8)	1–8
Artūrs Bērztīss	Chairman of the Australian Latvian Federation	See: Australia	4
Voldemārs Dulmanis	Chairman, Australian Latvian Federation		2,3
Dr. Rūdolfs Drillis	Professor, former Labor Union Executive	S (1)	1
Kārlis Dziļleja	ACEN: Lawyer, member of the Board, Latvian Reconstruction Committee, European Center, member of the Committee for a Free Latvia FEC: date of exile IX 1944, stipend: 150$/mo., since 11 IX 1961FRASH.		2–10
Kārlis Egevičs	No description		5
Pēteris Eglītis	Lawyer, President, Latvian Evangelic Lutheran Church Council	L (2–3)	1–18
Ojārs Gobiņš	Member of American Latvian youth association (was accredited to replace Kristaps Valters, Jr. Beginning with 30th Plenary Meeting)		2
Dr. Olģerds Grosvalds	Minister Plenipotentiary in France, member of the Latvian	See: France	2–8

Tab. 7F: LATVIA *(Continued)*

MEMBER ORGANIZATION: **Committee for a Free Latvia** ADDRESS: 270 Park Ave, New York 17 NY			
FIRST, LAST NAME of delegate to ACEN	AFFILIATION – all descriptions listed by the ACEN with session numbers	FUNCTIONS IN THE ACEN (L-Legal, P-Political, S-Social, E-Economic, I-Information, C-Cultural)	YEARS LISTED AS A DELEGATE BY ACEN
	Reconstruction Committee, European Center		
Vilis Hāzners	ACEN: Member, Committee for a Free Latvia (3); former member of the Latvian Army General Staff, Chairman, Committee for a Free Latvia, Chairman of Former Latvian Army Officers' Association, Vice Chairman, Board of Latvian Veterans" Association "Daugavas Vanagi" (8,9). FEC: council member 4,200$/y. (as of 1960)	C (3); S (8, 9); E (6–9) **GC (11–13, 17–18);** secr.: E-S (10, 15)	3–18
Jānis Jaunzemis	No description		6
Kārlis Karūsa	Lawyer		3
Ādolfs Klīve	ACEN: Former Member of Latvian Parliament, former Chairman of the Council of the Bank of Latvia (1–3), member of the Committee for a Free Latvia (8,9). FEC: FEC: council member 4,200$/y. (as of 1960)	I, P (8,9) P (1, 2); P-L (10)	1–18
Arvīds Krīpens	Former chairman, Latvian Association of Australia (1) former member of the Latvian Army General Staff, former Director, Latvian Military Academy, member of the Board, Latvian Australian Federation (8,9)		1, 6–11
Ričards Kronbergs	Member of the Board of the Latvian National Federation in Canada		4

Tab. 7F: LATVIA *(Continued)*

MEMBER ORGANIZATION: **Committee for a Free Latvia** ADDRESS: 270 Park Ave, New York 17 NY			
FIRST, LAST NAME of delegate to ACEN	AFFILIATION – all descriptions listed by the ACEN with session numbers	FUNCTIONS IN THE ACEN (L-Legal, P-Political, S-Social, E-Economic, I-Information, C-Cultural)	YEARS LISTED AS A DELEGATE BY ACEN
Rt. Rev. (Dean) Jēkabs Ķullītis	Former Member of Parliament; Representative of the Archbishop of the Latvian Evangelist Lutheran Church	C (2) S (1)	1–2
Professor Eduards Laimiņš	Former member of Parliament, former Cabinet Minister		12
Arvīds Līdacis	Member of the board of American Latvian Association		1
Roberts Liepiņš	Former Mayor of Riga City; former Cabinet Minister, diplomat	See: Germany	2–18
Boļeslavs Maikovskis	Lawyer, Vice Chairman of the Board of the American Latvian Humanitarian Association	C (8,9); See: IPU	5–11
Dr. Vilis Māsēns	ACEN: Diplomat; Doctor of Law; former Chairman and member of Committee for a Free Latvia (3); member of the Board, Latvian Reconstruction Committee, European Center (8,9). FEC: council member 4,800$/y. (as of 1960)	Chairman, General Committee ACEN (1–4); **GC (1–10)** L (8)	1–10
Gunars Meierovics	Member of the Board of the American Latvian Association		1–3
Dr. Pēteris Norvilis	Vice Chairman of the Board of the American Latvia Association, Chairman of the Latvian Humanitarian Association	C (8)	6–10
Alfrēds Puķīte	Chairman of Latvian War veterans association in the US		2
Pauls Ramans	No description		12–18
Onufrijs Rancāns	Member, Committee for a Free Latvia (2,3)	**alternate member of GC ACEN** (2); E (2–4)	2–3

Tab. 7F: LATVIA *(Continued)*

MEMBER ORGANIZATION: **Committee for a Free Latvia** ADDRESS: 270 Park Ave, New York 17 NY			
FIRST, LAST NAME of delegate to ACEN	AFFILIATION – all descriptions listed by the ACEN with session numbers	FUNCTIONS IN THE ACEN (L-Legal, P-Political, S-Social, E-Economic, I-Information, C-Cultural)	YEARS LISTED AS A DELEGATE BY ACEN
Olģerts Rozītis	No description		15 – 18
Dainis Rudzītis	Member of the Board of the American Latvian Association		6 – 18
Zigurds Rudzītis	No description		12 – 18
Jānis Saulītis	No description	See: CDUCE	5
Arnolds Skrēbers	No description		8 – 18
Konstantīns Sventeckis	Member of the Board of the Latvian American Association		3 – 4
Msgr. Eduards Stukelis	Prelate		1
Ādolfs Svenne	Chairman of the Latvian National Federation in Canada		1
Kārlis Tannis	Member, Latvian National Federation in Canada		2,3
Alexander Ūdris	Lawyer, member of the board of American Latvian Association		1
Viktors Upeslācis	Lawyer, Chairman of the Board of Canadian Latvian Federations;		6 – 18
Kristaps Valters, Jr.	Former chairman of the American Latvian Youth Association		1,2
Jānis Vinters	Teacher, member of the American Latvian Association		3 – 18
Arvīds Zāģeris	Member of the Board of American Latvian Association		4 – 15

Tab. 7G: LITHUANIA

MEMBER ORGANIZATION: Committee for a Free Lithuania ADDRESS: 270 Park Ave, New York 17 NY			
FIRST, LAST NAME of delegate to ACEN	AFFILIATION – all descriptions listed by the ACEN with session numbers	FUNCTIONS IN THE ACEN (L-Legal, P-Political, S-Social, E-Economic, I-Information, C-Cultural)	YEARS LISTED AS A DELEGATE BY ACEN
Juozas Audėnas	ACEN: Former Minister of Agriculture, Chairman (1–2); Secretary General (3) Vice Chairman (8) of the Lithuanian Peasant Populist Union, Deputy Delegate to the International Peasant Union (8–9). FEC: council member 3,600$/y. (as of 1960)	C (2) C, E (8,9) E (2,3); P-L (10); Vice chair: E-S (10)	1–18
Valteris Banaitis	Journalist		3–18
Kipras Bielinis	ACEN: Former Member of the Lithuanian Parliament, Secretary General of the Lithuanian Social Democratic Party, Delegation in Exile FEC: stipend: 275$/mo., since 1 I 1959; FEC: council member 3,600$/y. (as of 1960).	P (1,2) S (3)	1–12
Bronius Bieliukas	No description		14–18
Miss Birutė Bilevičiūtė	Professor of Economics	C (3); E (3)	3
Martynas Brakas	ACEN: Lawyer; Member of the Supreme Committee for the Liberation of Lithuania, member of the Committee for a Free Lithuania (L, P); FEC: council member 4,200$/y. (as of 1960).	L, P (8,9) I (3) L (4,6) Secretary L (3); L (1–3) S (1)	1–15
Juozas Brazaitis	Professor, journalist, former Deputy Prime Minister; and Member of the Supreme Committee for the Liberation of Lithuania	I (3)	3–18

Tab. 7G: LITHUANIA *(Continued)*

MEMBER ORGANIZATION: Committee for a Free Lithuania ADDRESS: 270 Park Ave, New York 17 NY			
FIRST, LAST NAME of delegate to ACEN	AFFILIATION – all descriptions listed by the ACEN with session numbers	FUNCTIONS IN THE ACEN (L-Legal, P-Political, S-Social, E-Economic, I-Information, C-Cultural)	YEARS LISTED AS A DELEGATE BY ACEN
Kajetonas Čeginskas	No description		12, 16–18
Mrs. Magadalena Galdikas	Former member of parliament	C (2); S (1)	1–2
Dr. Petras Karvelis	Chief of Foreign Service of the Executive Council of the Supreme Committee for the Liberation of Lithuania, former Minister of Finance of Lithuania; accredited delegate for 18–25th plenary meetings (2)	See: Germany	2–18
Dr. Domas Krivickas	Professor of International Law	L (1–2); E (2)	1–2
Juozas Lanskoronskis	Journalist, former military attaché of Lithuania in Paris;	See: Belgium	3–13
Jonas Makauskis	Former member of parliament		2
Dr. Vincas Maciūnas	No description		14–18
Juozas Miklovas	No description		10–13
Rev. Vincas Mincevičius	Journalist, Director of Lithuanian broadcasts in Vatican		3
Bronius Nemickas	ACEN: Lawyer, former Vice Chairman of the Supreme Committee for Liberation of Lithuania (1–3); Chairman, Lithuanian National Movement (8,9) FEC: stipend: 275$/mo., since 1 XI 1959; FEC: council member 3,600$/y. (as of 1960)	L, S (8,9) L (1–3)	1–18
Juozas Pažemeckas	former member of the Supreme Lithuanian Committee of Liberation		1–2

Tab. 7G: LITHUANIA *(Continued)*

MEMBER ORGANIZATION: Committee for a Free Lithuania ADDRESS: 270 Park Ave, New York 17 NY			
FIRST, LAST NAME of delegate to ACEN	AFFILIATION – all descriptions listed by the ACEN with session numbers	FUNCTIONS IN THE ACEN (L-Legal, P-Political, S-Social, E-Economic, I-Information, C-Cultural)	YEARS LISTED AS A DELEGATE BY ACEN
Dr. Jonas Puzinas	No description	Secretary C-I (15)	13–18
Vincas Rastenis	Chairman of the Lithuanian National Movement (1,2); Journalist, Chairman of the Lithuanian National Movement (3); Chairman, Lithuanian Independence Alliance (8, 9)	PR/I (1); Vice chairman I (2,3)	1–3, 8–13
Juozas Repečka	Lawyer	S (1)	1–2
Vaclovas Sidzikauskas	ACEN: Minister Plenipotentiary (1–3); Chairman of the Committee for a Free Lithuania. FEC: council member 4,800$/y. (as of 1960).	ACEN Chairman (7,12); ACEN Vice Chairman (6,18); **GC (1–18);** P chairman (1,2) P (4) L (3)	1–18
Kazys Šiliūnas	Lawyer		1–2
Jackus Sonda	No description		13–18
Antanas Trimakas	Professor, former Diplomat, Lithuanian Editor of the "Baltic Review" (1–2); Member of the Supreme Committee for Liberation of Lithuania (3); President of the Presidium of the Supreme Committee for Liberation of Lithuania (8,9). FEC: council member 4,200$/y. (as of 1960).	P (1,2, 6–9) Secretary S (1–3), S (1–4); chair: P-L (10)	1–10
Eduardas Turauskas	Minister Plenipotentiary	See: CDUCE; See: France	4–13, 18
Pranas Vainauskas	ACEN: Chairman, Lithuanian Christian Democratic Union, former minister of Commerce (1–3); member of the Supreme	S, E (8); S (1); E (2,3); E-S (10)	1–18

Tab. 7G: LITHUANIA *(Continued)*

MEMBER ORGANIZATION: Committee for a Free Lithuania ADDRESS: 270 Park Ave, New York 17 NY			
FIRST, LAST NAME of delegate to ACEN	AFFILIATION – all descriptions listed by the ACEN with session numbers	FUNCTIONS IN THE ACEN (L-Legal, P-Political, S-Social, E-Economic, I-Information, C-Cultural)	YEARS LISTED AS A DELEGATE BY ACEN
	Committee for Liberation of Lithuania (8,9) FEC: date of exile 1944, stipend: 275$/mo., since 1 IX 1961; FEC: council member 3,600$/y. (as of 1960).		
Jonas Valaitis	Former member of Parliament		1 – 3; 8 – 9
Vytautas Vaitiekūnas	Former member of the Supreme Lithuanian Committee of Liberation, journalist (1 – 3); lawyer, journalist, member of the Committee for a Free Lithuania (8,9). FEC: council member 4,200$/y. (as of 1960)	Secretary C (2 – 3); C (2 – 9); I (8,9); S (3); Vice chair: C-I (10)	2 – 18
Juozas Vilčinskas	Civil engineer, journalist.	See: Great Britain	3 – 18

Tab. 7H: POLAND (TWO ORGANIZATIONS WERE MEMBERS)

MEMBER ORGANIZATIONS: 1) Polish Political Council; **Polish Council of National Unity, PCNU (Korboński)** ADDRESS: 42 Emperor's Gate, London, SW 7 , GB Chelsea Hotel Apt. 705, 222 West 23rd Street, New York 11, NY 2) MEMBER ORGANIZATION: **Polish National Democratic Committee (Mikołajczyk) PNDC*** ADDRESS: 1402 Delafield Place, NY Washington D.C.			
FIRST, LAST NAME of delegate to ACEN	AFFILIATION – all descriptions listed by the ACEN with session numbers	FUNCTIONS IN THE ACEN (L-Legal, P-Political, S-Social, E-Economic, I-Information, C-Cultural)	YEARS LISTED AS A DELEGATE BY ACEN
Stanisław Bańczyk*	ACEN: Lawyer, Vice Chairman (1), Acting Chairman (2 – 9), Polish Peasant Party; Former Member of Parliament (2,3)	S (8,9); E-S (10)	1 – 18

Tab. 7H: POLAND (TWO ORGANIZATIONS WERE MEMBERS) *(Continued)*

MEMBER ORGANIZATIONS:
1) Polish Political Council; **Polish Council of National Unity, PCNU (Korboński)**
ADDRESS: 42 Emperor's Gate, London, SW 7 , GB
Chelsea Hotel Apt. 705, 222 West 23rd Street, New York 11, NY
2) MEMBER ORGANIZATION: **Polish National Democratic Committee (Mikołajczyk) PNDC***
ADDRESS: 1402 Delafield Place, NY Washington D.C.

FIRST, LAST NAME of delegate to ACEN	AFFILIATION – all descriptions listed by the ACEN with session numbers	FUNCTIONS IN THE ACEN (L-Legal, P-Political, S-Social, E-Economic, I-Information, C-Cultural)	YEARS LISTED AS A DELEGATE BY ACEN
	FEC: date of exile XII 1948, stipend: 275$/mo., since 1 XII 1949; FEC: meritorious exile 3,600$/y. (as of 1960)		
Bolesław Biega*	ACEN: Member, Central Committee (1), Vice Chairman (2–9) Polish Christian Labor Party; Vice Chairman (1–3) CDUCE; Former Secretary, Polish Underground Council of National Unity (1–9); Secretary General, Polish Council of National Unity American Division (2–3). FEC: council member 6,000$/y. (as of 1960)	S (4, 6–7,9); Chair: S (2–3); Chair: E-S (15); C-I (10); P-L (10); Chair: E-S (10	1–18
Adam Ciołkosz	Former member of parliament; chairman of Executive Board of the PCNU in London; was accredited as a delegate to the 18–21 and then 30–33 plenary meetings (2)	See: Great Britain	2
Władyslaw Furka	Social worker, former Underground Youth Leader in Poland (I)	I (8,9); C-I (10)	8–14
Feliks Gadomski*	Secretary General, Polish Democratic Party, former Judge (1,2); lawyer, member Presidium PCNU, American division; former director of Department in the Polish Government-in-exile, London.	ACEN Secretariat Staff member (3–9); ACEN Secretary General (13–18); S (1)	1–2

Tab. 7H: POLAND (TWO ORGANIZATIONS WERE MEMBERS) *(Continued)*

MEMBER ORGANIZATIONS:
1) Polish Political Council; **Polish Council of National Unity, PCNU (Korboński)**
ADDRESS: 42 Emperor's Gate, London, SW 7 , GB
Chelsea Hotel Apt. 705, 222 West 23rd Street, New York 11, NY
2) MEMBER ORGANIZATION: **Polish National Democratic Committee (Mikołajczyk) PNDC***
ADDRESS: 1402 Delafield Place, NY Washington D.C.

FIRST, LAST NAME of delegate to ACEN	AFFILIATION – all descriptions listed by the ACEN with session numbers	FUNCTIONS IN THE ACEN (L-Legal, P-Political, S-Social, E-Economic, I-Information, C-Cultural)	YEARS LISTED AS A DELEGATE BY ACEN
Bohdan Gajewicz	Lawyer, Vice President, Polish Council of Unity in the United States (L);	L (8,9)	7 – 15
Adam Galiński	ACEN: Lawyer, former leader of the Underground Organization in Eastern Poland, former inmate of the Soviet forced labor camp in Vorkuta FEC: date of exile 1959, stipend: 100$/mo., since 1 IV 1960.		7 – 18
Prof. Zygmunt Gross	No description		17 – 18
Bolesław Łaszewski	Chairman of the Freedom Movement, "Independence and Democracy" in the USA; President (1), former President (2 – 3), Association of the Polish War Veterans	C (1 – 2) P (1 – 2)	1 – 7
Jerzy Lerski	Former liaison officer between the Polish Government in Exile and the underground Government in Poland	See: Japan	1
Jan Librach	No description		6 – 7
Stanisław Jordanowski	No description		7, 13 – 18
Stefan Kaczorowski	Replaced Stanisław Wójcik for the 43rd and 44th Plenary Meetings		3

Tab. 7H: POLAND (TWO ORGANIZATIONS WERE MEMBERS) *(Continued)*

MEMBER ORGANIZATIONS:
1) Polish Political Council; **Polish Council of National Unity, PCNU (Korboński)**
ADDRESS: 42 Emperor's Gate, London, SW 7 , GB
Chelsea Hotel Apt. 705, 222 West 23rd Street, New York 11, NY
2) MEMBER ORGANIZATION: **Polish National Democratic Committee (Mikołajczyk) PNDC***
ADDRESS: 1402 Delafield Place, NY Washington D.C.

FIRST, LAST NAME of delegate to ACEN	AFFILIATION – all descriptions listed by the ACEN with session numbers	FUNCTIONS IN THE ACEN (L-Legal, P-Political, S-Social, E-Economic, I-Information, C-Cultural)	YEARS LISTED AS A DELEGATE BY ACEN
Edward Kleszczyński	No description		11 – 18
Pawel Kopocz	Former member of Parliament	S (1)	1
Stefan Korboński	ACEN: President, Polish Political Council, Working Committee in the U.S.A., former Acting Chief of the Underground Government of Poland (1) Lawyer; Member, Presidium Polish Council of National Unity American Division (2 – 3); former Chief of the Underground Government in Poland; former Member of Parliament. FEC: council member 6,000$/y. (as of 1960)	ACEN Chairman (5, 13, 18); ACEN Vice Chairman (7,12); **GC (1 – 18)**	1 – 18
Mrs. Maria Eva Mieroszewska	accredited a delegate for the eighth plenary meeting (1)		1
Michał Mościcki	ACEN: Former Minister Plenipotentiary; FEC: meritorious exile 3,600$/y. (as of 1960)	I (3)	2 – 7
Dr. Zygmunt Nagórski, Sr.	ACEN: Accredited a delegate for the tenth plenary meeting (1) FEC: date of exile 1945, stipend: 170.25$/mo., since 1 VI 1956.	Chairman PR/I (1) L (1)	
Adam Niebieszczański	Lawyer; Vice Chairman, Polish Council of National Unity American Division; Chairman, Polish National Party in USA (2 – 3);	Chairman L (1 – 3) L (1 – 5)	1 – 7

Tab. 7H: POLAND (TWO ORGANIZATIONS WERE MEMBERS) *(Continued)*

MEMBER ORGANIZATIONS:
1) Polish Political Council; **Polish Council of National Unity, PCNU (Korboński)**
ADDRESS: 42 Emperor's Gate, London, SW 7 , GB
Chelsea Hotel Apt. 705, 222 West 23rd Street, New York 11, NY
2) MEMBER ORGANIZATION: **Polish National Democratic Committee (Mikołajczyk) PNDC***
ADDRESS: 1402 Delafield Place, NY Washington D.C.

FIRST, LAST NAME of delegate to ACEN	AFFILIATION – all descriptions listed by the ACEN with session numbers	FUNCTIONS IN THE ACEN (L-Legal, P-Political, S-Social, E-Economic, I-Information, C-Cultural)	YEARS LISTED AS A DELEGATE BY ACEN
	Former Member, Polish Foreign Service (1 – 3)		
Stanisław Olszewski*	Chairman, Polish Democratic Party, Chairman, Executive Committee, Liberal Democratic Union of Central Eastern Europe		1
Zbigniew Ossowski	Accredited a delegate for the ninth plenary meeting (1)		1
Jerzy Panciewicz	Journalist; Chief editorial writer for Everybody's Daily in Buffalo, New York	I (3)	2 – 4
Otton Pehr	ACEN: Lawyer; Chairman, Polish Council of National Unity American Division; former Secretary General, Foreign Central Committee of the Polish Socialist Party; former Chief, Office of the Council of Ministers in the Polish Government in exile, in London (1 – 9) President, Polish Council of Unity in the United Sates (8,9). FEC: council member 4,200$/y. (as of 1960).	P (1) I, P, E (8,9) E-S (10); P-L (10)	1 – 10
Dr. Marian Piotrowski	Professor of Economics	E (8,9)	7 – 17
Michał Pluciński	Civil engineer	C-I (10)	7 – 17
Andrzej Pomian	Writer, journalist, former Lt.-Col. Of the Underground Army in Poland	C (8,9)	4 – 9, 18

Tab. 7H: POLAND (TWO ORGANIZATIONS WERE MEMBERS) *(Continued)*

MEMBER ORGANIZATIONS:
1) Polish Political Council; **Polish Council of National Unity, PCNU (Korboński)**
ADDRESS: 42 Emperor's Gate, London, SW 7 , GB
Chelsea Hotel Apt. 705, 222 West 23rd Street, New York 11, NY
2) MEMBER ORGANIZATION: **Polish National Democratic Committee (Mikołajczyk) PNDC***
ADDRESS: 1402 Delafield Place, NY Washington D.C.

FIRST, LAST NAME of delegate to ACEN	AFFILIATION – all descriptions listed by the ACEN with session numbers	FUNCTIONS IN THE ACEN (L-Legal, P-Political, S-Social, E-Economic, I-Information, C-Cultural)	YEARS LISTED AS A DELEGATE BY ACEN
Jerzy Ponikiewski	Journalist	I (8,9)	6, 8–11
Karol Popiel*	ACEN: Member of PNDC delegation (1) FEC: date of exile 1944, stipend: 275$/mo., 1 V 1950–30 VI 1958, since 1 I 1962; FEC: council member 4,200$/y. (as of 1960)	**GC (1)** See: CDUCE	1
Bolesław Rodowicz	Member Executive Committee, Association of Polish War Veterans, member Polish Democratic Party		3–4
Konrad Sieniewicz*	Secretary General, Polish Christian Labor Party, Secretary General, CDUCE, former Vice Director, Office of the Head of Underground Administration in Poland	P (1) See: CDUCE	1
Wacław Soroka	Accredited a delegate for the eleventh plenary meeting (1)	PR/I (1)	1
Wojciech Wasiutyński	No description		5–6
Jan Wepsiec	Accredited a delegate for the extraordinary Plenary Meeting on 3 XII 1954		1
Bolesław Wierzbiański	Journalist; Vice Chairman, Polish Council of National Unity American Division; President, International Federation of Free Journalists	P (2); I (3)	2–6

Tab. 7H: POLAND (TWO ORGANIZATIONS WERE MEMBERS) *(Continued)*

MEMBER ORGANIZATIONS: 1) Polish Political Council; **Polish Council of National Unity, PCNU (Korboński)** ADDRESS: 42 Emperor's Gate, London, SW 7 , GB Chelsea Hotel Apt. 705, 222 West 23rd Street, New York 11, NY 2) MEMBER ORGANIZATION: **Polish National Democratic Committee (Mikołajczyk) PNDC*** ADDRESS: 1402 Delafield Place, NY Washington D.C.			
FIRST, LAST NAME of delegate to ACEN	AFFILIATION – all descriptions listed by the ACEN with session numbers	FUNCTIONS IN THE ACEN (L-Legal, P-Political, S-Social, E-Economic, I-Information, C-Cultural)	YEARS LISTED AS A DELEGATE BY ACEN
Stanisław Wojcik*	Secretary General, Polish Peasant Party, former Member of Parliament; Secretary General, Polish National Democratic Committee (1); Former member, Polish Underground Council of National Unity (1–3); Lawyer (2–3)	P (2) L (2,3) E (2,3), Secretary E (2)	1–6
Zbigniew Stypułkowski	Lawyer, member of Exec Board of PCNU in London; former Member of Parliament, accredited a delegate 26–29 Plenary Meetings (2)		2
Franciszek Szwajdler	Former chairman of the province of Łódź, National Party, Chairman, Polish National Party in the U.S.A.		1
Władysław Zachariasiewicz	Executive secretary, Polish Immigration Committee, New York		1
Władysław Zaremba*	Member, Central Committee, Polish Peasant Party, former Vice President, Polish National Council in Exile (during the war)	PR/I (1)	1

*Due to a protest of unequal distribution of seats on the Polish delegation (only five for PNDC by the 2nd session) the PNDC (Mikołajczyk) did not nominate delegates since ACEN's third session. The original PNDC members that joined PCNU (Korboński) in 1955 are marked with an asterisk.

Tab. 7l: ROMANIA

MEMBER ORGANIZATION: **Romanian National Committee, RNC** ADDRESS: 157 W. 57th Street New York, NY			
FIRST, LAST NAME of delegate to ACEN	AFFILIATION – all descriptions listed by the ACEN with session numbers	FUNCTIONS IN THE ACEN (L-Legal, P-Political, S-Social, E-Economic, I-Information, C-Cultural)	YEARS LISTED AS A DELEGATE BY ACEN
George Assan	Former Under Secretary of Commerce; former Member of Parliament; former Minister Plenipotentiary (2)	L (3); E (2–3)	1–17
Dr. Asra Berkowitz	Former editor of "L'Indépendance Roumaine"	I (8,9); C-I (10)	8–12
Cornel Bianu	ACEN: Former Member of Parliament. FEC: council member 3,360$/y. (as of 1960)	E (2–3, 8–9); E-S (10)	1–12
Romulus Boilă	Editor of the newspaper "La Nation Roumaine"	See: France	5–9
Raoul V. Bossy	ACEN: Former Minister Plenipotentiary. FEC: council member 3,600$/y. (as of 1960)	C (2, 3); P (1–2, 4–6); Vice chair: P (2); Vice chair: I (3); See: LDUCEE	1–7
Alexandru Bunescu	Former Under Secretary for Reconstruction. FEC: council member 3,360$/y. (as of 1960)	Chair: E (2) E (2–4,8,9); S (1); E-S (10)	1–18
Brutus Coste	ACEN: Accredited to the first four plenary meetings. FEC: staff member of ACEN 6,847$/y. (as of 1960)	Secretary General of ACEN (1–11)	1–9
Prof. Anton Crihan	ACEN: Former Under Secretary of Agriculture; former Member of Parliament. FEC: council member 3,360$/y. (as of 1960)	S (1)	1–4
Grigore Constantinescu	Former Minister Plenipotentiary	See: Great Britain	3–18
Nicolae G.[eorge] Caranfil	Accredited to the first eight plenary meetings		1
Silviu Crăciunaş	Lawyer, writer		8–17

Tab. 7l: ROMANIA *(Continued)*

MEMBER ORGANIZATION: **Romanian National Committee, RNC** ADDRESS: 157 W. 57th Street New York, NY			
FIRST, LAST NAME of delegate to ACEN	AFFILIATION – all descriptions listed by the ACEN with session numbers	FUNCTIONS IN THE ACEN (L-Legal, P-Political, S-Social, E-Economic, I-Information, C-Cultural)	YEARS LISTED AS A DELEGATE BY ACEN
Carol Davila	Former Minister to the United States of America; former Member of Parliament	P (1 – 2) I (3)	1 – 9
Nicolae Dima	No description		18
Grigore Gafencu	Former Minister of Foreign Affairs; former Member of Parliament		1 – 3
Eftimie Gherman	ACEN: Former Member of Parliament; former Secretary General, Union of Romanian Mine Workers FEC: date of exile 1947, stipend: 112.25$/mo., since 1 XII 1961.		1 – 18
Emil Ghilezan	Former Under Secretary for Finance, Former member of parliament (1,2) accredited delegate to 18 – 25 Plenary Meetings (2)		1 – 2
George Ionescu	ACEN: Secretary General, RNC. FEC: council staff 4,200$/y. (as of 1960)		2 – 7
Mircea Ioannițiu	Former Private Secretary to H.M. King of Romania	L (1 – 2)	1 – 2
Dr. Sabin Manuilă	ACEN: Former Under Secretary, Presidency of the Council of Ministers. FEC: council member 3,360$/y. (as of 1960)	C (2,3); S (2 – 3) I (8 – 9); L-I (10)	1 – 10
Dr. Veturia Manuilă	Accredited to the eighth plenary meeting (wife of Dr. Sabin Manuila)		1
Naum Neagoe	Civil engineer, former Member of the National Liberal Party;	E (2); E-S (10)	8 – 18

Tab. 7l: ROMANIA *(Continued)*

MEMBER ORGANIZATION: **Romanian National Committee, RNC** ADDRESS: 157 W. 57th Street New York, NY			
FIRST, LAST NAME of delegate to ACEN	AFFILIATION – all descriptions listed by the ACEN with session numbers	FUNCTIONS IN THE ACEN (L-Legal, P-Political, S-Social, E-Economic, I-Information, C-Cultural)	YEARS LISTED AS A DELEGATE BY ACEN
Prof. Augustin Popa	ACEN: Former Member of Parliament (C, P). FEC: council member 3,360$/y. (as of 1960)	C (2, 3); C, P (8,9) P (2); PR/I (1, 3); Chair: P-L (15); chair: C-I (10); P-L (10)	1 – 18
Mihai Răutu	Former Under Secretary for Communications; former Member of Parliament	L (1 – 2)	1 – 5
Ion Stere	No description		11 – 17
Ion Vardala	ACEN: Former Diplomat. FEC: council staff 4,500$/y. (as of 1960)	L (6 – 9); P-L (10)	5 – 18
Dr. Virgil Veniamin	ACEN: Former Professor, Bucharest University; former Assistant Secretary General, RNC (1 – 3); former Assistant Secretary General, National Peasant Party (8,9). FEC: council member 3,360$/y. (as of 1960)	L (8,9); P-L (10) See: France	1 – 18
Constantin Vişoianu	ACEN: Former Minister of Foreign Affairs; President, RNC. FEC: council member 4,800$/y. (as of 1960)	**GC 1 – 18**	1 – 18
Iancu Zissu	Member, Central Committee; Independent Social Democratic Party	S (8,9); Vice chairman S (2 – 3); L (3); S (4, 6, 7); e-s (10)	1 – 16

Tab. 8 Party internationals' delegations to ACEN, 1954–1971

Tab. 8A: CDUCE

MEMBER ORGANIZATION: **Christian Democratic Union of Central Europe** ADDRESS: 471 Park Ave, New York 22, NY			
FIRST, LAST NAME of delegate to ACEN	AFFILIATION – all descriptions listed by the ACEN with session numbers	FUNCTIONS IN THE ACEN (L-Legal, P-Political, S-Social, E-Economic, I-Information, C-Cultural)	YEARS LISTED AS A DELEGATE BY ACEN
Mrs. Maria Andras	Former Officer in the Hungarian Ministry of Foreign Affairs accredited as delegate 17–25 plenary mtgs	S (2)	2
Bohumir Bunza	ACEN: Former member, Czechoslovak Parliament. FEC: international organizations staff 6,654 $/y. (as of 1960)	Secretary, P (1) PR/I (1)	1, 4
Benedikts Cevers	Secretary General, Latvian Christian Farmers' Party		1
Stasys Dziknas	No description		5–8
Dr. Tibor Horanyi	ACEN: No description. FEC: council staff 3,720$/y. (as of 1960)		4
László Kish	Member CDUCE		8–10; 16–18
Dr. Miha Krek	No description FEC: date of exile 1942, stipend: 275$/mo., since 1 II 1953; FEC: meritorious exile 3,600$/y. (as of 1960).		8–16
Rev. Donats Murnieks	No description		6
Denis Nemestothy	ACEN: No description. FEC: international organizations staff 3,360$/y. (as of 1960)		11–15
Istvan Paraezky	No description		6,7
Dr. Jaroslav Pechacek	No description		6

Tab. 8A: CDUCE *(Continued)*

MEMBER ORGANIZATION: **Christian Democratic Union of Central Europe** ADDRESS: 471 Park Ave, New York 22, NY			
FIRST, LAST NAME of delegate to ACEN	AFFILIATION – all descriptions listed by the ACEN with session numbers	FUNCTIONS IN THE ACEN (L-Legal, P-Political, S-Social, E-Economic, I-Information, C-Cultural)	YEARS LISTED AS A DELEGATE BY ACEN
Karol Popiel	Vice Chairman of CDUCE (8)	**GC (17–18)** See: Poland	7–18
Prof. Adolph Procházka	Chairman of the C.D.U.C.E. Executive Committee, former minister and member of parliament of Czechoslovakia (2–9); headed the delegation at the Third, Fourth and Twelfth plenary meetings, as well as at the Extraordinary plenary meeting on 3 December 1954 (1)	P (8,9) **GC (2–16)** See: Czechoslovakia	2–16
Dr. Ludovik Push	ACEN: Deputy Secretary general CDUCE. FEC: international organizations staff 6,000$/y. (as of 1960)		7–17
Jānis Saulītis	No description	See: Latvia	7
Konrad Sieniewicz	ACEN: Secretary General of CDUCE; Secretary General, Polish Christian Labor Party; former Vice Director (2–4) Office of the Head of Underground Administration in Poland (2). FEC: international organizations staff 7,543$/y. (as of 1960)	See: Poland	2–4, 18
Janusz Śleszynski	ACEN: Former Officer of the Polish Ministry of Foreign Affairs. FEC: international organizations staff 6,000$/y. (as of 1960)	Secretary L (1–2)	4–6
Paul Tigrid	Journalist, Czechoslovakia	P (2)	2
Edward Turauskas	Former Minister Plenipotentiary of Lithuania	See: Lithuania	3

Tab. 8A: CDUCE *(Continued)*

MEMBER ORGANIZATION: **Christian Democratic Union of Central Europe** ADDRESS: 471 Park Ave, New York 22, NY			
FIRST, LAST NAME of delegate to ACEN	AFFILIATION – all descriptions listed by the ACEN with session numbers	FUNCTIONS IN THE ACEN (L-Legal, P-Political, S-Social, E-Economic, I-Information, C-Cultural)	YEARS LISTED AS A DELEGATE BY ACEN
Adolf Venskus	No description	See: France	8 – 18
Dr. Vladas Villiamas	Vice Chairman, Lithuanian Christian Democratic Union	S (1); E (2)	1, 4

Tab. 8B: IPU

MEMBER ORGANIZATION: **International Peasant Union** ADDRESS: 201 West 79th Street, New York 24, NY			
FIRST, LAST NAME of delegate to ACEN	AFFILIATION – all descriptions listed by the ACEN with session numbers	FUNCTIONS IN THE ACEN (L-Legal, P-Political, S-Social, E-Economic, I-Information, C-Cultural)	YEARS LISTED AS A DELEGATE BY ACEN
Henrikas Blazas	ACEN: Secretary General, Central Committee, Populist Peasant Union of Lithuania (1 – 5, 7); Managing Editor of the Bulletin of the IPU, member of Lithuanian Populist Peasant Union (8,9). FEC: international organizations staff 6,000$/y. (as of 1960)	C (2) P (1,2) P (8,9)	1 – 5, 7 – 12
Béla Bokor	ACEN: Hungarian Peasant Association (2); FEC: international organizations staff 6,000$/y. (as of 1960)	S (1); E (2)	2, 7
Dr. Samuel Bellus	No description		4
Gerhard A. Bushmann	Member IPU	See: Germany	8
Jordan Dechev			10 – 18

Tab. 8B: IPU *(Continued)*

MEMBER ORGANIZATION: **International Peasant Union** ADDRESS: 201 West 79th Street, New York 24, NY			
FIRST, LAST NAME of delegate to ACEN	AFFILIATION – all descriptions listed by the ACEN with session numbers	FUNCTIONS IN THE ACEN (L-Legal, P-Political, S-Social, E-Economic, I-Information, C-Cultural)	YEARS LISTED AS A DELEGATE BY ACEN
Dr. Jani Dilo	Representative, Albanian Agrarian Democratic Party (1); Representative of the National Democratic Committee for a Free Albania; Representative of the Agrarian Democratic Party, Balli Kombëtar (2, 3). replaced in June 1957 by Aleksanders Ozolins (3)	Chairman of the Delegation (2, 3); S (2)	1–3
Dr. Vladimir Dostal	Member IPU		9
Dr. Milan Gavrilovic	ACEN: Delegate at the first four plenary meetings (1); Representative in the General Committee (9) FEC: date of exile 1944, stipend: 275$/mo., 12 VI 1950–1 VII 1952, since 1 II 1953; FEC: meritorious exile 3,600$/y. (as of 1960)	Chairman (10–18)	1, 9–18
Dr. Vladko Maček	ACEN: Delegate at the first four plenary meetings (1) FEC: stipend: 173$/mo., since 15 VII 1949; FEC: meritorious exile 3,600$/y. (as of 1960).		1
Dr. Halil Maci	Member IPU (9);	L (9)	4–5,7
Boļeslavs Maikovskis	Delegate for the fifth, sixth, seventh, and eighth plenary meetings (1)	See: Latvia	1
Stanisław Mikołajczyk	ACEN: Former prime minister of Poland, former member of the Polish parliament, President, Polish National Democratic Committee, President, International Peasant Union, Chairman	Chairman of the delegation (1). See: Poland	1–2

Tab. 8B: IPU *(Continued)*

MEMBER ORGANIZATION: **International Peasant Union** ADDRESS: 201 West 79th Street, New York 24, NY			
FIRST, LAST NAME of delegate to ACEN	AFFILIATION – all descriptions listed by the ACEN with session numbers	FUNCTIONS IN THE ACEN (L-Legal, P-Political, S-Social, E-Economic, I-Information, C-Cultural)	YEARS LISTED AS A DELEGATE BY ACEN
	of the delegation (1); President IPU, former Prime Minister; president PNDC, accredited to 16th meeting (2). FEC: council member 4,200$/y. (as of 1960)		
Ferenc Nagy	Former Prime Minister of Hungary, President, Hungarian Peasant Association, former member of the Hungarian Parliament (1)	See: Hungary	1
Aleksander Ozolins	No description (4, 5);	Chairman (4, 5)	4–5
Ivan Pernar	ACEN: No description FEC: date of exile 1945, stipend: 162.41$/mo., since 1 V 196; FEC: meritorious exile 2,248$/y. (as of 1960).		11–13
Istvan B. Racz	No description		4,5
Jani Shopov	Member IPU	S (9)	8, 9
Johannes Sikkar	Chairman, Estonian United Farmers' and Smallholders' Part; Member of the Central Committee of the International Peasant Union		3
Bohoslav Soumar	ACEN: Czechoslovak Republican Agrarian Party; Managing Editor of the International Peasant Union Bulletin (2,3). FEC: international organizations staff 3,925$/y. (as of 1960)	PR/I (1) L (2); S (2)	2–4
Stojan Stoykov	No description		5
Gyula Szentadorjany	ACEN: Member IPU. FEC: council staff 4,200$/y. (as of 1960)		8

Tab. 8B: IPU *(Continued)*

MEMBER ORGANIZATION: **International Peasant Union** ADDRESS: 201 West 79th Street, New York 24, NY			
FIRST, LAST NAME of delegate to ACEN	AFFILIATION – all descriptions listed by the ACEN with session numbers	FUNCTIONS IN THE ACEN (L-Legal, P-Political, S-Social, E-Economic, I-Information, C-Cultural)	YEARS LISTED AS A DELEGATE BY ACEN
Dr. Borislav Trifkovic	Member IPU		4–5, 7–8

Tab. 8C: LDUCEE

MEMBER ORGANIZATION: Liberal Democratic Union / **Liberal Democratic Union of Central-Eastern Europe, LDUCEE** ADDRESS: 4 West 57th Street, New York 19, NY, room 907			
FIRST, LAST NAME of delegate to ACEN	AFFILIATION – all descriptions listed by the ACEN with session numbers	FUNCTIONS IN THE ACEN (L-Legal, P-Political, S-Social, E-Economic, I-Information, C-Cultural); Delegation chairman	YEARS LISTED AS A DELEGATE BY ACEN
Dr. Oton Ambroz	journalist, member, Executive Committee, LDU	E, I (8, 9); C-I (10; E-S (10)	8–18
Nikola Balabanov	ACEN: Vice Chairman of the Executive Committee, LDU, former Bulgarian Minister Plenipotentiary (8,9) FEC: date of exile 1945, stipend: 184$/mo., since 1 IX 1951; FEC: meritorious exile 3,600$/y. (as of 1960)	Chairman (5, 6, 7, 11–18) C, P (8, 9)	5–18
Dr. Halim Begeja	Secretary General, Albanian Balli Kombëtar Organization	See: Albania	1
Raoul V. Bossy	Chairman of the Executive Committee, Liberal Democratic Union, former Romanian Minister Plenipotentiary (S, P)	Chairman (8, 9, 10), S, P (8, 9); See: Romania	8–10
Dr. Vratislav Busek	former professor, Charles University, Prague, member, Executive Committee, Czechoslovak	Chairman (2,3) L (1–2); S (2)	1–3

Tab. 8C: LDUCEE *(Continued)*

MEMBER ORGANIZATION: Liberal Democratic Union / **Liberal Democratic Union of Central-Eastern Europe, LDUCEE** ADDRESS: 4 West 57th Street, New York 19, NY, room 907			
FIRST, LAST NAME of delegate to ACEN	AFFILIATION – all descriptions listed by the ACEN with session numbers	FUNCTIONS IN THE ACEN (L-Legal, P-Political, S-Social, E-Economic, I-Information, C-Cultural); Delegation chairman	YEARS LISTED AS A DELEGATE BY ACEN
	National Socialist Party, Chairman of the delegation (1); President, Board of Directors, Liberal Democratic Union (1);		
Dr. Ferenc Durugy	former member, Hungarian Foreign Service (1); former Hungarian Minister Plenipotentiary (3); Secretary General, Liberation LDU (2, 3)	Chairman (4) I (3)	1–5
Quazim Emro	member exec committee, Balli Kombëtar Organization. He was replaced by Velaj Selaheddin on Sept. 24, 1956		2
Radu Florescu	No description		6–7, 10–13
Feliks Gadomski	Member, Executive Committee, Liberal Democratic Union of Central Eastern Europe	Secretary S (1); See: Poland	1
Dr. Nuci Kotta	ACEN: Vice Chairman of the Executive Committee, LDU, Lecturer at Colombia University. FEC: staff member of ACEN 6,460$/y. (as of 1960)	See: Albania	8–11
Dr. Imre Nemethy	No description		5–7
Dr. Stanisław Olszewski	Lawyer; Chairman, Polish Democratic Party; Chairman, Executive Committee, Liberal Democratic Union (2,3)	P (2); See: Poland; See: Great Britain	2–4
Selandin Velaj	No description	See: Albania	2
Vladas Zillinskas	No description		4–7

Tab. 8C: LDUCEE *(Continued)*

MEMBER ORGANIZATION: Liberal Democratic Union / **Liberal Democratic Union of Central-Eastern Europe, LDUCEE** ADDRESS: 4 West 57th Street, New York 19, NY, room 907			
FIRST, LAST NAME of delegate to ACEN	AFFILIATION – all descriptions listed by the ACEN with session numbers	FUNCTIONS IN THE ACEN (L-Legal, P-Political, S-Social, E-Economic, I-Information, C-Cultural); Delegation chairman	YEARS LISTED AS A DELEGATE BY ACEN
Stasys Zymantas-Zakevicius	Professor; General Secretary, Committee of the Liberal Exiles		3

Tab. 8D: SUCEE

MEMBER ORGANIZATION: **Socialist Union of Central and Eastern Europe*** ADDRESS: 69 Newman Street, London W1, England			
FIRST, LAST NAME of delegate to ACEN	AFFILIATION – all descriptions listed by the ACEN with session numbers	FUNCTIONS IN THE ACEN (L-Legal, P-Political, S-Social, E-Economic, I-Information, C-Cultural)	YEARS LISTED AS A DELEGATE BY ACEN
Karl Ast	No description		12–13
Valdemars Bastjanis	Former member of the Latvian Government; member of the central Executive Committee of the Social Democratic Party of Latvia in exile (1,2); member SUCEE (8,9)		2–9
Vilem Bernard	former member of Czechoslovak parliament; secretary, SUCEEE (1); Secretary of SUCEE (8, 9)	See: Great Britain	2, 4–13
Prof. Josef Kaminskas	ACEN: Chairman of the Lithuanian Social Democratic Party in exile; former member of Parliament (2); member SUCEE (8) FEC: stipend: 100$/mo., since 1 V 1960.		2–8
Dr. Georgi Petkov	ACEN: Former member of Parliament, Chairman of the Bulgarian Socialist Party in Exile (1)	Chairman (1, 3, 9–11,13); S (2, 9); E-S (10); P-L (10); L (2); See: Bulgaria	2–13

Tab. 8D: SUCEE *(Continued)*

MEMBER ORGANIZATION: **Socialist Union of Central and Eastern Europe*** ADDRESS: 69 Newman Street, London W1, England			
FIRST, LAST NAME of delegate to ACEN	AFFILIATION – all descriptions listed by the ACEN with session numbers	FUNCTIONS IN THE ACEN (L-Legal, P-Political, S-Social, E-Economic, I-Information, C-Cultural)	YEARS LISTED AS A DELEGATE BY ACEN
	FEC: date of exile 30 VI 1948, stipend: 275$/mo., since 22 V 1952.		
Dr. Zivko Topalovich	Vice Chairman SUCEE		8–13
Zygmunt Zaremba	Chairman of the S.U.C.E.E. and of the Central Council of the Polish Socialist Party;	Chairman (2); See: France	3–7

*No delegates were nominated for the first, since fourteenth sessions of ACEN

Tab. 8E: ICFTUE

MEMBER ORGANIZATION: **International Center of Free Trade Unionists in Exile** ADDRESS: 198 Avenue du Maine Paris (14e), France			
FIRST, LAST NAME of delegate to ACEN	AFFILIATION – all descriptions listed by the ACEN with session numbers	FUNCTIONS IN THE ACEN (L-Legal, P-Political, S-Social, E-Economic, I-Information, C-Cultural)	YEARS LISTED AS A DELEGATE BY ACEN
Franciszek Białas	No description		11–16
Valdis Bumpers	No description		4
Oldrich Dubina	No description		17–18
Arno Hais	ACEN: Treasurer of the ICFTUE, former secretary General of the Czechoslovak Socialist Trade Union (3); Vice president, ICFTUE, former Secretary General of the Czechoslovak Socialist Trade Unions, Treasurer, ICFTUE (8,9); FEC: date of exile 1948, stipend: 163$/mo., since 1 XII 1961.	See: France	3–17

Tab. 8E: ICFTUE *(Continued)*

MEMBER ORGANIZATION: **International Center of Free Trade Unionists in Exile** ADDRESS: 198 Avenue du Maine Paris (14e), France			
FIRST, LAST NAME of delegate to ACEN	AFFILIATION – all descriptions listed by the ACEN with session numbers	FUNCTIONS IN THE ACEN (L-Legal, P-Political, S-Social, E-Economic, I-Information, C-Cultural)	YEARS LISTED AS A DELEGATE BY ACEN
Alois Lisy	Member ICFTUE	E (8, 9)	8–18
Władysław Michalak	ACEN: former Secretary General, Christian Transport Workers Union of Poland (2,3); former Chairman of the Christian Transport Workers Union of Poland, Chairman of the Polish Christian Trade Union in Exile, member of the Council, ICFTUE FEC: date of exile 1946, stipend: 400$/mo., since 1 I 1958; FEC: council member 4,800$/y. (as of 1960)	Chairman (3–18) S (8,9); E-S (10)	2–18
Stefan Medey	former Member of the Hungarian Parliament		3–5
Frantisek Nemec	Vice President of the ICFTU, former Secretary General of the Czechoslovak Transport Workers Union		2
Karl Rudolf Pakalns	Teacher, former member, leadership of the Social Democratic Youth of Latvia Social Democratic Party in Exile, Member, Latvian Free Trade Union Group, Member, Latvian Free Trade Unionist Groups in the United States	P (8, 9) S (8)	5–10
Charles Peyer	Vice President of the ICFTUE, former Secretary General of the General Confederation of Labor of Hungary	See: Hungary	2
Jacques Serbeanu	No description		11–18

Tab. 8E: ICFTUE *(Continued)*

MEMBER ORGANIZATION: **International Center of Free Trade Unionists in Exile** ADDRESS: 198 Avenue du Maine Paris (14e), France			
FIRST, LAST NAME of delegate to ACEN	AFFILIATION – all descriptions listed by the ACEN with session numbers	FUNCTIONS IN THE ACEN (L-Legal, P-Political, S-Social, E-Economic, I-Information, C-Cultural)	YEARS LISTED AS A DELEGATE BY ACEN
Aleksander Skrodzki	Secretary General of the ICFTUE (8,9)		4 – 10
Jan Sykora	No description		4 – 7
Carlo Vajda	No description		6 – 7
Sacha Volman	Secretary, Executive Committee of the ICFTUE		2 – 3

*No delegates were nominated for the first session of ACEN

Tab. 9: ACEN representations abroad, 1956 – 1971
This table was prepared by the author based on ACEN archival collection at IHRC as well as ACEN publications. Delegations, representatives, correspondents

ACEN REPRESENTATION (PLACE, TYPE, DATES)	CHAIRMEN	MEMBERS (BY COUNTRY OF ORIGIN)
	ACEN OFFICES AND DELEGATIONS	
FRANCE, Paris 1956 – 1971	**ACEN Office 1956 – 1967** Director: Edmund Rehak (Czechoslovakia) **ACEN Delegation, 1956 – 1971** Chairmen: Dr. Paul Auer (Hungary); Karel Pusta (Estonia); Tsenko Barev (Bulgaria); Eduardas Turauskas (Lithuania); Virgil Veniamin (Romania)	**Albania:** Isuf Begeja, Lec Shllaku, Odhise Dhima; **Bulgaria:** Tsenko Barev; **Czechoslovakia:** Cornel Filo, Gen. Cenek Kudlacek, Edmund Rehak, Mrs. Marie Tumlirova; **Estonia:** Vahur Linnuste, Karel Pusta; **Hungary:** Dr. Paul Auer; **Latvia:** Dr. Olgerds Grosvalds, Karlis Berends; **Lithuania:** Stasys Backis, Jurgis Baltrusaitis, Eduardas Turauskas; **Poland:** Marian Czarnecki, Kajetan Morawski, Jerzy Żłobnicki; **Romania:** Romulus Boila, Virgil Veniamin; **CDUCE:** Seweryn Eustachiewicz, Adolf Venskus; **LDUCEE:** Nicolae George Caranfil, Witold Obrembski; **ICFTUE:** Eftimie Gherman, Arno Hais;

Tab. 9: ACEN representations abroad, 1956–1971 *(Continued)*

ACEN REPRESENTATION (PLACE, TYPE, DATES)	CHAIRMEN	MEMBERS (BY COUNTRY OF ORIGIN)
		M.D. Nemesthoty **IPU:** Abas Ermenji; **SUCEE:** Serban Voinea, Zygmunt Zaremba
GREAT BRITAIN, London 1956–1971	**ACEN Office 1957–1967** Director: Antoni Dargas (Poland) **ACEN Delegation, 1956–1971** Chairmen: Adam Ciołkosz (Poland); Dr. Jaak Taul (Estonia); Pauls Reinhards (Latvia); Vilem Svoboda (Czechoslovakia); Kazimierz Trebicki (Poland); Gregoire Constantinesco (Romania).	**Albania:** Tajar Zavalani, Mrs. Marie S.Zavalani; **Bulgaria:** Boris Potchedjiev, Prof. N. Dolapchiev; **Czechoslovakia:** Václav Holub, Vilem Svoboda; **Estonia:** Oskar Kerson; Dr. Jaak Taul, Aljonzo Rebane; J. Heinastu**Hungary:** Thomas Marffy; **Latvia:** Augusts Abakuks, Pauls Reinhards; **Lithuania:** Stepas Nenortas, Juozas Vilcinskas; **Poland:** Adam Ciołkosz, Antoni Dargas, Dr. Jan Starzewski, Kazimierz Trebicki; **Romania:** Gregoire Constantinesco; **LDU:** Dr. Stanisław Olszewski; **SUCEE:** Dr. Vilem Bernard
GERMANY, Bonn 1956–1968	**ACEN Office, 1956–1963** Directors: Aureliu Lapadatu Walter C. Banaitis **ACEN Delegation, 1956–1968** Chairmen: Gustav Hennyey (Hungary); Dr. Petras Karvelis (Lithuania); Minko Saliiski (Bulgaria); Elmar Reisenberg (Estonia)	**Albania:** Mark Traboini; **Bulgaria:** Jordan Reitschev, Minko Saliiski; **Estonia:** Gerhard A. Bushman, Lui Jakobsen, Elmar Reisenberg, Karl Selter; **Hungary:** Gustav Hennyey; **Latvia:** Col. Vilis Janums, Roberts Liepins, Jekabs Kiploks; **Lithuania:** Dr. Petras Karvelis, J. Norkaitis; **Romania:** D. C. Amzar, George Gallin; **ICFTUE:** Jonas Glenza
ARGENTINA, Buenos Aires 1956–1971	**ACEN Office, 1957–1967** Director: Dr. László Simon **ACEN Delegation, 1956–1971** Chairmen: Ceferino Iujnevich (Lithuania); Constantino Mihailescu (Romania); Stanisław Śliwiński (Poland); Zbigniew Kulpiński (Poland); Visvaldis Gusts (Latvia); Evald Talvari (Estonia)	**Bulgaria:** Dimitar Raikov, Ing. Dimitar Kristev; **Estonia:** Rev. Karl Lantee, Evald Talvari; **Hungary:** Gabriel Bethalm, Dr. Arno Bobrik, Dr. Janos Fercsey, Dr. László Simon; **Latvia:** Visvaldis Gusts, Prof. Leonids Slaucitajs; **Lithuania:** Jonas Cikta, Ceferinas Juknevicus, Caferino Lujnevich, Antanas Santaras, Prof. Vytautas Staugaitis; **Poland:** Zbigniew Kulpiński, Stanisław Śliwiński; **Roma-**

Tab. 9: ACEN representations abroad, 1956–1971 *(Continued)*

ACEN REPRESENTATION (PLACE, TYPE, DATES)	CHAIRMEN	MEMBERS (BY COUNTRY OF ORIGIN)
		nia: Radu Cutzarida, Constantino Mihailescu, Titus Mihailescu
	ACEN DELEGATIONS	
AUSTRALIA, Sydney, Melbourne 1957–1965	**DELEGATION** Aldur A. Urm (Estonia) Adam Dukats (Latvia) Arthurs Berztiss (Latvia) Meinhard Ots (Estonia) Frantisek Novy (Czechoslovakia)	**Albania:** Dr. Shelai Mitrovica, Prof. Luks Cuni; **Bulgaria:** Dimitar Chavdarov; **Czechoslovakia:** Frantisek Novy, Jan Viola; Peter Lansky; **Estonia:** Meinhard Ots, Aldur A. Urm; **Latvia:** Arturs Berztiss, Adam Dukats; **Lithuania:** Emilionas Kolakauskas, Vladas Jakutis; **Poland:** General J. Kloeberg, Tadeusz Saryusz-Bielski
BELGIUM, Brussels 1957–1971	**DELEGATION, 1957–1962** Chairman: Juozas Lanskoronskis (Lithuania) **REPRESENTATIVE, 1963–1971** Dr. Erno Tottosy (Hungary)	**Albania:** Rexhep Kumbarce; **Bulgaria:** Boyan Georgiev, Dimitar Rangelov; **Hungary:** Erno Tottosy, George de Barcza; **Latvia:** E. Ozols; **Lithuania:** Juozas Lanskoronskis, Rev. Julius Danauskas; **Poland:** Jerzy Drobnik; **LDUCEE:** Marian Piotrowski
BRAZIL, Rio de Janeiro 1957–1971	**DELEGATION, 1957–1966** Aldur Urm (Estonia) Jan Reisser, Dr. Miroslav Rasin (Czechoslovakia); Tadeusz Skowroński (Poland); Dr. Jan Reisser **REPRESENTATIVE, 1966–1971** Col. Edward Ressel (Romania)	**Czechoslovakia:** Dr. Miroslav Rasin; Dr. Jan Reisser; **Estonia:** Aldur Urm; **Latvia:** Dr. Peteris Olins, Dr. A. Rusins; **Lithuania:** Kazys Audenis, Johannes Abraitis, Dr. Fricas Majeris; **Poland:** Tadeusz Skowroński; **Romania:** Col. Edward Ressel
CANADA, Ottawa, Montreal, Toronto 1957–1969	**DELEGATION, 1962–1963** Chairman: J. Simanavicius (Lithuania) **CORRESPONDENTS, 1963–1969** Ottawa, correspondent: col. Stefan Sznuk (Poland); Montreal: Tudor Nenitesco (Romania); Toronto: George Nagy (Hungary)	**Czechoslovakia:** R. V. Frastacky; **Hungary:** George Nagy; **Lithuania:** J. Simanavicius; **Poland:** Col. Stefan Sznuk; **Romania:** Tudor Nenitesco

Tab. 9: **ACEN representations abroad, 1956–1971** *(Continued)*

ACEN REPRESENTATION (PLACE, TYPE, DATES)	CHAIRMEN	MEMBERS (BY COUNTRY OF ORIGIN)
CHILE, Santiago de Chile 1956–1963	DELEGATION, 1956–1957 Chairmen: Antonio Hadik (Hungary); Henry Helfant (Romania); Talivaldis Buss (Latvia) REPRESENTATION, 1959–1963	**Bulgaria:** Todor Aleksov, Stoyan Pavlov; **Czechoslovakia:** Dr. B. Mesany; **Hungary:** Dr. F. Rosthy Forgach; **Latvia:** Talivaldis Buss; **Lithuania:** Prof. J. Kakarieka, Prof. P. Stelingis; **Poland:** Prof. M. Poradowski; **Romania:** Henry Helfant
ITALY, Rome 1957–1971	DELEGATION Kvan Barev (Bulgaria) Witold Zahorski, Stanisław Janikowski (Poland) Ragip Frashëri (Albania), Vladimir Vanek (Czechoslovakia)	**Albania:** Ragip Frashëri, Dr. Athanas Gegaj; **Bulgaria:** Kvan Barev; **Czechoslovakia:** Albert Davidov, Vladimir Vanek; **Hungary:** Dr. Ferenc Simonfay; **Lithuania:** Prof. Zenonas Ivinskis, Dr. J. Gailius, Stasys Lozoraitis; **Poland:** Witold Zahorski, Stanisław Janikowski; **Romania:** Teodor Galiţă; **LDUCEE:** Kazys Lozoraitis
SWEDEN, Stockholm 1957–1969	DELEGATION Aleksander Warma (Estonia) Karlis Dzilleja (Latvia); Mrs. Ella Dickinson (Hungary); Wiesław Patek (Poland)	**Bulgaria:** Dr. Stemen Stamenov; **Czechoslovakia:** Dr. Emil Walter; **Estonia:** Heinrich Laretei, Arvo Horm, Aleksander Warma; **Hungary:** Mrs. Ella Dickinson, Dr. Georg Heler; **Latvia:** Janis Rutkis; **Lithuania:** J. Pajaujis, Prof Juozas Lingis; **Poland:** Wiesław Patek; **Romania:** Dr. Miron Giuroiu, Georges Serdici; **LDU** Dr. Janis Breikss; **ICFTUE:** Johannes Mikhelson; **SUCEE:** Bruno Kalnins
URUGUAY, Montevideo 1956–1971	DELEGATION, 1956–1966 Dr. Miroslav Rasin (Czechoslovakia); Jan Tarnowski (Poland); Alphonse Max (Bulgaria)	**Bulgaria:** Alphonse Max, Boris Zahariev; **Czechoslovakia:** Emil Novak, Ms. Hanus Paschova; **Estonia:** Dr. Evald Talvari; **Hungary:** Edmund Gaspar, Béla Simonsits; **Lithuania:** Casimir Cibiras, J. Vastakas, S. Tamosiunas; **Poland:** Dr. Jan K. Tarnowski, Roman Tustanowski; **Romania:** Petre Paunescu
	ACEN REPRESENTATIVES	

Tab. 9: **ACEN representations abroad, 1956–1971** *(Continued)*

ACEN REPRESENTATION (PLACE, TYPE, DATES)	CHAIRMEN	MEMBERS (BY COUNTRY OF ORIGIN)
DENMARK, Copenhagen 1957–1971	REPRESENTATIVE	August Koern (Estonia)
GREECE, Athens 1957–1971	REPRESENTATIVE	Radu Arion (Rumania)
PORTUGAL, Lisbon 1959	REPRESENTATIVE	Tibor de Bartheldy (Hungary)
SPAIN, Madrid 1959	REPRESENTATIVE	Francis de Marosy (Hungary)
SWITZERLAND, Geneva 1957–1971	REPRESENTATIVE	Béla Padanyi-Gulyas (Hungary) Dr. Joseph Vanek (Czechoslovakia)
JAPAN, Tokyo 1956–57; 1962–1970	REPRESENTATIVE, 1956–1957 Dr. Jerzy J. Lerski (Poland) CORRESPONDENT, 1962–1970 Eiichi Nobushima (Japan)	Dr. Jerzy J. Lerski (Poland) Eiichi Nobushima (Japan)
LEBANON, Beirut 1957–1971	REPRESENTATIVE	Dr. Zygmunt Zawadowski (Poland)
PHILIPPINES, Manila 1957–1971	REPRESENTATIVE	Romualdas G. Vildzius (Lithuania)
COLOMBIA, Medellin 1962–1971	REPRESENTATIVE	Rev. Myk Tamosiunas (Lithuania) Stany Sirutis (Lithuania)
MEXICO, Mexico City 1961–1971	REPRESENTATIVE	Jerzy Skoryna-Lipski (Poland)
PERU, Lima 1959–1963	REPRESENTATIVE	Grigore Cugler (Romania) Dr. Nicholas Mara (Hungary)
VENEZUELA, Caracas 1962–63	REPRESENTATIVE	Matei Ghica (Romania)
TURKEY 1959–1963	REPRESENTATIVES nominated but delegation not formed	S. Skarlev; A. Greimas; M. Sokolnicki
	ACEN CORRESPONDENTS	
INDIA, New Delhi 1962–1971	CORRESPONDENT	Rama Swarup

Tab. 9: ACEN representations abroad, 1956 – 1971 *(Continued)*

ACEN REPRESENTATION (PLACE, TYPE, DATES)	CHAIRMEN	MEMBERS (BY COUNTRY OF ORIGIN)
ECUADOR, Quito 1962 – 1971	CORRESPONDENT	Luis Cornejo Gaete
EL SALVADOR, San Salvador – 1971	CORRESPONDENT	Dr. Luis Roberto Hidalgo Zelaya
PARAGUAY, Asuncion – 1971	CORRESPONDENT	Dr. Carlos A. Levi Ruffinelli

ACEN Publications (1954 – 1971)

All works were published by the ACEN. The publication place, unless indicated otherwise, was New York. Some of the numbers of publications added by the ACEN do not follow chronological order, most likely due to delays in their production.

1954:

No. 1 *Assembly of Captive European Nations. First session, Plenary Meetings of September 20 and 21.*
No. 2 *Appeal to the Nations of the Free World. New York, December 20, 1954.*
No. 3 *Appel Aux Nations du Monde Libre, New York, le 20 Décembre, 1954.*
No. 4 *Llamado a las Naciones del Mundo Libre, Nueva York, 20 diciembre de 1954.*

1955:

No. 5 *Assembly of Captive European Nations. First Session. September 20, 1954 – Feb. 11, 1955. Organization, Resolutions, Reports, Debate.*
No. 6 *Assemblée des Nations Captives d'Europe.*
No. 7 *Charter and Rules of Procedure of the Assembly of Captive European Nations.*
No. 8 *Soviet Objectives at the Geneva Conferences.*
No. 9 *Assemblée des Nations Captives d'Europe. Session Spéciale, Strasbourg 1 – 4 juillet, 1955. Résolutions, rapports, débats.*

1956:

No. 10 *Assemblée des Nations Captive d'Europe. Deuxiéme Session (septembre, 1955-mars, 1956.*
No. 11 *Objectivos Sovieticos a la luz de las Conferencias de Ginebra.*
No. 12 *Assembly of Captive European Nations, First Session. Second Part. Feb. 12 – sept. 20, 1955. Organizations, Resolutions, Reports, Debates.*
No. 13 *Assembly of Captive European Nations. Origin, aims, views, general information.*
No. 14 *Assemblée des Nations Captives d'Europe. Origines, buts, activités, informations d'ordre general.*
No. 15 *Asamblea de Naciones Europeas Cautivas. Origen, propositos, puntos de vista, informacion general.*
No. 16 *Assembly of Captive European Nations. Second Session. September 22, 1955-November 11, 1956. Resolutions, reports, Organization.*
No. 17 *Assemblée des Nations Captives d'Europe. Deuxiéme Session Spéciale. Strasbourg. 12 – 15 Avril, 1956. Résolutions et Déclaratios, Débats. Délégués.*

1957:

No. 18 *Assemblée des Nations Captives d'Europe. Troisiéme Session. Novembre, 1956–Avril, 1957. Documentation, Organisation.*
No. 19 *Assemblée des Nations Captives d'Europe. Troisiéme Session Spéciale à Strasbourg. 26–30 Avril. 1957. Résolutions, Messages.*
No. 20 *Assembly of Captive European Nations. Third Special Session in Strasbourg. April 26–30, 1957. Resolutions, Messages.*
No. 24 *Assemblée des Nations Captives d'Europe. Quatriéme Session Spéciale a Strasbourg. 1957* (published in Starsbourg).
No. 25 *Assembly of Captive European Nations, Fourth Special Session in Strasbourg. 1957.* (published in Starsbourg).

1958:

No. 21 *Assemblée des Nations Captives d'Europe. Troisiéeme Session Spéciale* (Published in Paris).
No. 22 *Assembly of Captive European Nations. Third Session. November, 1956–September, 1957. Resolution, Reports, Organization.*
No. 23 *Assemblée des Nations Captives d'Europe. Quatriéme Session* (published in Paris).
No. 30 *Denial of Human Rights in Eastern Europe.*

1959:

No. 28 *Assemblée des Nations Captives d'Europe. Quatriéme Session Spéciale a Strasbourg* (published in Paris).
No. 29 *Assemblée des Nations Captives d'Europe. Cinquiéme Session* (published in Paris).

1960:

No. 26 *The New Colonialism. Four colored maps.*
No. 27 *Assenblée der Versklavten Europäischer Nationen* (published in Bonn).
No. 31 *Soviet Empire, 1917–1958—a pictorial exhibit* (photographic album)
No. 32 *Facts on the Captive Countries.*

1961:

No. 33 *Datos Relativos a las Naciones Cautivas* (published in Buenos Aires).
No. 34 *Realités des Pays Captifs* (published in Beirut).
No. 35 *Facts on the Captive Countries* (in Arabic.)

No. 36 *Facts on the Captive Countries* (2nd revised ed.)
No. 37 *Assembly in Captive European Nations. 4, 5, 6, 7 Sessions. September, 1957. September, 1961. Resolutions, Reports, Organization.*
No. 38 *El Nuevo Colonialismo* (published in Buenos Aires).

1962:

No. 39 *Les Nations Captives et la Liberté de l'Europe* (published in Paris).
No. 40 *Charter and Rules of Procedure of the Assembly of Captive European Nations* (published in London).
No. 41 *Self-determination for the Victims of Soviet Imperialism in Europe.*

1963:

No. 42 *Assembly of Captive European Nations. Eight Session. September. 1961 – september. 1962 resolutions, reports, Organization* (published in London).
No. 43 *The Western Choice in East-Central Europe.*
No. 44 *Le Choix a Faire par L'Occident en Europe Centrale et Orientale* (published in Paris).
No. 45 *Die Alternativlosung des Westens in Mittelosteuropa* (published in Bonn).
No. 46 *L'Alternativa Occidentale Nell'Europa Centro-Orientale* (published in Rome).
No. 47 *¿Que pueden Esperar los Obreros del Sistema Comunista?* (published in Montevideo).

1964:

No. 48 *Assembly of Captive European Nations. Ninth Session. September, 1962–September, 1963. Resolutions, Reports, Documents, Organization* (published in London).

Publication series:

"ACEN News": Fifty-seven issues (Nos. 1 – 101). Also as *Novedades de la ANCE* (in Spanish).

Hungary Under Soviet Rule, in association with the American Friends of the Captive Nations Vol. I (April–August, 1957); Vol. II (September, 1957 – August, 1958); Vol. III (Revolution to August, 1959); Vol. IV (August, 1959 – August, 1960); Vol. V (1959 – 1961); Vol. VI (1961 – 1962).

Spanish-language abbreviated, 59-page version of *Hungary Under Soviet Rule: Hungria Bajo la Dominacion Sovietica.*

Translations:

ACEN-prepared reports
a) on Communist takeover in the captive countries:
- in Portuguese (published in Brazil): *Como Foi Istaurada a Dominacao Sovieto-Comunista Sobre as Nacoes da Europa Centro-Oriental.*
- in Spanish (published in Argentina): *Las Naciones Cautivas de Europa*

b) on Soviet-captive nations trade:
- in Spanish (published in Argentina): *Comercio Entro La Union Sovietica y las Naciones Cautivas Durante*

c) Lawyers in the New Society
- in Spanish (published in Argentina): *Los Abogados en la "Neuva Sociedad."*

Ephemeric: ACEN Bulletins in Finnish, Swedish, and Arabic.

Mimeographed publications:

"A survey of Recent Developments in Nine Captive Countries"
1953–1955; February, 1956–Februbary, 1957; February, 1957–October 1957; October, 1957-March, 1958; March, 1958-October, 1959; March 1959-October, 1959; October, 1959-March, 1960; March, 1960-October, 1960; October, 1960-June, 1961-December, 1961; January, 1962-June, 1962; July, 1962-December, 1962.
Translation to French: "Etude sur la Situation Actuelle dans les Neuf Pays Asservis" 1953–1955; Février, 1956 – Février, 1957.

"East-Central European Papers" (Six Volumes).
"Official Reports of Debates" (13 volumes covering 13–44 Plenary Meetings of ACEN, in the period from 14 April 1955 to 28 June 1957).
"International Agreements and Pledges Concerning East-Central Europe."

Bibliography

Archives

Columbia University Libraries (New York, NY)
— Bakhmeteff Archive, Ferenc Nagy Papers,
Dwight D. Eisenhower Presidential Library (Abilene, KS)
— C. D. Jackson Papers, 1931–1967
— C. D. Jackson Records, 1953–1954
Harry S. Truman Library (Independence, MO)
— Charles Hulten Papers
Hoover Institution Archives (Stanford, CA)
— Brutus Coste Papers
— Christopher T. Emmet Papers
— Stefan Korboński Papers
— Sig Mickelson Papers
— Štefan Osuský Papers
— Arch Puddington Papers
— RFE/RL Corporate Files
Immigration History Research Center (Minneapolis, MN)
— Assembly of Captive European Nations
Józef Piłsudski Institute of America (New York, NY)
— Subject Archive, ACEN
National Archives College Park (College Park, MD)
— Record Groups: 59
— CREST
— Nixon Presidential Materials Project
Polish Institute of Arts and Sciences (New York, NY)
— Karol Popiel/PNDC Papers
Princeton University Library (Princeton, NJ)
— John F. Dulles Papers
Open Society Archives (Budapest, Hungary)
— Claire de Hédervary Collection: United Nations Special Committee Documents on the Problem of Hungary in 1956
— General Collection (HU OSA)
— Fekete Doboz Alapítvány Video Archive
Ossoliński National Institute, ZNiO (Wrocław, Poland)
— Gadomski Papers

Private collections

— Jadwiga Gadomska (Warsaw, Poland)
— John F. Leich (Canaan, CT)
— Christopher Simpson (Washington, D.C.)
— Ralph Walter Papers (Berlin, Germany)

https://doi.org/10.1515/9783110661002-016

Author's Interviews

in person: Zofia Korbońska, John F. Leich, Ralph Walter, János Horváth, Stanisław Gebhardt
via telephone/e-mail: Zbigniew Brzeziński, Paul B. Henze, John F. Leich, Ralph Walter

Published sources (print)

ACEN publications (see complete list in the Appendix)
— "ACEN News" (1955–1972)
— ACEN Sessions. Organization, Resolutions, Reports, Debate, 1–9 (1954–1963)
— *Hungary Under Soviet Rule* in six volumes: I (April-August 1957), II (September 1957–August 1958); III (Revolution to August 1959); IV (August 1959–August 1960); V (1959–1961); VI (1961–1962).
— *ACEN Seminars in Latin America. Lectures in the Seminar held in Buenos Aires, Argentina, September 8–14, 1963* (New York: ACEN, [1964?]).
— *ACEN Seminars in Latin America. Lectures of the Seminar Held in Medellin, Colombia, Nov. 29–Dec. 4, 1964* (New York: ACEN, [1965]).
Code of Federal Regulations (CFR), Title 3: The President, 1959–1963 Compilation (Washington: U.S. Government Printing Office, 1964).
Foreign Relations of the United States (FRUS)
— *FRUS, 1955–1957, vol. XXV: Eastern Europe* (Washington: GPO, 1990)
— *FRUS, 1952–1954, National Security Affairs*, Vol. II, part 2 (Washington: GPO, 1984)
— *FRUS, The Intelligence Community 1950–55. Organization of U.S. Intelligence* (Washington: GPO, 2007)
— *FRUS, 1952–1954, Vol. II, Part 2: National Security Affairs* (Washington: GPO 1984)
— *FRUS, 1958–1960, American Republics*, Vol. V (Washington: GPO, 1991)
Stefan Korboński, *Listy amerykańskie, 1953–1983*, ed. Roman W. Rybicki, Bartosz Nowożycki (IPN: Warsaw, 2019).
Polska emigracja polityczna. Informator, reprint, D. Piskorska (ed.), introduction Cenckiewicz Sławomir (Warszawa: Adiutor, 2004)
Public papers of the Presidents of the United States. Dwight D. Eisenhower, 1956, Containing the Public Messages, Speeches, and Statements of the President, January 1 to December 21, 1956 (Washington: GPO, 1958)
Wielkie Mowy Historii, vols. 1–4 (Warsaw: Polityka-Spółdzielnia Pracy, 2006).

Online Archives

Internet Archive https://archive.org
— Department of State Bulletin
— Wayback Machine (archive of web pages)
Association for Diplomatic Studies and Training
— Foreign Affairs Oral History Project, https://adst.org/oral-history/
HeinOnline, https://home.heinonline.org/
— Congressional Record, 1945–1989

CIA electronic reading room, www.foia.cia.gov
Council of Europe
— https://www.coe.int/en/web/portal/home
The National Film Archive's Digital Repository (Poland)
http://www.repozytorium.fn.org.pl
Hungarian Electronic Library (Magyar Elektronikus Könyvtár), http://mek.oszk.hu/indexeng.phtml
Mary Ferrell Foundation, https://www.maryferrell.org/pages/Archive.html
NATO Library, https://www.nato.int/cps/en/natohq/publications.htm
ProQuest Historical Newspapers, https://www.proquest.com/products-services/pq-hist-news.html
— "The New York Times" (1947–1989)
— "Chicago Tribune" (1947–1989)
United Nations, https://www.un.org/
— UN Digital Library, https://digitallibrary.un.org/
— Dag Hammarskjöld library, https://research.un.org/en/
United States Government
— Office of the Law Revision Counsel, House of Representatives, U.S. Code https://uscode.house.gov/
— U.S. Government Accountability Office, https://www.gao.gov
— U.S. Government information for all, https://www.govinfo.gov/
— The White House, https://www.whitehouse.gov/
— U.S. Department of State, Office of the Historian
Foreign Relations of the United States, https://history.state.gov/historicaldocuments
— U.S. Census, https://data.census.gov/cedsci/
— U.S. Government Publishing Office, www.gpo.gov
Wilson Center (Washington, D.C.), History and Public Policy Program Digital Archive,
— Radio Free Europe and Radio Liberty (A. Ross Johnson collection) https://digitalarchive.wilsoncenter.org/collection/104/radio-free-europe-and-radio-liberty
— Asian Peoples' Anti-Communist League (Syngman Rhee Institute)
https://digitalarchive.wilsoncenter.org/collection/193/asian-peoples-anti-communist-league

Reference & online materials

Słownik biograficzny Europy Środkowo-Wschodniej XX wieku (Warsaw: ISP PAN-Rytm, 2004).
Biographical Dictionary of Central and Eastern Europe in the Twentieth Century, ed. Wojciech Roszkowski, Jan Kofman (Abingdon OX-New York: Routledge, 2015).
Lawrence H. Officer and Samuel H. Williamson, "Purchasing Power of Money in the United States from 1774 to 2008," MeasuringWorth, 2009. URL http://www.measuringworth.com/ppowerus/.
Diccionario Biographico Ecuador, http://www.diccionariobiograficoecuador.com/tomos/tomo11/c7.htm
IPN, Poznański czerwiec '56, https://czerwiec56.ipn.gov.pl
IPN, Korboński, http://korbonski.ipn.gov.pl/portal/kor/1116/8545/Polityk_na_emigracji.html
Ukrainian Diaspora Electronic Library http://diasporiana.org.ua

Wilson Center, Cold War International History Project, https://www.wilsoncenter.org/program/cold-war-international-history-project
World League for Freedom and Democracy http://www.wlfdroc.org.tw/
NYS Department of State, Division of Corporations, www.dos.ny.gov/corps

Literature, Including Memoirs

Aldrich Richard, *The Hidden Hand. Britain, America and Cold War Secret Intelligence* (London: Gerald Duckworth & Co. Ltd., 2006).

Aldrich Richard, "OSS, CIA and European Unity: The American Committee on United Europe, 1948–60," *Diplomacy & Statecraft* 8/1 (1997).

Robert J. Alexander, *International Labor Organizations and Organized labor in Latin America and the Caribbean. A History* (Santa Barbara, CA-Denver, CO-Oxford, England: Praeger, ABC Clio, 2009).

Bailey Bernadine, *The captive nations, our first line of defense* (Chicago: Chas. Hallberg, 1969).

Beezley P. C., *The captive nations handbook* (Seattle: Captive Nations Council, 1966).

Beichman Arnold, "The story of Radio Free Europe," *National Review* 36/21 (1984).

Borhi László, Hungary in the Cold War, 1945–1956. Between the United States and the Soviet Union (New York, Budapest: CEU Press).

Brogan Patrick, *The Captive Nations: Eastern Europe, 1945–1990* (New York: Avon Books, 1990).

Broquetas Magdalena, San Martin, *Demócratas y nacionalistas. La reacción de las derechas en el Uruguay (1959–1966)*, Tesis de Doctorado en Historia, Facultad de Humanidades y Ciencias de la Educación, Universidad Nacional de La Plata, 2013).

Brown James F., *Radio Free Europe: An Insider's View* (Washington D.C.: Vellum/New Academia Publishing, 2013).

Butariu Miron, "Assembly of Captive European Nations. The Little United Nations – The Voice of the People," *Journal of the American Romanian Academy of Arts and Sciences* 10 (Davis, CA, 1987).

Carlson Peter, *K Blows Top: A Cold War Comic interlude starring Nikita Khrushchev, America's most unlikely tourist* (New York: Public Affairs, 2010).

Carruthers Susan L., *Cold War Captives. Imprisonment, Escape, and Brainwashing* (Berkeley–Los Angeles–London University of California Press, 2009).

Carruthers Susan L., Between Camps: Eastern Bloc "Escapees" and Cold War Borderlands, *American Quarterly* 57/3 (2005).

Collis Larry D., "The Free Europe Committee. An American Weapon of the Cold War," Dissertation Presented to the Faculty of the Department of Political Science, Carleton University, November 1973.

Kenneth Conboy, James Morrison, The CIA's Secret War in Tibet (Lawrence: Kansas: University of Kansas Press, 2002).

Congdon Lee W., Király Béla K. (eds.), The Ideas of the Hungarian Revolution, Suppressed and Victorious, 1956–1999 (Highland Lakes, NJ: Social Science Monographs, Boulder CO; New York: dist. Columbia Univ. Press, 2002).

DeWitt Copp, Marshall Peck, *Betrayal at the UN. The Story of Paul Bang-Jensen* (New York: The Devin-Adair Company, 1961).

Csicsery-Rónay István (ed.), *Nagy Ferenc miniszterelnök: visszaemlékezések, tanulmányok, cikkek* (Budapest: Occidental Press, 1995).

Cummings Bruce (ed.) *Child of Conflict: the Korean-American Relationship, 1943–1953* (Seattle: University of Washington Press, 1983).

Cummings Richard H., *Cold War Radio. The Dangerous History of American Broadcasting in Europe, 1950–1989* (Jefferson, North Carolina, London: McFarland & Company, Inc. Publishers, 2009).

Cummings Richard H., *Radio Free Europe's "Crusade for Freedom": Rallying Americans behind Cold War Broadcasting, 1950–1960* (Jefferson NC, London: McFarland & Company, 2010).

Defty Andrew, *Britain, America and Anti-Communist: The Information Research Department* (Oxfordshire: Routlege 2004).

Dorril Stephen, *MI6: Inside the Covert World of Her Majesty' s Secret Intelligence Service* (New York: Free Press, 2000).

Durin-Hornyik Veronika, "Le Collège de 'Europe libre et la préparation de la construction démocratique de l'Europe de l'Est (1948–1958)/The Free Europe University in Exile: Preparing for democracy in Central and Eastern Europe (1948–1958), *Relations internationales* 180/4 (2019).

Dziak Waldemar, *Korea, pokój czy wojna* (Warszawa: Świat Książki, 2003).

Epstein Julius, The Bang-Jensen Tragedy. A Review based on the Official Records, "American Opinion. An Informal Review" 3/5 (May 1960).

Europe: Nine panel Studies by Experts from Central and Eastern European Studies. An Examination of the Post-Liberation Problem of the Position of Central and Eastern European Nations in a Free European Community (New York: Free Europe Committee, 1954).

Faure Justine, Croisade américaine en 1950: La délivrance des "Nations captives" d' Europe de l' Est, "Vingtième Siècle. Revue d' histoire" 73 (2002).

Ferreira Roberto Garcia, "Espionaje politica: La Guerra Fria y la inteligencia political Uruguaya, 1947–64," *Revista Historia* 63–64 (enero-diciembre 2011).

Fousek John, *To Lead The Free World: American Nationalism & The Cultural Roots of the Cold war* (Chapel Hill: The University of North Carolina Press, 2000).

Gadomski Feliks, *Zgromadzenie Europejskich Narodów Ujarzmionych. Krótki zarys* (New York: Bicentennial Publishing Corporation-Nowy Dziennik, 1995).

Garrett Stephen A., "Eastern European Ethnic Groups and American Foreign Policy," *Political Science Quarterly* 93/2 (Summer 1978).

Gati Charles, *Failed Illusions: Moscow, Washington, Budapest and the 1956 Hungarian Revolt* (Stanford, CA: Stanford University Press, 2006).

Gaspar Edmund, *United States, Latin America: A Special relationship?* (Washington: American Enterprise Institute, 1978).

Gleijeses Piero, "Hope Denied: the U.S. Defeat of the 1965 Revolt in the Dominican Republic," *Cold War International History Project, Working Paper* 72 (Washington: CWIHP, 2014).

Griese Noel L., *Arthur W. Page. Publisher, Public Relations Pioneer, Patriot* (Atlanta: Anvil Publishers Inc., 2001).

Grose Peter, *Operation Rollback. America's Secret War behind the Iron Curtain* (Boston-New York: Houghton Mifflin Company, 2000).

Gross Feliks, "Political Emigration from Iron Curtain Countries," *Annals of the American Academy of Political and Social Science* 271: Moscow's European Satellites (September 1950).

Grow Michael, *U.S. Presidents and Latin American Interventions. Pursuing Regime Change in the Cold War* (Lawrence, KS: University Press of Kansas, 2008).

Gülstorff Torben, Warming Up a Cooling War: An Introductory Guide on the CIAS and Other Globally Operating Anti-Communist Networks at the Beginning of the Cold War Decade of Détente, Cold War International History Project, Working Paper no. 75 (Washington: CWIHP, 2015).

Harrigan John J., *Politics and the American Future* (New York: Random House, 1987), 420.

Hawthorne Daniel, *The ordeal of the captive nations* (Garden City, N. Y.: Doubleday, 1958).

Heikkilä Pauli, *Estonians for Europe. National Activism for European Integration, 1922–1991* (Brussels: Peter Lang, 2014).

Heiss Mary Ann, Exposing "Red Colonialism": U.S. Propaganda at the United Nations, 1953–1963, *Journal of Cold War Studies,* 17/3 (Summer 2015).

Hermes Walter G., *Truce Tent and Fighting Front* (Washington D.C.: Center of Military History, U.S. Army 1992).

Hershberg James G., Zubok Vladislav (transl.), "Russian Documents on the Korean War, 1950–53. Introduction," *Cold War International History Project Bulletin* 14/15 (Winter/Spring 2003–2004).

Jaroszyńska-Kirchmann Anna D., *The exile mission: The Polish political diaspora and Polish Americans, 1939–1956.* Athens: Ohio University Press, 2004.

Johnson A. Ross, "To the Barricades: Did Radio Free Europe Inflame the Hungarian Revolutionaries of 1956? Exploring One of the Cold War's Most Stubborn Myths," *Hoover Digest* no. 4 (2007).

Johnson A. Ross, Radio Free Europe and Radio Liberty. The CIA Years and Beyond (Washington D.C.: Woodrow Wilson Center Press and Stanford, CA: Stanford University Press, 2010).

Kádár Lynn Katalin (ed.), *Inauguration of Organized Political Warfare: Cold War Organizations Sponsored by the National Committee for a Free Europe*, ed. Katalin Kádár Lynn (St. Helena, Budapest: Helena History Press, 2013–distributed by Central European University Press, New York, Budapest).

Kaiser Wolfram, Co-operation of European Catholic Politicians in Exile in Britain and the USA during the Second World War, Journal of Contemporary History 35/3 (2000).

Kohler Foy D., Harvey Mose L. (eds.), The Soviet Union: Yesterday, Today, Tomorrow. A Report on A Colloquy of American Long-Timers in Moscow ([Coral Gables, FL: Center for Advanced International Studies, University of Miami, 1975).

Korbel Josef, *The Captive Nations*, Behind the headlines, v. 15, no. 5. (Toronto: Canadian Institute of International Affairs, 1955).

Korboński Stefan, *W imieniu Polski walczącej* (Warszawa: Rytm, 1999).

Korboński Stefan, *Warsaw in Exile* (New York-Washington D.C.: Frederick A. Praeger, 1966).

Kosicki Piotr H., Łukasiewicz Sławomir (eds.), *Christian Democracy Across the Iron Curtain: Europe Redefined* (Cham, Switzerland: Palgrave Macmillan, 2018).

Kula Marcin, *Paryż, Londyn i Waszyngton patrzą na października 1956 r. w Polsce* (Warszawa: ISS PAN, A. Marszałek, 1992).
Laville Helen, Wilford Hugh (eds.), *The U.S. Government, Citizen Groups and the Cold War. The state–private network* (London–New York: Routledge, 2006).
Łaptos Józef, "Projekty organizacji państw Europy Środkowo-Wschodniej (1942–1950). Analiza porównawcza," *Prace Komisji Środkowoeuropejskiej PAU* 3 (1995).
Łaptos Józef, *Europa marzycieli: wizje i projekty integracyjne środkowoeuropejskiej emigracji politycznej 1940–1956* (Kraków: Wyd. Nauk. Uniw. Pedagogicznego, 2012).
Leffler Malvyn P., Westad Odd Arne (eds.), *The Cambridge History of the Cold War*, vol. 1: *Origins* (Cambridge: Cambridge University Press, 2011).
Leich John F., "Great Expectations: The National Councils in Exile 1950–1960," *Polish Review* 35 (1990).
Lowe Peter, Wojna Koreańska (Warsaw: Bellona, 1995).
Lucas Scott, *Freedom's War. The American Crusade against the Soviet Union* (New York: New York University Press, 1999).
Łukasiewicz Sławomir, *Trzecia Europa. Polska myśl federalistyczna w Stanach Zjednoczonych, 1940–1971* (IPN: Warszawa, Lublin, 2010).
Łukasiewicz Sławomir, *Third Europe. Polish federalist thought in the United States, 1940–1970s* (Reno NV: Helena History Press, 2016).
Łukasiewicz Sławomir, *Partia w warunkach emigracji. Dylematy Polskiego Ruchu Wolnościowego "Niepodległość i Demokracja" 1945–1994* (Lublin-Warszawa: IPN, 2014).
Łukasiewicz Sławomir (ed.), *Tajny oręż czy ofiary zimnej wojny. Emigracje polityczne z Europy Środkowo-Wschodniej*, ed. Sławomir Łukasiewicz (Lublin-Warszawa: IPN, 2010).
Łukasiewicz Sławomir (ed.), *Jałta- rzeczywistość, mit i pamięć* (Warsaw: IPN, 2019).
Lurie Mark I., *Galantière. The Lost Generation's Forgotten Man* (West Palm Beach, FL: Overlook Press LLC, 2017).
Machcewicz Paweł, *Emigracja w polityce międzynarodowej* (Warszawa: Biblioteka "Więzi," 1999).
Machcewicz Paweł, *Poland's war on Radio Free Europe, 1950–1989* (Washington D.C.: Woodrow Wilson Press, Stanford CA: Stanford University Press, 2014).
Mania Andrzej, *Department of State i Foreign Service w polityce zagranicznej USA lat gorącej i zimnej wojny 1939–1989* (Kraków: Wydawnictwo Uniwersytetu Jegiellońskiego, 2019).
Mathias Jr. Charles Mc. C., "Ethnic Groups and Foreign Policy," *Foreign Affairs* 59/5 (1981).
Matthews John P.C., *Tinderbox: East-Central Europe in the spirng, summer, and early fall of 1956* (Tucson, AZ: Fenestra Books, 2003).
Marès Antoine, Wojciech Prażuch and Inga Kawka (eds.), *Les exilés polonais en France et la réorganisation pacifique de l'Europe (1940–1989)*, ed. (Peter Lang: Frankfurt am Main 2017),
Marinescu Aurel Sergiu, *O contributie la istoria exilului românesc: Activități în exil: ANEC și PNL*, (Bucharest: Vremea, 2005).
Mazurkiewicz Anna, *Dyplomacja Stanów Zjednoczonych wobec wyborów w Polsce w latach 1947 i 1989* (Warsaw: Neriton, 2007).
Mazurkiewicz Anna, Die "Stimme Freies Polen" aus München. Radio Free Europe, die amerikanische Deutchlandpolitik und die deutsch-polnischen Beziehungen, *Inter Finitimos. Jahrbuch zur deutsch-polnischen Beziehungsgaschichte* 6 (2008).

Mazurkiewicz Anna, *Uchodźcy z Europy Środkowo-Wschodniej w amerykańskiej polityce zimnowojennej, 1948–1954* (Warsaw-Gdańsk, IPN-University of Gdańsk, 2016).
Mazurkiewicz Anna, "'Narody ujarzmione'" – lobby polityczne czy projekt propagandowy? *Studia Historica Gedanensia* 5 (Gdańsk: Wydawnictwo UG, 2014).
Mazurkiewicz Anna, "'Join, or Die' The Road to Cooperation Among East European Exiled Political Leaders in the United States, 1949–1954," *Polish American Studies* 69/2 (2012).
Mazurkiewicz Anna, "Unwilling Immigrants: Transnational Identities of East Central European Exiles during the Cold War," *Studia Migracyjne – Przegląd Polonijny* 4 (158), (2015).
Mazurkiewicz Anna (ed.), *East Central Europe in Exile*, vol. 1–2 (Cambridge-upon-Tyne: Cambridge Scholars Publishing, 2013).
Mazurkiewicz Anna (ed.), *East Central European Migrations During the Cold War. A Handbook* (Berlin-Boston: De Gruyter, 2019).
Meyer Cord, *Facing Reality: From World Federation to the CIA* (New York: Harper and Row, 1980).
Mickelson Sig, *America's Other Voice. The Story of Radio Free Europe and Radio Liberty* (New York: Praeger, 1983).
Mikkonen Simo, Exploiting the Exiles. Soviet Émigrés in U.S. Cold War Strategy," *Journal of Cold War Studies* 14/2 (Spring 2012).
Mitrovich Gregory, *Undermining the Kremlin, America's Strategy to subvert the Soviet Bloc 1947–1956* (Ithaca-London: Cornell University Press, 2000).
Munters Vilhelms, *The own people's enemies* (Riga: Zvaigzne, 1965).
Nekola Martin, *Petr Zenkl: politik a člověk* (Prague: Mladá Fronta, 2014).
Nowak-Jeziorański Jan, *Wojna w eterze* (Kraków: Znak, 2005).
Osgood Kenneth A., *Total Cold War. Eisenhower's Secret Propaganda Battle* (Lawrence, KS: University Press of Kansas, 2006).
Osgood Kenneth A., Etheridge Brian C. (eds.), *The United States and Public Diplomacy. New Directions in Cultural and International History* (Leiden–Boston: Martinus Nijhoff Publishers, 2010).
Offner Arnold A., *Another Such Victory. President Truman and the Cold War 1945–1953* (Stanford University Press, 2002).
Paczyńska Irena (ed.), *Studia z historii Polski XIX i XX wieku ofiarowane Profesorowi Józefowi Buszce w pięćdziesięciolecie doktoratu* (Kraków: Towarzystwo Wydawnicze "Historia Iagellonica," 1999).
Paleček Pavel, "Protikomunistická propaganda ve studené válce. Výbor pro svobodnou Evropu a exil", PhD Dissertation (manuscript), Brno: Masaryk University 2010.
Parker Jason C., *Hearts, Minds, Voices. U.S. Cold War Public Diplomacy and the Formation of the Third World* (New York: Oxford University Press, 2016).
Anna Péczeli, Zsolt Pálmai (eds.), *Our Past and Present in the Shadow of the Cold War: The Legacy and re-emergence of a conflict between the United States and Russia* (Budapeszt: Antall József Knowledge Centre, 2017).
Pieczewski Andrzej, Komisja do Spraw Europy Środkowej i Wschodniej Ruchu Europejskiego (1949–1973) – głos emigracji w sprawie europejskiego zjednoczenia," *Studia Polityczne ISP PAN* 21 (2008).
Pisani Sallie, *The CIA and the Marshall Plan* (Lawrence: University Press of Kansas, 1991).

Małek Agnieszka, Praszałowicz Dorota (eds.), *The United States Immigration Policy and Immigrants' Responses: past and present*, (Peter Lang Edition: Frankfurt am Main 2017).
Pomian Jan, *Józef Retinger. Życie i pamiętniki pioniera jedności europejskiej* (Warszawa: Pavo, 1994 (reprint of 1972 edition).
Edward Prus, *Pannacjonalizm. Polityczna działalność emigracyjna byłych kolaboracjonistów z Europy wschodniej i południowo-wschodniej* (Katowice: Śląski Instytut Naukowy, 1976).
Puddington Arch, *Broadcasting Freedom: The Cold War Triumph of Radio Free Europe and Radio Liberty* (Lexington: The University Press of Kentucky, 2015).
Racz Barnabas, *Hungary and the United Nations 1956–1962: A Legal and Political Analysis* (Budapest: United Nations Association of Hungary, 2007).
Raška Francis D., *Fighting Communism from Afar: the Council of Free Czechoslovakia* (Boulder, CO: East European Monographs, 2008).
Reisch Alfred, *Hot Books in the Cold War. The CIA-Founded Secret Western Book Distribution Program Behind the Iron Curtain* (Budapest-New York: CEU Press, 2013).
Richardson John, *A New Vision for America* (New York: Ruder Finn Press: 2006).
Rowiński Jan (ed.), *Polski Październik 1956 w polityce światowej* (Warszawa: PISM 2006).
Scott-Smith Giles, "The Free Europe University in Strasbourg: U.S. State–Private Networks and Academic 'Rollback,'" *Journal of Cold War Studies* 16/2 (2014).
Scott-Smith Giles, *Networks of Empire. The U.S. State Department's Foreign Leader Program in the Netherlands, France, and Britain, 1950–70* (Brussels: Peter Lang, 2008).
Scott-Smith Giles, *The Politics of Apolitical Culture. The Congress for Cultural Freedom, the CIA and post-war American hegemony* (London–New York: Routledge, 2002).
Scott-Smith Giles, "A Radical Democratic Political Offensive": Melvyn J. Lasky, Der Monat, and the Congress for Cultural Freedom," *Journal of Contemporary History* 35/2 (2000).
Siwik Anna, *Polska Partia Socjalistyczna na emigracji w latach 1945–1956* (Kraków: Księgarnia Akademicka, 1998).
Siwik Anna, *Polskie uchodźstwo polityczne: socjaliści na emigracji w latach 1956–1990* (Kraków: Abrys, 2002).
Shain Yossi, *The Frontier of Loyalty. Political Exiles in the age of a nation state* (Wesleyan University Press, Hanover and London: University Press of New England, 1989).
Smal-Stocki Roman, *The Captive Nations: Nationalism of the Non-Russian Nations in the Soviet Union* (New York: Bookman Associates, 1960).
Smith Richard Harris, *OSS: The Secret History of America's First Central Intelligence Agency* (Guildford, CT: Lyons Press 2005).
Smith Tony, *American Mission. The United States and the Worldwide Struggle for Democracy* (Princeton, Oxford: Princeton University Press, 2012).
Sosin Gene, *Sparks of Liberty: an insider's memoir of Radio Liberty* (University Park, PA: The Pennsylvania University Press, 2005).
Stanek Piotr, *Stefan Korboński (1901–1989): działalność polityczna i społeczna* (Warsaw: IPN, 2014).
Stanek Piotr, "Powstanie i działalność Zgromadzenia Europejskich Narodów Zjednoczonych (ACEN) w świetle Archiwum Feliksa Gadomskiego," *Prace uczestników studium doktoranckiego. Historia* 9 (2007).
Stern John Allen, C. D. Jackson. *Cold War Propagandist for Democracy and Globalism* (Lanham: University Press of America Inc., 2012).

Stonor Saunders Frances, *The Cultural Cold War: The CIA and the World of Arts and Letters*, The New Press, New York 2001, 2013).

Szymczak Robert, "Hopes and Promises: Arthur Bliss Lane, the Republican Party, and the Slavic-American Vote, 1952," *Polish American Studies* 45/1 (Spring 1988): 12–28.

Taubman William, *Krushchev: The Man and His Era* (New York, London: W.W. Norton & Company: 2003).

Trachtenberg Marc, *A Constructed Peace. The making of the European Settlement, 1945–1963* (New Jersey: Princeton University Press 1999).

Tromly Benjamin, *Cold War Exiles and the CIA. Plotting to Free Russia* (Oxford: Oxford University Press, 2019).

Tyszkiewicz, Jakub, *Rozbijanie monolitu. Polityka Stanów Zjednoczonych wobec Polski 1945–1988* (Warsaw: PWN, 2015).

Ubriaco, Jr., Robert D., "Bread and Butter Politics or Foreign Policy Concerns? Class versus Ethnicity in the Midwestern Polish American Community during the 1946 Congressional Elections," *Polish American Studies* 51/2 (Autumn 1994).

Urban, George R., *Radio Free Europe and the Pursuit of Democracy: My War within the Cold War* (New Haven, CT: Yale University Press, 1997).

Urban, George R., *The Nineteen Days: A Broadcaster's Account of the Hungarian Revolution* (London: Heinemann, 1957).

Valkanier Elizabeth K., "Eastern Europe in Exile," *Annals of the American Academy of Political and Social Science* 317 (May 1958).

Van Dongen Luc, Roulin Stéphanie, Scott-Smith Giles (eds.), *Transnational Anti-Communism and the Cold War. Agents, Activities, and Networks* (New York: Palgrave Macmillan, 2014).

Walaszek Adam, Pezda Janusz (eds.) *The Polish Diaspora in America and the Wider World*, (Kraków: Polish Academy of Arts and Sciences, 2012).

Weiner Tim, *Legacy of Ashes. The History of the CIA* (New York-London-Toronto-Sydney-Auckland: Doubleday, 2007).

Wilford Hugh, *The Mighty Wurlitzer: How the CIA Played America* (London-Cambridge MA: Harvard University Press, 2008).

Wolański Marian, Thomas Lane, *Poland and European Integration. The Ideas and Movements of Polish Exiles in the West, 1939–91* (London: Palgrave Macmillan, 2009).

Wright Quincy, Subversive Intervention, *American Journal of International Law* 54/3 (1960).

Zahniser Marvin R., Weis W. Michael, "A Diplomatic Pearl Harbor? Richard Nixon's Goodwill Mission to Latin America in 1958," *Diplomatic History* 13/2 (Spring 1989).

Zake Ieva (ed.), *Anti-Communist Minorities: The Political Activism of Ethnic Refugees in the United States* (New York: Palgrave Macmillan 2009).

Ziętara Paweł, *Anders, Korboński, Sieniewicz... Szkice z dziejów Drugiej Wielkiej Emigracji* (Łomianki: LTW 2016).

Ziętara, *Emigracja wobec Października. Postawy polskich środowisk emigracyjnych wobec liberalizacji w PRL w latach 1955–1957* (Warszawa: LTW, 2001).

Subject Index

Neither the footnotes, nor the names listed in appendices were indexed.

https://doi.org/10.1515/9783110661002-017

Dunning John L. 281
Durán, Julio 250
Durin-Hornyik, Veronika 6
Düsseldorf 68